PUBLIC SPEAKING

Connecting You and Your Audience, 2e

MULTIMEDIA EDITION

Property of
FAMILY OF FAITH
LIBRARY

PATRICIA HAYES ANDREWS
Indiana University

JAMES R. ANDREWS
Indiana University

GLEN WILLIAMS
Southeast Missouri State University

Houghton Mifflin Company Boston New York

Guide to SpeechStudio and VideoLab Annotations in the Multimedia Edition

Chapter 9: Supporting Your Ideas with Evidence

Chapter 10: Organizing and Outlining Your Speech

Chapter 11: Delivering the Speech Effectively

Chapter 12: Using Language Effectively

Chapter 13: Using Presentational Aids in Public Speaking

Chapter 14: Speaking to Inform

Chapter 15: The Persuasive Process

Chapter 16: Arguing Persuasively

Chapter 17: Speaking on Special Occasions

Chapter 18: Communicating in the Workplace

Appendix A: Peer Evaluation and Feedback

Appendix B: Speeches for Review and Analysis

A Brief Guide to Using the New Multimedia Edition

This edition of *Public Speaking: Connecting You and Your Audience* features new media-based tools to enhance your learning and to make the learning process more enjoyable. The time you spend in class is always limited—usually 2 or 3 hours a week. You will spend far more time outside of class reading the text, thinking of speech topics, engaging in research, choosing your organizational strategy, and practicing your speeches. Whatever you do to enrich the way you spend this out-of-class time will enhance your ability to perform well during class and to function as a more thoughtful listener when your peers are asked to speak.

In the margins of this text, you will find dozens of annotations (printed in magenta), accompanied by CD-ROM and mouse icons. These annotations direct you to special exercises, quizzes, and activities that you can access either through the Online SpeechStudio or on the VideoLab CD-ROM that accompany your book. In all likelihood, your instructor will require you to complete many of these exercises as part of the class's regular assignments. In some cases, you may be asked to complete speaking worksheets and checklists, use forms you find on the Internet to evaluate peers' speeches, or use the outlining workshop to craft your formal speech outlines. In addition, you may elect to complete some of the exercises on your own so that you will be even better prepared for the graded speeches that you will present during class.

One of the most accurate predictors of strong classroom performance is something that learning theorists call "time on task." So, if you spend more time studying, devote more time to thinking critically and analytically, and spend more time actively grappling with the material, you will likely perform better. Some of the exercises in this text will allow you to prepare for specific speaking assignments, others will test your knowledge of key concepts, and still others will give you the chance to critically analyze student speeches. Here are some specific examples of the kinds of media-based tasks you may be asked to do or elect to undertake to enhance your learning:

- Go to the **Online SpeechStudio** and evaluate your level of communication apprehension by completing the self-assessment instrument.

- See if you can distinguish the habits of poor listeners from those of good listeners by taking the quiz that appears on the **Online SpeechStudio**.

- Using the **Online SpeechStudio**, challenge your own listening skills by completing the exercise that teaches you how to paraphrase as a way of improving your listening.

- Listen to a student speech on the **VideoLab CD-ROM** and complete the exercise that asks you to identify and assess the sorts of universal human needs and values that the speaker attempts to appeal to.

- To get ready for your first speech, complete the exercises on the **VideoLab CD-ROM** that teach you how to assess your audience's interests and attitudes and that show you how to construct an audience survey.

- How ethical are emotional appeals? View a speech on the **VideoLab CD-ROM** and then complete the exercise that invites you to assess the ethics of one speaker's appeals.

- Compare two speeches on the same topic on the **VideoLab CD-ROM**. Complete the exercise that asks you to assess the speakers' comparative credibility.

- What are you considering speaking about? Use the **Online SpeechStudio** exercises to help you survey your own interests, knowledge, and life experiences and to choose and focus your topic.

- View speeches on the **VideoLab CD-ROM** and respond to the questions that ask you to assess the effectiveness of the supporting materials that the speakers employ.

- Once you have decided how you want to organize one of your speeches, use the **Online SpeechStudio** to locate the exercises that will lead you through an outline draft. Then, check your work by using an outline check sheet.

- Having trouble with organization? Complete the exercises on the **VideoLab CD-ROM** that present you with scrambled outlines to unscramble, and get feedback on your efforts.

- What style of delivery do you prefer? View several speeches on the **VideoLab CD-ROM**, and then complete the exercises to allow you to consider the relative merits of different styles of delivery.

- Once you have chosen some presentational aids that you plan to use in a speech, go to the **Online SpeechStudio** and use the checklist you find there to assess their potential effectiveness.

- What makes for a good persuasive speech? Using the **VideoLab CD-ROM**, view a short persuasive speech and complete the assessment exercise.

- Use the **Online SpeechStudio** exercises to see if you can detect fallacies in inductive and deductive reasoning.

- Will you do a group presentation in class? If so, use the **Online SpeechStudio** to find evaluation forms that can be used with team and other sorts of group presentations.

- Has your instructor asked you to function as part of a group of peer critics during class? For guidance on how to approach this task, go to the **Online SpeechStudio** and complete the sample assignment for a peer-critic panel.

These are only a few examples of the nearly two hundred supportive learning exercises that are available to you as you strive to learn throughout the course of the semester. They are designed to supplement and enhance the text by giving you media-based opportunities for learning and by creating an interactive learning environment. As you work your way through any exercise, you will be given feedback on the quality of your work. For instance, if you are completing a quiz and you select the wrong answer, you will immediately learn that the response is wrong, and you will be given reasons for why the response is not the best, as well as be presented with questions and hints that will lead you in a better direction.

You will also be given many opportunities to listen to student speakers addressing diverse topics. As you complete many of the exercises, you will have the chance to practice thoughtful critical listening.

Many of the exercises ask for focused reactions. For instance, you may be asked to watch a portion of a speech and look specifically at how effectively the speaker introduces and concludes the speech (rather than offer a more global assessment). This progressive approach to speech criticism makes the task of critically listening to the speech more manageable and productive. Moreover, you may become better able to listen critically to peers and to offer thoughtful feedback during class as a result of practicing these skills outside of class. In short, the multimedia edition of this text offers several educational advantages to you by

- giving you multiple, media-rich opportunities for learning outside the classroom,
- providing you with the tools you need to be better prepared for your in-class performances,
- offering you excellent and immediate feedback as you strive to master the text and course content,
- providing strong connections between your in-class and out-of-class learning experiences,

- making learning dynamic, interactive, and enjoyable.

Taken as a whole, this media-enhanced edition will contribute to an enriched learning environment for both you and your classmates.

A Guide to Our Ancillary Package for Students

The multimedia edition of *Public Speaking: Connecting You and Your Audience* is accompanied by a number of distinguishing ancillary items designed to make the book an engaging learning tool, helping you to:

- Overcome your fear of speaking
- Practice your presentational skills
- Master your delivery
- Ensure your success as a speaker.

These ancillary items include the following material:

Companion Web Site for Students

Featuring Self-tests, PowerPoint Slides, Great Speeches Video Clips, and Reading List

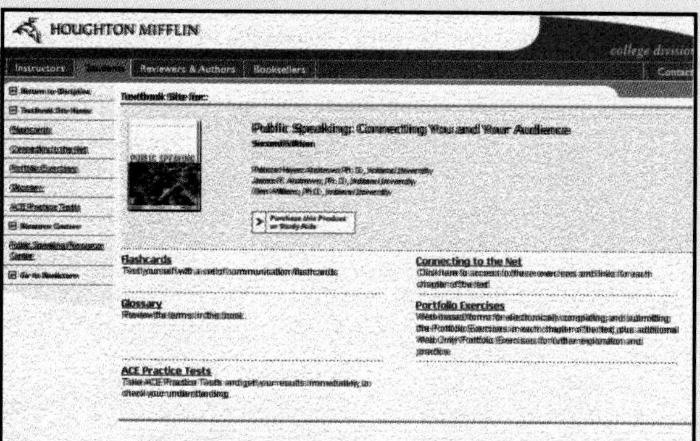

Online SpeechStudio

(Represented by the icon in the margins of the text). This online resource allows you to develop speech outlines and speeches within HTML-based forms. You complete assessment tools to help you develop your skills as a speaker, and these can be used by instructors as evaluation tools. The Online SpeechStudio helps you organize thoughtful and thorough speeches in the following ways:

- It offers you different types of speech design from which to choose when composing speeches using the tool.
- Each speech design features an outliner that allows you to identify a key point and enter supporting information in an essay box, enter a subpoint and that information, and so on until a speech outline is created.

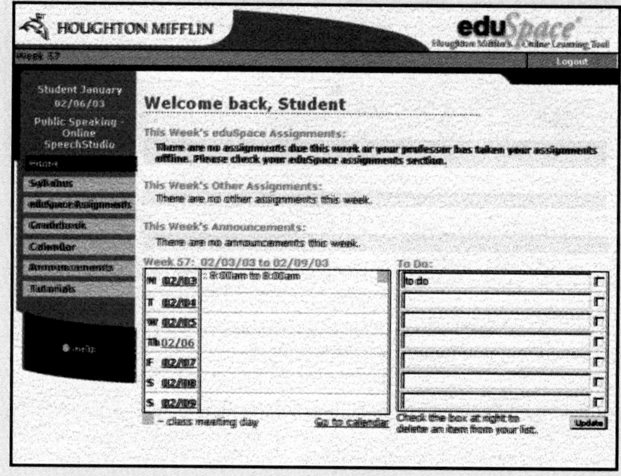

- A checklist at the end of each outliner prompts you to recognize the weaknesses of the speech, offering you valuable feedback.
- Self-assessments also help you to evaluate how ready you are to confront an audience, and whether or not you understand your audiences as thoroughly as possible.

Student VideoLab CD-ROM (represented by the ⊛ icon in the margins of the text) This technology tool uses digital video to create an interactive study tool for you that can be used both independently and in conjunction with the instructor. It allows you to watch speeches and follow along with outlines, a speech manuscript, and critical analysis, enabling you to see the book's concepts at work on screen.

Ten lessons, organized much like chapters in a book, detail different concepts covered in the text, such as listening, presentation, gesturing, and speech topic.

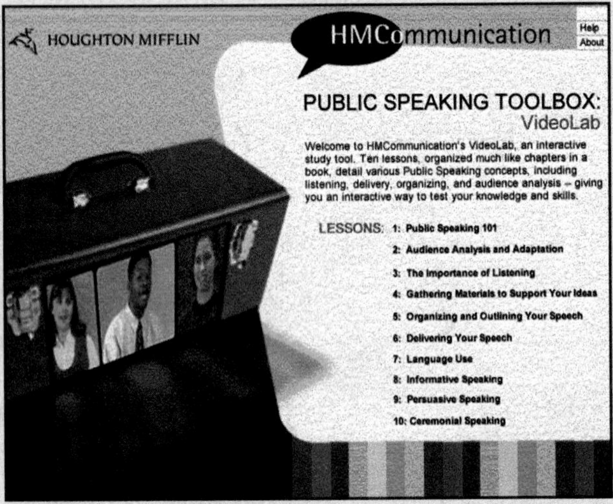

The Screening Room shows a digital video of a student speech in full on the left of the screen, while five options can be clicked on the right to examine specific aspects of the speech, such as:

Text: You can read the manuscript of the speech as it scrolls along with the corresponding video.

Outline: You can follow along with the speech outline as you watch the video.

Notecards: This view allows you to identify the key points of the speech by seeing what the speaker's notecards look like.

Content Analysis: This offers insight into the instructor's criticism of the speech, helping you understand important speech criteria and grading.

Delivery: This provides analysis of the overall discussion and delivery of the speech.

A series of three drills in each lesson provide an opportunity for assessment after viewing the speech in the Screening Room. The first drill examines the speech viewed in the Screening Room, asking several practice questions. A second focuses on another video, asking more practice questions. The third drill expands on a topic covered earlier in the lesson but not based on the Screening Room speech.

The Tips to Remember reiterate key points and highlight useful things to remember from the lesson.

The Next Step engages you in the application of the skills covered in the lesson.

PUBLIC SPEAKING

Connecting You and Your Audience

SECOND EDITION

PATRICIA HAYES ANDREWS
Indiana University

JAMES R. ANDREWS
Indiana University

GLEN WILLIAMS
Southeast Missouri State University

Houghton Mifflin Company Boston New York

We dedicate this work to three teacher-scholars who have been sources of inspiration for us and for generations of teachers and students of communication—as teachers, friends, colleagues, and role models: J. Jeffery Auer, late Professor of Speech Communication, Indiana University; Robert G. Gunderson, late Professor of Speech Communication, Indiana University; and Raymond G. Smith, late Professor of Speech Communication, Indiana University.

Sponsoring Editor: Adam Forrand
Associate Editor: Kristen Desmond LeFevre
Editorial Associate: Brigitte Maser
Senior Project Editors: Rachel D'Angelo Wimberly, Fred Burns
Editorial Assistant: Shanya Dingle
Senior Production/Design Coordinator: Sarah Ambrose
Senior Manufacturing Coordinator: Marie Barnes
Marketing Manager: Barbara LeBuhn

Cover Photography: Stefan May/Stone, Eyewire (four small images)

Acknowledgments: p. 2, Bob Daemmrich/Stock Boston, Inc.; p. 27, David Young-Wolff/PhotoEdit; p. 48, Tony Freeman/PhotoEdit; p. 76, Gary Walts/The Image Works; p. 99, David Young-Wolff/PhotoEdit; p. 118, AP/Wide World Photos; p.148, Mark Wilson/Newsmakers/Liaison; p. 168, Nancy Richmond/The Image Works; p. 184, Reprinted by the permission of the American Cancer Society, Inc. Netscape Communicator browser window copyright © 1999 Netscape Communications Corporation. Used with permission; p. 198, Associated Press; p. 222, Bob Daemmrich/Stock Boston; p. 256, Associated Press; p. 281, Associated Press; p. 309, Jim Erickson/The Stock Market; p. 336, Jeff Greenberg/PhotoEdit; p. 363, Robert E. Daemmrich/Tony Stone Images; p. 391, © Bob Daemmrich/The Image Works; p. 426, Tom Stewart/The Stock Market; p. 443, Walter Hodges/Tony Stone Images.

Copyright © 2002 by Houghton Mifflin Company. All rights reserved. 2004 impression.

No part of this work may be reproduced or transmitted in any form or by any means, electronic or mechanical, including photocopying and recording, or by any information storage or retrieval system without the prior written permission of Houghton Mifflin Company unless such copying is expressly permitted by federal copyright law. Address inquiries to College Permissions, Houghton Mifflin Company, 222 Berkeley Street, Boston, MA 02116-3764.

Printed in the U.S.A.

Library of Congress Control Number: 2002117741
Instructor's Annotated Edition ISBN: 0-618-37367-5
Student Edition ISBN: 0-618-37366-7

2 3 4 5 6 7 8 9 – WEB – 07 06 05

Brief Contents

Contents

CHAPTER 15 The Persuasive Process 363

CHAPTER 16 Arguing Persuasively 391

Spotlight On . . .

Preface

As we enter a new century, the most important skills are those that help us to communicate effectively with one another. Chief among these communication skills is public speaking. The ability and the right to speak in public has been central to creating and sustaining democratic ways of life for nearly four thousand years. Those who command public speaking skills share their insights and ideas, influence and persuade, and move others to act. And they do so in all kinds of contexts—in the court, in the Congress, and, certainly, in the classroom!

OUR APPROACH AND THEMES

Three convictions guided our writing of the second edition of *Public Speaking: Connecting You and Your Audience:*

- We are convinced that public speaking is both essential and pervasive. Students will make speeches in college, and will continue to speak in public as professionals and members of their communities.
- We believe that public speaking is a communicative partnership between a speaker and an audience. No speaker can succeed alone—the audience is crucial to the planning, delivery, and outcome of the speech.
- We are convinced that public speaking, while an important skill, is more than a skill. Truly effective public speakers have ideas or information worth communicating, can think clearly and reason soundly, and have the sensitivity and desire to connect with their listeners. Our overriding goal is to help students to become the best public speakers they can be.

Building the Speaker-Audience Partnership

One of the major themes of our book is the commitment to the speaker-listener partnership. From the earliest planning stages of a speech to the moments of reflecting on it afterwards, the listeners are central to everything a speaker does. Speakers need to consider the listeners' interests in tandem with their own. They need to ask: what are the listeners' likely values and beliefs regarding this topic? How can this speech help them learn? How can it encourage them to accept new ideas? How can it move them to act? We focus on helping students learn to ask themselves: *How can I connect with my audience?*

While we tend to speak of "the audience" as if it were a homogeneous group, the typical audience is made up of all kinds of people. Its members may be diverse in terms of race, religion, and gender. They may be from many parts of the world, and they may have widely varied interests and values. Being mindful of this diversity is crucial to connecting with any audience. In our book, we stress audience diversity and offer advice on understanding and responding to it.

Speaking ethically is also an overarching concern which is grounded in the speaker-listener partnership. Ethical speaking means keeping the audience's needs, concerns, and welfare at heart while setting forth to achieve specific speaking goals. Ethical considerations thus appear in nearly every chapter of our book as a constant reminder of their centrality to effective public speaking.

Involving the Reader

We believe that students will better learn how to prepare and deliver speeches if our book engages their interest and attention throughout. As we describe below, every chapter gives students ample opportunities for interaction and engagement with the text, including active pedagogy, integrated videos, plentiful samples of materials related to every step of the speech-making process, and engaging speech extracts and examples.

THE PLAN OF THE BOOK

We organized our book to help students develop their public speaking skills step by step. Of course, different instructors may choose to assign the chapters in a different order, and our book welcomes that kind of flexibility. We divide the text into five parts, beginning with an introduction to the key principles of public speaking and concluding with chapters devoted to special kinds of speeches. In addition, the appendix offers a selection of complete speeches for analysis.

Introducing Public Speaking

Part I gives an overview of the communication process and the basic principles of public speaking as they apply to both speaker and listener. Chapter 1 presents our model of audience-centered communication and introduces the concept of the speaker-listener partnership. Its preview of basic public speaking principles helps students immediately understand the key concepts and issues addressed throughout the course. We highlight the importance and pervasiveness of public speaking and discuss ethics as central to the speech preparation process. We conclude the chapter by describing several possible first speaking assignments (introducing a classmate, offering a tribute, giving a toast, or delivering a eulogy), so that students can begin to put public speaking principles into practice. Chapter 2 addresses the issue of communication apprehension (CA). Few books devote such attention to this widespread problem, but we strongly believe that students must understand the factors that may contribute to CA in order to apply the strategies that we suggest for managing it. Chapter 3 examines the importance of listening, particularly from the perspective of the audience, and gives the speaker insights into the audience's listening challenges. We offer guidelines for effective critical listening and suggest ways that the speaker can actually *help* the audience to listen more effectively.

Knowing Yourself and Your Audience

Part II continues our theme of audience-centeredness by helping students to discover what they need to know about their listeners and to plan a specific speech that addresses both their own goals and their audience's interests. We also guide students in using their own resources to decide what to speak about, how to choose an audience-centered purpose, and how to make themselves credible to listeners. Chapter 4 considers audience analysis by examining dimensions of audience diversity, such as age, gender, culture, education, and occupation. We then address certain universal human needs that tend to be shared by members of any audience. Chapter 5 moves beyond audience analysis to explain how to connect to listeners through audience adaptation. After examining situational factors that may influence adaptation, we describe specific methods of gathering information about listeners, with particular attention to administering an audience survey. The chapter concludes with a discussion of ethical considerations in audience adaptation. Chapter 6 is unique in combining an explanation of ethos and speaker credibility with instructions on selecting a speech topic. We discuss strategies for enhancing speaker credibility, as well as ethical considerations in choosing speech topics. Chapter 7 helps students understand the importance of speaking with a purpose, which should be assessed in light of the response sought from the audience. We offer guidance on how to distinguish different types of purposes and how to devise specific purposes and thesis statements.

Developing the Speech

Part III outlines the processes of gathering relevant materials, organizing ideas and information, and finding evidence to support those ideas. Chapter 8 provides in-depth coverage of the research process, including how to initiate a search for information, how to take notes and organize them, how to use the library, how to use the Internet, how to plan and conduct interviews, and how to quote appropriately and cite one's sources. Chapter 9 focuses on making ideas believable and using evidence to support those ideas. We discuss various types of evidence and present criteria that students can use to judge the quality of evidence both as they prepare their own speeches and as they listen to others' speeches. The next step in the speech preparation process is organizing ideas and information, the topic of Chapter 10. We present several different patterns of speech organization, discuss ways of introducing and concluding a speech, and highlight the function of transitions. We guide readers in developing outlines as they progress from the planning to the delivery of a speech. These three chapters set the stage for our exploration of effective presentation techniques.

Presenting the Speech

Part IV describes how a speaker's delivery and language can contribute to a successful, audience-centered speech. It also teaches students how to plan and use presentational aids. Chapter 11 focuses on delivery. While acknowledging diverse delivery styles, we promote the extemporaneous style in most speaking situations. We advance principles of good delivery and offer tips for responding to audience questions. We close the chapter by explaining the crucial distinction between "sounding good" and "being sound." Chapter 12 explores style and effective language. Consistent with our audience-centered model, we advise the use of language to promote audience understanding, to make ideas clearer to listeners, and to add interest to the speech. Chapter 13 discusses the functions of presentational aids, surveying the various options available and providing guidelines for their use. We devote a special section of this chapter to computer-generated presentational aids. Having learned how to present a speech effectively, students will be ready to consider particular applications of public speaking principles.

Types of Public Speaking

In Part V we turn our attention to specific speech types, as well as to special contexts in which public speaking often takes place. Chapter 14 explores speaking to inform. In addition to presenting the varied forms of informative speeches, we examine the overarching functions of informative speaking, show how to organize such speeches, and discuss the role of listener motivation in learning from them. We also consider ethical concerns specific to informative speaking. Chapters 15 and 16 address persuasion. In Chapter 15, we begin by examining persuasive issues that revolve around questions of fact, definition, cause, value, and policy; we then consider organizational strategies appropriate for addressing each of these types of issues. Next, we discuss different persuasive purposes; to stimulate, convince, and activate. We conclude the chapter by examining the use of emotional appeals in persuasive speaking, as always with attention to ethics. While Chapter 15 focuses on the role of emotion in persuasion, Chapter 16 addresses the logical side of persuading an audience. We look at how to construct a sound argument and how to use inductive and deductive reasoning. The chapter alerts both listener and speaker to common reasoning fallacies and distinguishes between reasoning and rationalization. In the book's final two chapters, we move on to a consideration of special speaking contexts. Chapter 17 examines speaking for ceremonial occasions. After a brief discussion of the functions of ceremonial speeches, we consider specific types: speeches of introduction, acceptance, and inspiration, and after-dinner speeches. While students may not make these kinds of speeches often in their lives, when they do, the event will probably be meaningful and memorable. Chapter 18 addresses communication in the workplace. Recognizing that team work is an increasing responsibility in organizational contexts, this chapter begins with a consideration of small group communication, group leadership, power and leadership, and team work. We discuss various kinds of public presentations made by groups and conclude with sections on proposal and sales presentations, which are often given in business and professional speaking contexts.

Appendix

The Appendix provides a variety of complete speeches for consideration and analysis. We offer an informative speech, a persuasive speech, and such ceremonial speeches as a tribute, a commencement address, an award acceptance speech, and a eulogy.

SPECIAL FEATURES

The second edition of *Public Speaking: Connecting You and Your Audience* offers a number of distinguishing features designed to make the book an engaging teaching and learning tool.

Integrated Videos and CD-ROM

A unique feature of this book is its integrated video program. Video segments accompany each chapter, and include the following:

- Comparisons of poorly prepared and improved speeches on the same topic, giving students the opportunity to critique the first speech before viewing the improved version
- A student's persuasive speech prepared using different appeals, to illustrate the relative effectiveness of rational and emotional appeals
- "Triggers" that invite students to complete a partial speech, in class or as a take-home exercise

- Interviews with a variety of students and professionals who discuss their experiences with preparing speeches, dealing with communication apprehension, adapting to audiences, and other public speaking issues

We also provide several complete speeches for viewing and discussion on a separate accompanying tape. The speakers featured in the video program include students from introductory public speaking classes, professional public speakers, professionals who speak publicly as part of their jobs, and political speakers. The videos also feature diverse speech types, including standard classroom informative and persuasive speeches, an awards presentation, a motivational speech, a speech of introduction, and a sales presentation. Some speeches were developed specifically for the video program and others were captured as the speaker spoke to a live audience. The video package that accompanies the Second Edition has been edited to offer some different student speakers, new speech topics, and a greater emphasis on speaker diversity.

The videos emphasize to students that public speaking is a critical life skill. In addition, the video program fosters a truly interactive, lively, and challenging classroom learning experience. It gives ample opportunities for discussion, critique, writing, speaking, and role-playing. The brief video segments lend themselves very well to use in the daily classroom. The models the videos provide and the active participation in speech criticism they promote better prepare students to make their own speeches, both in the classroom and beyond.

This multimedia second edition of *Public Speaking: Connecting You and Your Audience* is also accompanied by a free VideoLab student CD-ROM and EduSpace Online SpeechStudio access. These tools provide opportunities for students to further develop their understanding and skills outside of the classroom. The VideoLab offers ten videos of interactive sets of lessons based on student speeches. Students can review the presentation of the speech through five different perspectives (text, outline, notecards, content analysis, and delivery analysis) and engage in exercises that promote comprehension and success. The Online SpeechStudio guides students through the speech preparation process. With self-assessments, speech design outline designs, and checklists, this tool prepares students to deliver a solid performance in the classroom. The Online SpeechStudio is also a classroom management tool with all exercises and activities in HTML, with full e-mail and grade book functionality. Each tool is integrated into the text through point-of-use annotations for proper teaching and learning applications.

Although we make a number of recommendations for how and when all of these resources might be used, instructors are free to use all of our suggestions, some of them, or none of them. The book can stand alone or be used with the amount of video and technology supplementation that best suits you and your students' preferences.

Active Pedagogy

Students learn best when they are actively involved in the learning process. Consistent with this notion, our book's features take an active approach to pedagogy. Chief among these are the *Videos* and *CD-ROM* described above. In addition, we invite students to construct their own *Public Speaking Portfolios.* Portfolio items that appear in the margins of each chapter ask students to immediately apply concepts from the text. The Portfolios break down the speech preparation process into small, manageable steps and encourage students to become actively involved in preparing to speak from the moment they begin to read the book. Their incremental, developmental format encourages a hands-on, systematic approach to mastering public speaking. Portfolio activities may be used as an ongoing journal that the instructor checks from time to time, as homework assignments, or as a private record for students. The Instructor's Resource Manual includes advice on using the Portfolios.

In addition to the Portfolios, *Public Speaking: Connecting You and Your Audience* provides a variety of pedagogical features that direct students, clarify and reinforce the material, and summarize key points. Every chapter contains:

- A *Chapter Survey* to overview key topics addressed in the chapter.
- *Learning Objectives* to give students learning goals against which they can measure their personal progress.
- *Previews* to give readers a map of the material in each section of the chapter.
- *Keep in Mind* boxes to summarize key points within each major section.
- A running *Glossary* to define key terms in the margin, next to their first appearance.
- *Examples* to illustrate, highlight, and clarify principles discussed.
- A *Summary* to reiterate the chapter's core concepts.
- *Questions for Review and Reflection* to help students review the ideas presented in each chapter and to assist them in test preparation.

Further questions for application and analysis can be found in the Instructor's Resource Manual.

Real World Emphasis

One of the great challenges of teaching public speaking is convincing students that this skill will be valuable to them throughout their lives. In our book, we reinforce that message in several different ways. The video shows real speakers in diverse public speaking settings and presents interviews in which professionals talk about how often they speak and how important it is. The book is filled with complete speeches, speech extracts, and quotations from magazines, newspapers, and interviews to reinforce the real-world message.

Complete *Annotated Speeches* appear after nearly a dozen chapters. Our annotations model the process of critiquing a speech text and highlight how the speech applies the principles discussed in the preceding chapters. The *Speeches for Analysis* in the Appendix invite students to analyze and critique texts of student, professional, and political speeches.

Spotlight On ... boxes present speech extracts that demonstrate diverse principles, such as how to make an argument that appeals to the audience's need for safety and security, how to use humor in a speech, and how to use rhetorical questions. These boxes quote politicians, journalists, speech experts, business leaders, and students who share advice on how to speak effectively or testify to the importance of public speaking in their lives.

NEW FEATURES OF THE SECOND EDITION

Some of the major new features of the Second Edition include

Added Support for Instructors

- An Instructor's Annotated Edition
- Enhanced PowerPoint slides
- New videotaped student speeches for analysis and critique
- A revised and reorganized Instructor's Resource Manual with video exercises integrated chapter by chapter
- EduSpace Online Speech Studio: a tutorial and classroom management tool

Added Support for Students

- VideoLab student CD-ROM with interactive student speech video presentations, exercises, and applications
- EduSpace Online SpeechStudio access with self-assessments, speech design tutorials, and checklists for better-prepared speeches
- A companion web site with ACE quizzes and additional exercises to assess students' knowledge and progress
- *Ace Test Bank* allows students to self-test to assess their own understanding and progress
- A web page provides students with additional materials, exercises, and examples that supplement readings in the text

New Content

- First speaking assignment options presented at the end of Chapter 1
- An extended consideration of plagiarism as academic misconduct
- A section on practicing the speech as a strategy for managing communication apprehension
- A discussion of the listening process in terms of hearing, focusing, understanding and remembering
- A separate chapter on audience adaptation, including a major section on creating and administering an audience survey
- An expanded section focusing on evaluating Internet resources
- Tips for presenting speeches using extemporaneous, manuscript, memorized, and impromptu delivery
- Partial outlines illustrate how one topic can be approached from a variety of organizational perspectives
- A discussion of the kinds of issues that call for persuasion, including questions of fact, definition, value, cause, and policy

- Enhanced consideration of organizational patterns for persuasive speeches, such as the refutational pattern
- An expanded discussion of fallacies in reasoning with an added section on testing fallacies
- A new appendix on evaluating speeches and giving constructive feedback
- Four new speeches for review and analysis (appendix), plus eleven annotated speeches interspersed throughout the text
- A new chapter devoted to communication in the workplace, with an extensive consideration of group communication, leadership, power, and effective team membership
- A new section on team presentations
- *Connecting to the Net* boxes added to every chapter

ADDITIONAL SUPPLEMENTS

We designed our package to help instructors get the most out of the text. Toward that end, we offer an Instructor's Resource Manual that presents a specific approach to teaching the public speaking course. We offer sample syllabi for a variety of possible course structures. For every book chapter, we provide:

- Key points for lecture/discussion
- In-class activities and applications to help students learn the principles under consideration
- Activities and assignments for students to complete outside of class
- Guides to using the *Portfolios*
- Guides to using the Video Segments
- Short commentaries, teaching advice, exercises, and activities shared by accomplished public speakers and scholars from around the country

Other Ancillary Materials

We also offer a Print Test Bank with a full complement of multiple choice, true/false, and essay questions aimed at varying levels of Bloom's Taxonomy, from recall and application to analysis and synthesis. A Computerized Test Bank is available in Windows™ and Macintosh® versions. In addition, students can quiz themselves along the way by accessing the *Ace Test,* which provides sample questions aimed at determining if students are grasping fundamental concepts. PowerPoint slides are also available for instructors. Ask your Houghton Mifflin representative about the two additional videos that we offer: *Student Speeches* and *Contemporary Great Speeches.* Direct your students to the topic-specific workbooks they can purchase for extra help with two key areas of the course: *Overcoming Your Fear of Public Speaking* and *The Multicultural Activities Workbook for Public Speaking.* And be sure to visit the Communications homepage on Houghton Mifflin's College Division web site: **http://college.hmco.com.**

Support for Teachers and Teacher Training

We uniquely emphasize teacher training with two special supplements. Many basic public speaking courses are taught by inexperienced instructors and most course directors must grapple with training and developing graduate students as teachers. To support course directors in these training and development efforts, we offer a Teacher Training Video to introduce novice instructors to teaching. The video presents brief (90-second) trigger scenarios that portray problems that public speaking instructors commonly face, such as dealing with the high-CA student, managing in-class challenges to authority, making judgments about cheating and plagiarism, handling class discussions that go awry, finding ways of balancing being a TA (Teaching Assistant) with being a graduate student, eliminating sexism and other discriminatory behavior from the classroom, handling grade complaints, and other issues.

A brief TA Training Manual accompanies the video and offers advice on using it. We point to questions that each video segment raises and offer suggestions for different ways of approaching each problem. Course directors can use these questions and suggestions to lead TAs in discussing the scenarios or TAs may be asked to take up where the scenario concludes and to role-play appropriate ways of resolving the conflict (to be followed by discussion and critique). The manual and videos are aimed at new instructors and are ideally suited for use in teacher training programs.

Finally, for all instructors, an Instructor's Annotated Edition accompanies the second edition of our text. This special edition provides specific guidance on how significant concepts introduced in the book might be taught. Various icons that appear in the margins direct the instructor to assignments, video clips, activities, and other support features that offer specific advice for those teaching with our book. For the novice instructor, these pedagogical suggestions will help support his or her development as a teacher. For the experienced instructor, the IAE will point the way to the relevant ancillaries and will offer suggestions for alternative pedagogical strategies.

ACKNOWLEDGMENTS

Surely our book would never have come about without the support, encouragement, assistance, and guidance of many friends, students, colleagues, and others. First, we want to thank the wonderful staff at Houghton Mifflin Company. We are especially grateful to Adam Forrand, our Sponsoring Editor, who has guided us with incredibly innovative ideas, whose support for our project has been unwavering, and whose enthusiasm and commitment have been ongoing sources of encouragement and inspiration. We are also grateful to Kristen Desmond LeFevre, Associate Editor, whose many constructive suggestions, endless patience, and boundless energy kept us on task while keeping our spirits high. Adam and Kristen helped us rise to each new challenge and made us realize how fortunate we are to be part of the Houghton Mifflin team. We also extend our thanks to Rachel D'Angelo Wimberly, our Senior Project Editor, whose gentle probes made us mindful of each new deadline. She set the agenda for bringing the book to fruition.

We are indebted to the staff of the Sanders Group, who worked with us to create the extensive video component of our project. In particular, Larry Laswell, our neighbor, friend, and constant supporter, approved the project and has been with us as a creative source of support and enthusiasm throughout.

Alan Backler, a lifelong friend and colleague, helped us formulate the plans for the videos and offered insightful feedback on all phases of the project—and he kept us sane with his wonderful sense of humor. Finally, Sarah Jeffers, our producer, has been a delight to work with. Her excellent technical skills, her patience and perseverance, and her kindness and compassion have sustained us during our work. Although the video shoots could be exhausting, we always looked forward to working with the Sanders Group team!

We are also deeply grateful to the graduate students at Indiana University and Texas A&M University, who generously gave of their time and considerable talent by participating in our video project, giving scripted speeches and acting in the TA training video. In particular, we extend our thanks to Kari Anderson, Holly Baxter, Andy Billings, Sarah Bonewits, Josh Boyd, Martín Carcasson, Darryl Clark, Arne G'Schwind, Jeannette Heidewald, Jeff McKinney, Darryl Neher, Carolyn Novak, Claire Procopio, Kristy Sheeler, Karen Taylor, and John Tindell. Although we knew that our graduate students were very bright, we were amazed to see that they also possessed considerable acting ability—and, not surprisingly, excellent public speaking skills! We also thank the numerous undergraduates who volunteered to provide audiences for many of our taping sessions.

We would like to extend a special thanks to the reviewers whose thoughtful critiques helped us to refine and to realize our plans for this text:

> Bernard Armada, *University of St. Thomas;* Linda C. Atwell, *George Mason University;* Lisa J. Barr, *DePaul University;* Deborah Craig, *Southwest Missouri State University;* Barbara Franzen, *Central Community College;* Todd S. Frobish, *Iona College;* John Gore; *Indiana University-South Bend;* Robert Greenstreet, *East Central University;* Nichola D. Gutgold, *Pennsylvania State Berks-Lehigh Valley College;* Rita C. Hubbard, *Christopher Newport University;* Scott Jensen, *Webster University;* Sandra Lakey, *Pennsylvania College of Technology;* Rebecca Litke, *California State University-Northridge;* Dave McCowan, *Circleville Bible College;* Patricia Milford, *California University of Pennsylvania;* Nina-Jo Moore, *Appalachian State University;* Darrell Mullins, *Salisburg State University;* Kenna J. Reeves, *Emporia State University;* Chris Skiles, *University of Iowa;* Susan Smyth, *DeVry Institute of Technology;* Dee Stout, *Concorde Career College;* Beth Stewart, *Jackson State Community College;* Carl L. Thameling, *University of Louisiana at Monroe.*

We are indebted as well to the many friends and colleagues who supported us in varying ways throughout our work: Michael P. Hogan, Professor of English, Southern Missouri State University; Debbie Tindell, Research Assistant, Department of Psychology, Texas A&M University; Joe Schadler, Instructor and Technician, Speech Communication Instructional Laboratory, Texas A&M University; Elaine Gass, Reference Librarian, Texas A&M University; Maryann Hight, Instructional Services Coordinator, Indiana University; Emily M. Okada, Librarian for Instructional Services, Indiana University; Carolyn J. Smith, Humanities Bibliographer, Texas A&M University; Martin J. Medhurst, Professor of Speech Communication, Texas A&M University; Rick Rigsby, Professor of Speech Communication, Texas A&M University; Carolyn Calloway-Thomas, Associate Professor of Communication, Indiana University; and Tony Fehrenbacher, undergraduate student, Indiana University.

PATRICIA HAYES ANDREWS, *Indiana University*

JAMES R. ANDREWS, *Indiana University*

GLEN WILLIAMS, *Southeast Missouri State University*

PART I

Preliminaries: Introducing Public Speaking

Part I introduces the communication process and the basic principles of public speaking as they apply to you as a speaker and a listener. You will also learn how to manage the apprehension everyone feels when facing an audience. With this foundation in place, you will be ready to learn how to put these principles into action.

1 Public Speaking and the Communication Process

CHAPTER SURVEY

CHAPTER OBJECTIVES

After studying this chapter, you should be able to

1. **discuss the importance of developing public speaking skills for the classroom and for professional and community life.**
2. **explore how public speaking is important historically.**
3. **explain the meaning and importance of audience-centered communication.**
4. **know how ethical principles apply to public speaking.**
5. **list the key principles involved in preparing yourself to speak.**
6. **give a short speech.**

COMMUNICATION SKILLS IN THE TWENTY-FIRST CENTURY

Preview Communication is an integral part of our lives, occurring in a wide variety of settings. Public speaking has always been crucial in the conduct of human affairs and has a direct bearing on our own successes—interpersonally, at school and work, in our community, and in various groups to which we belong. In the contemporary world, with its increasing complexity and diversity, the ability to communicate effectively has become even more crucial.

What sorts of qualities do you especially value in your friends, family, business associates, and the other people in your life? How do these qualities affect your relationships with them? As we enter the twenty-first century, communication skills are becoming increasingly valued. Surveys reveal that most of us experience problems arising from poor communication, and we wish the people with whom we work, live, and interact could communicate more effectively.[1] Employers and professional groups also emphasize good communication skills and frequently offer training to bolster those skills.[2] What are these communication skills that concern us on so many levels? They include effective listening in the classroom, good teamwork, the

SPOTLIGHT ON... **Communication in the Corporate World**

Former Chrysler CEO Lee Iacocca

On public speaking: "Of course, the more common way to communicate with your people is to talk to them as a group. Public speaking... requires a lot of preparation. There's just no way around it—you have to do your homework. A speaker may be well informed, but if he hasn't thought out exactly what he wants to say *today, to this audience,* he has no business taking up other people's valuable time."

On adapting to audiences: "It's important to talk to people in their own language.... That's what Bob Hope is doing when he sends an advance man to scout his audience so that he can make jokes that are special to them and their situation. If you're watching on television, you might not understand what he's saying. Nevertheless, the live audience always appreciates it when a speaker has taken the trouble to learn something about who they are. Not everyone can afford an advance man, but the message is clear: public speaking does not mean impersonal speaking."

Lee Iacocca, *Iacocca: An Autobiography.* (New York: Bantam, 1984), pp. 54–55.

ability to perform well in a job interview, and the ability to stand in front of others and make a speech. This text focuses largely on speaking in public, although the principles we stress here apply to other communication situations as well.

Speaking with others in any **context** can be quite a challenge. Think of the time you tried to persuade your parents to lend you the family car. Or perhaps you've found yourself unable to articulate your ideas in a work group because of the domineering style of one of the group's members. Or perhaps you simply could not think of what to say when a recruiter asked, "Tell me about yourself," in a job interview.

context the situational factors and setting in which one speaks

Speaking in public, whether it be standing on a platform facing a large audience, addressing a small committee, or making a classroom presentation, presents a special challenge. It arouses our anxiety more than any other communication situation, yet it also offers us a unique opportunity to share our ideas and to influence others.

Your notion of what it means to give a *public* speech may not always be accurate. You might picture yourself in front of a large audience, but in most cases when you make public presentations, you are talking to much smaller audiences. Reporting on a recycling project in your dorm, describing a plan for a membership drive in a student organization, and making a short speech in a boardroom environment with only a half dozen employees and supervisors as your audience are just some of the other types of public speaking situations you are likely to encounter.

The Importance of Public Speaking

Whatever the context, speaking in public is becoming increasingly common. You will find that an ability to express yourself clearly and effectively will be of help to you right now and throughout your college career, both in classes and in organizations to which you belong, and the principles you learn as a public speaker can carry over to your written communication—papers and take-home exams—as well. Further, more and more colleges and universities are asking students to demonstrate proficiency in communication before they are allowed to graduate.[3] As a result, students are making oral presentations in classes as diverse as marketing, biology, history, and foreign language. Many students taking public speaking courses are already in the workplace. Many are

This speaker at a community meeting recognizes the importance of public speaking as he seeks to influence his listeners' beliefs and actions. *(The Syracuse Newspaper/ The Image Works)*

returning after years spent pursuing a career, raising a family, or working to save the money to go back to college.

Although administrators, board directors, and chief executive officers have always given speeches, in today's professional world, others are being called on to give speeches with considerable regularity. Organizations of all types are downsizing, eliminating many middle managers. As this happens, managerial work is being carried out by employees throughout the organization. A team leader whose group wants the company to make an investment in a new project will have to present the team's ideas to others higher in the organization. Successful professionals, whether they work in business, health care, education, law, or government, will inevitably need to make presentations sometime, somewhere, most likely many times in many places.

Whether you end up speaking in public frequently or rarely, when you do speak, the situation is usually quite important: Your professor asks you to teach the class one day—for 20 percent of your grade. You decide to run for student government and must give a speech on what you stand for. Your child's school music program is about to be eliminated, and you must appear before the school board to make a plea to save it. You are representing your fellow employees in arguing for less mandatory overtime. Your company is moving to a new computer system, and you must persuade your fellow employees that the benefits will outweigh the disruption of the changeover.

In a practical sense, being able to speak well in front of others is an important communication skill that you will need to function effectively across diverse situations throughout your life. In a more philosophic sense, the ability to speak well, to articulate your ideas persuasively, and to defend your beliefs against the attacks of others has long been the foundation of democracy, wherever and whenever it is found.

From the time of the Greeks, democratic governments have given citizens the *right* to speak. In addition, many who have played significant roles in advancing vital social, economic, political, and religious causes have also felt the *responsibility* to speak in public. The eloquent speeches of Winston Churchill and Franklin Roosevelt gave hope and inspiration to their embattled citizens during World

PORTFOLIO 1.1

The American Landscape

List the various opportunities you regularly have to listen to political leaders and to fellow citizens as they address social and political issues. Briefly answer the following:

1. What functions do those messages serve?
2. What impact do they have?
3. How does "free speech" differentiate our society from societies that are more restrictive?

War II. Think of Martin Luther King Jr.'s powerful message of peace in the midst of the violent reactions to the Civil Rights movement. President Ronald Reagan's moving tribute to the deceased astronauts of the space shuttle *Challenger* consoled a stunned and mourning country after the shuttle's explosion in 1986. In 1996 Jan License, a self-described rape survivor, recounted her terrible ordeal in a speech to the Republican National Convention in which she rallied support for victims' rights.

CONNECTING TO THE NET

Significant speeches have had an impact on human affairs throughout history. To gain some sense of the power of speech, go to **http://college.hmco.com/communication/andrews/public_speaking/2e/students/** and click on *Connecting to the 'Net.* From there, follow the link to *Historic Speeches.* Spend time browsing the speeches listed and select a speech that interests you. Why do you think the speech you selected was viewed as important at the time it was given? In what ways might the speaker have connected with her or his audience?

Public speeches are important. They sustain our democratic way of life; they provide opportunities for us to share our knowledge, life experience, and ideas with others; and they create a communication context in which ideas can be advanced and listeners can respond. Ideally, all who participate will grow from the experience, will come to understand more about the bases for their differences, and will begin to discover some emerging common ground. The public speech acts as a bridge between speaker and audience. This textbook will give you the materials you need—the fundamental principles of public speaking—to strengthen the span that connects you with your listeners (see Figure 1.1). Of course, you build a bridge for people to cross both ways, so the principles you learn should also help you improve your skills as a consumer as well as a producer of communication.

Speaking to Today's Audience

The speaker's task today is in many ways different from the problems that faced speakers in the past. Greek orators had to project their voices very well, or no one would hear them. Today we just assume that if we are speaking to a large crowd, a microphone will be there to amplify our voices. Speakers of the past could often count on a homogeneous audience. In fact, not very far back in history, most public speeches were given by men to men. Such homogeneity

FIGURE 1.1 **Basic Principles of Public Speaking**

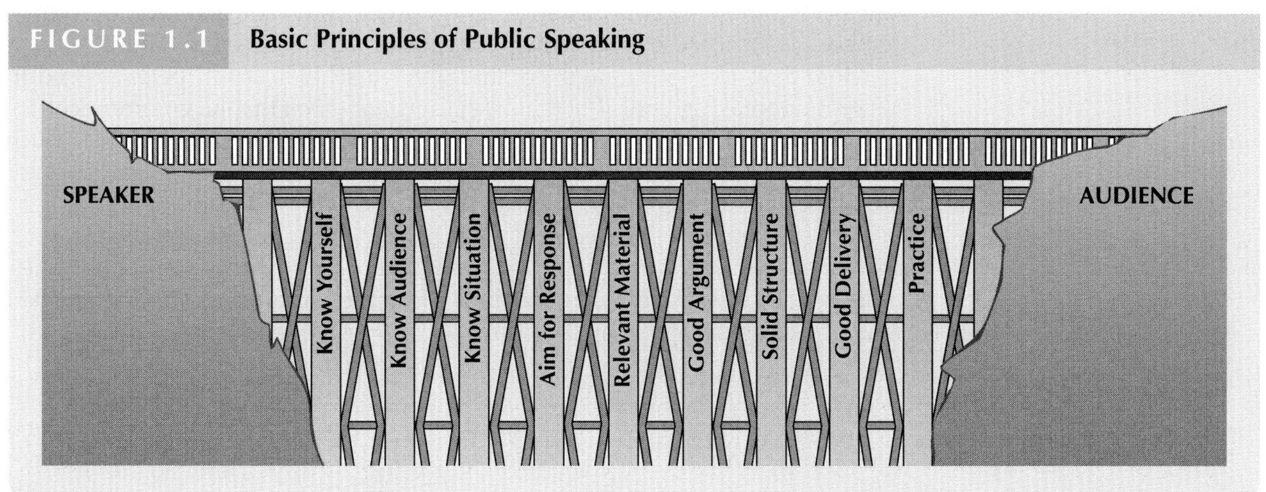

of sex—and race—simplified the speaker's task in that he could make certain assumptions about his audience that no speaker could make today.

Today we live in a world of increasing diversity where men and women of varied ages, races, religions, educational levels, and ethnic and regional backgrounds come together. During the 1980s, immigrants accounted for more than one-third of the U.S. population growth. In addition, for the first time, this increasing cultural diversity can be seen in all regions of the country.[4] When you make a speech in your classroom, your community, or your place of employment, your audience will almost undoubtedly be more diverse than it would have been even a decade ago. You can't assume that most of your listeners will be like you, sharing the same values, beliefs, and experiences. All listeners won't view fraternities and sororities in the same light that you do; all listeners won't trust the police to protect them; all listeners won't agree that the measure of success is the amount of money you make; all listeners won't interpret "moral values" in the same way, and some listeners may reject such values. One challenge for today's public speakers, then, is to acknowledge and adapt to the diversity of their audiences. To be effective, public speeches must be **audience-centered.**

audience-centered focused on one's audience—their characteristics, needs, and well-being

PUBLIC SPEAKING AS AUDIENCE-CENTERED COMMUNICATION

Preview Communication models that stressed the role of the speaker have been replaced by models recognizing that the aim of communication is to get a response from an audience. An audience-centered model of communication emphasizes communication as a partnership between the speaker and listeners.

The Audience-Centered Communication Model

Early communication models stressed the speaker and the importance of the choices he or she needed to make. Speakers had to decide what topics to address, how to support their views with evidence, whether to use note cards or manuscripts, and how to dress. Although all these factors are relevant to preparing a speech, the traditional view of communication minimized the importance of the audience by assuming that speakers who made good choices would succeed and that those who made poor choices were doomed to failure.

More than forty years ago, communication scholar David Berlo argued in his groundbreaking book *The Process of Communication* that all communication, including public speaking, should be viewed from a **process perspective.**[5] Such a process is a two-way, reciprocal exchange in which speaker and listener exchange messages and negotiate meanings.

process perspective communication viewed as a reciprocal exchange between speaker and listener in which meanings are negotiated

As a speaker, you share control with the audience. As a member of the audience, you send messages to the speaker. Because of cultural norms of politeness, you may send only certain kinds of nonverbal messages to the speaker while he or she is speaking, but during the question-and-answer period, you may also choose to speak—to ask questions, make arguments, or provide the speaker with information.

Figure 1.2 depicts the public speaking process from an audience-centered communication perspective. As you can see, this model is inherently listener

FIGURE 1.2 An Audience-Centered Communication Model

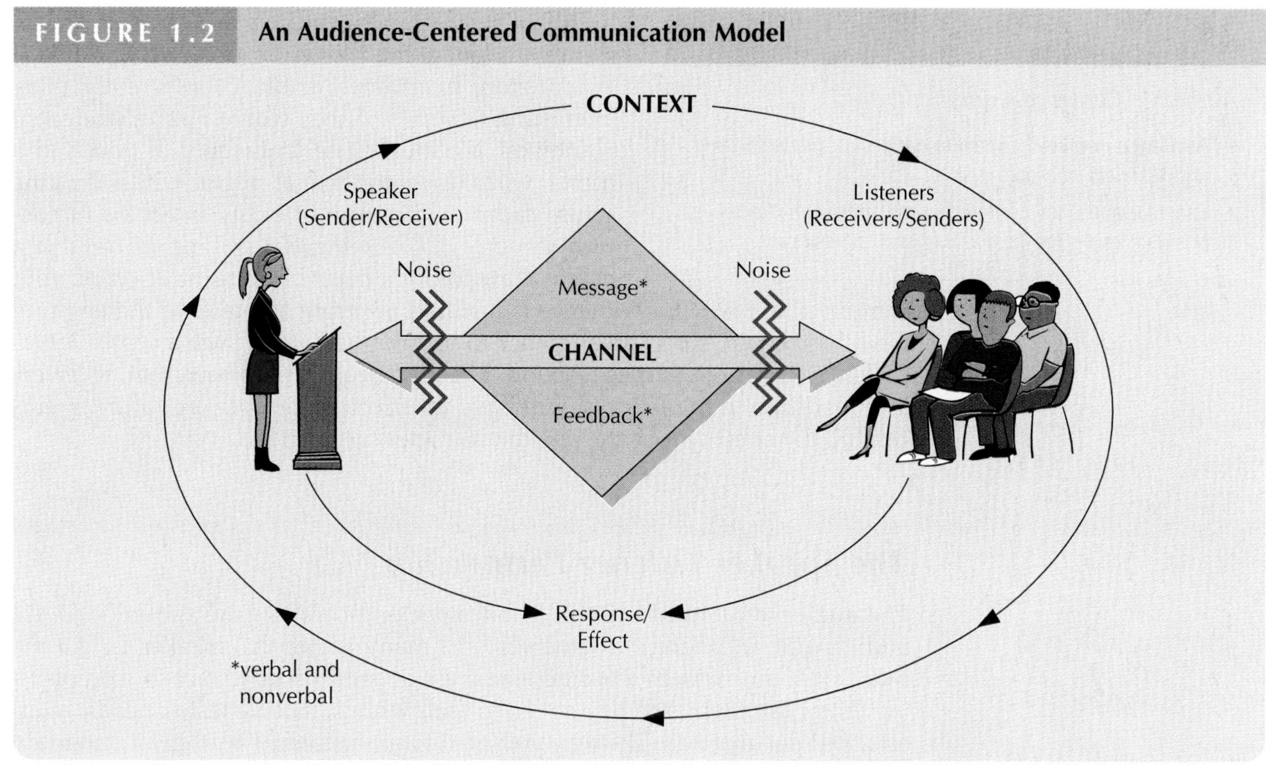

centered. Both speaker and listeners send **verbal messages** and **nonverbal messages**. Both speaker and listeners send and receive **feedback**. Good speakers are vigilant, watching for any kind of feedback they might get from the audience. They look for signs of interest or boredom; they listen to the audience for sounds of confusion or consent. If listeners appear confused, a good speaker will try to explain an idea in a different way or give another example. If listeners seem bored, a good speaker will try to come up with an interesting illustration or story related to the point she or he is making. So the speaker, while primarily a sender, is also a receiver who makes adaptations depending on the messages that come back from the audience. Listeners, while primarily receivers, are not passive—they feed information about their reactions to the speaker. Good speakers are adaptive and flexible, understanding that the communication process involves mutual control and choice making.

verbal messages messages created via language or code

nonverbal messages facial expressions, gestures, vocal qualities, and physical movements that reinforce or contradict one's verbal messages

feedback nonverbal and verbal reactions to another's message

Sometimes messages flow smoothly; other times **noise**—any interference, ranging from a squeaky microphone to conflicting attitudes—may intervene to distort or interrupt the message flow. A hot, stuffy room will offer a greater challenge to a speaker than a comfortable setting. Furthermore, all of us filter messages. We understand, believe, or act based partly on our own experiences, the values we hold, our age or sex, or our cultural practices. These factors will be discussed in detail in Chapters 4 and 5 on audience analysis and adaptation, but for now just remember that the situation in which the speaking occurs and the variety of backgrounds and interests of the listeners can influence the way the message is received, and a good speaker will try to anticipate the nature and extent of these influences.

noise any interference that distorts or interrupts message flow

KEEP IN MIND 1.1

Audience-Centered Communication

- Audience-centered communication connects speaker and listeners in a partnership.
- Effective audience-centered communication produces positive results for the speaker and the listeners.

All of this will be going on in a context. If you were a student at the University of North Carolina at Wilmington, hurricanes would be inherently more interesting to you than they would be to a student at Southwest Missouri State University. If you had a friend who was attacked at night while walking across campus, the issue of safety might be of concern to you. If, following the spiking of trees in a nearby state forest, a debate had been raging on your campus about whether violence is justified in trying to preserve the environment, you could expect an audience to be informed about such a controversy.

Ultimately, both parties respond. The message, as it has been sent, received, and modified in the process, will have an effect. If the speaker has been successful, the effect will be the one that the speaker intended.

The Speaker-Listener Partnership

The audience-centered view of public speaking connects the speaker and the audience in an ongoing partnership. In many ways, the speaker is like the owner of a business. In a business, success depends in large measure on pleasing your customers. You have to learn their whims, moods, tastes, needs, interests, and peculiarities. The way you treat your customers is often as important as the quality of the car, flowers, shirt, vegetables, or skis you are selling. Chances are, if your customers don't like or trust you and/or your products and services, they won't return. Similarly, if your audience doesn't like or trust you, if they doubt your integrity or competence, they are not likely to accept

Good speakers recognize that a partnership exists between the speakers and the audience; they engage listeners directly, connecting with audience interests and needs. (Bob Daemmrich/Stock Boston)

your information as accurate, find your ideas engaging, or be willing to vote for you or your cause. Effective public speaking is by definition audience centered. Public speeches are not static or unchanging. Instead they are dynamic—interactive and ever changing according to the situation and the audience.

FRAME OF REFERENCE

Speeches to entertain should be enjoyable and amusing, but they can also have interesting and useful things to say. Rosita Perez, a professional speaker, uses humor to help her convey her message.

Communicating Effectively

Communication is an effort on the part of the speaker to get the listener to respond in a particular way. Some might say that if the speaker gets what he or she is after, the speech is effective, and much of what follows in this book is designed to help you as a speaker get the response you want. Of course, there are situations where important ideas or values are planted by a speaker and only gain acceptance over time. But most of the speaking situations in which you'll find yourself will be those in which you have a concrete goal in mind: you will know what you want listeners to understand, believe, or do when your speech is over. But that's only part of the picture. The true **effectiveness** of a speech must be judged by the outcome for both parties in the speaker-listener partnership.

effectiveness the degree to which the speaker and audience benefit from a message

You communicate effectively when you obtain the response you hope for while respecting your listeners' needs, sensitivities, and rights. You must know something about their predispositions, tastes, prejudices, capabilities, and knowledge. If you hope to get a response from your listeners, you need to consider what characteristics they share as a group and what qualities individual members bring to the public speaking situation. Seeing public speaking as a mutually beneficial experience for both speaker and listener means that taking advantage of an audience—getting them to do something that is harmful to them, buy something that is useless, or act in some destructive way—is not effective communication. Public speaking is a way of promoting the public good, and as such it must occur within an ethical framework.

ETHICS AND THE SPEECH PREPARATION PROCESS

Preview Every speaker should be committed to communicating ethically. Ethical speakers examine their own motives. They insist on accuracy and are concerned with the way they acquire and present information. They see human communication as a transactional dialogue. They strive to adapt to and promote the interests of their listeners. They are alert to ethical dilemmas that may arise in different speaking situations. They stay in touch with the ethical standards of their community while remaining true to their own values and convictions. Communicating ethically is central to being an effective public speaker.

Renowned first-century Roman rhetorician Quintilian described the effective public speaker as "the good man speaking well."[6] Although your aim as a speaker is to get the audience response you are seeking, like Quintilian's "good man," you must also prepare and deliver your speech with an unwavering commitment to **ethical communication**. What do we mean by

ethical communication speaking honestly and truthfully with a thoughtful and genuine concern for the well-being of the audience and community

ethics a set of behavioral standards deemed to be good or desirable

ethical communication? **Ethics** are a set of behavioral standards generally considered to be good or desirable. Ethical communication means speaking honestly and truthfully, with a thoughtful and genuine concern for the well-being of the audience and the community. Ethical communication is not just something you tack onto a public speaking checklist. Rather, ethical speaking must grow out of your own values and character and the values of the community of which you are a part.

Characteristics of an Ethical Speaker

motives what compels a speaker to speak to an audience

transactional dialogue an exchange in which speaker and listener are viewed as equal partners in the creation of meaning

What, then, are the characteristics of an ethical speaker? Ethical speakers examine their **motives**—they do not slant the truth for the sake of their own gain. Ethical speakers insist on accuracy—they tell the audience what they believe to be truthful based on their own research and reflection. Ethical speakers are committed to communication as a **transactional dialogue**—they honor the right of all participants to raise questions, offer ideas, and make choices. Ethical speakers are concerned with the way they acquire information and are sensitive to the way in which they present it. They carefully examine the best interests of those to whom they speak, always thinking of the audience's rights, needs, and values along with their own. Finally, ethical speakers are concerned with the tension introduced by the need to adapt their ideas to the audience—they question how far they can adapt without compromising their own basic beliefs.

After reading these sections on ethics, go to **Drill 1.3: The Ethics of Public Speaking** on the **VideoLab** CD-ROM. View the three speech clips and respond to the corresponding question sets.

Ethical Issues in Public Speaking

Imagine having to speak to an audience you know to be opposed to your ideas. How far will you adapt? Suppose you have to speak on the same topic to several different audiences, each with different interests. How will your "core presentation" vary as you move from one audience to another? Or perhaps you are making a persuasive presentation. If you land this "deal"—persuade your audience to buy your product, invest in your idea, sign your contract—your career will likely soar. How will you make sure you present your case fairly, with a balanced concern for your audience's needs as well as your own?

When faced with these and other potential ethical dilemmas, some speakers might be tempted to exaggerate their case, make promises they cannot keep, or somehow severely compromise their stance in an attempt to please the audience. Grades, money, promotions, and votes can serve as powerful incentives for unethical communication.

As you can see, ethical issues permeate the public speaking process. For you, as a student, temptations abound. You may have a roommate who learns you are planning to speak on a topic he spoke on last semester and suggests that you use his outline as a foundation for your speech. You may discover an article that pretty much covers every point you want to make in your speech. Even though your instructor has asked you to read widely before starting to outline your speech, you find yourself tempted to use this article as the major basis of your presentation, leading you toward the ethical violation of **plagiarism**.

plagiarism presenting as new and original an idea derived from another source

Plagiarism is a very serious problem at colleges and universities. There are files of papers and speeches housed in fraternities and dorms. Material is for sale on the Internet, and, in reaction to this, web sites have been set up for instructors to consult so that they can cross-check topics. The fact that plagiarism is widespread, however, doesn't change the fact that it is academic dishonesty, and dishonesty is both unethical and dangerous. The risk of being discovered is great. In college, it can range from a lowered grade to dismissal. In other speaking situations, the credibility of speakers who are discovered passing off the work of others as their own is seriously damaged.

Students usually plagiarize in a variety of circumstances that can be avoided. If a speaker puts off preparing a speech until the last minute, there is not enough time to go through the process of narrowing a topic, doing research, organizing, and practicing that is necessary for a successful presentation. The speaker is then tempted to appropriate a magazine article as a speech. Most people feel apprehensive about giving a speech—that is normal. This, however, leads some novice speakers to seek out more experienced students for help. Sometimes, such help is in the form of a speech outline and notes from a friend who gave a speech in another class. In some cases, students plagiarize through ignorance or carelessness. They believe that they can simply repeat parts of articles or books or information found on the Internet as if it were their own, without indicating that the material is directly quoted. Or they may have taken notes in a careless way, so when they consult these notes, they don't even know that the notes are the words of another person, not their own.

KEEP IN MIND 1.2

Characteristics of an Ethical Speaker

Ethical speakers

- examine their motives.
- are committed to transactional dialogue.
- are sensitive to the way they acquire and present information.
- consider the best interests of their listeners.
- consider appropriate audience adaptation.
- recognize and confront ethical issues.
- are aware that speaking ethically is part of speaking successfully.

Following are some basic steps to take to make sure you don't plagiarize:

- Begin preparing your speech early.
- Pick a topic that interests you and that you will enjoy finding out more about.
- Research the topic carefully and thoroughly.
- In your speech, cite sources that you used.
- Be sure to identify direct quotes for your listeners.

There is no excuse for plagiarism. Don't ever put yourself in the position of behaving unethically and running the risk of ruining your college and future career.

Ethical Norms

In his book *Ethics in Human Communication,* speech communication scholar Richard Johannesen challenges us to examine the following account of political communication and to decide how ethical we believe it to be:

> Consider presidential candidate Walter Mondale's habit in 1983 of telling widely varied interest groups that *each* group's specific interests are "at the very core of my being." Commented *Newsweek* (October 3, 1983, p. 32): "In a single three-week period, Mondale used this same phrase to express his commitment to civil rights, his concern for quality education, and his fidelity to upholding 'the rights of unions.' Some joke that the core of his being must be very large, divided into small wedges, or rentable on short notice."[7]

PORTFOLIO 1.2

Truth and Its Consequences

How will truthfulness and the constant searching for the truth affect your interactions with others? To what degree will they enhance your development as an individual and as a speaker? Contemplate these matters and briefly sketch out your thoughts in writing.

We may disagree about the severity of the breach of ethics in this example. Some may think it is an exaggeration; others will see it as outright deception. But surely we have a common code that would disapprove of such a ploy. It is as if you had a relationship with someone who told you that you were the one he or she loved, that you were the most important person in his or her life, and then you discovered that he or she had told two other people the same thing. Of course, you would be angry and upset. Such behavior clearly violates **ethical norms**.

ethical norms a common code for what is and what is not ethical behavior

Speaking ethically is part of speaking successfully. Unethical public speaking practices—like all our actions—have consequences. In addition, unethical speaking practices have an effect on a speaker's reputation. Would it be easy to trust an unfaithful lover a second time? A student who is suspected of plagiarism might get off with a warning the first time but will be watched closely in the future. A salesperson might get a customer to buy an inferior product once, but when the overinflated promises aren't fulfilled, the customer isn't likely to come back. In short, what is ethical and what is successful are so closely related as to be inseparable.

As we turn now to an overview of the process of preparing yourself to speak, be aware that every phase of your preparation can have ethical implications.

PREPARING YOURSELF TO SPEAK

Preview The basic principles of public speaking will guide you in selecting a topic, establishing credibility, analyzing the audience, discovering relevant material, fashioning arguments, delivering the speech, and determining audience response.

PORTFOLIO 1.3

Getting to Know You

What can you do from day one of class to promote positive impressions of yourself? How will these considerations affect your communication with your classmates? How will these considerations affect your communication with your instructor?

As you think about the communication act in which you are going to participate, you will naturally think about preparing your speech for presentation. But what if you instead think about *preparing yourself to speak?* This is not just a trick of words; rather, it is a way of thinking about what you need to do to get ready to give a speech. It is a way of developing a strategy you can use each time you give a speech. *Preparing yourself to speak is the process of understanding and applying the principles of audience-centered effective speaking.* These principles are the subject matter of this entire book. The following sections of this introductory chapter will give you an overview of each of these nine basic principles, as well as a general idea of how they interact.

Know Yourself

You are your most important asset. Your own beliefs, ability, knowledge, and potential are the foundation on which any speech is built. However, very few people have speeches in their heads just waiting to be delivered. Getting ready to give a speech is hard work. Starting with what you know doesn't mean ending there.

Although you first need to canvass your own interests and concerns to find a topic to talk about, you also need to think of another dimension of yourself: your credibility. We've all heard the expression "If you could only see yourself as others see you." As a speaker, your task is to do just that—to try to see yourself as others do. We use the word **ethos**, a concept explored more than two thousand years ago by the philosopher-rhetorician Aristotle, to describe the

ethos The speaker's character, intelligence, and good will, as perceived by the audience speaker's character, intelligence, and values, as perceived by the audience. What you do to prepare for your speech and what you do during the speech affect how the audience perceives you. Being well prepared lets the audience know that you take them and the topic seriously and are in command of the facts. Being able to communicate directly and easily with your audience reassures them that you can be trusted. In short, in preparing yourself to speak, you must consider how you will be perceived.

In tracking your growth as a speaker, a reflective journal could be very helpful. You can keep such a journal by taking ten minutes or so after class each day to record your thoughts and impressions. Your journal can take a variety of forms. You could write one significant comment on the most important thing you've learned and how you might put your new knowledge to use in an upcoming assignment. You may want to reflect on what you see as your greatest challenge at this point in your development, then revisit this in a later journal entry as you assess how well you met the challenge. After some classes, you may be in a position to evaluate the progress you have made toward becoming a better speaker. Your instructor might want you to keep a journal based on the Portfolios included in each chapter of this book or to incorporate some of the Portfolio assignments into your journal. In any case, by writing down your reflections, you will not only clarify your goals and how well you are moving toward meeting them, but you also can sharpen your skills as a writer.

Know Your Audience

Speeches are given for audiences, to get people to respond in some way to ideas. The audience's needs, interests, beliefs, and knowledge must also play a part in your deciding what you will talk about and how you will put your speech together. Your knowledge of yourself needs to be supplemented by and compared with the knowledge of those who will listen to what you have to say.

Knowing an audience makes **adaptation** possible. If, for example, you planned to present a proposal first to the Engineering Department and then to Sales, you would adapt the content to mesh with the technical interests and concerns of the first group and the marketing priorities of the second. The point is that you must consider carefully the characteristics of the audience that are relevant to the speech you plan to give and take this understanding into account as you prepare to speak.

adaptation connecting one's message to the interests and needs of the audience, at a level appropriate to their knowledge and experience and in a style that they find comfortable

Know the Situation

The **setting** for a speech can influence how an audience responds to you. You may be speaking in a comfortable or an uncomfortable physical setting. Or you may be close to your audience or separated from them by an orchestra pit. You may be speaking directly to them or using a microphone. You may be talking to them first thing in the morning or right after lunch. Your audience may be there because they are interested in what you have to say or because they have to be. It is to your advantage to know in advance something about the setting in which you will be speaking so that you can anticipate potential problems.

setting the immediate environment in which the speech is presented

In addition to the setting, you will also need to consider the **temporal context** of your speech. Imagine, for example, that you are giving a class presentation on the role of government in student aid. The student newspaper has just published a story detailing proposed cuts in student aid programs. It is

temporal context previous, current, and anticipated events that affect what can or should be said and how it might be received likely that your audience will be aware of this turn of events and will be listening for what you have to say about it. You need to be aware of what is happening in your audience's world that is relevant to your topic so you can prepare yourself to speak as the context requires.

Aim for Audience Response

Think about the model of communication we presented earlier in the chapter. As a beginning speaker, your most critical task is to develop an *audience-centered perspective*—to understand that everything you do and say as a speaker is done and said because you hope to influence an audience. This principle is fundamental to everything else you will learn in public speaking.

Knowing what you want the audience to do will help you determine what ideas to include in your speech. For example, do you want your audience simply to understand a concept or to take a specific action? If you were speaking about the American Red Cross, the history of the organization might be interesting, but your audience would probably want you to provide good reasons for giving money to the Red Cross if you were to ask them for donations.

Remember, your aim in any speech is to get a specific audience response. One of the first things you should do in preparing yourself to speak is to determine your **specific purpose** as precisely as possible, since it will affect all your other choices.

specific purpose a precise statement of how the speaker wants the audience to respond to her or his message, which serves to direct the research and construction of the speech

Discover Relevant Material

As you begin to work on your chosen speech topic, you will most likely have some information already in your head. You may be building on your knowl-

Audiences respond to speakers who focus their attention on listeners. This audience at a rally to gain support for breast cancer awareness and education reacts enthusiastically to a speaker who addresses their concerns. (Gregg Mancuso/Stock Boston, Inc.)

edge of the stock market, your personal frustrations with parking on campus, or your experiences while biking through France. But even with this kind of initial experience or knowledge, to be a credible speaker you will have to learn a great deal more. Once you have decided on the specific purpose of your speech, you will need to explore potential sources of information for **supporting material** that develops and proves your points.

supporting material information presented in your speech to support your various points

Gathering pertinent information may begin with a computer search of the World Wide Web. You do need to exercise caution, however, when using information from the Web. Since it is relatively easy to post material to the Web, sites often present highly biased or even totally false information, rumors, or unsubstantiated gossip. Unless you know a source to be highly reliable (a government bureau, the *New York Times* or *Wall Street Journal*, a professional journal, and the like), it is best to confirm information through other sources. In addition, CD-ROM encyclopedias present useful information in the form of sound and pictures as well as written text. And, of course, you can find specific articles, books, and government publications in your campus or local public library. Whatever sources you use, they must be completely and correctly cited, as we describe in Chapter 8. The importance of using reliable sources is also discussed in Chapter 9. You may also want to interview experts, depending on the subject of your speech. Experts can be quoted as sources, and often they can direct you to additional resources.

Any topic of importance calls for research. All speakers, no matter how knowledgeable, can benefit from learning more about their topic. Obviously some will need to engage in more research than others, but few can talk "off the top of their head" and get away with it.

Present a Reasonable Argument

When you know what you want to accomplish in your speech, you will need to set about framing ideas and finding material that supports those ideas and builds a reasonable **argument**. You should seek information that will connect your topic with your audience's feelings, needs, and emotions—what is often referred to as **pathos**—and that makes logical sense to listeners—referred to as **logos**. Remember that this is a process: your purpose may change as you gather more information. As you learn more, what you hope to accomplish will become less tentative.

argument a series of ideas, each one supported by materials, used to advance a particular position about an issue

pathos emotional content that influences a belief or action

logos logical content that influences a belief or action

Consider the following example of how to develop an argument. You suspect that a pass/fail grading system rather than a normal grading system is not a good idea. This gives you a tentative *purpose:*

> *I want my audience to agree that it would not be in a student's best interests to elect to take courses pass/fail.*

You then ask yourself: Why do I believe this is so? Why should my audience agree with me? By answering these questions, you begin to form main ideas—ideas that will be convincing—such as:

> *Employers are suspicious of transcripts with pass/fail grades recorded in place of normal letter grades.*

You then set about researching the topic of pass/fail grades, looking especially for specific data or relevant information that will help you make this idea more believable to your audience—that is, you collect *supporting material.* (Note that you should be open to modifying your view if the material found does not support your initial hypothesis.) You might support this particular idea by

- citing a report in which a large percentage of employers surveyed said that they look carefully at transcripts to see how well students have done in courses that would be helpful to them on the job.
- reporting on an interview with a personnel director who said that in her opinion a recording of pass/fail instead of grades suggests that the student was trying to get around requirements in an easy way.
- quoting the director of the placement service at your school, who reported that employers tend to ask him a lot of questions about the pass/fail policy and why students would elect to take courses that way.

This process helps you build your argument. As you begin to find relevant material, this material helps you formulate ideas that further your purpose and provides data to make those ideas more convincing to your audience. Consulting several different kinds of sources and always looking for diverse perspectives will help you build the strongest, most compelling argument possible.

Give Your Message Structure

Well-organized speeches make it easy for the audience to follow the speaker's argument, they help the audience remember what has been said, and they give clear and convincing reasons for responding as the speaker wishes. If your audience perceives that you as a speaker are disorganized, if they cannot follow your ideas, they will have trouble accepting your information and arguments and trouble acknowledging your credibility.

For an audience to follow your ideas, your speech must have **structure**. Your ideas must relate to one another logically. Taken together, they must present the kind of **coherence** necessary to accomplish your purpose. As a speaker, you will need to plan carefully how to move the audience smoothly from one idea to the next by techniques such as devising smooth **transitions** between your ideas and selecting places where it makes sense to summarize what has been said before going on.

structure the organization and arrangement of ideas and materials within a speech

coherence the logical and orderly relationship of information and ideas to develop or support a larger point

transitions words, phrases, or sentences that help the audience perceive the relationship of ideas and the movement from one point to another

The speech must form a pattern that is clear to your audience. Using a meaningful pattern helps the audience take "mental notes" so that they will remember what you have said. The pattern also makes clear to them how everything in the speech fits together, points to the desired response, and contributes to your ethos as a speaker.

Speak Directly with Your Audience

The language you use and the way you use it can have a great impact on an audience and the way that audience responds to you. By choosing language suitable to the audience and the occasion and by developing a conversational and direct speaking style, you will promote understanding and belief on the part of the audience. **Suitable language** keeps both audience and purpose in mind—it is language that is precise, clear, interesting, and appropriate to the

suitable language language that is precise, clear, interesting, and appropriate to the audience and purpose context in which your speech takes place. Beginning speakers sometimes believe that speaking situations demand formal language, with the result that their speeches can sound stiff. We have often had the experience of talking with a student who describes a particular event or personal experience in an animated and natural way, then recounts the same story in a stiff, unnatural way to an audience. It helps to think of a speaking situation as an enlarged conversation in which you convey information to the audience in a way similar to the way you would talk with friends—similar, but not exactly the same. In speaking with an audience, you should be sure to omit the "fillers" we often use in informal conversation; avoid the "likes" and "you knows" that tend to clutter everyday speech.

Of course, all situations do not call for the same kind of delivery. Some formal occasions may call for **manuscript speaking**, in which you read a carefully prepared speech to an audience. At other times you may be asked to speak on the spur of the moment, with little or no time for preparation; this is **impromptu speaking**. On rare occasions, a **memorized speech** may be appropriate. Most often, however, you will be speaking **extemporaneously**—that is, with careful preparation but with minimal notes and a less formal, more direct, audience-centered **delivery**.

No matter how much work you put into preparing yourself to speak, what the audience finally sees and hears will determine their response. The best delivery does not call attention to itself: the audience is more aware of *what* is said than *how* it is said. Good delivery, in most of the contexts in which you will speak, should be conversational and relaxed. If the delivery is good, listeners can hear and understand what you say and will not find themselves distracted by mannerisms, inappropriate language, or a too-dramatic presentation.

manuscript speaking presenting a speech from a prepared text

impromptu speaking casual, off-the-cuff speaking, when there is little or no time for preparation

memorized speech a speech that one has committed to memory

extemporaneously speaking in a way that reflects thorough preparation but relies on an abbreviated set of notes

delivery the manner in which one presents a speech

Good speakers take every opportunity to connect with their listeners. Here Christine Todd Whitman waves enthusiastically to supporters as she celebrates with them her reelection after a close race for governor of New Jersey. *(Najlah Feanny/SABA)*

communication apprehension the feeling of anxiety that a speaker feels before and/or during a public presentation

Develop Confidence Through Practice

Being nervous just before and while you give a speech is normal. Everyone, however experienced or accomplished he or she may be, feels some **communication apprehension**, or speech anxiety. The ill-prepared speaker may deserve

As you begin to prepare for your first speech, go to **Lesson 1's Next Step: Preparing Yourself to Speak** exercise on the **VideoLab** CD-ROM. Complete this exercise, which asks you to prioritize the steps involved in getting ready to speak.

When you believe that you are ready to speak, go to the **Checklist for Speech Preparation** in the **SpeechStudio** and complete the speech preparation checklist. Is there anything you have forgotten to do?

FIGURE 1.3 **Preparing Yourself to Speak**

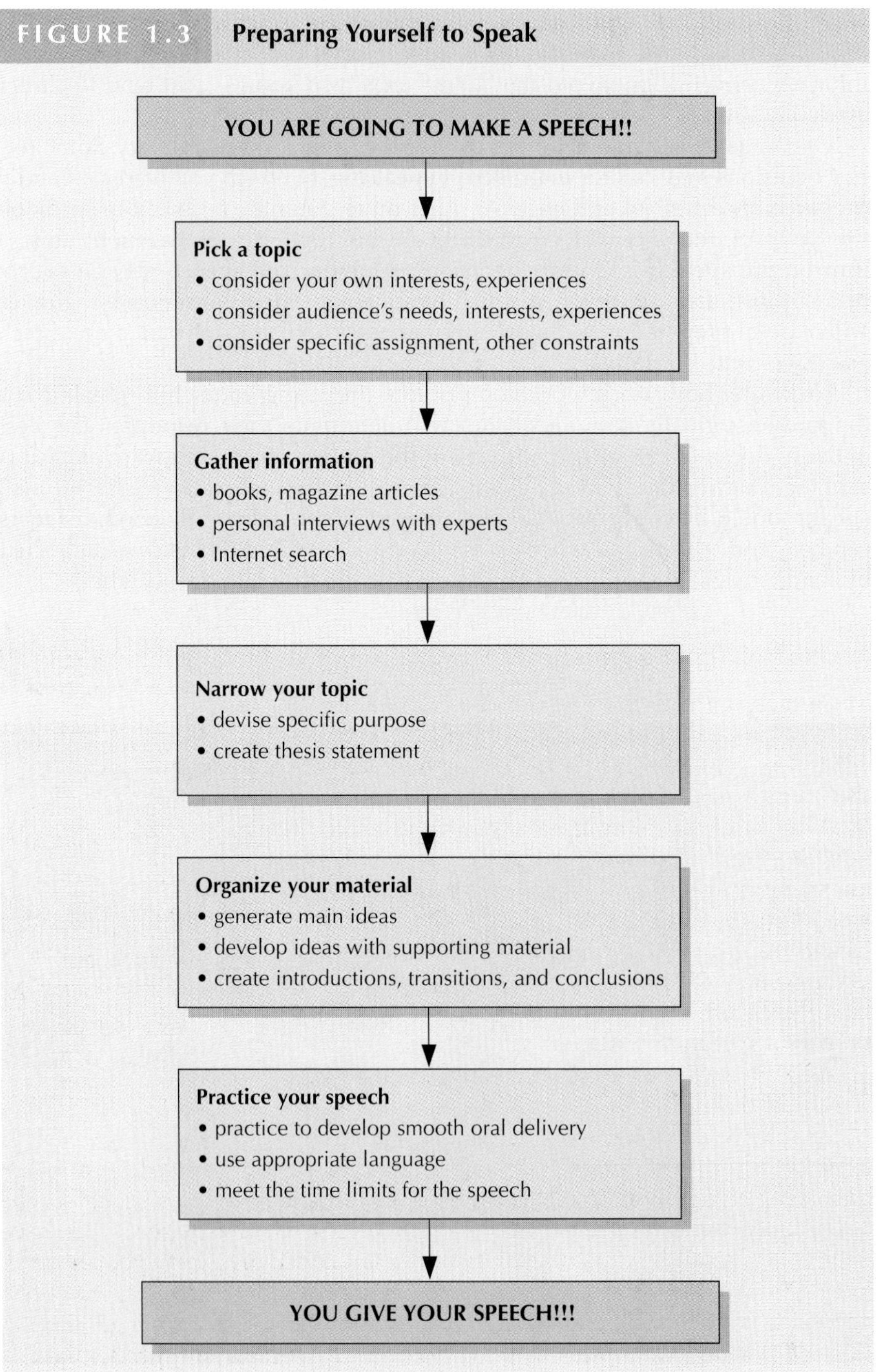
YOU ARE GOING TO MAKE A SPEECH!!
Pick a topic
• consider your own interests, experiences
• consider audience's needs, interests, experiences
• consider specific assignment, other constraints
Gather information
• books, magazine articles
• personal interviews with experts
• Internet search
Narrow your topic
• devise specific purpose
• create thesis statement
Organize your material
• generate main ideas
• develop ideas with supporting material
• create introductions, transitions, and conclusions
Practice your speech
• practice to develop smooth oral delivery
• use appropriate language
• meet the time limits for the speech
YOU GIVE YOUR SPEECH!!!

to squirm, but even with good preparation, effectively expressing ideas orally doesn't come naturally to anyone. For a summary of the steps involved in getting yourself ready to speak, see Figure 1.3.

As we will discuss in detail later in this book, there are many ways of reducing and managing speech anxiety. One of the most effective is repeated **oral practice**. Practicing out loud and frequently will show you what problems you may have putting any of your ideas into oral language. More important, oral practice will give you confidence in your ability to deal with these problems.

oral practice practicing one's speech aloud in conditions that simulate the actual speaking environment

PUTTING PRINCIPLES INTO PRACTICE IN A FIRST SPEAKING ASSIGNMENT

Preview In the following section, we suggest four possible first speaking assignments that can get you started: introducing a classmate, paying tribute to someone you admire, offering a toast, and delivering a eulogy.

All of the basic principles we have discussed will be developed in more detail in the chapters that follow, but your instructor may want you to speak right away—to get a feel for speaking with an audience. For this initial experience, we suggest four options. As with all speeches, you will need to prepare carefully, but these speeches require minimal research and may be a good way to get started.

For a variation on the speech of introduction, go to **Lesson 1's Screening Room** on the **VideoLab** CD-ROM and watch the speech of self-introduction, and rate the devices used to present a vivid, memorable introduction. Then complete accompanying **Drill 1.1**.

Introducing a Classmate

The people sitting around you in this class are going to make up the audience for the speeches you give in class. Knowing their interests, their experiences, and the kinds of knowledge they possess will be helpful as you plan your speeches. Listening carefully to what they talk about and the kinds of questions they ask will contribute to your knowledge of your listeners. This process of getting to know your audience can start right away through class introductions. By teaming up with one of your peers, you can learn about each other and then use this information to prepare a speech of introduction.

KEEP IN MIND 1.3

The Basic Principles of Public Speaking

- Know yourself.
- Know your audience.
- Know the situation.
- Aim for audience response.
- Discover relevant material.
- Present a reasonable argument.
- Give your message structure.
- Speak directly with your audience.
- Develop confidence through practice.

As you and your partner talk with each other, remember that you are not just gathering a random set of facts to pass on to the class. You will want to discuss topics such as family, hometown, travel, jobs, interesting personal experiences, hobbies, leisure activities, intellectual and academic interests, and goals for the future. Then you will have to put this information together in a speech. You have a purpose: you want your audience to understand what the person you are introducing is like and what is important to her or him. Organize what you have learned into a coherent presentation and practice the speech before giving it in class. Following is a simple example of how a short introductory speech might be structured:

As you prepare your speech of self-introduction, go to the **Outline Worksheet for a Speech of Self-introduction** in the **SpeechStudio**. This same format can be used for outlining a speech to introduce one of your classmates.

Purpose: I want my audience to understand that music and family are central to Howard's life.

When you feel that you are ready to present your speech, test your readiness by going to the **Checklist for a Speech of Self-introduction** in the **SpeechStudio** and evaluating your efforts by completing the self-assessment checklist.

Introduction: My new friend, Howard Krisler, has pursued many interests. In grade school he learned Spanish so he could communicate with a friend's grandmother who spoke only broken English. He also developed an interest in making music, so he took up the piano and then the French horn. In high school he wanted to experience Mexico, so he spent half his senior year there as an exchange student. When he returned he was soon on the road again, this time with his mom and his sisters, Maria and Chris, and their dog, Luna. The five of them traveled by motor home from their home in western Illinois to Massachusetts, where they attended the Berkshire Music festival. This was one of the best two weeks in Howard's life because it combined the two things he values most: his family and music.

Main Idea: Family has always been important to Howard.

> *Support:* Growing up in a single-parent family, Howard has always looked out for his two younger sisters, and helped take care of them while they were young.
>
> *Support:* Howard turned down a trip to Niagara Falls with friends, so he could be home for his sister's sixteenth birthday.
>
> *Support:* Howard saved his money and surprised his mother on her birthday with a mother's ring, something he knew she had wanted for a long time.

Go to **Drill 1.2: Giving Good Peer Feedback** on the **VideoLab** CD-ROM and respond to the questions that assess your understanding of how to give constructive feedback to your fellow classmates.

Transition: As you can see, Howard treasures his family. He's also very into his music.

Main Idea: Howard has long pursued his interest in music.

> *Support:* Howard began playing piano when he was seven, and he took up French horn in the fifth grade when he joined band.
>
> *Support:* Howard practiced religiously and became first chair his freshman year, a position he held throughout high school.
>
> *Support:* Howard also played in the marching band, the pep band, and the school orchestra, and he's still going; you'll see him here every halftime marching for us.

Go to the **Evaluation Form for a Speech of Self-introduction** in the **SpeechStudio** and read over the evaluation form. You may use this form (or another provided by your instructor) during class as you listen and respond to others' speeches. Be sure to write out some comments after you have completed the rating scales.

Conclusion: As you can see, Howard is someone who makes things happen, and he is most devoted to making good things happen for his music and for his family. I understood this best when I asked him why he chose to come to this university. He gave two reasons: It is close enough to home that he and his family can visit regularly, and the music program here is first rate. Howard will get his degree in Music Education and then move back close to home where he can always be near his family. In the meantime, you'll see him waving to them in the stands during halftime.

This three- to four-minute speech doesn't tell the audience everything there is to know about Howard, but it does focus on what seems important to him. It is not just a series of unrelated information.

Paying Tribute

When we pay tribute to a person or an event, we are remembering the values we hold dear, the bonds we share, our common aspirations, and our hopes and dreams. We are reinforcing our beliefs, taking time from our busy lives to celebrate someone we love or admire, a cause we believe in, or an event that has defined us as a community or a nation.

In preparing a **speech of tribute**, you must, as in any speech, have a clear, narrow purpose and well-structured ideas that support that purpose. In addition, you should consider the following guiding principles:

speech of tribute a speech in praise of a significant person or event

- *Make sure you are well informed.* In all likelihood, you will have chosen to pay tribute to a person or event because you know the person being honored or know a lot about the event being commemorated. Even so, you must make sure you know as much as possible about the subject and have gathered excellent factual information.
- *Choose vivid, colorful, memorable information to share.* In presenting a speech of tribute, one of your main purposes is to make the person's accomplishments come to life for the audience. It is one thing to say "He has always been a brave man." It is quite another to tell a story of how the person risked his life for others during the war in Vietnam.
- *Deliver your speech with warmth and sincerity.* Making a speech of tribute gives you the chance to communicate your feelings of admiration, affection, and pride. When you convey these emotions with sincerity, your audience will likely respond by appreciating your feelings and, ideally, sharing them.

An annotated sample of a student speech of tribute to the composer and singer Don McLean appears at the end of this chapter.

Offering a Toast

The **toast** is really a mini-tribute. You are likely to find yourself in several situations where you are called on to make a very short, straightforward speech of tribute. You might toast a coworker who has just had a baby, a friend who has just been admitted to medical school, or a pair of newlyweds on the occasion of their wedding.

toast a short speech of tribute and celebration

Some toasts are more informal than others. Even so, all toasts should be planned in advance and practiced aloud until you can deliver them smoothly and naturally. Try to use a bit of imagination. Avoid generic toasts such as "Best of luck to the lucky couple. May they have the happiness they deserve!"

Your toast should be brief. Choose a basic theme—the point that you want to make memorable and illustrate it with a short example. Then conclude your toast. Always emphasize something positive. Here is how one student toasted the "Teacher of the Year":

> I will always remember how much Miss Cagle cared that we learn. She was tough. You had to tremble when she returned one of your papers. You could not help but notice how she seemed to have written as much as you—all in bright red! You knew there would be drafts to follow. And you knew why she

was doing it. Because she was *determined* that we learn to write well, to be literate, and to grow in our love of literature. Miss Cagle is an extraordinary teacher. Congratulations to our "Teacher of the Year"!

Delivering a Eulogy

eulogy a speech of tribute to honor one who has died and to comfort those who mourn

When someone dies, it is customary in American culture for a speaker to eulogize him or her. A **eulogy** is often given by a minister, close friend, or family member. When a famous person dies, others may deliver eulogies. When former president Richard Nixon died, a number of political figures ranging from President Bill Clinton to Henry Kissinger delivered eulogies at his funeral.

Like a tribute, a eulogy may emphasize a person's important accomplishments. But unlike most tributes, it also may honor how the person lived his or her life, remember him or her, and stress personal qualities for which he or she was known. Also in contrast to most tributes, a eulogy may express the speaker's sense of loss and convey a tone of sadness. The speaker may also seek to comfort those in mourning. In *Spotlight on a Eulogy,* a grandmother is eulogized. The minister begins by quoting from the Bible (Proverbs 31). Appropriately, this moving eulogy is directed at her immediate family, seeking to comfort and sustain them.

Now that you have finished reading this chapter, go to **Lesson 1's Coach** on the **VideoLab** CD-ROM and review the list of "dos" and "don'ts." Remember that excellent preparation is the key to effective public speaking.

One of the most famous eulogies ever delivered was given by President Ronald Reagan in 1986. This eulogy was unusual in that it paid tribute not to an individual, but to a group of astronauts who died when the space shuttle *Challenger* exploded. President Reagan's eulogy appears in the Appendix.

Whatever your instructor chooses as a short first assignment, use it as an opportunity to begin to put the principles we have discussed here into practice and to get a feel for speaking with an audience.

SPOTLIGHT ON... A Eulogy

Delivered at the Funeral of Florence Griffin, July 28, 1997

"Strength and dignity are her clothing, and she laughs at the time to come." My first memories of Florence have to do with laughter. In March of 1987, Delma [Florence's daughter] invited me to Florence's 80th birthday party. After she overcame the surprise of the party, Florence introduced me to her children. "This is my son Dee, and my son Doyle, and my daughter Donnis, and my daughter Doris, and my son Dale ... well, you know how it goes!!!" I never knew there were so many names that started with "D"! I knew then that your mom—and probably your dad, too—loved children—and had a pretty good sense of humor!

As I picture Florence in my mind, I see her smiling—her pretty white hair framing a face full of kindness, gentleness, dignity. I know, like the virtuous woman in Proverbs, that Florence's children rise up and call her blessed. But I also know that she was blessed by her children and grandchildren and all the rest of her family. Over these years of her illness, you have taken such exceptional, loving care of her—and I know that Florence was grateful, and more than that, *moved,* by your devotion.

It all boils down to love, doesn't it? God put love in Florence's heart, and she shared it with you—and you shared it with her—and in that process, God himself is glorified. And it is with that glorified, loving God that Florence now resides—restored in strength, restored in vision, restored in life. "Strength and dignity are her clothing, and she laughs at the time to come." Florence is now laughing in the Lord, for which we give God thanks and praise. Amen.

—Susan Sides, Pastor of the Bernie United Methodist Church, delivered this eulogy on July 29, 1997, at the Rainey Funeral Home in Bernie, MO. This sermon was printed with the permission of the minister, Susan Sides, and Florence's grandson, L. Glen Williams.

SUMMARY

Public speaking has played a vital role in the history of humankind and is an important and increasingly common type of communication event in contemporary life. As we move further into the twenty-first century, it is imperative that we possess the ability to speak intelligently, thoughtfully, and engagingly.

As a speaker, you will likely consider your speech effective if you get the response you desire. However, your audience will consider the speech effective only if what they learn is satisfying or useful to them. A speech can be successful only if the speaker-audience partnership works for both parties. This means that, as a speaker, you must have an audience-centered approach to preparing and presenting your material. The increasing diversity of the U.S. population has intensified the need to adopt an audience-centered view of public speaking and the communication process. In this chapter, we have emphasized the ethical dimensions of public speaking. A good speaker will demonstrate his or her competence, integrity, commitment, and respect for the audience.

We have surveyed the guiding principles for preparing yourself to speak. We have stressed the importance of

- examining your own knowledge, ability, beliefs, and potential *(know yourself).*
- discovering the audience's needs, interests, beliefs, and knowledge *(know your audience).*
- understanding how the setting and other outside factors may influence the speech *(know the situation).*
- devising a clear purpose that reflects the desired response *(aim for audience response).*
- exploring potential sources of information *(discover relevant material).*
- devising clear, well-supported ideas that further the purpose of the speech *(present a reasonable argument).*
- arranging material in the speech in a way calculated to help the audience follow and understand your ideas *(give your message structure).*
- using language and delivering the speech in a manner suitable to the audience and the occasion *(speak directly with your audience).*
- practicing a well-prepared presentation frequently enough to give yourself oral command of the speech *(develop confidence through practice).*

QUESTIONS FOR REVIEW AND REFLECTION

1. Why has public speaking been viewed as important historically?
2. What is meant by *audience-centered* communication?
3. In what ways might audiences be more diverse in the year 2005 than they are today?

4. What are the most important things you should do to prepare yourself to make a good speech?
5. In what ways will public speaking be a needed communication skill for you in the professional life you hope to pursue someday?
6. As you learn to give speeches, what do you imagine your greatest challenge will be? How might you begin to grapple with it?

ENDNOTES

1. David A. Whetten and Kim S. Cameron, *Developing Management Skills,* 3rd ed. (New York: HarperCollins, 1994); Dan B. Curtis, Jerry L. Winsor, and Ronald D. Stephens, "National Preferences in Business and Communication Education," *Communication Education* 38 (1989): 6–15.
2. See, for example, "Speak for Success" and "Advanced Presentations Workshop," published for the American Bar Association (Boston: The Speech Improvement Company, n.d.). We might also note that abundant self-help books offer advice on how to improve one's communication skills. Although the advice might not always be well founded, the existence of such books suggests that many people believe they need to improve their skills.
3. See "Integrity in the Curriculum: A Report to the Academic Community," Association of American Colleges, Washington, D.C., 1985. See also *Spectra* (published by the Speech Communication Association), March 1995, p. 9, for a summary of the findings of a Department of Education study of the communication skills that faculty, employers, and policymakers believe are critical for college graduates to attain.
4. Sally J. Walton, *Cultural Diversity in the Workplace* (New York: Irwin Professional Publishing, 1994).
5. The process perspective is widely referred to as the "transactional perspective." David K. Berlo, *The Process of Communication* (New York: Holt, Rinehart & Winston, 1960).
6. Quintilian, *Institutes of Oratory* Vol. 2 (London: G. Bell & Sons, 1913), 391.
7. Richard L. Johannesen, *Ethics in Human Communication,* 4th ed. (Prospect Heights, Ill.: Waveland Press, 1996), p. 5.

The following speech of tribute was given by a student to fulfill an early speaking assignment. In this assignment, students were told that they could assume an audience and occasion if they wished.

Go to **Lesson 10's Screening Room** on the **VideoLab** CD-ROM to view this speech and complete the accompanying **Drill 10.1**. What are the strengths and weaknesses of this tribute?

A Tribute to Don McLean

Jenny Smith

Good evening, Ladies and Gentlemen. You and I are gathered here at the 1997 Grammy Awards to celebrate a common cause—to honor music. However, while you have been sitting in your seats enjoying the entertainment of the evening and the spectacle of this glorious event, I have been pacing backstage, nervous as hell about presenting this Lifetime Achievement Award.

In her opening, Jenny demonstrates her sincerity and admiration for her subject through the reference to her nervousness and a brief summary of the ways in which his impact has been recognized. Her choice of "immortal and inimitable" and "icon" vividly describes McLean and establishes him as worthy of tribute.

I wouldn't be so nervous if this man hadn't made music that touched me. If he were just an average man, if he never wrote songs with such messages and tone, if he hadn't ever made the impact on American culture that he did, I'd be as calm as I could ever be. However, if he had never made such an impact, he probably would not be receiving this honor. He has sung with such disparate musicians as Blood, Sweat, and Tears, Pete Seeger, and Dionne Warwick. He has sung about everything from Vincent van Gogh to Babylon, and twenty-five years ago this year, he sang about the day the music died. He is the immortal and inimitable Don McLean, and people everywhere consider him to be the icon of American folk music.

In this section, the speaker emphasizes the shared values that folk music promotes and illustrates how Don McLean exemplifies these values.

There are several definitions of what American folk music is. The *Smithsonian* magazine says folk music is simply the voice of man. Moses Ashe, the creator of Folkways Records, says it is oral literature. And folk legend Pete Seeger, himself, defines the art as being the voice of social injustice. Don McLean's music can be followed under any of these definitions, with his poignance, hallowing music, and lyrics. His undying "American Pie," essentially a tribute to his idol, Buddy Holly, is an eight-and-a-half-minute-long metaphor of a song. In it, Don delicately traced over a decade of rock and roll music and political sabotage, from the innocence of the sock hop in the mid-1950's, to the resistance of the draft, to the Rolling Stones. If folk music is, as the *Smithsonian* said, the voice of man, then Don McLean embodied that with this song. His voice spoke for millions, and Americans saluted and worshiped him.

Here Jenny demonstrates that she knows a lot about McLean and his history. She provides just enough information to help establish her as a credible source and to give the audience a snapshot version of his career.

It took Don McLean a long time to reach the status he did with "American Pie." When you hear him sing, "February made me shiver with every paper I'd deliver," you can rest assured that indeed, Don's first job was that of a paper carrier. As a hard-working young boy, Don was listening to music greats like Frank Sinatra, James Brown, and of course, his beloved Buddy Holly. Don started tinkering with the banjo and the guitar in his early adolescence, and it was after his father's death, when Don was only fifteen years old, when he left home and decided that his life was to be dedicated to music. His professional career began when Don started playing at undergraduate parties at Iona College and Villanova University. From there, he made his way into small coffee houses and clubs in upstate New York. Finally, he reached New York City, and after climbing the musician's corporate ladder, he rose to instant stardom with the release of "American Pie" in 1971. Amusingly, we can say that the only two jobs Don McLean has ever held were those of a paper boy and of a musician.

Using his words helps Jenny establish McLean as a real person, demonstrating his humility and his sense of humor. It also provides her with a transition into her point that his work continues to have an impact throughout the world.

Of his immediate success with "Pie," Don said, "I had to overcome the tremendous success of one song, which threatened to sink me completely. It really was hard to deal with. I look back, and I'm amazed that I weathered it. I'm sort of amazed by it. When people ask me today what 'American Pie' means, I tell them it means I don't have to work anymore if I don't want to."

But work, he did. After "Pie," Don went to work touring throughout the U.S. and the world, spending much of his time in the United Kingdom. It was at one of these U.K. concerts in 1972 that Charles Gimbel and Norman Fox were so overtaken by Don's glowing presence and moving lyrics that they left the show immediately and wrote, "Killing Me Softly," a Grammy award-winning single sung by Roberta Flack that reached number one in 1973. McLean made other impacts, as well. His song, "Vincent," about artist Vincent van Gogh, was seen by many throughout the world to be an even bigger hit than "American Pie." The song still plays every day, even now, at the entrance of the Vincent van Gogh museum in Amsterdam.

The next two paragraphs give specific details to reinforce the notion that not only is McLean successful but his impact is universal and enduring. Jenny also makes the point that his continuing career will produce even more great music.

Don has made eighteen albums. He earned twenty-five gold albums and twelve gold singles. He has been nominated for over four Grammy Awards, and he is still going strong. Though after his success in the early 1970's, he dabbled in other genres of music, like rock, pop, and country, McLean will always be a folk singer, singing about folk issues. The title track to his 1992 album, "Head Room," talks about, "what is going on in the country and how people feel, with seriousness and humor." He certainly has not lost his touch for making relatable, understandable, enjoyable music.

Finally, Jenny ends with tributes from other great folk musicians to reinforce her own assessment of McLean and suggests that this "Lifetime Achievement" will continue to fascinate listeners well beyond McLean's own lifetime.

Don McLean is thought of very highly among his fellow musicians. Pete Seeger said of him, "He is the finest singer and songwriter I have met since Bob Dylan." Pete Childs once said, "I can't imagine anyone listening closely to one of Don's songs, and failing to come away the better for it."

Don McLean has made an impact on all of us. For years to come, people will try to interpret the lyrics to "American Pie." Few, if any, will ever fully understand all that is to be derived from this epic display of music history, but they will always continue to be fascinated by Don McLean and his stories. In honor of his successes as a musician, in honor of his hard work, and in honor of the twenty-fifth anniversary of "American Pie," it is my pleasure to present this Lifetime Achievement Award to Don McLean.

Managing Communication Apprehension

2

CHAPTER OBJECTIVES

After studying this chapter, you should be able to

1. **define communication apprehension.**
2. **describe the factors that contribute to communication apprehension.**
3. **identify the physiological reactions speech anxiety may produce.**
4. **counter common misconceptions about communication apprehension.**
5. **harness your own communication apprehension and use it to your advantage.**

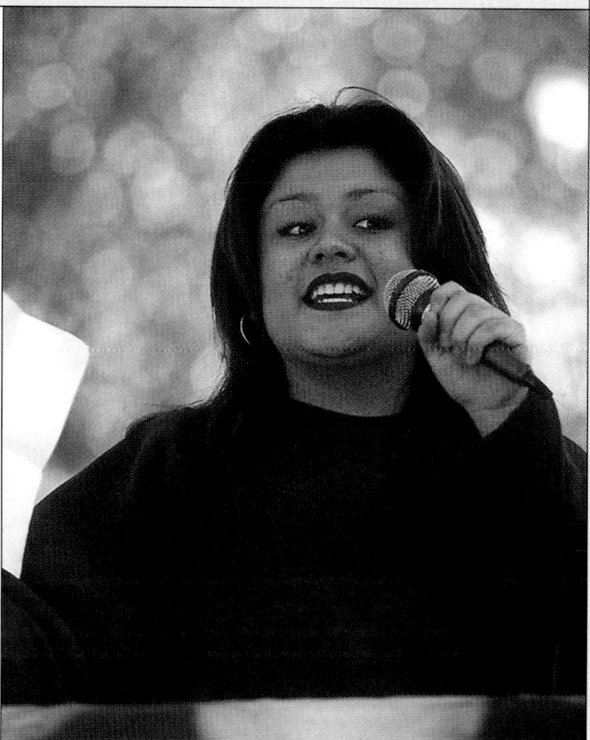

CHAPTER SURVEY

According to a commonly quoted survey, more people are afraid of public speaking than they are of dying.[1] This survey's results prompted Jerry Seinfeld to comment:

> According to most studies, people's number one fear is public speaking. Number two is death. Death is number two. Does that seem right? That means to the average person, if you have to go to a funeral, you're better off in the casket than doing the eulogy.[2]

However humorous this may sound, doctors at the Duke University Medical Center consider public speaking sufficiently stressful that they include it on a list of "mental stress tests." Physicians use these tests in identifying those most at risk for future heart problems.[3]

Few of us approach a chance to make a speech with sheer enthusiasm. Even if we have something we really want to say, even if we feel honored to have been asked to talk, even if we have volunteered to speak, we begin to experience some apprehension as the day of the speech draws near. We begin to ask ourselves questions that make our stomachs churn, such as: Will the audience like me? Will my mind go blank when I start to talk? Have I prepared sufficiently?

Whether you call it speech anxiety, stage fright, or communication apprehension,[4] you need to know about this phenomenon for several reasons. First, if unanticipated and poorly understood, communication apprehension can be debilitating to you as a public speaker. Second, there are many misconceptions about speech anxiety that, if left unclarified, will only intensify your apprehension. Finally, there are known strategies for dealing with communication apprehension that, if practiced, can help reduce your anxiety and allow your speechmaking to be not just bearable but a genuinely enjoyable experience.

WHAT IS COMMUNICATION APPREHENSION?

Preview Communication apprehension comes in many forms. For some, it is associated with interacting with others in interpersonal and small group communication settings. Most of us, however, are more likely to experience communication apprehension when we speak in public. At times, this apprehension can be severe.

Understanding the extent to which CA may affect you in diverse communication situations can be helpful in allowing you to develop strategies for managing it. Go to the **SpeechStudio** and complete the **PRCA-24**.

communication apprehension the feeling of anxiety that a speaker experiences before and/or during a public presentation. This term is synonymous with *communication anxiety* and *speech anxiety*

interpersonal communication a communicative exchange with one, two, or a similarly small number of individuals

Nearly all of us love attention. As children, we liked it when our parents paid attention to us. If a friend asks for our advice on a pressing personal decision and listens carefully to our ideas, we feel good. Likewise we enjoy having our siblings, peers, and instructors give us their undivided attention. It makes us feel important. Strangely enough, however, when a roomful of people turn their eyes on us as we are about to make a speech, we may become afraid.

Communication scholar James McCroskey, who has studied **communication apprehension (CA)** for more than twenty years, defines it as "an individual's level of fear or anxiety associated with either real or anticipated communication with another person or persons."[5] As this definition suggests, communication apprehension is not limited to public speaking situations. We may feel apprehensive about almost any kind of communication encounter. If, for example, you are preparing to have a conversation with a romantic partner who, you think, is about to suggest ending the relationship, if your professor has called you into her office to discuss your poor attendance record, or if a police officer has motioned you to pull off the road for a "conversation," you know what communication apprehension is all about.

In general, however, most of us tend to be more apprehensive about giving a formal speech in front of an audience than when engaged in most **interpersonal communication** and small group situations. In a sense, communication apprehension associated with speechmaking is akin to the "stage fright" we might experience when playing in a concert or performing in a play. On the student CD-ROM, you will find a quiz you can take to assess your own level of communication apprehension in four settings: group discussions, meetings, conversations, and public speaking.

Unfortunately, some individuals experience extreme communication apprehension in nearly every communication setting.[6] For example, one student in a public speaking course for people with high communication apprehension was so nervous about talking to strangers that whenever she wanted to order a pizza, she called her mother in New York City, who then phoned the pizza parlor in Bloomington, Indiana, and placed the order for her! A man enrolled in a similar class had passed up three opportunities for job promotions because his new position would require him to make speeches. (He passed the course and later accepted a promotion. As far as we know, he is making speeches with no ill effects.) Although such extreme forms of communication apprehension are rare, it would be foolish to underestimate the barriers created by speech anxiety—not only in the classroom, but in the world of work as well.

SPOTLIGHT ON... Communication Apprehension in the Business World

A Wall Street Journal Article on Fear of Public Speaking

In this garrulous, smooth-talking world, many executives and professionals are afflicted with what specialists call presentation phobia, or stage fright. A far cry from butterflies in the stomach, it's sometimes severe enough to slow careers to a stop.

The fear can strike not only the chief executive facing a hall of shareholders but also the manager asked to "say something about yourself" at a staff meeting. Bert Decker of Decker Communications, a San Francisco consulting firm, estimates that "roughly half the business population" labors under some form of anxiety and tries to avoid public speaking.

But as treatment becomes more effective and widely available, more people are getting help. "Of the full range of anxiety disorders," says Charles Melville, an Atlanta psychiatrist, "people can most predictably overcome a fear of public speaking."

Jolie Solomon, "Executives Who Dread Public Speaking Learn to Keep Their Cool in the Spotlight," *Wall Street Journal* (May 4, 1990), p. B3.

FACTORS CONTRIBUTING TO COMMUNICATION APPREHENSION

Preview Since we are all individuals, the factors that generate anxiety in public speaking situations vary from person to person. Some speakers bring their anxiety with them in the form of a poorly prepared speech. Others become anxious upon seeing the audience for the first time. Still others experience fear when they notice that their hands are shaking. However, several anxiety-producing factors affect nearly all of us, including poor preparation, inappropriate self-expectations, fear of evaluation, excessive self-focusing, fear of the audience, and not understanding our body's reactions.

Most speakers who have experienced communication apprehension would prefer to feel more confident when they speak. Often they don't really understand what it is they fear or why they feel anxious in some speaking situations but remain calm and confident in others. The factors that lead to communication apprehension may vary from person to person, but some factors, depicted in Figure 2.1, are there for all of us. Understanding the underlying causes of communication apprehension is the first step in learning to manage it effectively.

Poor Preparation

Unlike some factors that contribute to communication apprehension, poor preparation is a legitimate cause for concern. Any speaker who has prepared poorly and whose speech is disorganized, is poorly documented, or lacks an audience-centered purpose may well feel apprehensive as the moment to stand and speak approaches.

Of all the communication contexts, those involving speaking in public may contribute to the greatest sense of apprehension. Go to the **SpeechStudio** and complete the **PRPSA** to evaluate your feelings about making a public speech.

As you sit quietly before your speech, it is hard to be dishonest with yourself. If you are afraid you will lose your place because you have practiced only once with your note cards, if you think the audience will find you dull because you find your own speech uninteresting, or if you fear that some listener will ask you for more information after the speech and everything you know is contained in your ten-minute presentation, you may feel a sense of impending doom. But when you are well prepared, when you care about your topic, when you have done your homework and have done all you can to adapt your

FIGURE 2.1 **Factors Contributing to Communication Apprehension**

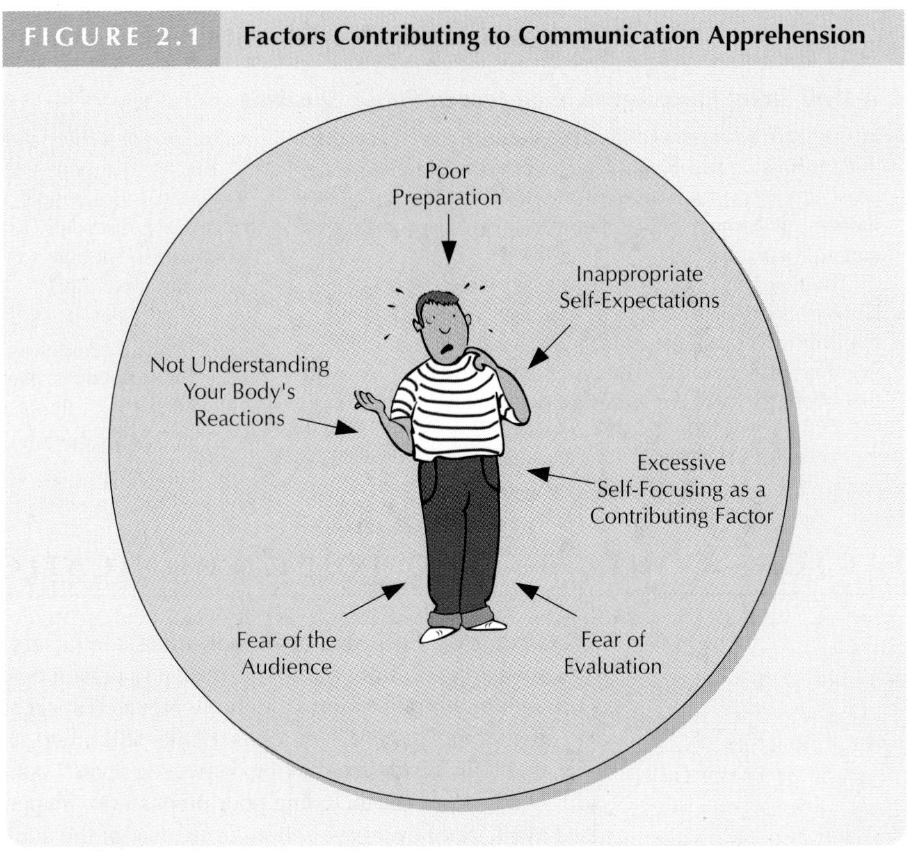

presentation to the audience, your speech anxiety should be significantly lessened, and it certainly will be far more manageable.

Inappropriate Self-Expectations

self-expectations the expectations you have for yourself in terms of your performance, including the extent to which you demand perfection from yourself

For some speakers, **self-expectations** may present problems. Suppose you are a perfectionist. You have high expectations for your own behavior, demanding much of yourself, especially in performance situations.[7] Suppose further that you begin to make a speech whose outcome is very important to you. You start with a humorous story, and the audience remains politely silent. Or you get your tongue twisted. Or you omit a point and have to go back to it. How do you feel? As a perfectionist, you might be tempted to see yourself as a failure or, at the very least, to feel disappointed in your performance even if, overall, it was quite well received.

If your self-expectations are unreasonably high, they will put you under a lot of performance pressure. No communicator is perfect. If you demand perfection of yourself, you will usually be disappointed. Equally important, you will most likely experience quite a bit of tension—both while preparing and while delivering your speech. High expectations of one's own behavior are commendable. Such expectations, however, should leave reasonable room for human error. Obviously, the other extreme—that is, low expectations—also should be avoided. In fact, not expecting to do well or not caring about the outcome of one's speech may well lead to poor preparation.

Fear of Evaluation

In almost any life situation, we dislike the idea of being judged. In fact, psychologists like Carl Rogers believe that we cannot have effective interpersonal relationships if we are critical or judgmental in our dealings with one another.[8] Every public speaking situation involves some element of evaluation. And although evaluation (if it is good) should offer positive as well as negative feedback, we tend to fix our attention on the negative parts and to fear the whole process.

Additionally, when we make a speech, the judgment seems largely one-way. It is not uncommon to hear listeners whisper to each other, "I thought George told us this guy is a good speaker. This speech sounds pretty recycled!" or "I can't believe how disorganized she is. She must have written her speech on the way from the airport!" Rarely will you hear a speaker muttering while leaving the podium, "Good grief! What a bunch of dunderheads! I'll never grace them with my presence again!" The strong potential for this one-sided evaluation is one of the common factors contributing to speech anxiety.[9]

In your public speaking class, evaluation is a given, since your instructor grades speeches. And since all of us like to be well thought of by peers and colleagues, you probably want other class members to evaluate your speeches positively. So the potential for evaluation apprehension to develop in your public speaking class is always present.

PORTFOLIO 2.1

What You Want and What You Get

What kind of self-expectations do you have for your own speaking? Do you demand perfection? Identify your self-expectations and then briefly answer the following:

1. How do your expectations affect your preparation?
2. How do your expectations affect your attitude during your delivery?
3. How do your expectations affect your assessment of how well you did as a speaker?
4. How realistic are your expectations?
5. How healthy are your expectations?

Excessive Self-Focusing

It's only natural to feel a little self-conscious when we stand up to give a speech. After all, we are all dressed up for the occasion and feel as if we are the center of attention. The audience is applauding, smiling, and looking at us thoughtfully and with anticipation.

If we are not careful, we may find ourselves thinking primarily about ourselves. How do I look? Is my hair okay? Is my tie straight? Do I look uncomfortable or confident? Besides contributing to our anxieties, these kinds of self-focused concerns represent a real problem in that our minds are directed to the kind of impression we are making and away from the ideas, thoughts, and information we hope to share. We may even forget what we are talking about as our minds continue to process self-directed questions.

Fear of the Audience

Throughout this book, we emphasize the importance of being audience centered. As speakers, we must recognize that we cannot be successful without the audience. We rely on their openness to our ideas, their good will, and their ability and willingness to respond. Knowing that we share control with listeners—that the outcome of our speech is mutually determined—can contribute to communication apprehension. We know, too, that some audiences are more or less responsive and supportive than others.

Anyone facing an audience of 600 of his or her fellow students, as this speaker at the University of Washington is, would be nervous. If you are like most of us, though, speaking even to a small group will cause some degree of communication apprehension. *(Jim Levitt/Impact Visuals)*

Specific audience characteristics may provoke some measure of speech anxiety. Here are some key audience dimensions to think about:

- *Status or power.* If we are speaking to a group of people whose status is greater than our own, we may feel uncomfortable.[10] Status and power may have a special impact in professional contexts in which the outcome of the speech matters a great deal.
- *Size.* Audience size also can be a problem.[11] Some speakers would rather speak to a smaller audience, whereas others enjoy the idea of speaking to a crowd. A few lucky speakers have no special preference.
- *Familiarity.* Some of us become apprehensive when we are asked to speak before a group of strangers, preferring the familiar and presumably more predictable kind of audience. By contrast, others dislike speaking in front of acquaintances, friends, or relatives; the pressure is on to perform well and not to disappoint anyone.
- *Perceived similarity.* When we believe that the audience's point of view is similar to our own, we will likely feel less apprehensive than if we believe that they oppose us in some important way. Most of us prefer speaking to listeners who share our values.

As we suggested in Chapter 1 and will stress throughout the book, gathering as much information as possible about an audience before making a speech helps you adapt your information, arguments, and evidence to their needs and come closer to realizing your purpose. Equally important, when you can anticipate the audience's size, point of view, status, and identity, you begin to reduce uncertainty and arm yourself with a realistic sense of what to expect. Having realistic expectations will help you manage your communication apprehension, as we will discuss later.

Not Understanding Your Body's Reactions

Finally, some speakers experience communication apprehension simply because they do not understand the **physiological reactions** anxiety may produce. Gaining some sense of what is happening to your body when you experience fear of public speaking will help you lessen and control your body's reactions.

physiological reactions bodily responses that accompany communication anxiety

Your body reacts to communication apprehension as it would to any fear-producing situation. If you were hurrying down a dark avenue on your way home from work one night and you became aware of quickening footsteps behind you, changes would begin to take place within your body. Your heart would beat rapidly, and your blood pressure would rise. The pupils of your eyes would dilate. Increased sugar in your blood would give you more than your normal level of energy. If you had food in your stomach, digestion might slow down or even stop. You would breathe more rapidly and less deeply. Even the hairs on your arms and legs would stand on end. In this situation, you might start walking much faster as you virtually flee to safety. Communication apprehension causes similar reactions. You may feel a great urge to take flight—or, at the very least, to get the speech over with quickly—so that you can go home and recover.

Some of your body's possible reactions to communication apprehension are listed in Figure 2.2. Each of us tends to have our own characteristic anxiety reactions. For example, you may find that you always have a dry mouth before you give a speech, or you may develop sweaty palms or cold hands. When you feel any of these anxiety reactions coming on, you may feel even more apprehensive. In turn, this apprehension generates still more nervous energy, which only aggravates the fear reactions you are already experiencing. The process is cyclical, as shown in Figure 2.3.

✔ KEEP IN MIND 2.1

Factors Contributing to Communication Apprehension

- Poor preparation
- Inappropriate self-expectations
- Fear of evaluation
- Excessive self-focusing
- Fear of the audience
- Not understanding your body's reactions

FIGURE 2.2 **Physiological Anxiety Reactions**

___ Parched mouth	___ The "you know" syndrome (also "um," "uh," and "okay")
___ Frog in the throat	___ Too much saliva
___ Shortness of breath	___ Shaking voice
___ Butterflies in the stomach	___ Nausea
___ Trembling legs (or hands)	___ Clammy hands
___ Inability to gesture	___ Icy hands
___ Frozen facial expression	___ Loss of memory
___ Red blotches on the neck	___ Flushed cheeks
___ Feeling light-headed or weak	___ Hot flashes
___ Clinging to the podium	___ Nervous pacing
___ Sudden urge to visit the restroom	___ Distracting gestures
___ Darting eyes (looking everywhere but at the audience)	

FIGURE 2.3 The Speech Anxiety Cycle

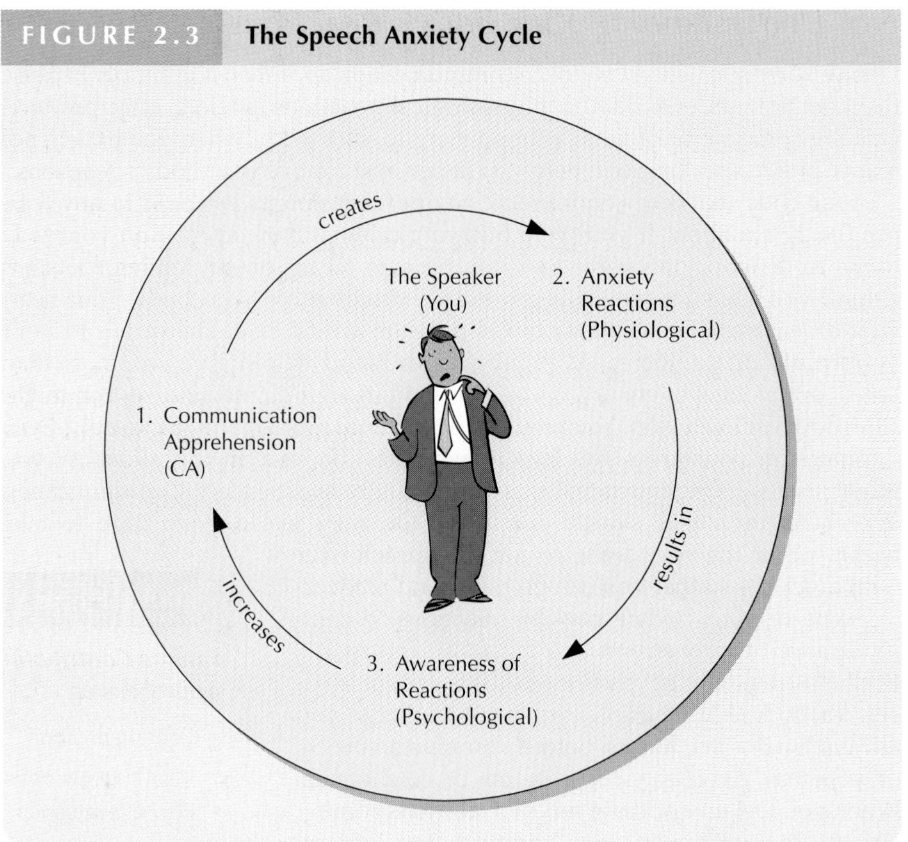

MISCONCEPTIONS ABOUT COMMUNICATION APPREHENSION

Preview We respond adversely to an awareness of our body's responses to speech anxiety in part because we labor under several misconceptions. We may mistakenly believe that everyone will be aware of the level of our apprehension, that it will get worse as we speak, that it will ruin the effect of the speech, and that the audience will be overly critical of what we do.

No one would argue that experiencing communication apprehension is pleasant. Yet when we better understand why our bodies are reacting as they are, we should be better equipped to grapple constructively with our anxieties. Unfortunately, misconceptions about communication apprehension are common. They stand in the way of our ability to manage communication apprehension effectively. Let us consider some of the most troubling of these misconceptions.

Misconception 1: Everyone Will Know

If you ever did anything naughty when you were a child, you probably remember feeling that as soon as your parents came home, they would know that you had been up to no good. Even if all the evidence had been removed, you still feared you would get caught. You believed your parents could read your mind.

Similarly, as public speakers, we imagine that the audience knows exactly what we are feeling, that they can hear our throbbing hearts, see our quivering limbs, and feel our sweaty palms. On the contrary, studies have shown that listeners, including trained speech instructors, are notoriously poor judges of the amount of anxiety speakers are experiencing.[12] In general, listeners rate speakers as significantly less anxious than speakers rate themselves. In fact, it is not uncommon for a speaker to think she "acted nervous," while audience members will comment on the degree to which she seemed confident and self-assured.

The speaking situation or environment may influence audience perceptions of a speaker's anxiety. For instance, if you are speaking in an auditorium, the distance between you and the listeners gives them little opportunity to even begin to assess your communication apprehension. Anytime you speak from behind a podium, you will be less visible. While this has some distinct disadvantages, it does mean that if your knees are knocking, no one will know the difference.

In many public speaking situations, however, no podium will be provided. Much public speaking in the contemporary professional world involves speaking to audiences in boardrooms and other small-meeting-room environments. In those settings, you may find yourself only a few feet from the audience. That's why it is so important to be able to manage your speech anxiety, as well as understand it.

Try to remember that most of your listeners will be thinking of things other than how you are feeling. Instead, they will be looking for useful information, interesting ideas, and practical advice. A good way for you to begin to manage your communication apprehension is to focus more on your message and less on yourself. As you become less self-conscious, you will begin to feel less apprehensive.

Misconception 2: Communication Apprehension Will Intensify as the Speech Progresses

Every speech you give is an opportunity to make a statement about a subject that matters to you. You may feel anxious before and during the early minutes of your speech. But as you continue to share your ideas and information—focusing more on your message and the listeners to whom you are speaking—your communication apprehension will diminish significantly. As your speech successfully progresses, you will realize that you have not passed out, that the audience does seem to be interested (or at least they are sticking with you), and that you do care about what you are saying. You will begin to relax.

Your ability to relax this way, however, is greatly dependent on two factors: your choosing a topic in which you are genuinely interested, and your preparing your speech to catch the audience up in your interest. Sometimes speakers settle on any old topic because they are rushed or they feel required to speak. In a public speaking class, for example, you may feel that you just have to make a speech on something convenient, easy to research, or pleasing to the instructor. But if you aren't interested in your topic and you don't put in the preparation needed to get a response from your listeners, you may find yourself getting more and more uneasy as your speech progresses.

In any public speaking situation—and the classroom is no exception—we are aware, at some level, of our personal responsibility for the outcome of the speech. We selected the topic, we have chosen to commit ourselves to a certain position, and we will be evaluated. If we know that we have not planned and prepared well, we may feel guilty. We may begin to tell ourselves that we deserve to be poorly received. These kinds of thoughts are far from reassuring. And the truth is that when we are not well prepared, we have every right to be worried.

In contrast, well-prepared public speakers who are discussing a topic of great concern to them and their audience can legitimately comfort themselves by saying, "I'm well prepared. I'm devoted to my position. I want to talk to this audience about it. They need to hear it." When you are prepared as a speaker, you will typically feel better as the speech progresses. Trembling hands, a quivering voice, and a dry mouth tend to disappear or diminish as you speak. By the end of the speech, you may wonder why you were so worried about what has proved to be a rewarding experience.

Misconception 3: Speech Anxiety Will Ruin the Effect of the Speech

Many people dread having an "attack" of communication apprehension because they believe they can be superior public speakers only if they are able to approach each speech with complete confidence. Although this notion makes sense for some performance areas—a saxophonist with a dry mouth might play a solo full of squeaky, sour notes—public speaking isn't necessarily one of them. In fact, speech anxiety actually has the potential to *enhance* your effectiveness as a public speaker.

It takes a great deal of energy to make a speech. Not only do you have to talk for a sustained period of time, but you may also have to enlarge and generally adapt your conventional speaking style. Although communication apprehension may produce some unpleasant physiological reactions that you might prefer to avoid, it also increases your available energy by increasing your adrenaline. Adrenaline helps you move more briskly, gesture more forcefully, and project your voice more vigorously. You need this energy for effective speechmaking.

productive anxiety nervous energy that can be used to make a more dynamic speech

When properly managed, communication apprehension can function as **productive anxiety**. How you choose to channel this extra energy will depend on you. Just remember, experiencing speech anxiety does not doom you to failure. Rather, productive anxiety is raw energy that you can tap into to increase the effectiveness of your performance.[13]

If you don't believe that speech anxiety can be productive, consider this: historically, some of the world's greatest speakers have had problems with speech anxiety. The great Roman orator Cicero wrote, "I turn pale at the outset of a speech and quake in every limb and in all my soul."[14] Other excellent speakers similarly affected by communication apprehension include Abraham Lincoln, Winston Churchill, William Jennings Bryan, John F. Kennedy, Jerry Garcia, and Maria Shriver. Not only does this list demonstrate that you can excel as a public speaker while experiencing some apprehension, but it should also reassure you that when you feel anxious about speechmaking, you are in very good company. It may even suggest that you will be a *better* speaker if you are armed with a little speech anxiety.

So you still don't believe that communication apprehension can be helpful? Many contemporary professionals who speak frequently as part of their jobs will tell you that if they don't experience some anxiety before speaking, they worry that they may be a bit "flat"—and less effective in getting their message through to the audience.

Misconception 4: The Audience Will Be Overly Critical

Most audiences are friendly. This does not mean that they will love you no matter what you say or do. Nor does it imply that they will agree with you before your speech is concluded. "Friendliness" here simply means that they are willing to give you a chance. No one has bolted the doors. Many listeners have *chosen* to spend their time listening to you. Moreover, anyone in the audience who has ever given a speech knows that it takes a certain amount of courage to stand up and speak in public. Certainly, in your speech class, every person understands this feeling, as each will have his or her turn giving speeches.

The same holds true for audiences outside the classroom. Your listeners will be familiar with the feelings that often accompany speaking in front of others. Audience members may take issue with your ideas or even heartily disagree with your proposed solution. Even so, they will typically behave politely, and they will certainly be sympathetic with, rather than critical of, any speaker who appears to be nervous. The nightmare of the audience that throws rotten tomatoes or barbed comments—or that boos, hisses, or applauds when you appear ready to conclude—is more likely to be the basis of a comic strip than the experience of a real-life public speaker.

Following the speech, audience members may raise questions or make comments. You should be more relaxed after your formal presentation is over and better able to cope with audience reactions, whatever they might be. Rest assured, that by and large, audience questions will grow from general interest, the desire to offer an opinion, or the need to acquire additional information—rather than the desire to embarrass or put you on the spot.[15]

> ✔ KEEP IN MIND 2.2
>
> ***Communication Apprehension: Myth vs. Reality***
>
> *Myth*
>
> - Listeners will know if a speaker has communication apprehension.
> - Communication apprehension will intensify as the speech progresses.
> - Communication apprehension will ruin the effect of the speech.
> - An audience is inherently hostile.
>
> *Reality*
>
> - Listeners tend to underestimate the speaker's communication apprehension.
> - A well-prepared speaker will relax as the speech progresses.
> - Communication apprehension may enhance a speaker's effectiveness.
> - Most audiences prefer that a speaker do well.

STRATEGIES FOR MANAGING COMMUNICATION APPREHENSION

Preview Once you understand communication apprehension, you can devise strategies for managing it. That is, you can use it as a resource. Strategies such as developing a positive mental attitude, being prepared, practicing your speech, anticipating the speech situation, practicing active listening, exercising for relaxation, acknowledging the potential benefits of communication apprehension, and maintaining a sense of humor will help you cope with your apprehension.

Every speaker needs to be aware of the array of strategies available for managing communication apprehension. As you give speeches, you may discover strategies that work especially well for you. For now, however, let's examine some of the communication apprehension management strategies that have been very helpful to many speakers.

Develop a Positive Mental Attitude

What do you think of when you imagine yourself making a speech? Do you picture yourself stumbling over your own words, dropping your note cards, freezing as you attempt to respond to an audience question, or perhaps fainting? In other words, do you envision yourself failing? These sorts of mental self-images are far from comforting. Research has clearly shown that people with high speech anxiety tend to have more negative thoughts prior to the delivery of a speech than people who are comfortable speaking.[16] It stands to reason, then, that having positive thoughts may help in managing or reducing anxiety.

When you think of making a speech as a "requirement" (as you may be inclined to do in a public speaking class), you are really viewing it as a kind of burden or load—something heavy and taxing, something you would prefer to avoid or clearly would not choose to do. What happens if you view it as an opportunity? If you can begin to think of making a speech as a chance to change minds, to share what you know, or to make a difference, you will become more enthusiastic, more challenged, more involved, and better able to anticipate success rather than failure.

When you speak in your future professional life, the same kind of reasoning options are available to you. Upon returning from a major conference, your boss may ask you to brief others in your department about new developments in the field. How will you view this speaking request? As a job requirement? A threat? Or as an opportunity? Will you dread the thought of having to speak? Will you sleep poorly the night before and wake up with a distinct sense of impending doom? Or will you recognize that your boss respects your opinion and wants to encourage you to share it with others?

Although having a positive attitude alone does not guarantee that you will make an effective presentation, researchers have demonstrated that **visualization**—a technique that asks the speaker to think positively about everything that occurs on the day of the speech from the time he or she gets up until after the speech has been presented—can greatly help reduce speech anxiety.[17] It's also a good idea to contemplate what you might do to reward yourself after the speech is over. In short, try to approach your speech with positive thoughts about yourself, your speech, and your audience.

PORTFOLIO 2.2

Envisioning Success

Positive visualization is a powerful tool for combating communication apprehension. From the moment you awake on the day you are to make your next speech, begin thinking positively about the entire day, anticipating that good things will happen. Phone someone who is encouraging and supportive of you. Practice your speech once or twice, focusing on what you like best about it. Recall challenges you've met successfully, and visualize yourself succeeding again as you present your speech. Continue to think positively and to anticipate success.

After your speech, jot down what you did that helped you approach your speech positively. Why do you think those things helped? Was there anything that you would not do again? Can you think of anything else you could do to manage communication apprehension before the speech? Jot down quick responses to each of these questions.

visualization a technique in which you anticipate good things transpiring before your speech, during your speech, and as a result of your speech

One way to manage communication apprehension is to develop a positive attitude, focusing on things you want to share with your audience. Here Ruth Batson concentrates on celebrating the accomplishments of Thomas I. Atkins, former executive secretary of the Boston NAACP and Boston's first African American council member. *(Globe Staff Photo/Thomas James Hurst)*

Be Well Prepared

There is no better psychological defense for dealing with speech anxiety than honestly being able to say to yourself that you are well prepared. You have selected a topic of interest and value to you as well as your audience. You have done your homework, conducting an audience survey and gathering and broadening your understanding of the subject. You have carefully organized your speech into a clear, coherent, and unified whole. You have reviewed and revised until you are satisfied that you have crafted a good speech. You have practiced by going over your speech—aloud—several times, timing yourself, and continuing to fine-tune your ideas. You have asked friends for feedback. You can reassure yourself that there is very little more you could have done.

When you prepare so carefully and responsibly, you are far less likely to be self-focused when you actually deliver your speech. Instead, you will be ready to lose yourself in the topic, to live in the moment, and to try to move the audience to grow, understand, and perhaps care as you do. You are truly prepared.[18]

Reminding yourself of your careful preparation can be reassuring and even liberating as you grapple with feelings of anxiety. Your delivery also will reflect your careful preparation, and the audience will sense that you have worked hard out of respect for their time and attention. Also remember that public speaking is an interaction between you and your audience. Just as you hope to speak well, they should be listening carefully. You and the audience *share* responsibility for the outcome of the speech. When you know that you have conducted yourself responsibly during your speech preparation process, you have every right to approach the speech's delivery with some measure of confidence.

Practice Your Speech

Once you have carefully prepared your speech, you are ready to practice. Practicing aloud is the final step in the speech preparation process and is absolutely essential to achieving a good delivery. Here are some specific guidelines that you may want to follow:

1. Before you practice aloud, read through your key word outline two or three times.
2. Practice your speech aloud all the way through. Don't go back and retrace your steps.
3. When you have finished one complete practice, sit down and look through your notes again, identifying spots that were difficult for you to get through. Read over those sections very carefully and revise/refine as needed.
4. Practice a second time—again trying to get through the complete speech. Make sure you are breathing deeply as you speak.
5. *Take a break.*
6. Practice only your introduction two or three times.
7. Practice only your first main point. Repeat as desired.
8. Practice your other main points, one at a time, until you get through the conclusion.
9. Now practice the complete speech one more time.
10. *Take another break.*

Taking breaks is part of the rehearsal process. You need to take a breather, to rest your mind and your voice, and to return to the process refreshed. When you are ready to begin again, you might consider some of the following options.

Practice in front of a small audience. Get their feedback, make changes, and practice once again. If you cannot find a suitable audience, try practicing in front of a mirror or taping your speech. However, try this only if you think you will be able to benefit. You don't want to dissect your delivery and fixate on the kinds of small mistakes we all make. The idea is to strive for general improvement in your fluency, poise, confidence, and use of nonverbals such as gestures and expression.

Practice again on your own for as many times as it takes until you feel comfortable with your notes and with your extemporaneous style. Make sure you practice as much as you need to, but don't over-rehearse by practicing until you have completely memorized your speech—unless your instructor has encouraged you to memorize all or part of it. You might even want to try practicing without using any notes two or three times. This can help you get the big picture, hopefully fixing the main ideas in your mind. Then, when you are able to use your notes again, you may feel more confident—and more grateful to have a set of notes.

Ideally, you should practice over a period of a few days, not a few hours. It is always a mistake to put off rehearsing your speech until the last minute. Prepare your speech in advance; give yourself ample practice time. Some speakers like to practice at odd times and places. For example, you might practice your introduction in your car on the way to work and your conclusion on the way home.

Following these steps will help you practice in a constructive way. No one can tell you exactly how many times to practice or what precise techniques will work for you. As you give more speeches over time, you will learn what approach to practicing works best for you as an individual.

Anticipate the Speech Situation

There are times in life when it's nice to be surprised, but before or during a public speech is not one of them. What happens if you thought you were addressing a few dozen people and it turns out to be a few hundred? Suppose you planned a very formal presentation and arrive at the speech site wearing your most professional attire, only to discover a half dozen listeners in jeans and sweatshirts. Or imagine you had planned to speak for half an hour but are told right before the speech that you have about fifteen minutes. What would you do?

If you are thinking that these situations are unusual or exaggerated, you are mistaken. Each is a speaking "crisis" that we have encountered in our own experiences as public speakers. You might find yourself in similar or equally uncomfortable situations unless you plan very carefully. How might you go about avoiding or minimizing such occurrences?

As we've said before, effective speakers are audience-centered. Gathering preliminary information about your listeners and the overall speaking situation helps you to focus on the audience right from the start and to avoid awkward situations. Whenever someone invites you to make a speech, try to obtain as much useful information as you can. Figure 2.4 previews some basic information you might want to collect about your audience and the speech situation. We'll return to this critical element of developing speeches in Chapter 4.

Go to **Lesson 1's Screening Room** on the **VideoLab** CD-ROM to view the speech of self-introduction and complete accompanying **Drill 1.1**. Consider the extent to which the speaker seems nervous. What strategies might be suggested to help her relax?

FIGURE 2.4 Collecting Information About Your Audience

Some Guiding Questions

1. Does the audience expect me to address a particular topic?
2. What is the audience composition?
   a. audience size
   b. age (range and distribution)
   c. sex (mixed or largely same sex)
   d. values (religious, political, economic, etc.)
3. What is the speaking environment like?
   a. size and arrangement of room
   b. availability of podium, blackboard, flip chart, microphone
   c. degree of formality
   d. location of building (do I need to get a map?)
4. Are there any time constraints?
5. Will questions follow the speech?
6. What is the anticipated length of the entire meeting? When should I arrive?
7. Can I arrive early or check out the setting ahead of time?

PORTFOLIO 2.3

Interacting for Relaxation

Make it a habit to arrive for class ahead of time to visit with your classmates and your instructor. If arriving early every day is not feasible, try to spend a few minutes after class mingling with others. Then the next time you are scheduled to speak to the class, arrive early and interact with classmates as they arrive.

Did doing so help you relax? Write a brief, journal-style entry in which you discuss how the interaction affected your apprehension about speaking that day. Was there a significant effect? In other words, did interaction counteract apprehension?

You can further anticipate the realities of the speaking situation by practicing your speech in the room where you will speak or in a similar environment. Practicing in the room might be especially important if you plan to use presentational support, such as an overhead projector. By incorporating your presentational aids into the practice sessions, you will become comfortable using them in this setting.

The more accurately you can visualize and/or access the speech situation in advance, the better you can plan and the less likely you are to be taken aback or surprised by what you find. Knowing what to expect reduces the ambiguity that can contribute to speech anxiety.

Practice Active Listening

active listening listening very carefully to gain information and understanding

Active listening[19] can be a powerful tool for managing communication apprehension. Rarely do you make a speech under circumstances in which you arrive, jump up and talk, answer a few questions, and leave. More likely, you will be part of an ongoing program, dinner, or business meeting. Other people will speak both before and after you. Listening to them will draw your attention away from your own anxiety.

Active listening also gives you another way to find out something about the audience or the occasion. You might discover, for example, that the listeners are celebrating a special anniversary or that they have been honored for some community project they sponsored. You might discover that they have a great sense of humor or that they are very inquisitive and ask a lot of good questions.

Certainly, you will be listening to other speakers before and after you make a speech in your public speaking class. Instead of fretting over your notes, work hard to listen carefully to those who speak before you. You will learn something, and hopefully you will find yourself a bit more relaxed when your time comes to speak.

Exercise for Relaxation

If you feel tense and nervous before you speak, you can do some simple physical exercises to relax. Of course, it would scarcely be appropriate for you to throw yourself on the floor and start doing pushups or deep knee bends. But, some subtler exercises might prove helpful.

deep breathing expanding the diaphragm to increase one's intake of air; doing so helps one relax and have good vocal support

One excellent way to relax is **deep breathing**. Deep breathing allows you to take in a large quantity of air, giving you a good supply of oxygen and the potential for vocal control. As babies, we all naturally breathe deeply, from the diaphragm and abdomen. Later in life, we often switch to more shallow chest breathing. Unfortunately, chest breathing takes in less air and so necessitates more frequent and rapid breaths. Singers and actors know about the importance of diaphragmatic breathing for good vocal support. Students of yoga also learn to breathe abdominally and with some subtlety.

Concentrating on pushing your abdominal cavity out as you inhale usually corrects poor breathing habits. Even if you have difficulty learning to do this kind of breathing on a daily basis, with a little determination and practice, you should be able to do it prior to a speech to help you relax. You will also want to continue breathing deeply and regularly *while* you are delivering your speech for better vocal support and ongoing relaxation.

Isometric exercise, which involves tensing and then relaxing a muscle of your choice, is another powerful relaxation technique. The principle behind isometric exercise is that by inducing tension and focusing on that tension for a few seconds, you are better able to relax not only the exercised muscle but the rest of your body as well.

isometric exercise tensing a muscle and holding it for a short time, followed by complete relaxation of the muscle

Try clenching and unclenching your fists, pressing your legs firmly together and then relaxing them, or squeezing the palms of your hands together as if you were trying to flatten a piece of clay. Alternatively, you can push your leg, arm, or foot against some immovable object, such as a wall, table, or even the podium. After you have pressed firmly, release the muscle, relaxing it as completely as possible. These isometric exercises are subtle—you can do them without being noticed, even in the middle of your speech. They can also be used before and after the speech.

Finally, performing **aerobic exercise** before your speech can help reduce communication apprehension. Aerobic exercise, such as walking, jogging, running, or swimming, is good for your cardiovascular system and thus is good for your general well-being as a person and a speaker. In addition, this kind of exercise uses up adrenaline and so helps reduce tension and bring communication apprehension into a manageable range.

aerobic exercise physical activity that increases one's heart rate and respiration and, as a result, lessens tension

Acknowledge the Potential Benefits of Moderate Communication Apprehension

Undoubtedly some people have serious problems with speech anxiety. For some, high communication apprehension can be extremely debilitating.[20] Most of us, however, can manage speech anxiety. As a beginning public speaker, it is only natural to wish that you could be perfectly calm and to admire any speaker you see who appears to be "cool as a cucumber."

Recall Misconception 3—that speech anxiety will ruin the effect of the speech. In most public speaking situations, you want a little anxiety. Your goal should not be to *eliminate* any traces of communication apprehension, but to *manage* it by using some of the techniques discussed here and others that may work for you. For instance, some speakers need to begin their day with meditation, prayer, a two-mile run, or a quiet walk. Everyone will benefit from getting a good night's rest and eating a light, nutritious meal before making a speech. Wearing comfortable clothes that make you feel good about yourself also will contribute to a positive mental attitude. Learn what helps you most, then simply accept that you will likely experience a spurt of adrenaline before and during the early minutes of your speech. But as you speak and gain experience as a public speaker, you will begin to feel more comfortable and confident and probably will welcome that adrenaline rush.

CONNECTING TO THE NET

For some additional tips on how to handle your communication apprehension and exercises that will help you find ways to reduce anxiety, go to **http://college.hmco.com/communication/andrews/public_speaking/2e/students/** and click on *Connecting to the Net.* From there, follow the link to Communication Apprehension.

FRAME OF REFERENCE

The context in which a speech is given helps determine what is appropriate. This speaker will choose language that fits the informal, relaxed setting.

Maintain a Sense of Humor

No matter how well you prepare for any speech, some things may happen that you did not anticipate. The microphone may fail. The person who introduces you may mispronounce your name. You may get something under your contact lens, or your earring may fly off. The point is that you have some control over your public communication activities, but as with the rest of your life, you do not have complete control. While this may seem somewhat intimidating, some degree of unpredictability makes speaking in public both challenging and interesting.

You need to maintain a sense of humor. Prepare well, do your best, be flexible, listen to others—but if something goes "wrong," look for the humor in it. What do you do if a dog wanders into the room in the middle of your speech? What happens if the fire alarm goes off? What if, heaven forbid, you lose your place for a minute? In most of these instances, you can maintain your composure, perhaps smile or even comment very briefly, and then go on with your speech. Even if, in your judgment, your entire speech goes badly—that is, *you* feel disappointed in your performance—you learned a few things about public speaking. Perhaps you learned what *not* to do, but at least you learned. And chances are, you weren't as bad as you thought.

Concentrate on what you learned. Look for the humor. Get ready to have another go at it. No matter how brilliantly or poorly you think you performed, it is crucial that you learn to view each speech as an opportunity to connect with an audience and a chance for personal growth. Figure 2.5 highlights the strategies for managing communication apprehension and thus breaking the speech anxiety cycle.

FIGURE 2.5 **Breaking the Speech Anxiety Cycle**

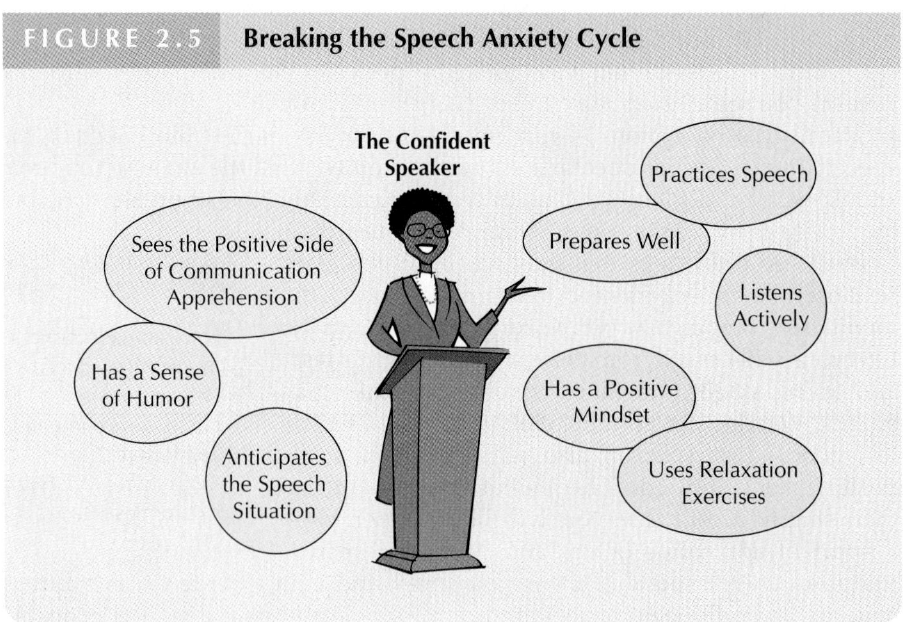

SUMMARY

Understanding communication apprehension is an important step toward being able to manage it and become an effective public speaker. As you learn more about what communication apprehension is, how your body is likely to react to it, and what you can do to manage it (rather than attempting to eliminate it completely), you will become better able to tackle each new speaking assignment.

Communication apprehension is not new—it's been around for as long as people have been talking to one another. Many factors contribute to communication apprehension, including poor preparation, inappropriate self-expectations, fear of evaluation, self-focusing, fear of the audience, and not understanding the body's reactions. Even so, many have learned how to deal with it and to cast aside misconceptions—by learning to believe, for example, that they can do well, that they are not alone, that the audience will give them a chance, and that they will feel more comfortable as a speaker over time.

Scholars have long pondered and studied communication apprehension, and from their research and observations, we have derived many useful insights about how to deal with speech anxiety in constructive and positive ways. For instance, striving to develop a positive attitude toward public speaking, anticipating the speech situation, and practicing active listening as others communicate prior to your speech may prove helpful. Many speakers also exercise for relaxation by breathing deeply or by doing isometric or aerobic exercises.

Successful speakers understand that there are potential benefits associated with communication apprehension, including having extra energy. They also learn to maintain a sense of humor. Most important, perhaps, they prepare very carefully. They have learned that careful, responsible planning and practice can go a long way toward helping them manage speech anxiety and giving them the best chance of making a speech that reflects positively on them and is worthy of the audience's time and attention.

QUESTIONS FOR REVIEW AND REFLECTION

1. What is meant by communication apprehension or speech anxiety?
2. To what extent is speech anxiety a significant problem for anyone making a public presentation?
3. Describe at least five factors that may contribute to communication apprehension. Which ones might be most likely to affect you?
4. What are some of the body's reactions to speech anxiety?
5. Describe the speech anxiety cycle and explain its significance.
6. To what extent are listeners likely to be aware of a speaker's feelings of apprehension?
7. In your view, will moderate communication apprehension help or hinder your speech? Why?

8. Do you view most audiences as basically friendly? How do you view your classroom audience?
9. What are some strategies available to you for managing speech anxiety? Which are most important? Why?

ENDNOTES

1. "What Are Americans Afraid Of?" *The Bruskin Report* 53 (July 1973), p. 8.
2. Jerry Seinfeld, *SeinLanguage* (New York: Bantam Books, 1993), p. 120.
3. "Mental Stress Test Indicator of Future Cardiac Problems," *Bloomington* (Ind.) *Herald-Times* (June 5, 1996), p. A6.
4. A great deal of research during the past three decades has focused on communication apprehension. See, for example, James C. McCroskey, "Oral Communication Apprehension: A Summary of Recent Theory and Research," *Human Communication Research* 4 (1977): 78–96. More recent articles include Ralph R. Behnke and Chris R. Sawyer, "Milestones of Anticipatory Public Speaking Anxiety," *Communication Education* 48 (1999): 165–172; Behnke and Sawyer, "Anticipatory Anxiety Patterns for Male and Female Speakers," *Communication Education* 49 (2000): 187–195; Amy M. Bippus and John A. Daly, "What Do People Think Causes Stage Fright? Naive Attributions About the Reasons for Public Speaking Anxiety," *Communication Education* 48 (1999): 63–72; and Rebecca B. Rubin, Alan M. Rubin, and Felecia F. Jordan, "Effects of Instruction on Communication Apprehension and Communication Competence," *Communication Education* 46 (1997): 104–114.
5. McCroskey, "Oral Communication Apprehension," p. 78.
6. James C. McCroskey and Virginia P. Richmond, "The Impact of Communication Apprehension on Individuals in Organizations," *Communication Quarterly* 27 (1979): 55–61. McCroskey distinguishes *trait communication apprehension* (a characteristic we carry with us across communication situations) from *state communication apprehension* (an anxiety response provoked by specific situations).
7. Marion Woodman, *Addiction to Perfection* (Toronto: Inner City Books, 1982).
8. Rogers was one of the first psychologists to stress this notion; see Carl Rogers, *On Becoming a Person* (New York: Houghton Mifflin, 1961).
9. James C. McCroskey, "The Communication Apprehension Perspective," in *Avoiding Communication: Shyness, Reticence, and Communication Apprehension*, eds. John D. Daly and James C. McCroskey (Beverly Hills: Sage, 1984), pp. 13–38.
10. A. H. Buss, *Self-Consciousness and Social Anxiety* (San Francisco: W. H. Freeman, 1980), pp. 14–16.
11. Joe Ayres, "Situational Factors and Audience Anxiety," *Communication Education* 39 (1990): 283–291.
12. Theodore Clevenger, Jr., "A Synthesis of Experimental Research in Stage Fright," *Quarterly Journal of Speech* 45 (1959): 135–159.
13. Joe Ayres and Tim Hopf, *Coping with Speech Anxiety* (Norwood, N.J.: Ablex, 1993), pp. 5–21.
14. Cicero, *De Oratore*, vol. 1, trans. E. W. Sutton (Cambridge: Harvard University Press, 1942), p. 29.
15. For an interesting discussion of how students with high communication apprehension often assume that the audience is overly critical, see Russell F. Proctor II,

Annamae T. Douglas, Teresa Garera-Izquierdo, and Stephanie L. Wartman, "Approach, Avoidance, and Apprehension: Talking with High CA Students About Getting Help," *Communication Education* 43 (1994): 312–321.

16. John A. Daly, Anita L. Vangelisti, H. L. Neel, and P. D. Cavanaugh, "Pre-performance Concerns Associated with Public Speaking Anxiety" (paper presented at the Annual Convention of the Speech Communication Association, Boston, 1987).

17. Joe Ayres, "Coping with Speech Anxiety: The Power of Positive Thinking," *Communication Education* 37 (1988): 289–296.

18. See Joe Ayres, "Speech Preparation Processes and Speech Apprehension," *Communication Education* 45 (October 1996): 228–235, for an interesting study on how the nature of speaking preparation is vital to the quality of the speech as delivered.

19. In the interpersonal communication and interviewing literature, *active listening* refers to a listening approach in which the listener participates in the conversation by summarizing, paraphrasing, and occasionally interrupting the speaker with clarifying, supportive questions. We are using the term in a different way here.

20. James C. McCroskey, *An Introduction to Rhetorical Communication,* 7th ed. (Boston: Allyn & Bacon, 1997), pp. 39–61.

3 Listening Effectively

CHAPTER SURVEY

The Importance of Effective Listening

Understanding Barriers to Good Listening

Guidelines for Improving Listening

Helping the Audience Want to Listen

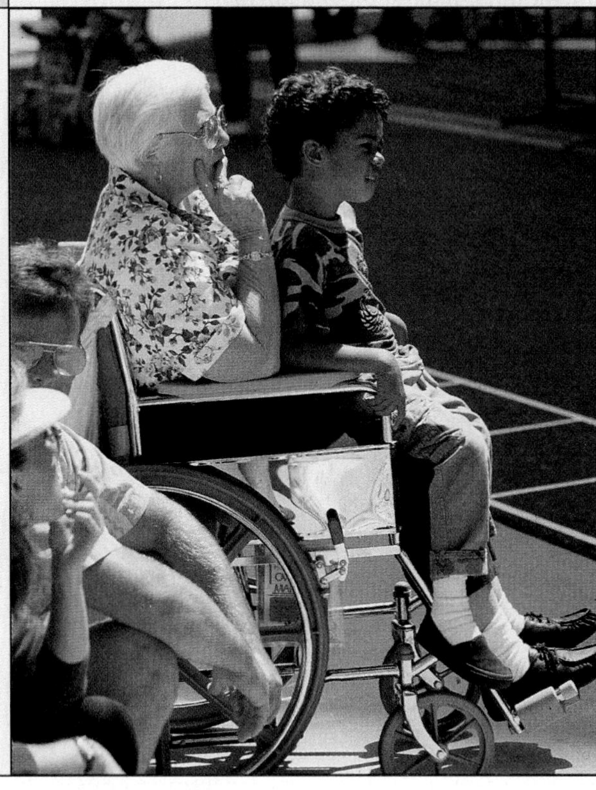

CHAPTER OBJECTIVES

After studying this chapter, you should be able to

1. **describe the importance of effective listening as part of the communication process.**
2. **explain why the speaker needs to know the listening challenges faced by audience members.**
3. **identify and describe common listening problems experienced by audience members.**
4. **list and discuss strategies for improving listening.**
5. **describe ways in which the speaker can help the audience listen more effectively.**
6. **apply the listening guidelines in this chapter.**

Throughout our lives, we are evaluated on the basis of how well we listen. The first-grader's report card assesses the extent to which he or she is attentive, follows orders, and listens when others are talking. As teenagers, our parents accuse us of daydreaming rather than listening; at the same time, we believe that they do not listen carefully to our points of view. Later, in college, we spend seemingly endless hours listening to lectures. In many instances, how well we listen may determine our final grade.

THE IMPORTANCE OF EFFECTIVE LISTENING

Preview Nearly every profession requires the ability to listen well. Those who listen well usually learn more, have better interpersonal relationships, more fully understand their own values, are better speakers, and are more likely to interact ethically with others than those whose listening skills are weak. Even so, effective listening remains a challenge. Most of us fall prey to varied listening problems at some time in our communicative exchanges with others.

Throughout our lives, listening effectively is important, and its significance only increases when we enter the professional world. Studies show that we typically spend about 70 percent of our waking hours in some form of communication: participating in meetings, exchanging ideas and information over email, giving and listening to others' presentations and briefings, writing letters, talking on the telephone, and so forth.[1] Much of this communication involves listening.

To test your skills and expand your understanding of listening, go to **Lesson 3** of the **VideoLab** CD-ROM and walk through the videos, exercises, and tips provided.

Diverse Purposes for Listening

We may listen for several different reasons. For instance, we may **listen for appreciation** when we want to enjoy what we are listening to, such as good music. We don't expect to be analytical or critical; we are simply listening for enjoyment. On other occasions, we may engage in **empathic listening** when we listen to a friend in a supportive way. Here we are striving to understand the other person's point of view or to identify with the feeling level of what he or she is saying.

Both of these are valuable reasons for listening, but in classroom settings and in business and professional life, we are more likely to engage in **informational listening** (in which we want to accurately record information and expand our knowledge about a subject) and **critical listening** (in which we analyze, assess, and evaluate ideas and information). In most public speaking situations, listeners are commonly involved in both informational and critical listening.

listen for appreciation listen with the simple goal of enjoying what is being heard

empathic listening listening, supportively, to another with the goal of understanding his or her point of view

informational listening listening to learn

critical listening listening analytically, carefully evaluating all that is said

To see if you understand the diverse purposes of listening, go to the **Next Step: Listening Purposes** exercise in Lesson 3 of the **VideoLab** CD-ROM and complete the exercise.

Understanding the Listening Process

Regardless of our goals as listeners, whether we are listening for information or analysis, we need to recognize that listening is a multi-step process, as illustrated in Figure 3.1.

- *Hearing.* The first step in the listening process is hearing what the speaker has said. This is the physiological part of listening. We hear more readily if the speaker's message is not impeded by competing sounds, such as a noisy air conditioner or chatting audience members. In addition, we can't hear the message if the speaker talks too softly or delivers the speech so rapidly that words and ideas are garbled. If hearing does not occur, listening is impossible.
- *Focusing.* Once we hear a message, our next task is focusing. When we focus on a speaker's message, we are able to concentrate on it, to filter out competing messages, and to attend to it in such a way that we begin to grapple with its meaning. It's usually easier for us to focus when we respect the speaker and view the message as important.

Do you know how important listening is? Go to **http://college.hmco.com/communication/andrews/public_speaking/2e/students/** and click on *Connecting to the Net.* From these, follow the link to the International Listening Association's web site. The ILA's "Listening Factoids" will give you the answers to some interesting questions. Do you know:

- how much of what we know we've learned by listening?
- the amount of time we are distracted, preoccupied, or forgetful?
- how much we usually recall immediately after we listen to someone talk?
- how much we remember of what we hear?

Look at the "10 Poor Listening Habits" as identified by the ILA. Do any of these habits describe your behavior as a listener?

- *Understanding.* The next stage of the listening process is understanding. Sometimes we hear and are able to focus on a speaker's message. Yet we do not *really* comprehend the speaker's meaning—perhaps because the message is unclear or—we have gaps in our background experience and knowledge base. When we cannot understand and interpret what a speaker means or we misinterpret his or her intended meaning, we falter as listeners.
- *Responding.* When we understand the speaker's message, we will respond in some way. The response range is considerable, including disagreeing, agreeing, questioning, feeling impressed or unimpressed, remaining indifferent or undecided, and so forth.

  All listeners respond internally, but each of us makes some choices about the kinds of *external responses* we make. We may respond nonverbally by smiling and nodding our heads in agreement, applauding with enthusiasm, or refusing to look at the speaker. We may respond verbally by asking questions, sharing our perspectives, or commenting on the speaker's interesting remarks.
- *Remembering.* Although we could complete the above steps and not recall much of what the speaker said a few days or weeks later, clearly the communication event will be viewed by both parties as more successful if, in the end, the listeners find some of the speaker's comments memorable. We may not remember the details, but hopefully we will remember the most important ideas. We can help ourselves remember by taking notes and by doing all that we can to participate as a full partner in the speaking-listening transaction.

Good Listening and Professional Life

Regardless of your chosen occupation, listening well, in the broadest sense, will be important to you. The intelligent doctor listens carefully to patients' complaints before diagnosing the causes of their illnesses. Investment counselors

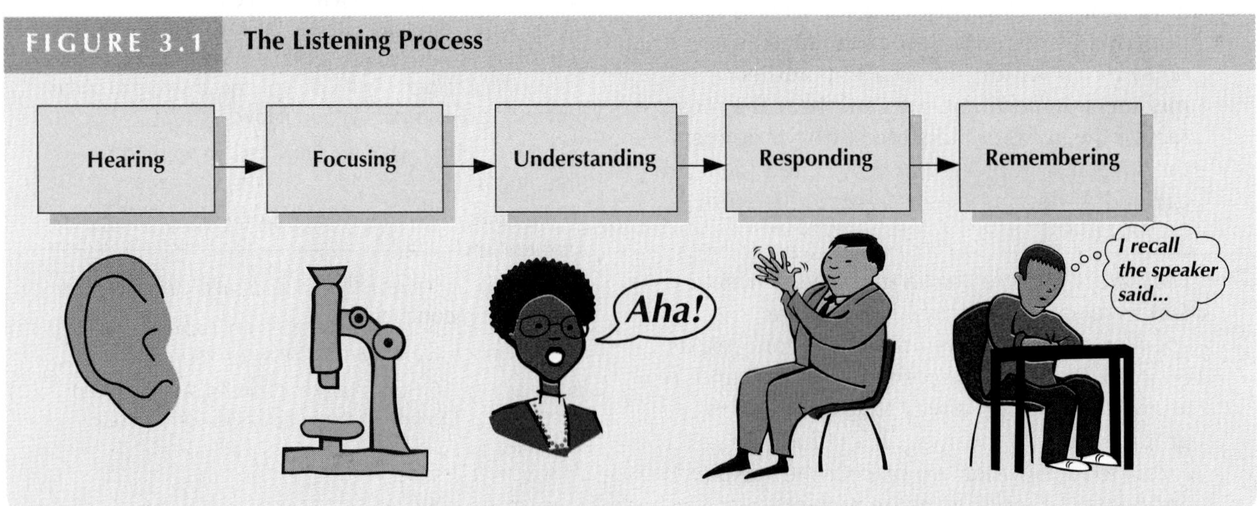

SPOTLIGHT ON... Listening and Leadership

Impressive listening skills have been identified as one common characteristic of credible leaders. . . . To serve others well, leaders must be in touch with them, listen to them, and respect them. . . . Leaders demonstrate that they value others when they listen to them, trust them, and are receptive to having others point out their own mistakes or other problems.

Being able to listen to the news, good and bad, is a basic ingredient for staying in touch. When things are going well, it's not all that difficult to hear the good news. It's how we react to news about mistakes and difficulties that may be the better indicator of whether or not constituents feel like keeping us in touch. From the constituent's perspective, the question is always, "Do they still shoot the messenger with bad news?"

James M. Kouzes and Barry Z. Posner, *Credibility: How Leaders Gain and Lose It, Why People Demand It* (San Francisco: Jossey-Bass, 1993), pp. 191–192.

listen to clients' accounts of how they currently manage their financial portfolios before suggesting any changes. The *good* car salesperson listens to customers' comments on what they are looking for in a vehicle before showing them around the lot. Assembly-line workers and construction workers have to listen to and master safety regulations if the company or crew is to remain accident-free. The wise manager listens to subordinates' concerns and ideas before moving forward with some bold, potentially costly venture. Across diverse occupations and situations, good listening is crucial.

In *Spotlight on Listening and Leadership*, business experts James Kouzes and Barry Posner emphasize the importance of excellent listening skills for those who aspire to upper-management positions in the business world.

To see if you understand the steps involved in the listening process, go to the **Next Step: The Process of Listening** exercise in Lesson 3 of the **VideoLab** CD-ROM and complete the exercise.

Positive Outcomes of Effective Listening

When we listen effectively, we increase our chances of experiencing positive outcomes, such as becoming well informed, maintaining good relationships with others, growing to better understand ourselves, improving our own speaking skills, and learning to participate ethically in the communication process.

- *Listening provides us with information.* Many of our ideas come from listening to others as we brainstorm, watching the news on television, and, of course, listening to formal presentations. Students who are good listeners usually perform better on classroom assignments.
- *Good listeners usually have better interpersonal relationships.* Listening to others, whether a friend or a public speaker, is an excellent way of showing we care about them—their problems, perspectives, and ideas. Furthermore listening is often reciprocated. Those to whom we listen are more inclined to listen to us.
- *Listening gives us a clearer sense of who we are and what we value.* Listening allows us to compare and contrast ourselves with others, helping us better understand our personal identity.
- *Those who listen are often better speakers.* By observing carefully, thoughtfully, and critically the way others communicate and what they say, we

PORTFOLIO 3.1

The Ideal Listener

Identify two people with whom you enjoy talking and use each person's name to head up a column. List the specific listening characteristics of each person that you find desirable.

Construct an inventory of general listening characteristics that others should find attractive.

can gain some understanding of what they find tasteful, sound, strategic, and interesting. And, of course, one of the best ways to analyze any audience is to listen to what they say about themselves whenever we have the opportunity to interact with them before or after a speech.

- *Listening well is an ethical responsibility for each of us as we participate as partners in the communication process.* How can we react thoughtfully to an argument we haven't really heard? How can we demonstrate our conviction that other people's views are valuable if we refuse to listen to them? How can we communicate a desire for dialogue or collaboration if we do not listen to others who are speaking?

In short, effective listening is both a practical imperative and an ethical responsibility.

Good Listening: Not an Easy Task

In spite of the importance of listening, many of us fall short of being the ideal listener. Right after listening to a public speech, we typically recall only about half of what was said; within a few weeks, our recall is reduced to only 25 percent.[2] This problem may be due in part to the fact that the average person speaks at a rate of about 125 words per minute, while our listening minds race on at a speed of 400 to 500 words per minute.[3] As listeners, we must discipline ourselves to use this lag time effectively, or we will find our mind wandering.

What does it mean to be an effective speaker? To distinguish between good and poor listener habits and attitudes, go to the **Next Step: Good Listeners vs. Poor Listeners** exercise in Lesson 3 of the **VideoLab** CD-ROM and complete the exercise.

Of course, general figures on listening can be misleading because we often listen much better under some circumstances than others. We listen more readily, for instance, to those whose views support our own. We listen better if we believe that the information the speaker is sharing is important. We listen more carefully if we know we are going to be evaluated on the basis of how well we have listened and how much we have learned. Any teacher knows that the best way to get students to listen is to utter the ominous words, "What I'm about to say *will be on the test!*" But often we do not have the luxury of listening under ideal conditions. We may not agree with the speaker, we may not see the relevance or usefulness of the information being presented, or we may be distracted by our own concerns.

Some people contend that ineffective listening is a chief cause of communication failure in the business and professional worlds. For instance, a study of more than one hundred Fortune 500 industrial organizations found that poor listening was one of the most important problems managers in charge of training confronted as they attempted to work with employees. These managers reported that poor listening contributed to ineffective performance and low productivity. They noted that listening among their employees was especially problematic during meetings, performance appraisals, and in any context involving superior-subordinate communication.[4] Figure 3.2 depicts several factors that contribute to poor listening.

KEEP IN MIND 3.1

Why Is Good Listening Important?

- Most communicative interactions involve listening.
- When we listen well, we are more likely to remember what we have heard.
- Professionals need good listening skills, regardless of specific occupation.
- Listening provides us with information.
- Good listening tends to improve interpersonal relationships.
- Listening provides us with a sense of our identity and values.
- Good listeners are often better speakers.
- Good listening is an ethical responsibility.

FIGURE 3.2 **Poor Listening**

Why do we listen so poorly? What can be done about it? For you, as a beginning public speaker, these questions are especially important. Not only do you need good listening skills for the reasons we have discussed previously, but when you come to speak in public, you will want your audience to listen to you.

UNDERSTANDING BARRIERS TO GOOD LISTENING

Preview To be effective as a public speaker, you must examine your audience to learn something about their needs, values, and ways of thinking. First, however, you must understand your audience as listeners. Quite apart from their specific characteristics, they are all listeners. If you are to be successful in communicating with your audience, you need to be knowledgeable about the listening process itself. In particular, you should be able to identify common listening problems. If you understand and anticipate these problems, you will be able to minimize, manage, or completely avoid them.

Passivity Syndrome

The average listener is unfamiliar with statistics on inefficient listening. Even if listeners could be introduced to such information, it is unlikely that it would have a significant impact. Why? First, most of us like to believe that we are exceptional. We may read the general statistics on poor listening and simply assume that they don't apply to us. Besides, we believe that listening is easy. After all, we've been doing it for years and for many hours every day (especially as students), so we are well rehearsed. In addition, many of us feel that our primary responsibility as listening audience members is to make sure that our bodies are

Everyone faces certain challenges as a listener. For a self-assessment of your own listening challenges, go to the **SpeechStudio** and complete the **Listening Problems Inventory** exercise.

in the seats at the appointed hour. From that point on, we believe, it is up to the speaker to make us want to listen; if he or she fails, too bad for the speaker!

passivity syndrome denying one's accountability as a listener and assuming that the burden of effective communication resides wholly with the speaker

This line of reasoning—known as the **passivity syndrome**—is rooted in a traditional view of communication that sees the speaker as acting and the listener as reacting, the speaker as controlling and the listener as being controlled. At a conscious level, few of us want to think of ourselves as being overly compliant, losing control, or failing to acknowledge the ethical responsibility inherent in the speaker-listener partnership. Yet these are all unfortunate extensions of the passivity syndrome.

listening actively attending to and processing the verbal and nonverbal elements of a message

The principle that should determine your approach to listening is simple: ***listening*** *is an active process.*[5] Anyone can make us hear just by turning up the volume. But no one can make us listen. We have to want to listen, and we have to be willing to work at it. Hopefully speakers will encourage us by presenting their ideas in an interesting, well-supported, organized, and effectively delivered manner. But say they don't. What if they are disorganized, speak in a monotone, or play with a pen? That doesn't let us off the hook. After all, most speakers have some weaknesses and, frankly, need our cooperation and assistance. Moreover, our attendance at a public speaking event represents a significant investment of valuable time. If we attend a public lecture because we hope to learn, to grow, to be stimulated, or to discover action strategies for dealing with a long-standing problem and we come away empty-handed, surely we must recognize that wherever the "fault" may lie, the outcome is, at least in part, our problem. Thus we should strive to listen effectively for our own sake as well as for the sake of the speaker.

Short Attention Span

How long can you listen to someone speak without starting to fidget or finding that your mind is wandering? Can you easily listen to your professor's forty-five-minute lecture and remain focused and attentive throughout? If you can, you have an exceptional **attention span**.

attention span the typical amount of time one can remain focused and attentive

sound bites brief excerpts of a longer message offered as a substitute for the longer message

Many people believe that our attention span is simply not as good, or as long, as it was five, ten, or twenty years ago. We seem to cope better with shorter messages—those ranging from five to fifteen minutes. Yet speeches and lectures often last much longer. Teaching experts increasingly advise instructors to break their lectures into small chunks, with no chunk lasting longer than fifteen minutes.[6] Some believe that television viewing has contributed to our listening patterns. That is, our attention span appears to follow the situation-comedy pattern: we can listen to a fifteen-minute chunk of information, followed by a "commercial" or some kind of break. Then we can take another ten minutes before needing a break, before the final eight to ten minutes.[7] In addition, television, radio, and newspapers give us much information in **sound bites**, so that we can get the quick gist of what someone has said without having to read or listen to the whole piece.

It may be true that teachers in a classroom setting can accommodate this kind of attention-span profile by stopping for discussion, showing video clips, interjecting exercises, and so forth. But other speaking contexts do not lend themselves as readily to this

PORTFOLIO 3.2

If I'd Only Listened!

Recall instances where you or others have exclaimed: "Oh! If I'd only listened!"

What are some of the more notable instances? What are some equally notable instances in which you or others listened and it paid off?

Divide a page into two columns and list the disasters in one column and the successes in the other.

kind of format. In fact, in most public speaking situations (other than workshops), we would be very surprised if the speaker stopped from time to time and began to ask us questions or broke us into small groups for discussion.

As listeners, we need to be aware of our own attention span. Even if the speaker is very good, we may not be accustomed to having to attend to any one speaker or message for thirty minutes or more. We need to acknowledge the challenge presented by listening to a longer presentation, and we need to be prepared to work hard to remain attentive. If we fade in and out of a speaker's presentation, we will soon lose the big picture and find ourselves hopelessly lost by the end of the speech. Some of the tips we will offer later on should help with the attention-span problem.

Stereotyping

Now that we have moved into the twenty-first century, we are thankfully leaving behind many sexual, cultural, racial, religious, and ethnic stereotypes. Even so, not all stereotypes have necessarily been abandoned. Many people still have a number of stereotypic expectations of women, Jews, homosexuals, African Americans, and many other groups within our culture.

The dictionary defines *stereotype* as "a conventional, formulaic, and oversimplified conception or image."[8] When **stereotyping**, we observe a few members of a particular category (Catholics, Japanese, retired persons, middle-schoolers, Democrats) and draw conclusions about others belonging to the same category. The difference between making a generalization about a group of individuals and stereotyping them is that when we stereotype, we leave no room for individual differences. We believe that each individual will fit the same mental mold we have created for the group.

stereotyping making assumptions about someone based on factors such as race or gender without considering the person's individuality

Stereotyping can interfere with our ability to listen effectively. When we are preoccupied with a speaker's gender, race, or ethnicity, we are focusing on dimensions that may have little or nothing to do with the speaker's message. We are not focusing fully on the information and ideas being communicated. For example, if you took your car to the repair shop and a female mechanic explained the likely source of your problem and the repair options, would her gender influence your ability to listen? Or suppose you were listening to a speech about the "glass ceiling" (an invisible barrier of alleged prejudices and discrimination that hampers women's ability to move beyond middle management). Who would you think was more credible (and easier to listen to), a male or a female speaker?

In examining our tendency to stereotype speakers in some situations, it may be useful to think of ourselves on the receiving end of other people's stereotypes. How does it feel? Reflect on the stereotypes that could be applied to you. Make a list of your personal qualities, organizational memberships, and other background characteristics that might be stereotyped by someone else. What sorts of stereotypes might be associated with you? More important, in what ways do you think you differ from these stereotypes? Table 3.1 provides an example of how one person completed this exercise.

As you think through this kind of exercise, you might reach some of these conclusions:

- Stereotypes abound.
- It is easier to think about stereotyping someone else than it is to examine how others may stereotype us.

TABLE 3.1 Self-Inventory: How Others Might Stereotype Me

My Background Characteristics	Common Stereotypes	What I Am Really Like
College professor	Aloof, superior, head in the clouds, boring	Warm, friendly, interested in students
Single parent	Overwhelmed, frustrated, depressed	Happy, loving, overworked
Methodist	Conservative Christian, regular churchgoer, methodical religious views	Flexible religious views, regular churchgoer
Woman	Emotional, passive, meek, dependent, tender	Active, loving, rational, emotional, independent

- Stereotypes may have some truth in them. You probably found that you have some things in common with your own stereotypes.
- All stereotypes have something wrong with them. Your variations from the stereotype are at least as great as your similarities to it.

In all communication situations—and public speaking is no exception—we need to be sensitive to and respect each person's uniqueness as an individual.

Environmental Distractions

Sometimes, as audience members, we behave as if we can listen only when the situation encourages or allows us to do so. We may become very sensitive to distractions in our surroundings, using them as easy excuses for our inability to listen. We complain, for example, that the room is too hot or too cold, is too large or too crowded, has poor acoustics, or is open to outside noise. Perhaps we sit in the last row and complain that the speaker's voice doesn't carry very well. We sit by an open window and then find ourselves distracted by a lawn mower, the shouts of children, or the beauty of the view. Clearly we are good at this blame-placing game. We tell ourselves that we had every intention of listening carefully but we were simply overwhelmed by environmental distractions.

There are times, of course, when speeches are made in rooms that are poorly ventilated, crowded, or noisy. Distractions are often real as well as imagined. Yet the fact that a listening situation is less than ideal does not mean that we are free to relax and daydream. In most instances, we can overcome **situational distractions** if we really want to. Think of a time when you wanted badly to listen to someone but, for one reason or another, the circumstances were difficult. For example, you get a phone call from a friend who is stationed overseas with the air force. You haven't heard from him in nearly a month, and you've been very concerned about his well-being. Although the connection is horrible—filled with cracks, squeaks, and a constant hum—you strain your ears and you listen. Because you are determined to hear what he has to say, you are able to cope with and overcome annoying distractions. Similarly, in most public speak-

situational distractions disturbances in the environment or medium that challenge our ability to listen ing situations, we have the ability to receive the speaker's message *if* we are determined and motivated to exert the effort required to listen.

Listening with the Eyes

Everyone is aware of the power of first impressions. When we first meet a person, we instantly begin to form an impression, leading to some level of evaluation. Sometimes the initial impression is quickly counteracted by subsequent events. On other occasions, early impressions have a more lasting impact. We know, for example, that recruiters rarely change their judgments of job applicants after the first five minutes, even though the typical interview lasts for thirty minutes.[9] One major component of the first impression is the individual's physical appearance. In fact, without additional information, appearance may be the sole basis for early judgments.

The public speaking situation represents a special problem in this regard since most public speakers are "on display" before they make their speeches. Seated at a luncheon table or on a speaker's platform, they can be viewed but have not yet spoken to the audience. Thus there is plenty of time for listeners to look at them and form early, and often stereotypic, impressions. How might you react if you saw a speaker who appeared to be approaching retirement or a speaker who looked much younger than you? What would you conclude about a speaker who wore sandals and casual attire at an event where everyone else was dressed formally? Would the speaker's body build or personal attractiveness influence the way you reacted? Obviously, to some extent, your reaction would depend on the topic and situation. For example, the speaker's body build might seem irrelevant if he was speaking about how to invest your money, but it might well be pertinent if he was talking about fitness.

When President Bush visited the ruins of the World Trade Center on September 14, 2001, he was greeted by a raucous crowd. To overcome listener distractions, Bush climbed atop a fire truck and grabbed a bullhorn.

"We can't hear you!" someone yelled.

"I can hear you," the president bellowed back. "The rest of the world hears you, and the people who knocked these buildings down will hear all of us soon."

Most listening situations are not as chaotic, nor as emotional, but audience members still need to overcome a variety of distractions to be effective listeners. (AP Photo/Doug Mills)

initial impressions images of a person formulated in our first few minutes around that person, based on her or his physical appearance, nonverbals, and brief remarks

The point is that some of our **initial impressions** of a speaker will be based on physical appearance. What is critical, then, is to recognize the first impression for what it is—and not allow ourselves to hear only what reinforces our first impression. Some listeners, for example, might be impressed by a speaker who appears in an Armani suit; they could be disposed to suspend their critical faculties and more readily believe what he says because he looks successful. If we allow ourselves to react only on the basis of first impressions, however, we have judged the speaker as if he were a contestant in a beauty pageant.

nonverbal communication facial expressions, vocal qualities, and physical movements that reinforce or contradict one's verbal messages

It is true, of course, that **nonverbal communication** is important and cannot be ignored, but what we observe with the eyes is only the beginning. We are there to listen to the speaker's complete presentation. Only then, on the basis of what we have heard and observed, can we formulate a reasonable reaction to the speaker and the speech.

Mental Games

Most of us are quite comfortable when we perceive our world to be in a state of balance. We enjoy chatting with people who seem similar to ourselves, and normally we prefer public speakers whose basic thinking is in line with our own.[10] This desire for harmony, consistency, and balance may not be conscious, but it can cause us to react defensively whenever we are exposed to ideas that challenge our world view. If the issue under discussion is relatively insignificant to us, we may take it in stride. However, when a public speaker questions our thinking on some matter central to our value system, we may be jarred into defensiveness. It can be painful to listen to a speaker discuss the dangers of smoking if you happen to be a smoker. It's hard to hear a speech about the billions of dollars U.S. citizens pay every year in credit card interest if you have reached the limit on all your credit cards. And a good speech on the virtues of volunteerism can be tough to take if you've never volunteered in your life.

On occasion, we may escape being subjected to distressing communication. We have seen members of our family turn off the TV in disgust when a politician whose views they abhor begins to make a speech. Others may utter comments of disrespect or begin to counterdebate while the TV speaker is talking.

In a live public speaking situation, the listener rarely pursues such options. Almost no one will interrupt a speaker to argue a point, and few of us will get up and walk out. Even so, it is always possible to turn the speaker off mentally. We may do this either by pretending to listen while turning our mind to other affairs or by engaging in mental rebuttal. Either represents a listening hazard.

pretending to listen simulating listening behaviors but not paying attention to the speaker's message

When we are **pretending to listen**, we feign attentiveness (and we are very good at that!) while allowing ourselves to fantasize, plan the evening ahead, or reflect on our day. Dogbert's account of how group members react to the boredom of meetings (see cartoon on the following page) is equally applicable to how listeners often respond to boring speakers.

Faking attention may be a polite way of not listening, but it wastes everyone's time (our own and the speaker's), and it is also less than honest, in that we are giving the speaker inaccurate nonverbal feedback. We may look attentive, but our mind is a world away.

mental argument mentally formulating rebuttals to the speaker's ideas and, in the process, losing track of the speaker's message as a whole

The second tactic, **mental argument**, is somewhat preferable in that we do remain actively involved in thinking about the speech topic. But it has nothing to do with listening to the speaker. As we carefully refute the speaker's ideas, we often lose the thread of the argument. When the speaker is finished, we may

DILBERT reprinted by permission of United Feature Syndicate, Inc.

know what was said up to a point, but the remainder of the speech escaped us because we got carried away with listening to our own reservations and counterarguments. It is hardly surprising, then, that during question-and-answer periods, listeners sometimes ask for information that the speaker has already provided. Other audience members will soon become impatient with those who waste everyone's time with unnecessary questions.

As effective listeners, we must allow the speaker to state his or her complete case so that we can make a sound judgment. Moreover, to function as **ethical listeners**, we must be prepared to give a speaker a fair and honest hearing before reaching conclusions. It is perfectly acceptable to recognize disagreement during the speech, but you should simply make note of it, put it aside, and listen to the rest of the argument. After having listened to a complete statement of the speaker's point of view, you are then equipped to react intelligently and justly to points raised along the way.

ethical listeners people who listen open-mindedly to a speaker before making any pronouncements about the integrity and value of the speaker's message

Poor Note Taking

Most of us have less than perfect memories. Even if we are striving to listen carefully and conscientiously, we will still have some problems with accurate and complete recall. Thus, many of us turn to some form of **note taking** to provide a more accurate record of what the speaker said.[11]

note taking a type of active listening that, if done correctly, can assist the comprehension and retention of a message

KEEP IN MIND 3.2

Audience Listening Challenges

- **The passivity syndrome**—failure to understand listening as an active process
- **Short attention span**—inability to attend to a long message
- **Stereotyping**—making assumptions about the speaker based on bias or prejudice
- **Environmental distractions**—failing to listen to a speaker because of distractions in the listening environment
- **Listening with the eyes**—being distracted from the speaker's message by some aspect of his or her appearance
- **Mental games**—pretending to be attentive or counterarguing
- **Poor note taking**—failure to take notes or using poor note-taking methods
- **Weak critical listening/thinking skills**—failure to assess the quality of the speaker's ideas and arguments

Interestingly, audience members do not consistently take notes. They are much more likely to do so if they are students listening to a professor than if they are members of a congregation listening to a minister or club members listening to a postluncheon speech. It seems that listeners are most likely to take notes if they feel they are supposed to be gathering information—perhaps for later use or for a test. Some researchers argue that most processing of ideas and information gathered during a speech or lecture occurs *after* the speech is over, emphasizing the importance of having a good set of notes for analysis and reflection.[12]

Note taking is also an excellent listening aid. Because it requires some action on our part, it reminds us that good listening is an active process. In addition, note taking takes time. Since we can think so much more rapidly than the speaker can speak, taking notes can help us synchronize our tempo with that of the speaker.[13] Finally, note taking helps us to remember. Our notes can help us ask questions after the speech and let us take home some recorded information to ponder and possibly use in the future.

Like any strategy for improving the outcome of a speech communication situation, however, note taking can be used adeptly or improperly. Listeners tend to move toward one extreme or the other—writing down too much or too little. For many listeners, a compromise approach works best, in which you record major ideas with occasional facts, phrases, or statistics to remind you of particularly striking or controversial examples or other evidence. If you use this approach, you end up with a basic outline of the speech, similar to the one the speaker has used. Such a set of notes will help you to reflect accurately and critically on what the speaker has said.

Weak Critical Listening/Thinking Skills

PORTFOLIO 3.3

Listening Made Easy

Think about speakers who have made listening easy for you.

Make a quick list of the things they did to make listening easy.

As you read the next section, compare your inventory with the pointers we provide.

We have already pointed to the importance of viewing listening as an active process. Part of this active process involves some critical reflection and reaction to what is being said. It also involves recognizing and believing that the listener's role is just as vital as the speaker's. We tend to forget that even when we are not talking we are still very much a part of the communication process. We can forget this especially in a public speaking setting in which constant recognizable feedback is not called for and in which overt interaction is minimal.

Many students in a public speaking class, for example, think that it is not important to be in class when someone else is speaking, except perhaps as a courtesy—so that there will be an audience to listen. But listening to speeches is as important as giving them. The dismissal of the listening process as unimportant is reflected by the type of comment that some students make (students who have not considered the effects of such comments on their ethos) when they ask instructors, "Did we do anything important when I was absent on Tuesday?" The implication is that if no assignments were given, no tests were taken, or no material was handed out, then the instructor only talked, so nothing important happened. But how students responded to that lecture might have been, or could be, vitally important for everyone.

The point is not so much that one is present as that one *does* something—not just that one hears but that one listens actively and critically.[14] **Listening critically** means assessing what you hear. You try to make what you hear relevant to what you need to know. You weigh it carefully before you decide whether to act or not to act. Since a speech is designed to get a response from you, you ought to ask yourself what the speaker's words are doing to and for you as you listen. The search for the answer to such questions can never be a passive one. You can be a productive listener only to the extent that you pursue a strategy aimed at getting the most out of listening to a speech.

Let us now lay out the tactics, most of which we have alluded to in the preceding pages, that should form your listening strategy. It's important to keep in mind that good listening and critical thinking are, of necessity, related. Effective listening provides the foundation for critical and constructive thinking.

listening critically analyzing what is being said in terms of whether it is accurate, reasonable, fair, and of consequence

What barriers to good listening are especially problematic for you? To what extent are those barriers based on sources internal to you, and to what extent are barriers sometimes created by the environment? Go to the **Next Step: Barriers to Listening** exercise in Lesson 3 of the **VideoLab** CD-ROM and complete the assessment of potential listening barriers.

GUIDELINES FOR IMPROVING LISTENING

Preview Listening effectively requires considerable effort. We must also approach listening strategically, by thinking about our attitude as well as about some of the things we can do to increase our chances of listening well. We would be wise to consider our own identity as we listen to someone speak. At the same time, we should strive to listen purposefully, to understand the setting, to think about the speaker's intended audience and purpose, and to examine our own knowledge about the speaker. Above all, we must remind ourselves of the importance of listening, approach listening critically and constructively, and recognize and practice listening as an active process.

Understand Your Identity as a Listener

We all bring who we are to a speaking situation, and who we are colors how we interact with the speaker and the speaking situation. For example, someone who thinks "It'll never happen to me," may not respond very well to fear appeals. Your background, your personal characteristics, and the roles you play in life all contribute to certain predispositions and biases that will influence your reactions. No one can totally eliminate bias, but you can, through self-analysis, discover some of the forces at work in yourself. Only by understanding your **identity**—what you bring to a speaking situation and who you are in relation to it—will you be able to listen in a realistic and fair-minded way.

Just as nearly everyone experiences listening challenges, everyone also possesses listening strengths. To assess yours, go to the **SpeechStudio** and complete the **Listening Skills Inventory** exercise.

identity what you bring to a speaking situation and who you are in relation to it

Listen with a Purpose

The speaker has a purpose in getting up to talk, and, as audience members, we ought to have one as we sit and listen. Do you want simply to better understand an opposing point of view? Do you hope to learn something? Can you relate the topic to your life and decide what aspect of it will be useful to you? If so, your main purpose may be to identify the practical aspects of the speech that pertain to you.

Your purpose may evolve as you listen. You may begin by thinking you just want information about a problem. But as you listen, you may decide that you want to get involved—to do something about the problem. In general, you can provide your own focus whenever you listen to someone speak. By **listening purposefully**, you can take from and respond to the message on your own terms while still maintaining a healthy respect for the speaker's position and purpose.

listening purposefully listening respectfully with the goal of gaining something from the message and responding appropriately to it

Understand the Setting

As we pointed out earlier, the setting of a speech imposes restrictions and expectations on a speaker. A political candidate who has bought thirty seconds of radio time is very limited in what he or she can say. A speaker at an outdoor rally and one in a classroom will be working under different **constraints**. When you listen, being aware of the limitations and **opportunities** of the particular setting will help you respond more appropriately to the speaker's efforts. If the speaker is given little time to speak, for instance, you might be less critical if his or her main points are not fully developed. In contrast, a speaker with ample time has ample opportunity to explain key points fully. In this situation, the speaker who fails to do so will be judged accordingly.

constraints things that limit or otherwise affect what you can or should say in a given situation

opportunities things that suggest what you can or should say in a given situation

Understand to Whom the Speaker Is Talking

Sometimes a speaker's words are aimed at more than one audience. For example, at a large state university, a series of racially motivated incidents resulted in several protest demonstrations and rallies on campus. At these rallies, students spoke to an audience of their peers—their **immediate audience**. However, these students knew that members of the press were present. Through the press, the speakers hoped to send powerful persuasive messages to a wider **target audience** composed of campus and community leaders. The types of appeals speakers make, the types of arguments they use, and even the topics they select may be puzzling to a listener who does not understand that public communication can have wide ramifications.

immediate audience those who constitute a speaker's audience at the speaking event

target audience those whom the speaker would most like to influence with the message

Consider the Speaker's Purpose

Understanding what the speaker hopes to accomplish by speaking (that is, the speaker's **purpose**) prepares us to listen effectively. Speakers do not always make their purpose clear, and some may even intend to mislead the audience. If a speech is poorly structured, it may not be easy to identify the goal or purpose. Knowing something about the setting, the speaker, and the general nature of the topic may help us identify the speaker's goal. Once we think we discern the basic thrust of the speech, we should write it down. Armed with this understanding, we are better positioned to make judgments about the quality of the ideas and information that follow.

purpose what a speaker hopes to accomplish by speaking

Examine Your Assessment of the Speaker

Often when we listen, we have some initial perceptions of the speaker's credibility. If we are not careful or honest with ourselves about these perceptions, we

SPOTLIGHT ON... The Power of Listening

Listen for More Than You Hear

Listening is powerful because it shows a genuine desire to understand the unique needs and feelings of others. . . . Kelleher's [Southwest Airlines' CEO] influence with people stems from his willingness to be influenced by them. People in the field, for example, are less resistant to change and more open to new ideas that come from the executive offices because they know that Herb [and the others on the executive team] will *listen* to what they have to say. More importantly, these people know that the company's executives will be influenced by what they hear. Listening that evokes some type of action or emotional response essentially shows people that they have been influential. People who feel that they have been heard are more willing to hear others.

Kevin Freiberg and Jackie Freiberg, *Nuts! Southwest Airlines' Crazy Recipe for Business and Personal Success* (New York: Broadway Books, 1998), p. 308.

will find ourselves overly influenced by the person speaking rather than by the quality of the message.

If, for example, you know the speaker is someone you don't like, then face up to that fact. You could fool yourself into believing that you won't take the desired action because it is too expensive, it isn't logical, or you are too busy. But the real reason might be that you just don't want to give the speaker satisfaction or pleasure by doing what he or she wants you to do. If the matter is not of vital importance, it may not make any difference whether you follow the course of action recommended. But suppose it is a very serious matter that could affect your health or well-being. Can you afford to base your decision on purely personal grounds? If you fool yourself, you will never even question whether you should act or not act solely on the basis of the credibility of the speaker. Thus you may lose the opportunity to listen effectively and, consequently, to act effectively.

Remind Yourself of the Importance of Listening

Because good listening does require effort, it's easy to become lazy and minimize its importance. So we may need to remind ourselves of how much we can learn, how we will have a chance to clarify our own positions, and why listening is an ethical responsibility for all of us who seek to become good communicators.

Although we have emphasized the importance of listening in the context of public communication, effective listening is a central life skill. In *Spotlight on the Power of Listening*, consultants Kevin and Jackie Freiberg describe the leadership philosophy of Herb Kelleher, chairman, president, and CEO of Southwest Airlines. Kelleher's views translate readily into many communicative contexts.

Listen Critically

A speaker who is really trying to communicate is attempting to get the listener to respond to the message in a specific way. The speaker may want you to vote, to volunteer, to agree with a point of view, to understand a certain perspective on a community problem, or to feel inspired or motivated. It may or may not be in your best interest to respond as the speaker wishes. As a listener, your major responsibility to yourself is to respond as intelligently as possible. This means that you cannot jump to conclusions. Instead, you must **suspend judgment** until you are convinced that you are making the best choice. You must listen critically, defending yourself against the appeals and pressures put on you by the event.

suspend judgment to avoid jumping to conclusions so that you can respond as intelligently as possible after processing the message in its entirety

Defending does not necessarily mean rejecting. You might, in the end, accept a speaker's arguments and respond as he or she desires. You might be skeptical of a television message, for example, but still end up buying the product or voting for the candidate. When you listen critically, you work to uncover and evaluate the basis of your own responses. As a listener, you should understand *why* you are reacting in a certain way to a speech and then ask yourself whether the basis for your reaction is sensible.

In examining your own motives, you should try to uncover the extent to which you are acting on the basis of the image or reputation of the speaker. It is important to determine how you are responding to the ideas in the speech, asking yourself how clear they are and how well **assertions** are supported by hard **evidence**.

assertions claims that one advances with an insistence that they are truthful

evidence fact and opinion used to support a particular perspective about a subject

Certainly you should consider the extent to which you are responding on the basis of your feelings—for example, because you feel sympathetic, frightened, hostile, or loving. You must ask yourself whether the speaker is attempting to manipulate your response by appealing to your feelings—for example, by associating your feelings of independence and self-esteem with smoking a particular brand of cigarette. As a critical listener, you will constantly probe the kinds of appeals the speaker is using and carefully reflect on the motives and feelings you bring to the speech situation.

Practice Listening as an Active Process

All the guidelines we've presented point to the hard work that must go into preparing yourself to listen and listening effectively. Here are some additional practical tactics that are a part of the **active listening process**.

active listening process preparing yourself to listen and listening effectively

- *Use nonverbal communication to show the speaker that you are actively engaged as a listener.* When you lean forward as the speaker talks, you express your interest. You also may smile or nod your head in agreement to show the speaker that you are amused, you are following his or her ideas, or you endorse his or her point of view. Through your facial expressions, you can show interest, confusion, or concern.

  As we have stressed throughout the book, effective communication demands thoughtful, responsible, and active participation by those involved in the process. When you are an audience member, you have an *ethical responsibility* to offer feedback. After the speech, you can ask questions and make comments, but during the speech, most of your feedback will be nonverbal. Based on your nonverbal feedback the speaker can begin to process your concerns, clarify your confusion, and anticipate some of the issues you may raise after the speech. In this way, you, as a listener, function as a responsible, active partner in the communication process.

You have already learned about such strategies as identifying main points and taking good notes as ways of enhancing your listening effectiveness. To explore another vehicle for achieving effective listening, go to **Drill 3.2: Active Listening—Learning to Paraphrase** on the **VideoLab** CD-ROM and complete the quiz that introduces you to paraphrasing.

- *Take notes as you listen.* As we noted earlier, effective note taking can help you follow the speech actively and record critical information and ideas for immediate and later use. In taking notes, you will want to jot down a basic outline of the speech, as well as specific questions you want to ask and statistics or examples you want to remember. Note taking is another way to remain actively involved during the speech.[15]

A good listener is actively engaged in the communication process. This student is taking notes and giving the speaker his full attention. (Michael Newman/PhotoEdit)

- *Identify main points.* Once you have discovered the speaker's purpose, you will need to start looking for main points. What are the key points the speaker wants you to remember? What are the reasons given for asking you to donate your time to a particular cause? What are the arguments advanced for persuading you that private education for elementary students is superior to public education?
- *Look for evidence.* As you are able to identify main points, take note of the evidence used by the speaker to support key ideas. Did the speaker cite credible sources of information? Were the statistics used clear and meaningful in helping you grasp the magnitude of the problem? To what extent did the speaker rely on personal experiences and opinions? If the speaker leaned heavily on personal knowledge, were you convinced that his or her personal experiences were sufficiently credible? Make note of the evidence (facts and opinions) that you want to remember, and jot down any information that you doubt or have questions about.
- *Examine the speaker's reasoning.* As the speaker advances arguments, consider the quality of her or his **reasoning**. Does the speaker seem to have jumped to some conclusion on the basis of too little evidence? Does he seem to attack someone's plan because he doesn't like the other person instead of arguing against the substance of the plan? Does she advocate a course of action (for example, changing your retirement plan or purchasing a specific kind of computer) primarily because a lot of other people are doing it? There may be plenty of good reasons for doing as the speaker suggests, but you need to be convinced that the substance of the speaker's arguments can withstand your critical scrutiny.

reasoning reaching a conclusion on the basis of supportive evidence

There is no better way to learn to listen well than to practice doing it. Go to **Drill 3.3: Practicing Listening** on the **VideoLab** CD-ROM. There you will have the chance to listen critically to a speech and to constructively assess its strengths and weaknesses. As you listen to the speech for the first time, you may want to experiment with using the **Checklist for Evaluating Speeches** in the **SpeechStudio**.

- *Minimize distractions.* Do all you can to stay focused on the speech. Note taking will help. Arriving early enough to get a good seat will help, too. Beyond that, put distractions—whether they come from the speaker or from the environment—in perspective. Remind yourself that your purpose is not to offer a critique of the speaker's gestures or hairstyle, nor to do an acoustical analysis of the room. Rather, you are there to listen to the ideas and information advanced by the speaker and to react as intelligently and thoughtfully as you can.
- *Suspend judgment.* Although we often react hastily to a speaker's comments, we should suspend final judgment until the speaker is finished. As you listen, you will, of course, make some judgments. You will listen

KEEP IN MIND 3.3

Guidelines for Listening

- Understand your identity as a listener.
- Listen with a purpose.
- Understand the setting.
- Understand to whom the speaker is talking.
- Consider the speaker's purpose.
- Examine your assessment of the speaker.
- Remind yourself of the importance of listening.
- Listen critically.
- Practice listening as an active process.

critically to every argument; you will scrutinize every piece of evidence. You will assess and reassess your perceptions of the speaker's ethos—his or her intentions, integrity, and competence—throughout the speech. Within the context of critical listening, however, you must strive for some measure of open-mindedness. Give the speaker a fair and reasonable chance.

Whatever your ultimate reaction to the speech, it should come at the end of the speaker's comments. Suspension of judgment might take you to the end of the planned speech, or you might want to wait until you've heard the speaker's responses to audience questions. The point is simply to wait until the end: maintain an open mind but never stop thinking, questioning, and examining the speech.

HELPING THE AUDIENCE WANT TO LISTEN

Preview Speakers need to do all they can to help their audience listen. It is up to you as a speaker to increase your chances of being listened to by involving the audience, minimizing and responding to distractions, stressing key ideas, and actively listening to the audience.

As you prepare for and deliver your speech, place yourself in the listeners' shoes. Ask yourself what you might do to help the audience listen more effectively. What are some things you can do (or avoid doing) to contribute to a positive outcome for both you and your audience? Following are some basic principles to keep in mind as you approach the prospect of speaking in public.

Involve the Audience

sustaining attention keeping the audience intellectually and emotionally involved in your speech

Seek ways to involve your audience throughout the speech. Nearly everyone knows that a good speaker needs to get the audience's attention during the speech's introduction, but **sustaining attention** presents an ongoing challenge. When the audience is intellectually and emotionally involved in your speech, they are more likely to be attentive.

Sometimes you can involve the audience through your delivery—by showing your enthusiasm and involvement, your sincerity and commitment. You can speak to them with directness and earnestness so that they know you really care about child abuse, the burning of African American churches, the importance of exercise, the dangers of driving while intoxicated, or the need for long-range financial planning for retirement.

Beyond an engaging delivery, you will also need to present clear, forceful arguments, accompanied by compelling evidence and sound reasoning. Or if your purpose is informative, you will want to give your listeners information that is new, that offers a different perspective or fresh insights. You will need to convince them that they *need to know* the information you're presenting or that

Good speakers use all the means at their command to arouse and hold listeners' interest. These storytellers at a Kwanza event being held in a New York state library use gesture, captivating language, and costume to connect with their audience and entice them to listen. *(Syracuse Newspaper/Albert Fanning/The Image Works)*

they or others they care about *would benefit from* the plan or course of action you are proposing. If you want to help the audience listen, you will need to keep asking yourself: Why should they want to listen to what I'm saying? How can I consistently remind them of the relevance, significance, and need for the information I'm sharing or the action I'm proposing?

Finally, you can involve listeners by *using clear and compelling language.* You connect with the audience when you use language that is understandable to them, and you gain and sustain their attention with language that is vivid, dramatic, and memorable. Here is how Cesar Chavez used powerful language to involve listeners in his moving speech on the dangers of pesticides:

> My friends, grapes are the most dangerous fruit in America. The pesticides sprayed on table grapes *are killing America's children.* These pesticides *soak* the fields, *drift* with the wind, *pollute* the water, and are *eaten* by unwitting consumers. These poisons are designed to kill life, and pose a very real threat to consumers and farm workers alike.
>
> This is a very technical problem, with very *human* victims. One young boy, Felipe Franco, was born without arms or legs in the agricultural town of McFarland. His mother worked for the first three months of her pregnancy picking grapes in fields that were sprayed repeatedly with pesticides believed to cause birth defects.
>
> The grape vineyards of California have become America's Killing Fields. These *same* pesticides can be found on the grapes you buy in the store.[16]

Chavez's use of vivid language, metaphor, and narrative made this speech one of the most stirring speeches of the twentieth century.

Like Chavez, you will want to consider your audience while you prepare and deliver your speech—consistently looking for opportunities to engage their interest and commitment along the way. In this way, you will be more likely to realize your purpose and help your listeners want to listen to your ideas.

Minimize and Respond to Distractions

Whenever you speak, you will want to minimize anything that might distract the audience. Potential distractions will vary from one speech situation to another, but in most speech settings, you'll want to make sure that neither your physical appearance nor your delivery detracts from your speech.

Sometimes these can interact. One speaker chose to wear his baseball cap to deliver his final speech, a very serious persuasive speech on advancing funding for research on Alzheimer's disease. Not only did the cap give the speaker a casual air, but he fiddled with the cap as he spoke, at times pulling it down so that the bill covered most of his eyebrows. A different speaker had her hair styled so that, during most of her speech, it covered almost half of her face. Not only was this a source of distraction for the audience, but it seemed to bother her, too, since she regularly brushed it aside, either with her hand or by tossing her head. In these examples, physical appearance contributed to distracting gestures and mannerisms that made it difficult for the listeners to focus on the information and ideas being advanced.

Some distractions may be introduced into the speaking environment through sources that are beyond the speaker's control. For instance, the microphone may die, your overhead projector may blow a bulb, or the room may be very hot. How you, as the speaker, react to these potential distractions is very important. You are, after all, the focus of attention and, for the moment, are responsible for creating a context in which you and your listeners can connect. To do this, you may need to stop for a few minutes and ask for assistance. The thermostat can be adjusted, windows opened, and spare bulbs found. Or you may need to abandon the podium and move closer to your listeners so that they can hear your message. You may need to use handouts rather than the overhead projector.

In managing distractions, three points are key. First, many distractions cannot be ignored. If the audience can't hear you speak, both you and your listeners are wasting your time. Second, the more you *anticipate* potential distractions, and the more *flexible* you are, the better are your chances of coping effectively when problems arise. For instance, if you have prepared and practiced your speech carefully, you can get by without using a podium. If you bring handouts as a backup, you can move forward without the benefit of an overhead projector. Finally, although you and your listeners share responsibility for the outcome of the speaking event, as the speaker, you are in a better position than the audience to ask for assistance or to take some corrective action. When you do so, both you and your listeners will benefit.

preview provide a glimpse of the major points one will be making in a speech or in a section of a speech

transitions words, phrases, or sentences that help the audience perceive the relationship of ideas and the movement from one point to another

internal summaries brief reviews of what one has presented in one or more areas of a speech, provided before moving on to the next area

signposts words that alert listeners to where you are in your speech, particularly in relation to its overall organization

Stress Key Ideas

You can help the audience follow your speech by doing all you can to emphasize key ideas. A *good introduction* is essential—one in which you set forth your purpose and **preview** your main points. But you will also need to work on good **transitions** so that the audience can see the relationship between what you've just said and where you are heading. **Internal summaries** can help, and occasionally, when an idea is really important, you may want to repeat it, perhaps using slightly different words. To help the audience follow your organizational pattern, you may want to use **signposts** (words such as *first, second,* or *finally*) to show listeners where you are in your speech. You can also *deliver main* *points so that you stress them*—perhaps by increasing your volume, slowing down just a bit, looking directly into the eyes of the audience, or pausing after you've shared something really important.

You may want to *use some presentational aids* to reinforce key ideas. Listeners have become increasingly visual over the past few decades and have shorter attention spans. Visually depicting a statistical trend, projecting main ideas onto a screen, or showing pictures or slides to emphasize the magnitude of the problem (such as the ravages of deforestation) can help the audience understand your points. In addition, using music, video clips, charts, or slides at strategic points during longer presentations will break up the material and help the audience refocus.

FRAME OF REFERENCE

Speakers who are well prepared and who focus their attention on their listeners will feel more confident and relaxed.

As you use presentational reinforcement (and deliver your comments effectively), you are also providing *variety.* When you walk to a screen or a flip chart to point to key ideas, you are moving and thus doing something a bit different. When you stop talking so that the audience can see a brief video clip or pause to let them listen to a bit of music, you have provided the kind of variety that can help them remain attentive during your entire speech. In many workshop and organizational settings in which professionals speak, presentational aids (increasingly including computer-generated graphics) are considered essential. They are part of audience expectations. By using them in this context, you are showing that you acknowledge and accept those expectations, and you are also showing the audience that you are well prepared. We discuss presentational aids in Chapter 13.

Actively Listen to the Audience

In the long run, you will help the audience listen to you if you show your willingness to listen to *them.* You can listen in several ways. Question the person who invited you to speak. Ask about the audience's knowledge, values, needs, and expectations before you begin to work on your speech. In this way, you can begin to learn about and "listen to" the audience before you develop your speech. Continue to listen to those with whom you interact right before you make your speech—during the early parts of a meeting, during lunch, and so forth. You might learn a few last-minute tidbits that you can incorporate spontaneously into your presentation.

Equally important is being attentive to other parts of the program or meeting that surround your talk. Speakers who whisper to the person next to them while business is being conducted or who read through their notes and ignore everything else that is going on risk being seen as rude and disrespectful. You can show your interest in the audience and the occasion by *active nonverbal listening*—nodding, smiling, and establishing eye contact with others who are speaking.

When it is your turn to speak, you can continue to "listen to" the audience by carefully observing their nonverbal feedback. If they are bored, confused, amused, or exasperated, you can probably pick up on that by watching their facial expressions. In some cases, you can make adjustments in your delivery, style, or content. You might, for instance, use an extra example to help clarify a difficult concept. Or you might use a little more humor with listeners who have really warmed to you and who seem to enjoy humor.

Finally, you can listen very carefully to audience questions and comments after the speech is over. Listening with sensitivity and thoughtfulness and responding with candor and concern for audience views go a long way toward

Both speakers and listeners can devise and implement strategies for improving listening processes and outcomes. Go to the **Next Step: Strategies for Enhancing Listening** exercise in Lesson 3 of the **VideoLab** CD-ROM for a review of the strategies available to both parties in the speaker–listener partnership.

FIGURE 3.3 Strategies for Effective Listening from Both Sides of the Podium

As a Speaker, You Will	As a Listener, You Will
• Be aware of barriers to effective listening • Seek to involve the audience • Show your own involvement • Minimize and respond to distractions • Emphasize key ideas by *previewing* *using internal summaries* *using good transitions* *signposting* *stressing main points through delivery* *using visual reinforcement* • Actively listen to the audience by *learning about listeners in advance* *showing attentiveness when others are speaking* *watching for nonverbal feedback* *being attentive and responsive to questions*	• Think about your identity as a listener • Listen with a purpose • Understand the setting • Think about the audience you're a part of by identifying the *immediate audience* *target audience* • Consider the speaker's purpose • Examine your assessment of the speaker • Remember the importance of listening • Listen critically • Practice listening as an active process by *using nonverbal communication to show your involvement* *taking notes as you listen* *identifying main points* *looking for evidence* *examining the speaker's reasoning* *minimizing distractions* *suspending judgment*

Now that you have finished reading this chapter, go to **Lesson 3's Coach** on the **VideoLab** CD-ROM and review the list of listening "dos" and "don'ts."

building your credibility and furthering the purpose of your speech. In essence, you are functioning as a role model for effective listening. Figure 3.3 presents a checklist of listening strategies for both speakers and listeners.

SUMMARY

Listening is important in every communication setting. It has long been recognized by teachers and business leaders as one key to successful performance in the academic and professional world. Listening well is equally important in more informal communication settings in our communities and homes.

The listening process has been studied extensively. Nevertheless, most observers agree that really good listening remains relatively rare. Yet it is essential for all who want to participate successfully in any communicative interaction to listen effectively.

Any good speaker will strive to understand the ways in which listening can be difficult for audience members. Some audience members may have trouble feeling active when they are in the listener's role, and they may find themselves distracted by the environment or the speaker's appearance or mannerisms. Listeners may also be burdened by skill deficits, including a limited attention span, poor note-taking skills, or weak critical thinking skills.

With genuine desire and effort, most audience members can learn to improve their listening skills. The good listener will know what he or she hopes to get out of the speech and will be aware of any personal biases that he or she may bring to the speaking situation or how impressions of the speaker's credibility might influence reactions to the ideas presented. Of course, each listener will want to listen actively and think critically throughout the speech.

Speakers will want to do everything possible to help audience members listen effectively. No speaker wants to raise unnecessary barriers or contribute to listeners' potential weaknesses. Toward that end, the effective speaker will use techniques designed to emphasize key ideas, try to engage the audience's attention throughout the speech, strive to minimize distractions, and behave respectfully toward listeners—seeking their feedback and responding to their questions with patience and candor.

QUESTIONS FOR REVIEW AND REFLECTION

1. Why is listening important in any communication situation?
2. Describe several different reasons for listening. Give an example of each.
3. Name and explain the five steps in the listening process.
4. What are the main advantages of listening effectively?
5. Do people generally listen well? Why or why not?
6. Describe your understanding of listening as an *active* process.
7. Name at least five problems that audience members often experience when listening to a public speech. Give an example of each.
8. List at least five tactics that should prove helpful for anyone wanting to improve his or her listening skills. Why is each important?
9. What are some ways that speakers can help audience members listen more effectively?
10. In your opinion, is listening more or less difficult in a public speaking setting as opposed to an interpersonal or small-group setting? What are some similarities and differences?
11. In your past experiences as a listener (in your home, in the classroom, with your friends, and so on), what have been your greatest listening challenges? Provide examples of each.

ENDNOTES

1. See, as examples, Deborah Borisoff and M. Purdy, eds., *Listening in Everyday Life: A Personal and Professional Approach,* 2nd ed. (Lanham, Md.: University Press of America, 1997); Stephen Covey, *The Seven Habits of Highly Effective People* (New York: Simon & Schuster, 1989); Ralph G. Nichols and L. A. Stephens, "Listening to People," *Harvard Business Review* 60 (1990): 95–102; and David A. Whetten and Kim S. Cameron, *Developing Management Skills,* 2nd ed. (New York: HarperCollins, 1991), p. 250.
2. Richard C. Huseman, James M. Lahiff, and J. D. Hatfield, *Interpersonal Communication in Organizations* (Boston: Holbrook Press, 1976), p. 7.
3. Andrew D. Wolvin and Carolyn Gwynn Coakley, *Listening,* 2nd ed. (Dubuque, Iowa: William C. Brown, 1985), p. 15.
4. Gary T. Hunt and Louis P. Cusella, "A Field Study of Listening Needs in Organizations," *Communication Education* 32 (1983): 368–378.
5. Carl Rogers and Richard E. Farson, "Active Listening," in *Organizational Communication,* 2nd ed., ed. Stewart D. Ferguson and Sherry Ferguson (New Brunswick, N.J.: Transaction, 1988), pp. 319–334.
6. Joan Middendorf and Alan Kalish, "The Change-up in Lectures" (manuscript, Indiana University, 1995), p. 6.
7. A. H. Johnstone and F. Percival, "Attention Breaks in Lectures," *Education in Chemistry* 13 (1976): 49–50.
8. *The American Heritage College Dictionary,* 3rd ed., s.v. "Stereotype."
9. Charles B. Stewart and William B. Cash, *Interviewing: Principles and Practices,* 9th ed. (Boston: McGraw-Hill, 2000).
10. Joseph A. DeVito, *The Interpersonal Communication Book,* 6th ed. (New York: Harper & Row, 1992), p. 64.
11. Carol A. Carrier, "Note-Taking Research: Implications for the Classroom," *Journal of Instructional Development* 6, no. 3 (1983): 19–25.
12. J. L. Fisher and M. B. Harris, "Effect of Note Taking and Review on Recall," *Journal of Educational Psychology* 65 (1973), 321–325.
13. Patricia Hayes Andrews and John E. Baird, Jr., *Communication for Business and the Professions,* 7th ed. (Boston: McGraw-Hill, 2000).
14. See K. Bosworth and J. Hamilton, eds., *Critical Thinking and Collaborative Learning: Underlying Processes and Effective Techniques* (San Francisco: Jossey-Bass, 1994); Rosabeth Moss Kanter, "Thinking Across Boundaries," *Harvard Business Review* 68 (1990), editor's foreword; and S. Holly Stocking et al. *More Quick Hits: Successful Strategies by Award-Winning Teachers* (Bloomington: Indiana University Press, 1998), especially "Fostering Critical and Creative Thinking," pp. 40–57.
15. For recent insights on note taking, see Rick Reis, Stanford Learning Lab, "Tomorrow's Professor Message #163: More Effective Note-Taking Strategies, April 15, 2000." <http://sll.stanford.edu/projects/newtomprof/postings/163.html> May 20, 2000); and Rick Reis, Stanford Learning Lab, "Tomorrow's Professor Message #172: Teaching Students to Take Better Notes," May 25, 2000. <http://stanford.edu/projects/tomprof/newtomprof/postings/172.html> (June 1, 2000).
16. César Chávez, "Pesticides Speech," in *Contemporary American Speeches,* 8th ed., ed. Richard L. Johannesen, R. R. Allen, W. A. Linkugel, and F. J. Bryan (Dubuque, Iowa: Kendall/Hunt, 1997), pp. 206–207.

The following speech was given by a student in a beginning public speaking class as one of the early speaking experiences. The assignment was to give a three- to five-minute, one-point speech that was audience centered and helped members of the audience listen effectively.

The Healthy Choice

Karen Kawalski

There are many ways that you and I are alike. We're all college students. Most of us are in the same age group. I'll bet we watch a lot of the same television programs. And I know all of us are looking forward to spring break. I am different from most of you in one way, however, even though growing numbers of people are becoming like me. The fact is that I'm a vegetarian.

In her introduction, Karen associates herself with common characteristics of her audience, suggesting that, while she may be different in one way (as a vegetarian), she is similar to them and shares many interests and goals (including being healthy). She also helps her listeners focus on what is important in her speech by directing their attention to the one argument for vegetarianism that she will develop: it is beneficial to health.

There are a lot of reasons why people become vegetarians. Some do so for religious reasons, some out of ecological concerns, some because they see the slaughter of animals for food as cruel and senseless. And there are different kinds of vegetarians, depending on what food they will or will not eat. But today I want to give you just one reason for considering whether you should be a vegetarian—your health. All of us want either to stay healthy or to improve our health. Getting sick just before finals would be a bummer. Also, people are living longer and we want those many years ahead to be as free from sickness and disease as they can be.

What you eat affects your health. Isn't that something that we all know? What we should also know is that eating meat can have bad effects. Eating meat, for example, is associated with heart disease, cancer, and bacterial infection.

The transition to the body again stresses the importance of her topic to her listeners and draws their attention to what will come with a brief preview of the examples of specific diseases she will relate to eating meat.

First, let's look at heart disease. Heart disease is the leading killer in America today and it is directly linked to eating meat. Saturated fat, which you take in when you eat meat, forms cholesterol along the arterial wall leading to the heart. [Here she showed a chart depicting the heart and clogging of arteries.] As this builds up, the artery becomes clogged, and the flow of blood is restricted. The heart pumps harder and harder—and the risk of a heart attack increases. Reducing that saturated fat by eating less meat pays off. In countries like the United States, Canada, and Australia, where a lot of meat is consumed, the mortality rate linked to heart disease is also high. In countries where meat consumption is low, such as Japan, the mortality rate is low. As a personal example, my friend Jenny was alarmed when she discovered that her cholesterol was abnormally high for a person her age. She became a vegetarian and her cholesterol level dropped 30 points in a year. So you can see that giving up meat could help you fend off heart disease.

Using the word "First" keeps her audience on track with her organization. The chart helps listeners to visualize the problem as well as providing some interest. A quick comparison between meat-eating countries and a non-meat-eating one supports the point. Karen's use of a specific example not only strengthens her case, it also demonstrates that someone like the listeners is at risk (since Jenny is presumably similar to most of the listeners, as is Karen herself).

Karen again signals a transition, saying "Second," which also helps the audience to follow. Her choice of very common meats that listeners would be likely to eat is a sign of her focus on the audience.

A similar transition—noting her "third" assertion—alerts listeners to the fact that a new example is coming. The example itself concerns a food that most listeners will have eaten from childhood, and Karen's assurance that the high count comes from a name brand is an effort to anticipate listeners' potentially skeptical response that the most dangerous meat must come from some small off-brand.

Karen's conclusion ties this short speech together for her listeners by referring to her opening remarks, reminding the audience that her major concern is their physical well-being, and quickly summarizing the risks she has enumerated in the body of the speech.

Second, there is the threat of actually eating cancerous materials when you eat meat. Cancer is commonly found in animals that we eat—inspectors often cut out cancerous tumors from cows just before they go to market. Chickens have certain forms of cancer that are hard to spot—to do so would cost a lot of money and take a lot of time, so these cancers can go undetected. In short, common foods can contain cancerous material. Accidentally eating food like that is one thing vegetarians don't have to worry about.

Third, harmful bacteria in meat is a danger to your health. Meat is, after all, part of a dead animal and so has a high bacterial count. Take, for example, the case of hot dogs. In one study carried out by a consumer advocacy group, researchers studied thirty-two brands of hot dogs bought in various supermarkets throughout the country. Considering that meat begins to rot when the bacteria level reaches 10 million per gram, they found that a whopping 40 percent had already begun to spoil. One brand—I won't mention the brand, but it is one that you'd know when you heard it—had a bacteria count of 140 million per gram. If you don't eat meat, you reduce the risk of poisoning yourself.

As I mentioned in the beginning of my speech, people can become vegetarians for many reasons—there are lots of good arguments for giving up meat. But what I've tried to point out to you today is that you need to think about yourself when you consider becoming a vegetarian. Why take chances with your health? Why increase the risk of suffering from heart disease, cancer, or food poisoning? Why not, instead, join the growing number of us who are becoming vegetarians and improve your chances of a healthier life?

PART II

Prepare: Knowing Your Audience and Yourself

In Part II, you will learn how to use your own resources to decide what to speak about and how to make yourself credible to your listeners. As a speaker, your most important consideration is your audience. This audience-centered approach will help you discover what you need to learn about your listeners and how to plan for the specific responses you hope to get from them.

4 Analyzing Your Audience

CHAPTER SURVEY

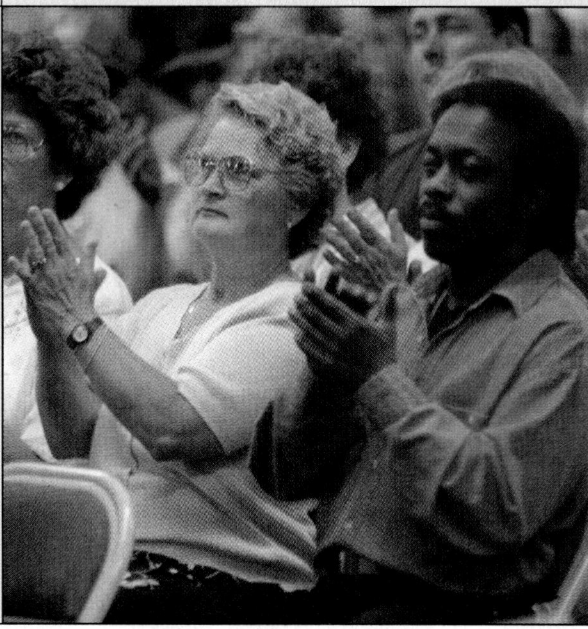

CHAPTER OBJECTIVES

After studying this chapter, you should be able to

1. **explain the role and significance of audience analysis in public speaking.**
2. **describe the diverse audience characteristics you need to consider as you prepare to deliver a speech.**
3. **identify human needs that are basic to all audiences.**

captive audience an audience whose members see no special reason to attend to the speaker

Listeners may come to a speaking event with a variety of motives. They may be there because they are a **captive audience** (the professor or boss says, "Be there!"), because they feel obligated to show up (a good friend is speaking and has made them aware of the event), because of mild curiosity, or because of passionate interest. Getting a general sense of *why* listeners are present—whether they really want to hear about your topic or not—may help you figure out how to approach your speech.

In every speaking situation, you should learn as much as possible about the audience's predispositions, tastes, prejudices, and knowledge. If you are asking listeners to make some commitment, you should know what the audience can or may be prepared to do about your request. In many cases, your audience will be diverse. You therefore need to consider what characteristics they share as a group and what qualities they, as individuals, bring with them to the communication situation.

UNDERSTANDING DIVERSE AUDIENCES

Preview As an audience-centered speaker, you must think carefully and analytically about your listeners because you cannot achieve what you want alone.[1] You and the members of your audience are in this together—that is, you form a kind of partnership. Knowing something about them will affect how you frame and deliver your message. As this chapter will show, there are a number of factors to consider when analyzing your audience.

Many elements go into making people what they are. These factors can influence the way listeners see events and how important they consider an issue, which in turn can mold their values, determine how attentive they will be to a speech, or suggest how much they will accept or reject change. Table 4.1 lists some audience characteristics that every speaker must consider.

Of course, making a comprehensive list of listener characteristics can seem overwhelming, and you cannot ever do a complete and exhaustive analysis of any audience. But trying to understand listeners and anticipate how they will react to messages is absolutely essential to effective, **audience-centered communication**. To anticipate intelligently, you must know as much as you can about your listeners and how they see the world, and you must understand how you and your listeners are the same as well as how you differ.

audience-centered communication thinking about one's audience throughout the process of communicating, from topic selection to message delivery

Age

The age of audience members will influence the way they receive messages. Some might argue that age is mostly a state of mind rather than a physical fact. Even so, our age often influences the sorts of experiences we have and the issues that most concern us.

To test your skills and expand your understanding of audience analysis, go to **Lesson 2** of the **VideoLab** CD-ROM and walk through the videos, exercises, and tips provided.

The Role of Experience. During the war in Vietnam, many students were in conflict with an older generation who had lived through World War II and the Korean War, when little significant public protest was raised. These older Americans believed they had fought for the American way of life, and they couldn't understand the reluctance of those who, fifteen to twenty-five years later, would not do the same thing. On their part, the students saw those who supported the war as "hawks" who seemed all too ready to sacrifice the lives

TABLE 4.1 Audience Characteristics
Age
Gender
Culture: race, ethnic origins, religion, geographic/cultural environment
Education
Occupation or profession
Income and assets
Group and organizational memberships

As you begin to think about possible topics for your next speech, always keep the audience's concerns in mind. To assist you in staying audience centered, go to the **SpeechStudio** and complete the **Audience Interest Worksheet**. If you have trouble responding to many of the questions, you will want to gather more information about your audience.

of young people. The "doves" taunted President Lyndon B. Johnson with the chant, "Hey, hey, L.B.J., how many kids did you kill today?"[2]

Students of today, caught up in a different set of problems, often regard the passionate divisions of the 1960s with mild curiosity or indifference. Even the Persian Gulf War (1991) may seem remote. Thus the famous generation gap occurs because people of different ages, seeing the world from different places, fail to understand how things might look from other people's point of view.

Of course, age and experience affect an array of other issues as well. Audience members who are over forty years old are more likely to be married, have children, and own homes than are audience members who are under twenty years of age. Each generation will have danced to different music, watched different movies, admired different political leaders, and used different technologies during their formative years.

Being "young" or "old" means, in part, living through different times. Although two people of exactly the same age can have widely divergent experiences, passing through a time in which certain events occur influences the way we feel about those events, as well as the way we process later events. In this sense, the shared experience of a generation unquestionably affects an audience's outlook. It is one of the age-related factors that a speaker should consider when thinking about his or her audience.

Matters of Immediate Concern. Another point to consider is that matters of immediate concern are different for different age groups. Getting a job, keeping a job, and living comfortably when you have retired from a job might be the three uppermost concerns for three different age groups. Thus matters have **saliency**, or great personal relevance or importance, partly because of age.

saliency great relevance or importance

This speaker is obviously connecting with his older audience whose values and experiences have influenced the ways in which they will respond to a message. (Spencer Grant/PhotoEdit)

SPOTLIGHT ON... **Age**

AMA President Lonnie Bristow Speaks on Medicare

One of the reasons Congress has been so reluctant to deal with Medicare realistically over the years is because, frankly, they've been scared out of their wits that the elderly would turn on them for doing anything at all to the program. It's like Social Security—in Washington it's the "third rail." Touch it and you'll die. Even when it's painfully obvious that things need to be done—must be done.

Well, without going so far as to even hint that any of us in this room today are "elderly," let me say that your support is critical. If you agree with me and America's physicians that the program now being considered by Congress is best for patients, best for the generations to follow, and yes, best for doctors, too, then speak out.

If I've done my job of "selling it here," then help us sell it everywhere. Write. Call. FAX. Send e-mail. Whenever it's possible, actually visit your Senators and Representatives.

Let them know you support the AMA's plan to transform Medicare. Tell them you want it for today, sure. But tell them that—even more important—you want it for tomorrow.

For your children's sake.

For your grandchildren's sake. . . .

I told you earlier that we—as a generation—were being called on—again—to make some sacrifices for the good of the nation.

Uwe Reinhart, the Princeton economist, once referred to the baby boomers as the "Pepsi generation." Then he referred to us as the "Iwo Jima Generation." And I don't have to explain that to anyone here.

And, it's—once again—our time.

I'm reminded of something I saw last night when I was driving home—here at Rossmoor. I turned a corner and my headlights shined [sic] on three deer. A stag, a doe and a fawn.

You know what their first instinct was?

No. They didn't run. That was their second act.

The first thing that the stag and the doe did was turn so that their bodies shielded the fawn from the approaching harm.

And that's what every older generation does. We shield our young from harm. We protect the generation we're leaving behind. It's an instinct as primal as food and shelter and warmth.

And that's what is being asked of us today. We are like those deer. . . . We are harvesting the accumulated wisdom and knowledge of a lifetime and sharing it with those who have it in their power to enact change to help the generations to come.

To protect the generations to come.

It is our time.

Vital Speeches of the Day 62: Lonnie R. Bristow, "A Time for Every Season: Medicare and Tomorrow's Generations," (December 15, 1995), p. 136.

Older people usually find questions related to the social security program salient, whereas college students may find the government's role in providing student loans more salient. Examine the speech in *Spotlight on Age.* It was delivered by Lonnie Bristow, president of the American Medical Association (AMA), to a group of older citizens. Consider how the speaker's topic, appeals, and language were probably influenced by the age of the audience.

Age and Values. Shared experiences and particular kinds of concerns have their impact on **values**.[3] Different age groups may have different values that are reflected in several ways. An effective speaker remembers that the worth or importance of values depends very much on whose values they are. We should all resist any inclination to dismiss a way of thinking or a model for living as stupid or irrelevant because it happens to differ from our own.

values those things that we consider good and desirable

For example, an investment counselor who is speaking to a group of retired citizens who lived through the Great Depression (1929) will need to recognize that, for these people, investing conservatively will probably be very attractive. Because of their shared experiences with poverty, job instability, and fuel and food shortages, this audience will probably value a low-risk approach to investing, which they will associate with a sense of safety, security, and responsibility—

Look through the various speeches in the **Screening Rooms** on the **VideoLab** CD-ROM. For which, if any, of these topics should the gender composition of the audience be taken into consideration?

values the speaker will need to honor, even if he or she does not completely agree with them.

Any speaker who fails to understand where audience values come from cannot be audience-centered and so will likely have difficulty connecting with listeners. This point should be kept in mind as we consider all facets of an audience's composition.

Gender

gender the roles, behaviors, and attitudes we associate with males and females

A person's **gender** is crucial to her or his very being. In some way, listeners respond to a speaker on the basis of their gender, and the gender composition of the audience is a factor that speakers will want to consider in developing a speech.

PORTFOLIO 4.1

A Matter of Sex

Look at the list of topics you're considering for an upcoming speech. Does your intended treatment of any of them involve any assumptions related to gender roles or attitudes that may constitute stereotyping? If so, how will you rethink and modify your message? List each potential problem, skipping several lines between entries. Beneath each entry, contemplate a corrective action.

Role Expectations. As men and women in our society move beyond prescribed gender roles and attitudes, expectations of how listeners will respond begin to change. One can no longer assume that women will want to hear about fashion and that men will want to hear about sports. Jokes that portray women as vain, silly, or nagging are considered in bad taste everywhere, as are those that portray men as insensitive, arrogant, tough, and unfeeling.[4]

In this new scene, however, both men and women may feel defensive about the roles they play or hope to play. As new options are opened up, some people may feel unsure either about exercising those options or about continuing to exercise traditional options. A woman who decides that she enjoys bringing up children and managing a household may wonder if she is inadequate because she doesn't want a career. A woman who has an aptitude for engineering may worry that she will be considered "unfeminine." A man who doesn't care to know anything about basketball might feel he isn't "masculine."

The Influence of Socialized Gender Roles. Even though artificial gender roles exert less influence now than in the past, such influence still exists. Although the speaker may not want to encourage such attitudes, he or she can't ignore them and their influence on the audience. It still is true that men and women have different outlooks and experiences. For example, gay women and men with long-time partners will encounter far greater barriers in adopting a child or obtaining housing than will a traditional married couple. Single women and widows have more difficulty obtaining credit than do single men and widowers. Furthermore, there are tastes and interests for which our culture tends to program men and women differently (for example, playing with dolls versus playing with trucks). If a speaker wishes to use the testimony of a Green Bay Packers star lineman, chances are that more men than women in the audience will know who he is. In this case, the speaker's responsibility is to avoid condescending to women who don't know the player and avoid making men who don't know him feel like misfits.

KEEP IN MIND 4.1

Age and Gender

The age of the listeners may influence their responses because of

- different life experiences.
- different immediate concerns.
- different values.

When considering the gender of listeners, the speaker should reflect on

- role expectations.
- the impact of socialized gender roles.
- avoiding stereotyping.

Sexual Stereotypes. Although all of the above is true, it is also good to remind ourselves that no category—such as sex, age, or race—automatically predetermines a listener's set of responses, interests, or life experiences.

Common assumptions based on the speaker's knowledge of listeners' **sexual orientation** provides an enlightening illustration. Homosexuals make up 10 percent of the U.S. adult population, and, regardless of stereotypes, they do not tend to work in certain industries. For example, a survey of more than four thousand gay men and lesbians conducted by Overlooked Opinions, a Chicago market-research firm, reported that 40 percent more homosexuals are employed in the finance and insurance industries than in the entertainment and arts industries, and ten times as many homosexuals are in the computer industry as in the fashion industry. There are also more homosexuals working in science and engineering than in social services.[5]

sexual orientation one's "emotional, romantic, sexual or affectionate attraction to individuals of a particular gender" (as defined by the American Psychological Association)

While the distinction between generalizing and **stereotyping** is sometimes hard to make, stereotyping is generally harmful. The sexual revolution of the 1960s should have taught us all one truth: although men and women do have concerns and experiences that are unique to their sex, there are also aspirations, attitudes, and aptitudes that are common to all humans and cannot be attributed to people strictly on the basis of gender.

stereotyping making assumptions about someone based on factors such as race or gender without considering the person's individuality

Culture

Listeners' responses to messages are also affected by their cultures. At one time, it was generally believed that Americans were a homogeneous people. The myth was that we arrived as immigrants, were melted in the pot for a generation or two, and emerged with a distinctively American character. Of course, there may be certain ways of looking at things that are especially "American." In recent years, however, we have come to realize that the melting pot concept is not quite accurate. Within the broader culture, there exist varied cultures that continue to be different and to influence us in many ways. For example, ethnic diversity has increased significantly in the United States since 1980, as Figure 4.1 shows.

FIGURE 4.1 The Increasing Ethnic Diversity of the United States

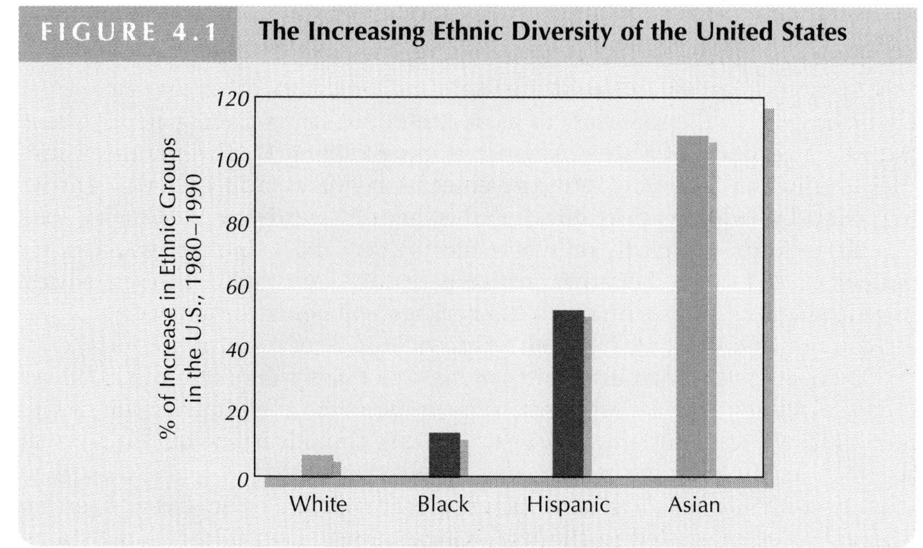

Culture includes dimensions such as race, ethnic origins, religion, and geographic/cultural environment. Although these various groups share some characteristics with the general U.S. culture, they may have marked differences that could affect their responses to spoken messages.

Race. Race is best seen as a matter of culture. Scholars commonly define intercultural communication as "interactions that involve people from other races and ethnic groups."[6] Race is principally a product of politics, social definitions, and personal preferences, rather than of biological, genetic, or inherited factors.[7] Understanding something of how race may be operating in a public speaking situation is very important.

racism the denial of the essential humanity of persons of a particular race

Over time, we have come to realize that, as each race has its own integrity, each also has its own perceptions and problems. Recognizing these racial influences is not **racism**. Racism denies the essential humanity of those who are different and thus severely limits the potential for communicating successfully. Racists can talk effectively only to other racists. Those who appreciate the distinctions between people of different races are better equipped to talk effectively with a wide and diverse audience.

For example, speakers must understand that African Americans and white Americans have different histories and cultural experiences in the United States. Communication between members of these different races can be extremely complicated and, too often, fraught with distrust.[8] The problem of how to find more jobs for minorities may cause some white listeners to fear that they are to be sacrificed in order to find jobs for unemployed blacks. The administration of justice might be viewed with great skepticism by urban African Americans who have been brutalized or bullied by white police.

 PORTFOLIO 4.2

Attempting to Empathize

Contemplate whether any of the speech topics you're considering revolve around views you've developed because of your race. Enter these in a column on the left side of a page.

Next, contemplate how persons of another race might think differently and what factors might influence their thinking. List these profiles in a center column, being sure to include every race in your class. Also acknowledge any discrepancies that might exist between individuals of a particular race and what might underlie those differences.

In a third column, contemplate how you will acknowledge your own influences as well as those others might have as you think about the topic and develop a speech.

Nevertheless, successful communication does occur in an overwhelming number of cases and situations every day.[9] A speaker must simply be sensitive to the racial influences operating in listeners' attitudes and approaches to issues.[10]

Ethnic Origins. The forebears of most Americans came from someplace else. With the exception of Native Americans, people emigrated from other countries to America beginning in the seventeenth century, and they are still arriving today. Depending partly on when they arrived, partly on what their habits and tastes were, and partly on where they settled, these immigrants had their outlooks colored by their own national history, customs, and experiences. Listeners who identify with their own heritage will be concerned with their living conditions here as well as their ties to their mother country.

Obviously speakers must avoid stereotypes. Poles will not find Polish jokes funny, and Italians will deeply resent the association of all Italian names with the Mafia. More important, however, speakers should realize that issues that seem to directly affect the mother country will shape the reactions of those who identify with a particular national group. For example, an Irish American is likely to be interested in the fate of Northern Ireland and to have strong opinions of which party operating there is right and what the outcome should be. A nation's particular viewpoints and values can influence even its transplanted citizens and their descendants.

Religion. Perhaps it is less accurate to talk of religious cultures than of religious beliefs that are associated with diverse cultures. In any case, a listener's religion, or his or her lack of religious beliefs, can influence that listener's reception and evaluation of a speech. On some issues, certain religious groups tend to take uniform stands. Catholics on the whole, for example, tend to oppose abortion; Jews tend to favor strong U.S. support of Israel; Quakers generally oppose war of any kind.

Religion can also have other kinds of influences on audience members. Some religions stress obedience and conformity, whereas others emphasize individualistic participation. Some religions stress personal salvation and hold political or social issues to be beyond any religious concerns. Others insist that all human matters should be of concern to the church, including political and social behavior. Church teachings can make a difference in the way people respond to a speech. Fundamentalists, for example, may be more open to messages that reflect conservative policies and values than those who have liberal religious views.[11]

Conventional wisdom once advised public speakers to avoid talking about religion. It was considered too personal and potentially explosive a topic. But there are many possible topics that could be so, given the right place and the right audience. If you choose to talk about religion, your speech needs to be designed with a specific audience in mind, just like any other speech.

In October 1983, Senator Edward M. Kennedy was invited by Rev. Jerry Falwell to speak to an assembled group of students at Liberty Baptist College in Lynchburg, Virginia. Kennedy chose as his topic "Truth and Tolerance in America." Recognizing that perceived differences between him and his audience could create almost insurmountable barriers to effective communication, Kennedy wisely chose to use humor in his introduction before going on to address the religious and political differences between him and his audience. *Spotlight on Religion* includes a portion of his introduction. By acknowledging religious differences, showing his respect for his audience and their beliefs, and appealing to transcendent values, Kennedy was able to move forward with an eloquent speech that was very well received.

Geographic/Cultural Environment. Finally, where a listener lives can make a difference in how he or she processes a public speech. Even though people might come from the same part of the country, their outlooks can differ depending on the kind of community with which they identify. Obviously, Newark, New Jersey, is not the same as Franklin, New Jersey; Chicago, Illinois, is not the same as Peoria, Illinois; and Dallas, Texas, is not to be confused with College Station, Texas.

PORTFOLIO 4.3

Locating That Which Transcends

To what extent have your religious beliefs (or lack of them) affected how you think and what you will say in a forthcoming speech? How might members of your audience differ in their beliefs, and how might those differences affect their response to your message? How will you acknowledge those differences as well as show respect for them? Establish three columns and enter abbreviated responses to each of these questions.

Listeners can be affected by their religious beliefs in a variety of ways. A speaker of one's own religion, speaking in a religious setting is likely to be especially effective. In other settings, speakers have to take into account the wide range of possible religious influences that might be at work.
(Alastair Halliday/The Image Works)

SPOTLIGHT ON... **Religion**

Senator Edward Kennedy Speaks at Liberty Baptist College

I have come here to discuss my beliefs about faith and country, tolerance and truth in America. I know we begin with certain disagreements, and I strongly suspect at the end of the evening some of our disagreements will remain. But I also hope that tonight and in the months and years ahead, we will always respect the right of others to differ, that we will never lose sight of our own fallibility, and that we will view ourselves with a sense of perspective and a sense of humor. After all, in the New Testament, even the disciples had to be taught to look first to the beam in their own eyes, and only then to the mote in their neighbor's eyes. I am mindful of that counsel. I am an American and a Catholic; I love my country and treasure my faith. But I do not assume that my conception of patriotism or policy is invariably correct—or that my convictions about religion should command any greater respect than any other faith in this pluralistic society. I believe there surely is such a thing as truth, but who among us can claim a monopoly on it?

There are those who do, and their own words testify to their intolerance. For example, because the Moral Majority has worked with members of different denominations, one fundamentalist group has denounced Dr. Falwell for hastening the ecumenical church and for "yoking together with Roman Catholics, Mormons, and others." I am relieved that Dr. Falwell does not regard that as a sin—and on this issue, he himself has become the target of narrow prejudice. When people agree on public policy, they ought to be able to work together, even while they worship in diverse ways. For truly, we are all yoked together as Americans—and the yoke is the happy one of individual freedom and mutual respect.

Alistair Press: Edward M. Kennedy, "Truth and Tolerance in America," in *Great Speeches for Criticism and Analysis,* 3/e; eds. Lloyd E. Rohler and Roger Cook (Greenwood, IN.: Alistair Press, 1998), pp. 312–313.

People who have grown up in the country may develop different habits and lifestyles than those who have grown up in the city. The horrors of muggings, of commuting on unreliable trains, or of always moving at a frantic pace seem terrible to the rural resident, whereas the city dweller imagines that the dullness and lack of stimulation in the country would bore him or her to death. Sometimes the reverse is true: the untasted excitement of the city lures one, and the longed-for peace and safety of the country lure the other. Each group will also have a specific set of problems. To urbanites, the following questions are important: How do we reduce crime? How do we improve mass transit? How do we keep food prices down? By contrast, the residents of a predominantly farming area will be more troubled by questions such as: How do we save the family farm? How do we reduce property taxes? How do we keep grain prices at a suitable level?

It's also true that different sections of the country have, through the course of our history, developed unique ways of looking at things. Easterners, westerners, southerners, southwesterners, and midwesterners have different ethnic mixes in their populations, different industries, different religious views, and different approaches to social and political problems. Westerners, for example, are proud of their rugged, independent individualism; New Yorkers value their cultural and artistic preeminence; and many Sunbelt communities are pleased with their image as safe, comfortable places for older citizens to live.

Beyond regional differences in the United States, those who grow up in cultures outside this country may see the world quite differently. Psychologists may not agree on whether the differences between Asians and Americans, for example, should be attributed to different social and religious practices, different languages, different geography, or different ways of thinking. Yet most agree that the differences are very real. In general, Asians pay more attention to context and relationship, while Americans rely more on formal logic. Some of the most recent studies have implications for the ways people communicate with each other, how they judge speaker credibility, and how they react to arguments opposing their own views.[12] In *Spotlight on Cultural Differences,* an article from the *New York Times* highlights some of these research findings.

Many intercultural communication differences may affect the nature and quality of the ways individuals interact. For instance, Americans tend to be more direct and explicit, whereas Asians tend to be more indirect and subtle.[13] Some cultures have an elaborate style of speaking. For instance, Arabic is full of assertions, proverbs, and exaggerations. By contrast, Japanese speakers have a succinct style, often using silence to convey meaning. Finally, many Western cultures use an instrumental style (which is speaker- and goal-oriented), whereas most Arab, Asian, and Latin American cultures use an affective style (which is more process- and receiver-oriented).[14] These culture-based differences provide further insights into the challenges that may exist when individuals from diverse cultures interact.

Major Cultural Factors That Can Influence Listeners' Responses

- Race
- Ethnic origins
- Religion
- Geographic/cultural environment

Education

Education provides us with specific knowledge, ways to solve problems rationally, an awareness of choices open to us, and ways of evaluating the best choices to make.

Acquired Knowledge. The educational level of a listener—his or her acquired knowledge—influences his or her reactions to messages. Two audiences might want to hear a lecture on the latest developments in high-energy physics. If one audience was a junior high school science class and the other was a college physics class, what they would expect from a speaker and what they would be prepared to deal with would be different. Even first- and second-year college students would likely differ in their levels of sophistication and their knowledge needs.

SPOTLIGHT ON... **Cultural Differences**

Based on Research by Dr. Richard Nisbett, University of Michigan

Presented with weaker arguments running contrary to their own, Americans were likely to solidify their opinions . . . "clobbering the weaker arguments." Asians, however, were more likely to modify their own position, acknowledging that even the weaker arguments had some merit. . . .

Asked to analyze a conflict between mothers and daughters, American subjects quickly came down in favor of one side or the other. Chinese subjects were more likely to see merit in both sides, commenting, for example, "Both the mothers and the daughters have failed to understand each other."

And Chinese subjects expressed more liking than Americans for proverbs containing a contradiction, like the Chinese saying, "Too modest is half boastful." American subjects . . . found such contradictions "rather irritating."

Erica Goode, "How Culture Molds Habits of Thought," *New York Times* (August 8, 2000), p. D4.

claims alleged truths put forward by a speaker

The Educated Response. How well audience members have been educated will determine not only whether they are familiar with the speech topic but also whether they can intelligently evaluate the message. Much public speaking takes the form of **claims.** One speaker claims that using a certain product will make us happier or healthier. Another claims that voting for a particular candidate will improve our economic situation. Educated listeners should be in a good position to make judgments about such claims. They should have specific facts at their disposal and should have had many intellectual experiences that they can relate to specific aspects of the message.

For example, suppose you hear someone argue that force must be used in response to a foreign policy crisis because, the claim goes, we are faced with the same kind of dangerous situation that Americans faced in the 1940s when they confronted the forces of Nazism. If, as an educated person, you take the time to think, you won't be tempted to agree automatically just because you know Nazism was evil. You will ask questions about the quality of the evidence. You will demand that the speaker prove to you that the situation before World War II was really similar to the present situation. You will also use your knowledge of world history to judge the case.

As you judge the speaker's argument, you will apply principles you have learned and knowledge you have acquired. If you find the speaker unconvincing, and if you cannot fully test the argument by your own knowledge and experience, you will suspend judgment. You'll wait and see—listen to other arguments, read more material, and assemble more facts—before you make a decision you want to act on. You will be acting as an educated person. For more on evaluating claims, see Chapter 16.

Education Versus Training and Intelligence. It is important to distinguish between education and training. Many people are *trained* in a skill by educational institutions, but they are not necessarily *educated.* They have not acquired much general information, nor have they learned to apply it in a variety of situations. One's training may range from relatively simple skills, such as driving a bus, to more complex ones, such as performing vascular surgery. But such mastery of skills does not necessarily produce an educated person.[15]

Training should not be confused with education, nor should education be confused with intelligence. Some very intelligent people have not had formal education, just as some who have attended good universities are not very bright.

Nevertheless, without embracing stereotypes about educated listeners, you can still expect most educated listeners to be more critical and to have more information about certain topics. For example, it would be hard to help an audience understand the accomplishments of Ronald Reagan's presidency if they had little knowledge of political, social, and economic events in the United States during the 1980s. A persuasive speech aimed at convincing the audience that *Macbeth* is Shakespeare's greatest tragedy would fail if audience members had never read any Shakespeare or did not possess even general knowledge about English literature at the beginning of the seventeenth century. As with all the characteristics we have been talking about, the precise role education plays in a public speaking situation depends on the specifics of the situation.

Occupation or Profession

The occupation of the listener also influences the way he or she views a message. The job you have can make a difference in the attitudes you hold and the way in which you grasp specific information. When people receive public messages, they sometimes ask themselves, "How is this going to affect my job?" A dairy farmer and an urban grocer both will be interested in a news story about the price of milk, but they will differ in their responses. It may be that their goals are incompatible; nothing a speaker can say about how milk prices should be set can completely satisfy them both. Similarly, when discussing the problem of how to improve our schools, a motel owner may be uneasy about the suggestion that schools be kept open all year, since that could mean that people would travel less in the summer and her or his livelihood would be threatened.

Attitudes and Skills. The occupations we hold make us feel differently about the world around us. Teachers, doctors, construction workers, dancers, postal clerks, and lawyers all deal with specific sets of problems. The constant practice of these problem-solving skills is what establishes people as experts. When experts function as listeners, they bring a whole set of competencies and attitudes with them to a speaking situation. An engineer, for example, will respond to technological information as a specialist, and the speaker must be aware of this.

Perceptions of Relevance. Finally, take the case of a technical specialist presenting a proposal to improve product design to a group of decision-makers in an organization. If the specialist focuses only on how a new design might make the product work more efficiently and neglects the cost associated with its implementation, the speaker's chances of being effective will be lessened. Within the audience, individual listener's perceptions and responses may vary significantly. The production manager might be worried about the cost, the sales manager might be concerned about how well the sales staff can understand the intricacies of the new product, and the advertising manager might be worried about how this change will affect the promotional campaign that is about to be launched. Thus the occupational interests, concerns, and goals of the listeners will be different from those of the speaker, even though all of them work for the same organization. If a speaker fails to anticipate and prepare for responses stemming from different occupational perspectives, his or her good idea might be impossible to sell.

 KEEP IN MIND 4.3

Educational and Occupational Factors

Listeners' education influences their responses according to their

- acquired knowledge.
- ability to apply knowledge.

Listeners' occupations shape responses through their

- attitudes and skills.
- perceptions of relevance.

Income and Assets

The income of listeners may influence their response. Again, the extent to which this factor is important and the precise ways in which it functions depend on the speaker's subject and purpose. The topic of a message may naturally interest some income groups and not others. How to devise tax shelters, for example, would probably have limited appeal to those of low income, who might also perceive the subject as an example of how the rich exploit the law to avoid paying their fair share.

How groups think their income level compares and should compare with that of others may have deep-seated effects on the communication process. People in the middle-income group, for example, may see themselves as burdened with taxes and yet excluded from the benefits of social welfare. Such

Advertisers target audiences they consider likely customers for their products. An ad for expensive watches, for example, would be aimed at readers who buy magazines featuring upscale products and services. (Courtesy of Rolex)

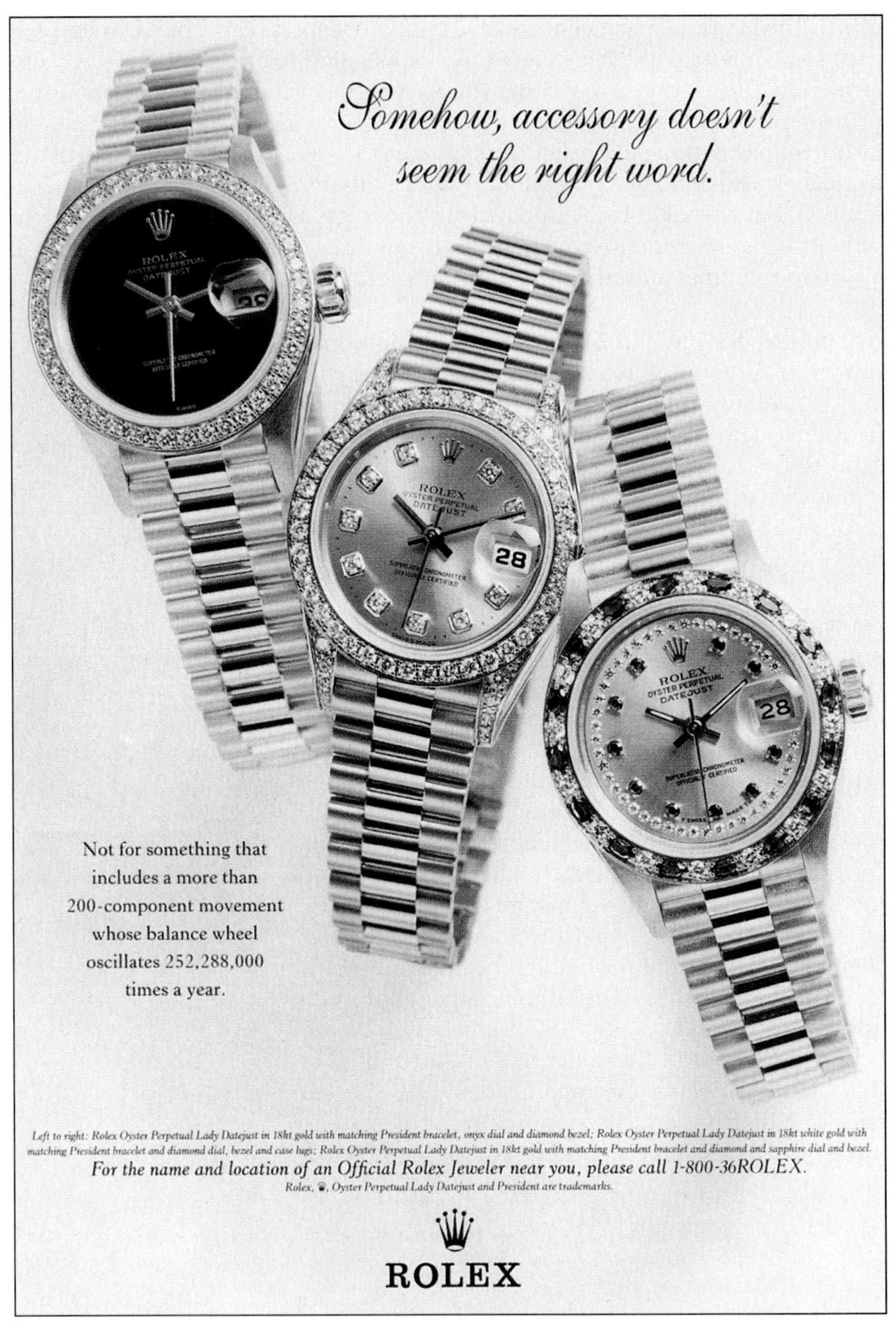

people may look on many political and social proposals with the jaundiced eye of those who are going to foot the bill.

Somehow, accessory doesn't seem the right word.
Not for something that includes a more than 200-component movement whose balance wheel oscillates 252,288,000 times a year.
Left to right: Rolex Oyster Perpetual Lady Datejust in 18kt gold with matching President bracelet, onyx dial and diamond bezel; Rolex Oyster Perpetual Lady Datejust in 18kt white gold with matching President bracelet and diamond dial, bezel and case lugs; Rolex Oyster Perpetual Lady Datejust in 18kt gold with matching President bracelet and diamond and sapphire dial and bezel.
For the name and location of an Official Rolex Jeweler near you, please call 1-800-36ROLEX.
Rolex, ♛, Oyster Perpetual Lady Datejust and President are trademarks.
ROLEX

Professional persuaders such as advertisers go to great lengths to try to see that their messages get through to the right income group. They carefully choose a mailing list (such as American Express Card holders) that will put their material in the hands of those who can afford to buy their product. They choose the kinds of magazines to advertise in, the time slots for their television ads, and the kinds of radio stations that will most likely reach the **target audience**. They are concerned with many factors besides income, but they want people who can afford to buy their products to know about those products.

target audience those whom the speaker would most like to influence with the message

The extent of financial resources available to listeners will surely help determine their receptiveness to any proposals that involve acquiring or spending money. The wise speaker will try to anticipate how listeners' income might influence their response to his or her message.

Group and Organizational Memberships

Diverse memberships held by listeners will have an impact on their response to speeches. A single listener may belong to the United Methodist Church, the Democratic party, the Parent Teacher Organization, the American Bar Association, and the Executive Board of the United Way.

Group Affiliations and Listeners' Feelings. Organizational associations contribute to the listeners' identity, the conception of who and what they are. Those who belong to the Sierra Club, for example, are clearly committed to preserving the environment. Staunch supporters of the club are likely to see the environmental aspects of a problem as others in the club would see them. Furthermore, such listeners might identify environmental dimensions to problems even when they are not immediately apparent, a possibility the speaker should be aware of.

One of the best ways to learn to give good speeches is to listen to others speak as often as possible. Even if they serve as imperfect role models, you can still learn a lot from observing them with a critical eye. Go to **Drill 2.1: Identifying Audience Centeredness** on the **VideoLab** CD-ROM, and after viewing the speech, respond to the questions presented.

In one situation, a speaker approached a city council with a proposal to build a small shopping center in a section of the community that lacked adequate shopping facilities. He chose to approach the topic in this way:

> There are two major advantages to moving forward with the Southside Mall. First, at a time when our community has been in a state of economic decline, this new Mall will bring hundreds of thousands of dollars of revenue to town. There is no comparable place for people to shop who live in the surrounding communities, so they will very likely come to our new Mall—bringing their purses with them! The other big advantage of building a Mall that will include more than 20 new businesses is *the addition of as many as 250 new jobs.* With unemployment at an all-time high, new jobs is what our community needs most.

Unfortunately for the builder, several environmentally minded members of the council were opposed to the project because building the strip would result in the removal of a wooded area and park. The builder had given scant attention to environmental consequences and could not respond to critical questions. His proposal was defeated, in large part because he had failed to consider the varied memberships and values of key members of the audience.

The Saliency of Key Group Memberships. Some memberships may be more important than others at certain times. When you attend a meeting of a particular group (a fraternity, a political club, United Way volunteers, or the Future Farmers of America), the reasons for being in that organization may be very important at that moment. You hear and respond to messages as a member of that group. At other times, and in other contexts, the goals of that group may seem less relevant.

You could be speaking on a topic—such as the importance of self-esteem—that would be appropriate for a national PTA rally or the Million Man March. Since these are very different audiences, though, with different interests, experiences, and goals, you would have to consider what factors would be most relevant to the specific needs of each audience. (*left:* Johnny Crawford/The Image Works; *right:* James Nubile/The Image Works)

✔ KEEP IN MIND 4.4

Income and Group Memberships

The income and assets of listeners may

- influence their perceptions of relevance.
- predispose them to act as members of target groups.

Group and organizational memberships influence listeners because

- affiliations may affect members' identity.
- memberships can determine the saliency of issues.

 CONNECTING TO THE NET

Check the web site of an organization of your choice (Red Cross, National Rifle Association, National Association for the Advancement of Colored People, American Civil Liberties Union, Sierra Club, and so on). In what ways does the group's message reflect its membership? From studying the web site, how would you describe the characteristics of members? Which demographics do you think are important in the group's appeal to members and nonmembers?

It is difficult, and not really necessary, to keep any one membership foremost in all our decisions. Whether we are active Democrats or Republicans will hardly matter as we decide how to respond to a manufacturer's plea to buy a specific brand of toothpaste. However, there are times when membership in a particular group is so important that all messages are evaluated by its standards or all irrelevant messages are screened out.[16] Consider two different examples.

- A young man might be a member of a fraternity. The membership may be so central to his life that he judges messages about where to eat (or what to wear or who he should vote for) by asking himself whether members of that group would eat that kind of food (or wear those clothes or vote for that candidate). None of these choices would seem to have any direct relationship to the goals and activities of the organization. Nevertheless, the listener may relate many issues to a particular group membership.
- Members and supporters of the National Rifle Association (NRA) are dedicated to the defeat of gun control legislation. So important is this to NRA members that they will often subordinate all other issues to this one. They might well end up voting for or against a political

SPOTLIGHT ON... **Esteem**

Excerpt from "Common Ground and Common Sense" by Jesse Jackson

I understand. I know abandonment and people being mean to you, and saying you're nothing and nobody, and can never be anything. I understand. . . . I'm a working person's person, that's why I understand you whether you're black or white. I understand work. I was not born with a silver spoon in my mouth. I had a shovel programmed for my hand. . . .

Every one of these funny labels they put on you, those of you who are watching this broadcast tonight in the projects, on the corners, I understand. Call you outcast, low down, you can't make it, you're nothing, you're nobody, subclass, underclass—when you see Jesse Jackson, when my name goes in nomination, your name goes in nomination. I was born in the slum, but the slum was not born in me. And it wasn't born in you, you can make it. Wherever you are tonight you can make it. Hold your head high, stick your chest out. You can make it. It gets dark sometimes, but the morning comes. Don't you surrender. Suffering breeds character. Character breeds faith. In the end faith will not disappoint. You must not surrender. You may or may not get there, but just know that you're qualified and you hold on and hold out. We must never surrender. America will get better and better. Keep hope alive. Keep hope alive. Keep hope alive. On tomorrow night and beyond, keep hope alive.

Jesse Jackson, "Common Ground and Common Sense," in *Great Speeches for Criticism and Analysis,* ed. L. Rohler and R. Cook (Greenwood, Ind.: Alistair Press, 1993), pp. 106–107.

1988 Democratic National Convention. In it, he used his own experience to inspire listeners who felt dispossessed to be proud of and to believe in themselves once again. In this portion of his speech, Jackson sought to persuade his listeners of their dignity, regardless of personal circumstances.

self-actualization need the desire to achieve to the full extent of our capabilities

Throughout the speech, Jackson aimed to convince his listeners that there was hope for them, no matter the circumstances under which they were born or the circumstances in which they currently found themselves. Of course, Jackson's impassioned delivery made the message even more compelling.

Helping Listeners Realize Their Own Potential

When people possess self-esteem and know that others respect them, they can begin to think about self-fulfillment. The **self-actualization need**, as Maslow calls it, recognizes that human beings want to make the most of themselves. Most people are in the process of becoming. We tend to strive for something; we have goals toward which we work. Most people, if they feel that striving is worthwhile, will continue to do so and will probably never be completely self-actualized. Not everyone, of course, will have the same ideal or the same ambition. Nevertheless, the speaker who realizes that people want to achieve the full extent of their capabilities will appeal to this very important need.

Belonging to an organized group and sharing common experiences can reinforce listeners' feelings of belonging and help a speaker elicit positive responses. (Richard Hutchings/PhotoEdit)

SPOTLIGHT ON... **Self-Actualization**

Excerpt from "Leaders for the 21st Century" by Norman Schwarzkopf

The wonderful thing about our country is that you can do anything that you want. . . . So, dare to live your dream! You know, it's the dreamers of the past . . . who have given us the greatest gifts . . . and so it will always be . . . a cure for cancer, a cleaner environment, an end of poverty, world peace. . . . So take your best shot and dare to live your dream.

Of course, you'll stumble along the way; we all do; but always remember that life is sort of like the 400-meter race: it's a staggered start. You can never tell who is ahead until the end of the race. So when you stumble, get back up and follow your dreams again! At the finish line of life, the winners are not determined by the quantity of the material goods that they have amassed but rather by the quality of what they leave behind.

Norman Schwarzkopf, "Leaders for the 21st Century," *Vital Speeches of the Day* 65 (June 15, 1999): 520.

In *Spotlight on Self-Actualization,* General Norman Schwarzkopf, in a commencement address at the University of Richmond, encouraged his student audience to seek self-actualization by living their dreams.

Of course, there are other ways that speakers might appeal to the audience's need for self-actualization. Some might encourage listeners to become attuned to their own spirituality, to seek a sense of empowerment in their work life, or to grow to experience a sense of inner peace.

Go to **Next Step: Using Monroe's Motivated Sequence** in Lesson 9 of the **VideoLab** CD-ROM. Watch the video clip and respond to the quiz to assess how the speaker uses the motivated sequence to appeal to universal listener needs.

SUMMARY

The speaker-listener partnership is central to the success of any public speaking venture. As you approach giving any speech, you will want to reflect thoughtfully and analytically on who your listeners are—considering the sources of their diversity while remaining mindful of the needs and values they likely share.

Audiences are rarely homogeneous, and that makes your task more challenging. You will want to avoid overgeneralizing and to fashion your speech so that you are as inclusive as possible. In analyzing your audience, you will consider such diverse listener factors as age, gender, race, religion, education, ethnicity, occupation, geographic/cultural environment, income, and group memberships.

At the same time, you must recognize that there are some universal human needs that all listeners share: basic physiological needs, as well as the need for safety and security, love and belonging, esteem, and self-actualization. You may engage these audience needs with a wide array of topics.

QUESTIONS FOR REVIEW AND REFLECTION

1. What are the major audience characteristics you ought to consider when planning a speech? Why is each important?

2. Think of a topic that you believe might be a good one to use in your public speaking class based on your interests and your perceptions of your fellow classmates' interests and values. How could this topic be adapted to a significantly older audience?

3. In your view, are there any topics that would be of greater interest to women than to men? How about the opposite? How might you broaden the appeal of a topic that you associate with either sex?

4. How might the location or geography of your hometown affect the kinds of issues that people who live there are interested in?

5. As a person who is currently cast in the role of college student, what are some topics that are of interest to you? Now imagine that you are pursuing the occupation of your choice in the future (attorney, teacher, salesperson, or computer analyst, for example). What sorts of topics would likely interest you as a member of that occupational group?

6. What is one group you belong to that is really important to you (sorority, church, or volunteer organization, for instance)? If a speaker were to address this organization, what sorts of topics would be of interest to most members attending the speech? Why?

7. According to Maslow's hierarchy, what are some of the most basic human needs that listeners share? Define each briefly.

8. Following are some possible speech topics:
   a. Gun Control
   b. Exercising for Fitness
   c. Finding the Career That's Right for You
   d. How to Excel as a First-Year College Student
   e. The Health Care Crisis
   f. Alternative Energy Sources
   g. Pain Management
   h. Becoming a Volunteer for the Local Humane Society

Which listener needs would you probably want to consider in speaking about each of these topics? Why would those needs be especially important?

ENDNOTES

1. Perhaps the first scholar to comment on the importance of audience-centeredness was Aristotle, who wrote, "A speech [situation] consists of three things: a speaker and a subject on which he speaks and someone addressed, and the objective *[telos]* of the speech relates to the last (I mean the hearer)." *Aristotle on Rhetoric: A Theory of Civil Discourse,* trans. George A. Kennedy (New York: Oxford University Press, 1991), p. 47.

2. For a brief account of the protests against the war, see James MacGregor Burns, *The Crosswinds of Freedom* (New York: Alfred A. Knopf, 1989), pp. 401–431.

3. See Patricia Hayes Andrews and Richard T. Herschel, *Organizational Communication: Empowerment in a Technological Society* (Boston: Houghton Mifflin, 1996), pp. 310–312. For a classic work on values, see Gordon Allport et al., *The Study of Values* (Boston: Houghton Mifflin, 1931).

4. See A. Cann and W. D. Siegfried, "Sex Stereotypes and the Leadership Role," *Sex Roles* 17 (1987): 401–408.
5. T. A. Stewart, "Gay in Corporate America," *Fortune* (December 6, 1991), pp. 43–56.
6. Myron W. Lustig and Jolene Koester, *Intercultural Competence: Interpersonal Communication Across Cultures,* 2nd ed. (New York: HarperCollins, 1996). These authors argue that "although it may be useful in some circumstances to use the terms *interethnic* and *interracial,* we believe these types of communication are most usefully categorized as subsets of intercultural communication" (p. 51).
7. Richard D. Alba, *Ethnic Identity: The Transformation of White America* (New Haven, Conn.: Yale University Press, 1990).
8. See L. Barna, "Stumbling Blocks in Intercultural Communication," in *Intercultural Communication: A Reader,* ed. L. Samovar and R. Porter (Belmont, Calif.: Wadsworth, 1988), pp. 322–330. Barna has found that individuals are often so steeped in their own culture that they don't recognize how it influences their thinking, views, beliefs, norms, and values, and they assume that others think, perceive, and value things similarly.
9. To help all communicators better understand and communicate with one another, researchers have studied how people in racially mixed groups interact. See, for example, Melanie Booth-Butterfield and Felecia Jordan, "Communication Adaptation Among Racially Homogeneous and Heterogeneous Groups," *Southern Communication Journal* 54 (Spring 1989): 253–272.
10. Lustig and Koester, *Intercultural Competence,* note several value differences between those of different cultures. For instance, they point out that "the fast, hectic pace of European Americans, governed by clocks, appointments, and schedules, has become so commonly accepted that it is almost a cliché. The pace of life in cultures such as India, Kenya, Argentina, and among African Americans is less hectic, more relaxed, and more comfortably paced" (p. 104).
11. Arnold D. Hunt, Marie T. Crotty, and Robert B. Crotty, eds., *Ethics of World Religions,* rev. ed. (San Diego: Greenhaven Press, 1991).
12. Erica Goode, "How Culture Molds Habits of Thought," *New York Times* (August 8, 2000), pp. D1 and D4.
13. See W. Gudykunst and S. Ting-Toomey, *Culture and Interpersonal Communication* (Newbury Park, Calif.: Sage, 1988).
14. See Carolyn Calloway-Thomas, Pamela J. Cooper, and Cecil Blake, *Intercultural Communication: Roots and Routes* (Boston: Allyn & Bacon, 1999), pp. 137–157.
15. See "Integrity in the College Curriculum: A Report to the Academic Community" (Association of American Colleges, Washington, D.C., February 1985) for a discussion of how all students need a broad-based liberal arts education in place of more narrow, specialized training.
16. George Cheney, "On the Various and Changing Meanings of Organizational Membership: A Field Study of Organizational Identification," *Communication Monographs* 50 (1983): 342–362; and George Cheney and Phillip K. Tompkins, "Coming to Terms with Organizational Identification and Commitment," *Central States Speech Journal* 38 (1987): 1–15.
17. Abraham H. Maslow, *Motivation and Personality* (New York: Harper & Row, 1954).

Adapting to Diverse Audiences

5

CHAPTER OBJECTIVES

After studying this chapter, you should be able to

1. **comprehend the situational factors that may influence the way the speaker adapts a message to an audience.**
2. **identify and acknowledge the values that audience members may share.**
3. **discover diverse ways of gathering information about an audience, including conducting an audience survey.**
4. **speak ethically while adapting effectively to the audience.**

CHAPTER SURVEY

It should be clear by now that your basic task as a speaker is to design a speech specifically for an audience. You must center your thinking on the audience; all that you do should be calculated to elicit a response from your listeners and to connect your message to them. To begin, you need to have a clear understanding of **audience adaptation**.

Adaptation is not saying what an audience wants to hear. Sometimes beginning speakers who think this feel a slight uneasiness or even moral outrage over this notion. But if you hope to accomplish something with an audience, you have to adapt. This does not mean that you should only reinforce and never try to change an audience's beliefs or attitudes, nor that you should always agree with an audience. *It means that you should recognize the essential humanity of all listeners and try to focus your message on their very real concerns, while understanding their level of knowledge and experience.*

audience adaptation connecting your message to the interests and needs of the audience, at a level appropriate to their knowledge and experience and in a style they find comfortable

SITUATIONAL FACTORS IN AUDIENCE ADAPTATION

Preview Adapting to an audience involves searching for relationships between you (the speaker), your message, and the audience, then using the results of such a search to bring together all those elements. To do this, you need to seek an understanding of diverse situational factors, including audience perceptions of you, your topic, and the occasion; audience size; and the physical setting for the speech.

To test your skills and expand your understanding of audience adaptation, go to **Lesson 2** of the **VideoLab** CD-ROM and walk through the videos, exercises, and tips provided.

Every speech is given in a specific situation. Even if you became a professional public speaker and you developed several presentations that you could deliver to diverse audiences, you would still need to make many changes in your message and how you presented it as you moved from one situation to another. Following are some of the key situational factors to consider.

Audience Perceptions of the Speaker

How does the audience perceive you? Do they view you as an expert or a novice? Do you have a reputation for making excellent presentations, or has the audience never heard of you? If you are unknown to them, what can you do to help them become better informed about your background?

In Chapter 6, we will discuss speaker credibility in considerable detail. For now, however, it's enough to recognize that your credibility as a speaker, what is known and unknown about you, and the audience's predisposition toward you are important to consider as you begin to adapt your message to the audience.

Audience Size

How large is the audience? In your classroom, you will probably be speaking to approximately twenty-five students. But in other speaking situations, you may speak to a much smaller group (for example, when you speak in a business boardroom environment) or a much larger group (perhaps at a political rally, a community meeting, or in a church).

While audience size may affect your communication apprehension (see Chapter 2), it will certainly influence how you prepare for your presentation in terms of your delivery, the use of visual aids, the kind of language you use, and so on. In general, you will want to speak more formally with larger groups.

Audience Feelings About the Speaking Situation

As you prepare to speak, you will want to consider the speaking context. To assist you in assessing your speaking environment, go to **Assessing Your Speech Environment** on the **Online SpeechStudio** and complete the exercise.

How does the audience feel about the occasion? Perhaps you are speaking on a day that is very special to the audience. They are eager to be there, and you can count on their attentiveness and good will. On other occasions, they may be neutral or even hostile toward the speaking occasion. Maybe you are a speaker at a required training session. Once you have finished your speech, the listeners can all go home.

Knowing how listeners view the occasion can help you plan your approach, your style of speaking, and the length of your speech. Many audiences are captive or are attending out of habit or politeness, and you will need to work very hard to engage their attention and interest.

Speakers and listeners must adapt to different speaking environments. A large audience may require the speaker to use electronic amplification and allows for little direct response from listeners. In a small, informal group the speaker can more easily see how listeners are responding and make immediate adaptations. (*left:* AP/Wide World Photos; *right:* Nancy Richmond/The Image Works)

The Speaking Environment

What kind of room are you speaking in? When you speak in your classroom, you are speaking in a familiar, comfortable environment. You know what to expect—whether there is an overhead projector or TV monitor, whether the lights can be dimmed, and so forth. As you begin to work on your speech, you will want to learn as much as you can about other physical settings where you may be speaking.

Go to **Lesson 9's Screening Room** on the **VideoLab** CD-ROM to view the first speech on women's gymnastics. Given the speaker's gender and the nature of the topic, how effectively does she adapt her speech to a mixed-gender audience?

Try to learn as much as possible about the basic speaking "equipment"—podium, technological support, microphone, and so on. Find out how large the room is. A small group in a very large room presents a different kind of speaking challenge from a large group crowded into a small room. Find out how much control you will have over the room's climate. Can you open windows? Darken lights? Pull down a screen? Ask listeners to move closer to you?

KEEP IN MIND 5.1

Situational Factors to Remember

In adapting to diverse audiences, consider such situational factors as:

- how the audience perceives you.
- audience size.
- audience views of the occasion.
- the kind of physical setting.
- audience views toward your topic.

Audience Views of the Speech Topic

What are the audience's attitudes toward your topic? How much do listeners know about it? What kinds of relevant experiences might they have had? If you are trying to persuade your classmates to consider camping in the wilderness next summer, you will want to know whether there are any campers in the room. If you want them to adopt a pet from the Humane Society, you will certainly want to know if they already own pets.

Beyond listeners' basic level of topic-relevant knowledge, you will want to reflect upon their **values** and how those values translate into attitudes and beliefs that are likely to influence their willingness to listen and their ability to respond positively to your message.

values those things we consider good and desirable

IDENTIFYING SHARED AUDIENCE VALUES

Preview Regardless of the situation, searching for and identifying audience values is a major step toward adapting your message to the audience. What values do you likely share with your listeners? How can those be used to establish common ground and make your message more compelling? Besides recognizing shared needs and values, you will want to think of what listeners believe and what attitudes they hold.

 PORTFOLIO 5.1

What They Value

What values do your listeners likely hold that seem especially relevant to a speech topic that you are contemplating? How will you ensure that they see the connection? What will you say or suggest that will connect with the value(s) you have identified?

When you catalog listener characteristics (age, gender, religion, and so forth), you are doing so, in part, to uncover audience values. You are especially interested in looking for areas of agreement (as well as potential conflict), and you will want to think about how listeners' value priorities might shape the way you approach your message. For certain audiences, patriotic values may be extremely important; for others, the need to get ahead; and for still others, the value of education. Of course, all listeners share certain basic human needs (such as the need for love and belonging), as we discussed in Chapter 4, and you will want to remember how these needs can be used to unify your audience.

attitudes learned predispositions to respond favorably, unfavorably, or in a neutral manner to particular objects or occasions

beliefs convictions that certain things are real or true

All of us possess a network of interlocking values, some of which conflict with others. For example, Americans tend to admire individualism as a trait while also placing great stress on the need for teamwork.[1] They profess the golden rule—do unto others as we would have them do unto us—while also valuing material success that often can be realized only at the cost of outwitting or outmaneuvering others. We hear of the "work ethic," the "business ethic," and the "Puritan ethic," all of which denote different sets of values at work in our society.

✔ KEEP IN MIND 5.2

Values Shared by Audience Members

Identify shared audience values by

- cataloging listener characteristics such as age, education, and gender.
- searching for areas of agreement.
- recognizing the presence of interlocking values, sometimes involving points of inconsistency or conflict.
- deciding whether or not listener values translate into attitudes and beliefs.

Once you have considered audience values, you will need to reflect further on how those values translate into listener **attitudes** and **beliefs**. For instance, you may determine that you and your listeners greatly value integrity and responsibility. Yet in an election year, you may discover that listener attitudes toward the political candidate you are promoting are negative. Whereas you see the candidate as honest, experienced, and trustworthy, your listeners may see her opponent as far superior. In this case, you would not try to change listener values (which you share). Instead you would try to identify the network of opinions and beliefs that may have contributed to those negative attitudes. For instance, you may discover that some listeners believe that women in general are poorly suited for high-level leadership positions. Or they may believe that your candidate's particular background experience is not relevant to the sort of leadership position she is seeking. Or they may see her voting record as having been inconsistent on environmental protection, which is a real priority for them.

Depending on how you analyze the nature of the problem—what specific discrepancies you uncover in listener beliefs, attitudes, and values—you will adapt your message in quite different ways. What is key here is that you are still supporting the candidate you believe in, but once you understand the nature of the audience's objections, you can proceed to adapt your message in specific ways so that you are able to address their very real concerns.

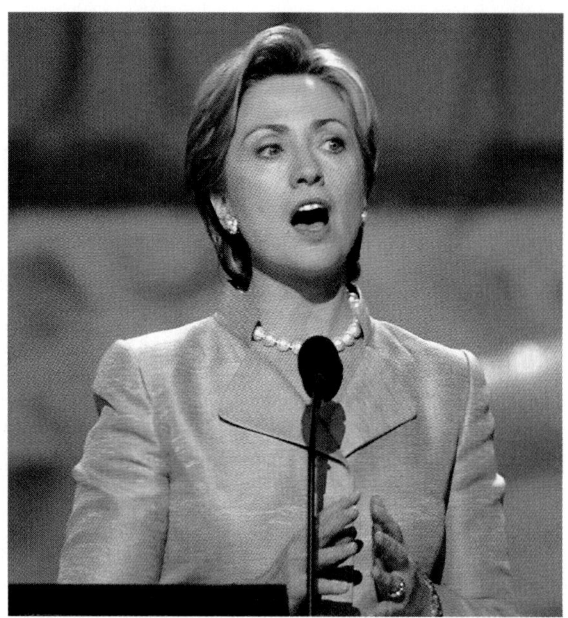

Audience attitudes and beliefs can vary widely in responding to the same speaker. Senator Hillary Clinton will be well received by her supporters and viewed negatively by her detractors. To be effective, she needs to understand how various reactions have the potential to affect her message. (Tannen Maury/ The Image Works)

GATHERING INFORMATION FOR AUDIENCE ADAPTATION

Preview There are different ways of collecting information about your audience. Approaching audience assessment from diverse perspectives may prove helpful. Information can be gathered through interviewing, administering an audience survey, conducting research on the Internet, and continuing to assess the audience before, during, and after the speech.

Once you have decided that gathering audience-relevant information is important, you must figure out how to do it. Some speakers use the help of others. Often professional public speakers, executives, and politicians hire people such as research assistants and even speechwriters to look into audience opinions, beliefs, and biases. Most of us, however, undertake this task on our own.

Interviewing for Information

A good place to begin is by contacting the person who asked you to speak. Usually this contact person is a member of the group or organization that will be addressed (or has worked with them closely) and knows the audience well.

You can interview this contact person either by phone or in person. Follow the basic principles of interviewing for information discussed in Chapter 8. Your goal is to find out as much as you can about the audience—their experiences, topic-relevant knowledge, values, and interests—as related to you, your topic, and the particular speaking situation.[2] Regardless of the specific topic, here are some of the general kinds of questions you might want to ask:

- How diverse is the audience in terms of age, sex, and the like?
- How many listeners will likely be present when I speak?
- Could you describe the room where I'll be speaking?
- How knowledgeable is the audience about my topic?
- What relevant experiences might audience members have had?
- How likely are they to be open to the sort of information I'm discussing or the proposal I'm making?
- Are there likely to be great differences of opinion or experience within the audience? If so, explain.
- How much time is available for my presentation? For audience questions?

Of course, you will want to adapt this basic interviewing format to the specific situation. Table 5.1. offers an extended illustration. In this example, assume that you have served for two years as a volunteer with the Big Brothers Big Sisters program in your college community. You have been asked to represent this organization and speak to a group of first-year college students, urging them to consider becoming a Big Brother or Big Sister. Before speaking, you might interview the program organizer, who has been working with this group for several weeks, and pose some of the questions listed in Table 5.1.

TABLE 5.1 Sample Interview Questions for a Speech on Volunteering for Big Brothers Big Sisters

1. How many students will likely be in my audience?
2. How diverse is the group in terms of gender, age, major, and so on?
3. Have these students heard presentations on volunteerism earlier in the semester? If so, what volunteer groups have been represented?
4. To your knowledge, are any students already volunteering? Any estimate of how many?
5. Has anyone else spoken on behalf of Big Brothers Big Sisters, or should I assume that the listeners know very little about the program?
6. I'd like to show a brief video of my Little Sister and me on a summer camping trip. If this seems like a good idea to you, I'll need a VCR and a monitor. Will that represent a problem?
7. How much time do I have to make my presentation? I'd like to leave plenty of time for questions. Does that seem reasonable with this group?
8. Is there anything else you can think of that I need to know or anticipate?

Administering an Audience Survey

You can also construct and administer an audience survey, with the permission of the contact person and the cooperation of the group, aimed at gathering insights into the same sorts of issues. This approach to gathering information can be especially valuable in your own public speaking class. Public speaking instructors often ask students to create a brief questionnaire, administer it to the class, use the results for audience adaptation, and write a critical analysis of the process.

Although survey construction can be fairly complicated, you can learn to design a very basic questionnaire that will serve as a valuable analytical tool.[3] Following are some principles to follow as you design your audience survey:

- *Use the survey to collect relevant* ***demographic information*** *about the audience.* For some topics, for instance, you may want to know the age or major of your classmates. For others, you may want to know their political affiliation or religion.
- *Use different kinds of questions to gather the kind of information you need.*[4] Some questions may ask audience members to check the appropriate answer from among several choices. Others may ask them to write a few sentences.
- *Limit your audience survey to a few good questions that can be answered in the time your instructor has set aside during class.* Besides respecting the time constraints of the class, you are more likely to get more accurate and better developed responses from your classmates if you do not overwhelm them with questions.
- *Be sure to use the results of the survey as you craft your speech and adapt your message to your audience.* Administering an audience survey is not just an academic exercise. It is one of the most direct means available of finding out about your audience's knowledge, opinions, and values. Because your classmates remain anonymous as they complete the survey, they are more likely to respond with candor than if they had to identify themselves.

demographic information factual information gathered about listener characteristics

An excellent way to analyze your audience is to administer an audience survey. Go to the **Audience Analysis Questionnaire** on the **Online SpeechStudio**, where you will find a sample survey. You may want to complete the questions yourself as a kind of self-survey.

When you conduct an audience survey, you may choose to probe listener attitudes regarding a specific topic, or you may survey their views on a wide variety of topics. For an example of the more general approach, go to the **Audience Attitudinal Questionnaire** on the **Online SpeechStudio.** You may complete this survey yourself.

Devising Good Questions for an Audience Survey

Whether you are interviewing for information or constructing an audience questionnaire, you should include both closed and open questions (see Chapter 8). Closed questions yield limited information, and open questions may be hard to tabulate and are time-consuming to complete. The key is balance.[5]

There is no magic formula for constructing an audience survey, but here are some tips to guide you:

- *Begin the survey with closed, fixed-choice questions to collect basic demographic and other factual information.* For example:

What is your class standing?

Freshman ____ Sophomore ____ Junior ____ Senior ____

Are you registered to vote?

Yes ____ No ____ Not sure ____

If you are registered to vote, are you registered as a(n):

Democrat _____ Republican _____ Independent _____ Other _____

Should license taxes for sport-utility vehicles (SUVs) be higher than those for other vehicles?

Yes _____ No _____ No opinion _____

Should our campus become pedestrian-only?

Yes _____ No _____ No opinion _____

Through these kinds of questions, you can collect "bottom-line" information very quickly. However, the responses give you no insight into how strongly listeners identify with the choices they make. One person might be registered as a Republican, but she might be disillusioned with the Republican party and is considering becoming an Independent. Yet she would likely check "Republican," and you would count her as such.

- *Use scale questions to acquire more precise information from respondents or to gain an understanding of how firmly committed they are to their opinions and beliefs.* For example:

How many servings of fruits and vegetables do you usually eat each day?

Seven or more ____ Five or six ____
Three or four ____ One or two ____ None ____

Indicate the extent to which you agree or disagree with the following statements:

I believe that capital punishment should be abolished.

Strongly agree ____ Somewhat agree ____
Somewhat disagree _____ Strongly disagree ____
Not sure ____

I get at least eight hours of sleep each night.

All of the time ____ Most of the time ____
Rarely ____ Never ____ Not sure ____

Scale questions allow you to gain more precise information and to measure degrees of commitment.

- *You will also want to include some open questions on your survey to provide greater depth of response.* For instance:

How do you feel about the proposal to make this campus pedestrian-only by the year 2003?

If you voted during the last election, why did you do so?

If you didn't vote during the last election, why did you not do so?

In your view, why, in general, do fewer U.S. citizens vote now than at any time in the past?

Through open questions, you give the audience the freedom to respond as they choose. By examining their responses, you may grow to better understand

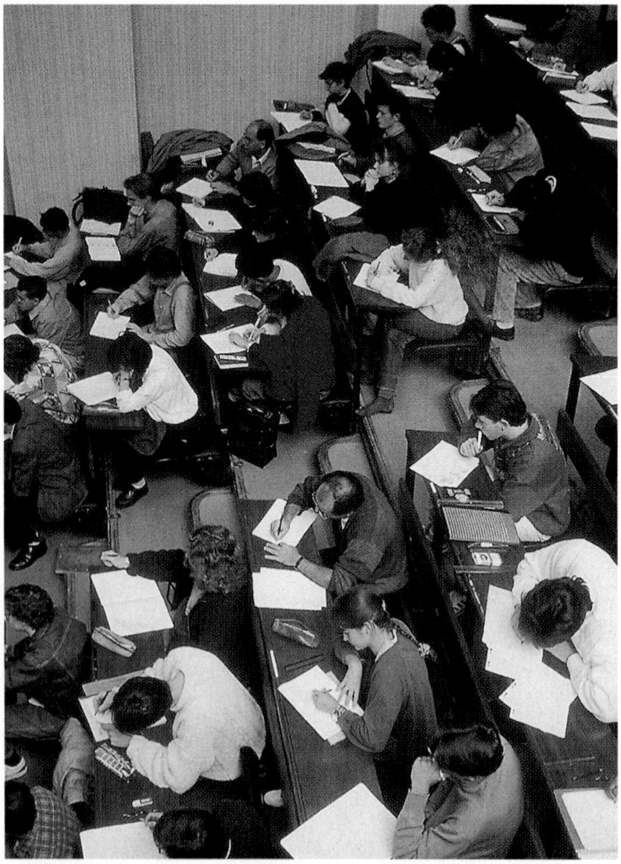

Getting written responses from listeners through an audience survey can provide valuable information a speaker can use to adapt his or her message. (Ultrike Welsch/PhotoEdit)

why they believe as they do and how they justify their actions and opinions. At the same time, you may find that some listeners will give you irrelevant information and some will simply refuse to write out a response. When used in combination with other questions, however, open questions should enrich your survey's results.

- *Finally, avoid leading or loaded questions.* Make sure you phrase your questions with neutrality and objectivity so that you do not lead respondents in a particular direction. If you were giving a speech about drinking on campus, you might ask this question on your audience survey: "Describe your drinking habits." A leading version of the same question might read, "Describe the last time you drank excessively." The second version assumes that the respondent does in fact drink excessively. By contrast, the first version invites the respondent to describe an array of behaviors ranging from complete abstinence to extreme drinking. All survey questions should be written in the most neutral way possible.[6]

Table 5.2 is an example of an audience survey used by one public speaking student who was interested in giving a persuasive speech on vegetarianism. After studying the following results of her survey, she decided to change her basic approach.

1. Definitions of vegetarianism varied widely among audience members. About one-third believed that a person is a vegetarian if he or she does not eat red meat. Two class members believed that vegetarians do not eat any animal products (such as milk or eggs). The speaker knew that she would have to take some time early in the speech to clarify her definition of vegetarianism.

TABLE 5.2 Sample Audience Survey on Vegetarianism

1. Please check the categories that most accurately describe you:

   Sex:
   Male ____ Female ____

   Major:
   Liberal arts ____ Business ____ Health care professions ____
   Music ____ Engineering ____ Other ____

2. How would you describe a vegetarian?

3. Are you a vegetarian?

   Yes ____ No ____

4. Do you have a close friend or relative who is a vegetarian?

   Yes ____ No ____ Not sure ____

5. Do you agree or disagree with the following statement? *Vegetarians can enjoy a nutritious and flavorful diet.*

   Strongly agree ____ Somewhat agree ____ Undecided ____ Somewhat disagree ____ Strongly disagree ____

6. If you are a vegetarian, please explain your reasons for becoming one.

7. In your view, what are the main reasons that people choose to become vegetarians?

2. Only two students (other than the speaker herself) out of a class of twenty-four students were vegetarians. In addition, six other students, or 25 percent of the class, said that they had a vegetarian friend or relative. The speaker realized that she could not count on much direct experience among the audience.

3. Sixty percent of the class did not believe that vegetarians can enjoy a healthy, flavorful diet.

4. The reasons the two students gave for becoming vegetarians were primarily related to their own health rather than moral objections to consuming meat.

5. Students tended to view vegetarians as having taken a rather extreme approach to a healthy diet. Some cited dangers. Two or three seemed hostile toward vegetarians—one calling them "kooks" and another referring to them as "granola." In general, men were more negative than women. Nearly 70 percent of the women discussed animal rights as one reason for vegetarianism. Students' majors seemed unrelated to their responses.

Take the opportunity to assess your knowledge of audience survey construction. Go to **Next Step: Building an Audience Survey** in Lesson 2 of the **VideoLab** CD-ROM and complete the quiz and exercises that follow.

The speaker's own commitment to vegetarianism grew from a deep ethical conviction regarding animal rights. Based on the survey results, however, she felt that converting this particular audience to her point of view would be unrealistic, given their initial views and the short time available for persuading them. Instead, she decided to make them aware of the problems (both to animals and humans) associated with factory farms (with a specific focus on poultry farms). She would acknowledge inhumane killing, but she would go well beyond that to discuss dangerous working conditions; the extreme poverty of the work force; and the unsanitary conditions under which the chickens are bred, fed, and killed—making them unsafe for consumers. Her specific purpose in this speech was to get her audience to purchase only free-range chickens—for the welfare of the workers, the animals, and the consumers.

Had the speaker not conducted the audience survey in this instance and set forth to give her original speech, she surely would have been doomed to failure. As it was, her speech was extremely well received, and five or six students said that they were going to purchase only free-range chickens in the future.

As you can see, the audience survey is an extremely helpful tool that enables a speaker to gather the kind of information he or she needs to adapt a message to the concerns, experiences, and priorities of an audience.

CONNECTING TO THE NET

For advice on and practice with putting your own audience survey together, go to **http://college.hmco.com/communication/andrews/public_speaking/2e/students/** and click on *Connecting to the Net.* From there, follow the link to Audience Surveys.

Other Ways of Gathering Preliminary Information

Still other avenues for collecting information about the audience exist. For instance, you might consider *attending a meeting of the group* that you will address and see for yourself what their concerns, interests, and values appear to be. This strategy is practical only if you have the time and the opportunity. If you live far away from the town where you will speak, you probably will not make such a visit. But if you live right down the street, you might consider meeting with the group to get acquainted. Your contact person should prove helpful in arranging this.

You also can learn much about the organization or group by *conducting research on the Internet.* Suppose you were speaking to the local chapter of the American Red Cross. You might begin by visiting the organization's national web site (www.redcross.org). By doing this, you would learn a great deal about the history of the Red Cross, its mission and scope, its major projects, and its national leadership. At the same time, you would find a link to your own local Red Cross chapter, where you could learn how long the chapter has been in your community, what services it has provided, the size of its staff and volunteer force, and so forth.

Thus, through various avenues—using the resources available to you through the Internet, the community, your contact person, and the group itself—you should be able to craft your speech with an excellent sense of your audience.

Once you have surveyed your audience, you will want to take what you have learned about it and draw some conclusions about how best to approach your speech. To do this, go to **Using What You've Learned Through Your Audience Assessment** on the **Online SpeechStudio** and respond to the questions posed.

KEEP IN MIND 5.3

Methods of Gathering Information About an Audience

Gather information for audience adaptation by

- interviewing for information.
- conducting a soundly constructed audience survey.
- attending meetings of the group.
- exploring the Internet.

ONGOING STRATEGIES FOR AUDIENCE ADAPTATION

Preview Sometimes we may assume that audience analysis is done only before the day of the speech. Of course, much analysis will be done in advance. But a resourceful speaker can continue to assess and adapt to the audience immediately before, during, and even after a speech.

Many speeches are made in the context of conferences, business meetings, and other ongoing events. When you arrive at a conference or meeting room and begin to interact with the audience during a meeting or meal that precedes your speech, you may learn a good deal about their interests and priorities. You may discover that the audience looks a little different than you had imagined. They may be younger, they may sound more conservative, or they may express interests you had not thought of or learned about in advance. Based on what you learn immediately preceding the speech, you may choose to make minor adjustments in your presentation.

Similarly, it is even possible to adapt to the audience while you are speaking. To some extent, all effective speakers do this. If they sense that the audience is bored by too much background information, they may cut out some of it and move on to an assessment of current problems. They may use more humor if the audience seems to enjoy it, or move closer to listeners and speak more informally if they sense that the podium is creating a barrier.

Sometimes speakers turn a speech into a dialogue, where the audience asks questions from the very beginning. As the speaker answers the questions, he or she constructs the speech. One speaker who uses this approach is Mike Bryson, coordinator of the Indianapolis Substance Abuse Program. Bryson describes his approach in *Spotlight on Letting the Audience Set the Agenda.*

FRAME OF REFERENCE

HIV educator, Mike Bryson, stays in direct contact with his audience by inviting them to ask questions whenever they arise in listeners' minds as he speaks.

SPOTLIGHT ON... Letting the Audience Set the Agenda

When I'm talking about HIV [the most common topic that he addresses], I know there are certain things I feel I really need to cover, but I'm also trying to gauge my audience to get some type of feeling for what *they* might want to hear, where *their* interests may be. So, if possible, I do parts of my presentation and accept questions as I go along. I feel that helps in my effectiveness because I involve the audience. I get a feel for where they're coming from, what they want to hear. . . . It's a big concern when you're up there, knowing whether you're holding the interest of the people there.

Interview with Mike Bryson, Coordinator of the Indianapolis Substance Abuse Program.

Finally, based on your perceptions of how much you are "on target" with your planned remarks, you may choose to shorten your speech so that you can focus your attention on the audience's concerns during a question-and-answer period after the speech. In *Spotlight on Saving Genuine Time for Audience Concerns*, General John Stanford, former superintendent of schools in Seattle, describes a speaking occasion in which his decision to move on to audience questions salvaged what was otherwise a very unsuccessful speech.

In short, audience analysis and adaptation is an ongoing process. From the moment you learn you are to make a speech until the moment you stop interacting with listeners, you can continue to learn more about them and make appropriate adjustments in your strategy, style, and response. And from this experience, you may reflect on what you have learned, how your speech was received, and what things you'd like to change if you were to give it again. This kind of reflective analysis will help you grow as a public speaker.

KEEP IN MIND 5.4

The Continuing Quest for Information About the Audience

You can continue to gather information about the audience by

- arriving early for your speech and observing and interacting with listeners on the spot.
- remaining attentive to how listeners are responding during the speech and making adjustments.
- trying other interaction formats.

SPOTLIGHT ON... Saving Genuine Time for Audience Concerns

A tough speaking experience for me was when I spoke with a group of textile manufacturers—CEOs of textile corporations. . . . There were maybe one hundred fifty people, but the room was very narrow, and so the people were spread all the way out through that room. I did not feel in contact with the people who were in the back of the room, and I came to give my leadership speech about "love them and lead them." And while I was trying to give them my love them and lead them speech, I noticed that they were not engaged. I mean, this . . . is my most powerful speech! I was just on fire, but I was not reaching those people. We stopped this leadership speech, and we went into the question-and-answer period. The question-and-answer period lasted longer than the speech; it lasted forty-five minutes. And what they wanted to talk to me about was education. Education—how do you make it work? How do I make it work as a parent? How do I make it work as a school board member? How do I help in the school and [with] the teachers? What should I do? So they were not interested in my leadership stuff. And I sensed that during the speech. But it was very clear that they loved the question-and-answer period.

Interview with General John Stanford, former superintendent of schools in Seattle.

SPEAKING ETHICALLY AND EFFECTIVELY

Preview In adapting to audience interests, needs, and values, you must maintain the highest concern for ethics. Your message must grow from your true beliefs about the subject at hand. Ethical speakers will also acknowledge and respect listener diversity, avoid stereotyping, and engage audience emotions responsibly.

While adapting to your audience, it is important to remain true to your own values. Do not lose your own perspective. Although you need to see the listeners' perspective, your own point of view should not be overwhelmed by your considerations of the audience. *Being open-minded does not mean being empty-minded.* You don't want to lose your own convictions merely to please an audience. You must try to understand the people you want to influence, but understanding is not the same thing as agreeing. To sell oneself or one's ideas for any price, including audience acceptance, is pandering—and that is something quite apart from speaking effectively.[7]

Using your speech topic as a frame of reference, go to the **Logistics, Occasion, and Audience Analysis Worksheet** on the **Online SpeechStudio** and complete the worksheet. By doing this, you will synthesize all you have learned about your audience and your speaking context.

Acknowledging Diversity and Avoiding Stereotyping

From the list of diverse audience characteristics that were discussed in Chapter 4, you should grapple with those that apply to your specific speaking situation. The setting and the topic may suggest the obvious ones, but successful speaking will involve going beyond the obvious.

One thing to bear in mind is that people are not always aware of all of their own interests. When we are thinking of buying a new car, for example, our role as consumer may conflict with our role as parent: we might want to buy a car that is inexpensive and gets good gas mileage, but that same car may be too cramped for the children on a long trip.

Because of this fact, the speaker has every right to emphasize one aspect of listeners' lives over others, even though he or she is aware of certain audience characteristics. For instance, in speaking to a community group, you may choose to remind them of their responsibility to the homeless, even though you know that your listeners are well-off and are more easily focused on their children, their jobs, and even their leisure pursuits. You may point out that, in the long run, a community with many homeless people will not provide a safe environment for children or a prosperous economy for small businesses. The listener, who may be preoccupied with the immediate considerations suggested by the setting and the topic, may overlook aspects of his or her own life that are, indeed, relevant to the speaking situation, but the effective speaker can point these out.

A key to effective public speaking is successful and ethical audience adaptation. Go to **Drill 2.2: Adapting Persuasive Messages to Diverse Audiences** in Lesson 2 of the **VideoLab** CD-ROM. Respond to the questions to assess different ways in which the speech might be adapted to different audiences.

FRAME OF REFERENCE

Superintendent of Schools John Stanford brings his experience and expertise to bear in talking about the accomplishments of the Seattle public schools and the challenges facing public education in the United States.

As we noted in Chapter 4, a speaker should not stereotype.[8] As much as we know or seem to know about listeners, we cannot overgeneralize about people. We should not assume that all older people have the same view of sexual morality, for example. Older people may live together without being married because of the threat of serious income loss due to social security regulations or because of tax benefits. Many young people are surprised to think of grandmothers and grandfathers doing such a thing, just as many older people may be surprised to learn that all young people do not believe in premarital sexual relations.

Labels often deceive us into stereotyping as well. All women and men who believe in feminism, for example, do not believe in the same thing. Feminism to one woman may mean the freedom to pursue a career and be married at the same time—in short, to be treated as equal to men. To another, it may mean the rejection of all traditional male-female relationships. So as we try to construct a profile of listeners and adapt to their needs, we should remember that we are talking about *trends* in behavior among certain groups. We can never predict with absolute certainty that particular listener characteristics will predetermine their responses.

Engaging Audience Emotions Ethically

Go to **Lesson 6's Screening Room** on the **VideoLab** CD-ROM to view the first speech on Native American symbols. Consider the speaker's use of emotional appeals from an ethical perspective. Do you think she is speaking ethically? Why or why not?

As a speaker, you must realize that emotion is not an evil force. We are upset, angry, happy, excited, or apprehensive only when we care about something. If we hear a message that excites no emotion at all or that does not arouse our interest, we will probably judge that message to be irrelevant. The presence of emotion means that a topic is important.

Quite often we tend to think of logic and emotion as separate things. The former is "good," the product of education and intelligence, and the latter is "bad," the result of primal passions that should be kept under control. But without feelings, both learning and persuasion are more difficult to achieve. If you were asked to take action, and if you felt that the action would make you feel content, you would be more likely to take it than if you thought the action would be a waste of time because it did not matter to you.

Of course, not all feelings are constructive. Greed may cause a business executive to continue an unsafe or unhealthy way of manufacturing a product because costly changes would reduce profits. Or excessive love may lead to smothering. Since emotions can go either way, your duty as a speaker is to use emotion constructively—say, by arguing for something positive, such as a fire safety device to protect loved ones. In this case, the feeling of love is channeled into a constructive action.[9]

KEEP IN MIND 5.5

Audience Adaptation and Ethics

Speak ethically and effectively by

- remaining true to yourself.
- acknowledging diversity and avoiding stereotyping.
- engaging audience emotions ethically.

SUMMARY

It is one thing to analyze an audience and quite another to adapt your message effectively to what you think you have learned. After considering the particulars of the situation in which you will be speaking (audience size, physical setting, and audience attitudes toward you, the topic, and the occasion), you will need to gather critical information about your listeners. You can do this by interviewing the person who invited you to speak, conducting an audience survey, observing the audience in their natural environment, and exploring the Internet.

Learn all that you can about listener values, beliefs, and attitudes. Audience adaptation is an ongoing process. Immediately preceding and even during and following the speech, you can make adjustments as you assess, watch, listen, and reflect on the communication experience.

As an ethical public speaker, you must honor diversity, avoid stereotyping, and use emotion constructively to engage listeners' interest and commitment.

Most important, as you prepare your speech and deliver your message, stay true to yourself and your own convictions, while recognizing and respecting the convictions and feelings of your audience.

For a review of some basics of audience adaptation, go to **Coach: Tips to Remember** in Lesson 2 of the **VideoLab** CD-ROM. Watch and reflect on the video clips that demonstrate both strong and weak audience adaptation techniques.

QUESTIONS FOR REVIEW AND REFLECTION

1. What is your understanding of the meaning of *audience adaptation*?
2. What are some key situational factors you will want to consider as you analyze your audience and anticipate the speaking situation? Consider the topic you plan to use for your next speech. Which of these situational factors might be especially important in this speaking context?
3. As you continue to think about your speech topic, identify one person you would like to interview. Write down several open questions you would like to ask this person.
4. As you continue to prepare for your next classroom speech, conduct an audience survey. Use the guidelines offered in this chapter and the advice of your instructor in constructing your survey. Then compile the results of your survey and write a short summary of what you have learned about your fellow classmates. Note especially the ways in which this information will influence your approach to your topic and help you better adapt to your audience.
5. Besides conducting a survey, what are some other audience adaptation methods you can use before, during, and after you make a speech?
6. What are the major stereotypes associated with the following groups: football players, sorority members, accountants, lawyers, and college professors? For each category, offer at least one example of someone you know who violates the stereotype.
7. What are some ethical issues that you will want to think about as you adapt your ideas to an audience?

ENDNOTES

1. See Peter F. Drucker, "The Coming of the New Organization," *Harvard Business Review* 66 (1988): 45–53, for a team-focused discussion of the modern American organization. Also see David A. Whetten and Kim S. Cameron, *Developing Management Skills,* 4th ed. (New York: HarperCollins, 1997), for an interesting discussion of values commonly espoused in the American workplace.
2. There are many excellent books on interviewing. See, for examples, Jeanne Tessier Barone and Jo Young Switzer, *Interviewing Art and Skill* (Boston: Allyn & Bacon, 1995); Arnold B. Kanter, *The Complete Book of Interviewing: Everything You Need to Know from Both Sides of the Table* (New York: Times Books, 1995); and Charles J. Stewart and William B. Cash, Jr., *Interviewing: Principles and Practices,* 9th ed. (Boston: McGraw-Hill, 2000).
3. Priscilla Salant, *How to Conduct Your Own Survey* (New York: Wiley, 1994).

4. Jeane M. Converse and Stanley Presser, *Survey Questions: Handcrafting the Standardized Questionnaire* (Newbury Park, Calif.: Sage, 1986). Also see Floyd J. Fowler, Jr., *Survey Research Methods* (Newbury Park, Calif.: Sage, 1993), for an excellent discussion of how to construct survey questions.

5. Stanley L. Payne, *The Art of Asking Questions* (Princeton, N.J.: Princeton University Press, 1980). Also see Robert W. Eder and Michael M. Harris, eds., *The Employment Interview Handbook* (Thousand Oaks, Calif.: Sage, 1999); even though this book is focused on the employment interview, it contains an excellent section on questioning as related to structured and unstructured interviews (pp. 143–216).

6. For additional information about survey construction, see Paul Rosenfeld, Jack E. Edwards, and Marie D. Thomas, "Improving Organizational Surveys," *American Behavioral Scientist* 36 (1993): 414–426; and Sam G. McFarland, "Effects of Question Order on Survey Responses," *Public Opinion Quarterly* 45 (1981): 208–215.

7. Many excellent books address communication ethics. Among them are James A. Jaska and Michael S. Pritchard, *Communication Ethics: Methods of Analysis,* 2nd ed. (Belmont, Calif.: Wadsworth, 1994); and Matthew W. Seeger, *Ethics and Organizational Communication* (Cresskill, N.J.: Hampton Press, 1997).

8. See Carolyn Calloway-Thomas, Pamela J. Cooper, and Cecil Blake, *Intercultural Communication: Roots and Routes* (Boston: Allyn & Bacon, 1999), especially "Stereotypes and Prejudice," pp. 79–103.

9. For an excellent discussion of the relationship between ethical communication and the use of emotional appeals, see Richard L. Johannesen, *Ethics in Human Communication,* 4th ed. (Prospect Heights, Ill.: Waveland Press, 1996), pp. 127–129.

On November 10, 2001, two months after the September 11 destruction of the World Trade Center, President George W. Bush addressed the United Nations General Assembly in New York. The terrorist attack had been deplored throughout the world, but there were countries in which anti-American feelings were strong and countries who actively or indirectly aided the terrorists. Further, since the terrorists were Islamic extremists, there were some in America who blamed all Muslims and some in Muslim countries who feared that America and the West would identify all Muslims with the murderous actions of the terrorists. The President's task was to speak to those various audiences so that they joined with the United States to combat the violence represented by the September 11 outrages, while still preserving fundamental human values.

The Coalition Against Terrorism

George W. Bush

We meet in a hall devoted to peace, in a city scarred by violence, in a nation awakened to danger, in a world uniting for a long struggle. Every civilized nation here today is resolved to keep the most basic commitment of civilization: we will defend ourselves and our future against terror and lawless violence.

The president begins by asserting that all the nations' representatives assembled for his speech are "civilized," which he defines as opposed to terror and lawlessness.

The United Nations was founded in this cause. In a second world war, we learned there is no isolation from evil. We affirmed that some crimes are so terrible they offend humanity itself. And we resolved that the aggressions and ambitions of the wicked must be opposed early, decisively, and collectively, before they threaten us all. That evil has returned, and that cause is renewed. A few miles from here, many thousands still lie in a tomb of rubble. Tomorrow, the secretary general, the president of the General Assembly, and I will visit that site, where the names of every nation and region that lost citizens will be read aloud. If we were to read the names of every person who died, it would take more than 3 hours.

By reminding the delegates that the United Nations was founded in response to the inhuman cruelties of World War II, Bush equates the terrorist attack with such atrocities as the Holocaust.

Those names include a citizen of Gambia, whose wife spent their fourth wedding anniversary, September the 12th, searching in vain for her husband. Those names include a man who supported his wife in Mexico, sending home money every week. Those names include a young Pakistani who prayed toward Mecca five times a day, and died that day trying to save others.

Using specific examples, President Bush stresses the fact that the victims were not only Americans, but citizens of many countries and people of many faiths.

The suffering of September the 11th was inflicted on people of many faiths and many nations. All of the victims, including Muslims, were killed with equal indifference and equal satisfaction by the terrorist leaders. The terrorists are violating the tenets of every religion, including the one they invoke.

Last week, the sheikh of Al-Azhar University, the world's oldest Islamic institution of higher learning, declared that terrorism is a disease, and that Islam prohibits killing innocent civilians. The terrorists call their cause holy, yet, they fund it with drug dealing; they encourage murder and suicide in the name of a great faith that forbids both. They dare to ask God's blessing as they set out to kill innocent men, women, and children. But the God of Isaac and Ishmael would never answer such a prayer. And a murderer is not a martyr; he is just a murderer.

Using a respected Islamic authority, the president reinforces his point not only that all terrorists are not Muslims, but also that those who committed the September 11 attacks were not themselves true to the Islamic faith, as they claimed to be.

Time is passing. Yet, for the United States of America, there will be no forgetting September the 11th. We will remember every rescuer who died in honor. We will remember every family that lives in grief. We will remember the fire and ash, the last phone calls, the funerals of the children.

Showing American resolve, the president appeals to his domestic audience while, at the same time conveying the seriousness of America's determination—a message to the terrorists themselves and those countries that might be inclined to aid them in any way.

And the people of my country will remember those who have plotted against us. We are learning their names. We are coming to know their faces. There is no corner of the Earth distant or dark enough to protect them. However long it takes, their hour of justice will come.

By alluding to the terrorists' verbal assault on the United Nations, and particularly the Arab states, Bush appeals again to those who might view the struggle as the United States versus Islam to view it as a terrorist war against all "civilized" peoples.

Every nation has a stake in this cause. As we meet, the terrorists are planning more murder—perhaps in my country, or perhaps in yours. They kill because they aspire to dominate. They seek to overthrow governments and destabilize entire regions. Last week, anticipating this meeting of the General Assembly, they denounced the United Nations. They called our secretary general a criminal and condemned all Arab nations here as traitors to Islam. Few countries meet their exacting standards of brutality and oppression. Every other country is a potential target. And all the world faces the most horrifying prospect of all: these same terrorists are searching for weapons of mass destruction, the tools to turn their hatred into holocaust. They can be expected to use chemical, biological, and nuclear weapons the moment they are capable of doing so. Civilization itself, the civilization we share, is threatened. History will record our response, and judge or justify every nation in this hall.

The civilized world is now responding. We act to defend ourselves and deliver our children from a future of fear. We choose the dignity of life over a culture of death. We choose lawful change and civil disagreement over coercion, subversion, and chaos. These commitments—hope and order, law and life—unite people across cultures and continents. Upon these commitments depend all peace and progress. For these commitments, we are determined to fight. The United Nations has risen to this responsibility. On the 12th of September, these buildings opened for emergency meetings of the General Assembly and the Security Council. Before the sun had set, these attacks on the world stood condemned by the world. And I want to thank you for this strong and principled stand.

Bush singles out Arab countries in an effort to disassociate Islam from al Qaeda.

I also thank the Arab Islamic countries that have condemned terrorist murder. Many of you have seen the destruction of terror in your own lands. The terrorists are increasingly isolated by their own hatred and extremism. They cannot hide behind Islam. The authors of mass murder and their allies have no place in any culture, and no home in any faith.

Here the president issues a clear threat to those who might try to evade the struggle against the terrorists or, especially, those who would provide them assistance.

The leaders of all nations must now carefully consider their responsibilities and their future. Terrorist groups like al Qaeda depend upon the aid or indifference of governments. They need the support of a financial infrastructure and safe havens to train and plan and hide.

For every regime that sponsors terror, there is a price to be paid. And it will be paid. The allies of terror are equally guilty of murder and equally accountable to justice.

The president explains that the actions of the United States are aimed at the terrorists and not the people of any country whose government harbors terrorists. He emphasizes that

In this war of terror, each of us must answer for what we have done or what we have left undone. After tragedy, there is a time for sympathy and condolence. And my country has been very grateful for both. The memorials and vigils around the world will not be forgotten. But the time for sympathy has now passed; the time for action has now arrived.

We have a responsibility to deny any sanctuary, safe haven, or transit to terrorists. Every known terrorist camp must be shut down, its operators apprehended, and evidence of their arrest presented to the United Nations. We have a responsibility to deny weapons to terrorists and to actively prevent private citizens from providing them.

These obligations are urgent, and they are binding on every nation with a place in this chamber. Many governments are taking these obligations seriously, and my country appreciates it. Yet more is required, and more is expected of our coalition against terror.

We're asking for a comprehensive commitment to this fight. We must unite in opposing all terrorists, not just some of them. In this world there are good causes and bad causes, and we may disagree on where the line is drawn. Yet, there is no such thing as a good terrorist. No national aspiration, no remembered wrong can ever justify the deliberate murder of the innocent. Any government that rejects this principle, trying to pick and choose its terrorist friends, will know the consequences.

The war against terror must not serve as an excuse to persecute ethnic and religious minorities in any country. Innocent people must be allowed to live their own lives, by their own customs, under their own religion. And every nation must have avenues for the peaceful expression of opinion and dissent. When these avenues are closed, the temptation to speak through violence grows.

And, finally, this struggle is a defining moment for the United Nations itself. And the world needs its principled leadership. It undermines the credibility of this great institution, for example, when the Commission on Human Rights offers seats to the world's most persistent violators of human rights. The United States depends, above all, on its moral authority—and that authority must be preserved.

The steps I described will not be easy. For all nations, they will require effort. For some nations, they will require great courage. Yet, the cost of inaction is far greater. The only alternative to victory is a nightmare world where every city is a potential killing field.

The outcome of this conflict is certain: there is a current in history and it runs toward freedom. Our enemies resent it and dismiss it, but the dreams of mankind are defined by liberty—the natural right to create and build and worship and live in dignity. We stand for the permanent hopes of humanity, and those hopes will not be denied. We're confident, too, that history has an author who fills time and eternity with his purpose. We know that evil is real, but good will prevail against it. This is the teaching of many faiths, and in that assurance we gain strength for a long journey.

It is our task to provide the response to aggression and terror. We have no other choice, because there is no other peace.

We did not ask for this mission, yet there is honor in history's call. We have a chance to write the story of our times, a story of courage defeating cruelty and light overcoming darkness. This calling is worthy of any life, and worthy of every nation. So let us go forward, confident, determined, and unafraid. Thank you very much.

Vital Speeches of the Day 68: George W. Bush, "The Coalition Against Terrorism," (December 1, 2001), pp. 101–104.

this is not a war in which all Islamic people are America's enemies. This is a message he hopes to convey to several segments of his audience: reminding his fellow Americans that all Muslims are not enemies, reassuring friends and skeptics among the Arab governments of that position, promising Muslims throughout the world that we have no quarrel with them, and assuring the Afghan people that we will not simply abandon them.

President Bush attempts to unite his diverse audiences with a definition of terrorism as the deliberate murder of innocent people.

There were those who believed that the United States should bypass the United Nations and act regardless of what the U.N. might do. Here the president appeals to the U.N. to take action in its own best interest, although what follows makes it clear that America will proceed in its fight against terrorism in any case.

6 Enhancing Your Credibility and Selecting Your Topic

CHAPTER SURVEY

CHAPTER OBJECTIVES

After studying this chapter, you should be able to

1. **explain what ethos is, how it is formed, and how it affects a speaker.**
2. **understand the ways in which the context of a speech can influence ethos.**
3. **enhance your ethos in your own speechmaking.**
4. **conduct a self-inventory.**
5. **revise and narrow your topic so that it is manageable.**
6. **determine how ethical considerations affect your choice of a topic.**

As a speaker, you are an important resource for your speech. The audience will make judgments about what you say based on their perceptions of you. You bring to the situation your own experiences, interests, and values. You will be making choices based on what you care about and what you think is ethical.

In this chapter, we will consider some of the ways that you can enhance your own credibility as a speaker, as well as important choices you have to make concerning what to talk about and what is ethically acceptable.

UNDERSTANDING ETHOS

Preview Ethos is determined by the listeners' perceptions of the speaker's character, intelligence, and good will. The more positive the speaker's ethos, the more credible he or she is. Although there are variations, the primary factors that determine ethos are trustworthiness, competence, objectivity, and dynamism.

Have you ever responded negatively to a speech and realized later that it wasn't the content of the speech that bothered you, but rather the person delivering it? Perhaps the speaker's voice irritated you. Perhaps the speaker was a member of the "opposite" political party or was a politician—and you distrust politicians. Or have you ever followed someone's advice not so much because you were convinced by the array of facts presented or because you carefully weighed the consequences of taking certain actions, but just because the person giving the advice seemed trustworthy? For good or ill, listeners may react to a message on the basis of *what they think about the speaker and not on what the speaker says.* The perception we have of a speaker forms the speaker's ethos.

Students of the communication process have been thinking about the issue of a speaker's personal ethos for a long time. More than two thousand years ago, the Greek rhetorician and philosopher Aristotle studied the art of public speaking, and his work *Rhetoric* has probably had the greatest impact on our thoughts about public speaking.[1] Aristotle observed that the speaker's character, intelligence, and interest in the audience's well-being are very important to successful communication. He argued that the kind of person the speaker is will be clear to the listeners and will affect their reactions.

Later theorists, beginning with George Campbell in the eighteenth century and continuing in the work of credibility researchers in our own time, have refined and modified Aristotle's original concept. They have reasoned that listeners might not always know precisely what the speaker's character is and have suggested that ethos depends on what an audience *thinks* about the speaker. For modern students of communication, ethos is associated with listeners' perceptions, so we define **ethos** as listeners' perceptions of the speaker's character, intelligence, and good will. Ethos describes the speaker *as the audience sees him or her.*

ethos the audience's perception of a speaker's character, intelligence, and good will

Who, after all, is the real person who addresses an audience? We make judgments about people—who is honest, who is smart, who cares about us, and who is reliable—on the basis of what we know or hear. You have probably disagreed with a friend over a mutual acquaintance. You might think the person is kind

The integrity and sincerity of this law student at the University of Texas enhances her ethos as she speaks out for diversity in higher education. (Bob Daemmrich/The Image Works)

and intelligent, whereas your friend thinks the same person is thoughtless and arrogant. Although someone can behave differently at different times and in different places, both of you cannot be right in describing that person's essential character. The person has an ethos for you that depends on *your* perception.

When we talk about ethos, we are not talking so much about a speaker's essential character as an audience's *beliefs* about the speaker's character. The speaker may not be intelligent, but the audience may think he or she is. The speaker may have the good of the audience at heart, but the audience may not think so. This means, of course, that ethos is both relative (it depends on who the audience is) and fluid (it can change as the audience or the situation changes). A speaker's ethos will not be the same for every listener. It can even change in the course of a single speech.

Clearly *ethos* is not the same thing as *ethics*, but the two are related in two important ways.[2] First, the audience's perception of whether a speaker is ethical will greatly affect the speaker's ethos. Second, a person who is ethical is more likely to establish a good reputation that will positively influence his or her ethos. Perhaps the same person, living by the same code of ethics, is reported to have said or done something that listeners thought violated the code. Then the speaker would have a negative—or, at least, a less positive—ethos. The speaker's ethics might not change, but the speaker's ethos would change because of the audience's interpretation of that person's ethics.

Primary Factors of Ethos

Scholars have taken the definition of ethos and tried to identify specific qualities that influence our perceptions of a speaker.[3] From their research, we can name four major qualities that cause listeners to see a speaker as a good, intelligent person who sincerely cares about their welfare.

- Trustworthiness
- Competence
- Objectivity
- Dynamism

trustworthiness an audience's perception of a speaker's reliability, honesty, sincerity, and good will

Trustworthiness. Not surprisingly, we are more likely to listen to and act on the advice of people who we think are honest and concerned about us. Integrity and sincerity are qualities that inspire trust. Suppose, for example, you were trying to determine where to attend college. You might consider cost, distance from home, kinds and quality of academic programs, size, and so on. Having narrowed your list to a few possibilities, you are then interested in finding a place where you—with your particular strengths and weaknesses, personality, tastes, and interests—can succeed and be happy. An older friend whom you trust—a teacher, a counselor, a Girls Club leader—assures you that Mid-State University and Centerville College are friendly, supportive places where you would fit in well and says that you should choose one of them. You are likely to take this advice if you believe that the person will always be honest with you and cares about you.

Public figures often rely on perceptions of their trustworthiness when trying to persuade and reassure listeners. In 1986, for example, a highly publicized scandal erupted over a secret government arms-for-hostages deal with Iran and the use of profits from the deal to support, without congressional approval or knowledge, rebel (contra) activities in Nicaragua. Ronald Reagan, called by the press "the great communicator," had consistently high personal public approval ratings. In his 1987 State of the Union address, President Reagan tried to capitalize on perceptions that he could be trusted when he referred to the Iran-contra affair. After a section of the speech in which he identified positive features of the year gone by—couched in inclusive, plural terms ("Our inflation rate is the lowest in a quarter of a century"; "We can also be heartened by our progress across the world")—Reagan moved to the first person to explain and justify actions taken with regard to Iran. In the passage that follows, he essentially asked the American people to rely on his personal integrity in judging the motives for the actions taken and to trust him to find the truth and do the right thing:

> But though we've made much progress, I have one major regret. I took a risk with regard to our action in Iran. It did not work, and for that I assume full responsibility. The goals were worthy. I do not believe it was wrong to try to establish contacts with a country of strategic importance or try to save lives. And certainly it was not wrong to try to secure freedom for our citizens held in barbaric captivity. But we did not achieve what we wished and serious mistakes were made trying to do so. We will get to the bottom of this and I will take whatever action is called for.[4]

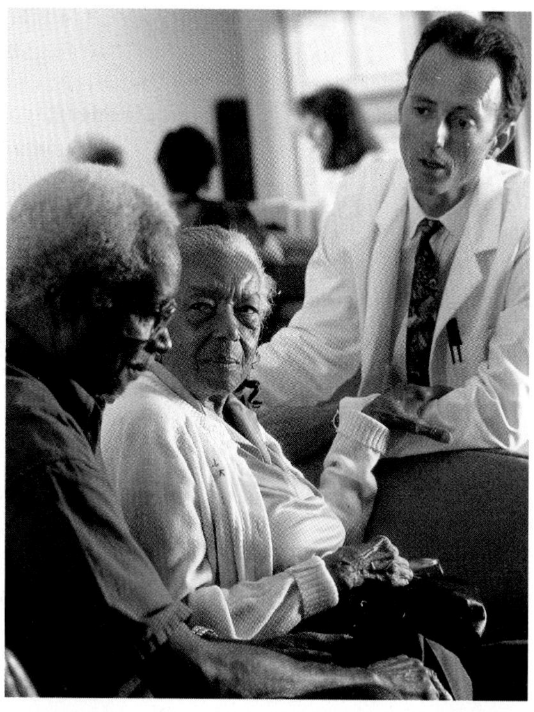

Most listeners will respond positively to physicians speaking on medical matters. Because of their assumed competence, trustworthiness, and objectivity, doctors will normally have a positive ethos in such situations. (Steven Peters/Tony Stone Images)

Trustworthiness is often directly related to, or interacts with, the second principal factor in shaping ethos: competence.

Competence. Listeners tend to listen more closely and be persuaded more easily by someone they see as a believable and knowledgeable source. Thus competence is often associated with trustworthiness. To return to the example of choosing a college, the person who recommends a particular college may be influential because of her honesty and sincere concern for your welfare. But you would also want that person to have some knowledge about higher education generally and your possible choices specifically.

competence an audience's perception of a speaker's intelligence, experience, and education or training relevant to the speech topic

Janice Payan, vice president of U.S. West Communications, gave the keynote address to a conference of Hispanic American women in Denver. If her message—that success can come if women will believe in themselves and work hard to achieve their goals—was to be believed, Payan needed to convince her audience that she knew what she was talking about. That she was an executive at a major company proved her business ability, but was she competent to give advice to women who faced many cultural and societal obstacles to success? She answered that question as she related her own experience.

> If you're thinking, "that's easy for *you* to say, Payan," then I'm thinking: "little do you know. . . ." If you think I got where I am because I'm smarter than you, or have more energy than you, you're wrong. . . .
>
> I am more like you and you are more like me than you would guess. I'm a third-generation Mexican-American . . . born into a lower middle-class family

> right here in Denver. My parents married young; she was pregnant. My father worked only about half the time during my growing-up years. He was short on education, skills, and confidence. There were drug and alcohol problems in the family. My parents finally sent my older brother to a Catholic high school, in hopes that would help him. They sent me to the same school to watch him. That was okay.
>
> In public school I never could choose between the "Greasers" and the "Soshes." I wanted desperately to feel that I "belonged." *But I did not feel that I had to deny my past to have a future.* Anybody ever feel that way? . . .
>
> For all my suffering in high school, I finished near the top of my graduating class. I dreamed of attending the University of Colorado at Boulder. You want to know what my counselor said? You already know. That I should go to a business college for secretaries, at most. But I went to the University of Colorado anyway. I arranged my own financial aid: a small grant, a low-paying job, and a *big* loan. I just thank God that was an era when jeans and sweatshirts were getting popular. That was all I had!
>
> . . . During my freshman year, I received a call that my mother had been seriously injured in a traffic accident. Both of her legs were broken. So was her pelvis. My younger brother and sister were still at home. My father was unemployed at the time, and I was off at college. So who do you think was elected to take on the housework? Raise your hand if you think it was my father. No??? Does anybody think it was *me?* I am truly amazed at your guessing ability. Or is there something in our Hispanic culture that says the women do the housework? Of course there is. So I drove home from Boulder every weekend; shopped, cleaned, cooked, froze meals for the next week, did the laundry, you know the list. And the truth is, it did not occur to me until some time later that my father could have done some of that. I had a problem, but I was part of the problem. I *did* resist when my parents suggested I should quit school. It seemed better to try doing everything, than to give up my dream. And it was the better choice. But it was also very difficult.[5]

In so speaking, Janice Payan convinced her audience that she knew about their hardships from firsthand experience and that, therefore, she was competent to speak to them.

objectivity an audience's perception of a speaker's openness and fair-mindedness in considering diverse points of view

Go to **Lesson 8's Screening Room** on the **VideoLab** CD-ROM to view the speech on milk additives. To what extent does the speaker present both sides of the controversy in an objective and fair-minded manner?

Objectivity. Listeners will also form impressions of a speaker's objectivity, or open-mindedness. Audiences value speakers who seem to be willing to enter into a dialogue with them, who are willing to consider various points of view, who can treat opposing ideas and values fairly and respectfully, and who can search for common bonds that unite different groups. Of course, open-mindedness is not the same thing as empty-mindedness; a speaker has the right and the obligation to take a clear position and argue for it forcefully. What can damage your ethos as a speaker is the impression that you are distorting, exaggerating, or dismissing the arguments, feelings, or values of those with whom you disagree. Thus to say that you are seen as objective is not to say that you take no position. Rather you are objective in that you will listen to other voices, consider the ideas of others fairly, and remain open to the possibility that you can change your mind if others' arguments are compelling enough.

In many situations, a speaker's objectivity is seriously doubted because of the speaker's known beliefs or because of the setting in which the speech takes place. In such cases, the speaker often has to try to appear objective. In Barbara

Jordan's keynote address to the Democratic National Convention in 1976, for example, partisanship was naturally expected. Jordan tried to overcome such perceptions and suggest her objectivity by addressing concerns larger than immediate political ones.

> I could easily spend this time praising the accomplishments of this party and attacking the Republicans but I don't choose to do that.
>
> I could list the many problems Americans have. I could list the problems which cause people to feel cynical, angry, frustrated; problems which include lack of integrity in government; the feeling that the individual no longer counts; the reality of material and spiritual poverty; the feeling that the grand American experiment is failing or has failed. I could recite these problems and then I could sit down and offer no solutions. But I don't choose to do that either.
>
> The citizens of America expect more. They deserve and they want more than a recital of problems.
>
> We are a people in a quandary about the present. We are a people in search of our future. We are a people in search of a national community.
>
> We are a people trying to solve the problems of the present: unemployment, inflation—but we are attempting on a larger scale to fulfill the promise of America. We are attempting to fulfill our national purpose; to create and sustain a society in which all of us are equal.[6]

Of course, Ms. Jordan was not and could not be completely objective. She believed in her party and what it could do for the people. But she tried to get beyond partisanship by emphasizing common bonds and addressing common problems.

Dynamism. Finally, audiences look positively on those speakers who are energetic and enthusiastic—who are dynamic. However, being dynamic is not just being greatly enthusiastic; it is achieving the right tone for the audience and the situation and avoiding extremes in behavior. Any speaker who seems bored, who talks in a colorless monotone while rooted to one spot, or who is more fixed on his or her notes than on the listeners will obviously be viewed negatively by an audience. Likewise the ethos of a speaker who is too loud, too physical, or too intense will suffer in the eyes of the audience. A dynamic speaker takes the middle ground—neither ignoring nor overwhelming the listeners. Being audience centered, this speaker talks with them, shares a sense of personal enthusiasm and conviction, and looks to them for their responses. Naturally, audiences tend to react positively to a speaker with these dynamic qualities.

dynamism an audience's perception of a speaker's enthusiasm, energy, and genuine interest in the issues being discussed

Perhaps the best way to summarize the nature of ethos is to consider the various factors that have been discussed in this chapter as a kind of filter: Everything the speaker says, does, or stands for passes through it. What comes out is what the audience thinks the speaker is—the speaker's ethos.

Contextual Factors Influencing Ethos

Although ethos is important, it is not important in the same way and to the same degree in every situation. At times, some elements of a speaker's ethos are not critical. For example, suppose you are studying for an exam and go to a review session being conducted by a graduate student you don't know. If you really want to understand the material, you won't care how dynamic the graduate student is.

SPOTLIGHT ON... Credibility

Credibility is an essential quality in a candidate for office. Following are excerpts from George W. Bush's speech accepting the Republican nomination for president in July 2000. Note how he emphasizes his trustworthiness by contrasting the fundamental American values represented by his small-town background with the Washington perspective, and his competence by references to his accomplishments as governor of Texas. Objectivity is suggested by his reference to bipartisanship.

In Midland, Texas where I grew up . . . there was a restless energy, a basic conviction that, with hard work, anybody could succeed, and everybody deserved a chance. . . . This leaves me with more than an accent, it leaves an outlook. Optimistic, impatient with pretense. Confident that people can chart their own course. That background may lack the polish of Washington. Then, again I don't have a lot of things that come with Washington.

The largest lesson I learned in Midland still guides me as Governor. Everyone . . . has an equal claim on this country's promise. So we improved our schools . . . moved people from welfare to work . . . budgets have been balanced . . . we cut taxes. . . . We accomplished a lot.

I don't deserve all the credit, and I don't attempt to take it. I worked with Republicans and Democrats to get things done.

George W. Bush, "Acceptance Speech," *The New York Times*, Friday, August 4, 2000, p. A20.

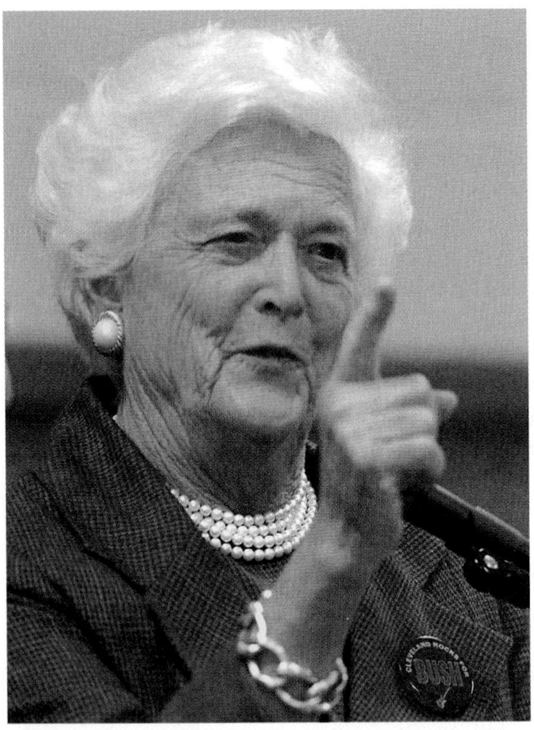

Barbara Bush established her ethos as the wife of the President of the United States and yet, at the same time, was generally perceived positively because she avoided public political statements and was viewed in a more "motherly" role. (AP/Wide World Photos)

You assume (probably unconsciously) that the speaker knows what she or he is talking about—that she or he is competent.

Depending on context, certain aspects of the speaker's ethos may be more important than others. For example, you may know something about a speaker's political views and therefore distrust or dislike the speaker. But if the topic being addressed is how to buy real estate and the speaker is a successful real estate agent, you might be willing to put your political differences aside. Depending on what is relevant, the speaker's ethos changes as the context changes.

Finally, ethos from one area may spill over into another, causing good or bad effects for the speaker. Advertising, for example, often tries to capitalize on the ethos of popular people. Nike seeks the endorsements of popular basketball players, assuming that their ethos will spill over and enhance sneaker sales. Spillover isn't always beneficial, however. A listener may form such a bad image of a particular source—say, from a report of drug use—that every message from that speaker will be discounted. The speaker's ethos has been damaged, regardless of the relevance of his or her personal qualities to the subject matter. A sponsor will quickly drop a popular personality involved in a personal scandal because the sponsor is afraid that the person's unacceptable behavior will tarnish the image of the product.

There are also factors that constrain a speaker and influence her or his ethos. Barbara Bush, for example, in giving a commencement address, was constrained by the fact that she was the wife of the president of the United States. On the one hand, her ethos as first lady served her well. On the other hand, to maintain that ethos, she had to avoid taking positions that could be interpreted as indications of her husband's views. Hillary Clinton's ethos as she ran for the Senate in New York in 2000 was both helped and hurt by her being associated with her husband's policies and personal problems as president. Indiana University's famous basketball coach Bob Knight, known for his fiery temper and passionate style of coaching, was constrained by media portrayals of his more tempestuous moments. For those who saw only his highly publicized outbursts, no explanation on his part could excuse him. For the thousands of students and supporters who gathered to hear his farewell speech after he was fired by the university in 2000, the integrity of the basketball program, the coach's blunt honesty and unpublicized philanthropy, and the ineptitude of the administration in dealing with the situation all reinforced their loyalty to Knight. These are only a few examples of the many ways in which ethos changes with the situation.

Primary Factors Influencing a Speaker's Ethos

Listeners' perceptions of a speaker's character, intelligence, and good will can be influenced by

- the extent to which they find the speaker trustworthy.
- whether they believe the speaker is competent.
- how objective the speaker appears to be.
- whether the speaker is dynamic.

CREATING YOUR OWN ETHOS

Preview You can shape your own ethos in the course of a speech. The content, structure, and clarity of your speech, how you deliver it, and the ways in which you relate to your audience will all contribute to your ethos.

As we've seen, listeners may have some prior sense of a speaker's ethos. Further, speakers may do various things to enhance that ethos. In many communication situations, however, the speaker is almost neutral. If you know nothing about a speaker, he or she carries neither a positive nor a negative ethos for you. If you know only a little about a speaker, you will form an impression based on what you *do* know. You may think of the speaker positively if he or she matches you in readily observable psychological, social, and cultural characteristics. For example, people tend to identify with someone who is their own age and sex or who attends the same place of worship or belongs to the same organization. One of the purposes of introducing a speaker is to help the audience establish ties with him or her, as well as to establish the speaker's authority as a credible source of information on a given topic. Even with little introduction and in situations such as your classroom where speakers have no established image in the minds of their audience, ethos is still a factor.

What can you do as a beginning public speaker in situations such as a speech classroom? In some classrooms, students may know one another well, so that whoever is speaking on a particular day will have an already established ethos. In other classrooms, especially at large universities or at institutions where many students go to school part-time while holding down jobs, students may never see one another except when they meet in class. In these situations, listeners most likely will evaluate speakers as they communicate. Each speaker's ethos will be formed in the minds of the listeners as the speech unfolds.

Shaping Listeners' Perceptions

You must shape listeners' perceptions of you as you give a speech. The content of your speech, how you deliver it, your level of commitment to the audience's well-being, the kinds of authority you rely on, how well structured and clear your message is, and how interesting your overall presentation is all contribute to the development of your ethos. But the basic principle of effective speechmaking is that it must center on the audience.

- *Show your audience that you share their concerns.* Showing concern for the problems faced by an audience can influence their perceptions of you. Establishing common ground with an audience helps promote identification between you and the listeners. We feel a natural attraction for and sympathy with people we perceive to be like ourselves; they seem to be trustworthy. For example, a student speaker talking about grading developed a positive ethos partly because he showed that he understood the pressures to succeed that students may experience.

  > My parents, maybe like yours, are proud of me. They are happy that I got into this university and expect that this is the beginning of a successful career for me. At the end of my first semester, they were just as anxious as I was to see how well I did. I remember how nervous I was the day my grades arrived. I thought I had done pretty well, but I wasn't absolutely sure of a couple of courses. Well, I came home from my summer job and my mother was waiting in the kitchen. My father had just come home, too, and both of them were looking at me and at the envelope on the table. Talk about pressure! I opened the grade report, sighed with relief, and passed it on to my parents. Well, that was the first semester. The end of the second semester was much the same—and I still have six more to go!
  >
  > My parents, of course, are only part of the problem. I want to get into an MBA program when I graduate, just as many of you want to go to graduate school or law school or medical school. And all of us want eventually to get good jobs. When someone says to us, "Grades don't matter—it's what you learn," we say, "Yeah, right." We know that grades do matter—to our family, to our opportunities for moving on to the next academic level, to our chances for good jobs and economic security in the future. And the temptation to say to ourselves: "I'll do anything it takes," is very strong. None of us is a saint, and many of you might have faced the question I have: does "anything it takes" mean cheating?
  >
  > Well, today I'm going to give you my answer to that question because I've come to realize that the person who gets cheated most is the person doing the cheating.

  In this case, the students in the audience appreciated the fact that the speaker chose a topic with which they could identify. He showed that he understood and shared the pressures and motivations they felt. He was honest enough to admit that he had been tempted. He was someone listeners could trust.

- *Bolster your own ethos with the ethos of authorities.* Sometimes you will have to give speeches on issues about which you cannot be considered an expert, and this lack of expertise can represent a threat to your ethos. In these circumstances, support from acknowledged experts gives the audience confidence in you. (Chapter 9 will explore support in more detail.)

  Consider, for example, Meredith, a student speaker who wanted to convince her audience that milk injected with the hormone rBST poses a threat to both cows and humans. She began her speech with testimony from attorney Andrew Kimbrell of the Foundation on Economic Trends that "the American dairy industry is in a mess. It has become so insensitive that cows are suffering from . . . infections such as bovine leukemia and the bovine equivalent of AIDS. We've increased production so much that we've destroyed the cow's immune system." Meredith then developed the point that practices focusing on this hormone cause extreme pain and suffering to the cows. She quoted John Webster, professor of animal husbandry at Bristol University, who observed that cows are worked as "a high performance machine, as highly tuned as a racing car, and like a car that's pushed flat out, it goes bust more easily." After a vivid description of the cow's environment, Meredith reinforced her conclusion with the testimony of an authority: "Unable to stretch their legs, or even turn around, the victims of factory farms exist in a relentless state of distress. According to veterinarian Dr. Bruce Feldman, 'When animals are intensively confined and under stress, as they are on factory farms, their autoimmune systems are affected and they are prone to infectious diseases.'" Meredith's further development included testimony from the Consumers Union, medical expert Dr. Stuart Levy of Tufts University, cancer researcher Dr. George Tritsch, and Dr. Richard Burroughs, a former senior scientist at the Food and Drug Administration. Meredith was not, of course, a scientist. But by citing the testimony of such experts, she enhanced her own credibility. You can see an annotated version of this entire speech in the Appendix (page 471).

- *Strengthen your ethos with personal experiences.* As we've already seen, you are likely to be seen as trustworthy and competent when you've had some personal experiences that qualify you to offer opinions or give accurate information. A student aiming to help her audience understand life on an Indian reservation, for example, explained her special qualifications this way:

A speaker's confidence, often demonstrated through personal commitment and dynamism, contributes to a strongly positive ethos. (Robert King/Liaison/Newsmakers/Online USA)

When I was a sophomore in high school, I joined a group from my church who, joined by others from other churches, spent three weeks of their summer vacation on an Indian reservation in Arizona. We didn't go as tourists, we went there to help the people who lived on the reservation with projects to improve their communities—helping to repair homes or paint school rooms. In those three weeks I began to learn a little about life on the reservation—and a lot about myself. The experience was such a good one for me that I went back again the next year—and every year for the last four years. In that time, I've come to learn much more about the people of the reservation. I've shared some of their problems; I've got to know some of their kids as they moved from being children to becoming teens. And I've come to respect the values they hold and the traditions they uphold.

It is not always possible for you to speak about issues with which you have direct experience. You can talk about anorexia, for example, without having been anorexic. One way to strengthen your ethos in such a case is to bring in the testimony of others, as you might do when trying to make up for your lack of expertise. One student, for example, wanted his listeners to know that the job market, which had been considered dismal, was beginning to improve. So he cited the experience of another student.

I recently talked with a friend of mine who will graduate at the end of this semester in accounting from IU's School of Business. He's 21 years old and will start work in June as an auditor for Price Waterhouse in Chicago and a salary of $35,000 a year. Is his experience unusual? Here's what he told me: "I did eight interviews and got four offers, but I could have had more—I ruled out two of them early on. I'd say 90 percent of my friends have jobs, and most had them relatively early. Basically, if you do your part right, you should have nailed down a job by November, which makes Christmas break a lot more fun."

- *Strive to be clear and interesting.* Clear and absorbing messages will inspire confidence in you. Listeners appreciate speakers who make their ideas understandable and who make an effort to keep the audience interested. Unfortunately, some speakers jump back and forth from point to point, and some students give dull and uninteresting speeches, perhaps sharing information that is hardly news to anyone. In these cases, the speakers' ethos has suffered.

  As an audience-centered speaker, you should gain the audience's attention and interest in the introduction to your speech. Doing so will create an immediately positive impression and improve your ethos. Coming to a conclusion in a timely manner also will reflect well on you by showing your concern for the audience's comfort and well-being. As you will see when you read Chapter 10, introductions and conclusions take careful and thoughtful preparation.

- *Show your audience that you have considered different opinions.* If you can show that you are aware of opposing points of view, you will demonstrate that you are both informed and willing to consider various possibilities. For example, a highly publicized controversy raged over a plan by the Department of Natural Resources to allow a special two-day deer hunt in a state park in order to deal with deer overpopulation. A

PORTFOLIO 6.1

The Other Side

As you consider various potential topics for a speech, briefly answer the following:

1. Do other sides or viewpoints exist? If so, what are they?
2. How might you acknowledge and respond to each of them?
3. How might acknowledging and responding to them affect your ethos?

student who wished to argue in favor of the hunt began by showing that she was aware of the emotional nature of the issue and explained how she had explored the question thoroughly and carefully.

> When I read in the paper about the proposed deer hunt in Brown County State Park, my first reaction was to think of Bambi. How could anyone imagine shooting Bambi? The more I read about the problems caused by overpopulation, such as an increase of disease and starvation among the herd, the elimination of low-level plant species, and the resulting threat to small animals in the park, the more I became convinced that the shoot might be necessary. Then I read about alternative proposals—like tranquilizing the deer and moving them to other parks, or sterilizing female deer. I wasn't at all sure how I came down on this.
>
> I decided that I was going to try to find out all I could. Two leading activists fighting the hunt are students here at the university, so I decided to talk to them. I also went to talk to the regional head of the DNR. I considered what each had to say, looked very carefully at all the literature they all gave me, and did a lot of reading about related issues.
>
> Today, I'm going to take you through the process I went through, examining the evidence and considering competing claims. I think that you'll finally come to the same conclusion that I did. For the sake of the entire ecological system in the park, including the deer themselves, the hunt should go on.

Go to **Lesson 9's Screening Room** on the **VideoLab** CD-ROM to view the two speeches on women's gymnastics. Think about which speaker is more credible as well as the factors that either enhance or diminish the credibility of either.

- *Develop a dynamic, audience-centered delivery.* Delivery can certainly affect ethos. One student with a very well prepared speech concerning the need for more funding for safety on campus suffered because the listeners simply couldn't hear her. Sitting in the back and straining to catch what she said was a very irritating experience and lowered the listeners' opinion of the speaker. Likewise a speaker with many vocalized pauses—"uhmm," "you know," "like"—can irritate listeners or sound unprepared or unintelligent. Finally, a speaker who rushes through a written manuscript without looking up will not be perceived as one who cares much about how listeners respond.

  If you are a dynamic speaker, you are in touch with your audience. Dynamism interacts with other primary ethos factors, since someone who is boring or detached does not appear to care about his or her audience and rarely is perceived as competent.

Obviously, these are only a few facets of delivery. As we'll see in Chapter 11, many other presentational skills can help or hinder a speaker's ethos during the course of a speech.

The principles of effective speaking that you are learning here are audience centered. As such, they will tend to enhance your relationship with listeners, contributing to a positive ethos. As we have seen, ethos is both fluid and relative. However, as a speaker,

CONNECTING TO THE NET

How can you improve your own ethos in upcoming speeches? For additional suggestions and practical exercises on how you might strengthen your ethos, go to **http://college.hmco.com/communication/andrews/public_speaking/2e/students/** and click on *Connecting to the Net*. From there, follow the link to Improving Your Ethos.

KEEP IN MIND 6.2

Guidelines for Improving Your Own Ethos

- Show your audience that you share their concerns.
- Bolster your own ethos with the ethos of authorities.
- Strengthen your ethos with personal experiences.
- Strive to be clear and interesting.
- Show your audience that you have considered different opinions.
- Develop a dynamic, audience-centered delivery.

you can take steps to build a positive ethos with your audience. One of the first steps is to pick a topic that is interesting to you and that you can make interesting to an audience—a topic that, with the proper amount of effort on your part, will help demonstrate your credibility to an audience.

FINDING A SUITABLE TOPIC

Preview As you start thinking about a topic, first focus your attention on what you know and care about. Taking an inventory of your intellectual and educational interests, your career goals, your leisure activities, and your personal and social concerns will help you come up with potential speech topics.

Deciding what to talk about may or may not be one of your initial concerns as a speaker. In some situations, the topic of your speech will be predetermined. For example, an employer may ask an employee to make a presentation on how to market the company's latest product, or a community forum may ask a health professional to speak on whether the local hospital should be sold to a private concern. Sometimes, however, a very broad and nonspecific topic will be suggested. For example, the health professional may be asked to speak on whatever she or he believes to be an important public health issue; the employer may want a report on the most interesting new developments in the employee's department. These situations demand that the speaker refine the vague suggested topic and come up with something far more specific. Regardless of specificity, however, the speaker was invited because of his or her expertise, and the invitation determines the topic.

Early on in your public speaking class, you may be assigned a very specific topic that doesn't require much preparation or specialized knowledge, primarily to help you get comfortable speaking before a group. You may be asked to give a short speech describing a person you greatly admire, telling about a recent job, demonstrating a simple skill, or introducing yourself or another person in the class. Normally, however, you will not have so narrowly defined a topic assigned to you either in or outside of your class.

Your typical class assignment will be to give a speech to your classmates, and neither circumstances, setting, nor audience demands will determine your topic. Your first task, then, will be to define the best topic.

What Matters to You?

A good way to start thinking about a topic is by thinking about yourself. The fundamental question to ask is, *What things do I already know and care about?* This doesn't mean, What can I already give a speech about? Don't try to find a speech ready-made in your head; don't try to limit yourself to topics on which you are already an expert. That kind of thinking could lead you to imagine that you don't have anything to talk about. What you really mean is that you don't know enough to get up and give a speech on this topic at this particular moment—and of course you don't! Giving a good speech takes a lot of work, and part of that work is learning more about the topic. Research is essential to support your personal perceptions and experiences. Keep in mind that one of the real benefits of a course in public speaking is that it will give you the opportunity to learn more about things you want to learn more about.

Conducting a Self-Inventory

By doing a **self-inventory**—taking a thoughtful look at what you really know and care about—you can come up with a list of more topics than you might have thought possible. Your intellectual and educational interests, your career goals, your leisure activities and interests, and your personal and social concerns all offer possible topics. In the following discussions of each of these categories, try to answer the questions and see what topics you can come up with that are personally meaningful and exciting to you.

self-inventory a list of topics that you care about and know something about

Begin by **brainstorming**—writing down anything that comes to your mind under a category without thinking about whether the topic would be interesting to your audience, whether you will be able to get enough material, or anything else. Just put down all the possibilities that come to you. When you have come up with a number of ideas, you can proceed to a **self-analysis** in which you evaluate possible topics critically, considering your own capabilities, limitations, and personal characteristics.

brainstorming the process of thinking creatively and imaginatively, temporarily suspending critical judgments of what is produced

self-analysis the evaluation of potential topics in terms of your capabilities, limitations, and personal characteristics

Intellectual and Educational Interests. A good place to begin your self-inventory is by thinking of what you enjoy learning about or what you would like to know more about, asking yourself questions such as:

- What do I like to read?
- What interesting things have I learned from television?
- What specific courses, or issues covered in courses, have particularly interested me?

One student listed the ten books she'd most enjoyed reading in the past year, as shown in Figure 6.1. Her self-analysis revealed that she was drawn to books by Irish authors or about Ireland, so she thought of a possible topic: Irish storytelling—humor and humanity.

FIGURE 6.1 **Self-Inventory: What Do I Like to Read?**

Best books I read last year	Anything in Common?
biography of Nora Joyce	4 bios/memoirs
The Dead School by Patrick McCabe	lots of fiction
Moo by Jane Smiley	mainly Irish authors
Interview with the Vampire by Anne Rice	
Paddy Clark Ha Ha Ha by Roddy Doyle	
Emma by Jane Austen	
Angela's Ashes by Frank McCourt	
Liar's Club by Mary Karr	
Jackie O's bio	
Book of Ruth by Jane Hamilton	

FIGURE 6.2 Self-Inventory: What Do I Like to Watch on TV?

What do I most enjoy watching on TV?

Sitcoms: Friends / Frasier
Drama: ER / Homicide
Nature: National Geographic / all animal shows on the Discovery channel

If I had to choose one kind of show, what would it be?

Nature programs: particularly sea animals

What animal do I find particularly interesting?

Sharks

What are some possible topics focusing on sharks?

Sharks may be the last survivors of the prehistoric past
Swimmers need to take precautions to prevent shark attacks

Another student, focusing on his favorite television shows, organized and analyzed his brainstormed thoughts in a different way to come up with potential topics, as shown in Figure 6.2.

Courses in your major field of study can also be a source of topics. Figure 6.3 shows some examples of topics generated by students from their majors. In each case, the topic grew from something the student had heard about in a course.

Career Goals. Students will usually have an ultimate career goal in mind; many may already be pursuing a career. The major question to start with here is, *What do I hope to do with my life?* Follow up on this question by brainstorming possible issues that such a profession might raise. Figure 6.4 shows how one student who planned to be a lawyer brainstormed professional issues to get to a broad topic: the professional ethics of lawyers.

Asking yourself why you might want to pursue a particular career should lead you to think about interesting aspects of a field. Figure 6.5 gives

FIGURE 6.3 Self-Inventory: Topics Based on Major

Major	Topic
Physics:	How weather develops
English:	You are what you read: books and our view of the world
Psychology:	Experiencing cognitive dissonance in our daily lives
Business:	Smart investments can help you repay your college loans

some examples of speech topics generated by students on the basis of their career goals.

Giving a speech related to a career has the added bonus of providing you with information you can use in the future. Ned, for example, hoped to start his own business. He had accumulated a great deal of practical experience and had decided he was ready to strike out on his own. Here is how he began his speech on beginning a small business:

> I had a very bright idea. It was an idea that would give me some practical experience, help me make a lot of money, and be a lot of fun as well. I decided that I could start my own business.
>
> I had worked in the summers for my uncle in his greenhouse and learned quite a bit about gardening. I had also taken a course on landscape architecture and helped my uncle on several landscaping projects. All I needed was to find a place to locate—there was a small barn in pretty good shape on the edge of town that I could rent and fix up; a couple of willing workers—I knew two guys who had worked part-time for my uncle and would be interested; and some

FIGURE 6.4 Self-Inventory: Issues I Might Face in My Chosen Career

What are some issues that a lawyer faces?

Do you take any client who can afford to pay?
What if you think someone is guilty and you have to defend him?
Is it right to approach a potential client when that person is suffering a tragic loss?
What do you do if your personal interests conflict with a client's best interests?
What can you do about the widespread mistrust of lawyers?

What do these issues have in common?

They all raise serious ethical concerns

FIGURE 6.5 Sample Speech Topics Based on Career Goals

Career	Topic
Teacher:	The characteristics of a good teacher
Engineer:	The deteriorating infrastructure
Accountant:	Simplified tax laws
Research chemist:	Generic drugs and how they affect the consumer
Marketing analyst:	Consumer choices among similar products
Television producer:	The role of viewers in network programming

> equipment—which my uncle was willing to lend me to get started. So, I had all I needed to start a landscaping business, right? Well, when I started to think about how to put my bright idea into action, I found out that I was dead wrong!
>
> I was going to give a speech telling you about my idea and how I was going to become an entrepreneur. Well, as I began to gather information, I found out that it was going to be a lot harder than I thought. I didn't have the slightest idea how to fill out the required social security forms for my potential employees. I didn't know what kinds of insurance I had to have for them or what kind of insurance I had to have to protect myself against lawsuits. I didn't know what taxes I was liable for and how to keep accurate tax records. I didn't know the best ways to let people know that I was in business and how to get them to hire me once they did know I existed. In short, I discovered that starting a small business is fraught with many pitfalls—pitfalls that I'm going to tell you about today.

Not only did Ned give an excellent speech on the pitfalls of opening your own business, but he also gained insights into what he had to know to achieve his goal. These insights influenced the courses he elected to take before he graduated.

Your possible career choice could open up a host of topics for you to explore and also help you understand more about the field you have chosen.

There are many ways of conducting a self-inventory as you begin to search for good speech topics. Try your hand at taking a self-inventory by going to the **Online SpeechStudio** and completing the **Self-Awareness Worksheet**.

Leisure Activities and Interests. Things you do for pleasure or enjoyment are another source of topics. Begin with the basic question, *What things do I do for fun that others might like to learn more about or participate in?* Then develop a list of possible topics based on your particular leisure interests. Marsha, who answered the question by indicating that she is a sports enthusiast, an avid movie-goer, and a mystery fan, generated the lists shown in Figure 6.6.

Sometimes you may think that your hobby or interest won't be very interesting to someone else. But leisure activities can be made very compelling. Take, for example, the student who began his speech this way:

> I was in a room filled with groups of four people sitting around small, square tables. At my table were four men. Each was intently studying the objects he held in his hand. No one laughed, no one smiled, no one made small talk about the weather or politics. The first man, sitting across from me, spoke briefly and calmly. The man to his left then spoke. The first man looked across the table at me, his gaze so intense I felt like he was boring a hole in my head—he probably was trying to read my mind or send me a psychic message. I hoped that I didn't look as panicked as I felt. I hoped that the sweat that was now congealing on my clammy forehead wasn't noticeable. I took a deep breath and spoke. The man across from me seemed to relax just slightly. I thought that he approved of what I had said.
>
> Now you might find this hard to believe, but I was playing a game—if bridge can properly be called a "game" and if participating in a bridge tournament can be called "playing."

From describing the intensity of the players, the student went on to discuss the strategies that developed, the mental agility demanded, the financial stakes involved, and even the intrigues among players who wanted desperately to win. On the face of it, a speech about bridge might sound as exciting as renewing a driver's license. But even those in the audience who didn't understand the basics of the game were caught up in the drama of the tournament. This

FIGURE 6.6 Self-Inventory: Topics Based on Leisure Activities

I'm a sports enthusiast	I'm an avid movie-goer	I'm a mystery fan
How basketball developed historically	How to produce special effects	Sherlock Holmes
Scandals in college athletics	Stunt men and women	Female detectives
Psychology of spectator sports	The first sound movies	Mystery and history
Outlawing boxing	Why movies cost millions to make	Police procedurals
Provisions of Title IX	History of horror films	The real-life mystery of Agatha Christie

student speaker's love of bridge and his experience in competition led him to give a fascinating speech.

A word of caution about choosing topics that deal with your hobbies or leisure activities: speeches designed for particular audiences and settings may be very interesting or important in some circumstances, yet very ordinary or trivial in others. For example, you may be teaching children to play tennis. In the course of your instruction, you may want to show them how to string a racket. That's information that could be important to them and relevant to the setting in which you are speaking. If your instructor gives you a short speaking assignment to give you the experience of speaking before a group, and if you are instructed to demonstrate to the class how to do something, the topic "How to String a Tennis Racket" might or might not be appropriate.

Normally, however, such a topic would seem trivial. The major problem with such a speech—and this is something that should be avoided in any speech on any topic—is that it would present no challenge either to the speaker or to the audience. It would demand little preparation by the speaker, and it would give the audience little to take away from the speech. To return to the example of the speech given by the bridge player, that absorbing, compelling speech about human interactions in a highly charged, competitive situation captured the audience's attention. How excited would they have been by a speech on how to bid a hand of bridge?

You can begin to look for topics by asking yourself such questions as: What are my life's goals? What activities do I most enjoy? What societal problems concern me most? Go to the **Online SpeechStudio** and complete the **Personal Interests Worksheet** to examine your interests as broadly as possible.

Personal and Social Concerns. Here are two major questions to start you thinking of topics in this category:

- *What is going on in my life that bothers or concerns me?* All of us know of things that we would like to change. We've all been upset by people or events that have affected our lives or the lives of people we care about. All of us have values or ideals that we wish would influence the behavior of others. Sometimes these concerns are very much a part of our daily lives. Begin a list of things that frustrate or upset you—things that you would like to change as you go through a typical day—and then consider the possible speech topics you might generate from such a list. Figure 6.7 shows how one student went about this process.

- *What is happening outside my immediate world that is unfair, unjust, or in need of correction? What good things going on in the world deserve more support?* Consider the larger world of which you are a part. Read

FIGURE 6.7 **Self-Inventory: What Is Going On in My Life That Concerns Me?**

Concerns	Possible Topics
Registering for classes is frustrating	How to streamline registration
It's hard to meet degree requirements in four years	Flexible degree requirements
Balancing work, study, and classes	Going to school and holding a job
Getting into medical school is a constant worry	Preparing for admission to professional schools
What am I going to do this summer?	Ways to spend a profitable summer
Student athletes get a bad rap	Unfair stereotypes of student athletes

FIGURE 6.8 **Self-Inventory: What Is Going On in the World That Concerns Me?**

Concerns	Possible Topics
The number of homeless seems to be growing	Providing housing for the homeless
Excessive drinking among my friends	Alcoholism on college campuses
Rape and sexual abuse	Child abuse; rape
Materialism and warped contemporary values	Values Americans hold
Possibility of war in the Middle East	The Middle East peace process

Once you've discovered some topics of interest to you, you are ready to reflect on how much you already know about each topic and what you will need to learn by conducting additional research. Go to the **Online SpeechStudio** and complete the **Personal Knowledge and Experience Worksheet** as you begin to focus on one specific speech topic.

newspapers and newsmagazines. Watch television news broadcasts and documentaries. Write down issues that capture your interest. Jot down matters that you believe need some kind of public action. Ask yourself what kinds of things give you particular concern. Consider what topics these concerns might lead to. Figure 6.8 shows how one student used his social concerns to generate possible speech topics.

KEEP IN MIND 6.3

Conducting a Self-Inventory

Ask yourself:

- What are my intellectual and educational interests?
- What are my career goals?
- What are my favorite leisure activities and interests?
- What personal and social concerns are important to me?

From Interests to Topic

All of the categories mentioned in the previous section are offered as starting points for you to consider as you search for your own topics. Ultimately, you will have to transform generalized topics like the ones in the sample lists into a clear and specific statement of your speech purpose—the final step in shaping your topic to fit the audience and the occasion. Devising a good speech purpose is so important that we devote Chapter 7 entirely to it. But for now, you need to take the next step in topic selection: evaluating potential topics before selecting one. To do that, you need some guidelines for refining and narrowing your topic.

Go to the **Online SpeechStudio** and complete the **Personal and Audience Interests Worksheet** to see how *mutual* interests can converge and lead you to a promising speech topic.

NARROWING THE TOPIC

Preview The potential speech topics that emerge from your self-inventory are just that—potential. Now you can narrow and refine your choices by understanding how the situation, time constraints, and audience factors will determine a topic that is suitable to both you and your listeners.

Any topic must be appropriate for the audience and the occasion. It must stretch listeners' present understanding or perception of your topic and add to it. As you refine the purpose of your speech (Chapter 7), do research (Chapter 8), develop ideas and supporting material (Chapter 9), and organize your speech (Chapter 10), you will probably find that you need to adjust your topic somewhat. To start with, however, you need to consider your audience very carefully and to decide more precisely what you hope to accomplish. Chapters 4 and 5 discussed audience analysis in full. For now, let's review two guidelines for considering your audience and the situation that will help you choose and refine a final topic from your self-inventory.

1. Consider the situation.
   - *Will my audience be familiar with any immediate events or information that will help me choose a topic?*
   - *Can I choose a topic to highlight recent events that may be of serious concern to my listeners?*
   - *Could I encourage my listeners to be less apathetic toward events that matter deeply to me?*
   - *Do I have sufficient time to cover the topic adequately?*
2. Consider the audience.
   - *What does my audience already know?*
   - *What common experiences has my audience had?*
   - *Where do my and my audience's interests meet?*
   - *How diverse is my audience?*

Even if you and your audience are mutually interested in a particular topic, chances are it will be too broad to address effectively in a single speech. One way of narrowing your topic is to go to the **Online SpeechStudio** and complete the **Topic Focusing Worksheet**.

Figure 6.9 summarizes the possible topics generated from the examples given in this chapter. Let's use this list to see how to apply the guidelines in specific cases.

Ruiz, a physics major, was interested in how weather developed. For him, situational factors proved decisive in narrowing his topic. When he asked himself if his audience would be familiar with any immediate events that would help him choose a topic, he realized that the weather had been in the news

FIGURE 6.9 Possible Topics from Self-Inventories

Possible topics derived from intellectual interests
- Irish storytelling—humor and humanity
- Sharks may be the last survivors of the prehistoric past
- Swimmers need to take precautions to prevent shark attacks

Possible topics derived from career interests
- The professional ethics of lawyers
- How weather develops
- You are what you read: books and our view of the world
- Experiencing cognitive dissonance in our daily lives
- Smart investments can help you repay your college loans

Possible topics derived from leisure activities
Sports:
- How basketball developed historically
- Scandals in college athletics
- Psychology of spectator sports
- Outlawing boxing
- Provisions of Title IX

Movies:
- How to produce special effects
- Stunt men and women
- The first sound movies
- Why movies cost millions to make
- History of horror films

Mysteries:
- Sherlock Holmes
- Female detectives
- Mystery and history
- Police procedurals
- The real-life mystery of Agatha Christie

Possible topics derived from problems and social concerns
- How to streamline registration
- Flexible degree requirements
- Going to school and holding a job
- Preparing for admission to professional schools
- Ways to spend a profitable summer
- Unfair stereotypes of student athletes
- Providing housing for the homeless
- Alcoholism in America
- Child abuse; rape
- Values Americans hold
- The Middle East peace process

lately because of particularly bad spring floods and that, therefore, his listeners would be familiar with some of the effects of weather. However, when he asked himself if this topic would be of serious concern to his audience, he knew that since few of them lived in a part of the country that was subject to flooding, they might not see much relationship between the effects of the floods and themselves. Then he asked himself how he could encourage his listeners to be less apathetic toward these events, which mattered deeply to him. If, he reasoned, his audience could understand that disasters caused by weather can have consequences for everyone, they would find his topic interesting. Lastly, he asked himself how much he could say about the weather in five to seven minutes, the time allotted for his speech. This kind of thinking helped him decide to talk about how natural disasters in a distant part of the country could affect his audience.

Here's how he began his speech:

> Have you been watching the news stories about the huge floods along the Red River this spring? I have, and come summer, I'm going to be watching something else: the price of my favorite breakfast cereal, Wheaties. Although those may not seem connected, they are. Every spring, melting snows fill the rivers to capacity and beyond, and late this winter there was an awful lot of snow in Minnesota and North Dakota, where the Red River flows. The Red River isn't the only thing these states have in common: they're also among the top five wheat-producing states in the United States. So as you can imagine, the floods will probably affect wheat production—blow it out of the water, you might say. It happens all the time: Florida has a deep freeze in December, and in early January your orange juice costs twenty cents more. There's a drought in California, and all of a sudden iceberg lettuce costs twice as much as it used to, if you can find any.

Marsha, the student with sports interests, first looked at the possible topics she had generated in her self-inventory:

How basketball developed historically
Scandals in college athletics
Psychology of spectator sports
Outlawing boxing
Provisions of Title IX

To narrow her choice among these topics, Marsha first looked for situational factors that might single out one topic over the others. In asking herself whether she could relate any of the topics to current events that would be familiar to her audience, she realized that the basketball season was nearing its end and that her school team had a very good chance of making the National Collegiate Athletic Association (NCAA) tournament. So from a situational point of view, basketball seemed a very good topic for her audience.

Marsha then looked at all her topics again from the point of view of audience factors: What did her audience already know? What experiences did they have in common? Where did her own interests meet her audience's interests? How diverse was her audience? She guessed that since basketball was a very popular sport at her college, and since the school team had a long history of league championships, either the basketball topic or the "psychology of spectator sports" topic would likely be of more interest to her audience than would a speech on boxing. Her school had not been involved in sports scandals, so although this topic could be interesting, it didn't seem as relevant to the audience as basketball. Title IX, providing equal sports opportunities for women, might be interesting and controversial, but she thought it would still be less interesting to her listeners than basketball. Finally, her audience would consist of about an equal mix of men and women, who might not share the same enthusiasm for and tastes in sports, but she felt that most of them would have some interest in basketball. Thus, after considering both situational and audience factors, Marsha finally decided to give her speech on how basketball developed historically. Figure 6.10 uses Marsha's experience as a model for the steps to take in selecting and narrowing your own topic.

Note that even when you have completed these steps, your topic will still be somewhat tentative because doing research and shaping a specific purpose usually can further refine any topic. But by following the process we have explained here, you will have gone from a broad range of interests to a concrete topic for a speech.

The subject of your speech is not all that you must consider as you choose and narrow a topic, however. Ethical considerations may also play a role.

PORTFOLIO 6.2

Putting Potential Topics to the Test: What's Right for You, Your Audience, and the Situation?

Conduct a self-inventory along the lines of what has been suggested. Then review the topics you have listed. Which will be interesting and beneficial to your audience? Will you simply be telling them what they already know, or will you present new information and helpful insights? Cross off any topics that your classmates likely will not find interesting or worthy of their attention.

Now contemplate the situation. Does your topic choice fit the assignment? Do you have time to cover the topic? If not, how might you narrow it? Cross off any topics that are inappropriate, given the assignment and the time allowed.

FIGURE 6.10 **Model for Narrowing Your Topic**

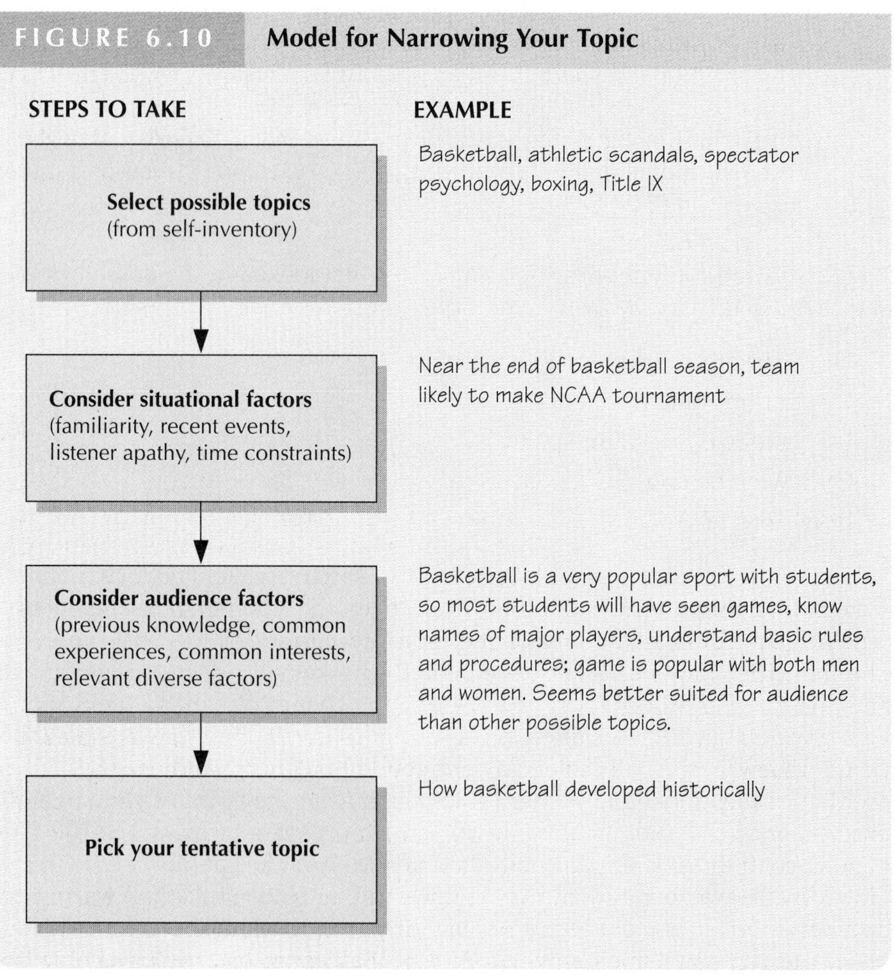
STEPS TO TAKE
EXAMPLE
Select possible topics (from self-inventory)
Basketball, athletic scandals, spectator psychology, boxing, Title IX
Consider situational factors (familiarity, recent events, listener apathy, time constraints)
Near the end of basketball season, team likely to make NCAA tournament
Consider audience factors (previous knowledge, common experiences, common interests, relevant diverse factors)
Basketball is a very popular sport with students, so most students will have seen games, know names of major players, understand basic rules and procedures; game is popular with both men and women. Seems better suited for audience than other possible topics.
Pick your tentative topic
How basketball developed historically

about them. However, an audience-centered speaker approaches topic selection, if not in an absolutely objective manner, at least in a fair-minded way. If you select as a speech topic "HMOs and the Decline of Health Care in America," you have clearly taken a position hostile to HMOs. Such a position is certainly acceptable, but you have the ethical obligation to be open to the possibility that what you learn in your research may modify your initial point of view. An ethical speaker allows for change as part of the speech preparation process and avoids using the topic as a filter to screen out any information that might enlarge, limit, or redirect it. Once you have gone through such a process and come to a conclusion based on a thoughtful and fair examination of relevant information, you can be more confident in taking a strong, well-reasoned stand on an issue.

Giving a Topic a Fair Shake

Look again at the topics from your self-inventory that have passed the test outlined in the previous portfolio. For each topic, determine whether you can meet your ethical obligation to treat the topic fairly by suspending your own biases and remaining open to competing ideas. Cross off any that seem problematic.

Taste and Judgment

Generally you should avoid topics that audiences might find embarrassing or offensive, understanding that putting listeners in such a position violates ethical norms. An audience-centered perspective is crucial here. *You* might find certain topics appealing, amusing, or of great importance. Thinking of what an audience might feel about a particular topic, however, may cast it in a different light.

For example, imagine a student in your public speaking class giving a speech that advocated converting to the speaker's religion. Although the student has the right to hold particular beliefs, a classroom audience will likely be made up of people whose beliefs differ and who could well be offended by a speaker trying to convert them. The likelihood of offense increases when the audience is a captive one: listeners in a classroom did not choose to come to hear that particular speech, nor can they simply leave. Attempting to force one's beliefs on an audience will likely be viewed as a tasteless effort showing a lack of judgment on the part of the speaker. Moreover, trying to change a deeply held faith, ingrained skepticism, or even habitual indifference is not a practical goal to expect to accomplish in a short speech. In a public speaking class, you need to be especially wary of issues on which the audience is already deeply divided before you begin to talk.

As you begin to think about possible speech topics, you will want to stay focused on ethical concerns. To assist you in doing this, go to **Next Step: Ethical Considerations in Topic Selection** in Lesson 1 on the **VideoLab** CD-ROM and complete the exercise.

It might be, however, that a topic that simply gives information about religious beliefs or practices and does not attempt to change listeners' convictions would be acceptable to the same audience. In any case, different audiences may view the same topic in different ways. As a speaker, you must consider every audience separately and fully understand its members' particular tastes and dispositions when selecting a topic.

Characteristics of Ethical Speakers

Ethical speakers

- inform themselves about their topic.
- select their sources carefully.
- strive for objectivity and fair-mindedness.
- exercise good taste and judgment.

Speakers face other ethical concerns. They must consider, for example, how they use evidence, and they need to determine how to deal ethically with opposing arguments. Ethical questions must be raised and answered in many contexts during the preparation process.

SUMMARY

This chapter has focused on you as a speaker, considering first how an audience may perceive you—your ethos—and then what you can do to influence listeners' perceptions. *Ethics* derive from a set of behavioral norms, whereas *ethos* derives from perceptions. The ethos of a speaker will tend to be positive to the extent that an audience views that speaker as trustworthy, competent, objective, and dynamic. Since ethos depends on perceptions, a speaker's ethos will not necessarily be the same for all people at all times and may vary with the situation.

Although some speakers' ethos is predetermined because of their reputation or position, many speakers face audiences who have no prior perceptions of them. Essentially, these speakers can improve their own ethos by giving a good speech. If speakers give good speeches, audiences will tend to trust them and consider them authorities.

Preparing yourself to speak begins with the choice of a topic that has the potential to enhance your ethos and contribute to your effectiveness as a speaker. In this chapter, we looked at how you can examine your own resources to find a suitable topic and then narrow the topic.

Doing a self-inventory when choosing a topic might be a helpful first step. The next step is to narrow the topic so that it is manageable in the time limit, meets the expectations of the assignment or occasion, and can be made interesting to an audience. Since the audience is central to the development of your speech, you will need to pay particular attention to how the topic will reflect the listeners' knowledge and experience.

In choosing a topic, you also must remember your ethical obligations to be accurate and fair-minded and to exercise good judgment in accommodating the tastes and standards of the audience.

Much of what follows in this book will help you give good speeches. You, just like any other speaker, have an ethos, and that ethos will be working for or against you. What you do will make a difference in your ethos. A good speech starts with you; you are your first resource.

QUESTIONS FOR REVIEW AND REFLECTION

1. What determines a speaker's ethos?
2. Define each dimension of ethos. In your judgment, which dimensions are most important?
3. Compare and contrast ethos and ethics. Why is each important to a public speaker?
4. How can you, as a speaker, improve your ethos while making a speech?
5. What is meant by finding a "suitable" topic?
6. What are the four things to consider when looking for a speech topic? Give a specific example of how each of these categories might relate to you personally (for example, you might have an intellectual interest in medical advances or in the history of jazz).

7. As you narrow a basic speech topic, what are some factors you will need to keep in mind? Why is each important?
8. In your view, which of the following topics would be of greatest interest to your fellow classmates and why?
   a. Habitat for Humanity: A Worthy Cause
   b. Ethics and the Internet
   c. How to Start Your Own Business
   d. How to Interview Effectively to Get the Job You Want
   e. Reasons to Consider Becoming a Vegetarian
   f. Pet Store Pets: Why You Should Not Even Consider Buying One
   g. The Best Mystery Writers of the Decade
   h. Walking: The Best Way to Exercise
   i. The Dangers of Cocaine
   j. Learning to Manage Your Time More Effectively
   k. Why Everyone Should Read Shakespeare
9. What are the major ethical considerations in selecting a topic for any speech?

ENDNOTES

1. *The Rhetoric of Aristotle,* trans. George Kennedy (New York: Oxford University Press, 1992).
2. See Richard L. Johannesen, *Ethics in Human Communication,* 4th ed. (Prospect Heights, Ill.: Waveland Press, 1996).
3. Gary Cronkhite and Jo Liska, "A Critique of Factor Analytic Approaches to the Study of Credibility," *Communication Monographs* 43 (1976): 91–107; J. C. McCroskey and T. J. Young, "Ethos and Credibility: The Construct and Its Measurement After Three Decades," *Central States Speech Journal* 32 (1981): 24–34; Jack L. Whitehead, "Factors of Source Credibility," *Quarterly Journal of Speech* 54 (1968): 59–63.
4. Ronald Reagan, "State of the Union Address," in *Three Centuries of American Rhetorical Discourse,* ed. Ronald F. Reid (Prospect Heights, Ill.: Waveland Press, 1988), p. 743.
5. *Vital Speeches of the Day* 56: Janice Payan, "Opportunities for Hispanic Women," (September 1, 1990), pp. 698–699.
6. Barbara Jordan, "Keynote Address to the Democratic Convention," *Vital Speeches of the Day* 39 (1976): 654.

The following speech illustrating positive ethos was given by Christopher Reeve, an actor who became an activist for people with disabilities after a riding accident left him paralyzed from the neck down. Reeve spoke to the Democratic National Convention in Chicago on August 26, 1996. The speech was televised in prime time, so that it reached millions of viewers in addition to the delegates attending the convention. His own disability and stories of his efforts to continue an active life, his reputation for trying to help others with disabilities, and the courageous act of speaking at all that night when his breathing had to be supported by a respirator all contributed to a very positive ethos going into the speech.

America Is Stronger When All of Us Take Care of All of Us

Christopher Reeve

Reeve redefines a theme that Republicans had emphasized, family values, in terms of his own theme: that America is a family whose members have responsibility for each other.

Over the last few years, we've heard a lot about something called family values. And like many of you I've struggled to figure out what that means but since my accident I've found a definition that seems to make sense. I think it means that we're all family, that we all have value. And if that's true, if America really is a family, then we have to recognize that many of our family are hurting.

Note Reeve's personalization of statistical data.

Just take one aspect of it, one in five of us has some kind of disability. You may have an aunt with Parkinson's disease. A neighbor with spinal cord injury. A brother with AIDS. And if we're really committed to this idea of family, we've got to do something about it.

Reeve associates legislation to aid the disabled with civil rights laws. He also strengthens his own ethos by acknowledging the budget constraints of applying the ADA, yet reframes the issue by stressing that research to help the disabled is a sound *investment.*

First of all, our nation cannot tolerate discrimination of any kind. That's why the Americans with Disabilities Act [ADA] is so important and must be honored everywhere. It is a civil rights law that is tearing down barriers both in architecture and in attitude. Its purpose is to give the disabled access not only to buildings, but to every opportunity in society. I strongly believe our nation must give its full support to the caregivers who are helping people with disabilities live independent lives. Sure, we've got to balance the budget. And we will. We have to be extremely careful with every dollar that we spend. But we've also got to take care of our family and not slash programs people need. We should be enabling, healing, curing. One of the smartest things we can do about disability is invest in research that will protect us from disease and lead to cures. This country already has a long history of doing just that.

Reeve uses statistics to support his contention that research is an investment by showing that the cost of research would reduce high maintenance costs.

When we put our minds to a problem, we can usually find solutions. But our scientists can do more. And we've got to give them the chance. That means more funding for research. Right now, for example, about a quarter-million Americans have a spinal cord injury. Our government spends about $8.7 billion a year just maintaining these members of our family. But we spend only $40 million a year on research that would actually improve the quality of their lives, get them off public assistance, or even cure them. We've got to be smarter, do better. Because the money we invest in research today is going to determine the quality of life of members of our family tomorrow.

During my rehabilitation, I met a young man named Gregory Patterson. When he was innocently driving through Newark, New Jersey, a stray bullet from a gang shooting went through his car window, right into his neck and severed his spinal cord. Five years ago, he might have died. Today because of research he's alive. But merely alive is not enough. We have a moral and an economic responsibility to ease his suffering and prevent others from experiencing such pain. And to do that: we don't need to raise taxes. We just need to raise our expectations.

Here Reeve refers to his own rehabilitation; reminding his audience of his own very intimate experience with disability bolsters his ethos.

America has a tradition many nations probably envy; we frequently achieve the impossible. That's part of our national character. That's what got us from one coast to another. That's what got us the largest economy in the world. That's what got us to the moon. On the wall of my room when I was in rehab was a picture of the space shuttle blasting off, autographed by every astronaut now at NASA. On top of the picture it says, "We found nothing is impossible." That should be our motto. Not a Democratic motto, not a Republican motto. But an American motto. Because this is not something one party can do alone. It's something that we as a nation must do together.

Reeve appeals to listeners' patriotic pride by using the astronauts' motto as an example. He underscores that such a motto is nonpartisan.

So many of our dreams at first seem impossible, then they seem improbable, and then, when we summon the will, they soon become inevitable. If we can conquer outer space, we should be able to conquer inner space too. The frontier of the brain, the central nervous system, and all the afflictions of the body that destroy so many lives, and rob our country of so much potential. Research can provide hope for people who suffer from Alzheimer's. We've already discovered the gene that causes it.

He makes the transition to the next idea by extending the notion that nothing is impossible, then uses the "space" metaphor to describe genetic research.

Research can provide hope for people like Muhammed Ali and the Reverend Billy Graham who suffer from Parkinson's. Research can provide hope for millions of Americans like Kirk Douglas, who suffer from stroke. We can ease the pain of people like Barbara Jordan, who battled multiple sclerosis. We can find treatments for people like Elizabeth Glazer, whom we lost to AIDS. Now that we know that nerves in the spinal cord can regenerate, we are on the way to getting millions of people around the world like me up, and out of our wheelchairs.

Reeve uses well-chosen examples to appeal to a wide audience. Further, his reference to the "millions of people around the world like me" impacts positively on his ethos.

Fifty-six years ago, FDR dedicated new buildings for the National Institute of Health. He said, "the defense this nation seeks, involves a great deal more than building airplanes, ships, guns and bombs. We cannot be a strong nation unless we are a healthy nation." He could have said that today. President Roosevelt showed us that a man who could barely lift himself out of a wheelchair could still lift a nation out of despair. And I believe and so does this Administration in the most important principle FDR taught us: America does not let its needy citizens fend for themselves. America is stronger when all of us take care of all of us. Giving new life to that ideal is the challenge before us tonight. Thank you very much.

Quoting President Franklin D. Roosevelt is especially effective: FDR is revered by most Democrats and regarded as one of the greatest U.S. presidents ever. As a polio victim, he offers a powerful example of what a disabled person can accomplish. Reeve's conclusion ties FDR with the speech's theme of mutual responsibility as a core value. He links his ethos with that of a respected historical figure.

Vital Speeches of the Day 62: Christopher Reeve, "America Is Stronger When All of Us Take Care of All of Us," (1995–96), p. 719.

7 Speaking with a Purpose

CHAPTER SURVEY

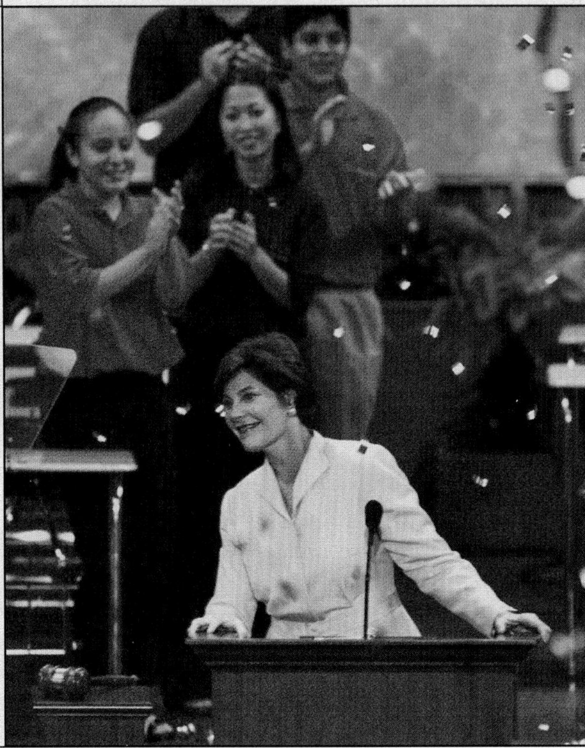

CHAPTER OBJECTIVES

After studying this chapter, you should be able to

1. **understand what is meant by a general purpose.**
2. **distinguish between the goals of informative and persuasive speeches.**
3. **devise a good specific purpose for your speech.**
4. **understand how purposes can relate to one another.**
5. **write a clear thesis statement.**
6. **appreciate the ethical implications in devising a purpose.**
7. **understand how speakers' and listeners' purposes relate to one another.**

After giving a poor speech, a student came to talk to his instructor, one of the authors of this textbook. The student, whose name is David, told this story.

Two weeks before he was scheduled to give a five- to seven-minute informative speech, he had not yet chosen a topic. He had not been able to figure out what he would talk about. He admitted that he was clueless.

As he sat in his political science class, he had a bright idea. His professor was explaining how a president is elected in the United States. David had taken fifteen pages of notes and read two chapters on the subject. That seemed to him to be a lot of information. Why not, David thought, just summarize his notes and develop a short speech? He felt great relief as he decided to speak on presidential elections.

Although David's choice of a speech topic may seem sensible, it wasn't. Randomly choosing a topic can prove disastrous. In this kind of situation, the array of choices involved are largely random because they are inspired chiefly by ready convenience and not by the demands of the communication setting. This topic, for one thing, was too broad to be addressed adequately in the available time. The lecture-based information was also much too technical to be useful to David's specific listeners. In short, David had a difficult time because he did not choose the speech topic based on audience interests and potential benefit. This "boiled-down" version of a lecture failed to connect with his public speaking classmates. Matters were made worse by the fact that David hadn't taken the time to come up with a clear purpose for his speech. He thought only about giving information—"talking about presidential elections"—instead of what controlling idea he wanted the audience to understand and what, specifically, he hoped their response to his speech would be.

Beginning with his own interests and ongoing learning, David should have asked himself, "What might this audience find interesting or need to know?" Many worthy topics might have emerged from this kind of reflection. David might have chosen to speak about political action committees, campaign finance reform, or the evolution of the national party convention to its present form and function. These worthy topics would have grown from what David already knew, but they also would have needed to be fashioned to connect with the interests of the audience. Naturally David would have to have done additional research to deepen and strengthen what he already had learned and to make sure that he could inform listeners in an accurate and interesting way. These possible topics would have needed to be shaped by a clear understanding on David's part of how he hoped to influence the audience's behavior and thinking.

In any communication situation, we are compelled to make choices. In public speaking situations, most basically and obviously, we have to decide whether to talk or to listen. Once committed to speaking, we start selecting what to talk about. Or once committed to listening, we start selecting what to listen to, as well as choosing the specific ways we will try to listen carefully and constructively. *Both speaking and listening involve a whole series of choices, and the option that is open to us is whether we want those choices to be random or reasoned.* As we pointed out in Chapters 4 and 5, you must consider the audience for your speech and what you can bring to the situation as you move on to select and narrow possible topics. Once you have a tentative topic identified, you are ready to make more focused choices regarding precisely what you hope to accomplish in your speech.

GENERAL PURPOSES

Preview Public speaking is always purposeful—that is, a speaker always aims to get responses from listeners. Sometimes the principal kind of response you want from an audience is understanding, so you give an informative speech. At other times, you want to influence the way listeners feel, what they believe, or how they act. In those cases, you give a persuasive speech.

Just as speakers contemplate the situation, their own interests, and those of the audience in selecting a topic, they must use those considerations to formulate a specific purpose and a thesis statement. We discussed purpose in Chapter 1 and suggested that the purpose of communication is to get a desired response from an audience. As you refine your topic, you try to translate it into a specific statement of the audience response you anticipate. Everything that can be done to ensure successful public communication rests on having a clear conception of purpose. The first step in crafting a purpose is to determine the nature of the response you want from an audience; this is your **general purpose**.

general purpose what the speaker generally hopes to accomplish by speaking, such as audience understanding, agreement, conviction, or action

In most classroom situations, you will be assigned a general purpose. It is also true, as we discussed in Chapter 6, that you may be asked to speak at work or in a setting related specifically to your interests or expertise. In such cases, although you will not have a choice of general purpose, you will have to make many other choices growing from the general purpose. Let us now consider the two general purposes that will account for most of the public speaking you will be called on to do.

Informative Purposes

When we talk about informing people, we naturally think about giving them information. But you need to remember that an audience-centered speaker does not think in terms of giving. *An audience-centered speaker thinks about what she or he is trying to get from an audience.* So what do you want to get when you give an informative speech? You want to get *understanding*—an informative speech is a speech to gain understanding.

This is not just playing with words. A very important concept is involved. Have you ever been in a class where the instructor gave a lecture that contained a lot of information but you were confused about what it meant? Or have you gotten directions from someone and then found that you couldn't reach your destination because those directions were not clear to you? Has a supervisor ever given you instructions on how to do a job, and then you found

A lecture in a college classroom is largely informative since the instructor's goal is to help listeners understand new material.
(Ulrike Welsch/PhotoEdit)

yourself unable to complete the task because you weren't able to follow those instructions? If anything like this has happened to you, you have experienced the difference between just giving information and getting understanding. The person attempting to communicate with you in these cases was unsuccessful not because he or she didn't "give information," but because that person failed to make you understand.

General Purposes and Audience Response

- *Informative speeches* aim at audience understanding.
- *Persuasive speeches* aim to reinforce feelings, change beliefs, or induce action.

When you are asked to give an informative speech, you are being asked to give a speech that will result in listeners understanding something that they did not understand before. After you have finished speaking, listeners will not just have *heard* something new; they will have *learned* something new. We discuss informative speaking further in Chapter 14.

Persuasive Purposes

Persuasion surrounds us; it intrudes on almost every aspect of our lives. We are urged to give our time to worthy causes, our money to producers of all kinds of goods and services, our votes to politicians, our energy to working harder, and a phone call to Mother to let her know how we're doing. We're asked to take seriously beliefs or values we hold, to accept new ideas, and to defer to the judgment of others.

As with an informative message, a persuasive message aims to get something from an audience. Persuasion is more than telling listeners what they ought to do or believe. It is more than simply giving an audience facts or statistics. It is more than offering your opinion. It is more than asking, recommending, or demanding. We often hear advertisers, or politicians, telemarketers, or salespersons give substantial reasons why we should take the action they recommend, but we don't always do what they would like us to. We are not persuaded.

specific purpose a precise statement of how the speaker wants the audience to respond to his or her message. This statement directs the speaker's research and construction of the speech

Persuasion is an effort to get a response from an audience. As a speaker, you want listeners to feel more strongly about things that presumably matter to them, to agree with you, or to take some definite action. We discuss persuasive speaking further in Chapters 15 and 16.

A general purpose, then, points you in the direction you want to go. The next step is to refine that general purpose into a **specific purpose** that spells out precisely the response you want from your audience given the topic you have chosen.

One of the hardest tasks you will face in devising a realistic purpose and thesis statement is overcoming the time constraints that are always imposed on a speaker, not only in your classroom, but in virtually any situation you are likely to encounter. *Spotlight on Speaking Campaigns* offers some suggestions for accomplishing long-range purposes when it is possible to give multiple speeches on a related topic over time.

PORTFOLIO 7.1

Establishing a Realistic Purpose

What response do you hope to elicit with various speech topics you're considering for presentation to the class? Given your classroom audience, consider whether each response is realistic.

Contemplate and briefly answer the following:

1. What, ultimately, would you like the audience to understand, accept, believe, feel, and/or do?
2. What might you do that takes the audience a step in the right direction? In other words, what is a realistic goal for your most immediate speech?
3. What subsequent messages will be needed to accomplish your ultimate goal?

SPOTLIGHT ON... **Speaking Campaigns**

Long-Range Purposes and Speaking Campaigns

It is sometimes more effective to try to accomplish a **long-range purpose** through a series of speeches. To get changes in environmental protection laws, many people spent years educating the public—merely trying to get people to understand the nature and gravity of the problem—before they could urge any direct action. In the classroom situation, you may be able to use the speaking assignments as a sustained **campaign** aimed at an ultimate goal.

One student speaker wanted to urge revisions in the school curriculum that he knew might not be popular. He decided to tailor his three speaking assignments to this general topic with a long-range goal in mind. He began with an informative speech, then moved to a persuasive speech to convince his audience that he had a good plan for change, and finally delivered a persuasive speech that directed them toward an action they could take.

FIRST SPEECH

I want my audience to understand how curriculum changes are brought about and curriculum decisions are made.

SECOND SPEECH

I want my audience to agree that requirements should include more courses that help them to write and speak more effectively.

THIRD SPEECH

I want my audience to volunteer to work for the Student Committee for an Improved Curriculum.

long-range purpose the ultimate goal a speaker hopes to accomplish as a result of presenting a series of speeches on a particular topic

campaign a series of messages aimed at moving listeners closer to a specific position or course of action

It is not always possible to plan a sequence of speeches, depending on the organization and assignments of a particular public speaking course. Speaking opportunities outside the classroom also might not allow for a series of presentations. But in this case, the speaker was able to give a series of speeches and had a better chance of bringing student listeners around to his position than if he had tried to do everything in only one speech.

CRAFTING A SPECIFIC PURPOSE

Preview Specific purposes are statements of the desired audience response. They are shaped by the speaker's goal, the situation in which the speech is given, and the potential benefits to the audience. Although speakers may need to accomplish many things in a speech, the purpose is the ultimate response that the speaker hopes to achieve.

Beginning students of public speaking often tend to hurry over the specific purpose without realizing how it determines so much that will happen. Without a clear specific purpose as a foundation, you can make a potentially interesting topic confusing and cluttered. You must know what you want to accomplish so that all your preparation moves you toward that end.

Purpose and Response

Successful speakers plan the desired audience response carefully and never allow themselves to be vague or unclear about their purpose. For example, a

The purpose of any speech is to get a response from an audience and an effective speaker plans carefully to get the desired response. The listeners at this "Promise Keepers" rally responded enthusiastically to the speaker's message. (B. Kraft/SYGMA)

speaker turned in a preliminary statement of purpose that read, "My purpose is to talk about modern technology." Such a statement, of course, is not a purpose at all. It says something very vague about what the speaker will do, but it doesn't specify a response. Furthermore, "modern technology" is a broad and nonspecific idea unless it is related directly to what the speaker hopes the audience will understand. With the purpose stated in this way, the speaker would have had a very difficult time choosing what to include and what to exclude in such a speech.

In this case, the student's immediate concern was giving an assigned informative speech. She knew, however, that she also had a persuasive speech assignment coming up. After much thought about the possibilities, she came up with two specific purposes that were related to each other, reflected her interests, and were designed to fulfill the informative and persuasive assignments. These specific purposes were as follows:

- *For an informative speech:* I want my audience to understand how modern technology makes learning easier.
- *For a persuasive speech:* I want my audience to agree that modern technology creates psychological problems for some workers.

Both of these statements are specific purposes because they state the desired audience response, and both purposes relate to the topic of "modern technology," but both would have to be developed differently.

Purpose and the Situation

The specific purpose is also shaped by the particular demands of the situation. Suppose you are to give an informative speech in class and your topic is the problem of crime. You would—after considering the factors influencing the audience, the relationship of crime to the audience, and the amount of time available for the speech—decide that the audience should know more about how crime can affect them directly. In trying to gain understanding, you could devise several goals that could be accomplished in a limited amount of time.

Following are some examples of informative specific purposes that might be set by a speaker addressing crime:

- *Specific purpose:* I want my audience to understand the economic impact of crime.
- *Specific purpose:* I want my audience to understand the kinds of crimes committed on college campuses.
- *Specific purpose:* I want my audience to understand some of the major causes of crime.

Since each of these specific purposes is informative, they specify what the speaker wants the audience to understand, and they also define what he or she hopes to accomplish. If, however, you were alarmed by the increase of crime on campus, you might want to advocate some plan of action that students could take, and you would therefore give a persuasive speech based on one of the following statements:

- *Specific purpose:* I want my audience to sign up to take a self-defense course.
- *Specific purpose:* I want my audience to agree that a workshop on crime prevention should be included as part of freshman orientation.

Purpose and Audience Benefits

In devising a specific purpose, you need to consider what the listeners should gain and how they are expected to respond. The benefit to the audience ought to be apparent in the speech. Too often speakers are not aware of this basic principle. A speaker at a large university, for example, addressed a crowd gathered to protest proposed fee hikes for state colleges. The listeners had come because they wanted to know what to do to stop the increases and to show support for those who were fighting to keep fees as they were. The speaker, however, delivered a long, angry attack on student apathy and implied that such ignorant, unresponsive people deserved whatever they got at the hands of an unsympathetic legislature.

> Most of the time in life we get just what we deserve. Most of you are uninvolved, you don't know what's going on, you're not reading the papers and not following politics that take you beyond your campus. You're *never* going to be able to do anything about politicians and lawyers and college administrators who have their own interests at heart—not yours. You aren't doing anything to educate yourself about the economics of this state and the political battles going on in the state legislature—nothing at all. You're too busy with school, work, and social life. You haven't taken the time and made the effort to prepare for this kind of debate—so you can expect to get just what you deserve—which is precious little! You're basically apathetic—and that, frankly, makes me think it's a waste of time even to talk to you!

Clearly this speaker could have pursued other options. He could have talked about the need to become active, or he could have tried to get his audience (already motivated to act) to understand what direct actions they could take to put pressure on lawmakers. He could have used a wide range of appropriate purposes. Instead he probably decided just to "get up and talk about apathy." The result was that he irritated and alienated an initially friendly audience and injected a depressing note into what should have been an enthusiastic show of unity and determination.

If you were about to go to the grocery store, you would have some clear goal—at least to buy food, at best to buy particular items. Your goal would be to buy something, not just to shop. Shopping is the process, the means to an end. In the same way, "talking about" something isn't an end in itself. Instead you talk with an audience to benefit them and to obtain a desired reaction from them.

Purposes and Multiresponses

Beginning speakers sometimes have difficulty seeing the differences between informative and persuasive speech purposes. Indeed sometimes speakers must be informative before they can be persuasive. Public service ads, for example, are designed to help people understand the dangers of smoking or how to prevent the spread of AIDS, in the hope that understanding will eventually lead to changes in behavior.

Some speeches promote understanding, reinforce ideas and feelings, seek agreement, and call for action—all within one speech. The specific purpose of such a speech, however, is what the speaker hopes to accomplish. The more minor purposes are secondary to the major specific purpose. Let's consider an example.

A student interested in Native American culture in the Southwest chose to talk about pueblos to fulfill a persuasive speaking assignment. She considered several possible purposes before deciding on this one: *I want my audience to sign up for the special Christmas charter tour to the Southwest.* In the speech, the audience was given information that would help them understand what pueblos are and how they are built. The speaker then attempted to reinforce the listeners' feelings that it would be good to get a complete break from the routine of school. She next presented evidence in an effort to gain agreement that a charter tour would be the most economical, affordable way they would ever have to make a trip to the Southwest. Finally, she encouraged them to take direct action by signing up to go on the tour. In other words, she aimed at a whole range of responses preceding the ultimate desired one.

But if the listeners understood something about how pueblos are built but did not sign up for the tour, if they agreed that it would be fun or cheap to go on the trip but did not sign up, or if they enjoyed the talk very much but did not sign up, the speaker would not have been satisfied. Her purpose was to get them to take a specific action. To do that, she would have had to go beyond gaining understanding to help the audience see how the trip would directly benefit them. The cross-cultural experience might be one that would ultimately make a student more attractive to an employer, for example. The trip might be combined with an independent study course to earn college credit, or it might introduce the student to an area of study, such as anthropology or history, that he or she could pursue as a major. Although much of the speech was informative, its persuasive goal called for different, more motivational material. We will discuss this notion in more detail in Chapters 15 and 16.

Two important points are being made here. *First, sometimes speakers have to inform before they can hope to persuade.* How, for example, could listeners be asked to agree that genetic research is safe and desirable if they did not understand anything about the kind of research that is going on? How could listeners be expected to agree that nuclear energy is more efficient than electrical energy if they did not understand at least a few fundamental principles that explain how each works? *Second, sometimes speakers have to persuade before they can hope to inform.* For example, how could a speaker get an audience to understand how energy for our daily lives is produced if the listeners were not convinced that such information was important to them? Getting an audience to understand how to conserve energy would be very difficult if that audience didn't agree that energy should be conserved. But all this is preliminary to achieving the specific purpose of the speech, which ultimately is either a persuasive or an information one.

No matter what range of responses is called for, audience-centered considerations lead to the conclusion that what determines the purpose of a speech is the communicator's hoped-for end result. In other words, no matter how many other purposes are met, the result is negative if the end result is not the achievement of the specific purpose.

KEEP IN MIND 7.2

Developing the Specific Purpose Statement

The specific purpose is a statement of the desired audience response shaped by

- the speaker's goal.
- the speaking situation.
- the benefits to the audience.
- the ultimate response to be gained.

TESTING SPECIFIC PURPOSES

Preview How will you know if your purpose is appropriate? Make sure that it aims for a specific response from the audience, reflects the realities of the situation, is clear, and is ethical.

strategy a plan that attempts to identify the best steps for achieving your goals

Because specific purposes are the foundations on which all **strategy** is built, we've devoted a great deal of space in this chapter to describing them carefully. Let's consider some quick ways to test the specific purposes you develop. Basically, there are four principles that suggest questions you can ask yourself to determine whether you have a sound purpose.

1. *A good specific purpose asks for an audience response.* Ask yourself, "Does the purpose call for a response from the audience?" Here are some ideas that are *not* specific purposes:
   - What you should know about your taxes.
   - I want to talk about the need for tax reform.
   - Tax reform.
   - My views of tax reform.

These might be topics or titles, but they do not designate the response you want from the audience. Compare these ideas with statements that *do* call for a response.

AN INFORMATIVE SPEECH

NO: *What you should know about your taxes.*

YES: *I want my audience to understand that taxation is a means of producing revenue and effecting social policy.*

A PERSUASIVE SPEECH TO INTENSIFY LISTENERS' FEELINGS

NO: *I want to talk about the need for tax reform.*

YES: *I want my audience to feel more strongly that taxation should be fair.*

A PERSUASIVE SPEECH TO INDUCE LISTENERS' AGREEMENT

NO: *Tax reform.*

YES: *I want my audience to agree that tax loopholes should be eliminated.*

A PERSUASIVE SPEECH TO GET LISTENERS TO TAKE A SPECIFIC ACTION

NO: *My views of tax reform.*

YES: *I want my audience to agree to urge their representatives to support a federal flat tax.*

2. *A good specific purpose is realistic.* Ask yourself, "Does the purpose reflect the realities of the situation?" The audience, the setting, and the occasion should influence the purpose of your speech. Consider the following specific purposes:
   - I want my audience to understand the history of Russia.
   - I want my audience to take up quilting as a hobby.

The first purpose is an absurdly broad topic to be explained in a short period of time. The second is most likely not a good choice for a speech in class, although it might be realistic for another group. Here is how these ideas might be restated:

NO: *I want my audience to understand the history of Russia.*

YES: *I want my audience to understand the major immediate causes of the disintegration of the Soviet Union.* (A more manageable purpose, but still not easy to accomplish in a short time.)

NO: *I want my audience to take up quilting as a hobby.*

YES: *I want my audience to understand why quilting is a folk art.* (Could be interesting for a group unlikely to or be able to participate in quilting.)

3. *A good specific purpose is clear.* Ask yourself, "Is the purpose clear?" An audience can often be confused by a strategy that grows out of a vague purpose. Communication is almost invariably unsuccessful when speakers are not clear about what they want to accomplish.

   I want my audience to understand about the Japanese tea ceremony is not a good purpose because, although it is couched in the appropriate language of a purpose, it shows that the speaker does not know precisely what he or she wants the audience to do. The phrase "understand about" is a clue that the purpose lacks clarity and is as vague as that suggested by "talk about." If you were speaking on this subject, you might want your audience to know how the ceremony is performed, how persons are trained to do it, or why it is such an important ritual in Japanese life. Maybe you would even ask them to go see a ceremony performed in a room on campus. All these would be purposes that reflect a clear conception of the response you desire from your audience.

FRAME OF REFERENCE

Speakers constantly face a variety of ethical choices. The speaker's purpose should be consistent with the speaker's values and be one that he or she believes is in the best interest of the audience.

NO: *I want my audience to understand about the Japanese tea ceremony.*

YES: *I want my audience to understand the intricate ritual that is followed in the Japanese tea ceremony.*

YES: *I want my audience to understand the ways in which the Japanese tea ceremony reflects Japanese culture.*

YES: *I would like my audience to attend a Japanese tea ceremony next Friday night at the International Student Center.*

4. *A good specific purpose is ethical.* Ask yourself, "Is the purpose ethical?" So far, in discussing specific purposes, we have been concerned with issues of clarity, realism, and audience centeredness (as reflected in the response the speaker is seeking). All of these are important criteria, but they could all be fulfilled and still the purpose could be unethical.

   In any communication situation, as we have already discussed, speakers may seek goals that are not in the best interests of the listeners or of society at large. The following specific purpose, for example, is not ethical: *I want my audience to learn how to cut their income taxes by failing to report cash.* Cheating on your income tax is not only socially irresponsible, but it is clearly illegal. Obviously this is not an ethical purpose.

   Even if legality is removed as an issue, ethical judgments about speaker purposes can be made.[1] For instance, suppose a speaker wanted to advance this purpose: *I want my audience to understand how to go about purchasing term papers over the Internet.* You won't be sent to jail for doing this, but the action you are advocating is so clearly plagiarism that this purpose violates both ethical norms and the specific regulations of every college or university in the country.

   Sometimes ethical boundaries are less clear. Suppose a speaker wanted smokers in his audience to switch from smoking cigarettes to smoking cigars. Nearly everyone is aware that smoking in general is not good for anyone's health. But both forms of smoking are legal, and the speaker might try to argue that cigar smoking is less harmful to one's health, less expensive (unless one gets into exotic brands), and more socially acceptable than cigarette smoking. We might decide that this is not an ideal purpose, but we would probably judge it as more ethical than one that enticed nonsmokers to take up smoking.

   The point here is that, like other aspects of public speaking, our specific purposes often have ethical consequences. As speakers, we need to think about who we are, who our listeners are, what we have to gain or lose, and how our audience might benefit or be hurt by the information that we are sharing with them or the actions we are urging them to pursue.

KEEP IN MIND 7.3

Characteristics of Specific Purposes

A good specific purpose

- asks for an audience response.
- is realistic.
- is clear.
- is ethical.

DEVISING A THESIS STATEMENT

Preview The thesis statement grows from your specific purpose. It is a clear declarative statement that embodies the principal idea of your speech. It should be focused without being cluttered with too much detail.

After you have worked out a specific purpose, you need to formulate a declarative statement that sums up the thesis of your speech, sometimes called the central idea or overriding idea of the speech. You should think of this as your speech in a nutshell. A good thesis statement will help while you're doing research and as you draft the speech. If you are successful in achieving your specific purpose, the **thesis statement** is what listeners will carry away with them—what they will remember as the heart of your speech.

thesis statement a single, simple declarative sentence that expresses the principal idea of a speech and that the speaker would have the audience understand and/or accept

Guidelines for Constructing a Thesis Statement

There are three basic guidelines to keep in mind when constructing a thesis statement.

1. ***The thesis statement is a single, complete declarative sentence that embodies the idea that you want the audience to understand and/or accept in order to accomplish your specific purpose.***

   It is important to emphasize that the thesis is a *declarative* sentence—an idea you want to convey to your audience—not a question or a phrase that simply announces the topic. *How can we improve our public schools?* and *Improving our public schools* are not thesis statements. Most likely, your answer to the question is really the thesis statement, as in, *The massive infusion of federal money into underfunded school districts in poor areas is the best way to improve public education.*

   The thesis statement grows from your specific purpose. In effect, it answers the question, "What do listeners have to understand (or feel or believe) if I am going to get the response I want?" Let's go back and look at some of the specific purposes we suggested earlier for an informative speech on crime and see what thesis statements might grow out of them.

   Specific purpose: *I want my audience to understand the economic impact of crime.*

   Thesis statement: *Crime costs taxpayers millions of dollars each year in law enforcement and judicial costs.*

   From this specific purpose: *I want my audience to understand the kinds of crimes committed on college campuses.*

   Comes this thesis statement: *Although theft is the most prevalent crime committed on college campuses, personal assault and rape are also serious problems.*

   Specific purpose: *I want my audience to understand some of the major causes of crime.*

Thesis statement: *Crime in America is the result of both economic and social problems.*

2. ***The thesis statement should be clear and specific without being so detailed as to include all your main ideas.***
   The thesis statement is not a summary of all the main points in a speech, but instead it includes these ideas in an overriding concept. Earlier we gave the statement that follows as an example of a specific purpose for a persuasive speech: *I want my audience to agree that modern technology creates psychological problems for some workers.* Compare a good thesis statement (clear and direct) growing from this purpose with a poor one that tries to include all the individual ideas and ends up as a kind of summary of the speech.

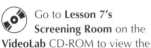

 Go to **Lesson 7's Screening Room** on the **VideoLab** CD-ROM to view the speech on corporate welfare. See if you can identify the speaker's specific purpose and thesis. You may want to repeat this exercise with other speeches.

Good: *Technological advances can induce stress among workers as they intensify feelings of insecurity and isolation.*

Poor: *Technology can cause psychological damage because it can lead to downsizing and thus the fear of job loss, can increase demands on workers' productivity, can take away special skills needed to perform some tasks and so become increasingly boring and repetitive, and can make contact with other people unnecessary, resulting in feelings of isolation.*

Note also that the thesis is not a presentation of the specific information you will present in your speech. Another poor thesis statement for this speech might be one that neglects the driving idea of the speech in favor of giving information that will be used in the speech: *A recent survey conducted for the* Wall Street Journal *shows that close to half of all workers in nonprofessional jobs believe that technology is harmful to them.*

KEEP IN MIND 7.4

Testing Thesis Statements

The thesis statement should

- reflect the specific purpose.
- be a declarative statement.
- be clear and specific.
- be focused and limited in scope.

3. ***The thesis statement, growing from the narrowing of the topic and the clarity of the specific purpose, should be focused and limited in scope.***
   You want to be sure that you don't try to accomplish too much or too many different things in one speech. If you have a good specific purpose, this is unlikely to happen. But if you find yourself developing a broad thesis statement—*A school voucher system will improve public education and should be coupled with national standardized tests to measure student achievement and content examinations for teachers*—you are probably taking on too much for a single speech. Such a thesis statement should alert you to potential problems that you can avoid by reworking your specific purpose.

 **PORTFOLIO 7.2**

The Bottom Line

What is the general purpose of your next speech? What is a specific purpose that will

1. achieve the general purpose?
2. identify a precise goal that is suitable for the situation?
3. identify a precise goal that is of genuine benefit to your audience?
4. identify a precise goal that is realistic in terms of what can be expected?
5. seek a goal that is in the best interests of the listeners and society?

Use these considerations to create and test the bottom line in your next speech.

Avoiding Common Mistakes

As you try to put these guidelines into effect when developing your own thesis statement, you should try to avoid the most common mistakes made by students when devising thesis statements. Your thesis statement should

- not be written as a question or a topical phrase.
- not be a preview of the speech.
- not be too complex and hard to follow.
- not present excessively detailed information.
- not present too many ideas for a single speech.

 CONNECTING TO THE NET

Would you like some practice in devising thesis statements? Do you need some help in constructing the thesis statement for your next speech? If so, go to **http://college.hmco.com/communication/andrews/public_speaking/2e/students/** and click on *Connecting to the Net.* From there, follow the link to Thesis Statements.

FROM TOPIC TO PURPOSE TO THESIS: REVIEWING THE PROCESS

Preview As a way of reviewing the procedure we have been describing, let's consider one example and follow the process step by step. We'll take as our example Marsha, a speaker mentioned in Chapter 6, who generated a list of possible topics based on her leisure interests.

STEP 1: Select Possible Topics (from Self-Inventory). You might remember that, as a part of her self-inventory, Marsha generated the following list of possible topics based on the fact that she was an avid movie-goer:

- How to produce special effects
- Stunt men and women
- The first sound movies
- Why movies cost millions to make
- History of horror films

STEP 2: Consider Situational and Audience Factors. Several recent horror films, such as *I Know What You Did Last Summer 2, Scream 3,* and *Scary Movie,* were very popular, and many students had seen them. Also, Marsha was scheduled to give this speech in mid-October, and she knew that soon old horror movies would be running constantly on TV. Few in her audience would not have seen films such as *Halloween, Friday the Thirteenth,* and *Nightmare on Elm Street.*

STEP 3: Pick Your Tentative Topic. Given the situational factors, Marsha chose as her tentative topic: the history of horror films.

STEP 4: Determine the General Purpose. Marsha's assignment was to give an informative speech, so she would attempt to gain audience understanding.

STEP 5: Craft a Specific Purpose. Marsha had to determine exactly what response she wanted from her audience. After conducting and evaluating an audience survey, she finally crafted this specific purpose: *I want my audience to understand why horror films are so popular.*

STEP 6: Write a Thesis Statement. As she began to gather material, she considered what the principal idea of the speech was. She experimented with several possibilities and finally decided that the most interesting aspect of horror films was the way in which they play on deep-seated human fears. So she devised this thesis statement: *From the very beginning, horror films have fascinated audiences because they tap into basic human fears.*

Marsha's purpose was still somewhat tentative. She could modify it as she gathered and organized material for the speech. However, she had gone through the process from topic selection to specific purpose to thesis statement carefully and thoughtfully and had a purpose that met the criteria for a good specific purpose: it was conceived in terms of response, was realistic and clear, and had no negative ethical aspects.

AGREEMENT AND CONFLICT IN SPEAKERS' AND LISTENERS' PURPOSES

Preview Audiences are also concerned with the purpose of messages aimed at them. In public speaking situations, both speakers and audiences have purposes. Here we consider the ethical obligations of the speaker and the notion of the listeners' purposes.

In many communication contexts, both speaker and listener have compatible purposes. Advertisers who are trying to persuade people to buy automobiles are listened to by people who want to buy automobiles. A lecturer who wants the audience to understand the anatomy of the inner ear rightly expects to find that medical or audiology students who are listening want to understand.

Ethical Choices in Crafting Purposes

We have often pointed out that the speaker must be audience-centered. This means that the speaker must take into account the characteristics and interests of the audience, as we've already discussed. But it also means that the speaker must bear in mind the audience's welfare. This very important ethical dimension should guide the speaker's choices.

Consider negative campaign ads. Many voters are convinced that politicians often choose to distort the facts to destroy an opponent rather than explain their own positions clearly to help inform the audience. Unfortunately, these strategies often work, but success is achieved by abandoning the ethical standards that are based on a genuine concern for the audience's well-being. Goals are not to be achieved by any means; the means must be ethical. A student who develops a strategy for achieving good grades may identify a host of helpful tactics: taking careful notes, summarizing the notes at the end of each week, and planning far in advance. The student also could cheat. Doing so, of course, would put the student beyond acceptable ethical behavior even if it would help him or her get a better grade.

Speakers have ethical choices to make when planning their strategies and determining the purposes of their speeches. The critical touchstone for making

Listeners' and speakers' purposes may be in direct opposition. These Planned Parenthood supporters are unlikely to respond positively to the message aimed at them by the "Right to Life" advocate. (Bob Daemmrich Photos)

such choices is the audience-centered ideal: the speaker must ask whether the purpose of the speech will have beneficial or harmful consequences for the audience and whether the audience's best interests are being sacrificed for the speaker's personal gain.

Successful businesses soon learn that a reputation for honesty, fair dealing, and service results in more profits in the long run than does a "buyer beware" strategy designed to grab the quick buck.[2] Similarly, a speaker should realize that cheap tricks designed to mislead an audience into acting in ways that benefit the speaker are both counterproductive and unethical. It is in this audience-centered, ethical context that speaking with a purpose should be understood.

Go to the **VideoLab** CD-ROM to complete **Drill 1.1: Identifying Speech Components**. Pay particular attention to the questions that probe purposes, specific purposes, and thesis statements. You may also want to complete the first drill in other lessons of the VideoLab in order to further test your knowledge in this area.

Reinforcing Purposes

Listeners need to recognize that it is often in their interests, as well as the speaker's, to be informed, persuaded, and entertained. As we have noted, listening is an active process. Sometimes that process involves listeners working hard to help the speaker do what he or she has set out to do. Listeners cannot be, and cannot expect to be, passively acted upon. They may sometimes have to overcome boredom, fatigue, initial lack of interest, and other distracting factors so that they can interact with the speaker and the message as constructively as possible. Only then will all participants in the public speaking situation be satisfied.

Conflicting Purposes

The listener does, however, need to be aware that her or his purpose can be in conflict with the speaker's. It may be true, for example, that the listener may want to buy a car and the speaker may want to sell one. But the salesperson may want to make the best profit possible from the sale, and the listener may

PORTFOLIO 7.3

Reading Between the Lines

When you listen to others, do you go beyond the content, trying to discern the speaker's motive for speaking? Think back on speeches you've heard that you did not size up in terms of the underlying motive. What seems to have been the speaker's specific purpose? Do the hoped-for consequences seem desirable for you and for others the speaker wishes to affect?

KEEP IN MIND 7.5

Listeners' Purposes

- It is often in the listener's best interest to work to help the speaker achieve his or her goal.
- Careful listeners will try to discern their own purposes before going along with the speaker.

wish to spend as little as possible. Listeners, for their own defense, need to define precisely what they want to accomplish in the communication exchange.

In public speaking, of course, the listener can't always think ahead. When you come into a speech class, you are not sure what topics will be discussed that day. Faced with a speech on the role of women in intercollegiate athletics, for example, many listeners may not know what purpose they bring to the class. If they hope to be successful, speakers will try to relate their speeches to their audience. As listeners perceive and evaluate such efforts, they can begin to decide what they ought to be getting out of the speech.

To benefit from a speech, listeners will try to formulate a purpose for themselves. If, for instance, someone in your class gives a speech on pollution control legislation, factors such as your awareness of national problems or your geographic location could shape your initial interest in the question. If the speaker successfully engages your attention so that you begin to be aware of how pollution is directly harming you, you may begin to form a purpose, such as "I am listening to this message to find out how I can stop pollution in this town." Of course, the listener's purpose, unlike the speaker's, will be somewhat open-ended and subject to modification as the speech goes on.

Whatever purpose the listener finally discerns, he or she should be cautious in deciding whether it has been accomplished. Speakers may well press for an immediate response to their messages. Careful listeners, however, will refrain from doing anything immediately until they have thought about whether their own purposes have been achieved. Ethical considerations play a role here, since it is partly the listeners' responsibility to consider whether the speaker's purpose is ethically motivated.

SUMMARY

Speeches aim at getting responses from audiences. The principal kinds of responses that speakers aim for in most cases—both in the classroom and in professional settings—are the general purposes: informative and persuasive. The goal of informative speeches is to gain audience understanding, while the goal of persuasive speeches is to reinforce audience feelings, change beliefs, or elicit action.

Based on the topic that you have chosen, you will be able to create a specific purpose that states precisely the response you want from your audience in a particular situation. A specific purpose is the foundation on which the thesis statement is built. The thesis statement, the guiding idea of the speech that you want your listeners to take away from it, should be carefully crafted to be precise and inclusive without being cluttered with too many details. It is not a summary of your speech. As you go through the process of crafting a specific purpose and thesis, you should be mindful of the effects your ideas will have on the audience. You must consider the ethical implications of what you are trying to do.

The listeners also have purposes in a speaking situation. As a listener, you hope to derive as much benefit as you can from a speech, so it is in your best interest to help the speaker achieve her or his goal. As a good listener, however, you also need to be aware of your own purposes and consider carefully whether you want to respond as the speaker hopes you will.

QUESTIONS FOR REVIEW AND REFLECTION

1. What are the general purposes of public speaking? Define each.
2. What is meant by a specific purpose? Why is it important for every public speaker to have a specific purpose?
3. What is a thesis statement, and why is it important for a speaker to develop one?
4. What are the criteria you ought to use to evaluate your specific purpose? Why is each criterion important?
5. Here are three specific purposes. Which is best and why?
   - I want my audience to understand the hazards of relying on credit cards.
   - I want to give my account of my bicycle tour of France.
   - I want to persuade my audience that General Motors vehicles are the best on the market.
6. Suppose someone decides to give a speech with this specific purpose: *I want my audience to vote to repeal the state law that requires motorcyclists to wear safety helmets.* Using the criteria for evaluating purpose statements discussed in this chapter, is this an effective purpose statement? Why or why not?
7. Following are three thesis statements. Which one is the best and why?
   - Would you like to do something that is both fun and useful this summer?
   - Volunteering to work for Habitat for Humanity this summer will be a rewarding personal experience and will provide a very useful public service.
   - If you volunteer to work for Habitat for Humanity, you will get good physical exercise, learn new skills, meet interesting people, get to work with kids your own age, provide homes for needy and deserving people, and earn the gratitude and respect of the people you help.
8. Can a single speech have multiple purposes? Why or why not?
9. Describe your understanding of the relationship between speaker and listener purposes.
10. What can listeners do if and when they decide that their purposes differ from those of the speaker?

ENDNOTES

1. See *Communication Quarterly* 38 (Summer 1990), special issue on communication ethics.
2. See Kenneth R. Andrews, "Ethics in Practice," *Harvard Business Review* 67 (September–October 1989): 99–109.

PART III

Produce: Developing the Speech

With your audience in mind and a clear idea of what you hope to accomplish, you will learn in Part III how to gather relevant material. You will discover how to formulate ideas, how to make those ideas understandable and believable, and how to structure that material to suit the topic and the audience. On the basis of this thorough preparation, you will then be able to explore the most effective ways to present your speech.

8 Discovering Relevant Material Through Research

CHAPTER SURVEY

CHAPTER OBJECTIVES

After studying this chapter, you should be able to

1. **understand the importance of research in the development of your speech.**
2. **understand how the speech preparation process assists in the development of your speech.**
3. **use library resources efficiently.**
4. **use the Internet to find reliable sources.**
5. **conduct an interview to gather information.**
6. **document your sources accurately and know how and when to cite sources in your speech.**

Not long ago, a friend decided to purchase a new car. His excitement turned into frustration when the salesperson insisted that the price on the sticker was fair and could not be lowered. Moreover, his trade-in would bring only a fraction of the original price, even though it was only a few years old. Our friend suspected that the salesperson could provide a better deal, but he was powerless to argue because he had no information. Wisely, he said he would consider the deal and perhaps return.

Our friend consulted a colleague who recently had bought a new car. She handed him the book *Consumer Guide 2000: New Cars*, which proved invaluable. It provided an overview of the makes and models our friend liked, and it rated each vehicle according to road tests and reports from owners of the previous model. On the basis of reliability, warranty, price, and safety, the book's editors indicated which vehicles they thought were the best buys. The book also disclosed manufacturers' prices for vehicles and optional equipment, and it alerted readers to advertising expenses that some dealers charge, as well as to the types of taxes that might accompany a particular model.

In addition to consulting the printed guide, our friend located helpful information on the World Wide Web. He found several sites listing prices for new automobiles and their optional equipment, as well as information about the market value of his trade-in, including formulas for determining the added value of various options and deductions for excessive mileage. He pasted the relevant information into a new document and printed it out.

Armed with this information, our friend was ready to do business. His next visit to the dealer produced very different results. He was able to negotiate a much better price and receive more for his trade-in. In addition, he exposed the advertising charge, and the dealer agreed to drop it from the price. As a result, our friend now is driving a new vehicle, confident that he bargained effectively.

Our friend's experience illustrates a simple point: knowledge is power. Similarly, the well-informed public speaker is a powerful speaker. Being knowledgeable about your topic allows you to formulate better ideas and to be confident in their accuracy. At the same time, your audience will feel that you know your subject and will accept you as a credible source. In fact, you have an ethical obligation to be informed and to reveal your sources. By fulfilling this basic obligation, you can rightfully be considered responsible and trustworthy.

This chapter will help you to be accountable as a speaker. We focus on various possibilities for finding information relevant to your topic, including consulting print and electronic media and interviewing experts and others who have useful information, knowledge, and experience. First, though, we consider how you can effectively and efficiently conduct your investigation, providing suggestions for taking notes and beginning the construction of your speech. These hints may help make a sometimes overwhelming process more manageable and perhaps even satisfying. Finally, this chapter explains how to integrate source material into your speech, how to reveal sources during your presentation, and how to document sources.

SEARCHING FOR MATERIAL

Preview You begin building a speech by carefully constructing a thesis statement and purpose. With such a focus in mind, you quickly survey material for relevant sources and formulate the main ideas of the speech, refining them and expanding them as you work.

As we pointed out in Chapter 7, you need to formulate a thesis statement to guide your investigation. The thesis should express your central idea. Often, too, a thesis can foreshadow the main areas that you will develop.[1] For example, an informative speech concerning recent changes in the monitoring of tap water in the United States might have the following thesis: *A newly passed water bill will make our water safer to drink because it increases funding for research, provides upgrades for facilities, and requires stricter certification.* Given this thesis, you will then decide precisely what response you want from your audience and arrive at a specific purpose, such as: *I want my audience to understand why tap water is now safer to drink.*

Once you have chosen a topic and have carefully crafted your specific purpose statement, you are ready to move forward by conducting research. To get started as efficiently as possible, go to the **Online SpeechStudio** and complete the **Research Strategy Worksheet**.

You may need to conduct some initial investigation to establish and/or fine-tune the thesis and purpose. As noted in Chapter 7, some probing may be necessary. An article that presents a general overview of the subject may give you some ideas. You also may need to determine how easily and readily you can get information—factors that may rule out certain choices.

Focus is important because it will direct your search for information, allowing you to discern what is or is not relevant and to know which sources are most appropriate. For example, if you are speaking on a very current issue, such as advances in genetic engineering, you will need to consult sources that provide the latest information, such as journal articles and recent newsmagazine articles. Books will not present the latest information because many of them are written a year or more before their publication date. If you wanted to explore the origins of the study of genetics, however, books might be the most valuable sources.

Finding Relevant Information: A High-Speed Pursuit

Once you have a thesis and a purpose in mind, you can proceed speedily. High speed is especially recommended as you initially search printed and online materials for information. Rather than painstakingly reading through an article that has a promising title, for example, skim it. Don't read every word, but try to detect which ideas and information are valuable. Indexes that provide abstracts can help you determine if a given source may be relevant. You also can evaluate potentially relevant books quickly by scanning the table of contents and then skimming promising chapters and sections. Likewise, you might search the subject index for relevant key terms and skim the pages on which those terms appear. This quick survey will help you locate the most valuable works.

Keep your mind free to focus on the material. Rather than trying to keep a mental record of which sources are valuable and which are not and where you found what information, make quick notes regarding the usefulness of a source and, if it's not apparent in the title, the nature of the content. If you have a printout of potential sources, you can make these quick notations beside each entry and cross out any useless ones. Once you have identified which sources are valuable, you can extract information and ideas from those sources.

Beginning Your Investigation

- To focus your investigation, identify your thesis and specific purpose early.
- Use the thesis to help yourself formulate ideas.
- Use the thesis to help as you discern valuable sources and important information.

THE CREATIVE ENTERPRISE OF BUILDING A SPEECH

Preview As you compile material for a speech, you can proceed most productively if you establish a method for gathering, recording, and organizing material through the use of note cards.

As you prepare yourself to speak, you gradually compile information from a variety of sources. Your speech consists of information and ideas arranged into a coherent form and made more understandable and appealing through good style and appropriate word choice. Your mind will operate on all these levels as you sift through material that may or may not make it into your final speech.

From the moment you begin contemplating your topic, you begin formulating ideas for your speech on the basis of what you already know or believe. You begin envisioning what areas you will discuss, what material you will include, what the purpose and thesis of the speech will be, and what might provide an intriguing introduction or a moving conclusion. This is not busywork; you have actually begun the process of writing the speech and should take advantage of these thoughts. You will not want any ideas to escape beyond recall.

While researching your topic, you need to record more than information. You also need to note the idea the information suggests or supports and where it should appear in your speech. Jot down other thoughts that come to you—possible sources to consult, the design of a presentation aid, what might be a good title or a good analogy, and so forth.

This process of preparation is crucial to being able to present an effective message. Perhaps you have encountered a dynamic, outgoing speaker who seemed to have "a way with words." If that speaker strayed aimlessly or did not support his or her points, however, he or she did not present an effective message. The quality of a speech is directly related to the quality of critical thought that goes into its preparation.

The Compilation Process

A good speech is built by **compiling**; it is constructed gradually from a variety of materials. Starting the process early is essential. As already noted, once the topic is identified, it still may take some time to establish a focus. Even without a specific focus, however, your mind sets to work. As you undertake the process, you go through several crucial stages. Let us consider these stages, how they interact with each other, and how vital they are to your success.

Once you have identified your topic, **sensitivity** will begin to work for you. Sensitivity refers to an awareness of relevant materials in your environment

compiling building gradually and carefully from a variety of materials

sensitivity an awareness of relevant materials in your environment and the significance of those materials

Speech preparation should include time for reflection, time to think about the ideas you are developing and time carefully to absorb and sift through the information you gather as you do research. (Mark Richards/PhotoEdit)

that otherwise might pass unnoticed. Not only will you notice items for your speech, but you will notice them more quickly.[2] This phenomenon is akin to the experience of encountering a new word or expression, only to find it later popping up everywhere. Similarly, you will notice information pertaining to your speech suddenly appearing in various places.[3] Once you notice what appears to be relevant material, your mind will take in the information and ideas, adding them to existing ideas.

reflection cognitively processing and testing information and ideas

assimilate to associate new information and ideas with those within your long-term memory

accommodate to build new structures of meaning from information and ideas encountered in your environment

Your mind also needs time for **reflection**—time to think about and evaluate the information, to test ideas, and to begin making sense of all that you've found. You will associate findings with other information and ideas you have encountered, as well as those within your long-term memory, and you will begin to **assimilate** them into your existing thoughts or **accommodate** them into new structures of meaning. Assimilation and accommodation may occur quickly and accurately,[4] or you may have to wait and return to your thoughts later. As cognitive psychologists have noted, when your thinking is "stuck," your mind probably cannot be forced to produce;[5] it probably needs a brief rest. Once you are no longer fixated on the "problem," your mind can operate quietly in the background, making associations and generating new ideas.[6]

When you return to the task after a period of time, you often will find new ideas flowing from your mind and a new, improved understanding of the subject and the goals for the speech. You do not have to be "on task" for these ideas to emerge; they may emerge as flashes of inspired thought while you are barely thinking about it. As cognitive psychologists explain, "The classic example of coming up with great ideas while taking a shower may simply reflect the importance of releasing oneself from fixated retrieval processes."[7] When these flashes appear, jot them down as soon as possible to prevent them from escaping and also to free your mind from the burden of trying to retain them. In this manner, your mind will continue working creatively.

Along with quiet time, you may also benefit from some intensive thinking. Write down whatever pops into your head without stopping to analyze or critique it. Later, after this brainstorming session, you will have something to review and evaluate.[8] In addition to writing thoughts down, you can try to explain or work through something aloud, perhaps in the presence of a friend. You may surprise and impress yourself with what rolls off your tongue. As with other inspirations, you will want to record these as soon as possible.

incorporation determining if and where specific information and ideas belong in a speech

In addition to allowing time for your creative processes to work, you also need to set aside time for **incorporation**. Incorporation involves deciding if and where specific information and ideas belong in the speech and then fitting them in. This process continues as you search for materials, an area to which we now turn.

Productive Note Taking: Drafting as You Do Research

As you gather information and explore the ideas and opinions of others, you seek to determine what is relevant. In doing so, you shift your attention from the particular information and the idea it suggests to the theme and/or purpose of your speech.[9] To keep your information aligned with your theme, you need to take notes methodically.

To maximize efficiency and avoid frustration, establish a system for taking notes and for recording information about the sources. Whether you use a laptop computer, an electronic note pad, or a pen and index cards, you will need to establish a system that allows you to record information and ideas consistently.

Index cards are commonly used to record source information and notes from your reading and interviews, as well as from radio broadcasts you have heard or telecasts you have seen. Devise a format for *source cards* and a format for *note cards,* and stick to it. The format should be comprehensive and allow you to find, at a glance, whatever element you are looking for—whether it is the page number for a quotation, the title of a source, or the publication date. Many people find the following system useful.

For source cards, familiarize yourself with the format of whatever style guide (such as MLA, APA, or *The Chicago Manual of Style*) you will be using and write the source cards so that you will not have to restructure them later as you type your bibliography (see sample entries in Figure 8.6 later in this chapter). You also should assign each source a code. Doing so, as we explain below, will allow you to take notes more efficiently and productively (see Figure 8.1).

Design a consistent format for recording source information. Place the bibliographic information in the central part of the card, the code you assign in the upper left or right corner, and the call number at the bottom of the card if it is material from the library. If you are photocopying an article, make sure all source information appears on the card or photocopy. If it is material from an interview, place the person's address, phone number, email address, and/or fax number there in case you need further contact.

Source cards likely will require less space than note cards. Hence, a three-by-five-inch card should suffice. For note cards, four-by-six-inch index cards should work well, since you will limit each card to a single idea and the information on which that idea is based (see Figure 8.2). To format consistently, record information in the center of the card, and *be sure to place quotation marks around any material that you are recording word for word from the source.* Place the code you have assigned the source and the specific page number or numbers (if it is printed material) in parentheses in a bottom corner. Enter the idea suggested by the information as a heading in the upper right or left corner.

This heading is more than a descriptor; it should relate the information to the goals of your speech. Obviously you have some sense of why the information is valuable. Force yourself to write it down, even if you believe it will be obvious later. Use a concise phrase to articulate the idea. You might often enter the information before writing the idea because you may not have fully determined the meaning and the best wording. Before moving on, articulate the idea, even if it is only an approximation. You can revise it later. The point is

FIGURE 8.1 Sample Source Card

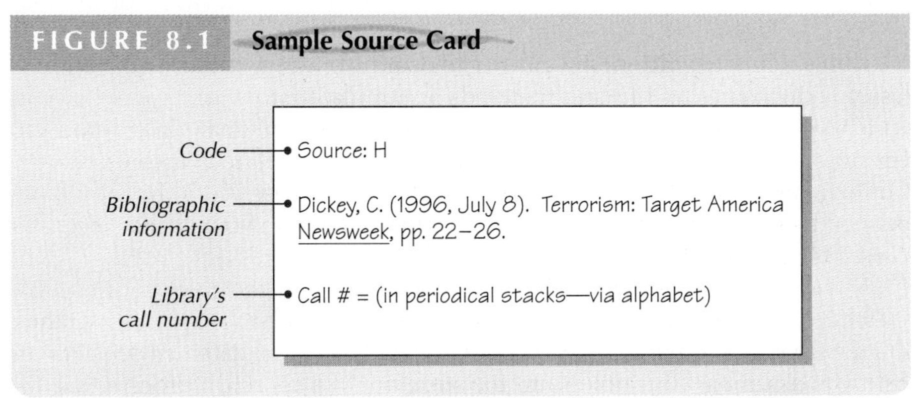

Code
Source: H
Bibliographic information
Dickey, C. (1996, July 8). Terrorism: Target America
Newsweek, pp. 22–26.
Library's call number
Call # = (in periodical stacks—via alphabet)

FIGURE 8.2 Sample Note Cards

Not useful (not processed and not documented):

information about Cryptosporidium

"People with poor immune function may wish to boil their tap water before drinking it, a government report advises. Certain transplant recipients, people infected with HIV, and some cancer patients may be particularly vulnerable to Cryptosporidium, the waterborne parasite responsible for more than 400,000 illnesses and blamed for as many as 100 deaths in Milwaukee two years ago. What about the rest of us? For most Americans, Cryptosporidium poses no danger, according to the report, issued by the Environmental Protection Agency and the Centers for Disease Control and Prevention (CDC)."

Useful (processed and documented):

Code → Source: G

Idea supported by source → Some people should boil their water

Direct quotations indicated → "Transplant recipients, people infected with HIV, and some cancer patients may be particularly vulnerable to Cryptosporidium," a "waterborne parasite" responsible for "more than 400,000 illnesses" and "blamed for as many as 100 deaths in Milwaukee two years ago."
(Boiling the water kills the parasite.)
(The parasite "poses no danger" for "most Americans," according to the EPA and the Centers for Disease Control and Prevention.)

Page number → p. 48

As you begin to do research, you will want to keep accurate and useful records of what you have read. Go to the **Online SpeechStudio** and complete the **Research Overview Worksheet** to help you structure your note taking.

PORTFOLIO 8.1

Taking a Stab at It: Getting Started

Think about the topic you will explore in a forthcoming speech and construct a tentative thesis. Then enter in one column the main areas you will research. In another column, identify where you need to fortify your knowledge and understanding.

that you will want to think about the meaning and relevance of all that you encounter.

Think of how inefficient it would be to operate otherwise. Rather than mindlessly taking notes and letting the cards accumulate into a large pile that you will have to sort out later, begin making sense of your material as you go. Group the cards into categories, noting what related areas emerge. Contemplate the idea in the heading on each card; these ideas that you have penned likely will be a subpoint or a sub-subpoint within your speech, perhaps even a main point.

As you group and arrange the cards, create a rough sketch of your speech. Watch it grow and evolve as you continue to sort through the cards and arrange them with one another and with the thesis and purpose statements. This will help you assemble your notes into the structure of a speech, a process that we will discuss fully in Chapter 10. You will soon begin to see the outline of the speech emerge.

After sorting your materials, you will have new substance to ponder. **Revision** is essential for quality. Upon reexamination, you will evaluate what you have produced, retaining the good, modifying what needs to be rewritten, and deleting faulty or extraneous material. Revision, as composition theorist Jean Wyrick notes, is not an "autopsy";[10] it does not merely occur after you have a complete first draft of your speech. Instead it occurs anytime you reassess what you have done, whether it is a word, or a sentence, or a title. No set formula exists for when and how often this should occur, but it must occur from time to time throughout the drafting process if you expect to produce a quality message. Revision is part of the ongoing process; the key to good preparation is working through multiple drafts.

revision critiquing your own writing and modifying it by adding, deleting, or altering material

As you prepare yourself to speak, there is a constant flow between information and ideas as you check them against each other.[11] You develop and revise your speech as you evaluate content and arrangement, detect and repair weaknesses, recognize the need for more material, try out the best phrasing for an idea, assess the fit with the goals (as well as assess the fitness of the goals), and so on. Preparing the speech, as with any act of composition, involves intense, multidimensional cognitive activity.[12]

Quintilian, an early teacher of speechmaking, emphasized the importance of revision, noting that "correction takes the form of addition, excision, and alteration" and that "erasure" is "as important a function of the pen as actual writing."[13]

✔ KEEP IN MIND 8.2

Beginning the Speech Preparation

- Adequate preparation is crucial to effective speechmaking.
- In compiling a speech, you will work through several creative and critical stages.
- Productive note taking will help you draft your speech.
- Subjecting your work to critical examination and revision is part of the ongoing process.

INVESTIGATING IN THE LIBRARY

Preview Today's library has a wide variety of resources for a speaker seeking information. The library holds extensive collections of books, documents, and periodicals that modern technology makes easily accessible. Librarians and various reference materials can assist you in your quest for information.

Some students find the library's size and layout and the complexities of its holdings overwhelming. But the resources of a library are invaluable to a speaker, and you can learn to use them effectively.

Librarians are one of the most helpful resources the library offers. Librarians do more than loan materials and shelve returned materials. Professional librarians are schooled in the latest information and communication technologies and systems, and they use this knowledge and skill daily. They know the way around their own holdings and resources, but they also know how to locate and retrieve information located in other libraries and information sites. In addition, they work cooperatively with other librarians in the academic, public, and private sectors to classify and organize materials and databases so that information is well managed and easily retrieved via a common interface. Scholars, researchers, practitioners, students, citizens, government officials,

Through the library, speakers have vast amounts of printed material and electronic resources available to them as they prepare to speak. (Rafael Macial/ PhotoResearchers)

manufacturers, and others rely on librarians. Never hesitate to ask a librarian for help.

Today's library is more than a repository of books, documents, and periodicals. Its walls are but an illusion. Libraries are internetworked with other libraries and information sites via the Internet, and a Library's staff of professionals can help you locate and retrieve the latest information about your topic.

catalog a library's written inventory of its holdings, often available in written and electronic form

Despite its own vastness via its connection to other libraries and information sites, the library has become increasingly user-friendly and efficient. For example, the library's **catalog** of holdings is likely available in electronic form, accessible from computer terminals located throughout the library. The user can simply search the holdings file for a particular author or title or for works on a particular subject. The user can locate all this from a keyboard and often can even conduct searches from home via a modem. Rather than writing down each promising entry, the user can print it out. In addition, the same server that contains the catalog may also feature various reference materials, such as encyclopedias and databases, as well as indexes to periodicals. These indexes, along with others available online or on CD-ROM, simplify your search for information and allow you to print out your findings.

Borrowing books and other materials also has been made much easier. Now most libraries bar-code each book and issue each user an identification card that likewise can be scanned into an electronic record. As an added convenience, this information is recorded in the catalog of holdings so that users can see whether the item is available or on loan.

The Library's Infrastructure and Holdings

The holdings at your campus library probably range from the general to the specific, including books, periodicals, newspapers, and reference materials. Some are available in print form, and others exist on microfilm or microfiche that you can photocopy. An increasing number of materials are available as electronic files that you can save to a floppy disk, print out, or export to your email address.

The books available in your library are cataloged by author, title, and subject/keyword. If you discover one relevant book, scan the spines of neighboring books for titles that seem promising. Even if the book is on loan, you may wish to visit its location on the shelves to scout the area. In addition, be mindful that most collections are shelved according to Library of Congress (LOC) subject headings. Hence you can also use LOC subject headings to determine where relevant books would be located. Simply consult the *Library of Congress Classification Outline*, available in the reference area. Once you find a book you wish to borrow, go to the **circulation desk**, where a librarian will oversee the loan.

circulation desk the department within a library that oversees the loan and return of materials

Your library also subscribes to numerous **periodicals**, which include popular magazines and newsmagazines, academic journals and trade journals. As noted earlier, indexes and abstract services are an efficient way to find relevant articles. Various specialized indexes and abstract services exist in a variety of media. If an electronic form is available, you will want to use it. Rather than having to search year by year in a printed index, you can use an electronic index to search a span of ten years or so simultaneously, and you can often combine two or more terms or concepts to focus the search. For example, if you were researching drug use among teens, you could enter "teenagers" and "drugs." The returned list would consist of works that featured both terms (see Figure 8.3). In addition, the electronic medium allows

periodicals journals, magazines, and similar printed materials that are published at regular, set intervals

FIGURE 8.3 A Sample Search

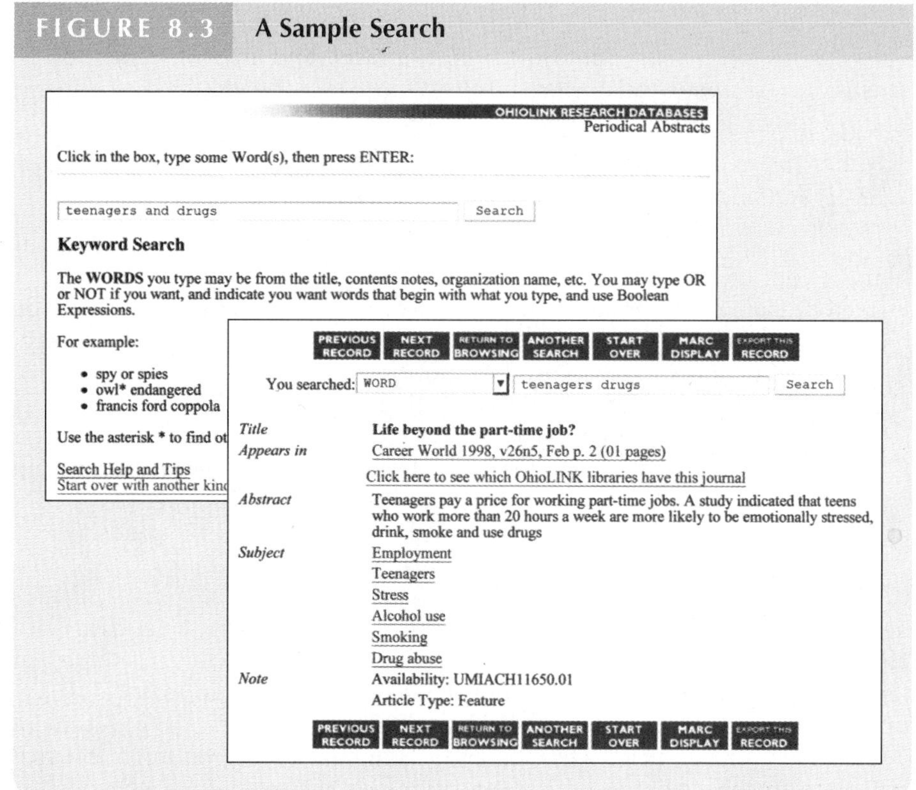

you to print out anything that appears relevant. Some of these databases list only titles, whereas others may provide an abstract of the article, and still others may provide the full text.

reference librarian a librarian who works in the reference area and assists with locating and retrieving information

A **reference librarian** can help you select and use the appropriate index for your search. Help sheets also should be available, as well as onscreen help. Once you have found a promising work, consult the library's catalog of holdings to determine availability, location, and form.

Your library likely subscribes to various local, regional, and national newspapers. Determine your library's holdings and how best to search for articles. You may need to use the newspapers' respective indexes, or your library might have an index that covers more than one newspaper, such as the *National Newspaper Index,* which indexes articles from the *Christian Science Monitor, Los Angeles Times, New York Times, Wall Street Journal,* and *Washington Post.*

Your library also has a number of reference materials, such as various indexes and abstract services (described previously), bibliographies, atlases, encyclopedias, almanacs, dictionaries, and other similar works. Reference librarians can help you determine which resources might be useful and can help you use a particular resource.

Your library likely has numerous government documents. Most college and university libraries are a depository for publications by the U.S. government. Topics range from the American antelope to zero tillage, and much of the literature presents census data and other statistical information. In addition, you may find literature produced by states, counties, and even some cities. And you may find publications from foreign governments and international organizations. The library's catalog might list recently acquired holdings, but you may need to use indexes in the Government Documents area, especially for older materials. In addition, you may find the indexes there more current and helpful, especially the *American Statistics Index* and the *Monthly Catalog of U.S. Government Publications.* Some indexes, abstracts, and information, such as census data, may be available on CD-ROM.

Using the Library

Once you understand the way libraries are set up generally and the particular setup of your library, you can proceed with minimal assistance. Self-service help is often available at information kiosks that display the floor plan and provide brochures that will brief you on holdings, resources, services, and how to proceed.

If you are having difficulty locating information and need professional assistance, visit the reference desk; a reference librarian can help. The librarian's role is to help you locate information, not to do your work for you. For example, it is not the librarian's job to decide your topic and focus. The librarian can help you only if you know what you are looking for. Reference librarians often work on weekdays and may or may not be available at night or on weekends.

If professional help is not available, consult *The American Library Association Guide to Information Access: A Complete Research Handbook and Directory.*[14] This helpful book, located in the reference area of your library, provides assistance on how to research thirty-one general topic areas. Each section lists relevant Library of Congress subject headings and relevant reference materials, electronic sources of information, scholarly and popular periodicals, government publications, and agencies, associations, and organizations you might contact, as well as any specialized libraries that might exist.

PORTFOLIO 8.2

Going Electronic

Glance over the computerized indexes listed and described in Figure 8.4. Which index or indexes appear best suited to the topic of your next speech? What keywords should you use to search the database?

Some campuses, especially large universities, have specialized libraries for particular disciplines or special collections. For example, the school of business may have its own library. In addition, if your campus has the papers of a famous writer or political figure or a famous person's personal library, it likely will house these collections separately.

The computerized indexes listed in Figure 8.4 may prove valuable if you are researching one of the respective subject areas. Before asking your reference librarian about the availability of one of these indexes, describe the information you need and ask what indexes or databases might best assist you. Your library may have resources superior to these listed in Figure 8.4.

Mastering the library's resources can take a little time and effort, but it will be one of the most important skills you can learn, not only for doing research for a speech but also for your entire college career and beyond. As you get started, you may encounter some stumbling blocks. The trouble-shooting guide that follows addresses four of the most common problems faced by beginning researchers.

KEEP IN MIND 8.3

Library resources include

- reference librarians.
- newspapers.
- reference materials.
- government documents.

Efficient use of the library is promoted by

- familiarizing yourself with the basic setup of your library.
- consulting librarians when you need help.
- learning to use computer indexes.

A Trouble-Shooting Guide

Help! I don't know how to start!

If you do not know where to begin, try the reference desk, help sheets, or the *ALA Guide to Information Access* (in the reference collection).

Help! What I need is gone!

If an item you need is not in the library's collection or is missing (for example, a lost book or an article cut from a periodical), you can obtain it via interlibrary loan. Fill out a request form at the interlibrary loan office, and the staff there will identify a library that has the material and obtain it from that library. If it's a book, the library will ship it. If it's an article from a periodical, the library will photocopy it and send or fax the pages, sometimes charging a small fee to recover its costs.

Help! Someone has checked out a book that I need!

If the electronic catalog indicates that a book is on loan, you can have it recalled. The person who has the book will be notified and told to return the item. How soon you will be able to get it depends on the time allotted for return, how quickly it is returned, and how quickly you can be notified.

Help! The item I need is not on the shelf!

Another person may be using the item, or it may be waiting to be reshelved. Ask a librarian at the circulation desk how to proceed. Most libraries will allow you to request a search for an item, and they will contact you when the item is located or determined to be lost or missing.

FIGURE 8.4 Examples of Computerized Indexes

Agriculture:

AGRICOLA (1970 to present) indexes agricultural literature from around the world, including journal articles, books, government documents, reports, proceedings, publications from state extension services and experiment stations, and FAO documents.

Business:

Wilson Business Abstracts (1982 to present) indexes and abstracts leading business magazines and trade and academic journals, as well as relevant articles in the Wall Street Journal and the New York Times.

Education:

ERIC (Educational Resources Information Center) (1966 to present) indexes education-related publications as well as unpublished materials, such as conference papers, lesson plans, and bibliographies. It provides an abstract for most items indexed.

Engineering:

COMPENDEX*PLUS (1987 to present) indexes literature pertaining to engineering and technology from around the world. It indexes nearly 5,000 journals as well as government publications, conference papers and proceedings, and books.

INSPEC (1969 to present) indexes and provides abstracts to literature from around the world regarding physics, electronics, electrical engineering, computer science, and information technology. It covers approximately 4,200 journals, as well as books, reports, dissertations, and conference papers and proceedings.

See also Science Citation Index, described below under "Science."

Environment:

Environmental Periodicals Bibliography (1972 to present) provides titles to articles in over 300 periodicals devoted to environmental topics.

Biological and Agricultural Index (1983 to present) indexes journals from the fields of ecology, environmental science, and forestry.

Applied Science and Technology Index (1983 to present) indexes journals from such fields as environmental engineering and waste management.

Health:

Consumer Health and Nutrition Index (1984 to present) indexes articles from journals, magazines, and newspapers.

INVESTIGATING ON THE COMPUTER

Preview Computer technology can help you obtain information and assistance. The Internet has become increasingly rich with information and easy to navigate. Email also can prove valuable in many ways.

Personal and networked computers have become commonplace. Your campus likely has a local network of computers with a central server that is tied into the Internet. As a result, you can move around locally and can travel into cyberspace as well. All you need is an account and a password to log on to the campus system, and then you can use your access in many productive ways. Let us examine some of the possibilities.

Internet a global network of computers that enables the widespread and efficient exchange of textual, visual, and audio information

Using the Net

Net, abbreviated from ***Internet***, refers to the internetworking of computers from around the world. Advances in software and hardware and a common interface

FIGURE 8.4 (Continued)

History:

America: History and Life (1982 to present) indexes and provides abstracts of periodical articles about the history and culture of the United States and Canada.

Historical Abstracts (1982 to present) indexes and provides abstracts of periodical articles pertaining to world history except for that of the United States and Canada. It also includes some recent books.

Literature, Folklore, Language, and Linguistics:

MLA International Bibliography (1981 to present) indexes and describes journal articles, books, and dissertations from around the world pertaining to critical works of literature and research in the areas of language and linguistics.

Politics, Government, and Economics:

PAIS (Public Affairs Information Service) International (1972 to present) indexes articles, books, pamphlets, and government publications from around the world.

Popular Topics:

Periodicals Abstracts (1988 to present) indexes articles in popular magazines.

Psychology:

PsycLIT (1974 to present) indexes and provides abstracts for articles in psychology journals from around the world.

Science:

Science Citation Index (1986 to present) indexes and provides abstracts to over 600,000 articles, reviews, and other published material in journals devoted to science and engineering.

Sociology:

Sociofile (1974 to present) indexes and provides abstracts for articles, books, conference papers, and dissertations from around the world.

Technology:

See COMPENDEX*PLUS and INSPEC, described above under "Engineering."

allow people from around the globe to communicate and to exchange information almost instantaneously. As a result, the Internet has grown exponentially. New sites appear every minute, adding to the millions already there. Organizations, companies, corporations, agencies, schools, colleges, universities, libraries, repositories, interest groups, and politicians have scrambled to establish a presence.[15] On the Internet, you can encounter information and opinions on any topic imaginable, not only in textual form but also as images, sound, and video.

Locating and Retrieving Information on the World Wide Web

The creation of the **World Wide Web** and advanced yet easy-to-use software (such as Netscape and Internet Explorer) have tamed the wilds of cyberspace. Web-browsing software that acts like the Macintosh or Windows operating system allows users to peruse the entire Internet and locate and retrieve information with ease.

World Wide Web an area of the Internet where information is organized and linked via hypertext and hypermedia

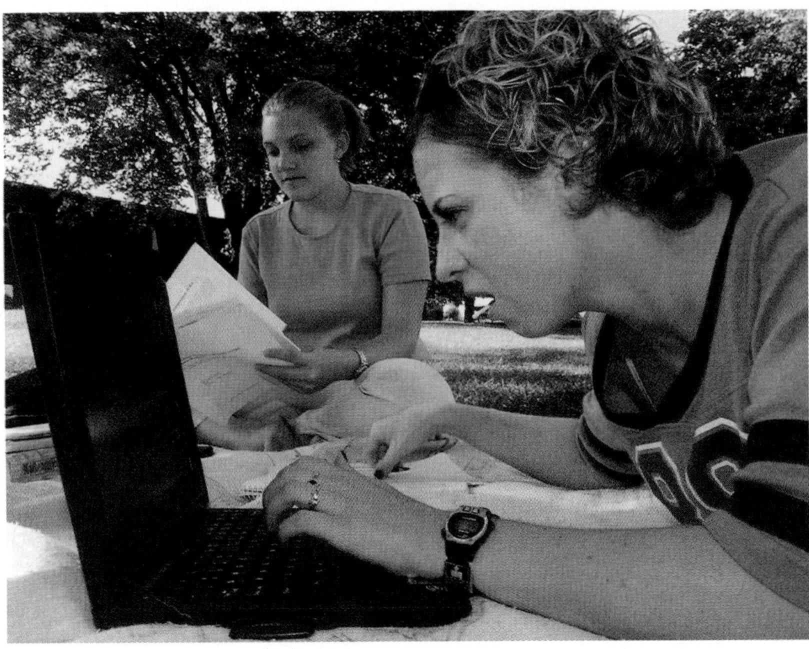

The World Wide Web can provide great quantities of information useful to a speaker, but these sources have to be approached with caution to be sure that they are reliable and accurate. (Associated Press AP)

To locate information for your speech topic, you can proceed in various ways. You might locate information by conducting a keyword search and examining links, exploring various links between pages and sites, or traveling directly to a page for which you know the address. Let's explore each of these options.

If you are starting from scratch, with no information or leads about particular sites, you could begin with a search—usually an option on the menu bar. You may choose among several popular web **databases**, such as Lycos or Yahoo! To initiate a search, simply enter in the designated bar a keyword or two that best describes your subject. For example, if you are interested in ozone depletion, you could enter "ozone layer hole." Once you have designated the term or terms, the **search engine** will go to work, scanning an index of sites that have titles or abundant information that matches the keyword(s) you have supplied. In a matter of seconds, it will return a listing of web pages. Once the list appears, simply scroll through it and click on any entries that appear promising, and you will travel directly to that site or file. To return to the list, simply click on the appropriate menu button to take you back until you return to the list.

database categorized groupings of data stored in electronic form on a computer or on a computer disk, such as a CD-ROM

search engine a software robot you can use to search the Web via keywords

To conduct an effective search on the Web, you need to be aware of a few factors. First, search engines often provide a superficial view of what might be available and often return an incomplete listing of their findings. Each engine uses different criteria for a search and will return information based on those criteria. As a result, each searching mechanism will generate a somewhat or completely different list. If you do not find what you want with one engine, launch a search from another database (such as those listed in Table 8.1). For best results, use several different search engines. You also might vary the keywords, using the same engine to search a new term or terms. Keep in mind that merely retrying the same descriptors with the same engine will not yield new results, at least not as long as the sites or files that are available remain the same. Sites or pages that disappear in the days to come obviously will not make the list again, and new sites or files that appear may better match the criteria used by the engine and thus bump off ones that appeared previously. This manner of searching by keyword(s) can be effective; simply proceed by trial and error.

Rather than explore by keyword, you might find it more helpful to explore by subject heading. Most databases offer this alternative, providing shortcuts to information sites for various common subjects. For example, among its many subjects, Yahoo! includes "Health," "News & Media," and "Government." If you wanted to know about a particular piece of legislation, you could click on "Government," and with a couple of more clicks, you would have that information. If you wanted to examine news coverage around the country about a particular news item, Yahoo!'s "News & Media" would provide direct links to major media outlets.

Yahoo! is not the only database providing access to current news information. Most databases offer news, and many are affiliated with a particular news organization. For example, MSN.com offers MSNBC News, GO.com features ABC News, and iWon provides news from CBS and Reuters.

In addition to searching databases by keyword or subject, you can search for relevant information via links that you encounter. Links are a central component of the Web. Web space is governed by hypertext transfer protocol (HTTP), and documents on the Web are written in hypertext markup language (HTML). Within a web page the user will find **hyperlinks**—highlighted words and phrases that, with a click of the mouse, establish a link to another file or site. A page also may contain **hypermedia**, graphical buttons or image maps that contain links to other files and other sites. Because of this format, users often read a little from a file and then click their way on to another locale. Authors of web pages understand this form and design their sites accordingly.

Links may lead you to sites that prove fruitful. Keep in mind that every file has its own unique **Uniform Resource Locator (URL)**, which will enable you to return directly to that particular file without having to retrace your steps and travel through various layers. You can simply use the Open Location command and enter the URL. To maximize efficiency, most software will allow you to record a URL with a simple command, often called a bookmark or a favorite. You will want to establish a bookmark (via the menu bar) for each file that is valuable or jot down the URL that is indicated on the Show Location line. Keep in mind that you will need the URL for your bibliography of sources if you use material from that site.

hyperlinks highlighted words and phrases in a web page that designate a link to other relevant material on the Web

hypermedia graphical buttons or image maps that designate a link to other relevant material on the Web

Uniform Resource Locator the specific address of a web site that allows a user to travel directly to that site

TABLE 8.1 Common Search Engines/Databases

AltaVista.com	*HotBot.com*
AskJeeves.com	*iWon.com*
Dogpile.com	*Looksmart.com*
Excite.com	*Lycos.com*
GO.com	*MSN.com*
GoTo.com	*NorthernLight.com*
Google.com	*Yahoo!.com*

PORTFOLIO 8.3

An Effective Launch

Look over the plan for your forthcoming speech and the areas you intend to address. Should you explore the Internet? If you already know the Uniform Resource Locator (URL) for a relevant organization's web pages, travel directly to it. Also launch a search using keywords or examine the subject areas provided by the search agency. In any case, explore the various links you encounter and bookmark the best ones.

The URL provides another way to investigate your topic. If you obtain the URL of a particular web site that likely will have information you can use, travel directly there as described above: use the Open Location command and enter the URL. For example, if you wish to know the latest figures for the incidence of diabetes, you could visit the web pages of the American Diabetes Association, located at www.diabetes.org. In addition to the information that they provide, the association's web pages can help you locate information about various local incidence rates because they feature links to the web pages of agencies and organizations in states throughout the country.

Most URLs are kept simple so that users can remember the address or be able to guess what it might be. The web page of the American Cancer Society, for instance, is www.cancer.org (see Figure 8.5). To guess more accurately, be aware that the last three letters designate the organization's kind of Internet membership. These codes include the following:

.com (commercial companies)
.edu (educational institutions)
.gov (government agencies)
.mil (military institutions)
.org (nonprofit organizations)

Advances in software not only assist you in locating information, but they also simplify its retrieval and use. Since the information is sent to your com-

FIGURE 8.5 Sample Web Page

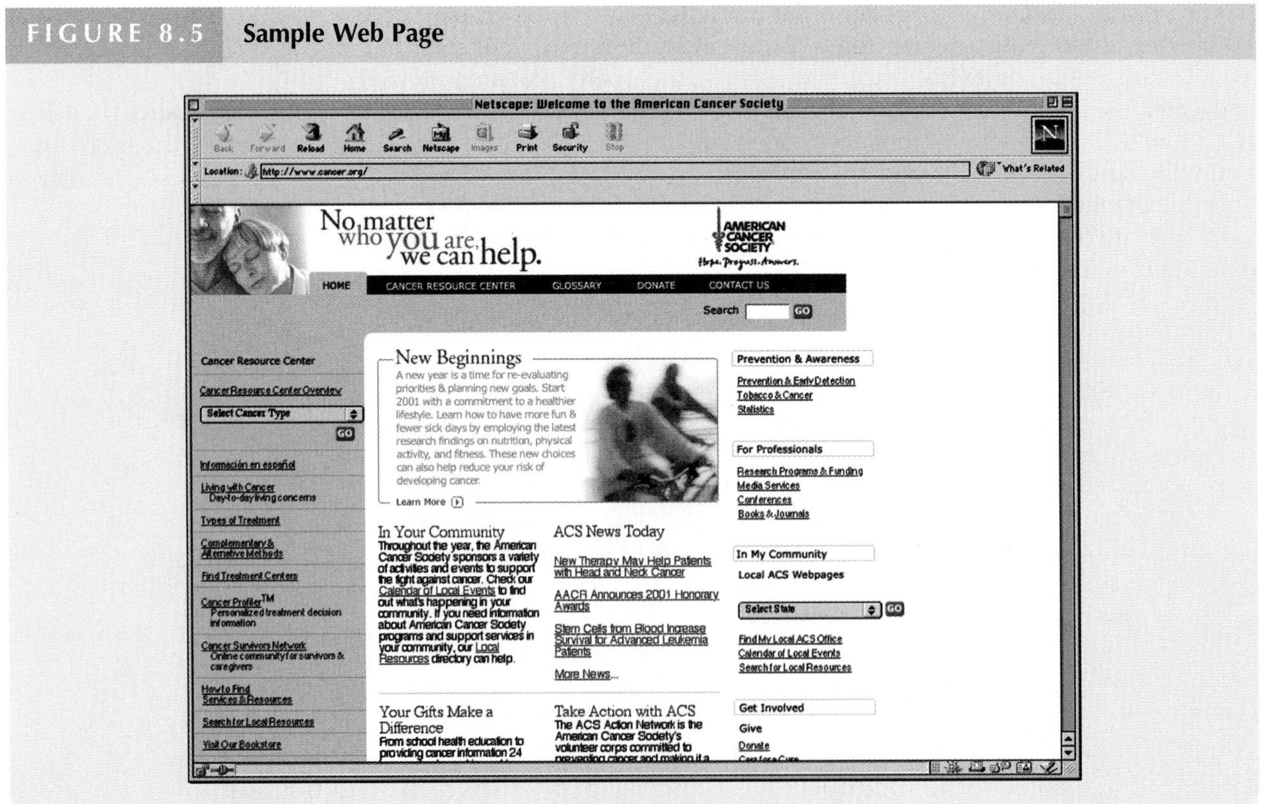

puter and stored on your clipboard, you may have the option to save it to a file on the hard drive or on a floppy disk, cut and paste it into a word-processing document, or send it to your electronic mailbox. Options and procedures will vary, but the computer support personnel at your school should be able to advise and instruct you. If you are using a computer in a lab, you will want to save permanently not to the hard drive but to your own floppy disk, or you can email the file to your electronic mailbox. Before you do so, be sure to evaluate the material, as described in the next section.

Evaluating Internet Resources

Michael Gorman, writing in the *Library Journal,* compared the Internet to a library where all the books have been stripped of their indexes and their pages ripped out and scattered. "The net," he wrote, "is even worse than a vandalized library because thousands of additional unorganized fragments are added daily by the myriad of cranks, sages, and persons with time on their hands who launch their unfiltered messages into cyberspace."[16]

Gorman's observation ought to serve as a warning to everyone who uses the Net to gather information. Anybody with a minimum of skill can set up shop on the Net at very little cost. What that person chooses to put on the site is not subject to review for accuracy or fairness. It is easy to anticipate bias in some cases: A political candidate's own web page obviously will be designed to promote that candidate, and web pages put up by opposing groups just as obviously will try to make the candidate look bad. Hate groups are often so blatant in their attacks on minority racial or religious groups that their prejudices can readily be identified. But aside from examples of blatant bias, it is not always easy to tell how reliable a web source is.

The basic rule to keep in mind is this: *Don't take anything you find on the Net at face value.* This means that you have to evaluate the material you get from the Net. How do you go about doing this? Here are four critical questions that you should answer before you use information taken from the Net in a speech.

1. **What is the source of this information?** Think of this: You would certainly dismiss a story coming from a supermarket tabloid that told you aliens had landed in Arizona. What is more, you would be suspicious of any information you got from that tabloid, even if the information was more plausible than the alien story. Supermarket tabloids are simply not credible, and most educated people will dismiss information that comes from them unless it is confirmed by a reputable source. The trouble is, on the Net we don't have as clear an understanding of the source. So you have to get beneath the surface. Look carefully to see if a group sponsors the page. What do you know about that group? Don't be fooled by the name. You will know what to expect right away if you see that the Ku Klux Klan, the Democratic National Committee, or the National Rifle Association is the publisher of the page. But the name does not always tell you much. Take, for example, a group publishing a web page in the summer of 2000: Citizens for Better Medicare. That name suggests an admirable goal. But you wouldn't find on the web page the fact that this group was formed by the global drug industry to lobby against the Clinton administration's proposal to provide drug coverage for the elderly.[17] If the publishing group is not readily identifiable, try to

determine who the author is. Is any author named? If so, is that person a relevant authority?

2. **What is the purpose of the page?** Some web pages are designed to give information, while others advocate certain policies or ideologies. It is not always easy to tell the difference, since advocacy groups frequently try to give the impression that they are just giving you the facts. The purpose of the page is sometimes given as a mission statement or a "who we are" link. The purpose is closely associated with the source, of course. The National Library Association, for example, attempts to give information on how best to use Internet resources, and nonpartisan government agencies produce statistical information on a wide variety of subjects. Other groups attempt to go beyond just presenting information and hope to persuade users. This does not mean, of course, that information gained from advocacy groups is not useful or accurate. For example, the American Association of Retired Persons (AARP) tries to influence public policy affecting older Americans, and consumer groups advocate policies that will affect the buying public. These are not bad things. But whoever uses the information provided needs to be aware that those who produce it have an agenda, and it is a wise and ethical consumer who tries to understand what that agenda is.

3. **How well balanced and accurate is the content?** If you can't be sure of the biases of those providing the information, careful study of the page will give you substantial clues. Are a variety of viewpoints acknowledged? Are the claims made supported by good arguments and credible evidence? What about the links to other pages—does this page send you to other credible sites? Is there any information presented that you know to be inaccurate or misleading? You should judge a web site in the same way that you would judge any attempt to persuade you to do or believe anything. In the chapters that follow, we'll be very specific about what makes a sound argument, how to detect fallacies, and what kind of evidence is both effective and ethical. You will want to apply all of this information to material you find on the Net. But for now, at least ask yourself if the content that is presented seems fair, and if it is convincing to you, why and how it is.

4. **How current is the site?** Check to see how recently the site was updated. If a site is maintained regularly, the information is more likely to be up-to-date. Regular updating also indicates that the site is still active. A page that has been abandoned for a long time should be viewed with suspicion.

If it turns out that you can't answer most of these questions after close inspection of the site, that in itself should raise doubts in your mind about the site's credibility. Be skeptical of a source that doesn't identify itself or its purpose, that makes unsubstantiated claims, or that is out-of-date. The thing to remember is that the Internet is not a "one-stop" research source. Information should be cross-checked with other sources. By all means, use the Internet in your research, but don't use it thoughtlessly and don't use it exclusively.

CONNECTING TO THE NET

Go to a site that is relevant to the topic of a speech you are planning to give. Ask the questions listed in the text. How well does this site measure up? In what ways and how well does it answer or fail to answer the questions?

To learn more about the complications of evaluating web sites, go to **http://college.hmco.com/communication/andrews/public_speaking/2e/students/** and click on *Connecting to the Net.* From there, follow the link to Evaluating Internet Resources.

Using Email

email electronic messages you can send and receive via a local network or the Internet

Electronic mail, or **email**, has become extremely popular because of its efficiency and versatility. Once you have a computer access account at your school, you will have an electronic mailbox and address. In a matter of minutes, support personnel can teach you how to send messages and how to open and manage the messages you receive.

To use email effectively, you will need to be aware of standard practices. For example, people expect users to check their mail frequently and to respond promptly. Further, messages should be kept short, simple, and to the point. Since email is used for its quickness, receivers generally do not want to be burdened by lengthy messages or by inquiries that require elaborate responses.

Although email can enable you to communicate quickly and efficiently, you may experience some disruptions from time to time. For example, the system's server might crash or undergo maintenance, making the system unavailable for use. Another problem you may experience is heavy traffic during peak hours of use, making it difficult to log on, and if you do succeed, the system may run at an annoyingly slow pace. For the most part, though, email is a reliable and useful means to communicate and to obtain information.

As a student working on a speech, email can assist you in a number of ways. For example, you may want to consult your instructor about the focus of your speech, possibilities for research, or some other matter related to the speech. You also can send and receive messages beyond the local network. You might, for example, use email to request information from a relevant person or agency that may be able to email you a response. For instance, email enabled a student who was researching new antidepressant medications to consult experts at the University of Maryland's School of Medicine. The student went to the school's web pages, clicked on a button that allowed for inquiries, and composed a brief question. Within a few hours, he had a very helpful reply. Be mindful, though, that not all sites that allow inquiries are as prompt or as helpful. You should continue your search for information elsewhere while awaiting a reply. Also, before making any request for information, be sure that it is not information you can find with relative ease in printed material or on that agency's web pages.

An electronic mailing may be appropriate for requesting and arranging an interview by phone or face to face. In addition, it can allow you to acquaint the person with the questions you wish to ask. You may even find that an email conversation will suffice if it yields all the information you had hoped to gather in an interview.

Email presents other advantages as well. A message can be printed out if you need a hard copy. It also can be saved to a file for later reference and can even be pasted into a word-processing document. This versatility, coupled with its speed, has prompted more and more people to use email as a communication medium.

Other Means of Connecting, Locating, and Retrieving

Two other principal online tools that users may encounter are telnet and FTP. Usually these operate in the background of a web browser, but you may find yourself using them directly to locate and retrieve information as you research your topic. Telnet allows a user to connect with a remote host and view the information available there. For example, your library's system may allow

KEEP IN MIND 8.4

Using the Internet

- The local computer network and the Internet can prove extremely valuable for the speaker.
- The World Wide Web and its browser software have simplified cyberspace, making it easier to locate and retrieve information.
- Users can evaluate a site by asking questions about the source, purpose, and currency of the site and the balance and accuracy of its content.
- Email is a great way to communicate and to store retrieved information.

you to telnet to the catalogs of other libraries that have their catalogs online. Similarly, your campus system may allow you to telnet to various databases, such as the Educational Resources Information Center (ERIC). Availability will vary from school to school. Once you arrive at a telnet host, it will likely present text files that are organized by directories and subdirectories. Simply work your way through the menus, exploring what is available. Rather than having the luxury of a bookmark utility, you will need to keep track of how you proceed, recording the choices you make as you explore the various menus. If you wish to explore other remote sites, your local system might have Hytelnet, which provides a subject directory of various telnet sites and can help you connect with the host.

FTP (file transfer protocol) is a method of retrieving a file from a distant host that, like telnet, usually operates unnoticed in the background of your browsing software. Sometimes, though, you may need to use FTP to retrieve a file from a remote site. Whereas the process used to require substantial know-how, it has been simplified by various user-friendly programs. Often a file is compressed for transfer. If so, you will need to decompress it before you will be able to use it. Again, various programs exist that simplify the process. Simply contact your local computer support personnel for assistance.

INVESTIGATING THROUGH INTERVIEWS

Preview Interviewing can provide valuable information for your speech. Determine if persons with expert knowledge or direct experience are available to help you. Prepare carefully by gathering the information you need and generating good questions. The interview must be conducted professionally and the information gathered efficiently, and it must be followed up appropriately.

One of the most useful resources you can tap is people who have personal experience with your topic or who have studied the topic and are recognized experts. For example, a student at San Jose State University in San Jose, California, investigated gang activity in schools. He interviewed students, counselors, and gang members at a local high school to determine the number of active gangs, the approximate number of members, the reasons people join gangs, and gang rituals, activities, and rules. He combined this information with that found in newsmagazines, newspapers, and broadcasts to provide a good overview of teenage gangs. A student at Southwest Missouri State University investigated crime on campus and interviewed two campus police officers. One acquainted her with the various types of theft and told her which were the most common on campus; another discussed violent crime. She discovered, among other things, that opportunity theft was the most common type of crime on campus and that the campus was, by and large, a safe environment because of the security measures taken by the university and increased awareness among the community. A student at Texas A&M University decided to explore alternatives to chemical pesticides and was able to contact a professor on campus who had studied the introduction of natural predators as a means of pest control. The professor functioned as a source and critiqued her working bibliography, suggesting additional sources she should consult.

As these examples illustrate, interviews with laypeople and experts can furnish material that relates your speech to the local community and can provide specific examples of human interest.

Preparing the Interview

Determine whom you should interview. Perhaps you need to consult an expert who knows the latest developments, literature, history, trends, and issues related to your topic. Or perhaps you need a layperson who has direct experience and can provide insight or recount real-life experiences. Maybe you would benefit from interviewing both types. Once you know what type of person can best help you, you can begin searching for a person who meets that profile.

We are quick to rely on experts. After all, they are the ones with expertise.[18] But you should also consider who else might help you explore your topic. For example, the student speaking about pest control through natural predators found that nonexperts also could provide information and insights. In her speech, she used as an example comments made by a woman who lived in the country. The woman told her that a couple of chicken snakes lived under her house, but that didn't bother her because she had not seen any mice since the snakes took up residence. Similarly, another person reported that the rat problem in his barn no longer existed since Barney, a tomcat, showed up. Another student, speaking on welfare reform, found that he did not have to limit interviews to experts. Local law enforcement officials, for example, claimed that when monthly welfare checks arrived, disturbances and violent crime escalated. The police found that recipients who liked to party then had the money to do so, and often those parties got out of hand. Local police also maintained that children's needs often were not met because money was spent on alcohol rather than on the food, clothing, and medicine for which it was intended. These officials argued that assistance should be provided in some form other than cash.

As soon as you have determined whom you might interview, make an appointment. Obviously you will want to contact the person early to improve your chances of getting an appointment when you need it. Acquaint the person with your project and goals. Explain who you are, what you are doing, and how you believe he or she may be able to help you. If the person feels unable to provide the assistance you need, he or she might refer you to someone who can.

When making the initial contact, you may have to work through a secretary or other gatekeeper to schedule an appointment. Establish a friendly, cordial tone and respectfully explain your goals and needs and how you believe the person with whom you wish to speak can help you. Once an appointment is set, you may request a fax number, mailing address, or email address so you can provide a set of questions in advance of the interview. The person will then have time to consider her or his responses and thus provide better information.

To devise a set of questions, consider why you think the person can assist you. For example, the student who interviewed campus police officers knew

PORTFOLIO 8.4

Who? What?

Look over the plan for your forthcoming speech and the areas you intend to address. Should you interview someone? If so, whom? What helpful information and insights might he or she provide? List the possibilities.

that the police could provide statistical information about crime on campus, so she raised these questions:

- What is the most prevalent type of crime on our campus?
- How likely is it that an individual will be the victim of a violent crime?

She also realized that police officers could provide expert testimony, so she asked the following:

- Should we feel safe on campus?
- What precautions might we take to protect ourselves and our property?

As you can see from these sample questions, you should design some questions that ask for a simple "yes" or "no" response or a brief explanation and other questions that encourage a longer response, where the person might provide his or her opinion and elaborate on why he or she holds that opinion. The first type of questions, which limit the response, are called **closed questions**. Questions that encourage elaboration are called **open-ended questions**.

closed questions questions that encourage a limited response

open-ended questions questions that encourage a detailed response and elaboration

In devising questions, you should have a general knowledge of the topic and know what types of information and materials are available. In other words, you should have surveyed some general readings on the subject or otherwise have acquainted yourself with the topic. Doing so will help you construct better questions and avoid wasting the interviewee's time asking for information that you could easily locate at the library or via the Internet. Consider how the interviewee might respond if it were obvious that you had not done your homework. For example, the student researching alternative means of pest control was familiar with what constituted those basic means, such as genetics and the breeding of insect-resistant varieties, mixed crop stands that pair desirable with undesirable foliage, and the use of natural predators. If she were to have asked the professor to identify the various alternatives, he likely would have wondered why she had not done some initial research. Instead her questions to him included the following:

- How long have you studied natural predators?
- What types of predators have you researched, and what have been the results?
- How effective are natural predators compared to other means of pest control?
- What do we need to understand about natural predators that is commonly misunderstood?
- How widespread is the current use of natural predators in agriculture? In gardening?
- How extensively do you predict that natural predators will be used by farmers? By gardeners?

Note how the student combined closed and open-ended questions, allowing the interviewee some freedom and latitude. In addition, note how the student kept the questions simple and to the point. You should also note that if you are addressing a controversial topic, you will want to keep all questions nonthreatening and nonconfrontational. For example, the student who interviewed individual gang members was careful when inquiring about whether the gang had committed any crimes.

Conducting the Interview

FRAME OF REFERENCE

To get useful information from an interview, the interviewer must be prepared. Having some background knowledge and a set of well-thought-out questions will help you conduct a successful interview.

To produce the best results, you need to be taken seriously, and you can encourage such perceptions by being professional. Things such as dressing appropriately and arriving on time will have an impact on the impression you make. You should begin the interview by thanking the person and otherwise establishing a cordial and respectful tone. After the brief "thank you," quickly get down to business by reminding the person of the nature of your project and how you believe she or he can help you. For example, when interviewing the entomology professor, the student reminded him that she was researching the subject for a class in public speaking, that she was preparing speeches that explored alternative means of pest control, and that she wanted to include the latest developments in the use of natural predators. Once she had clarified her goals as a speaker, the professor understood how he could help her. He saw the amount and depth of information she needed—enough for a quick overview for part of an informative speech plus persuasive materials for a follow-up persuasive speech.

During the interview, you might want to mention some of the sources that you have consulted. Doing so not only indicates that you have done your homework, but it also indicates what you already know and do not know. Also, the interviewee may be able to critique your sources and point out additional works you should consult. Within your questions, you might even have the person react to something you have read. For example, the student researching alternative pest control might have asked the following: "In a recent article in *BioScience,* David Pimentel suggests that natural enemies play a major role in keeping the populations of many insects under control.[19] Is this accurate?" The interviewee may even supply you with pamphlets or other materials produced by the agency or organization for which he or she works.

For note taking during the interview, you might ask if the person minds if you use a tape recorder. Be mindful that some individuals may feel uncomfortable or be distracted by the recorder. Others may refuse to be taped. Note taking with pen and paper may be less distracting and should suffice. When taking written notes, you can write notes on one side of a page, reserving the other side for answers to follow-up questions or for your reflections on what has been said. Also leave plenty of space between questions so that if the person pursues an angle that you had not considered, you will have room to record it.

Sometimes an interviewee gives anecdote after anecdote and explores tangent after tangent, not all of which may appear useful. Nonetheless, always show appreciation for what the person has to say. When you get the opportunity to speak, let him or her know that what he or she has said is interesting, then note that you want to explore further or take up another item on the list. Your courtesy and respect will kindle the person's enthusiasm and keep him or her talking, but you may need to nudge the interviewee back on track from time to time.

Also show respect by allowing the person to have his or her say, even when you disagree with what is being said. You can question specific statements, but do so with diplomacy and tact. Accurately record statements made during the interview. Repeat key phrases you wish to quote or if you need verification, and repeat paraphrased material to check your accuracy.

Conclude on schedule. As you wrap things up, make sure you have the person's name and title entered correctly—perhaps request a business card. Remember to thank the person for her or his time, and likewise thank the secretary on the way out, simply smiling and waving if the secretary is busy or on the phone.

KEEP IN MIND 8.5

Conducting an Interview

Obtain valuable information and assistance through interviews by

- identifying the interviewee and contacting him or her early.
- preparing well for the interview.
- conducting the interview professionally.
- taking good notes and verifying information and quotes.
- reviewing your notes soon after the interview.
- following up the interview with a note (or notes) of appreciation.

After the Interview

As soon as possible after the meeting, review and check your notes to make sure you recorded accurately the person's statements and her or his positions on given issues. Later, transfer the notes to note cards, or if you have a good set of notes from the interview, you may simply number each entry, articulate its idea on an individual note card, and then, in the content area of the card, designate the number of the entry in your interview notes.

Sometime soon after the interview, send a quick thank-you note to the person interviewed. If a secretary was involved in scheduling the appointment, be sure to praise her or him in the letter and send a personal thank-you to the secretary.

QUOTING AND CITING SOURCES

Preview Once you have gathered information from a variety of sources, you need to use these sources effectively. You also need to use the correct form for citing sources in your bibliography.

Although you probably have a great interest in your topic, you may not be an expert. It is rare for a student in a beginning public speaking class to be an expert on the topic that he or she has selected for an informative or persuasive presentation. Even if a student can be regarded as an expert, she or he would still need to seek additional information and opinions. As discussed in Chapter 6, speakers who discover the best sources available on a topic and who cite these sources during a presentation will bolster their ethos, and their audience will more likely accept their message.[20]

Quoting Material

When you incorporate material into your speech, you might quote the source verbatim, or you might choose to paraphrase it if you can say it as well or better. In either instance, you will need to reveal, or cite, the source *during* your presentation whenever you present material from that source. As we discussed in Chapter 1, one of the most serious ethical violations that a speaker can commit is plagiarism. So you must be sure that material taken from a source is always properly acknowledged and that the audience is never given the impression that quoted or paraphrased material is your own original material.

Quote information when

- you wish to bolster your own ethos by associating your ideas with that of a recognized authority.
- the information you are presenting is so startling or unusual that the audience will doubt its accuracy unless a respected source is cited.
- you support an unpopular position and wish to blunt its unpopularity by citing the opinion of a source whom the audience will respect.
- the material is expressed so eloquently that you could not say it better. (This may enhance audience retention if it is especially memorable.) **Eloquence** is the ability to capture appropriate thoughts and feelings in words. Eloquence does not have to be in a grand style; some of the most eloquent statements are simple, as when Abraham Lincoln explained that the Civil War was being fought to ensure "that government of the people, by the people, for the people, shall not perish from the earth."

eloquence the ability to capture with words the thoughts and feelings appropriate to the occasion and the audience

Citing Sources During Your Presentation

As we have noted, to avoid plagiarism you must attribute any quoted or paraphrased material or ideas to their original source. When you cite sources during your presentation, you do not need to provide complete bibliographic information. Simply provide enough information to acquaint the audience with the source and whatever else seems important, such as the date or time of the information. For example, you could simply say, "*Time* magazine reported last month that . . ." or "In a recent interview, Attorney General John Ashcroft stated that . . ." or "Dr. Robert Wharton, professor of entomology here at Texas A&M, recently informed me of new developments in . . ." You will then provide full bibliographic information in your bibliography (see Figure 8.6), and you should be ready to provide this information to anyone in your audience who might ask for it.

Revealing sources during your presentation does more than safeguard against plagiarism; it fulfills your ethical obligation and bolsters your effectiveness. Ethical speakers recognize their duty to reveal the sources of the information and ideas that they have consulted and incorporated. Fairness requires that we recognize what others have contributed to our knowledge and thinking and that we give them rightful credit.

Go to **Lesson 2's Screening Room** on the **VideoLab** CD-ROM to view the speech on child protection. Examine the speaker's use of source citation and evaluate its effectiveness.

Not only are you doing the right thing by revealing your sources, but you are also doing the smart thing in terms of your effectiveness and reputation. If two speakers asserted that "violent crime has dropped dramatically over the past few years," how would you perceive the speaker who revealed the source versus the one who did not? How would you perceive a speaker who drew on a reputable source versus a speaker who made reference to a questionable source? As Professor William Norwood Brigance observed a half century ago, "One is known by the company he [or she] keeps; and when listeners find that you have been keeping company with eminent people of ideas and with expert collectors of information, they are impelled to accept you and your ideas."[21] In short, by citing your sources, you will meet your ethical responsibility,

KEEP IN MIND 8.6

Citing Sources

To be responsibly and fully informed, bolster your ethos, and meet your ethical obligations, you should

- consult external sources extensively.
- give credit to the sources you use.
- provide complete source citations in your list of references.

FIGURE 8.6 Sample Bibliographic Entries and Format Information

The following entries (based on the APA Publication Manual, 4th ed.) will illustrate how to format your bibliography. Ask your instructor if other official styles (such as MLA or Chicago/Turabian) are permitted or preferred.

The last entry illustrates an item for an **annotated bibliography,** a bibliography that also features a brief description of the material and how it is relevant to the speech. Some instructors require students to submit an annotated bibliography to display the research under way.

Article in a journal:

Duck, S.W. (1990). Relationships as unfinished business: Out of the frying pan and into the 1990s. Journal of Social and Personal Relationships, 7, 5–28.

Article in an annual publication: [with multiple authors]

Duck, S.W., & Pond, K. (1989). Friends, Romans, countrymen, lend me your retrospective data: Rhetoric and reality in personal relationships. In C. Hendrick (Ed.), Review of social psychology and personality, vol. 10: Close relationships (pp. 17–38). Newbury Park, CA: Sage Publications, Inc.

Article in a magazine: (See sample annotated entry—last entry below.)

Kaye, E. (1996, May). To die for. Esquire, 125: 96–103.

Article in a newspaper: [with no author specified]

Bush library gets $900,000 in gifts. (1996, April 29). Fortnightly. p. 3.

Book:

Curtain, H. (1994). Language and Children: Making the Match. New York: Longman.

Chapter in a book compiled by an editor:

Wrage, E.J. (1993). Public address: A study in social and intellectual history. In M. Medhurst (Ed.), Landmark essays on American public address (pp. 53–60). Davis, CA: Hermagoras Press.

Pamphlet:

Merck & Co., Inc. (1994). High cholesterol puts you at risk for heart disease: Can you risk ignoring it? [Pamphlet].

Information obtained via the Internet:

Article from a periodical available online:

Walsh, J. (2000, May 22). Can these schools be saved? *Salon.com* [online].
Available: http://.salon.com/news/feature/2000/05/22/intro/index.html

[Note: The date should be the date published. If that date cannot be determined, provide the exact date of your search.]

Material from a web page:

Murray-Rust, D.M. (1995). "Quakers in Brief" [online].
Available: http://www.cryst.bbk.ac.uk/~ubc09q/dmr/intro.htm [Accessed 18 November 2000].

[Note: Be sure to include author/agency. If the entry is untitled, create a title and place it in brackets. Date = the date you found the information as well as the last date it was updated. Make sure the Uniform Resource Locator (URL) is accurate & complete. Also include the name of the site administrator, if one is listed (e.g., <mailto:hsoi@tamu.edu>). Your instructor should be able to retrace your steps, see how recent the information is, and see who authored it. If any of this information is not provided at the web site, note so in brackets.]

Interview:

Wharton, Dr. Robert A., Professor of Entomology, Texas A&M University. Personal interview. 1996, March 25.

and you will impress the audience with how well you did your homework and the quality of the material on which you have based your assertions. The audience will see that you were well prepared to speak.

To ensure that you cite your sources orally during your presentation, cite them parenthetically in your speaking outline in a manner akin to the way you would say them. If, for instance, you were making reference to the attorney general in the manner described earlier, you might write (Ashcroft, interview) in your speaking outline. For the formal outline that you submit to your instructor, cite sources according to whatever style guide you are using, unless you are instructed otherwise.

Even the most thorough research will be unappreciated by the audience unless the speaker *orally* cites his or her sources of information. Go to **Next Step: Citing Sources Correctly** in Lesson 4 of the **VideoLab** CD-ROM and take the quiz to test your understanding of oral source citation.

SUMMARY

As a speaker, you must be informed. A careful and extensive investigation of relevant material will allow you to gather the information you need. You must seek out reliable information and sift through this material very carefully. Then you should organize your conclusions and the information on which they are based into the structure of a speech. Sketching your thoughts into outline form (discussed comprehensively in Chapter 10) will facilitate this process, and you probably will compose multiple drafts. To be most productive, you need a clear focus. Your initial research, a well-formulated thesis, and a clear purpose will assist you in achieving this focus.

Once you have found the most helpful sources, you can begin to take notes. The best notes are those that make sense of the information and relate it to the overall speech. Notes on cards limited to a single idea allow you to group the cards into subject areas and to arrange and rearrange them into the structure of a speech. In addition to notes from sources, you should jot down whatever inspirations you have. In this manner, you will take advantage of your cognitive processes, which begin to work from the moment you begin contemplating a topic. As you prepare yourself to speak, you will think and rethink your ideas. The ability to critique and refine your own thinking is central to producing an effective message.

To meet your responsibility as a speaker, you must research your topic thoroughly, seeking out information and ideas from trustworthy sources. Part of your accountability to your audience is revealing your sources, and to do so, you should cite them during the presentation and provide complete documentation in a formal list of references.

Research includes information obtained at the library, through interviews, and on the Internet. Today's library allows users to find a substantial amount of material quickly and easily, and its staff of professionals can help you with your search. Interviewing an expert will not only provide authoritative information and opinion, but such interviews also will help you sharpen your own thinking. Interviews with laypersons can provide additional information and insights, as well as real-life examples that add color and authenticity to your speech. Research via the Internet can be very useful. The amount of material available online increases daily and becomes easier to locate and retrieve. Just be sure to evaluate this material carefully. In addition, your email account can help you to contact potential sources, manage and store findings from the Net or from a database, and consult your instructor if you have a quick question about your speech.

QUESTIONS FOR REVIEW AND REFLECTION

1. In what ways does the specific purpose help you when you are preparing to speak?
2. How will a working thesis statement help you to formulate ideas and find relevant material?
3. Identify the various stages you will go through when you are compiling speech materials.
4. What are the important do's and dont's in recording information?
5. Why is revision so important in speech preparation?
6. Describe at least three important library resources and explain how they could be helpful to you in preparing a speech.
7. How would you go about finding information using the World Wide Web?
8. How can email be useful to you when preparing a speech?
9. What is the role of interviewing in speech preparation?
   a. How would you prepare for an interview?
   b. What are the guidelines for conducting an interview?
   c. How would you follow up an interview?
10. Under what circumstances should you quote material in your speech?
11. How should you cite sources as you deliver a speech, and why is it important to do so?

ENDNOTES

1. See Richard A. Katula and Celest A. Martin, "Teaching Critical Thinking in the Speech Communication Classroom," *Communication Education* 33 (1984): 160–168.
2. See Stephen K. Reed, *Cognition: Theory and Application*, 3rd ed. (Pacific Grove, Calif.: Brooks/Cole, 1992), p. 223.
3. See Ilan Yaniv and David E. Meyer, "Activation and Metacognition of Inaccessible Stored Information: Potential Bases for Incubation Effects in Problem Solving," *Journal of Experimental Psychology: Learning, Memory, and Cognition* 13 (1987): 187–205.
4. See John B. Best, *Cognitive Psychology*, 3rd. ed. (St. Paul: West, 1992), p. 445.
5. See Ronald A. Finke, Thomas B. Ward, and Steven M. Smith, *Creative Cognition: Theory, Research, and Applications* (Cambridge, Mass.: MIT Press, 1992), pp. 149–150.
6. See Best, *Cognitive Psychology*, p. 445.
7. Finke, Ward, and Smith, *Creative Cognition*, p. 166.
8. See Peter Elbow, *Writing with Power: Techniques for Mastering the Writing Process* (New York: Oxford University Press, 1981).

9. See Linda Flower and John R. Hayes, "A Cognitive Process Theory of Writing," *College Composition and Communication* 32 (1981): 380–381.
10. Jean Wyrick, *Steps to Writing Well: A Concise Guide to Composition*, 6th ed. (New York: Harcourt Brace, 1996), p. 103.
11. See Sondra Perl, "Understanding Composing," *College Composition and Communication* 31 (1980): 363–369.
12. See Flower and Hayes, "Cognitive Process Theory," pp. 365–387.
13. Quintilian, *The Institutio Oratoria of Quintilian*, trans. H. E. Butler (New York: G. P. Putnam's Sons, 1922), pp. 109–111.
14. Sandy Whiteley, ed., *The American Library Association Guide to Information Access: A Complete Research Handbook and Directory* (New York: Random House, 1994).
15. See Patricia Hayes Andrews and Richard T. Herschel, *Organizational Communication: Empowerment in a Technological Society* (Boston: Houghton Mifflin, 1996), p. A1.
16. Michael Gorman, "The Corruption of Cataloging," *Library Journal* 120 (September 15, 1995): 34.
17. *New York Times* (June 28, 2000), p. 1.
18. See Thomas M. Lessl, "The Priestly Voice," *Quarterly Journal of Speech* 75 (1989): 183–197.
19. See David Pimentel et al., "Environmental and Economic Costs of Pesticide Use," *BioScience* 42 (1992): 750–756.
20. See John C. Reinard, "The Empirical Study of the Persuasive Effects of Evidence: The Status After Fifty Years of Research," *Human Communication Research* 15 (1988): 3–59.
21. William Norwood Brigance, *Speech: Its Techniques and Disciplines in a Free Society*, 2nd ed. (New York: Appleton-Century-Crofts, 1952), p. 211.

9 Supporting Your Ideas with Evidence

CHAPTER SURVEY

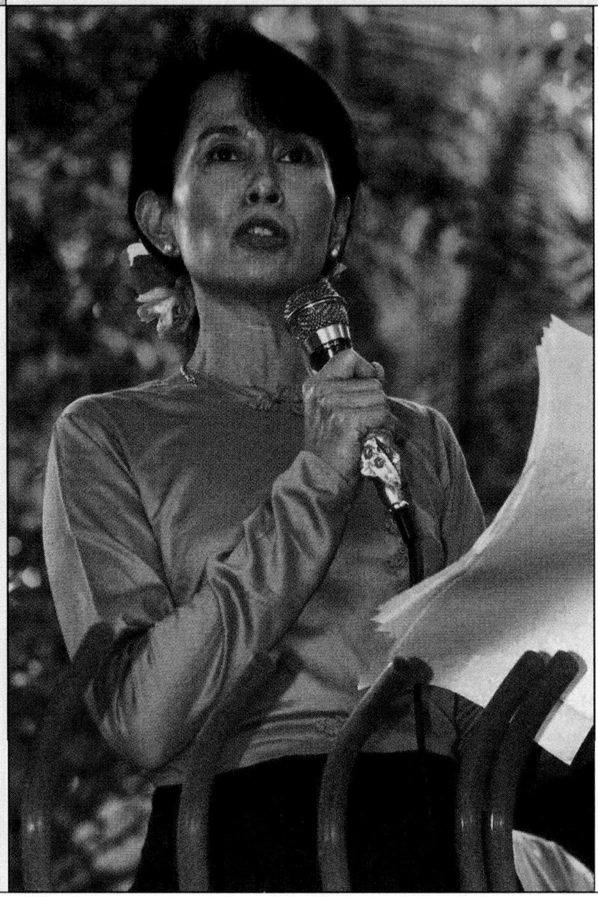

CHAPTER OBJECTIVES

After studying this chapter, you should be able to

1. **understand the importance of making ideas believable.**
2. **identify the principal types of evidence used to support ideas: examples, statistics, testimony, and comparison and contrast.**
3. **apply tests to determine the quality of different kinds of evidence.**
4. **choose evidence carefully to support your ideas.**
5. **use repetition, restatement, presentational aids, and delivery to present evidence effectively.**

To test your skills and expand your understanding of support materials, go to **Lesson 4** of the **VideoLab** CD-ROM and walk through the videos, exercises, and tips provided.

Supporting ideas is something we do every day. When we urge a friend to see a movie that we've seen by telling him that it is very good, we are likely to add something like, "It's your kind of humor," "It has a lot of action," or "Matthew was with me, and he thought it was great, too." If we're recommending a particular course to someone we know, we'll probably tell the person something specific about it, such as the nature of the instructor and the amount and type of readings and assignments. If we're explaining to friends how to get to our house when they come to visit, we'll probably draw them a map.

In our routine communication situations, we develop ideas—we bring in evidence to make those ideas believable or understandable—when we feel that it is necessary. Giving a speech, unlike informal conversation, requires more varied information, chosen carefully to support ideas we want the audience to understand or accept.

MAKING IDEAS BELIEVABLE AND UNDERSTANDABLE

The need to use evidence to support ideas varies with the situation, the audience, our relationship to the listeners, and the complexity of the idea. Sometimes a friend will just take your word for an assertion you make about the quality of a film you've seen. Sometimes that friend might need you to give her an example of what you thought was so exciting about the movie, or she might ask you to compare it with another film you've both seen. What will help some listeners understand an idea may not be enough information for others. The amount of proof you need to make an idea believable for some audiences may not be enough for others.

In Chapter 8, we discussed gathering relevant information. We pointed out that your task is to search for information that will help you achieve your desired response. Now we want to turn to the kinds of information that will most benefit you as you develop your speech.

SUPPORTING IDEAS WITH EVIDENCE

Preview Good evidence can give life to ideas and arguments, making them more memorable and convincing. There are four major kinds of useful evidence: examples, statistics, testimony, and comparison and contrast.

Suppose you were speaking to your classmates. You might assert, "We need to revitalize our scholarship program here at the university." On the basis of that assertion alone, the audience would be unable to determine whether your idea was sound. You would need to support the assertion with evidence. **Evidence** is the body of fact and opinion pertaining to a subject.

evidence fact and opinion used to support a particular perspective about a subject

In most of your speeches, you should use several different kinds of evidence. Some kinds of speeches, such as technical reports, rely heavily on statistical evidence, often reinforced with presentational aids (see Chapter 13). But even a technical speech can be enhanced by the use of examples, comparison and contrast, and the opinions of experts. In almost every public speaking situation, you will communicate more effectively if you use good and varied kinds of evidence. And, as we have pointed out, you should substantiate that evidence by citing the source of it.

The main forms of supporting material we will discuss are

- examples.
- statistics.
- testimony.
- comparison and contrast.

Examples

One of the problems that you may face is how to take an idea that is abstract and make it concrete or how to take something that is generalized and make it specific. Using examples, often in the form of **narratives**, or stories, is one of the most effective ways of doing that.

narratives stories that give an account of events as they happened

Examples are used naturally in informal kinds of communication settings. If you were to say to a friend that a particular course is very interesting or very boring, you would probably use an example or narrative to explain what you meant. You might describe a test, the content of a lecture, an anecdote told in class, or another bit of information that would make the generalization clear.

Narratives are effective forms of evidence. We could talk about the atrocities committed during the Holocaust by indicating the numbers of people killed or imprisoned. The enormity of the crime, however, becomes more apparent through the experience of reading books or watching film versions of real and fictional accounts, such as *Playing for Time, Sophie's Choice, The Diary of Anne Frank, Schindler's List,* and *Life Is Beautiful.* Characters are seen as people. Anne Frank is not a number but a person who hid for years from Nazi persecutors, only to be discovered at last and sent to die in a prison camp. In this case, a real little girl—a concrete example—makes the abstraction of numbers both more terrible and more real.

Charitable organizations often use examples as a way of translating the abstractions of poverty, disease, and misfortune into reality. They might talk about a specific family made homeless by a flood, a specific child who will not get enough to eat, or a specific person stricken with a disabling disease.

There are two principal kinds of examples that a speaker can use to support ideas: specific examples and hypothetical examples. Either kind may be extended or brief.

specific example a real-life case or instance

Specific Examples. A **specific example** deals with a real case; it is something that actually happened. The following excerpt from a student speech shows the use of a specific example:

> Fad diets not only waste your money, they can be dangerous. Last semester a girl in our dormitory tried to live on nothing but water, apples, and eggs for several weeks. One day she passed out in a class and had to be taken to the hospital. Not only had the diet done her body a great deal of harm (her blood count and potassium levels were dangerously low), but she also fractured her arm when she fainted and fell against a chair in the classroom.

We often see narratives used to make widespread problems more concrete. At the 1992 Democratic National Convention, Elizabeth Glaser used her own experience as an example to urge her audience to support AIDS research. Glaser began her speech by telling her own story.

> I'm Elizabeth Glaser. Eleven years ago, while giving birth to my first child, I hemorrhaged and was transfused with seven pints of blood. Four years later I found out that I had been infected with the AIDS virus and had unknowingly passed it to my daughter, Ariel, through my breast milk and to my son, Jake, in utero.
>
> Twenty years ago, I wanted to be at the Democratic Convention because it was a way to participate in my country. Today I am here because it is a matter of life and death. Exactly four years ago my daughter died of AIDS. She did not survive the Reagan administration. I am here because my son and I may not survive four more years of leaders who say they care but do nothing.
>
> I am in a race with the clock.[1]

Actor Christopher Reeve uses his experience with spinal cord injury as an example to urge audiences, lawmakers, and medical researchers to support spinal cord injury research. (© Martin Simon/Corbis SABA)

Glaser's use of herself as evidence demonstrates how specific examples taken from real life can be extremely compelling narratives. On some occasions, however, speakers may choose hypothetical examples instead.

Hypothetical Examples. A **hypothetical example** is one that represents an action or an event that could very plausibly take place in the way it is described but is not an account of a particular incident or event. Although it is in a sense a "made-up" example, it must not seem exaggerated or distorted if it is to be effective. The following excerpt from a student speech shows the use of a hypothetical example:

hypothetical example an action or event that could easily and plausibly occur

> Everyone has suffered from careless and irresponsible actions of others. Imagine how angry you would feel, for example, if you got up one morning, hurrying to get to an early class, only to find that someone had parked and blocked your car. Somehow you managed to arrive at class just in time, only to discover that the instructor didn't show up—not even a message left on the board! It's when these kinds of things happen to us that we begin to wonder if there are *any* unselfish people left in the world!

Another student, participating in a speech contest, began her informative speech with a hypothetical example as a way of attracting the audience's attention.

> Last week I walked into my favorite restaurant, sat down, and pulled out a pack of cigarettes, fully intending that this time I was going to smoke. But no sooner had I lit up when, of course, the waiter runs up to me to tell me, "This is a smoke-free restaurant!" "That's okay, this is an Eclipse—it's a smoke-free cigarette."

PORTFOLIO 9.1

Consider This

Examine the working outline for your next speech.

1. What areas will benefit from specific examples? Where might you locate them? Jot down your needs and your ideas for obtaining material.
2. What areas will benefit from hypothetical examples? Jot down your needs. Next, begin sketching out ideas for plausible examples.

> Now is this scenario true? Well, not really. I don't smoke. But R. J. Reynolds has spent the last 10 years in developing the technology that reduces secondhand smoke by more than 90 percent. Since 1993, it's tested Eclipse in more than 20 states among 12,000 smokers. And . . . this last June, R. J. Reynolds began selling Eclipse in Germany, Sweden, and the United Kingdom, and that Mecca of America—Chattanooga, Tennessee!

Throughout history, speakers have used hypothetical examples effectively. For instance, Angelina Grimke, a nineteenth-century crusader for the abolition of slavery and for women's rights, sought to characterize the experiences of Northerners who refused to condemn slavery based on their contact with Southern slaveholders. She did not single out any particular persons; rather she pictured a hypothetical group who exemplified their reactions. "Many persons go to the South for a season," she said, "and are hospitably entertained in the parlor and at the table of the slaveholder. They never enter the huts of the slaves; they know nothing of the dark side of the picture, and they return home with praise on their lips of the generous character of those with whom they have tarried."[2]

Because things that are real are so much easier to identify with, examples can be a very potent means of support. As speakers, then, we must use examples properly. As listeners, we have to exercise a great deal of care in evaluating arguments supported by examples.

typicality the degree to which a particular example is normal

Thinking Critically About Examples. The best test of an example is the test of **typicality**. If a speaker is trying to support a specific generalization by the use of examples, listeners must ask themselves whether these examples really represent the normal course of events. If a speaker were to describe, as a specific example, a newspaper article in which a student was arrested for shoplifting and then argued from that example that students don't have any values, the listener should be very skeptical. Such a specific example simply does not support such a sweeping generalization. It would be as if someone argued that because one college professor was arrested for hit-and-run driving, all professors are criminals.

These kinds of distortions in the use of specific examples produce stereotyping, in which one group member's behavior is generalized to an entire group. It is up to both the speaker and the listener to look very carefully at the relationship between an example and the conclusion to which that example leads.

The listener also should feel compelled to make a judgment about the importance of an example. Occasionally an example will show that certain actions *could* take place but not necessarily that they *frequently* take place; that might be enough to support a generalization. One speaker, for instance, argued that a cafeteria in a dormitory should be closed pending a thorough investigation by the board of health. She supported that assertion with three specific examples of students who had suffered from ptomaine poisoning in a week, citing as her source the campus and local newspapers. Whether those cases were typical might be a secondary consideration. Even if only three out of five hundred students were poisoned, the seriousness of the matter would be more crucial than the number of representative cases.

✔ KEEP IN MIND 9.1

Using Examples

Here are some tips for using examples as evidence:

- Distinguish specific from hypothetical examples.
- Avoid overgeneralizing or stereotyping. Test examples for typicality.
- Recognize that an example's importance might, on occasion, be more critical than its typicality.
- Cite your source.

While examples often function as a "human interest" form of support, they are perhaps most compelling when used in tandem with other forms of evidence, such as statistics.

Statistics

In the business and professional world, it is hard to imagine anyone presenting a persuasive speech or a technical report without using statistics for support. Some speakers may be intimidated by the thought of using statistics. Yet **statistics** simply provide a numerical method of handling large numbers of instances. When used appropriately, they provide some of the most precise information available to public speakers.

statistics a numerical method of interpreting large numbers of instances to display or suggest factors such as typicality, cause and effect, and trends

Understanding Statistical Support. Statistics offer a way of showing how some things are related to others. They may tell us about the typicality of an occurrence and thus validate the examples used. In a speech dealing with the problems of rehabilitating criminals, for instance, a speaker gave an extended example dealing with the experience of a young man who left prison only to become a repeat offender and return to prison. This example was coupled with statistical information showing how often this kind of experience was repeated.

Statistics also might be used to show cause-and-effect relationships, or at least correlations between certain phenomena. One student, in a speech dealing with the relationship between smoking and health, used statistical information to show that the incidence of lung cancer increased as the number of cigarettes smoked increased.

Statistical information can be helpful in pointing out trends over time. For example, we can better appreciate how quickly and significantly the price of building a new home has increased if we can see the year-by-year costs. If we contend that crime is becoming a more serious problem in suburban and rural areas, we must show the crime rate over a period of time and specific information on the number of crimes committed.

Finally, statistics—particularly those that are accompanied by a presentational aid—can highlight or reinforce an important point the speaker is making. For instance, a student made a speech in which she argued that the television news work force is controlled by white men and women and that minority men and women are dramatically underrepresented. To highlight the extent of underrepresentation, she put the statistical information into a presentational aid, depicted in Figure 9.1.

The example below illustrates how an economist, Ed Rubenstein, used statistics to show the high cost of crime in the United States. (Normally, you should cite the sources of such information. Dr. Rubenstein, however, is a distinguished economist whose audience was unlikely to be concerned that he would have been careless or misleading in presenting such evidence.) You can see in this illustration how dramatic and significant statistics can be in establishing the relevance and importance of a topic.

> Polls show that Americans regard crime as the number one social problem facing the nation. We fear being a victim of violent crime, or having our property violated, far more than we fear being unemployed or suffering a loss of income. . . . We know . . . that the national crime rate—crimes per capita—has tripled over the past 30 years. And at least 71 percent of all violent crimes

FIGURE 9.1 **TV News Work Force**

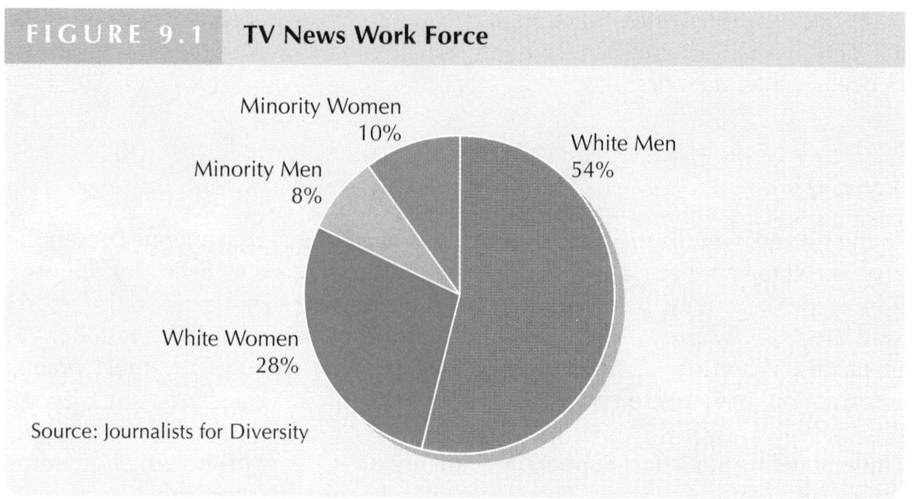

(rape, robbery, assault, personal theft) involve some kind of economic loss. The direct costs in one sample year, 1992—in cash, cars, and personal property—came to $18 billion. But this is merely the tip of the iceberg. Crime victims suffer trauma, depression, and fear that inevitably affect their ability to work and help others. These problems last a lifetime. The total costs to crime victims can, therefore, easily reach $250 billion to $500 billion each year.

Then there are the public costs. State and local governments spend about $80 billion per year on public safety. That includes police, courts, prisons, and parole systems. There are about 700,000 policemen and an even larger number of national security guards. We have, in effect, become a police state, incarcerating 1.1 million people. Our incarceration rate has doubled since 1980. It is the world's highest—4 times greater than Canada's, 5 times England's, 14 times Japan's.[3]

Statistics, then, are one important way of making ideas more understandable and believable. They should, however, be used responsibly by the speaker and viewed critically by the listener. One should not assume that a statistic "proves" something conclusively. It is part of the total structure of evidence and should be considered in light of other supporting material.

mean a mathematical average calculated by adding a set of numbers and dividing the total by the number of figures that have been added to obtain the sum

mode a numerical figure that occurs most frequently in a particular set of numbers

median a number that is halfway between the largest and smallest number in a particular set of numbers

Using Averages Reliably. The speaker and the listener both must recognize that statistics can sometimes be misleading. *Average,* for example, is a notoriously vague concept, even though it seems to give an air of statistical weight when it is used. Many people just assume that the words *mean* and *average* are synonymous, but they aren't.

Averages can be computed in different ways, such as by adding up a list of figures and dividing by the number of figures (the **mean**), by choosing the figure that occurs most often (the **mode**), or by choosing the figure that is the midpoint between the two extreme figures (the **median**). These three methods of computing an average may lead to quite different conclusions. The mean is the arithmetic average, but it is not necessarily the best or the preferred average to quote. If there are extreme scores in the distribution of numbers, the mean will reflect a greatly distorted version of the real central tendency.

Consider the following array of numbers: 20, 22, 25, 18, 26, 29, 26, 21, 23, 24, 17, 19. Here the mean is 22.5, a sensible indication of that distribution's central tendency, or true average. But suppose the numbers being examined were salaries, as follows: $78,000; $67,000; $26,000; $22,000; $20,000; $20,000; $24,000; $21,000; $19,000; $25,000; $28,000. Here the mean is about $32,000. If you were going to work for a department with that salary distribution, however, you would not expect to make $32,000 because nine out of the eleven persons earn only $28,000 or less. You can see that the two high salaries in the distribution distort the mean, causing it to be much higher than the true average.

If you have reason to believe that the mean would not fairly represent the true average of the distribution you are discussing, it would be better for you to use the mode or the median. Both of these statistics are unaffected by extreme scores. When large numbers of scores are involved, the mode and the median are often quite similar.

Descriptive Versus Inferential Statistics. Still other issues should be considered when using statistics or listening to speakers using statistics. First, most statistics quoted in speeches are **inferential** rather than **descriptive**; that is, they deal with probabilities rather than with observable facts. If you pointed out that "25 percent of all teachers in this country belong to a union," you would be using a descriptive statistic. But if you observed, on the basis of a survey of several hundred teachers, that "over 80 percent of all teachers are dissatisfied with their retirement plans," you would be using an inferential statistic. It is inferential in the sense that you sampled the opinions of some group you believed to represent the views of a larger population and you generalized from the small group to the larger population. Let's look at another example: Political polls taken during a campaign are inferential—they make inferences about what voters will do based on a representative sample. When the votes come in and are counted on Election Day, the fact that one candidate got 51 percent of the vote and the other got 49 percent is a descriptive statistic—it describes what actually happened.

inferential used to calculate a probability

descriptive observable

Not all inferential statistics are potentially suspect. However, it is important to recognize that whenever you generalize from a sample to a larger population, there is always some **margin of error**. That margin may be quite small, perhaps one in one thousand, but it does exist. Whether or not an inferential statistic is sound depends on the size and representativeness of the sample on which the statistic is based.

margin of error possible error or slight miscalculation associated with inferential statistics

If you want to know how students at your college feel about a particular issue, you need to gather the opinions of a cross section of the entire college, including first-year students through seniors, women and men, different ethnic and racial groups, and students proportionately representing various ages as well as different majors in the arts, business, the sciences, and other fields. In addition, if there are ten thousand students in your school, your sample size ought to number in the hundreds, not between ten and twenty-five. When inferential statistics are based on adequate and representative samples, they can function as excellent pieces of evidence.

By contrast, if you asked ten students who happened to be in the cafeteria at lunchtime what their opinions on academic advising are, then you reported your findings as, "Seventy percent of students at this college don't believe that advising is adequate," you would be using a poorly grounded inferential statistic. Of course, you should provide, and your audience should want to know, the source of such a statistic. Telling them that this statistic was the result of a poll of ten people in the cafeteria would make you look ridiculous and render such evidence ineffective. In most cases, it is unrealistic to expect that you will be able to carry out the kind of survey needed to make broad generalizations. For such information, you will have to do extensive research. If you want to generalize about your own particular class, however, you can much more easily get a representative sample from which you can draw a confident inference. If everyone responded to your survey, you would obtain a descriptive statistic. See Chapter 4 for a discussion of how you can survey your audience to adapt your message to them.

PORTFOLIO 9.2

What the Numbers Say

1. Which areas in your forthcoming speech require or would benefit from statistics? How? To show typicality? Cause and effect? A trend? Jot down your needs along with ideas for locating your statistical information.
2. Examine the ideas you jotted down. Will you be using these statistics responsibly? Note any problems that you detect with reliability.

Go to **Lesson 3's Screening Room** on the **VideoLab** CD-ROM to view the speech on gun control. Pay particular attention to the ways the speaker uses statistics as evidence. Evaluate how effectively you think he uses statistics in his speech. Be sure to explain the basis of your assessment.

Thinking Critically About Statistics. Sometimes speakers use statistics in ways that can be baffling to listeners. For example, in presidential campaigns, both candidates usually try to use statistics to defend their own views of how the economy is faring. In 1992, there was controversy over what Bill Clinton claimed was his success as governor in creating jobs in Arkansas. Using statistics derived from the previous two years, Clinton pointed to dramatic increases in jobs. By contrast, the Bush campaign, using statistics covering a ten-year period, claimed that Arkansas had fared worse than the rest of the nation. Both sides were technically right, but they were using different sets of figures to prove their points. The media consistently pointed out that the two campaigns were projecting how much programs would cost, whether or not they would lead to tax increases, how many people would be employed, and the like, based on statistics that each side had carefully selected to reinforce its own position.

All of this shows that statistics must be approached cautiously. If the listener can figure out where the statistics came from and how they have been computed, he or she will have a much better idea of how seriously to take them. However, this is usually not possible, and both the speaker and the listener should carefully evaluate the place of statistics in the total pattern of evidence.

Like other forms of evidence, statistics should be used only when they provide needed support. No speech should be "padded" with statistics simply because they seem impressive. Moreover, too many statistics can overwhelm the listeners. When you need to use many statistics, you might want to present some visual representation or summary of the statistics to help the audience follow you. One student gave a speech that involved a number of statistics relating to smoking and lung cancer. To help the audience remember the most important of those statistics, he used a number of presentational aids, such as the one depicted in Figure 9.2.

FIGURE 9.2 **Percent of Lung Cancer Deaths Caused by Smoking**

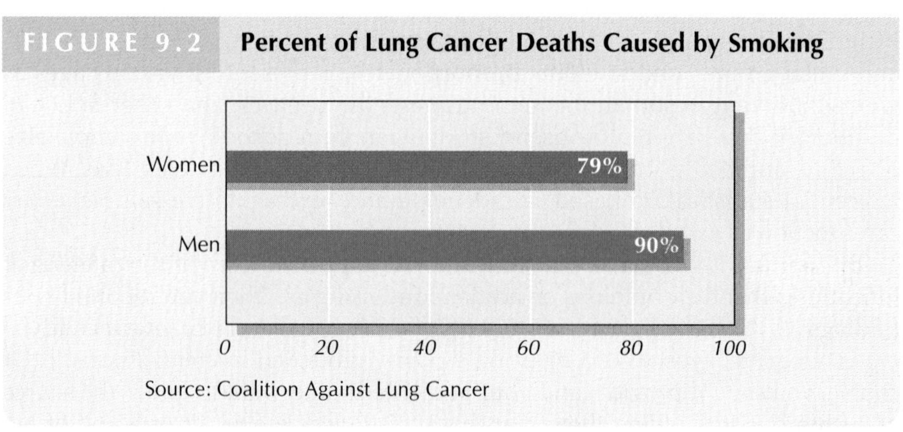

In general, every attempt should be made to present the statistics clearly and meaningfully. One speaker made health statistics meaningful to listeners by using an **analogy**: "According to Dr. Richard A. DeVaul at Texas A&M University's College of Medicine, 100,000 people die annually in the United States from adverse drug reactions. This is the same as if a 727 airliner crashed every day, killing all aboard—approximately 274 individuals per day."[4]

KEEP IN MIND 9.2

Using Statistics

Following are some tips for using statistics as evidence:

- Watch out for averages; distinguish the mean from the median and the mode.
- Recognize the difference between inferential (probable) and descriptive (observable) statistics.
- Use statistics with caution. Check sources and try to discover how statistics were computed.
- Use statistics as evidence only when they are needed.
- Present statistics clearly and meaningfully.
- Use only current statistical information.
- Cite your sources.

It may also be helpful to translate a statistic into audience-specific terms. Instead of saying that a new school will cost $7 million, you might point out that each taxpayer should expect a property tax increase of about $100 per year over a ten-year period. In this way, the audience can understand what the proposal would mean to them personally. And if you are a listener and the speaker does not clarify the impact of a statistic on you and other audience members, question the speaker when you have a chance.

analogy a comparison based on resemblance

Finally, statistics change rapidly. Although all evidence should be as recent as possible, nothing is more useless or boring than outdated statistics. Always gather statistical information from current sources and cite those sources in your speech.

Testimony

Another way to support your ideas is to offer supporting evidence based on opinions or testimony. Whereas statistical evidence seems more "factual" or "objective," testimonial evidence tries to illuminate information by offering interpretation and judgment. There are three kinds of testimonial evidence: personal testimony, lay testimony, and expert testimony.

Personal Testimony. Regardless of the kind of speech you are making, you are quite likely to offer your **personal testimony** from time to time. For many topics and in many speaking situations, this is entirely appropriate. We have pointed out in previous chapters that a speaker's ethos or personal appeal can have a significant impact on listeners. However, you should avoid overreliance on your own testimony to the exclusion of other kinds of support. Equally important, you need to ask yourself a fundamental question: *To what extent am I perceived by my audience as being a credible source of information on this subject?*

personal testimony testimony based on your own personal experiences and beliefs

If you have high credibility with your listeners, then your personal views may be the most potent source of support. If, for example, you are an oral surgeon discussing tooth implants, a company vice president talking about business trends in your industry, or a college student discussing social pressures to drink on college campuses, your personal experiences and views will likely be considered quite credible. Dr. Randolph D. Smoak, Jr., of the American Medical Association advances his opinion based on personal experience. In doing so, he makes a persuasive case against the tobacco industry.

> Let me finish today with my story. As you heard in Professor Daynard's introduction, I am a general surgeon. I have removed cancerous lungs. I have

removed cancer of the throat, larynx and voice box, tongue, jaw, and gums of hundreds of patients whose faces I will never forget. I have watched the tears roll down the faces of my patients and their families as I have told them of their cancer. I have heard their words of regret for not overcoming their addiction to tobacco. So, I must tell you I had great difficulty one year ago watching seven leaders of the tobacco industry raise their hands and swear before this nation and God that they do not believe nicotine is addictive.

Who knows? They may honestly believe that. But I have raised my hand with a scalpel too often not to know—they are dead wrong.

In South Carolina—tobacco country—where I practice, chewing tobacco is still very popular. In fact, its use is growing. Kids walk with the perfect circle of a chew can in the back pocket of their fading blue jeans. I've operated on a bunch of these great kids later in their life—some when they are in their 20's or 30's. And I can tell exactly what part of the Carolinas they are from without even glancing at their chart. In certain counties, they chew here on the side and back. Other counties, they place the chew up front here between the teeth and front lip. And so on. Wherever they place their chew—that's where I'll find the cancer. I know nicotine is addictive. I know, firsthand; it causes terrible, terrible cancer.[5]

In other speaking contexts, using personal testimony to support our ideas may be less effective. This can be a particular problem for you as a college student. You will often choose to speak about something of great interest to you, but you may have no direct experience or expertise with the topic. For instance, you may be very concerned about how to deal with the problem of homelessness or how the United States can play a more constructive role in bringing about peace in the Middle East. However interesting these subjects might be to you and your audience, neither of you would assume that you are an expert in these matters. In this case, you need to go beyond your personal views and gather other kinds of supporting evidence.

lay testimony testimony offered by ordinary people based on their experiences and beliefs

Lay Testimony. Another kind of opinion evidence is **lay testimony**. Suppose you wanted to argue that most students are dissatisfied with the food being served in the dormitory cafeteria. To support this argument, you might cite the results of a recent student opinion poll in which 85 percent of the students polled indicated that they found the cafeteria food to be "extremely poor." Of the remaining 15 percent, only 2 percent found the food to be "satisfactory." In this case, lay opinion is excellent evidence because the matter being judged does not require the testimony of an expert and your personal views would not be enough.

In short, lay testimony can be very effective as evidence as long as the audience needs to know what people in general think, and as long as the information has been gathered in a valid and reliable way. Often, as in TV talk shows, for example, lay testimony—what the average person thinks—is combined with expert testimony to give the lay testimony more weight.

PORTFOLIO 9.3

A Matter of Experience

1. Return to your working outline for your next speech. Which areas will benefit from including your own experiences? Is there something you can mention in the introduction? To develop a main point? To bolster the conclusion? Sketch out the possibilities.

2. Now determine which areas of your working outline will benefit from including others' experiences. Sketch out the possibilities for using lay testimony throughout your speech.

Expert Testimony. Perhaps one of the most effective ways of being persuasive is, in a sense, to borrow the ethos of someone to whom the audience will respond positively. Many speakers try to support their own ideas by using **expert testimony**. Again, this is a common practice in everyday settings. For example, if you were studying for an exam with a friend and you disagreed over a specific point, the disagreement could be settled by one of you saying, "Kevin [who is generally regarded as the best note taker in class] let me copy this from his notes, so I'm sure it is right."

expert testimony the views of someone who is especially well informed about a particular subject

In public speaking, expert testimony is one of the most frequently used forms of support when one is dealing with important, often complicated issues. For one thing, it is impossible for most of us to make very well informed judgments on many issues. In such cases, we rely on those whom we regard as experts or on those whom we have some particular reason to trust. For example, in the 2000 presidential race, some very knotty issues such as social security, tax policy, education reform, and military preparedness were debated. Both candidates used expert testimony to support their various plans—plans that were often too complex for most of us to understand. So, for example, George W. Bush used an education expert from Texas to testify in TV ads to the success of his education reforms. Similarly, to refute the charge that military preparedness had decreased, Al Gore relied on testimony from the chairman of the Joint Chiefs of Staff. Most voters find such complicated issues hard to untangle and may rely on the testimony of experts in making decisions.

Thinking Critically About Expert Testimony. Both the ethical speaker who wants to present accurate and relevant information and the critical listener need to evaluate expert testimony carefully. By raising questions about the nature of the testimony, we seek to determine whether it is or is not enlightening or persuasive.

It is, of course, essential that any authority we quote be considered an authority by the audience. So we need to begin by asking, Is the authority I am quoting known to my listeners? It is all very well to use the testimony of a brilliant nuclear physicist regarding the future of scientific research, but if the audience does not know the physicist by name, the impact of his or her testimony will not be great.

What the Experts Say

Look once again at your working outline. Which areas need the testimony of experts? Note the areas as well as possible sources to contact.

Testimony by experts is often the most compelling kind of testimony. Here the head of the Food and Drug Administration, Dr. David Kessler, and the former Surgeon-General of the United States, C. Everett Koop, testify before Congress in a hearing on the tobacco settlement.
(Kenneth Lambert/ Newsmakers/Liaison)

If there is any doubt in your mind about whether your listeners are familiar with the expert you are quoting, identify the authority during your speech. You might say, for instance, "Dr. Linda Hoffer, head nurse at the Cleveland Clinic's Cancer Care Center, has pointed out that the most fatal kind of cancer is cancer of the liver." Specifying the authority's position clarifies her expertise and enhances the credibility of your argument.

Sometimes speakers provide only vague references to their sources, perhaps by saying, "Political analysts have noted that . . ." or "One member of the New York City police department said that . . ." In such cases, listeners are uncertain about whom you are quoting. "Political analysts" could mean political science professors, media consultants, or political spin-doctors. The police officer could be a rookie cop or the chief of police. Audience members who are also good critical listeners are unlikely to be impressed or persuaded by such ambiguous references to authorities. And, during a question-and-answer period, some listeners may try to pin you down about the identity of your sources.

Another important question that might be asked of testimony is—How timely is it? People's ideas change as a situation changes. For example, a political figure may have commented on the relations between the United States and Russia in 1976 in a way that would not represent that person's views in 2000, when so much in Russian political, economic, and social life has changed. We've all probably had the experience of finding that an initial impression we had about a person, an event, or an experience in our lives has changed over time. It is important, therefore, to understand the circumstances in which testimony is given.

When using testimony, one must also be sure to use it in context. Suppose, for example, a noted financial expert had written this: "Mining stocks are generally a good investment these days, as long as you avoid any association with companies that have been in business for less than two or three years." Suppose a speaker, representing a company that had been in business for six months, quoted this financial expert as saying, "Mining stocks are a good investment these days." The quotation, taken out of context, clearly misrepresents the expert's views.

Perhaps the most critical factor in evaluating testimony is the nature of the authority. Ask yourself if the person being quoted is a relevant authority. One of the most common misuses of expert testimony in public communication occurs in advertising. Often someone who is an authority in one field is used to give testimony in a field in which he or she has no particular expertise or experience. A famous tennis player may know a great deal about the best kind of equipment to use for tennis, but he or she does not necessarily know more about what kind of toothpaste is best to use or what kind of shampoo is best for the hair. This sort of shift of authority occurs frequently, and it should be avoided by speakers and received critically by listeners.

prestige testimony the views of a popular, famous person who, though not an expert on the subject addressed, expresses a genuine commitment to a cause

Of course, there may be speaking situations where it is acceptable, and even desirable, for a person with high credibility and/or visibility to speak on behalf of an important cause. This kind of **prestige testimony** would be appropriate when the speaker is lending his or her good will, fame, popularity, or high regard to a worthy cause but is making no claim to expertise. For instance, every year in Bloomington, Indiana, former IU basketball coach Bob Knight spoke to many audiences seeking support for the Indiana University library. No one would regard Knight as an expert on university libraries, nor did he claim to be one. He hoped, rather, as a person with high visibility and a genuine commitment to the university, to speak out persuasively in support of a cause in which he strongly believed.

Finally, whenever possible, quote those individuals who have nothing to gain from the position they are taking. One would expect the president of General Motors to advocate purchasing GM products. Similarly, NASA officials would support added government expenditures for space exploration, and the Democratic party chairperson would advocate support for Democrats. Although these people are authorities in their fields, quoting them (and especially if you lack more objective evidence) may not further your cause, because they may be seen as biased.

In all these areas of concern, it might not always be possible for the listener to make an informed judgment about testimony. The listener might not always be able to tell when the testimony was given, what the total context was, or even how expert or objective the authority is. However, the listener should be somewhat skeptical. As for the audience-centered speaker, he or she will make every effort to be sure that the testimony used is recent, consistent with its meaning in context, and relevant.

KEEP IN MIND 9.3

Using Testimony

Here are some tips for using expert testimony:

- Make sure the expert is known to the listeners.
- Identify unknown experts by name during the speech.
- Use timely testimony.
- Understand the broader context of the testimony.
- Quote only relevant authorities.
- Quote experts who are not motivated by self-interest.
- Cite your sources.

Comparison and Contrast

One of the principal ways that human beings learn things is by comparison and contrast. We compare the unknown to the known. We look for similarities and differences between a new experience and an old one. We try to see ways in which new problems that need to be solved are similar to or different from old ones that have been solved. Comparison and contrast are not strictly evidence, but they are a form of support for ideas, and they often incorporate other kinds of evidence to enhance clarity or persuasiveness.

As you develop your assertions, you will want to remember to support each main idea with high-quality evidence. Go to the **Online SpeechStudio** and complete the **Outline Worksheet for Supporting an Idea**. Once you have fully developed one main idea, repeat the exercise with the others.

Techniques of Comparison and Contrast. One of the most frequently used ways to make ideas more understandable or believable is by comparing the familiar with the unfamiliar. A student giving a speech in which she hoped to help the audience understand styles of architecture, for example, compared a famous example of a particular architectural style, St. Paul's Cathedral in London, with a more familiar example of a similar design on a nearby university campus.

One of the most striking uses of comparison occurred in the 1992 presidential campaign. Ross Perot, in countering the Clinton campaign's focus on how well the governor had done in Arkansas, told voters that to claim that one who had succeeded in running Arkansas would likewise succeed in governing the United States was like comparing the successful management of a mom-and-pop grocery store to overseeing Wal-Mart.

If you wished to condemn a course of action, you might well compare that course of action with one taken in the past that led to unhappy results. A returning student in one class argued that a new plan by the registrar to "streamline" the drop and add process was very similar to one tried years before, when he was taking his first college classes. He described the similarities in the plans and then recounted the frustrations students had had with long lines, missing the first day or two of classes, closed classes, and the like.

Comparisons are often made to simplify difficult concepts. We have all experienced traffic control firsthand. It's relatively easy to understand how a police officer at an intersection manages the flow of cars. In some ways, this management is like certain kinds of functions performed by the brain. Thus a speaker who wants to explain the process by which the brain controls specific actions might compare it with the way in which the traffic officer controls traffic.

As you continue to develop your speech, you need to make sure that the evidence you gather is both varied in type and sufficient in quantity. To guide you through the evidence-gathering process for one of your main ideas, go to the **Online SpeechStudio** and complete the **Checklist for Supporting an Idea**.

Contrasts can be an effective way to stress the value of your approach or plan versus the approaches of others. For example, a returning student who had some experience in selling real estate gave a speech in which she reviewed all the steps one had to go through in selling a house. She contrasted what the sellers would have to do if they tried to sell the house themselves and compared this with the services provided by a realtor.

Read the 1980 speech excerpt that follows: In it, Senator Edward Kennedy spoke to the Democratic National Convention. He devoted a large portion of his speech to contrasting the Democratic and Republican parties. After defining the Democratic party as that of the common man and woman—the party of farmers, mechanics, and laborers—he went on to paint a contrasting view of the Republicans as the excerpt shows.

> The 1980 Republican convention was awash with crocodile tears for our economic distress but it is by their long record and not their recent words that you shall know them.
>
> The same Republicans who are talking about the crisis of unemployment have nominated a man who once said—and I quote: "Unemployment insurance is a prepaid vacation plan for freeloaders." And that nominee is no friend of labor.
>
> The same Republicans who are talking about the problems of the inner cities have nominated a man who said—and I quote: "I have included in my morning and evening prayers everyday the prayer that the federal government not bail out New York." And that nominee is no friend of this city and of our great urban centers. . . .
>
> The same Republicans who are talking about preserving the environment have nominated a man who last year made the preposterous statement—and I quote: "Eighty percent of air pollution comes from plants and trees." And that nominee is no friend of the environment.
>
> And the same Republicans who are invoking Franklin Roosevelt [who was quoted by Reagan in his acceptance speech] have nominated a man who said in 1976—and these are his exact words: "Fascism was really the basis of the New Deal." And that nominee, whose name is Ronald Reagan, has no right to quote Franklin Delano Roosevelt.
>
> The great adventure which our opponents offer is a voyage into the past. Progress is our heritage, not theirs.[6]

Thinking Critically About Comparison and Contrast. Although the listener may find comparison and contrast helpful and persuasive, the basis of comparison should be carefully considered. Speakers and listeners should ask the question, *Are the persons, events, places, or objects being compared really comparable in essential ways?* Some may be similar in obvious or superficial ways, but comparison on such bases could be misleading. They also should ask, *Are the points on which contrasts of two approaches or plans based essential points?* Contrasts may, in reality, be superficial, so plans may appear to be different but are not as different as they seem.

Assume, for example, that a speaker is urging the rejection of a plan (plan B) because it is similar to a plan (plan A) the group has already rejected. The nature of the similarities is very important if the comparison is to be valid. If plan A costs $5,000 to put into operation and plan B also costs $5,000 to put into operation, and if plan A was rejected because no money was available for the operation, the comparison is a good one: plan B, like plan A, is too costly and therefore should be rejected. If, however, plans A and B are similar except that plan B does not involve any expenditure of funds, the comparison is not a good one because financial considerations are central.

The speaker who urges a particular form of government for one country by pointing out that that form of government has worked well for another country might be setting up a false comparison if the histories, cultures, and values of the two countries are not similar. So care must be exercised in using comparisons. Speakers and listeners should try to satisfy themselves that the things being compared are really similar in ways that are essential to the argument. A. Thomas Young, a successful businessman, advanced a bold comparison in a 1992 speech.

> Whether in Washington, New York, or Peoria, most people seldom set out with the deliberate intent of breaking the law. They are drawn into it, almost as a boa constrictor defeats its prey.
>
> Most of us probably think a boa crushes its target in the powerful folds of its body. Actually, this snake places two or three coils of its body around its prey. Each time the victim exhales its breath, the boa simply takes up the slack. After three or four breaths, there is no more slack. The prey quickly suffocates.
>
> This deadly phenomenon of a victim becoming the unwitting accomplice of its own destruction is not confined to the world of reptiles. It exists in the human behavior that characterizes all walks of life anywhere on the globe. The boa we have to face—and sometimes fail to face—is following our ethical values; each lapse is another coil of the snake.[7]

Using Comparison and Contrast

Following are some tips for using comparison and contrast:

- Compare the familiar with the unfamiliar.
- Use comparison to simplify difficult concepts.
- Use contrast to stress the value of one approach over another.
- Make sure the persons, events, or objects being compared are appropriately comparable.

To identify different types of evidence used by several speakers, go to **Drill 4.2: Identifying Supporting Materials** on the **VideoLab** CD-ROM.

TESTING EVIDENCE

Preview Now that we have examined several different kinds of evidence, let's look carefully at how to determine its quality. There are several criteria to use when testing evidence: accuracy, recency, completeness, source reliability, audience appropriateness, and ethical considerations. All evidence, regardless of type, should be carefully scrutinized.

Not all evidence is of equal quality. Simply collecting a great deal of information on a subject is not enough. As you read, talk with individuals, and ponder the information you've unearthed, you need to make judicious decisions about what should be included in your speech and what should be omitted.

Accuracy

accuracy the degree to which information is agreed on by experts or is otherwise verifiable

Naturally, you want to determine the **accuracy** of your evidence. Accurate information is redundant and verifiable. You should, for example, be able to examine several independent sources and discover essentially the same factual or statistical information. For instance, doctors should be able to agree on the major causes of heart disease. Statistics describing the number of teenage pregnancies or the cost of a college education should be relatively consistent in different sources. When serious inconsistencies occur, you should question the accuracy of your sources.

Recency

recency the degree to which information is current and up-to-date

You should also strive to obtain the most recent information possible. Of course, the significance of **recency** as a criterion for evaluating information depends on the subject being discussed. In many professional settings, crucial decisions must be based on the most recent information that can be gathered. So if you are addressing economic trends, consumer demands, or productivity figures, you know that relevant data change rapidly, and you need to be armed with the most recent information you can obtain. Advances in technology have made recent information far more accessible. Because so many audience members are computer literate and have access to twenty-four-hour news channels on television, the burden on the speaker to be up-to-date is even more pressing.

Completeness

completeness the degree to which you have been thorough in locating information

You should also test information for **completeness**. Although you cannot know all there is to know on a subject, the more thorough, complete, and well rounded your knowledge is on a topic, the better your speech will be.

Completeness and accuracy are clearly related. As you check for accuracy, you will consult numerous sources, making your evidence more and more complete. Having complete information will also help you during the question-and-answer period. You may speak for only twenty or thirty minutes, but you may be questioned for another twenty minutes or so after the speech has ended.

Source Reliability

reliability the degree to which an information source can be considered credible

It is also important to assess the **reliability** of your sources of information. We have already addressed this concern, but we want to stress here that if you find an impressive piece of testimony or a compelling statistic, you must ask yourself about the credibility of the magazine, newspaper, web site, or other source in which the information appears.

The same considerations apply to the people you interview. Ask yourself, *Are they promoting a position out of self-interest? Are they known to possess some bias on the subject I'm discussing?* In general, whenever you doubt a source's objectivity, trustworthiness, or competence, it is best to disregard the information and look elsewhere.

Audience Appropriateness

Regardless of the quality of the evidence you find, it should not be used if its **appropriateness** to the audience and the situation is in question. Rarely should a human interest story or personal narrative find its way into a technical report. Yet the same kind of evidence is almost a necessity in sermons, political speeches, and after-dinner speeches. Humorous anecdotes can provide excellent support for many topics, but with really serious subjects, such as addressing the problem of poverty, AIDS, or child abuse, humor would be considered tasteless. The kind of speech you are giving, the topic you've selected, and your perceptions of the audience's needs and values should guide you in your selection of appropriate evidence.

appropriateness the degree to which information can be understood and appreciated by an audience

CONNECTING TO THE NET

Would you like more help in evaluating source material that you might use as evidence? Go to **http://college.hmco.com/communication/andrews/public_speaking/2e/students/** and click on *Connecting to the Net.* From there, follow the link to Evaluating Source Material.

Ethical Considerations

In a sense, ethical considerations in using evidence are related to all the other evidence tests we've discussed. If a speaker uses evidence that he or she knows to be inaccurate, incomplete, biased, or tasteless, that speaker does not have the audience's best interests at heart. Sometimes speakers lose track of their responsibility to the audience. They want, more than anything, to get the audience to respond, vote, contribute, or commit. They want these things so badly that they use evidence in ways that they know to be unethical—perhaps by quoting expert testimony out of context, visually distorting statistics, or portraying unusual examples as typical.

Although anyone can unwittingly make mistakes in using evidence, a speaker's ethical obligation is to scrutinize his or her own intentions carefully, guarding against the temptation to "get the job done" even if the audience is somehow misled in the process. A commitment to audience-centeredness is a commitment to ethical public speaking.

KEEP IN MIND 9.5

Testing Evidence

Following are some criteria for testing evidence:

- Accuracy
- Recency
- Completeness
- Source reliability
- Audience appropriateness
- Ethical considerations

MAKING EVIDENCE COMPELLING

Preview Even the best evidence may have little impact unless it is presented effectively. In this last section of the chapter, we consider restatement and repetition, the use of presentational aids, and good delivery as ways of enhancing the presentation of evidence.

There are many ways that we can go astray in presenting evidence—by speaking too quickly, using too many statistics, or failing to emphasize critical information. Choosing excellent evidence is the first step in creating a good speech. Presenting it effectively follows. Often ideas can be furthered by repeating or restating them, or by visually reinforcing them, or by delivering them well.

Repetition and Restatement

When you're reading a book, you can move at your own pace. If you begin to daydream, you can go back to the page, reread the part that the daydream obscured, or quickly scan the last few pages to remind yourself what is happening. With a speaker, of course, this is impossible. So the speaker needs to take into account the less than 100 percent attention of the audience.

As an audience-centered speaker, you want to make sure that the audience follows you, remembers what you say, and sees the direction in which you want to go. This means that you'll have to say things more than once and in different ways. The communicative devices of **repetition** and **restatement** are pretty common. For example, how many times have we given directions in which we repeat crucial elements to make sure the listener goes the right way? In a speech, the speaker does the same thing. A speaker might, for example, present the idea, "The best way to defend yourself from attack is by being prepared," then simply restate it as, "If you know what to do beforehand, you can defend yourself." After developing the idea of preparedness, the speaker could then restate the idea one final time as a transition while also looking ahead: "So we've seen that preparing for an attack is the best defense. Let's consider what you would do if you were actually faced with an assault."

repetition repeating, word for word, key elements presented in a message

restatement restating, with slightly different language or sentence construction, key elements presented in a message

Repetition and restatement are especially important ways of communicating complex evidence as well as evidence, that is absolutely central to the case you are making. Thoughtful listeners will likely recognize the importance of information that is stressed through repetition.

Presentational Aids

In helping the audience follow and remember, and in attempting to be persuasive, a speaker will do well to engage as many of the listeners' senses as possible. The fact that we talk about the audience as "listeners" indicates that the principal sense that the audience members use is their sense of hearing. But the speaker has ample opportunities to engage the audience's sense of sight as well.

The use of presentational aids may range from the simple device of listing the major ideas on the blackboard as one talks about them, to using prepared charts, to employing various kinds of equipment such as slide projectors, opaque projectors, overhead projectors, and video players. Modern technology allows speakers to present material visually to an audience through computer projections and videodiscs.

Speakers often do not fully exploit the potential of visual material and do not realize how important it is and how often it can be used. Almost every speech can benefit from some type of presentational aid. In Chapter 13, we will focus on presentational aids in detail, discussing the range of opportunities available to speakers and offering specific suggestions for their use.

Take the opportunity to practice your assessment skills. Go to the **VideoLab** CD-ROM and complete **Drill 4.3: Assessing the Use of Supporting Materials**, which asks you to evaluate several pieces of evidence used by a number of speakers.

> ✔ KEEP IN MIND 9.6
>
> ***Making Evidence Compelling***
>
> You can make evidence compelling by
> - using restatement and repetition.
> - using presentational aids.
> - using compelling delivery.

Style of Presentation

Even the best evidence may not have much impact if it is delivered in a listless or ineffective way. A compelling piece of expert testimony (perhaps one with some dramatic effect) should be delivered with appropriate emotion. Statistics should not be rattled off, but should be presented with emphasis and with pacing that allows the audience to absorb their meaning and impact. Comparison may be reinforced by gestures portraying contrast. A vivid example can be made more meaningful to listeners if it is shared with a sense of urgency, concern, or excitement.

One of the great advantages of speaking about ideas as opposed to writing about them is that you have the chance to show the audience how you feel through the way you talk about your ideas. You can vocally underline an important fact or statistic. You can show your distaste, enthusiasm, or sorrow through your facial expressions and voice. You can show the audience how significant your evidence is by gesturing with force and conviction.

In short, the way in which you deliver the supporting material you use in a speech is critical to its success in making ideas believable and understandable. Delivery is a major concern for speakers, and we discuss it in detail in Chapter 11.

At some level, good evidence may speak for itself. Yet if your audience is to be informed, convinced, or moved to act in certain ways, you will need to present your evidence in such a way that it is clear, powerful, and memorable.

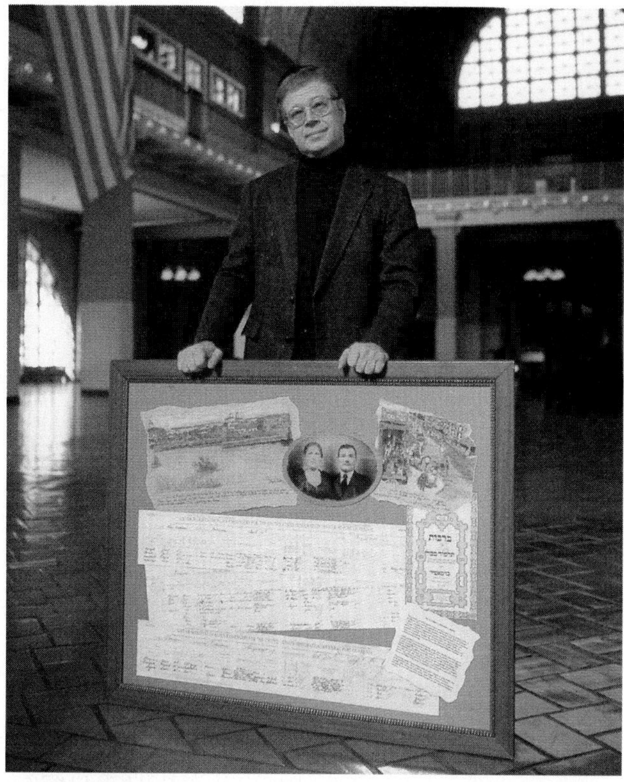

A good speaker will try to find ways to make evidence compelling. Rafael Guber presents information about how to find your ancestors through an interesting presentational aid that engages listeners. (Ken Schles)

Go to **Lesson 4 Coach: Tips to Remember** on the **VideoLab** CD-ROM for some reminders of how supporting materials can be used more or less effectively.

SUMMARY

Even if your ideas have merit, they need to be developed and supported if they are to be understandable and believable to your listeners. Using good evidence is critical. For most speech topics, several different kinds of communicative evidence might be used effectively:

- Specific or hypothetical examples that are typical and important
- Statistics that accurately show how things are related and what trends have occurred over time
- Testimony that is authoritative, timely, and in context
- Comparisons of the familiar with the unfamiliar; comparisons that simplify difficult concepts and that compare things that are essentially similar; contrasts that focus on essential differences

Regardless of the specific kind of supporting material used, you will want to carefully examine its accuracy, recency, completeness, source reliability, appropriateness to the audience and the situation, and ethics. These evidence tests can be applied as you prepare a speech for presentation and also when you are in the audience.

To present your evidence in a way that will be memorable and understandable, you may want to consider using some repetition and restatement, as well as presentational aids that support your ideas and engage your listeners' senses. Of course, delivering your ideas and evidence effectively also is essential. Even the best evidence can fail to be compelling if it is not delivered effectively.

QUESTIONS FOR REVIEW AND REFLECTION

1. Why should speakers use evidence?
2. What are the four kinds of evidence that speakers might use? Briefly define each.
3. Compare and contrast the specific example with the hypothetical example. Which do you think is generally better to use in speechmaking?
4. Contrast the three different kinds of averages—mean, median, and mode. Under what circumstances might the mode or median be preferable to the mean as a measure of the true average?
5. If you were going to use expert testimony in a speech, what criteria would you use in choosing this kind of evidence?
6. How might comparisons be effective as evidence?
7. What are some basic tests for evidence? Why are they important?
8. How might using restatement and repetition, presentational aids, and style of presentation help you support your ideas?

ENDNOTES

1. Elizabeth Glaser, "AIDS: A Personal Story," in *Public Speaking,* 3rd ed., eds. Michael Osborn and Susan Osborn (Boston: Houghton Mifflin, 1994), p. B17.
2. Angelina Grimke, "Address at Pennsylvania Hall," in *Man Cannot Speak for Her,* vol. 2: *Key Texts of the Early Feminists,* ed. Karyl Kohrs Campbell (New York: Praeger, 1989), pp. 27–28.
3. *Vital Speeches of the Day* 62: Ed Rubenstein, "The Economics of Crime," (October 15, 1995), p. 19.
4. Taken from *Healthwise,* Richard A. DeVaul's weekly radio program, broadcast on Texas A&M's National Public Radio affiliate, KAMU, 90.9 FM, September 12, 1996.
5. *Vital Speeches of the Day* 62: Randolph D. Smoak, Jr., "The AMA's Tobacco Fight," (February 1, 1996), p. 247.
6. *Vital Speeches of the Day* 46: Edward M. Kennedy, "Principles of the Democratic Party," (1979/80), pp. 714–715.
7. A. Thomas Young, "Ethics in Business," *Vital Speeches of the Day* 58 (1992): 726–727.

Kate Schnippel was a senior and member of the Indiana University speech team when she gave this speech at a regional contest at Ball State University in October 1996. Her specific purpose was to get her audience to understand the advantages and disadvantages of a new tobacco product.

Smokeless Cigarettes

Kate Schnippel

Last week I walked into my favorite restaurant, sat down, and pulled out a pack of cigarettes, fully intending that this time I was going to smoke. But no sooner had I lit up when, of course, the waiter runs up to me to tell me, "This is a smoke-free restaurant!" "That's okay, this is an Eclipse—it's a smoke-free cigarette."

Kate begins her speech with a hypothetical example, followed by statistical information suggesting the effectiveness of the new technology. She then gives specific examples of where the new cigarette is sold and finishes her introduction with a preview. You should note that throughout her speech, Kate is careful to cite the sources for her information.

Now is this scenario true? Well, not really. I don't smoke. But R. J. Reynolds has spent the last 10 years in developing the technology that reduces secondhand smoke by more than 90 percent. Since 1993, it's tested Eclipse in more than 20 states among 12,000 smokers. And according to the July 5, 1996 *Chattanooga Herald,* this last June, R. J. Reynolds began selling Eclipse in Germany, Sweden, and the United Kingdom, and that Mecca of America—Chattanooga, Tennessee.

So now people all over the world can buy a smoke, which doesn't. But Eclipse promises to do much more than change the vocabulary we use to describe cigarettes. In fact, it might finally be the middle ground between nonsmokers and smokers that will allow both to stay inside. In order to understand this, we first need to understand what Eclipse is, secondly, examine how the process works, and finally, take a look into its future implications, both the negatives and the positives.

In 1988, R. J. Reynolds introduced a new smokeless cigarette called Premier. It spent more than $500 million in developing the technology, which it explained in a self-published book entitled *New Cigarette Prototypes That Heat Instead of Burn Tobacco.* But smokers concluded that Premier tasted like dung, and R. J. Reynolds quickly retreated in the tobacco-industry version of the Crystal Pepsi flop.

Here Kate compares the failure of Premier to the better-known Crystal Pepsi failure.

To avoid similar consumer rejection with Eclipse, R. J. Reynolds initiated smoker discovery groups. The May 31, 1996 *New York Times* explains that smokers would meet every 2 weeks with a company representative to comment on the flavor and their ability to smoke different prototypes. The resulting Eclipse resembles Premier in technology, but so far has scored much higher with smokers. The July 28, 1996 *New York Times* tells us that Eclipse must only win 1 percent of the $45 billion cigarette industry's market in order to be R. J. Reynolds' most successful new product since the 1970s. And it has shown the first signs of success in Chattanooga, despite the fact that manufacturing costs make Eclipse cost about 10 cents more per pack than most premium brands. The June 8, 1996 *Financial Times* tells of one store that sold more than 500 packs in 3 days. And converts enjoy the 90 percent reduction in secondhand smoke. They said that when you cut the smoke, you cut the smell that used to linger in their clothes, their cars, and their apartments.

Statistical information used to show the positive reception of Eclipse is combined with specific examples of what subjects in the focus groups liked—reduction of secondhand smoke and elimination of the smell.

As Kate describes the process, she uses the teakettle comparison devised by R. J. Reynolds, along with a presentational aid in the form of a diagram. From *Popular Mechanics,* Kate draws a comparison between the process used by Eclipse and brewing coffee.

The June 8, 1996 *All Things Considered* on National Public Radio explained that to encourage these conversions, R. J. Reynolds has hit Chattanooga, Tennessee, with sales representatives and cardboard displays picturing steaming tea kettles. Now the smoke, the water vapor rising from these steaming tea kettles, is supposed to give the concrete image to the fact that whereas normal cigarette smoke is 80 percent nicotine and tar, the smoke from Eclipse is 80 percent water vapor. R. J. Reynolds has also been passing out free videos with every package of cigarettes [holds up video]. Now in the videos, Barbara takes smokers through a step-by-step process of how you, too, can enjoy an Eclipse. I've watched the video. R. J. Reynolds is not in Hollywood for a reason. So, I'll spare you Barbara's bad acting and go through the process myself in the second step.

The first thing you have to do is light the cigarette, but instead of actually igniting tobacco, what you do is you heat a carbon tip. Once the carbon tip is warm it can then warm the air that will travel through the Eclipse. Initially, you also set fire to a small amount of paper covering and powdered tobacco. The paper covering produces the only ash residue of Eclipse. The 25 milligrams of tobacco gives smokers exactly what they expect. Their first few puffs are real tobacco smoke. But the July 15, 1996 *Marketing News* warns us that the real smoke also has real biological activity, which means it does contain cancerous agents.

Go to **Lesson 5's Screening Room** on the **VideoLab** CD-ROM to view this speech on smokeless cigarettes. After viewing the speech and reading the analysis of it on pages 219–21 of this textbook, think carefully and critically about your *own* reactions to the speaker's use of evidence. In what ways might her use of supporting material have been further strengthened?

Now glass fibers separate the carbon tip from the rest of the cigarette. The glass insulation is to ensure that only the warm air, not the flame itself, will travel through the tobacco, which has been specially treated with glycerin. The September 1996 *Popular Mechanics* explains that the glycerin helps to extract both the flavor and the nicotine from the tobacco. When you brew coffee, hot water pulls the flavor from the coffee grounds. When you smoke an Eclipse, hot air pulls the flavor and the nicotine from the tobacco leaves. The final step of the process is to inhale and pull the vapor through the filter, delivering nicotine to your body in the same way that a normal cigarette would.

The July 20, 1996 *Boston Globe* explains that during the 6 or 7 minutes of smoking, nicotine immediately enters your body and begins to speed your body systems and your heart rate, same as always. But the 6 or 7 minutes is only approximate because smokers can't tell when Eclipse is finished. The cigarette does not burn down. This is a completely smoked Eclipse. When smokers find it difficult and must draw harder or more puffs upon the cigarette, it's probably time to quit. They can then lay it down and it will extinguish itself. Fortunately, it's much easier to tell when we've finished with the second point than when we've finished with an Eclipse, so now let's move on and discuss the future of this new technology.

As Kate lists the disadvantages of Eclipse, she develops one of the most serious problems—the use of the technology to deliver illegal drugs—as a specific example supported by expert testimony. Statistical evidence indicates health risks that still exist.

Like all wonder products, Eclipse has a downside and it's the fact that it answers the dreams of children, too—the ones that used to have to brush their teeth before talking to their parents or sneak outside of the school to avoid those smoke detectors. But Eclipse leaves no smell and produces virtually no ash. Eclipse also recalls a debate first introduced by the National Institute on Drug Abuse with the release of Premier in 1988. Both versions of the smokeless cigarette, Premier and Eclipse, contain a chamber where hot air can pass through a drug—officially tobacco. Yet the January 25, 1989 *Alcoholism and Drug Abuse Week* tells of anecdotal and experimental evidence that users can replace the tobacco with Crack. The January 6, 1989 *Journal of the American Medical Association* warns that smokeless cigarettes provide a highly efficient way to take drugs while avoiding detection.

Finally, Eclipse seems to increase our risk of heart disease. Because smokers cannot tell when the Eclipse cigarette is done, they usually take more and deeper puffs upon this device than they would with a traditional cigarette. Perhaps this is why, according to the April 28, 1996 *Durham Herald Sun*, that Eclipse has been shown to increase levels of carbon monoxide in the blood stream well above that from normal cigarettes, and the levels from normal cigarettes already lead to the death of more than 300,000 Americans each year. Well, the cigarette industry is currently embroiled in many lawsuits and it's unsure whether Eclipse is going to hurt or help their future. R. J. Reynolds has been reluctant to announce health benefits precisely because the benefits of Eclipse link all other cigarettes to health risks. But the June 26, 1996 *Raleigh News and Observer* points out that scientists are interested in Eclipse precisely because it seems to be better for our health. So we should now look at the positive implications of this new technology.

First, families and friends of smokers are rejoicing at the release of Eclipse. The June 3, 1996 CNN News tells us that even though most smokers have accepted the personal risk in smoking, they really don't like jeopardizing the lives of their loved ones every time they exhale. Yet Eclipse largely eliminates the concern that environmental smoke also causes cancer and once again makes smoking more of a personal decision. Eclipse also seems to offer benefits to smokers, too.

Kate moves to potential benefits, offering as specific examples the reduction of secondhand smoke, possible health advantages, and eliminating the dangers of fires. She concludes with a very brief summary of the main points she covered in the speech.

The *Atlanta Journal* of August 24, 1996 reported recent skin painting tests on mice that show that Eclipse did not produce malignant tumors, unlike even low-tar cigarettes. Burning tobacco produces tar, which contains cancerous agents. But Eclipse only warms the tobacco, never releasing these harmful compounds.

Finally, R. J. Reynolds' Barbara just can't get over how Eclipse won't burn holes in her carpet, her furniture, or her clothes. But with thousands of house fires every year caused by cigarettes, perhaps all of us should pause and consider a technology that allows a cigarette to extinguish itself before catching our homes on fire.

And so today we've cleared some of the "water vapor" surrounding R. J. Reynolds' new smokeless cigarette, Eclipse. We've discovered what it is, how it works, and finally, what it promises for our future. And so the next time you're in a smoke-free zone and you see somebody light up, don't yell. Watch. Maybe they have a smoke-free cigarette.

10 Organizing and Outlining Your Speech

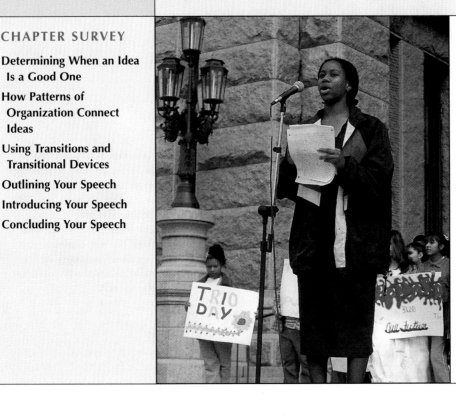

CHAPTER OBJECTIVES

After studying this chapter, you should be able to

1. **evaluate the quality of ideas.**
2. **select and apply appropriate organizational patterns and sequences.**
3. **understand how to construct and use good transitions.**
4. **understand and apply the principles of outlining.**
5. **plan effective introductions and conclusions.**

To test your skills and expand your understanding of organizing and outlining your speech, go to **Lesson 5** of the **VideoLab** CD-ROM and walk through the videos, exercises, and tips provided.

Many speakers carefully select and focus their topics, judiciously choose a specific purpose and thesis, seek out good supporting materials, and still never experience success in their public speaking endeavors. Part of their failure may be related to bad luck, but more commonly a good measure of it is related to some significant problem with the way they have organized and outlined their ideas. This chapter is devoted to helping you understand how good ideas for a speech are crafted and how they are organized in a structure that will help you achieve your purpose.

DETERMINING WHEN AN IDEA IS A GOOD ONE

Preview When deciding whether an idea is a good one, a speaker should consider how well it is designed to get the desired audience response. A good idea is clear, simple without being oversimplified, appropriate to the demands of the situation, and, above all, sensible.

All of us have probably been guilty at one time of saying something like, "Well, I know the answer to that, but I just can't put it into words"; "I understand it myself, but I just can't explain it"; or "I know what I want to say, but it just doesn't come out right." All of these comments are often ways of fooling ourselves. The reality is that if we can't say it, we probably don't know it, and if we can't explain it, we probably don't truly understand it. If you are to be successful at communication, you have to admit that putting an idea into accurate, correct, and clear language is the only way to be sure that you truly understand the idea yourself.

Some speakers are able to use especially strong structure to help the audience listen and learn. Go to **Drill 5.1: Keys to Good Informative Organization** on the **VideoLab** CD-ROM and respond to the questions that invite you to react to an informative speech on smokeless tobacco. Pay attention to the speaker's organization.

Organizational patterns for persuasive speeches often differ from those in informative speaking. Yet, some patterns work for both. Go to **Drill 5.2: Keys to Good Persuasive Organization** on the **VideoLab** CD-ROM and respond to the questions.

Clarity of Ideas

To be clear, an idea must first of all be complete. Consider, for example, Carlos, who was giving a speech on the benefits of space exploration. In his preliminary outline, the main ideas read like this:

Specific purpose: I want my audience to agree that substantial funds should be channeled into space research.

Thesis statement: Investment in space research will pay off.

Main ideas:

I. Accomplishments

II. Medical

III. They will advance

IV. Space relation to earth

V. Altering environment

These are not clearly stated ideas. Points I and II are simply one-word notations that don't convey specific meaning. To be a complete idea, point I might read like this:

I. In the past, space research has resulted in very practical benefits.

If this were the idea, the speaker's job would be to prove how beneficial the program had been in the past. In this case, Carlos reconsidered his initial thoughts and realized that this one idea could be the entire speech. He decided that he could reasonably go back and change his purpose. However, he did not wish to neglect the fact that he was arguing for future policy and therefore had to show in some way that positive good would come out of the program. He decided that he would develop ideas along these lines. He rewrote his thesis statement and specific purpose in this way:

Specific purpose: I want my audience to agree that the space program is of great benefit to all of us.

Thesis statement: It is to our advantage to continue funding the space program.

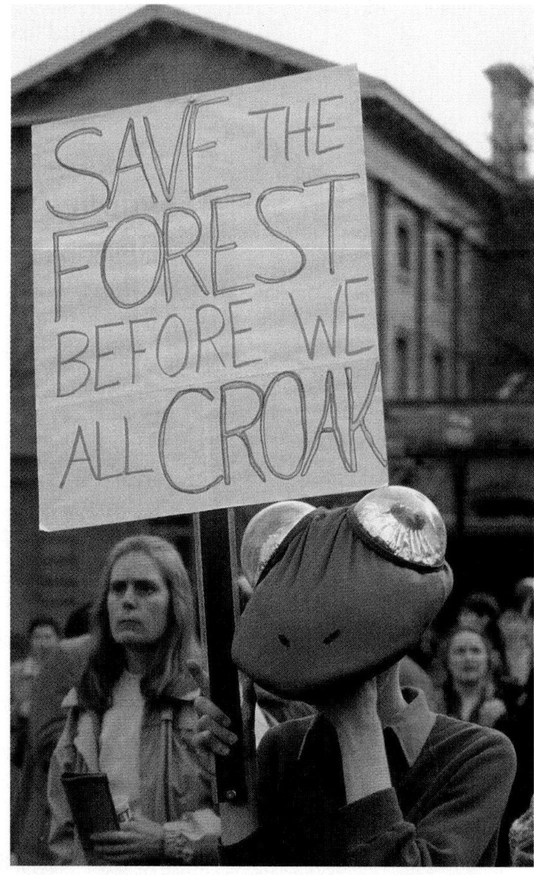

These environmentalists feel strongly about the depletion of the forests. They are trying to convey, as simply and clearly as possible, that destroying trees can have serious consequences for their audience. (Paul Conklin/PhotoEdit)

Then Carlos reexamined the remaining four notations on his outline and began to develop those in light of his restated purpose. His first idea became the following:

I. In the past, space research contributed considerable knowledge of how the human body functions.

Under that point, he could use information about the medical advances made as a result of space research. He then consolidated points IV and V into one idea:

II. Our increased knowledge of space has contributed to our understanding of earth itself and its environment.

The point that Carlos had listed before under III, "They will advance," is a complete sentence but obviously is not a clear idea. What he had in mind here was that, in the areas in which some knowledge had been gained in the past, there would be even greater advances in the future. He finally developed this notion into a third main idea:

III. The kinds of knowledge that can be gained by continuing research could be of direct practical advantage to us as inhabitants of earth.

After having gone through this process, Carlos decided that this was about all he could accomplish in one speech and therefore omitted the last two ideas. He now had a set of ideas that were clear and related to the purpose of the speech.

Simplicity of Ideas

Audiences must understand ideas if they are to respond to them. An idea must be directly and simply stated, without distortion. Your objective is to establish *balance*—to communicate ideas accurately, yet simply and intelligently.

With the specific purpose in mind, you should ask yourself whether the idea is as basic as it can be. If your idea cannot be simplified in order to be understood, then you may wish to reexamine the specific purpose to see if it is appropriate to the audience. You might be trying to do too much in the time allotted and need to focus more sharply.

Furthermore, speakers often try to include too much information or even a whole series of ideas within one idea. The idea is, after all, the essence; it is what the audience must grasp and respond to. Let's consider two examples, Barbara and Jeff.

Barbara had as her specific purpose, "I want my audience to become actively involved in political campaigning," and her thesis was, "Political involvement leads to positive results." Her first idea read like this:

I. People who take an interest in politics can restore idealism to the process as well as learn valuable skills themselves and make a practical impact.

This idea tries to fit in too much. It is not, in reality, a single idea. It is a complex and interrelated set of ideas. Barbara needed to sort out the idea from the material necessary to develop the idea. A revised form of this might be the following:

I. There are direct benefits to society when citizens participate in politics.

II. There are direct benefits to individuals who participate in the political process.

If Barbara can induce her audience to agree that there are important benefits to be gained from participating in the political process, and if she can inspire them to become actively involved, she will have achieved her purpose. To accomplish this, of course, she'll have to take the next step of developing the ideas. She'll have to enumerate the benefits that come from participation, show that they are indeed beneficial, and make them real and motivating for an audience.

Jeff came up with a main idea that could be improved through simplification:

Specific purpose: I want my audience to understand the roots of our American legal system.

Thesis statement: The rule of law is the basic principle on which the American justice system is built.

In this speech, Jeff will be discussing aspects of English history that bear on the development of the U.S. legal system. He planned to begin his speech with this idea:

I. Since Charles I was defeated by the parliamentary forces, English monarchs have been deemed to be accountable to the law.

This idea is accurate and perhaps clear enough, but it presents certain problems that could be solved by simplification. First, it buries the main point within a historical context. Second, in doing this, Jeff emphasizes historical elements with which his listeners probably won't be familiar and that might tend to distract them from the point. One way to recast this idea would be the following:

I. The principle that no one is above the law was established in England in the seventeenth century.

This statement emphasizes the point—no one is above the law—and does not obscure it with unnecessary historical detail. It helps the audience understand how basic principles developed historically and how they shaped our legal system. As Jeff develops the idea, he will explain in detail the historical situation that brought it about, but the historical situation is subordinate to the idea he wishes to promote.

Simplicity, then, goes hand in hand with clarity as a basic characteristic of a well-stated idea. Of course, clarity and simplicity are relative concepts. Since ideas grow out of and are adapted to the rhetorical situation, simplicity and clarity will be defined, in part, by the context.

Situational Considerations

We have already considered in Chapter 7 the notion that a speech is designed for a specific audience and that the speech is also influenced by the occasion that prompts it and the setting in which it occurs. Thus the ideas must be appropriate for the listener and the context.

The level of **complexity** of any idea will be significantly influenced by the audience's relationship to the topic. If, for example, you have as your specific purpose, "I want my audience to understand the types of scientific data that were gathered during Pathfinder's exploration of Mars," you can further that purpose by using ideas that are highly technical, sophisticated, and complex. A speech to a colloquium in the Astronomy Department might call for exactly those kinds of ideas. A speech in a beginning public speaking class would call for a different level of complexity.

complexity the quality of being intricate or complicated

PORTFOLIO 10.1

Out with It

What are the main areas you'll present in your next speech? What is the point you'll be making in each area? Is the idea complete? Clearly expressed? Simple? Sensible? Draft each idea until it is well stated and sensible.

Ideas That Make Sense

You also need to ask yourself whether your ideas are sensible, then consider how an audience might view them. Speakers sometimes propose main ideas that are just not reasonable. Consider, for example, whether the following ideas make sense:

1. Most people would probably like to learn to throw the javelin.
2. Whether or not you subscribe to the student newspaper will be one of the most important decisions you will ever be called upon to make.
3. People who participate in college athletic programs need special tutoring since they do not have the intellectual abilities of other students.

These ideas are not sensible. The first idea confuses the speaker's own interests with those of the audience. The second idea seriously overstates the case. And the third idea overgeneralizes on the basis of stereotypes.

Sometimes ideas will not be sensible to listeners if they appear to be romantic, sentimental, or idealized, or if they seem too cynical or pessimistic. For example, the idea that students come to college primarily to develop and sharpen their intellectual and artistic powers rather than to prepare themselves for a career may not seem sensible to the average college audience. Perhaps what the speaker is talking about is what he or she believes college students *ought* to do, or what he or she believes the true goals of a university *ought* to be. In other words, the speaker is being too idealistic. The speaker could keep the concept behind the idea intact but would need to rephrase it in light of probable audience reaction.

KEEP IN MIND 10.1

Good Speech Ideas

Main ideas should be

- clear.
- simple.
- grounded in the situation.
- sensible.

A good speech is planned to carry its audience through an orderly progression of ideas, making it easy to follow. You can evaluate the structure of a speech by keeping in mind a few key points to listen for as an audience member. To practice, go to the **Online SpeechStudio** and complete the **Worksheet for Structural Analysis**.

HOW PATTERNS OF ORGANIZATION CONNECT IDEAS

Preview To make a set of ideas reasonable and coherent for your audience, you need to put the ideas together so that they accomplish the specific purpose of the speech. To do this, you will use such basic patterns of organization as chronological or sequential, spatial, categorical, climactic, cause-and-effect, and problem-solution.

When you have developed a good idea or series of ideas, you then face the job of putting them together in some order. There are many organizational patterns from which to choose, several of which we will discuss in later chapters dealing with informative, persuasive, and business and professional speaking. Here, however, we introduce several of the most commonly used organizational patterns.

Chronological or Sequential Order

Ideas can be arranged in a logical time sequence. This is often called a **chronological pattern**. If the subject matter of a speech deals with historical development, then a time sequence is sensible. If, for example, you wanted your audience to understand the events that led to the breakup of the Soviet Union, you could very easily use a chronological approach that traced the events through time.

chronological pattern an organizational pattern in which ideas are arranged in a logical time order

If you have chosen a speech topic that would work well with a chronological or sequential pattern, go to the **Online SpeechStudio** and complete the **Outline Worksheet for Chronological/Sequential Pattern**.

Here is how one student, giving a speech that was basically a historical account, arranged his ideas in a chronological pattern:

Specific purpose: I want my audience to understand how the Nazis came to power in Germany.

Thesis statement: Nazism grew because of social and political unrest.

I. In 1919, the Treaty of Versailles created several serious problems for Germany.

II. Financial crises encouraged the National Socialists to attempt an unsuccessful coup in Bavaria in 1923.

III. By 1930, the National Socialist party had emerged as a major political party.

IV. The violent election campaign of 1933 brought the Nazi party to power.

Once you think you have fully developed your speech using a chronological or sequential pattern, go to the **Online SpeechStudio** and complete the **Checklist for Chronological/Sequential Pattern**.

Similar to the chronological pattern is the **sequential pattern**, which you would use if you wanted your audience to understand some step-by-step procedure or occurrence. For instance, if you wanted listeners to learn how a skilled craftsperson weaves a rug, you could begin with the first step that the worker takes and follow the process in order, step by step.

sequential pattern an organizational pattern in which the various steps of a process or a phenomenon are identified and discussed, one by one

Spatial Order

Ideas can be arranged in a pattern governed by space relationships. This **spatial pattern** is effective when a topic is, by its nature, geographical, or when a topic demands progression that moves from one physical area to another. If, for example, you were describing the facilities at the university library, you could do this by telling students where they should go from place to place, from the main entrance to the top floor.

spatial pattern an organizational pattern in which ideas are arranged with regard to their natural space relationships

If you have selected a topic that would work well with a spatial pattern, go to the **Online SpeechStudio** and complete the **Outline Worksheet for Spatial Pattern**.

The following is an example of how one student arranged ideas in a spatial pattern determined by geography:

Specific purpose: I want my audience to understand what natural disasters affect different parts of the country.

Thesis statement: The threat of natural disasters is present throughout the United States.

I. On the eastern seaboard, hurricanes can ravage coastal areas.

II. In the Midwest, flooding and tornadoes threaten lives and property.

III. In California and on the West Coast, earthquakes have caused widespread devastation.

Once you have developed your speech using a spatial pattern, go to the **Online SpeechStudio** and complete the **Checklist for Spatial Pattern**.

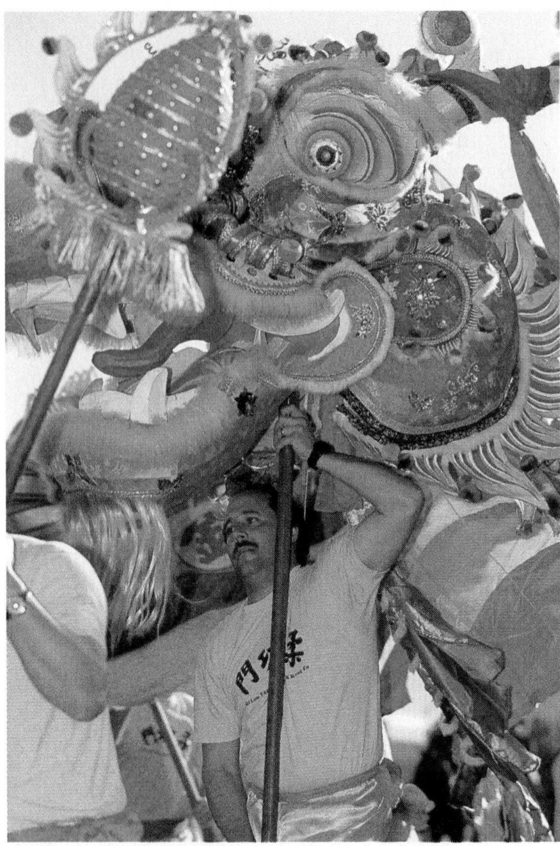

If you were speaking about the lunar calendar used by the Chinese, you might use a categorical pattern. If your topic focused on your experiences during Chinese New Year, you might use a spatial pattern. (Gary A. Conner/PhotoEdit)

If your topic would benefit from a categorical pattern, go to the **Online SpeechStudio** and complete the **Outline Worksheet for Categorical Pattern**.

Categorical Order

Ideas can also be arranged in a pattern that emphasizes distinct topics—a **categorical pattern**. If you are advocating a position that offers several benefits to the listeners, those benefits could form individual categories. For example, if you were giving a speech on the benefits of higher education, you could develop ideas related to the intellectual, social, or economic advantages of education. These categories are interrelated yet suggest independent ideas.

The following example shows how one student arranged her ideas categorically:

Specific purpose: I want my audience to vote at the next election.

Thesis statement: It is important to register and vote.

I. The results of the election could influence the amount of taxes that you pay.

II. Aid to higher education could be affected by the outcome of the election.

III. Your vote can make a difference.

IV. It is easy for you to register and vote.

See Chapter 14 for an extended illustration of how one might take the same basic topic and arrange it in a variety of ways, using chronological, spatial, and categorical patterns of organization.

Climactic Order

Another way of arranging ideas is to use a sequence that goes from simple to difficult, from least important to most important, or from emotionally neutral to emotionally intense. When the **climactic order** reflects audience needs and priorities, it can be an especially effective way to arrange ideas if the goal is to gain audience agreement or action. If, for example, you are addressing a topic with which the audience is not familiar, you might want to start with a very simple idea so that the audience is not puzzled or confused. As you assess your ideas or arguments, you would then arrange them to build up to your strongest argument or most compelling idea.

Like a playwright, a speaker may wish to build on the listeners' interests and concerns until a climactic moment is reached. The following is an example of ideas patterned climactically, from least to most important, with rising emotional intensity:

Specific purpose: I want my audience to agree that action to stop environmental pollution must begin now.

Thesis statement: Stopping environmental pollution should be a top priority for our community.

categorical pattern an organizational pattern in which several independent yet interrelated ideas are used to advance a larger idea

climactic order an organizational pattern in which the points being made in a speech are arranged so that they build in intensity

If you have developed your speech using a categorical pattern, go to the **Online SpeechStudio** and complete the **Checklist for Categorical Pattern**.

I. Pollution of air and water in this community has direct consequences for your health and your pocketbook.

II. Pollution effects can drastically alter the standard of living in this country.

III. Pollution can ultimately lead to the destruction of human life on this planet.

You can also use this pattern in reverse, so that you begin with your strongest information or argument, follow through with other important ideas or arguments, and then return briefly to review the best one again.

When you think you are ready to develop your speech using a climactic pattern of organization, go to the **Online SpeechStudio** and use the **Outline Worksheet for Climactic Pattern** to assist you in constructing your outline.

Once you have a good draft of your outline that is organized according to a climactic pattern, go to the **Online SpeechStudio** and complete the **Checklist for Climactic Pattern** to assess your efforts.

Cause-and-Effect Order

Ideas can be arranged in an order that leads from cause to effect or from effect to cause. This **causal pattern** is a useful one for speakers who want an audience to understand how an idea or event has unfolded, or for speakers who want to suggest changes in a chain of relationships that will bring more desirable outcomes.

causal pattern an organizational pattern in which ideas are arranged to reveal cause-to-effect or effect-to-cause relationships

If, for example, you wanted your audience to understand why urban violence occurs, you could arrange ideas so that they would show the relationship of an event or circumstance (unemployment, poverty, broken homes) to another event or circumstance (young people with nothing to do, desire for material goods, lack of family support), thus forming a chain of events that has violent behavior as its final link.

The following is an example of ideas arranged in a causal pattern by a neighborhood association president who argued that the lack of traffic lights and signs produced harmful results and urged the city council to take action.

Specific purpose: I want council members to agree that a better system of traffic lights and signs is needed in this community.

Thesis statement: The present system of traffic control is inconvenient and dangerous.

I. *Effect:* Pedestrians, young and old alike, have been struck and killed at unguarded crossings.

II. *Effect:* At the main mall entrance, several accidents have resulted when oncoming traffic has failed to stop for the red light.

III. *Effect:* Traffic jams causing long delays occur every weekday during rush hours.

IV. *Effect:* Directions showing turn lanes, painted on the street, are completely worn away by the end of winter.

V. *Cause:* The real culprit contributing to this safety hazard is poor traffic control procedures.

If you think you have chosen a speech topic that would work well with a cause-and-effect pattern of organization, go to the **Online SpeechStudio** and complete the **Outline Worksheet for Cause-and-Effect Pattern**.

Once you believe you have fully developed your speech using a cause-and-effect pattern, go to the **Online SpeechStudio** and complete the **Checklist for Cause-and-Effect Pattern**. Is there anything you have forgotten to do?

Quite often the cause-and-effect pattern may be incorporated into various organizational patterns that address problems and go on to propose solutions.

Problem-Solution Order

Finally, ideas can be arranged in a **problem-solution pattern**. This arrangement lends itself well to some topics. It appeals to an audience that wants a careful,

problem-solution pattern an organizational pattern in which a problem is identified and one or more specific solutions are proposed

PORTFOLIO 10.2

Structuring Your Speech

Examine the patterns of organization. Which one seems most appropriate to the content and purpose of your speech? If none appears appropriate, what alternative pattern might you use?

If you have selected a speech topic that lends itself to a problem/solution pattern of organization, go to the **Online SpeechStudio** and complete the **Outline Worksheet for Problem/Solution Pattern**.

Once you feel confident that you have fully developed your speech using a problem/solution pattern, go to the **Online SpeechStudio** and complete the **Checklist for Problem/Solution Pattern**. Have you forgotten to include anything?

Go to **Lesson 7's Screening Room** on the **VideoLab** CD-ROM to view the speech on corporate welfare. Try to identify the organizational pattern the speaker used. How well did this pattern advance his purpose? Might any other pattern have worked more effectively?

logical, well-grounded solution to a problem. This pattern is especially useful when there are many ways to deal with a problem and when the solution advocated by the speaker has certain drawbacks. Through a problem-solution pattern, a speaker may be able to show that her or his solution, even with its disadvantages, is still the best possible solution to a difficult problem.

Following this pattern, your first idea would deal with the nature of the problem: what it is and whom it affects. Your second idea would establish the criteria for solving the problem. Your third idea would describe the possible solutions to the problem. Your fourth idea would offer the best possible solution. When you use this pattern, you need to make clear the relationship between the criteria for the solution and the best possible solution. After all, the solution that most nearly meets the criteria will be the best one.

The following is an example of ideas from a student speech that fall into a problem-solution pattern:

Specific purpose: I want my audience to agree that prostitution should be legalized and regulated by law.

Thesis statement: Prostitution should be made legal under strict controls.

I. *Problem:* Illegal prostitution is a serious issue in many American communities today. (This point would be developed by specific reference to legal, moral, and health problems.)

II. *Criteria for solution:* Any solution to these problems must take into account the concerns of various parties to the problem. (This point would be developed by describing the sensibilities of the community, the difficulties of law enforcement, the protection of the public, and the individual rights of those involved.)

III. *Possible solutions:* There are at least three options for dealing with prostitution. (This point could be developed by discussing possibilities such as: Prostitution could be kept as a totally illegal act, as it is in most places now; it could be kept illegal, and enforcement could be made stricter and punishment more severe; it could be legalized without any restraints; or it could be legalized only under careful government supervision.)

IV. *Best solution measured against criteria:* Legalization under supervision is the best solution. (This idea would be developed by showing how it meets the needs of society and would deal with the more serious aspects of the problem.)

KEEP IN MIND 10.2

Principal Organizational Patterns

You can arrange your speech according to the following patterns:

- Chronological or Sequential
- Spatial
- Categorical
- Climactic
- Cause-and-effect
- Problem-solution

This list of organizational patterns is not exhaustive, but it does include the principal ways in which you can arrange your ideas. Although we tend to associate problem-solution and cause-and-effect patterns with persuasive speaking, both can be used with informative speeches as well. For example, a speaker could discuss a problem, articulate its causes, and then go on to help the audience understand three different solutions that have been proposed by different experts, without advocating any one of them.

In addition, there are many variations on persuasive organizational patterns, depending on whether the topics addressed are related to issues of fact, cause, value, or policy. Additional examples of these (and other) patterns can be found in Chapters 14, 15, and 18.

USING TRANSITIONS AND TRANSITIONAL DEVICES

Preview Transitions and transitional devices can add clarity and smoothness to a speech. Without strong transitions, even a well-organized speech may strike listeners as confusing or disorganized. When crafted well, transitions can contribute significantly to the impact of the speaker's overall message.

As a responsible speaker, you need to help the audience see the relationships among your ideas. Once you have drafted your speech, you must consider how you will progress from one idea to another so that listeners can see the connections.

A **transition** is a bridge from one idea to another. Listeners can't be expected to pay complete attention to the speaker, nor can they be expected to understand the sequence of ideas and information as clearly as the speaker does. You must alert your listeners to a new idea about to be introduced and help them see how it relates to your overall message.

transition a sentence or two in a speech that quickly reviews an idea that has just been discussed and previews the next one, while displaying their connection in light of the thesis

In addition to alerting listeners to the progression and relevance of the main ideas in your speech, you also need to assist them as you develop those ideas. To do so, you can rely on transitional devices. Let's examine transitions and transitional devices, when to use them, and how to craft them.

Transitions

These structural elements are small but mighty. They are, perhaps, the most unappreciated and underutilized components of effective speechmaking. A transition links one major idea with another in a speech, showing their relationship to each other. However, a transition does more than showing how an idea fits into a speech. It also reinforces an idea that a speaker wishes to share.

Let's examine the transitions that one student provided in a persuasive speech in which he wanted his audience to agree that steel-framed homes are superior to wood-framed homes.

Thesis statement: Steel-framed homes are a better choice than wood-framed structures.

The first main idea read:

I. Steel-framed homes are more durable than wood-framed homes.

Following the development of this idea, the student used the following transition:

As you can see, then, steel-framed homes are better than wood-framed homes because they're stronger and provide superior protection against natural disaster. The benefits don't end there, though; steel-framed homes are also better for the planet.

The choice of an organizational pattern is a strategic decision that every speaker must make. To review many of the diverse pattern options available to you, go to the **Online SpeechStudio** and review **What Pattern to Use When**.

This transition led to the second main idea:

II. Steel-framed homes are extremely environmentally friendly.

This example illustrates that transitions not only connect ideas to one another, but they also reinforce and reiterate those ideas. A transition is a quick glance back at the idea just discussed and then a quick look forward to the next main idea. The transition helps the speaker achieve his or her specific purpose while advancing the speech's thesis. In a sense, it functions as a miniature review and preview of ideas.

Sometimes, in lengthy speeches, this reviewing and previewing should be done more extensively. When this is the case, the speaker can rely on an internal preview or an internal summary, both of which are extended transitions.

Internal Previews

internal preview a quick look ahead at what will be covered while devloping a particular point of a speech

When moving from one idea to the next, you can give your audience a very brief **internal preview** of the point you are about to make. For example, a speaker moving from the point, "Pollution of air and water in this community has direct consequences for your health and your pocketbook," to the point, "Pollution effects can drastically alter the standard of living in this country," combined a simple restatement of the previous idea with an internal preview in this way:

> Pollution, then, can cost you both your health and your money. But its effects are even more far-reaching. If pollution isn't controlled now, drastic steps will have to be taken that could curtail your ability to travel, determine at what level you heat or cool your home, or restrict the food available to you. Let's consider now the ways in which our standard of living is at risk because of pollution.

Internal Summaries

internal summary a brief review of what has been presented in one or more areas of a speech before moving on to the next area

Sometimes getting from one idea to another has to be more elaborate because the material is complex. In these cases, you may use an **internal summary**, briefly going over the information covered so far before moving on to the next point. A speaker explaining the background of the American Revolution, for example, used an internal summary in her transition:

> We've seen how the Stamp Act in 1765 aroused the first successful organized resistance on the part of the colonists to the British government. Then, British attempts to deal with the problems of taxation and defense, coupled with a growing spirit of independence in the colonies, caused an ever-widening breach between North America and Great Britain. Now let's see how the events in the months preceding the Declaration of Independence led the young colonies to a final break with the mother country.

That kind of transition—a short summary of what has been said—helps keep the audience mentally on track. It also reinforces ideas.

Sometimes internal summaries can be brief phrases embedded in new ideas. Let's go back to the

Transitions may seem like a small detail, but they are very important in helping your audience follow your speech and should therefore be planned carefully. For assistance with devising good transitions, go to **http://college.hmco.com/communication/andrews/public_speaking/2e/students/** and click on *Connecting to the Net.* From there, follow the link to Good Transitions.

student's speech about steel-framed homes and examine the transitions used to develop the first main idea:

I. Steel-framed homes are more durable than wood-framed homes.
   A. Steel-framed homes are virtually fireproof.
   B. Not only are steel-framed homes fireproof *[transitional device]*, but they are also hurricane resistant.
   C. In addition to being fireproof and hurricane resistant *[transitional device]*, they are also tornado resistant.

These sample transitions illustrate how words and phrases can help listeners process information and ideas as they are advanced by the speaker.

PORTFOLIO 10.3

Connecting, Reinforcing, and Smoothing Out

Look at the working outline for your next speech. Where do you need transitions or transitional devices? Mark the areas with large ">T" in the margin. Make quick notes about which type of transition or transitional device would work best.

Transitional Devices

Transitional devices help listeners understand and follow developing ideas through the use of linguistic markers. Transitional devices consist of words and phrases such as "for instance" and "on the other hand."

transitional devices words and phrases that help listeners understand and follow the flow of ideas in a speech

In some instances, you may merely want to provide verbal markers to alert your audience to the fact that you're moving from one idea to another by enumerating each point or by signaling the next point to be made. If so, you can rely on transitional devices known as **signposts**. You might, for example, tell your listeners that you have three good reasons for asking them to volunteer for a Habitat for Humanity project. Your transitional devices might be as simple as this: "*The second reason* for you to sign up now is because the need is so urgent in our community." As you move into the third reason, you might say: "*A final reason* for volunteering is that you will derive great satisfaction from knowing you have really made a difference in a family's life."

signposts simple transitional devices, often consisting merely of enumeration

Other signposts include words such as *next*, *another*, and *finally*. Here are some examples:

"*The next* good reason is . . ."

"*Another* reason you should sign up is . . ."

"*Finally*, you should join now because . . ."

Taken together, transitions and transitional devices help listeners follow your speech, by making the right connections and following the progression of your ideas. In any speech, you will use a variety of these devices.

KEEP IN MIND 10.3

Using Linguistic Markers

Speakers can increase the clarity and smoothness of their speeches by using

- transitions.
- internal previews.
- internal summaries.
- other transitional devices.

OUTLINING YOUR SPEECH

Preview An outline emerges from careful preparation. Working outlines include your first thoughts, full-sentence outlines contain fully developed ideas and support, and key word outlines serve as notes for speakers. You should be guided by three basic principles: each point of an outline contains only one idea, the outline shows the relationship between ideas and support, and the outline uses a consistent set of symbols.

As you have learned by now, a good speaker will try to understand the nature of the audience and the situation, devise a sensible, reasonable purpose that will generate sound ideas, and put those ideas together in a meaningful way—a process designed to prepare you to speak effectively. This process of preparation can be visually represented through an outline.

An outline is built as the speaker goes through the operations necessary to get ready to speak to an audience. What we have already discussed will now help you generate an outline: when you've defined a clear purpose, designed ideas to further that purpose, and arranged ideas (through note cards) in an effective sequence, you've already begun to outline.

Types of Outlines

There are three types of outlines.

working outlines early drafts of your speech outline, representing your work in progress

full-sentence outlines outlines in which ideas and their development are articulated completely and precisely

key word outlines abbreviated outlines that serve as a speaker's notes while she or he presents a speech

- **Working outlines** reflect the first steps in the organizational process. These are the preliminary sketches that will develop into main ideas and accompanying support.
- **Full-sentence outlines** emerge from the preparation process when ideas are fully and clearly developed.
- **Key word outlines** are speaking outlines that serve as notes for you to use as you deliver a speech.

As we saw at the beginning of the chapter, incomplete thoughts can be molded into clear, direct, and complete ideas. This distinction holds between a working outline and a full-sentence, formal outline. Let's go back and look at the example we used earlier. In a working outline of a speech on space exploration, the speaker came up with a short list of notations that evolved into main ideas. He transformed his working outline into a full-sentence outline, as shown in Table 10.1.

Of course, these are not fully developed outlines of the entire speech, only of the main ideas. But they show the value of the full-sentence outline, which encourages you to develop complete thoughts. It forces you to consider precisely what ideas you want your audience to understand or believe. It shows the relationship between and among ideas and information and thus ensures that you understand what materials you need and how they will fit together.

You will find it useful to create a working outline as you begin to develop your speech. Go to the **Online SpeechStudio** and use the **Working Outline Worksheet** to assist you in crafting your working outline.

When you think your working outline is in good shape, go to the **Online SpeechStudio** and use the **Checklist for a Working Outline** to test your perceptions.

TABLE 10.1 Working and Full-Sentence Outlines

Working Outline	Full-Sentence Outline
I. Accomplishments	I. In the past, space research contributed considerable knowledge of how the human body functions.
II. Medical	II. Our increased knowledge of space has contributed to our understanding of earth itself and its environment.
III. Advancements	III. The kinds of knowledge that can be gained by continuing research could be of direct practical advantage to us as inhabitants of Earth.

Basic Principles of Outlining

First, each point in your outline should contain only one idea or piece of information. Here is a poor example:

I. Excessive salt in the diet leads to water retention and has also been linked with high blood pressure and depression.

This example is poor because it contains several different points in a single statement. Following is an improved example that conforms to the principle.

I. Salt should be minimized in the diet.
   A. Excessive salt intake leads to water retention.
   B. High blood pressure and excessive salt intake have been linked.
   C. Depression is often associated with excessive salt.

Second, your outline should accurately reflect relationships between ideas and supporting material. The main ideas are listed with Roman numerals, the subpoints that support those ideas with capital letters, the material that develops the subpoints with Arabic numbers, the support for these with lowercase letters, and a final level with numbers in parentheses (see Figure 10.1). The outline thus becomes a visual representation of the supporting relationships between ideas and evidence or explanatory material. Consider the following poor example:

I. Too much salt leads to high blood pressure.
   A. Excessive salt intake causes water retention.
   B. Depression and excessive salt use have been linked.
   C. Salt substitutes should be explored.
   D. Salt should be minimized in the diet.

The main idea in this illustration is that salt should be minimized in the diet. Yet that point has been made subordinate to the one claiming that salt leads to

One way of learning about outlining is to go through the process of organizing the basic parts of someone else's speech. Go to **Lesson 5 Next Step: Scrambled Outline I** on the **VideoLab** CD-ROM and work through the scrambled outline you find there, organizing it in a logical way.

For another opportunity to organize the elements of a scrambled outline, go to **Lesson 5 Next Step: Scrambled Outline II** on the **VideoLab** CD-ROM and complete the exercise. Again, your goal is to find the most logical way to arrange the parts of this speech.

FIGURE 10.1 Outline Form

BODY

I. MAIN IDEA
   A. First main subpoint
      1. Support for this subpoint
         a. First piece of specific information
         b. Second piece of specific information
   B. Second main subpoint
      1. First supporting statement
      2. Second supporting statement
         a. Specific information
         b. More specific information
            (1) Very detailed support
            (2) More detailed support
         c. More specific information
   C. Third main subpoint
      1. First supporting statement
      2. Second supporting statement

II. SECOND MAIN IDEA
   A. First main subpoint
      1. Support for this subpoint
      2. More support
   B. Second main subpoint
      1. Support for this subpoint
         a. First piece of specific information
         b. Second piece of specific information
      2. More support for the second subpoint

III. THIRD MAIN IDEA
   Etc. . . .

high blood pressure. In fact, none of the subpoints is related directly to the main point. Depression, for example, has nothing to do with high blood pressure.

Here is a better approach to this outline:

I. Salt should be minimized in your diet.
   A. Diets containing too much salt produce several negative effects.
      1. Adults often develop high blood pressure.
      2. All age groups tend to become obese.
      3. Adults, especially women, tend to become depressed.
   B. Minimizing salt in the diet does not mean that food must taste "flat."
      1. Several good salt substitutes exist.
      2. Other herbs and spices can be substituted for salt.
      3. Popular foods such as salsa can be used creatively to enhance flavor.

Third, use a consistent system of symbols and indentations. Learning a system will help you fix in your mind the relationships between ideas and supporting material that the outline represents and is important in organizing your speech into a coherent structure. Figure 10.1 illustrates how the system looks when outlining the body of the speech.

Fourth, write out transitions and relevant portions of introductions and conclusions. Moving from one point to another should be very carefully planned. Writing out transitions will help you be sure that the connections you make are clear. Some speakers like to write out their introductions and conclusions as well, whereas others prefer to indicate the main ideas and supporting material in sentence form as in the body of the speech. You may wish to write out parts of your introductions or conclusions; for example, you might write out a compelling example to be sure that you have all the details right.

When you move to writing the note cards from which you will speak, however, you should try to write out as little as possible so that you won't be tempted to read your notes and thus lose contact with your listeners. Certainly it makes sense to write out and read direct quotations and specific statistical information, but you will stay focused on the audience if you have practiced enough so that you don't need to rely on your notes too much.

Figure 10.2 presents a fully developed outline that illustrates these principles of outlining. Figure 10.3 presents a key word outline that shows how a speaker might prepare a speaking outline to use when delivering a speech. Because the transitions in this speech are fairly complex, the speaker decided to write them out. With briefer, simpler transitions, this practice might not be necessary.

Normally a list of sources or works consulted is required at the end of an outline. Various forms of bibliographic citations are illustrated in Chapter 8. Your instructor will probably tell you which form she or he prefers.

When the speaker delivered the speech shown in Figure 10.2, she did not use this outline as a set of notes. It is far too detailed and would have distracted her from her audience. Instead, she prepared the key

KEEP IN MIND 10.4

Outlining a Speech

Different types of outlines have different functions:

- Working outlines indicate preliminary thinking.
- Full-sentence outlines contain fully developed ideas.
- Key word outlines are used as notes by a speaker.

The basic principles of outlining are the following:

- Each point contains only one idea.
- Outlines reflect the relationship between ideas and supporting material.
- Outlines use a consistent system of symbols.
- Transitions and relevant portions of introductions and conclusions are written out.

FIGURE 10.2 A Fully Developed Outline

Title: PREVENTING DATE RAPE
General Purpose: Speech to Persuade (actuate)
Specific Purpose: I want my audience to take steps to prevent date rape.
Thesis Statement: You can protect yourself against date rape.
Organizational Pattern: Problem-solution

INTRODUCTION

In this introduction, the speaker used the technique of telling a startling story that related the problem to the audience. Because the story centered on the speaker's best friend, it helped establish her credibility as someone who really cared.

I. College students are at risk from "date rape."

A. My best friend from high school is named Amy. When Amy was a freshman in college, she went on a date to a fraternity party, where she drank quite a bit. Later that evening, she went to her date's room, where he forced her to have sex, and then was taken to a shower room, where two other men had sex with her. She was found later by police, lying in a hallway at the fraternity house next door with her skirt pulled up and her undergarments removed. After this experience, Amy left school and tried to kill herself. Two years later, she is still in therapy and has never been able to return to college.

She further reinforced the idea that this was relevant to the audience by using statistical data.

B. This is not an isolated instance.

1. *Public Health Reports* recently reported that 84 percent of the rapes committed on college campuses are committed by someone the victim knows.
2. Approximately half occur on dates.

She provided additional support for the idea that this could be a problem for this audience.

C. Chances are that many of you in this audience could find yourselves in a date rape situation.

1. The *Newsweek* article also reported that one out of nine college women had been raped—and of these, eight out of ten knew their attackers.
2. Four out of five of these sexual assaults were committed by male students.

Her transition to the body of the speech incorporated a brief statement of her purpose and a preview.

Transition: Today I'd like to tell you how you can avoid date rape. If all of us are to avoid being involved in date rape—as an aggressor or as a victim—we need to understand what date rape is, what is being done by colleges to prevent it, and what each of us can do to prevent it.

BODY

The first main idea is stated as a full sentence that defines rape. It is supported with a citation from a magazine and further elaboration.

I. Rape occurs when one of the persons involved is not willing to have sexual contact.

A. An article in *Parents Magazine* explained that if the victim says "no" and then sexual contact occurs, it is considered rape or some form of sexual assault.

B. When people are on a date or with an acquaintance—no matter how well they know each other or what their relationship is—if one person forces the other to have sex, that is rape.

1. In this instance, it would be called "date rape" or "acquaintance rape."

The transition uses testimony to move to the need for specific policies.

Transition: Since date rape so often affects college students, Aileen Adams, in *Sexual Assault on Campuses: What Colleges Can Do,* has recommended that "all colleges distribute a clear institutional policy against rape to let students know that this will not be tolerated on campus under any circumstances."

The second main idea is supported by pointing to specific examples of programs set up by universities. The student was sure to include an example from her own

II. Universities are making it clear that date rape is wrong by taking specific steps to stop it.

A. Universities are setting up special programs.

1. At the University of Oregon a special educational project is aimed at men as well as women students.

word outline shown in Figure 10.3, which she used to make sure that she didn't forget any major points, but which did not restrict her ability to stay in contact with her audience. She put her key word outline on a series of three-by-five-inch note cards and numbered the cards so that they would not get out of order.

FIGURE 10.2 (continued)

BODY (continued)	
university. The point was further developed by evidence that Greek organizations had established projects to combat rape.	2. At Indiana University a group called "Men Against Rape" presents programs devoted to changing male attitudes toward rape, and a student group, "Peer Presenters," gives presentations on date rape to students. B. Greek organizations have set up special projects to combat date rape. 1. UCLA requires rape awareness workshops as a part of the rush process. 2. SAGA (Sexual Awareness Greek Association) at the University of Florida conducts mandatory programs on sex roles and rape education at fraternity and sorority houses.
The transition quickly sums up the previous point and states the next.	**Transition:** We have seen that date rape is a serious problem for college students and that colleges and universities are taking steps to prevent it, but what each of us does individually may be the most important factor in preventing date rape. III. Date rape can be combated by both men and women. A. Men need to realize that rape is a serious matter.
The third and final main idea asserts a solution and develops the idea by introducing specific actions that women can take to solve the problem.	1. Men should forget the old myth that when a women says "No" she means "Yes." 2. Men must take women's statements seriously or risk going to jail—rape is a crime. B. Everyone should control the consumption of alcohol. 1. *Newsweek* reported that 50 percent of victims and 75 percent of aggressors had been drinking before the incident occurred. C. In the event that a woman finds herself in a threatening situation, she should take specific actions. 1. Firmness in saying "No" is essential: a recent issue of *Health* suggested a phrase like "No, get your filthy hands off me." 2. An article in *Nation's Business* suggested that screaming is one of the best deterrents. 3. Resisting with physical force can also be an effective tactic. a. *Psychology Today* reports that women who screamed or physically resisted were less likely to go into long-term depression after the event. b. The article in *Health* suggested kicking the assailant in the groin or hitting him with a closed fist in the eyes, and then running away.
Transition to the conclusion makes reference to the story in the introduction.	**Transition:** No woman wants to be in a position similar to that of my friend Amy, and no man wants to be guilty of an act that is both indecent and illegal.
CONCLUSION	
The conclusion first summarizes the main points quickly. *The speech ends with a startling statement and a challenge to the audience.*	I. Understanding what date rape is and how to prevent it can be important to all of us. A. I've tried today to explain that many rapes are committed by people who know the victim. B. Preventing date rape is a major concern on college campuses throughout the country, many of which are taking steps to stop it. C. All of us, both men and women, must act responsibly to prevent rape and decisively to escape from a rape situation if it occurs. II. It is shocking to realize that a rape occurs every six minutes—do everything you can to make sure it doesn't happen to you/yours.

Some speakers prefer to use a sheet of paper instead of note cards for their key word outline. When using note cards, you can easily carry them with you as you speak, gesturing and moving with ease. However, you do have to move from card to card without getting confused or losing your place. If you use a

FIGURE 10.3 A Key Word Outline

① **Introduction**
College students are at risk from date rape
Share personal story of friend raped in frat house
Statistics from *Public Health Reports:*
84% of rapes on campus by person known; half on dates
1 of 9 college women are raped; 8 of 10 knew attackers
4 out of 5 of these assaults by male students

② **Transition:** Today I'd like to tell you how you can avoid date rape. If all of us are to avoid being involved in date rape—as an aggressor or as a victim—we need to understand what date rape is, what is being done by colleges to prevent it, and what each of us can do to prevent it.

③ **Body**
I. Rape: when one of the persons involved is not willing to have sexual contact
If victim says no, it's rape
Date or acquaintance rape

Transition: Since date rape so often affects college students, Aileen Adams, in *Sexual Assault on Campuses: What Colleges Can Do,* has recommended that "all colleges distribute a clear institutional policy against rape to let students know that this will not be tolerated on campus under any circumstances."

④ II. Universities taking steps
Oregon program
Indiana "Men Against Rape"
Greeks: UCLA rape awareness; U of Florida SAGA—Sexual Awareness Greek Association

Transition: We have seen that date rape is a serious problem for college students and that colleges and universities are taking steps to prevent it, but what each of us does individually may be the most important factor in preventing date rape.

⑤ III. We can act individually to prevent date rape
Men must understand "No"; force is a crime
All can control consumption of alcohol (75% drinking)
Women:
Firm NO. "Get your filthy hands off me"
Scream
Kick assailant in groin, hit in eye, run away

⑥ **Transition:** No woman wants to be in a position similar to that of my friend Amy, and no man wants to be guilty of an act that is both indecent and illegal.

⑦ **Conclusion**
Understanding date rape important to all
Rapes committed by acquaintances
Prevention a major concern on college campuses
You can act to prevent rape
Rape every six minutes: don't let it happen to you/yours

sheet of paper, you can see the entire outline at a glance, but you will probably need to rest the outline on a table or podium because carrying it around while you speak may look awkward and restrict your gestures. Practice with each method to see which you prefer, and seek guidance from your instructor.

Different speakers use different organizational approaches. Outlining is the most common method used, but for an alternative method, go to the **Online SpeechStudio** to try your hand at another approach, using the **Structuring Worksheet**.

INTRODUCING YOUR SPEECH

Preview Although speech introductions may be structured in different ways, the most effective introductions will capture and hold the listeners' attention, stress the relevance of your topic, establish your credibility as a speaker, clarify your purpose, and provide a preview of your ideas.

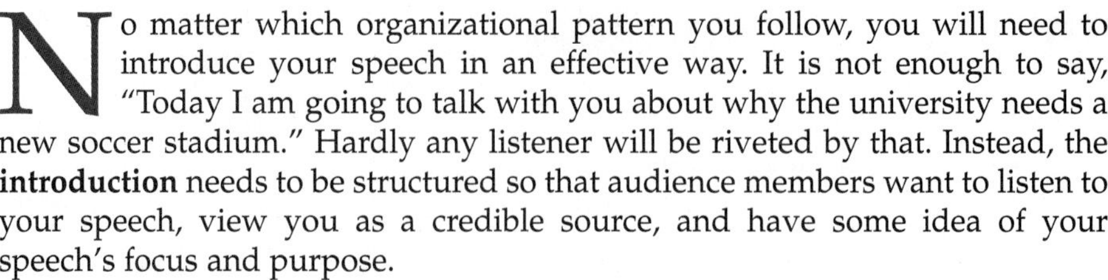

No matter which organizational pattern you follow, you will need to introduce your speech in an effective way. It is not enough to say, "Today I am going to talk with you about why the university needs a new soccer stadium." Hardly any listener will be riveted by that. Instead, the **introduction** needs to be structured so that audience members want to listen to your speech, view you as a credible source, and have some idea of your speech's focus and purpose.

introduction the beginning of a speech, in which a speaker stimulates interest, discloses the focus and intent of the speech, enhances her or his ethos, and previews what is to follow

Capturing and Maintaining the Listeners' Attention

When you first get up to speak, listeners will usually give you their full attention. But that attention may prove to be fleeting. Let's consider several approaches to maintaining the audience's attention and how some speakers have used them.

- *Establish common ground.* Audiences tend to listen to speakers with whom they share common experiences, problems, or goals. Karen, giving a speech on student loans in a class with several other working students, began her speech this way:

  When I get to this class at 8:00 A.M., I have had four hours' sleep. I work full-time as a waitress at Nick's and don't get home until about 2 A.M. Like many of you, I need to work to support myself while going to school. Some of you have full-time jobs and some are part-timers. Some of you also have families to care for as well as working and going to school. And I know that at least one of you is also a single parent. For us, getting an education and making ends meet is not easy.

- *Arouse curiosity.* Another way of holding listeners' attention is through the use of an intriguing or startling statement or series of statements that pique the audience's curiosity. Luis began his speech this way:

  This might be a pretty grisly thought, but imagine this room filled with blood—blood from the floor right up to the ceiling. Imagine what kind of pump it would take to fill this room with blood. Well, today I'm going to talk about a device that pumps blood at a rate that will surprise you. And before this speech is over, I'll tell you how long it would take this pump—your heart—to fill this room.

FRAME OF REFERENCE

Getting and keeping an audience's attention in your introduction is a crucial step for a speaker. This speaker's unusual visual aid both gains attention and makes a point central to her speech about transplanting organs.

- *Tell a story.* An interesting story—whether it is emotional, humorous, puzzling, or intriguing—commands attention. The story can be real or hypothetical. It can be a personal story that reveals something of your own experience, or it can be something you have read. Beth began her speech by relating a personal story:

  When I was in high school, I had a friend named Jerry. Jerry was tall, good-looking, an athlete and a good student. He was also a really nice, friendly guy—no one thought of him as stuck up or conceited. We were finishing our senior year, and Jerry had been accepted to a great university. Everything seemed to be going just right for Jerry. A bunch of us were having an end of the year party. Late in the evening we began to wonder where Jerry was. We called him at home, but just got an answering machine. The

> next morning we found out why Jerry didn't come to the party. He had gotten his father's shotgun, gone to his room, and shot himself. This great guy with every reason to live had taken his own life. Another victim of the greatest killer of young people: suicide.

- *Use rhetorical questions.* Rhetorical questions don't seek immediate responses. Rather, they are intended to get listeners thinking about an issue or idea. Lin began his speech by raising questions that challenged listeners to consider how they might deal with ethical dilemmas:

> This is an honors public speaking class, and, as honors students, we're all used to getting good grades. Grades are very important to us and we can be very competitive—even compulsive, some people might say. Well, you might not kill for an "A"—but, what would you do for an "A"? Would you consider taking a peek at the answers to someone's exam if you had the chance to do so and were sure you wouldn't get caught? Would you tell a professor that he or she made a mistake in grading an exam if it meant that your grade was lowered? Would you let a friend write a short paper for you and turn it in as your own? If you were in a class where grading was done on a curve, would you give someone else in the class a misleading or incomplete answer to a question when studying together for an exam? Can you think of any time when you've done something to get a grade that you wouldn't like anyone else to know about? If we're perfectly honest with ourselves, we know that these questions are not so easy to answer in a "socially approved" way. Maybe you've never cheated or plagiarized or lied to a friend—but, have you never been tempted?

- *Begin with a memorable quotation.* Sometimes someone has said or written something that captures the thesis of your speech. The idea has been expressed so well, perhaps by a person whom the audience respects and admires, that you know it will get the listeners' interest and attention right away. An esteemed scholar, scientist, or political figure can be quoted. Or you can use the words of a popular entertainer, author, athlete, or singer or other well-known and highly respected figures.

  Hannah, discussing self-esteem problems, started her speech by quoting these Janis Joplin lyrics: "Down on me, down on me, / Looks like everyone in the whole round world / Is down on me." Micah wanted his listeners to realize that trying to understand how the universe came about was very important, and so he began with this quotation from a famous physicist:

> Stephen Hawking said, "If we do discover a complete theory of the universe it should in time be understood in broad principle by everyone, not just a few scientists. Then we shall, philosophers, scientists and just ordinary people, be able to take part in the discussion of the question of why it is that we and the universe exist. If we find the answer to that, it would be the ultimate triumph of human reason—for then we should know the mind of God."[1]

- *Use humor.* Some speakers like to begin a speech with a humorous story, but you need to approach humor with caution. No matter how funny a story might be, it must be relevant to the point you want to make. Just telling a few jokes is not a good way to begin a speech, and a joke that falls flat is embarrassing. Humor should never be disrespectful or aimed at ridiculing someone or something, so you need to be careful. Bruce Lockerbie, dean of the faculty at the Stony Brook School, used humor in addressing his audience of students and teachers. He was introducing a talk on the need for people who are totally committed to the educational process.

> There's a story about a chicken and a pig who were passing a church, when they noticed the signboard and its weekly message: "What have you given to God today?" The chicken looked at the pig, the pig looked at the chicken, and each agreed that it had been a long time since either one of them had given God anything.
>
> "Pig," said the chicken, "I think we ought to mend our ways."
>
> "I agree," said the pig. "What exactly do you have in mind?"
>
> The chicken thought for a moment, then said, "Pig, you and I ought to give God a plate of ham and eggs."
>
> "You can't be serious," replied the pig.
>
> "Why not?" said the chicken, offended that his suggestion had been rebuffed. "Don't you think God would be pleased at our token offering?"
>
> "That's just the point," the pig retorted. "What for you may be a token offering, for me is total commitment!"[2]

Of course, these techniques are not mutually exclusive—you can use several at once. You might, for example, tell an interesting story that also establishes common ground and arouses curiosity. And you will want to deliver the introduction effectively. For example, pausing after telling a compelling story, posing an engaging rhetorical question, or sharing a memorable quotation may help listeners ponder what you are about to say. The key factor is capturing and holding the audience's attention and interest.

Stressing Relevance

saliency great relevance or importance

Either consciously or unconsciously, your listeners will soon ask themselves why they should care about your topic. Even when we find something very interesting, we soon begin to wonder whether it has any relevance to us. In the introduction, you should take the time to establish the **saliency** of your topic, answering for your audience the question, "Does this have anything to do with me?"

Kelly knew that many students weren't very interested in politics and didn't care much about who was elected in the upcoming congressional elections. Her purpose was to get her audience to understand the major policy decisions that faced the next Congress and what difference these decisions could make to them. She began her speech this way:

> Some of you who are on scholarships might find that you are paying more taxes on their value next year than you are this year. Some of you who are helping to finance your education by working at McDonald's for minimum wage might get a raise next year. Your grandparents might be able to get home health care and not be forced into nursing homes in a couple of years. Your little brothers and sisters may have better teachers as they go through school. The city streets may

> be safer or more dangerous. The job you want when you finish college might be a lot harder to get in a couple of years. What Congress decides to do about a whole host of policy questions can affect you directly in your everyday lives. Who runs Congress is a lot more than "just politics"—your money, your future, your life is at stake here, and you can do something about it.

Establishing Credibility

The audience should know of any special relationship that you have with the topic that would enhance your **ethos**. Of course, credibility is an ongoing issue throughout any speech, but for every speaker, the introduction represents an especially critical time for establishing her or his credentials. For seasoned professionals, this process may be less daunting. We expect doctors to know about medicine, attorneys to know about law, and accountants to be able to answer questions about our taxes. For student speakers, however, establishing ethos can be somewhat more challenging.

ethos the audience's perception of a speaker's character, intelligence, and good will

Yet student speakers can establish their ethos in compelling ways. Let's look at how one student did it. In her speech urging students to volunteer for a summer work project, Carmen began by relating her own experience:

> Last year I took a different kind of summer vacation. I didn't go to the beach to try to get a fabulous tan. I didn't go to a lake and learn to water ski. I didn't go to a big city to visit museums and see shows. I went to a hot, dry desert. There was no air conditioning anywhere. After a night spent sleeping in a sleeping bag on a bare floor, I got up, had breakfast, got into an old truck with about a dozen other kids and took off over a dusty road to a house that badly needed repair. In the hot sun I helped plug cracks in the wall, learned how to mix and apply plaster, and stripped and painted peeling boards.
>
> I did this for nothing. Well, that isn't right. I didn't get paid money, but I did get something a lot more valuable. Working as a volunteer in a remote town in an Indian reservation, I learned so many things about a different culture. I made close friends among the people I worked with. I helped to make a real difference in real people's lives. I came back from this experience a different—and richer—person than I was when I went. I am going to tell you today how you can enrich your life, too.

Clarifying Your Purpose

Sometimes you might discuss a subject of such interest or significance that the most appropriate introduction is to go directly to the purpose of your speech. This is especially fitting if the audience is aware of your subject in advance, already wants to learn about it, and views the subject as serious. Under these conditions, listeners are likely to take a "let's get on with it" attitude.

The audience, for example, could have gathered to hear you talk about how to make profitable and safe investments. They will want you to get to the point quickly, so you might simply say, "I am here to help you make the most money in the safest ways through sound investment. I want you to understand two important things about investing: the risk factors and the kinds of profits you can reasonably expect to make."

Usually such a situation occurs when you have been asked to speak as an expert, and that situation is rare in a classroom setting. However, it can happen. Karla, for example, gave a speech on job interviews to a class made up mostly of college seniors. She began this way:

> If you're like me, you're starting to get a little nervous about finishing school and getting a job. Most of us are in the process of lining up interviews, and we all know that when you go on an interview you're competing against a lot of other people who also want that job. My purpose today is to give you some sound guidelines that will help you do the very best you can in that interview.

Providing a Preview

preview a glimpse of the major points one will be treating in a speech or a section of a speech.

Before moving into the body of your speech, you should give a **preview**. The preview introduces your main ideas and focuses the audience's attention on the structure of your speech. In previewing, you are also signaling what you feel is most important—those things you want the audience to remember and reflect on long after you have finished speaking. If, after giving your preview, you follow through with your plan, you will have further enhanced your credibility by demonstrating your careful organization and preparation.

Consider, for example, the speech given by the student whose purpose was to get her audience to register and vote in the next election. After relating her topic to the audience and clarifying her purpose in her introduction, she went on to preview the ideas she had developed:

> While all of you know that an election is coming up, chances are that many of you are not very interested in it. Many of you probably don't care enough to vote. That attitude is pretty typical of people our age. When it comes to politics, many of us are likely to shrug our shoulders and say "What difference does it make who wins?" We think we know the answer to that question: "No difference." But actually who wins can and will make a very real difference to each and every one of us in this room. Today I'm going to show you how your life will be directly affected by the different policies advocated by different political candidates.
>
> First, I'll explain how the results of the election could influence the amount of taxes that you and your parents pay. Second, I'll show you how aid to higher education could be affected by the outcome of the election. Third, I'll give you some quick examples of a whole range of other issues related to your everyday life that could be settled by this election. Finally, I'll explain how simple the process of registering and voting is and how your vote can make a difference.

PORTFOLIO 10.4

A Public Viewing

Look at the main points you refined in Portfolio 10.1. Using them as a guide, construct a brief preview for an introduction. In a similar fashion, use the points to guide your construction of a review for a conclusion. In this way you will emphasize each point several times in your speech.

KEEP IN MIND 10.5

Effective Introductions

Engage listeners' attention by

- establishing common ground.
- arousing curiosity.
- telling a story.
- using rhetorical questions.
- beginning with a memorable quote.
- using humor.

Stress relevance.

Establish your credibility.

Clarify your purpose.

Provide a preview.

Craft the introduction after outlining the speech.

Keep the introduction brief.

Final Tips About Introductions

Remember the power of first impressions. Part of your first impression as a speaker will be based on the way you introduce your speech. Craft your introduction with care. Most speakers wait until after they have outlined the body of the speech to develop the introduction. For instance, they may experiment with several different attention-getting devices before they settle on the one they feel is most compelling.

The length of the introduction varies with the needs of the speaking situation. Some very formal events require the speaker to offer an introduction that refers to the events at hand and acknowledges or thanks several significant persons related to the event. Usually, however, introductions should be reasonably brief, and especially so in the classroom context. We have all heard speakers who ramble on for some time, then say, after ten minutes or so, "What I'd like to talk about today is . . ." This can be a signal for the audience to tune out. So in most speaking situations, you should keep your introduction brief.

Go to **Drill 5.3: Creating Powerful Introductions** on the **VideoLab** CD-ROM. After observing the clips of three speech introductions, complete the quiz to assess their effectiveness.

CONCLUDING YOUR SPEECH

Preview Carefully planning your speech's conclusion is an essential part of preparing to speak. By summarizing your main ideas, challenging your audience, appealing to your audience, visualizing the future, using good quotations, or referring to the introduction—or by using a combination of these techniques—you can craft an effective ending for your speech.

Many speakers don't really conclude their speeches—they simply stop talking. Others may stumble through their concluding remarks, reducing the effectiveness of the presentation. The **conclusion** is very important. If you construct it carefully, you will bring your speech to a strategic close and create a final positive impact.

conclusion the ending of a speech, in which the speaker can summarize what was covered and attempt to create a lasting impression of what was offered in the speech

Summarizing Your Ideas

One of the most common techniques used to conclude a speech is to present a **summary**. Summaries are especially important when the speech is complex or rather long. The summary reinforces your ideas and reminds the audience of your most important points. When combined with the preview in your introduction and the development of each main idea in the body of your speech, the summary provides a final chance to reiterate key ideas and help the audience remember them.

summary a brief account of what was presented in a speech, provided to refresh the audience's memory and to reinforce the thesis and other points made

Let's look back at the speaker whose purpose was to get her audience to understand how different natural disasters threatened different parts of the country. Here is the way this speaker used a summary in her conclusion:

> Today I've tried to help you understand that natural disasters of different kinds pose threats to all parts of the country. If you live on the East Coast, giant waves could wash away the foundation of your house or hurricane winds could blow off its roof. Tornadoes in the Midwest, even if they didn't touch down on your property, could still wipe out essential services and utilities. From breaking the

> china in your cupboards to demolishing a freeway, earthquakes would be an ever-present danger if you lived in California.

Challenging Your Audience

Most of the time, summaries do not stand alone. Often they are—or should be—accompanied by some other interesting concluding device. One such device that can be very effective is a challenge to the audience to act on what you have said. Following is an example of such a challenge in a speech given by management expert Karl D. Bays, speaking on "Perspectives on Productivity":

> I hope you'll remember some more ancient values that apply just as effectively to the work of management. I'm talking about the values of hard work, creativity, self-fulfillment and service to other people.
>
> Those may be older values than the latest organizational methods and marketing theories. But they're old because they work. They apply to the job of management and to the jobs of the people you'll manage in the future. They're values that can help us, as managers, in improving productivity.
>
> The world needs your skills, your abilities and your productivity. It needs your zest and curiosity, your courage and generosity. And I feel that you, as managers, have an opportunity to deliver all that, and more. I'm an eternal optimist about the progress that we, as managers, can create. And I'm so glad you're planning to take part. I wish you all the best of luck.[3]

Appealing to Your Audience

In your conclusion, you can make a final attempt to move your audience to act or believe more strongly about your proposition. In the early 1990s, Senator Jesse Helms gave a speech urging unity among conservatives and ended with an emotional appeal in the form of a personal story.

> I recall that Easter weekend three decades ago when our family embarked on a journey across our state to attend a sunrise service on a mountain top in western North Carolina. . . . Indelible on my mind is the memory of our little girl, possessing all the charming impatience that goes along with being four years old. She couldn't see over the heads of the adults all around her. . . . She spotted a boulder, but her little legs—and the thick soles of her new Easter patent-leather shoes—frustrated her efforts to scramble up to her own private vantage point. So she implored her Daddy to help her. . . .
>
> I climbed up first, then with whispered cautions to "hold hands tight," I extended my hand to the seven-year-old who, in turn, held tight to the hand of her little sister. And there we were—the three of us on top of the boulder at the precise moment that the rays of the sun slashed through the darkness. . . . "You see, Daddy," she said triumphantly, "I'll betcha if we all hold hands tight, we could go anywhere."
>
> Isn't that it? Isn't that the very essence of our gathering here today?—to signal our awareness that if we hold hands tight, with God who gave us liberty, and the truth that set us free, and with honor and decency and courage, we can go anywhere. If we can rekindle our faith—we can climb that boulder. If we hold hands tight. It's up to us.[4]

Visualizing the Future

In a speech in which you advocate some important changes, **visualizing** the results of such changes is an especially appropriate and powerful way to conclude. Some of the student speakers quoted above used this technique when visualizing how much easier it would be to balance work and school if students could get adequate loans, how good we would feel about ourselves if we gave up our free time to help others, or how much less stressed we would be if we knew how to prepare for an important interview. President John Kennedy, speaking at a ceremony naming the Amherst College Library after Robert Frost, praised the role of art in American life, imagining what the country could be like.

visualizing envisioning for the audience what could transpire

> I look forward to a great future for America, a future in which our country will match its military strength with our moral restraint, its wealth with our wisdom, its power with our purpose. I look forward to an America which will not be afraid of grace and beauty, which will protect the beauty of our natural environment, which will preserve the great old American houses and squares and parks of our national past, and which will build handsome and balanced cities for our future.
>
> I look forward to an America which will reward achievement in the arts as we reward achievement in business and statecraft. I look forward to an America which will steadily raise the standards of artistic accomplishment and which will steadily enlarge cultural opportunities for all our citizens. And I look forward to an America that commands respect throughout the world not only for its strength but for its civilization as well. And I look forward to a world which will be safe not only for democracy and diversity but also for personal distinction.[5]

One of the most famous speeches that visualizes the future is Martin Luther King's "I Have a Dream" speech in which he describes his vision of racial harmony. (Topham/The Image Works)

Ending with a Quotation

Ending your speech with a good quotation can help reinforce your thesis and restate the major points you made. Poetry, plays, songs, speeches, and literary works can all supply effective quotations. In the early 1990s, Lowell Weicker, Republican senator from Connecticut, spoke from the pulpit of the United Church on the Green in New Haven when the issue of a constitutional amendment to allow school prayer was before the Senate. Senator Weicker, who opposed the amendment, used biblical passages to sum up his viewpoint.

> The Apostle Paul wrote that "faith without works is dead." And in the Old Testament text read this morning, Isaiah seems to be saying that prayer without actions to match is not heard. . . . Isaiah is explaining why the Lord is ignoring Israel's many prayers, fasts, and solemn observances. As I read it, the people's piousness is an abomination to God until they first act on His social agenda. Isaiah writes: "Is not this the fast that I have chosen? To loose the bands of wickedness, to undo the heavy burdens, to let the oppressed go free? Is it not to deal thy bread to the hungry, and that thou bring the poor that are cast out to thy house?"
>
> This, I believe, should be the agenda of each of us as individuals, and indeed for me as a Senator. It pains me to see the Congress diverted into these moral crusades when there is so much real suffering in our land, when so many people are losing their livelihoods and so many going without the necessities of life. And when there are so many people denied the justice which should be accorded them by law.
>
> Let us rededicate ourselves to taking up this agenda. Let us get involved in our public and private lives to shape a fairer society. Then, and only then, does God promise to hear our prayers. "Then shalt thou call, and the Lord shall answer," writes Isaiah. "Thou shalt cry and He shall say, Here I am."[6]

Referring to the Introduction

You can achieve a sense of symmetry and reinforce your major theme by coming back to the introduction in the conclusion of your speech. This commonly happens when a speaker uses both a preview and a summary, but you can find more interesting ways to do this, often by using one of the techniques we have already discussed. For example, Beth, who began her speech by telling her audience about her friend Jerry, who committed suicide, returned to her point that what you see on the surface may not be what is going on inside someone. She did this by using two quotations—first a short observation of Thoreau's and then a poem by Edwin Arlington Robinson.

> My friend Jerry is not a unique case. The nineteenth-century naturalist and writer Henry David Thoreau observed that most men live "a life of quiet desperation," lives we don't know much about. If we want to have friends in the deepest sense of that word, we need to try to get closer to people, to be there for them in bad times as well as good, to really listen. Edwin Arlington Robinson wrote about human relationships and exposed our lack of understanding. Let me conclude with one of his short poems, "Richard Cory."

Whenever Richard Cory went to town,
  We people on the pavement looked at him:
He was a gentleman from sole to crown,
  Clean favored and imperially slim.

He was always quietly arrayed,
  And he was always human when he talked;
But still he fluttered pulses when he said,
  "Good-morning," and he glittered when he walked.

And he was rich—yes, richer than a king—
  And admiringly schooled in every grace;
In fine, we thought that he was everything
  To make us wish that we were in his place.

So on we worked, and waited for the light;
  And went without the meat, and cursed the bread;
And Richard Cory, one calm summer night,
  Went home and put a bullet through his head.

The speech's conclusion should create a final impact. To try your hand at organizing one speaker's conclusion, go to **Drill 5.4: Creating Powerful Conclusions** on the **VideoLab** CD-ROM and complete the exercise. Then, view the video clip to check your work.

Most speakers use a combination of techniques. Beth referred to the introduction and used quotations. Senator Weicker not only quoted from the Bible but also challenged his audience. Senator Helms appealed to the audience's emotions while envisioning the future. Karl Bays summed up the traditional values he had been discussing and then challenged his audience to follow them.

For a review of the basics of outlining, go to **Lesson 5 Coach: Tips to Remember** on the **VideoLab** CD-ROM and read through the tips provided.

Final Tips About Conclusions

Just as the introduction of your speech contributes to the audience's first impression of you, the conclusion represents your last chance to reach out to listeners and reinforce your speech's purpose. The conclusion should be brief; this is no place to introduce new information or to tack on something you forgot to say earlier.

Speakers sometimes have trouble ending their speeches. A speaker may say, "Let me leave you with this thought," then ramble on for several more minutes. Or the speaker may pepper his or her remarks with signposts such as "finally" or "in conclusion"—but not stop talking. When a speaker uses these verbal markers, listeners take him or her seriously. If the speaker uses them and continues to speak, listeners may become frustrated or bored, and they will probably stop listening. Even a good speech (and a good speaker) can lose considerable ground if the conclusion is poorly crafted and delivered. The last word is your last opportunity to connect with your audience, and it should never be lost.

KEEP IN MIND 10.6

Effective Conclusions

Effective conclusions summarize your main points.

Effective conclusions may also include

- challenges to your audience.
- appeals to your audience.
- visualizations of the future.
- memorable quotations.
- reference to the introduction.

Because conclusions are so important and potentially memorable, they should

- be brief.
- never ramble.
- not introduce new information.
- be crafted carefully.

SUMMARY

In preparing a speech, you design ideas with a specific purpose in mind, being sure that they are clear, simple without being oversimplified, appropriate to the situation, and sensible. Ideas have to be organized in a coherent and reasonable fashion. The principal patterns of organization discussed in this chapter are chronological or sequential (arranged in a time or step-by-step order), categorical (a pattern that emphasizes distinct topics), climactic (arranged according to importance, size, or degree of simplicity), causal (moving from causes to effects or from effects to causes), and problem-solution (a logical progression that moves from perceived difficulties to an examination of alternatives to a best solution). Ideas are held together by carefully constructed transitions and transitional devices that help the audience follow your ideas and see the connections between them.

As you prepare yourself to speak, an outline will begin to emerge. Working outlines incorporate preliminary thoughts, full-sentence outlines contain fully developed ideas and support, and key word outlines serve as notes for speakers. As you build an outline, you should be sure that each point contains only one idea, that the outline depicts relationships between ideas and support, and that you use a consistent set of symbols and indentations in writing the outline.

Once you have chosen the basic organizational pattern, worked on good transitions, and outlined the body of your speech, you are ready to think about how to begin and conclude your comments. Your speech's introduction should help you capture and hold the audience's attention, show them why your topic is relevant to them, and establish your credibility. Equally important, you should advance the speech's purpose and preview your main ideas.

Crafting an effective conclusion also is important. Conclusions allow you to summarize your main points, challenge your audience, appeal to listeners, and visualize the future. Memorable quotations and references to the introduction also can be effective.

When the audience perceives your speech as well planned and structured, they will be more likely to view you, the speaker, as a credible source of information and a person whose ideas and proposed initiatives are worthy of their consideration.

QUESTIONS FOR REVIEW AND REFLECTION

1. In what ways does the purpose of your speech influence the main ideas?
2. What makes an idea a good one? Consider the topic for your next speech and generate two main ideas that you might use. How well do these ideas fit the criteria for good ideas?
3. What are the principal patterns of organization? Why would you choose one pattern over another? Take the tentative ideas you came up for your next speech and arrange them in at least two different patterns. Which seems best to you and why?
4. What is the function of transitions? What are the different kinds of transitions and transitional devices that you might use? Briefly define each.

5. What are the different kinds of outlines, and what purposes do they serve?
6. Why is it important to restrict each point in the outline to one idea?
7. How does the outline reflect relationships between ideas and supporting material? How does the use of a consistent set of outlining symbols help make this relationship clear?
8. What are the major components of the speech introduction? Why is each important?
9. Give some examples of how you might capture the listeners' attention in your introduction.
10. What should you accomplish in the conclusion to your speech? What are some techniques that will help you do this?

ENDNOTES

1. Stephen William Hawking, *A Brief History of Time* (New York: Bantam Books, 1988), p. 189.
2. D. Bruce Lockerbie, "Teaching Who We Are," *Vital Speeches of the Day* 48 (May 15, 1982): p. 476.
3. Karl D. Bays, "Perspectives on Productivity: Let's Not Forget the Managers," *Vital Speeches of the Day* 48 (October 15, 1981): 27.
4. Jesse Helms, "The Uniting of the Silent Majority," in James Andrews and David Zarefsky, *Contemporary American Voices* (New York: Longman, 1992), p. 321. *Vital Speeches of the Day* 48: Jesse Helms, "The Uniting of the Silent Majority" (July 1, 1982), p. 555.
5. John F. Kennedy, "Amherst College Speech," in Andrews and Zarefsky, *Contemporary American Voices*, p. 166.
6. Lowell Weicker, "Prayer in the Public Schools," in Andrews and Zarefsky, *Contemporary American Voices*, pp. 325–326.

The following speech was given by a student in a beginning public speaking class. It is a good, audience-centered speech, although you may see ways in which it could be improved. Note Cindy's organizational pattern and the way in which she uses transitions to help the audience follow as she moves from point to point. Also focus on her development of ideas as she combines personal experience with other forms of support.

Losing Weight, Looking Great?

Cindy Myles

Introduction: Cindy begins with a story related to a popular sport; her audience would likely be aware of and interested in the Olympics, so this device will help gain their attention and interest.

World-class gymnast Christy Henrich had the future planned. She anticipated making the U.S. Gymnastics Team and aspired to go on for a medal. Her dreams came to a halting stop one day when a judge casually mentioned that Henrich was too fat to make the Olympic Team. At that time, Christy was 4'10" tall and weighed 93 pounds. As a result of the judge's comment, Christy went on a severe dieting program. Over the next four years, she dropped 33 pounds. You can do the math for yourself, but that put her at a whopping total of 60 pounds before she died of multiorgan failure.

Then Cindy tells of a personal experience to attract further attention and to enhance her own ethos by relating her topic to her personal experience. This also relates more directly to the audience since Jenny could be any one of them or someone they know, and not a professional gymnast.

Extreme dieting is not unique to athletes and dancers. My junior year of high school, I befriended Jenny Wolf. Jenny was a slightly overweight, healthy-looking girl. She came from a normal family, had a supportive group of friends, and performed well in school. Jenny and I did not have any classes together and I would only run into her occasionally. I saw her for the first time of my junior year sometime around Thanksgiving. She looked wonderful. She had lost about 20 pounds, and it was obvious that she had been exercising. I commented that I thought she looked great but didn't want to probe into her diet or exercise plan for fear that it might offend her. I didn't see Jenny again for about another two months, and when I did it was obvious that she had a problem. Jenny had gone from slightly overweight to absolutely gorgeous to definitely sickly. She was clinging to a water bottle as if it were her life support. And I heard over the next few weeks rumors that she had taken up jogging every day regardless of the weather. I wasn't a doctor but I knew enough about eating disorders to wonder if Jenny was anorexic.

And what did Jenny Wolf have in common with Becky Schiffron, Dora Israel, Rene Hardy, Shannon Graff, Francie Block, and Kevin Melinowski? Well, the answer is both simple and scary. They were all victims of anorexia nervosa, they all graduated with me, and they were the seven sick people in my graduating class that I knew were sick. There must have been even more that I didn't know about. And how does one handle such a situation? Do you confront the person? Do you go see a counselor? Do you tell the parents? Well, like most people confronted with such an issue, I had no idea who to turn to for help. And like most people confronted with such an issue, I wondered why it had to be my friend.

Transition: Here Cindy explicitly states that this is a problem that can have a direct impact on her audience and then previews the two main points that she wants to make in the speech.

Anorexia nervosa is a serious problem facing people of all ages in every community. Today, I would like to do two things. First, I would like to help you understand more about the disease, and second, I want to let you know what you can do to help locally.

Cindy starts by raising a question. She will do this for each of the subpoints she

What exactly is anorexia? Many people have heard of anorexia nervosa but very few know the exact definition. According to the Department of Health and Human Services, anorexia is the refusal to maintain body weight at or above a minimally normal weight for age and height, leaving body weight to less than 85 percent of that expected. It is an intense fear of gaining weight, and the Anorexia Nervosa and Bulimia Association calls it an obsession, often accompanied by extreme exercise.

wishes to make, imposing a structure on the speech that will help the audience follow it. Then she defines anorexia, using a definition from an authoritative source.

Why do people become anorexic? The causes of anorexia are not exactly known. There are four potential causes that researchers have cited.

First, and probably the most obvious, is family pressure. Many families believe that their children are going to be the model kids. They are going to get great grades in school, they are going to be perfect, and they are perfectionists often, and these children become dependent on the family for all of their decision making. They want some aspect of their life that they can control all by themselves and so many of them turn to controlling their eating habits because it's the easiest thing for them to get a grip on.

Cindy tells listeners that she will explain four causes and takes them up one at a time. The causes are explained generally and fairly clearly, but perhaps a specific example for the first, third, and fourth causes would have driven the point home more forcefully. However, Cindy was giving a speech that had to fit in an assigned time, so this might have been the best place to make generalizations and minimize support. The second point is reinforced with statistical data but could have been strengthened by citing a source.

The second, and another obvious cause of anorexia nervosa, is the media. Our media portray females as very very thin and there's an emphasis on this ideal shape. To blame it solely on the media is a definite oversimplification, but the media are probably a cause of anorexia. A recent survey of fifth- and sixth-graders disclosed that 73 percent of girls and 43 percent of sixth-grade boys wanted to be thinner. Children that young can only get this idea from the media that they see.

The third cause of anorexia nervosa can be low self-esteem or a poor body image, and this is often accompanied by a life crisis. If your life is turning upside down and you're searching for something to get a hold of, why not get a hold of your eating habits?

Fourth, and finally, many people turn to anorexia nervosa to find a sense of triumph over helplessness. In our society obesity is like a plague. There are so many people you see who are overweight and people feel like they are achieving a social success and a social victory by getting a hold of their eating habits and staying thin.

The causes of anorexia, then, arise from pressures in our everyday lives, pressures that cause some of us to take actions that can destroy our lives. What exactly are the effects of this disease?

Transition: Cindy moves from causes to effects by using the simple structural device of raising a question again.

Anorexia has many severe physical and mental effects. The physical, with treatment, are relatively easy to cure. One is weight loss, which brings about coldness and an irregular heartbeat, and hormonal imbalances which can cause dry skin, brittle hair, dental problems, and amenorrhea. And for those of you who don't know, amenorrhea is the loss of the menstrual cycle in females. Twenty-five percent of the women who have severe cases of anorexia never regain the ability to menstruate, which makes them infertile. So anorexia can be a cause of infertility. Also, anorexia can bring about malnourishment which can cause a tingling in the hands, feet, and face and often is accompanied by dizziness.

She wants to tell her audience what the physical and mental effects are, so she simply goes through them quickly. They are not difficult to understand or visualize. The only one that might be unfamiliar to an audience is amenorrhea, so she stops to define it for her listeners. To help her audience follow and remember, however, she might have used a presentational aid that listed the effects.

The mental effects of anorexia nervosa are much longer lasting and difficult to cure. All recurrences of anorexia nervosa can be attributed to these mental effects. They include a poor self-image, a fear of judgment, the striving for perfection, a need for control, and finally, in 40 to 80 percent of anorexia victims, there is depression.

While you can witness the effects of this disease on individuals, the overall statistics are terrifying. Anorexia is the third most common chronic illness among teens. In fact, the National Center for Health Statistics reported that 1 out of every 200 girls in America between the ages of 12 and 18 will have

Cindy wants to reemphasize that these effects are a serious threat to people in the listeners' age group. She does so with statistical data

derived from an authoritative source. Since the data might be hard for listeners to follow, here too she might have used a presentational aid.

some form of anorexia nervosa. This implies that 0.5 to 3 percent of all teens will contract an eating disorder. Like Christy Henrich, 60 to 70 percent of athletes are anorexic and 10 to 15 percent die as a result of this disorder. Anorexia is 90 percent a female disease, but don't forget the men. Men constitute 10 percent of the victims; 4 percent are adult males and 6 percent are adolescent boys.

Transition: Cindy returns to using a question and rules out some obvious, but misguided, ways to try to help before moving to ways to treat the disease.

So, when the statistics are so overwhelming and the prevalence is so high, the question becomes: What can you do to help? Well, many people believe that monitoring a person's eating habits is the way to go. They force-feed or try to put the person on a diet which they can watch and actually plan out for the victim. Well, this is not the way to help if you are a friend or family of an anorexic victim. Explaining to the person that he or she looks ill or questioning the motives behind becoming anorexic is also not the way to go. This is only going to lower their self-esteem and make them feel guilty for having the disease. Neither method is going to result in an improved condition.

After reviewing treatment, Cindy goes on to stress what listeners can do—again relating this issue to her audience.

The recommended treatment for anorexia nervosa is three-fold. First, the help of a trained professional such as a doctor or nutritionist is necessary; a doctor or nutritionist can provide the diet restrictions and the correct eating habits. Second, individual counseling has proven very effective. And, third, the team approach has been used to include more people and a larger support group for the victims. That is where friends and family come in: an anorexic victim needs emotional support, and that's what you and I have to give them.

To support the notion that personal help is necessary and to show how it might be done, Cindy uses a specific example and then relates this example to the personal ones she used earlier in this speech.

Many communities have begun programs of their own. For example, in Victoria, Canada, they have established a 24-hour hotline where victims and friends and families of victims can call and talk about the problems that they are having as a result of anorexia nervosa. They have also established two support groups in Victoria. One is exclusively for the sufferers of anorexia nervosa and the other is for the friends and family members. A lot of people who have this disease or know someone with this disease think they are going through it alone. That is not the case. Just from the seven people in my graduating class, I knew that they thought they were going through it alone.

Transition to the conclusion brings the audience back to the point that this is a problem relevant to the audience.

Of course, it would be best if treatment was not needed—if the disease could be prevented. Education about anorexia in the schools, starting at a junior high level, would surely help. Kids need to be aware that this disease is out there. They need to be aware of the symptoms and how they can detect them, and they need to be aware of coping strategies so if someone they know contracts this disease they know where to go or how to help them. But such a step is too late for many women and men in our age group, people who may be our friends and family—maybe even some of us.

Victims of anorexia nervosa should not have to face this disease or the healing process alone. They need the support, love, and encouragement to overcome the illness and prevent it from recurring. The earlier the detection, the better the chances are for a full recovery. Christy Henrich never got this chance. Her environment was not supportive enough. It is up to us to create an environment in each community so that anorexia nervosa victims do not continue their disease and that the mortality rate decreases.

The conclusion repeats the role the audience can play in helping people with this disease and returns to the examples used in the introduction.

Jenny Wolf received the help that she needed and has made a successful adjustment to college. She has regained half of the weight that she lost and has maintained this weight through healthy exercise and a great eating program. Together, we can make all victims of anorexia nervosa success stories like Jenny Wolf. Hopefully, we will not be able to list as many names of anorexia nervosa victims in our college graduating class as I could in my high school class.

PART IV

Present: Presenting the Speech

Part IV discusses how language and delivery contribute to a successful, audience-centered speech. It also describes how to use presentational aids to engage your listeners and to achieve the response you want from your audience. Having learned how to prepare yourself to speak effectively, you will be ready to consider particular applications of public speaking principles.

11 Delivering the Speech Effectively

CHAPTER SURVEY

CHAPTER OBJECTIVES

After studying this chapter, you should be able to

1. **describe and apply the basic characteristics of good delivery.**
2. **deliver an effective extemporaneous speech using a key word outline.**
3. **distinguish between several alternative styles of delivery and describe the strengths and weaknesses of each.**
4. **anticipate audience questions and various ways of responding to them.**
5. **distinguish ethically sound from ethically questionable delivery.**

After all of the preparation, investigation, thought, and work that go into your speech, you ultimately must present yourself to an audience. You may have taken days or even weeks to analyze your audience, investigate your topic, and organize and practice your speech. In the end, you may deliver your speech in only a few minutes. Even so, the actual delivery of the message is the climax and culmination of the public speaking experience.

Delivery is one of the most obvious aspects of public speaking, and one that draws the initial focus of both speaker and listener. If, for example, one were to ask an audience what they thought of a speech that had just been given, the most likely responses would be something like: "I think he had a very nice voice"; "I think she should have moved around more"; and "I couldn't always hear him." We know, of course, that delivery is not *the* defining factor in public speaking. An engaging delivery cannot compensate for a speech that is poorly structured or lacking in substance. Even so, most of us recognize the importance of delivery, and sometimes it frightens us. We may feel pretty comfortable preparing the speech, doing the research, organizing our ideas, preparing the outline, and so forth. But when faced with the necessity of "standing and delivering," we may become very apprehensive.[1] The more we know about delivery, the better are our chances of learning to present speeches effectively in diverse settings. Delivery may be a small part of the entire speech process, but it is a very noticeable and influential part.

To test your skills and expand your understanding of effective delivery, go to **Lesson 6** of the **VideoLab** CD-ROM and walk through the videos, exercises, and tips provided.

PRINCIPLES OF GOOD DELIVERY

Preview Certain basic principles of effective delivery are applicable across a wide variety of public speaking situations. You will want to adapt your delivery to the specific situation and to audience expectations. In general, effective delivery is associated with proper attire; good eye contact; effective gestures, movement, and facial expressions; and an effective speaking voice.

Should you use a podium? Should you move much during your speech? How quickly should you speak? Will vocal projection be a problem? Is it ever appropriate to sit down while making a speech? There are no absolute answers to any of these questions. You should adjust your style of delivery to the demands of the speaking situation.

Understand the Situation and Audience Expectations

What is appropriate in one situation may be inappropriate in another. For example, the speaker who stands stiffly behind a massive podium and reads a manuscript to a small group of five or six people is not adapting well to the speech setting, which seems to call for a more direct, conversational speaking style. Above all, using a delivery style that allows you to connect with the audience is crucial, as illustrated in *Spotlight on Connecting with the Audience: President Clinton's Delivery.*

The more you know about what audience members need, like, and are accustomed to, the better able you are to deliver your speech effectively. How do speakers usually approach this group? Is formality expected, or does the group like to sit in a circle and have the speaker "chat" with them? Perhaps this is a business organization, and they fully expect you to use visuals. In what kind of room will you be speaking? Is there a podium, and is it commonly used by others speaking to the group?

To assess a student speech on Native American symbols using persuasive speech, go to **Lesson 6's Screening Room** on the **VideoLab** CD-ROM. After viewing the speech, respond to the questions that ask you to critically analyze the speaker's presentation.

One woman embarrassed herself when she arrived to give her manuscript speech and discovered that there was no podium anywhere in the building. Since she did not want to have to hold the manuscript in front of her and read from it, she asked the president of the organization she was addressing what could be done. The best he could do was produce a large cardboard box, which he turned upside down and placed on top of a table to create a makeshift podium. Unfortunately, the box did little to add to the seriousness of the speaker's remarks on alcohol abuse: it boldly advertised Red Dog Beer.

Dress for the Occasion

How should you dress when you make a speech? Your appearance can influence audience perceptions of your ethos. Although there are no precise rules for attire, listeners generally expect speakers to look well groomed and to be nicely

SPOTLIGHT ON... Connecting with the Audience: President Clinton's Delivery

From the* New York Times, *February 2, 1997

Remember how Bill Clinton electrified a joint session of Congress in 1993 by brandishing a prototype of a national health care card and calling for "health care that can never be taken away, health care that is always there"?

That speech still stands as one of the most impressive formal addresses of his Presidency. And perhaps it was no accident that Mr. Clinton could hold that Congress in his sway even though he was winging it for seven minutes as the wrong text scrolled across the Teleprompter. But he might not be as dramatic Tuesday when he delivers his State of the Union Address.

For Mr. Clinton has a curious split personality when it comes to oratory. Speaking extemporaneously, he can be arresting, eloquent, and amusing. . . . His turns of phrase twang with a delicious backwoodsiness. During the campaign, he said of the Republican budget proposal: "It is their dog. And it was a mangy old dog, and that's why I vetoed that dog." And at the pulpit of a church, Mr. Clinton can burn with a preacher's passion that rivals the Rev. Jesse Jackson's.

But put this President in the most stately settings of government with a written text and a Teleprompter and his eloquence sometimes fades. Connectedness is the key to his best oratory, his aides say. Mr. Clinton needs the synergy of the crowd; he needs to feel people's enthusiasm or their pain.

Alison Mitchell, "State of the Speech: Reading Between the Lines," *New York Times* (February 2, 1997) p. E5. Copyright © 1997 by The New York Times Company. Reprinted by permission.

dressed. How listeners themselves are dressed provides one clue. You would not want to be wearing jeans and a polo shirt if audience members were wearing suits and ties. However, in your public speaking class, wearing nice jeans and a shirt on your speaking day is probably quite appropriate. Check with your speech instructor for further guidance. In other speaking situations, you may ask the person who invited you to speak about the formality of the occasion and the practices of audience members.

When you go to the trouble of looking good and dressing well, you are conveying to the audience that you take the occasion seriously, thus enhancing your ethos. As we discussed earlier, when you speak, you are the center of attention. You want to feel confident about the way you look and to dress comfortably. Avoid pants that are too tight or shoes that hurt when you stand up for more than five minutes. Also avoid any attire that detracts from your speech, such as a flamboyant blouse or a baseball cap.

Every speaking environment will offer opportunities as well as constraints. As we noted in Chapter 2, the more you can anticipate about the speech situation, the more likely you will be to manage your communication apprehension and deliver a good speech that fits the occasion and the audience. Still, there are a few principles of good delivery that, if applied with flexibility, can serve as useful guidelines.

Establish Eye Contact

Have you ever talked with anyone who couldn't look you in the eye? Did you feel that the person was uncomfortable? Nervous? Ashamed? Preoccupied? Dishonest? In U.S. culture, when a communicator cannot or does not look us in the eye, we often respond negatively.[2] Our response is no different in public speaking situations. As listeners, we prefer speakers who make **eye contact**.

eye contact looking into the eyes of those with whom you are communicating

Of course, there are cultural variations in practices and reactions to eye contact. For instance, Puerto Ricans consider it disrespectful to make prolonged eye contact with superiors.[3] In Japan, meeting participants often look down or close their eyes while others are talking. By doing so, they show their attentiveness to and even agreement with the speaker.[4]

Regardless of cultural differences, our eyes can be very expressive. As we squint, smile, laugh, frown, or scowl, we communicate many emotions: concern, commitment, joy, or anger. When we fail to establish eye contact, we must rely solely on our words, voice, gestures, and facial expressions to convey emotions. In U.S. culture, we clearly place ourselves at a disadvantage if we do not use our eyes to communicate.

Another reason for establishing eye contact is to convey a positive ethos. Once again, cultural norms differ on this point, but in general we are more likely to believe a speaker who looks us in the eye while defending his or her point of view.[5] When we establish eye contact with our listeners, we come across as more truthful, candid, and open, and thus less likely to mislead.

Finally, looking at the members of the audience gives us a chance to watch their reactions to our speech. How can we see those yawns or glazed expressions if we never look at the listeners? How can we clarify what we're saying if we haven't noticed that they seem confused? Or, on a more positive note, how can we benefit from appreciative smiles and nods of encouragement if we aren't looking? If we are not aware of audience reactions, we cannot respond to them. Almost all audience feedback will be nonverbal until after the speech is over. So if we "close our eyes," we miss out on an important chance to make our speech more of a dialogue and less of a monologue.

As you establish eye contact with your audience, remember to share your attention with everyone. Avoid focusing on only a few people (the most friendly faces or your speech instructor), looking only at one section of the room, or staring at some audience members as if in a trance. Also avoid darting your eyes or glancing up and down from the outline as if bobbing for apples. Table 11.1 highlights several patterns of eye contact to be avoided. Of all the principles of effective delivery, establishing eye contact may be the most important.

TABLE 11.1 Ineffective Eye Patterns

1. *The Bobber:*	Bobs up from notes, like that little dog folks used to display in the back glass of their cars.
2. *The Stargazer:*	Looks above and beyond the audience at a spot on the back wall.
3. *The Obsessor:*	Limits eye contact to one, two, or a few individuals. The intensity of the gaze can become uncomfortable for the victim(s), while those excluded feel very much left out.
4. *The Obliterator:*	Limits eye contact to one side of the room—obliterating all on the other side.

Source: Adapted from Professor J. Michael Hogan, Pennsylvania State University.

 PORTFOLIO 11.1

The Windows to the Soul

Respond to the following questions:

1. What is your typical level of eye contact when talking with a friend?
2. What is your typical level of eye contact when talking with someone you do not know very well?
3. What is your typical level of eye contact when talking in front of a group of people?

In light of your answers, note where any deficiencies might lie and how you might improve your level of eye contact to derive the benefits discussed in the text.

Reinforce Ideas Through Gestures, Movement, and Facial Expressions

gestures the expressive use of your hands

movement the expressive use of your body

facial expressions the expressive use of your face to convey emotion

Most of us use numerous **gestures** in daily conversations. We wave our hands, point, and pound on the table to stress a point. Our **movement** can also communicate to others. We pace, slouch in our chairs, move closer to someone to express liking or intimacy, or move farther away to create distance or convey aloofness. We communicate a great deal with our faces, too. Through **facial expressions**, we smile broadly, scowl, raise an eyebrow, or clench our teeth to communicate determination, anger, or stubbornness. Yet the person who is quite animated in daily conversation may become rigid and immobile when making a speech.

The act of standing before others and making a speech can make many people acutely uncomfortable. Suddenly they don't know what to do with their hands, their feet, or their bodies. So they do nothing, standing lifelessly behind the podium. Only their head moves from time to time, but their arms and hands are never seen, and their faces are masklike. Other speakers react differently. As if they have been supercharged, they dart around the front of the room or continuously pace back and forth, punching the air with sharp, repetitive gestures. Figure 11.1 shows speakers who represent the two extremes.

Clearly such extremes are to be avoided. Taken together, your movements, gestures, and facial expressions should reinforce the points you are making. Through gestures, you can accent an idea, demonstrate a relationship, depict contrast, illustrate size, and so forth. Suppose you are giving a speech comparing the experience of attending a Big Ten university with that of attending a small, private college. As you make a verbal transition from one kind of school to the other, you might move (perhaps from right to left) and gesture (by extending first your right and then your left hand), thus reinforcing the contrast.

Your words and actions should be mutually reinforcing. If you were talking to a friend about something that mattered to you, you might say, "I *really* want you to consider doing this!" At the same time, you might lean forward, look

Good Delivery Avoids Extremes in Gestures and Movement

FIGURE 11.1 **Delivery Problems**

into her or his eyes, and nod your head. Some public speakers might use very similar words in speaking to an audience, but with a deadpan face, little eye contact, and no movement or gestures. No audience is likely to be moved by such a bland and contradictory appeal. If what we say and how we say it contradict each other, listeners will place more faith in our nonverbal behavior.[6]

Perhaps you are uncertain about whether your movement, gestures, and facial expressions are appropriate. If so, you need to watch yourself speak in front of a mirror or on a videotape, or ask someone to watch you practice your speech and give you feedback. Here are some questions you might want to consider to guide your thinking:

- Do I gesture enough? Too much?
- Does my movement seem to reinforce the flow of the speech?
- Are my gestures distracting in any way?
- Do I rely too much on any one gesture?
- Does my face seem to convey the meaning or feeling I am trying to communicate?
- Are there different gestures, movements, or facial expressions that might convey my intended meaning more effectively?

Although some basic gestures and movements can be planned and rehearsed in advance, most should occur spontaneously as you interact with your audience. Thus your movement will vary as you give the same speech at different times, in different rooms, and to different audiences. For instance, natural conversational gestures will work well if you are speaking to an audience of 25 or fewer. But if you are speaking to 150 people assembled in an auditorium, you will need to enlarge your gestures so that they can be seen by everyone.

Finally, even if you feel that you cannot gesture very much or very often, make sure that your movements are not perceived as nervous or distracting. Some speakers pace nervously. They play with their earrings, stroke their hair, chew gum, hang on to the podium, or tap a pencil they forgot to leave behind. Still others use such exaggerated gestures that they look foolish or melodramatic. Whenever a gesture calls attention to itself, you should eliminate it.

Strive for an Effective Speaking Voice

One of the most obvious aspects of any speaker's delivery is, of course, his or her voice. Have you ever listened to a speaker whose voice drove you crazy? Perhaps she or he spoke in a monotone, stumbled over words, or inserted "you know" between every sentence. Or maybe the speaker had a pitch problem (too high and squeaky or too low and unvarying), spoke at a breathtakingly rapid pace, or seemed to be shouting at the audience. Clearly our voices can get us into a lot of trouble as public speakers. But they can also be used fully and compellingly to convey our ideas. When we use our voices effectively, we can emphasize key ideas, display a wide variety of emotions, and improve our credibility.

You will want to consider seriously how you can best use your voice. You might try speaking into a tape recorder and playing it back to see what your voice sounds like to others. Obtaining feedback from friends also could be helpful, since they are likely to notice peculiarities that might sound "normal" to

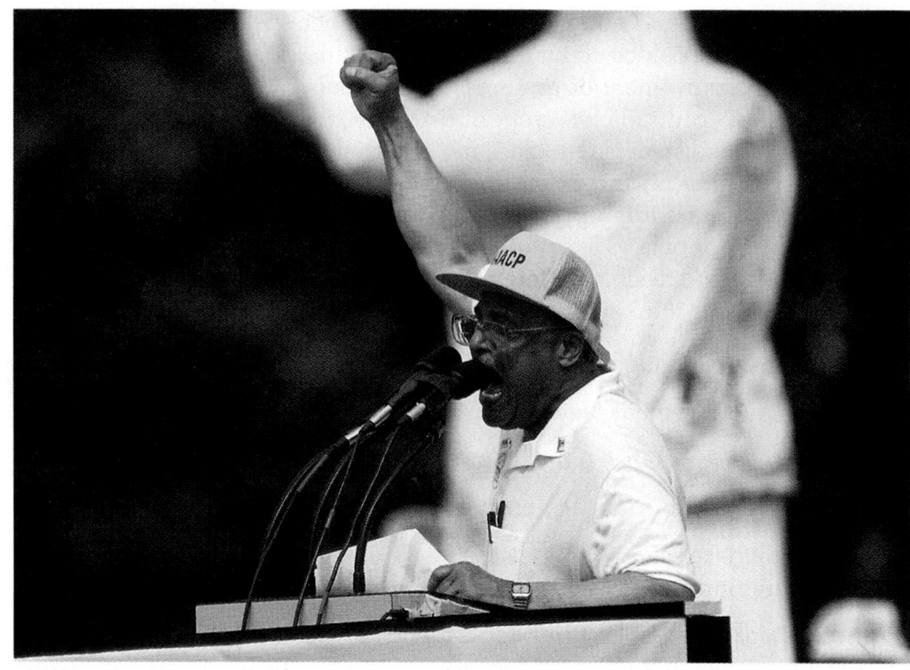

A speaker's gestures and expression will reflect his or her engagement with the topic and the audience. Here, Benjamin Hooks, Executive Director of the NAACP, forcefully addresses a large labor rally in Washington, D.C. (Rob Crandall/Stock Boston)

you. You can modify some features of your voice by recognizing their importance, monitoring their operation as you speak, and paying special attention to them in oral practice. These features are volume, rate, pitch, clarity, and variety.

Volume. It should be apparent that no idea will be understood and no idea will be motivating if it cannot be heard. Nor will an audience be able to concentrate on your message if you are so loud that they are uncomfortable.

volume the degree of softness or loudness in your vocalizations

Your **volume** may directly influence the audience's attentiveness. One speaker, who later reported that he wanted to be "emphatic" and "forceful," shouted his speech to an audience of about twenty people in a small classroom. In discussing the speech, the listeners concentrated almost entirely on the volume, describing the speaker as "obviously very nervous," "too aggressive," "too emotional," and even "insulting." Members of the audience could hardly reconstruct the speaker's thesis or remember the main points he made, so unnerved were they by the loud delivery. At the other extreme, speakers whose voices come out in soft whispers usually cause an audience first to strain to hear and then to lapse into bored inattention.

The degree of loudness or softness should be determined by the setting in which the speaking takes place. Naturally a small room calls for a quieter voice than does a large lecture hall or an outdoor setting. As you gain speaking experience, you will learn to attend to listeners' needs and increase or decrease your volume as the situation demands. Practice is critical in helping you ready yourself for the actual speech situation. Standing up and giving your speech, at a volume that seems realistic for the actual presentation, will help you monitor your own voice and begin to get a feel for speaking loudly or softly enough for the listeners to understand and be comfortable. If you are concerned that you are not being heard, ask your listeners. They will appreciate your asking, and they will give you accurate feedback.

Rate. It is not uncommon for a beginning speaker to sit down after giving a speech, look at the clock, and be amazed to find that the planned ten-minute speech took only five minutes. Several miscalculations in planning could account for such a result, but often the problem is that the speaker has rushed through the speech. In his or her anxiety to "get it over with," a speaker can forget that an audience needs time to follow, to absorb, and to react.

The needs of the listeners are paramount. Just as they can't keep up with a too-fast speaker, they'll lose interest in a too-slow one. Rate and fluency can be interrelated. Often speakers who have not practiced or prepared enough drag through a speech, stumbling along with "um's" and "ah's," pausing too frequently or too long, and filling in gaps with the ubiquitous and irritating "you know." In fact, some research suggests that listeners may perceive speakers who speak more quickly (though not breathtakingly fast) as really knowing what they are talking about, thus potentially enhancing their ethos.[7]

Your **rate** should largely be determined by your estimate of the nature of the listeners' response. As we pointed out earlier, listening to a speech can be contrasted with reading a book. The reader can slow down or speed up as his or her needs dictate. The speaker, however, cannot be stopped and replayed by the listeners, just as the listeners cannot skip ahead to the speaker's next point. When speaking, you must anticipate the listeners' reactions and be prepared to adjust to the feedback you receive. This means that your focus is on the members of your audience and on their responses to the material, not exclusively on the material you are presenting.

rate the degree of quickness or slowness in your vocalizations

As you plan for and react to listeners' responses, you will modify your speaking rate as the situation demands. In addition, the material itself will influence your rate. A speaker describing the last few laps of the Indianapolis 500, for example, will undoubtedly speak at a faster rate than will a speaker who is describing the feelings of someone who is coping with a significant loss. To increase the potential for achieving your desired response, strive to speak at a rate that is appropriate to the mood of the speech.

Finally, your speaking rate can be used to emphasize key ideas. **Pausing** gives the audience the opportunity to absorb information and ideas. At the same time, by using silence to reinforce a compelling statistic, quotation, or narrative, you are saying to the audience, "Let's stop to contemplate this for a minute. This is important." Similarly, you may slow down or use restatement to emphasize an idea. When you vary your rate—by pausing, slowing down, or using restatement or repetition at critical and strategic moments—you enhance your chances of delivering a memorable speech.

pausing using vocal silence during a speech for emphasis, dramatic effect, or to signal a transition

Pitch. Sometimes a speaker's voice is simply unpleasant to listen to. It may be squeaky or raspy, or it may be pitched so low that you can hardly distinguish one word from the next. **Pitch** refers to the degree to which a voice is high or low. Sometimes a speaker's vocal pitch can be too high, too low, or too unvarying. When the pitch is too high, listeners tend to cringe. When the pitch is too low, listeners may be unable to hear what the speaker is saying. An unvarying pitch is a **monotone**—a vocal quality guaranteed to end all sleepless nights.

pitch the highness or lowness of a speaker's voice

monotone use of the same vocal pitch without variation

Rightly or wrongly, listeners often draw conclusions about speakers who possess pitch problems. A high pitch may be associated with immaturity, tension, or excitability. A low pitch or a monotone may cause listeners to view the speaker as being bored or unengaged. Clearly a speaker's pitch can present an array of problems.

What can you do about pitch? Start by tape-recording your voice and listening to what you hear. If you are not satisfied, you may want to use some vocal exercises to improve your pitch or to seek assistance from someone trained in voice therapy. Here are a few pointers to keep in mind:

- Your pitch will vary throughout your life. It will be higher when you are younger and lower later in life. Working with it is an ongoing process.
- If you are tense, your pitch tends to rise. Use the relaxation techniques outlined in Chapter 2 to help manage your communication apprehension and control your pitch.
- Strive for some variety in your pitch. In general, you want your voice to be interesting, and you want to use all aspects of your voice to emphasize those things that you most value. When used with variety, vocal pitch, rate, and volume can combine to help you do that.

The importance of effective nonverbal communication can hardly be overstated. Go to **Drill 6.2: The Importance of Nonverbal Communication** on the **VideoLab** CD-ROM; after viewing the video clips, evaluate each speaker's use of nonverbal communication. To what extent does the delivery of each reinforce or contradict his or her verbal message?

Vocal Clarity. To be effective in informing or persuading, you must be understood. One speaker baffled an audience for some time until they finally understood that he was not referring to his "buddy" but rather to his "body." Another speaker discovered in the discussion following his speech that many listeners interpreted his mispronunciation of key words as a sign that he didn't know what he was talking about. To achieve **vocal clarity**, you should aim to achieve three important qualities.

vocal clarity the degree to which your vocalizations can be readily understood

articulation the manner in which you produce individual sounds in words and phrases

pronunciation the manner in which a word is pronounced, in terms of sounds and acccents

disruptive mannerisms vocal habits and conventions that clutter your speaking and might distract listeners

- *First, strive for distinctness in* **articulation**. Dropping the endings of words, slurring sounds, and running words together can interfere with the meaning of a message.
- *Second, try to achieve accurate* **pronunciation**. Every speaker should feel confident that the words he or she uses are pronounced correctly. This means going to the dictionary whenever you have the slightest doubt. Practice aloud so that you are comfortable with the words you are using, and especially check the pronunciation of words used in quoted material.
- *Third, do all that you can to achieve freedom from* **disruptive mannerisms**. It is pointless and distracting to keep saying "you know." One speaker obscured the clarity of his message by concluding almost every statement with the unnecessary question "Right?" Also, there are regional mannerisms that clutter speech and thus reduce clarity, such as the question "Hear?" at the end of a sentence, or the unnecessary and ungrammatical "at" tacked on to statements such as, "He didn't know where I was *at*." Such mannerisms are distracting to listeners.

Variety. In supporting the ideas being communicated, the speaker's voice should be adapted to the needs of the audience, the setting, and the content of the speech itself. Unvaried volume and unvaried rate will not only negatively affect the listeners' attention, but they also may distort the basic meaning of the ideas being discussed. To develop **variety**, cultivate an awareness of your own voice. Learn to listen to yourself and begin to appreciate what listeners will hear as you speak. Through practice and careful attention to your own behavior, you can develop a voice that will be pleasing to listeners.

variety the degree to which you vary your voice to add expressiveness to vocalizations

Vocal variety is vital for effective public speaking. To emphasize some ideas or key words of your speech, you may slow down or project your voice more forcefully. You can deliver background information that is already largely understood at a brisker pace. Not every word or phrase in your speech is of equal importance. Through the way you use your voice, you can stress those things that matter most and, you hope, will be most memorable. Varying your voice will not only help the audience know what you value most; it also will make the speech more interesting and "listener-friendly."

A good speaking voice is an important part of the total process of delivery, but it is only one part. Speakers continuously work on vocal quality. Your voice will be different in the morning than in the evening. If you have been talking a good deal before your speech, your voice may sound strained or harsh. As you grow older, your vocal quality will change. Striving for good breath support is important. As we pointed out in Chapter 2, diaphragmatic or deep breathing is one way to deal with communication apprehension. It also provides excellent vocal support. Achieving good vocal quality is a lifelong task.

PORTFOLIO 11.2

A New, More Fluent You

Do you habitually insert unnecessary words, phrases, or other vocalizations into your sentences? Do you have a habit of saying words indistinctly? Ar there any words you always mispronounce? Do you ever speak too rapidly?

Make a list of any of these "problems" in your own speaking and ask your friends and classmates if they would add any. Once you become more sensitive to any undesirable speaking habits, you can begin to eliminate them.

Sometimes focusing on a specific aspect of a speaker's delivery can allow you to refine your critical listening skills. Go to the **Online SpeechStudio** and use the **Guide to Evaluating Voice and Articulation** to assess the way a speaker uses his or her voice.

Remain Flexible

No matter how carefully you plan and practice in advance, some speaking situations will surprise you. **Flexibility** is the key to responding successfully to these situations. You will find larger (or smaller) audiences than you expected, podiums missing, dead microphones, or previously unannounced time constraints. You may have to cut a portion of your speech at the last minute. If you are speaking from a key word outline, you will find it much easier to adapt to the situation. Suppose you expected to find an audience of about thirty traditionally clad businesspeople and you found in their place a group of five or six people wearing jeans and sneakers. Rather than standing behind a podium and speaking formally, you might want to consider sitting on the edge of a table and "chatting" with them.

flexibility the degree to which you can adapt your speechmaking to new elements in a speaking situation

The foundation of flexibility is spontaneity and open-mindedness—a willingness to recognize that there are many different ways to give a good speech and an ability to discover a "better" way whenever a situation seems to demand it. Contrary to stereotypes, it is not always appropriate for public speakers to stand, they do not have to use a podium even if one is provided, and they can engage the audience in dialogue if those practices seem fitting and consistent with the audience's norms and expectations.

Sometimes adapting to the peculiarities of a speaking situation may involve some risk. After all, if you've planned to do it one way and the situation you're in seems to suggest something different, you may fear that your attempt at spontaneity will fail. Yet every public speaking venture is accompanied by some risk. Determining what is appropriate always calls for judgment. As your experience as a public speaker increases, you will feel greater confidence in exercising your judgment and acting accordingly. Regardless of the risk, however, adapting your speech to the conditions under which you are speaking is almost always the best route.

Practice Your Speech

Sometimes speakers think that once they have carefully researched their topic, organized their thoughts, and prepared their outline, all they need to do is read through the outline silently a few times—and they will be ready to go. Nothing could be farther from the truth. If you have not practiced your speech aloud several times, chances are you are not prepared to speak.

In Chapter 2, we discussed the specific steps to take in practicing your speech. Reviewing that section might be wise. Here are a few reminders:

- Practice delivering your speech aloud with your key word outline. But first read through your notes silently several times until you feel ready to begin.
- Practice your speech all the way through—noting sections that are rough, rereading your notes, and then practicing again.
- Break the speech into parts and practice major sections, such as the introduction, several times in a row.
- Always take breaks. Avoid practicing so much at one time that you begin to lose your energy, voice, or concentration.
- Tape-record (either audio or video) your speech and play it back. Avoid dissecting your delivery. Focus on major issues.
- Practice in front of a small audience and ask for their constructive feedback.
- Over a period of time, practice your speech again several times, all the way through, but guard against memorization.
- Be sure to incorporate your visual aids into your practice sessions. If possible, visit the room where you will speak and practice using the equipment there.
- Be sure to time yourself several times. If your speech is too long, make appropriate cuts. For instance, you might cut a section that is less important, use fewer examples, edit long quotations, or plan to tell the audience that you will be glad to address an issue more fully during the question-and-answer period. Remember, if your speech is too long or too short, you may violate the audience's expectations and damage your credibility.

It's important to remember that practicing your speech is something you do *before* the beginning of class. Sometimes speakers read through their notes while their classmates are speaking. Don't fall into this trap. Practice sufficiently beforehand, so that you will be better able to function as a supportive, attentive audience member.

KEEP IN MIND 11.1

Basic Principles of Effective Delivery

- Understand the situation and audience expectations.
- Dress for the occasion.
- Establish eye contact.
- Reinforce ideas through gestures, movement, and facial expressions.
- Strive for an effective speaking voice.
- Remain flexible.
- Practice your speech.

SPEAKING EXTEMPORANEOUSLY

Preview In most public speaking situations, the extemporaneous style of delivery is best. Using the extemporaneous style and speaking from a key word outline allow you to be completely involved in your speech while maintaining the flexibility you need to be adaptable and dynamic.

Sometimes people confuse extemporaneous speaking with impromptu speaking, believing that you don't have to do very much to prepare for an extemporaneous speech. In fact, **extemporaneous speaking** requires a great deal of preparation. To give an extemporaneous speech, you must engage in thoughtful, thorough research, organize and outline your ideas carefully, practice your speech several times without memorizing it word for word, and deliver it using limited notes.

When delivering a speech extemporaneously, you commit key ideas to memory, but words, phrases, and examples vary during practice sessions as well as during the presentation of the speech. Thus, you have the advantage of being well prepared and the ability to adapt to the situation when changes seem prudent.

FRAME OF REFERENCE

In the extemporaneous speech, the speaker has practiced thoroughly and prepared well. In this kind of speech, the speaker uses notes yet still maintains contact with listeners.

Preparing and Using a Key Word Outline

We discussed outlining in Chapter 10. The formal outline you give your instructor anticipates the language you will use. It represents the fully developed, carefully crafted speech you will deliver. But it is *not* the outline you will use when delivering your speech extemporaneously. If you were to use this kind of outline, you would essentially be using a manuscript. As with a manuscript (see pages 271–273), you would probably be tempted to be glued to it, diminishing your directness and eye contact with the audience.

When you deliver a speech extemporaneously, you should use a **key word outline**, discussed in Chapter 10. This outline keeps you on track and reminds you of your main points, but it does not provide so much information that you are tempted to use it as a crutch. You will stick to your main ideas, but you will be encouraged to speak directly with your audience, to watch for their responses, to move as you speak, and to make changes that seem justified by the situation.

For example in class you will typically speak on a day when several other people are speaking, too. Should someone refer to a piece of evidence or an event that is relevant to your topic, you may decide, during your speech, that you will make some reference to what that speaker has said. For example, you might say, "Joan has already made us keenly aware of how poorly our campus is equipped to serve disabled students. Well, our campus has another problem that affects all of us: it is not a very safe place to go to school."

Whenever you are able to do some last-minute fine-tuning, you show others in your audience that you have been paying attention to what has been said immediately preceding your speech. Doing so helps you better connect with your audience and may improve your ethos. Figure 11.2 provides an example of a key word outline. (See Chapter 10 for another example.)

Learning to speak extemporaneously requires effort and practice. We have all seen extemporaneous speakers who flounder for precise words (and may

extemporaneous speaking the presentation of a thoroughly prepared speech using an abbreviated set of notes

key word outline an abbreviated outline that serves as a speaker's notes during a speech

Go to **Lesson 9's Screening Room** on the **VideoLab** CD-ROM to view the first speech on women's gymnastics. After viewing the speech, evaluate the extent to which the speaker used effective extemporaneous delivery. What did she do well, and in what specific ways might her delivery be improved?

FIGURE 11.2 Key Word Outline

Speech topic: Understanding and coping with stress

INTRODUCTION*

Share personal story
Define stress
Relate to college audience
State purpose
Preview main points

I. Major causes of stress
   A. Internal (self-esteem)
   B. Job/school related (too challenging)
   C. Relationship (loss)
      1. Breakup with boyfriend
      2. Father's death
   D. Situational (moving)

II. Effects of stress
   A. Irritability
   B. Poor concentration
   C. Sleeplessness
   D. Loss of appetite

III. What to do?
   A. Develop realistic expectations
   B. Relax
   C. Take care of self
   D. Avoid dramatization
   E. Strive for balanced life
   F. Keep perspective/sense of humor

CONCLUSION*

Revisit personal story
Summarize
Challenge

* Some speakers prefer to write out their introductions and conclusions. As long as this does not encourage you to read rather than speak with an audience, this might be a better strategy for you.

never find them), ramble, or use poor examples. With the help of your instructor's feedback and guidance, these potential problems, should they occur, will decrease with experience.

KEEP IN MIND 11.2

Keys to Effective Extemporaneous Delivery

Extemporaneous delivery

- requires careful preparation.
- is based on a key word outline.
- allows the speaker to remain direct, involved, and flexible.

Reasons for Using Extemporaneous Delivery

With extemporaneous speaking, you have considerable control over what you say and do, especially as you are speaking. You can make changes, clarify or elaborate with examples or illustrations, omit a minor point if time is running short, or refer to the audience.

Extemporaneous speaking demands total involvement from you. You can't just read from a manuscript or rely on an overly detailed outline. Nor can you "zone out" or speak from a hastily prepared outline. Speaking extemporaneously from a key word outline demands a carefully constructed set of notes as you speak, encourages you to remain audience-centered, and makes it possible for your speech to be an intellectually and emotionally creative process.

ALTERNATIVE STYLES OF DELIVERY

Preview Besides the extemporaneous style of delivery, speakers can choose from several other presentation styles. Among the alternatives are the impromptu, manuscript, and memorized styles. The style you choose will depend on your preference, the demands of the speaking situation, and audience expectations.

When it comes time to give your speech, you need to choose the type of delivery you want to use. Most speakers need to develop the ability to use different delivery styles since different topics or occasions call for different approaches. You would not want to speak to a large, formal meeting with a casual, off-the-cuff style, nor would you want to speak to your classmates about the need to support the football team by writing out and then reading a manuscript to them. It is important to fit the delivery style to the situation.

There are four major styles of delivering a speech: *impromptu, manuscript, memorized,* and *extemporaneous* (which we have already discussed). Although the extemporaneous style is appropriate in most public speaking situations and is generally preferred by audiences, each of the others deserves some attention.

Go to **Drill 6.2: Identifying Delivery Components** on the **VideoLab** CD-ROM and view the speech video clips that demonstrate diverse styles of presentation. How effectively does each speaker use the style of delivery he or she has chosen? Complete the quiz to test your perceptions.

The Impromptu Speech

Impromptu speaking is off-the-cuff and casual, delivered with little or no preparation or organization. In general, you should never choose to make an impromptu speech if you are given time to prepare in advance. There may be occasions, however, when you find yourself in a situation where impromptu speaking is the only option.

impromptu speaking casual, off-the-cuff delivery when a speaker has little or no time for preparation

For instance, as you participate in professional and social groups and organizations, you may be called on to articulate your point of view, make a brief report, or explain a procedure. Requests for these "speeches" often arise within a meeting when someone needs information. It's important to recognize these requests as serious speaking opportunities, even if there is little time to prepare for them. For instance, the president of your sorority may say to you, "Jen, you attended the national conference this summer. Didn't they talk about some new guidelines for recruiting new members? Can you give us some idea of what they said?" In some of your classes, instructors may occasionally hold unannounced discussions or debates, and you may be asked to make brief, spontaneous comments or to defend your point of view without advance planning.

Your speech instructor also may choose to hold occasional rounds of impromptu speeches. These speeches are usually designed to help you get accustomed to standing up and speaking in front of your classmates without having to worry about formal evaluation. They also give you a chance to "think on your feet." Impromptu speeches can be creative and enjoyable in this context.

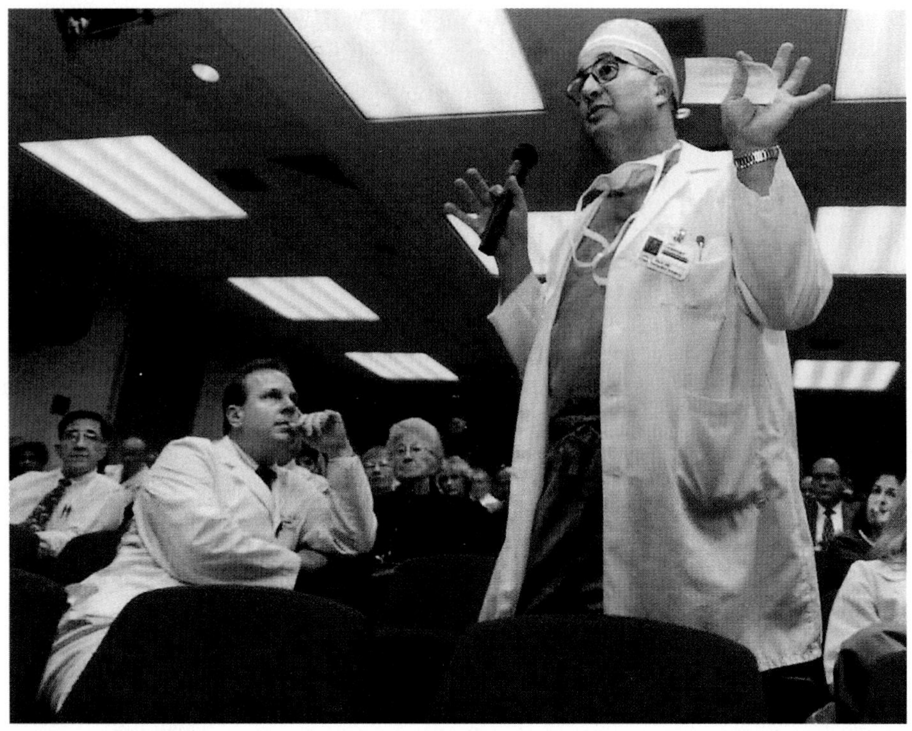

Much impromptu speaking occurs in informal public settings. Here a physician explains the position of the medical staff in an open board meeting of the Geisinger Medical Clinic in Danville, Pennsylvania. (Associated Press)

Tips for Giving Impromptu Speeches. When giving an impromptu speech, you have limited control over what you say and how well you say it. Even so, here are a few things you can do to succeed:

- *Anticipate the possibility that you might be called on to speak, and make some preparations.* If you are taking a class and the instructor knows that you have had a specific experience relevant to a topic being discussed, you might be asked to share your experience. What might you share? Jot down a few notes and take them to class with you.

  Similarly, when you are going to a meeting, examine the meeting agenda to see what items are of interest to you or relate to your knowledge and experience. Even if no one has asked you to speak, you might be expected to share your views. You also may have issues that you want to address. If so, prepare in advance.
- *Practice active listening.* In meeting contexts, it is critical that you follow the flow of the conversation. If you are daydreaming and you suddenly hear someone say, "Kevin, does this plan make sense to you based on your experience?" you will be hard-pressed to say anything, much less offer a coherent view. As in other communication situations, good listening and effective speaking go hand in hand.
- *Manage communication apprehension by reminding yourself that no one expects you to be perfect when you are asked to speak impromptu.* Give it your best shot and don't worry about small mistakes.
- *Use whatever small amount of preparation time you are given to your advantage.* For instance, you may be asked immediately before a meeting to make some brief remarks. Other business will precede your comments.

In this case, you have some time to review what you know, make a few notes, and organize your thoughts. Use your notes when you speak.

- *Use basic principles of speech organization.* Even an impromptu speech should have an introduction, a body, and a conclusion. Within the body, you will want to follow some basic structure, such as chronological or categorical order. Your organizational pattern can be simple yet easy to follow. It may be helpful (for both you and your listeners) to offer a preview and summary.
- *Speak briefly and concisely.* Regardless of the situation, impromptu speeches should not consume too much time. When people gather together—for a class, a conference, or a business meeting—there is usually a planned agenda. When someone is asked to make impromptu comments, he or she is doing so as a relatively spontaneous addition to an already full schedule. Even in a classroom context, we expect student responses to instructor questions to be concise, allowing time for others to participate. Keeping it brief is a must.
- *Think of the impromptu speaking occasion as providing a golden opportunity to practice and develop your delivery.* When you have more time to prepare for other, more formal speeches, you will speak even more effectively.

Even when making an impromptu speech, the speaker should follow some basic principles of good public speaking. Go to the **Online SpeechStudio,** where you will find the **Guide to Evaluating Impromptu Presentations**. You can use this during class the next time your instructor assigns a round of impromptu speeches.

The Manuscript Speech

At the other end of the delivery continuum is the **manuscript speech**. Although you are unlikely to give manuscript presentations in your public speaking class, some occasions seem to invite the use of a prepared manuscript. For instance, you may be representing an organization and addressing an important, controversial topic, and the press will be covering your comments. Accuracy may be quite important in these situations, and the manuscript provides a record of what you said.

manuscript speech a speech presented using a prepared text

Some settings may call for manuscript speeches largely because of their formal nature. When giving a speech as a class representative at commencement, you would probably write out the speech. Or you could be called on to make some formal remarks at the installation of officers of an organization to which you belong. The president of the United States uses a manuscript when delivering such important speeches as the State of the Union address.

Using a manuscript allows you to exercise control. You can time your speech accurately, choose your words carefully, and decide precisely how you will treat each aspect of the speech. The underlying principles of good public speaking also apply to the manuscript speech: being well prepared, having experience, practicing, and working from a good copy are important.

FRAME OF REFERENCE

This speaker is using a manuscript, well suited to a more formal situation. Manuscript delivery needn't prevent the speaker from staying in contact with the audience. This speaker has practiced his speech extensively and so is able to look up from his manuscript at his audience.

Tips for Giving Manuscript Speeches. Delivering a manuscript speech presents special challenges related to eye contact, movement, the use of your voice, and flexibility. Here are some guidelines to follow:

- *Use a manuscript for the right reasons.* Use a manuscript to enhance the care with which you choose your words and structure your sentences. Use it to control time and to allow you to select interesting, colorful language. Don't use it as a crutch to hide behind or as a way to manage your anxieties.

- *Use good oral style.* Even though you are speaking from a manuscript, you should use language that is more characteristic of oral than written style. This means that you will choose words and construct your sentences in ways that are accessible to the audience. See Chapter 12 for an extensive discussion of the effective use of language in public speaking.
- *Practice extensively.* You must know the material well enough to look at the audience and get back to the manuscript without losing your place. Even when using a manuscript, you must remain connected with the audience. You need a clean, double-spaced copy printed in an easily readable font.
- *Look for opportunities to move and gesture.* When you speak from a manuscript, you may feel compelled to stand in one place—behind the podium and close to your script. You may even feel tempted to lean on the podium or to grasp it as if you were trying to anchor yourself in a strong wind. Don't succumb to these temptations. With planning and practice, you can speak from a manuscript and still move from side to side and toward or away from your listeners, and you can certainly use appropriate gestures. The key is anticipation, preparation, and practice. The more comfortable you are with your manuscript, the freer you will feel to move and gesture in natural and content-reinforcing ways.
- *Use your voice effectively.* Some speakers sound artificial or flat when delivering a manuscript speech. Their inflection may be less animated than in normal speaking, or they may sound somewhat singsong, as if they are doing a poor job of reading some bad poetry. Yet, audiences have come to hear speakers speak, not read! To avoid falling into this reading trap, commit yourself to using your voice in ways that add variety, color, and emphasis—just as you do when speaking extemporaneously. You may

Go to **Lesson 5's Screening Room** on the **VideoLab** CD-ROM to view the speech on the case for olestra. The speaker is using manuscript delivery. Identify the ways in which he uses this delivery style effectively. Also offer some specific suggestions for ways that he might improve.

Formal settings often call for manuscript speeches. Here a Gropo Folklorio member speaks at a Cinco de Mayo festival in Los Angeles. (David Young-Wolff/PhotoEdit)

want to write self-directives on your manuscript, such as "slow down," "pause here for emphasis," or "project this/maybe repeat." You can also underline or otherwise highlight key words and phrases.

- *Maintain flexibility.* Rather than adapting to the moment or reacting to audience feedback, speakers often feel compelled to read from their manuscript, word for word, with no deviations, no matter what. Yet one of the hallmarks of effective delivery is flexibility. Your manuscript is not intended to be a straitjacket. It can be changed. You can add different examples. You can (and often should) include spontaneous comments. You may commit small portions of it to memory so that you can feel free to gesture and move more readily. When you plan to use your manuscript with flexibility, you are more likely to remain connected with the audience and you can monitor their reactions and feedback.

PORTFOLIO 11.3

Manuscript? Memorized? Extemporaneous?

Contemplate, in light of your career path, intended level of community involvement, and special occasions that may arise, when you may be asked to speak. When would an extemporaneous presentation be appropriate? When should you use a manuscript? When should you memorize your remarks?

The Memorized Speech

There are few situations where giving a **memorized speech** is a preferred option. Some students who enter speaking contests, such as the American Legion Oratorical Contest, or intercollegiate speaking contests are required to memorize their speeches. Similarly, more formal or ceremonial occasions might call for a short memorized speech: you might not want to use notes or a manuscript when you are proposing a toast at a wedding or paying tribute to a close friend or relative. Also, when giving an extemporaneous speech, you might want to memorize the introduction, the conclusion, or a striking piece of poetry for you use during the course of the speech.

memorized speech a prepared speech presented from memory, without the assistance of notes

Tips for Giving Memorized Speeches. When you find yourself in a speaking situation in which you plan to speak from memory, keep these pointers in mind:

- *Stay focused on your specific purpose and the key ideas you want to convey.* When you memorize, you may be tempted to focus on the specific words you plan to use. You may try to memorize, literally, word for word. But don't forget that a memorized speech, like any speech, is audience centered. The response you are trying to get from your audience should remain foremost in your mind. In a memorized speech, as in any other, you need to have a firm command of the ideas you want understood. For example, you plan to say, "Incredible as it seems, starvation is a problem in the United States," but you get only as far as, "Incredible as it seems," and suddenly you can't remember the next word. If you remember the point you wish to make, you can continue even if the words aren't exactly what you had originally intended. Saying "Incredible as it seems, people in this country are going hungry," makes the point and enables you to go on.

- *Speak in the moment.* Sometimes when speakers deliver a speech from memory, they go on "automatic pilot." They appear to forget the immediate situation and simply recite the words that they have drummed into their head. Under these conditions, their mind may wander or even go blank. The speech has become a performance rather than a communicative exchange with an audience.

Go to **Lesson 2's Screening Room** on the **VideoLab** CD-ROM to view the speech on child protection. This speaker is using a memorized style of delivery. Identify the ways in which her delivery is effective. Also think of specific ways that she might further enhance her delivery.

If you stay focused on your listeners and remember your specific purpose, if you remain centered on ideas rather than on exact words, and if you look for ways to adapt as you speak, you will more likely stay tuned in to the moment and maintain your poise, focus, and flexibility. An audience-centered speaker never forgets that she or he is involved in a communicative interaction and is not just putting on a show.

- *Practice, practice, practice!* To be effective, all speakers must practice, regardless of the style of delivery they plan to use. But the memorized speech may require even more practice—and especially so if the memorization is part of a speaking contest and the speaker must memorize a fairly long text. When faced with such a situation, you should read through the text several times, then practice it in sections before you try to deliver the entire speech. Practice sessions should be distributed over time rather than crammed into a few hours. Getting plenty of rest between practice sessions is essential. Remember, too, that even in speech contests, there is usually some room for varying your exact words. Stay focused on what you are trying to accomplish with your audience even if you forget the precise words you intended to use.

KEEP IN MIND 11.3

Alternative Styles of Delivery

- Impromptu
- Manuscript
- Memorized

RESPONDING TO AUDIENCE QUESTIONS

Preview Often after you make a speech, you will be asked to entertain questions. The question-and-answer period is particularly important because it allows you to interact informally with the audience, to provide additional information, to build your credibility, and to deal with aspects of your topic not addressed in the speech itself.

forum period the question-and-answer period following a speech that allows for a dialogue between speaker and audience

Some speakers give little thought to the **forum period**. Instead they focus all their attention on the preparation and delivery of the formal speech. Yet many speakers damage their credibility when attempting to respond to audience questions. They reveal their ignorance, defensiveness, or prejudice through thoughtless or insensitive answers.

The forum period is a potentially crucial aspect of the public communication event. It is a time when the speaker and the listener exchange roles—when the listener does the speaking and the speaker does the listening. It is a dynamic time when the audience-centered model of communication seems to come to life.

Preparing for the Question-and-Answer Period

Although you can't anticipate everything listeners might ask, you can make some good guesses. You should expect questions about controversial points you make in your speech. You also should know what other points of view audience members might have. Think about arguments that they might use to challenge your ideas and how you would answer them. Be absolutely sure of your sources. Know as much as possible about how your information was gathered and by whom in case your data are questioned. Consider which parts of your speech might be most difficult to understand because of their technical nature or because they are outside the realm of listeners' experience. Try to think of additional examples or analogies or different ways to restate your explanations.

The more you know about your topic, the better prepared you will be to deal with questions. If all you know about a topic can be contained in a short speech, you are not thoroughly prepared. Gather and assimilate a lot more information than can fit into your speech. This will be very helpful to you in answering audience questions.

Conducting the Question-and-Answer Period

Before you conduct the forum period, make sure you conclude your speech. We have all heard speakers who simply stop speaking, scratch their heads, and mumble, "Well, I guess that's about it. Do you have any questions?" The question-and-answer period follows the conclusion, but it is not a replacement for it.

Decide where you will stand as you receive audience questions. Some speakers return to their seats as soon as they conclude their remarks. It's as if they are saying, "Whew! Glad that's over!" This sort of behavior does not invite a dialogue with the audience. What are some alternatives? One option is to remain behind the podium. This conveys a sense of formality, maintaining some distance between you and the audience. Another option is to stand at the side or in front of the podium, where you can interact more directly with the audience. Finally, in informal settings, you might sit on a table and move into a "chatting" mode. Any of these options might work well depending on the situation in which you are speaking, the audience's expectations, and your own preferences.

The following general guidelines may help you conduct the question-and-answer period. If you handle audience questions well, you can make your message more compelling.

- *Listen carefully to each question posed.* If you can't hear the questioner very well, ask her or him to stand and repeat the question. Or (if you have not already done so) move away from the podium and stand closer to the audience. As you listen, provide a few nonverbal cues, such as nodding your head, to let the questioner know that you are following the point being raised.

- *If appropriate, repeat each question so that everyone can hear it and keep track of what is happening.* In repeating the question, you may need to rephrase it, since audience members often phrase their questions in awkward or rambling ways.

- *Do not allow one person to dominate the forum period.* If many people raise their hands at once, make sure you call on ones who have not spoken previously. If someone who has already posed a question raises his or her hand again, you might ask, "Is there anyone with a question who has not yet spoken?" Occasionally a persistent questioner may try to engage you in a dialogue for an extended period of time. If that happens, you might ask that person if he or she can remain after the formal meeting is concluded so that you can talk more.

- *Don't try to fake your way through a response.* If you don't know the answer to a question or are not familiar with a related topic, say so. For example, someone may ask you if you have read a particular book that relates to

KEEP IN MIND 11.4

Conducting the Forum Period: Guidelines for the Speaker

- Anticipate and prepare for possible questions.
- Listen carefully to each question posed.
- Repeat questions when appropriate.
- Discourage those who would dominate.
- Never fake your way through a response.
- Respect time limits.
- Actively encourage listeners to participate.

your presentation. If you haven't but you say that you have, you will find yourself in an even tougher spot when the listener next asks, "How did you interpret the author's comments on the postmodern view of Jung's works?" Admitting that you do not know something is not the end of the world. Besides, you can use it as an opportunity to learn from the listener, to jot down a note or two, and to show the audience that you respect them.

In addition, if a listener poses a challenging or important question that you cannot answer, offer to find out the answer and get back to him or her. It's easy to get a listener's email address following your talk—then, do your research and follow through with a thoughtful response. When you do this, you are behaving responsibly and respectfully toward the listener. At the same time, you are learning more about your topic—which may prove useful as you go on to address similar issues in the future.

- *Respect time limits.* Question-and-answer periods cannot go on forever. Like speeches, they have time constraints. Sometimes you will be asked to speak briefly and leave plenty of time for audience questions. Other times you will have only a little time left for interaction with the audience. Ask in advance what the audience expects or desires, then follow through, cooperating with listener norms and expectations.

On most speaking occasions, the speech itself is followed by a time when the speaker responds to audience questions. Go to the **Online SpeechStudio**, where you will find a form called **Evaluation Form for Question-and-Answer Sessions.** You can use this form to assess a speaker's ability to conduct the question-and-answer period effectively.

- *If appropriate, actively encourage listeners to participate.* Sometimes you may deliver a speech that generates a strong audience response. Or perhaps you have presented a lot of new information and you want to find out whether listeners have followed you. In these cases, you may want to solicit audience participation. You may begin in a very general way with, "What questions do you have?" Though useful in some situations, this approach doesn't provide any clues as to the kind of questions or comments that might be appropriate. In addition, some listeners are reluctant to speak up in front of others, so you may have to encourage them in various ways.

  For instance, ask a more specific question, such as, "What do you think of the idea of making condoms widely available in public schools?" That kind of question signals an area of potential controversy and might make listeners think, "This may be a good topic for us to pursue."

  You also may target someone you know who has experience with or ideas on the subject. You might ask that person to share his or her perspective as an involved parent, educator, or academic adviser. Of course, you will want to make sure that you do not embarrass anyone. Ask questions only of those who are clearly listening and who have established and maintained eye contact with you.

  Finally, you may encourage listeners to talk by moving from behind the podium, desk, or table (if such a barrier exists) and leaning against something or sitting on a table or desk. This will reinforce the notion of informal information and idea exchange and remove potential status barriers. As you continue to encourage listeners to interact with you, they will see that you are interested in engaging them in a dialogue.

PORTFOLIO 11.4

Opening the Dialogue

Think ahead to your next speech and the material you'll be presenting. Now try to anticipate what questions your audience might have. Write them out, along with your responses. Also prepare a set of questions (in case they're needed) that you might use to stimulate discussion after your speech.

"SOUNDING GOOD" VERSUS "BEING SOUND"

Preview One of the speaker's ethical obligations is to try to present a message of substance, and good delivery is no substitute for sound ideas. Having good delivery means staying audience-centered, avoiding behaviors that distract from the message, and promoting the listeners' belief and understanding.

Sometimes we find ourselves in the uncomfortable situation of thinking that someone sounded good but not being sure of what he or she said. Sometimes delivery is so striking that it takes us away from the content of the communication. This may be a purposeful act on the part of the speaker, or it may be an accident. In either case, it is not good delivery.

Beyond Delivery: Listening to the Message

The immediacy of a public speaking situation—in which the speaker and the listener actually encounter each other and the audience witnesses the speech's presentation—sometimes gives unwarranted influence to delivery. The speaker who is poised, has a good voice, is articulate, and appears confident and friendly may impress us. Sometimes, however, such a speaker is merely **facile**—he or she can speak easily but might not be saying very much. One thing that this book has been designed to do is to prepare you to distinguish between a speaker who is sound and a speaker who just sounds good.

facile speaking with ease and fluency, but lacking substantive content

A sound speaker's ideas pass the rigorous tests that grow out of the principles embodied in the preceding chapters. As much as we might admire the ease and grace with which someone can address an audience, we need to be on our guard against the slick, superficial person who is out to sell himself or herself and not to grapple with important ideas.

The Foundation of Ethical Delivery

Ethical delivery grows out of an audience-centered approach to public speaking. A speaker whose constant and consistent attention is on himself or herself is liable to be far more concerned with what he or she looks like or how he or she moves than with how the audience is reacting to what is being said. After all, when you speak, you are not putting on an "act": you are trying to get a response from a specific audience, and you are concerned for their well-being. Good delivery reflects this kind of mental state.

ethical delivery speaking honestly and truthfully, with a thoughtful and genuine concern for the well-being of the audience and community

Second, as noted earlier, good delivery does not call attention to itself. The best delivery is one that the audience doesn't notice at all. It is the type that the audience will not respond to by obliterating content or meaning because of a physical action on the part of the speaker. This means, for example, that you will want to exhibit speaking behaviors that are appropriate to the situation, such as using a conversational type of voice when speaking to an audience of fifteen or twenty people sitting close to you. Of course, no speaker should intentionally use dramatic gestures, striking movement, or interesting vocal patterns to distract the audience from weak content. Not only is this kind of strategy ethically questionable, but it also can backfire. Your delivery should reinforce your remarks rather than compete with them for attention.

CONNECTING TO THE NET

Would you like some help in polishing your delivery? For some suggestions on making your presentation, go to **http://college.hmco.com/communication/andrews/public_speaking/2e/students/** and click on *Connecting to the Net.* From there, follow the link to Effective Delivery.

Go to **Lesson 6 Coach: Tips to Remember** on the **VideoLab** CD-ROM and watch the video clips that illustrate and recap some of the basics of effective and less effective delivery.

Finally, ethical delivery is that which best promotes the listeners' trust and comprehension. When you make a speech, your body, voice, and gestures must be in tune with the mood and nature of your message. It is not always easy to judge the best way to integrate your delivery into a speech situation. Practice delivering your speech and then seek constructive feedback. Never forget that what is happening in front of your audience is all that the audience really knows about you and the topic at that particular moment. A speaker may have some very good and compelling reasons for urging an audience to take an action, but if the speaker, through a dull and lifeless delivery, doesn't seem to care at all, the message may be lost.

SUMMARY

The delivery of your speech represents the climax of the speech preparation process. There are many different ways to deliver a speech, ranging from the formal memorized or manuscript presentation to the very informal impromptu speech. For most public speaking situations, however, the extemporaneous style, involving meticulous research and preparation and delivered from a key word outline, is best.

When you speak extemporaneously, you are more likely to speak with flexibility, adapting to audience expectations and to the physical environment in which you deliver your speech. As you speak, you are encouraged to establish eye contact with members of the audience, to use appropriate reinforcing gestures, and to use your voice effectively. This is not to say that you cannot have good delivery when, for instance, you deliver a speech from a manuscript, but other forms of delivery do present special challenges.

Although we often think of a speech as completed when the speaker has delivered his or her conclusion, many times the conversation with the audience will extend for many minutes while listeners ask and the speaker responds to questions. The question-and-answer period is a very important part of any public speech. When you receive audience questions, you have the chance to show them how well informed you are, how well you can think on your feet, how carefully you listen, how open you are to their ideas and diverse points of view, how you handle conflict, and how honest you are in responding to difficult questions. To be most effective in this situation, you should anticipate and prepare for possible questions from your audience.

Ethical delivery grows from an audience-centered approach to public speaking. Good speakers try never to distract the audience through their presentational style. They do all they can to promote audience belief and understanding. They know that good delivery is essential. And good, ethical delivery not only sounds good, but grows from a sound foundation—a carefully constructed, well supported, and reasoned speech. Both speaker and listeners must be mindful of the distinction between sounding good and being sound.

QUESTIONS FOR REVIEW AND REFLECTION

1. Define each of the following styles of delivering a speech:
   a. Extemporaneous
   b. Impromptu
   c. Manuscript
   d. Memorized

   Discuss the advantages and disadvantages of each delivery style.
2. Why is a key word outline useful in delivering a speech? Can you think of any potential disadvantages to using such an outline?
3. Your friend has to make an important presentation at his fraternity awards dinner. He comes to you and asks you for advice on how to deliver his speech. What three things would you stress? Why are they important?
4. You have heard many people give speeches (classroom speeches, lectures, political speeches, after-dinner speeches, speeches at memorial services). Given your experience as an audience member, what are the things that most annoy you about some speakers' delivery habits or styles? What are some delivery characteristics you especially admire?
5. Suppose you have been asked to deliver a eulogy or speech of tribute. Now imagine that you have been asked to speak briefly to your fellow volunteers at a Red Cross fundraiser—to make spontaneous remarks that will motivate them. How do you think your delivery would vary as you move from the first to the second speaking situation?
6. You have given a speech, and now it is time for audience questions. How would you deal with each of these situations?
   a. An audience member is hostile.
   b. An audience member asks three questions in a row.
   c. Someone asks you a question you do not know the answer to.
   d. No one asks you a question.
7. You have just given a speech in your public speaking class. As you leave the room, one of your classmates comes to you and says, "Wow! You have the most impressive speaking voice! I could listen to you speak all day long." Would you consider this to be good or bad news? Why?
8. What is the difference between sounding good and being sound?

ENDNOTES

1. See, as examples, Joe Ayres, "Speech Preparation Processes and Speech Apprehension," *Communication Education* 45 (July 1996): 228–235; Joe Ayres and Tim Hopf, *Coping with Speech Anxiety* (Norwood, N.J.: Ablex, 1993); Ralph R. Behnke and Chris R. Sawyer, "Anticipatory Anxiety Patterns for Male and Female Speakers," *Communication Education* 49 (April 2000): 187–195; and Thomas Robinson II, "Communication Apprehension and the Basic Public Speaking Course: A National Survey of In-class Treatment Techniques," *Communication Education* 46 (1997): 188–197.

2. For a classic work on nonverbal communication, see Edward T. Hall, *The Silent Language* (Garden City, N.Y.: Doubleday, 1959). More recent works include Edward T. Hall, *The Dance of Life* (New York: Doubleday, 1983), and Mark Knapp and J. Hall, *Nonverbal Communication in Human Interaction* (Philadelphia: Harcourt Brace Jovanovich, 1997).
3. See, for example, Edward T. Hall and M. R. Hall, *Understanding Cultural Differences* (Yarmouth, Maine: Intercultural Press, 1990), and M. Lustig and J. Koester, *Interpersonal Competence: Interpersonal Communication Across Cultures,* 2nd ed. (New York: HarperCollins, 1996).
4. Carolyn Calloway-Thomas, Pamela J. Cooper, and Cecil Blake, *Intercultural Communication: Roots and Routes* (Boston: Allyn & Bacon, 1999); Virginia P. Richmond et al., *Nonverbal Communication: The Unspoken Dialogue* (New York: Harper & Row, 1989).
5. Virginia P. Richmond and James C. McCroskey, *Nonverbal Behavior in Interpersonal Relations,* 3rd ed. (Boston: Allyn & Bacon, 1995).
6. Albert Mehrabian, *Silent Messages: Implicit Communication of Emotions and Attitudes,* 2nd ed. (Belmont, Calif.: Wadsworth, 1982).
7. Richmond and McCroskey, *Nonverbal Behavior,* pp. 68–70.

Using Language Effectively

12

CHAPTER OBJECTIVES

After studying this chapter, you should be able to

1. **use good style to promote understanding through the use of clear, interesting, and appropriate language.**
2. **make language choices that reflect the characteristics of good oral style.**
3. **discern ethical considerations in the use of language.**
4. **explain how style can influence listeners' responses.**

CHAPTER SURVEY

Style is a very difficult term to define, partly because we use it in so many different ways. If we refer to a person as having style, the context of our reference will tell whether we mean that person dresses very well, sings in a unique way, or plays basketball with a special flair. When we talk about a speaker's **style**, we may also mean many different things. We might say that a speaker's style is the unique or specific type of image he or she creates for the audience. The speaker's use of language, movement and gestures, and appearance on the platform all affect the way he or she is perceived by the audience. In its most general sense, style covers much that has been discussed in this book. Our speaking style is influenced by the way we think, by the way we put arguments together, and by the way we relate to the audience.

This chapter focuses specifically on one aspect of style: language—how to choose it and how to use it. For the moment, let's consider style to be the use and choice of language. Let's look at style as it relates both to the understanding of messages and to persuasion.

style a speaker's choice and use of language

To test your skills and expand your understanding of effective language use, go to **Lesson 7** of the **VideoLab** CD-ROM and walk through the videos, exercises, and tips provided.

USING STYLE TO PROMOTE UNDERSTANDING

Preview Every speaker has a personal style, but style is also concerned with how the speaker chooses to use language. Language choices can help speakers connect with listeners or can create barriers when misunderstandings occur. When choosing your language, it is critical to remain audience-centered.

One thing that is often difficult for us to appreciate as speakers is that we and our listeners do not always speak exactly the same language. All of us may speak English, but we do not choose and use language in the same ways. We may come from different backgrounds that provide us with different words or different meanings for words.

Regional uses of English, ethnic uses of language, and generational uses of language can be confusing to those outside a particular linguistic group. When your grandmother talks about going out to purchase a CD, she is probably planning to go to the bank to get a certificate of deposit, not to the local music shop to purchase a compact disc. Sometimes language uses are very specific and unusual. For instance, on a certain New Jersey campus, "making out" or "necking" is called "grouching." Students who attend that institution might say that someone has given them a "little grouch" when they have received a kiss. No one else would have the slightest idea of what they meant. Most listeners would probably assume they have encountered someone who was grumbling or complaining.

As you consider the ways in which appropriate language choices will help you connect with your audience, be aware that oral style and written style are not the same. Unless the situation calls for a manuscript speech, you will typically give much more informal speeches. These should not be written out and read to an audience. If they are, they will sound stilted and may suggest that you are not sincere or don't care as much about the listeners as you do about the speech. Most speeches you give will be characterized by good oral style, which is more informal, simpler, and more repetitious than written style. Also—and this is very important—oral style is more spontaneous. It allows you the flexibility to adapt your language as you speak. The advice we offer in this chapter is directed toward helping you make careful and effective language choices, but it should not be taken as encouragement to write speeches instead of preparing yourself to speak.

The Symbolic Nature of Language

Words are symbols. They are abstractions that allow us to talk about persons, places, things, actions, and ideas without providing every detail. The more abstract our words, the more details we omit. The names for things often provide no more than the titles of broad categories. Although we may think of such titles as fairly concrete, when we use them, we leave out many potentially distracting details. You call what you drive a car, but that word is a category that ignores the car's color, design, make, model, age, rust spots and chips, and other details that distinguish it from other people's cars.

Of course, some words are more abstract than others. The dictionary defines *abstract* as "not concrete or specific, without reference to a specific instance." That definition suggests the potential for problems in communication that grow from abstractness in language. As we speak more abstractly, ideas can become more and more difficult to grasp, and the chances of misunderstanding increase. If the word *car* omits detail, consider how many more details are omitted when we speak of *education, home, love, patriotism,* or *ambition.*

Whatever the complications that grow from the abstractness of language, the corresponding advantages are clear. We can communicate more easily because we do not get bogged down in details. Abstraction allows us to manipulate great chunks of the world verbally. It permits us to talk about the absent, the past, and the future, and it allows us to conceptualize ideas—such as *love, honor,* and *beauty*—that may lie beyond concrete experience. Abstracting is also a powerful source of identification. Politicians have long known that speaking in general, more abstract terms makes it easier for others to endorse their ideas. Most of us favor *family values, responsive government,* and *responsible citizenship.* Yet we all recognize that those words can mean many different things.

When we use words that are highly abstract, we must remember that as we lose detail, we tend to ignore differences. So we talk of students without acknowledging their very real differences in background, social skills, age, cognitive style, maturity, and so forth. Yet honoring very real differences is important if we are to avoid stereotyping and seek true understanding. The vigilant listener will ask questions of the speaker to clarify his or her intended meaning. Remaining aware of the symbolic nature of language is important for both speakers and listeners.

Vague? Volatile?

Contemplate the words or expressions you've considered using in a forthcoming speech. Will any be confusing in the way you're using them? Are any too abstract? Are any too highly charged? What substitutions might you make? Jot down words and expressions to avoid, as well as suitable substitutes.

Denotative and Connotative Meaning

Besides being symbolic, the words speakers use have both denotative and connotative meaning. **Denotative meaning** derives from words that carry less emotional baggage—those that tend to be more objective and less susceptible to a wide variety of interpretations. Often denotative words describe the relationship between the word and some object to which it refers. For example, the denotative meaning of *pencil* is "a writing implement consisting of a thin rod of graphite or similar substance encased in wood or held in a plastic or metal mechanical device." Its meaning is relatively objective; there are likely no personal interpretations and feelings. When we hear the word *pencil,* few of us feel fear, joy, or anger.

denotative meaning meaning that is considered objective or universally agreed on

connotative meaning the subjective or emotional meaning or association that a person has for a particular word or phrase

Connotative meaning derives from emotionally charged words that suggest a range of subjective and emotional interpretations, depending on the listener. In some instances, the same word can be denotative for one person and connotative for another. The word *cat* for many people might simply denote a four-footed, furry feline. To one who is severely allergic to dander, however, the word *cat* is emotionally charged and thus connotative. In our culture, many words carry obviously emotional meanings. Describing someone as *disgusting,* for example, clearly suggests strong negative feelings about that person. For many U.S. citizens, the word *American* provokes emotional responses.

Denotative or connotative meaning is infused into language by the context in which words appear and by the perceptions of the listener. Nonetheless, in our

KEEP IN MIND 12.1

Language and Understanding

To promote understanding,

- be familiar with the meaning of style in the context of public speaking.
- be aware of language differences between speakers and listeners.
- acknowledge the symbolic nature of language.
- distinguish denotative from connotative meaning.

society, some words seem to be more emotionally charged than others: *mother, honor, free enterprise, racist,* and *neo-Nazi* are some examples. All of these words are liable to conjure up a wide variety of intense personal responses.

As speakers, we must heighten our sensitivity to language. We cannot assume that our language choices will automatically be those that our listeners would make. Nor will our language necessarily be understood by listeners unless we strive to make ourselves clear.

USING LANGUAGE CLEARLY

Preview The most profound idea, clever remark, or astute observation will have little impact if your listeners cannot grasp it. Clear speakers use language with which the audience is familiar; speak with specificity, concreteness, and precision; avoid the use of clichés, empty words, and distracting language; and construct their sentences with a concern for good oral style.

We need to keep in mind that a speech, being oral, is very different from a written presentation. You know that if you are reading a page and you come across words that you have never seen before, you will either figure out the meaning from the context, ask a friend or expert what the words mean, or look up the words in a dictionary. Indeed a good book often challenges the reader and contributes to his or her own knowledge of the language. But a speech is a different matter.

When you are giving a speech, the listeners can't stop you and get you to run through a section of your speech again, nor can they stop you so that they can rush out and look up a word. As speakers, we need to be sensitive to the differences between oral and written communication contexts and do all we can to achieve **clarity** and to make ourselves readily understood. If our speaking is to be clear in a meaningful sense, it cannot simply be clear in the long run, after minutes of speculation, or after several trips to the dictionary. Rather it must be instantly intelligible.

clarity the degree to which a speaker's language is instantly intelligible to his or her audience

Of course, good writing is also clear, although the writer's sentences, depending on the audience, can be more complex and his or her vocabulary more sophisticated than the speaker's. Some writers fail to appreciate the value of clarity. A concern over obscure, unintelligible, and pompous language led the editors of the scholarly journal *Philosophy and Literature,* published by the Johns Hopkins University Press, to initiate the Bad Writing Contest. This contest attempts to locate the "ugliest, most stylistically awful passage" found in a scholarly book or article published in the last few years. *Spotlight on Bad Writing* features some recent winning sentences. It is hard to imagine any audience for whom these sorts of messages would be enlightening. The message is simple: neither writers nor speakers should confuse obscure expression with profound thinking.

On other occasions and in other contexts, lack of clarity may more accurately be attributed to lack of care, thought, or vigilance in choosing words and constructing sentences or phrases. Among the so-called best newspaper headlines of 1997 were the following: "Police Begin Campaign to Run Down Jaywalkers," "Drunk Gets Nine Months in Violin Case," "Lung Cancer in Women Mushrooms," "Clinton Wins on Budget, But More Lies Ahead," and "Killer Sentenced to Die for Second Time in Ten Years." Similarly, a careful reading of

SPOTLIGHT ON... **Bad Writing**

Winners of the Johns Hopkins University Press Bad Writing Contest

From an English professor:

"The lure of imaginary totality is momentarily frozen before the dialectic of desire hastens on within symbolic chains."

From an art historian:

"To this end, I must underline the phallicism endemic to the dialectics of penetration routinely deployed in descriptions of pictorial space and the operations of spectatorship."

From a philosopher:

"Since thought is seen to be 'rhizomatic' rather than 'arboreal,' the movement of differentiation and becoming is already imbued with its own positive trajectory."

From a historian:

"When interpreted from within the ideal space of the myth-symbol school, Americanist masterworks legitimized hegemonic understanding of American history expressively totalized in the metanarrative that had been reconstructed out of (or more accurately read into) these masterworks."

From a professor of comparative literature (and first-prize winner):

"The visual is *essentially* pornographic, which is to say that it has its end in rapt, mindless fascination; thinking about its attributes becomes an adjunct to that, if it is unwilling to betray its object; while the more austere films necessarily draw their energy from the attempt to repress their own excess (rather than from the more thankless effort to discipline the viewer)."

From the 1997 "Bad Writing Contest," *Philosophy and Literature,* Johns Hopkins University Press, 1997.

the same year's classified ads reveals some of these: "Dog for sale: eats anything and is fond of children"; "Honest man. Will take anything"; "Wanted: Man to take care of cow that does not smoke or drink"; and "We will oil your sewing machine and adjust tension in your home for only $3.00." As you can see, lack of clarity can be amusing—and certainly open to interpretation.

Clarity and Familiarity

One way to promote clarity is to use words with which the audience is familiar. Once one of us was giving a lecture in which he described a political speech as "pedestrian." After the lecture was over, one student was somewhat puzzled and frustrated. "I thought a pedestrian was someone who walked across the street," the student said. "How can a speech be pedestrian?" This is an extreme example; we should be able to assume that a college student would know the meaning of *pedestrian* (that is, banal or unextraordinary) in this context. Nevertheless, the instructor might have said, "This was a very pedestrian, ordinary speech; there was nothing unusual, striking, or interesting about it." Such restatement would have explained the unfamiliar word and reinforced the idea.

Technical Language. A speaker should always remember that technical words may be unfamiliar to an audience. A chemistry major will have no difficulty understanding what a *reagent* is and an accounting major understanding a *trial balance*. For someone training to be an auto mechanic, a *fuel injector* is an ordinary object, and its function is readily understood. A nutritionist knows what *carbohydrates* are, a laboratory technician what *red blood cells* represent, and a teacher what a *grade curve* is. In other words, technical language doesn't have to be words such as *aerodynamics, quantum mechanics,* or *iambic pentameter.*

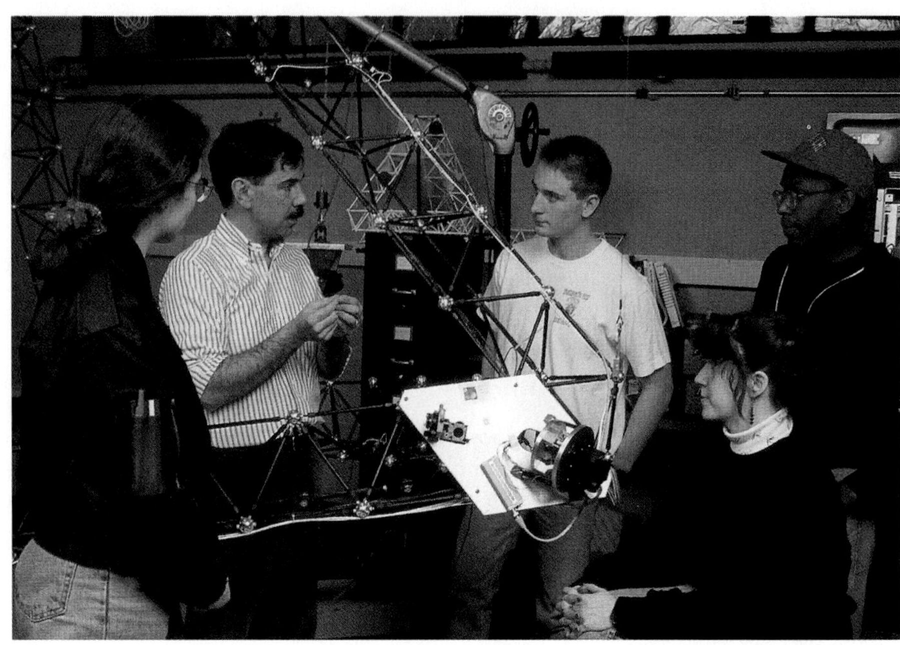

A speaker's language should be appropriate for the listeners. This aeronautics professor will be likely to use technical language when speaking with students who are familiar with technical terms. In speaking to a general audience, the professor would choose language more easily understood by listeners with less specialized knowledge. (Christopher Morrow/Stock, Boston, Inc.)

technical language any language that has a very precise meaning within a particular field of endeavor

jargon technical language; often carries a negative connotation when used to describe incomprehensible or pretentious language

Any language that has a very precise meaning within a particular field of endeavor is **technical language**. It's easy for us to forget that language we consider to be ordinary may be considered technical by an audience. Whenever we use language in ways that exclude some people who lack technical expertise, we diminish the opportunity for dialogue.

Technical language is also known as **jargon**, as in "medical jargon" or "computer jargon." But another meaning of jargon is gibberish, so jargon is often thought of as meaningless technical language. Jargon used in this way carries with it the implication that its user does not want to communicate with the audience, but, rather, to impress listeners with his or her knowledge. Or it may be that the user is not very clear in his or her own mind and is using jargon to cover up this lack of clarity. Using jargon to impress an audience or to hide fuzzy thinking is clearly unethical. Furthermore, language used inappropriately for audiences who are not part of a particular technical community is almost certain to be ineffective.

acronym letters that stand for names or titles, often derived from the initial letters or parts of a series of words

Abbreviations and Acronyms. The same, of course, is true of technical or specialized abbreviations or substitutions for longer words or titles that are commonly used in specific contexts. The best example of this is the way in which we use **acronyms**, letters that stand for names or titles. Anyone in an audience who is interested in broadcasting will know what is meant by the FCC, but others in the audience may not know that this refers to the Federal Communications Commission. Many college students will know what a GPA is, but their parents, friends, or others not associated with the university may not know that it refers to grade point average. As speakers, we need to be conscious of the fact that our language grows out of our experience and knowledge and sometimes needs to be translated for listeners.

Concreteness and Specificity

Words that are chosen for their concreteness and specificity increase clarity. Telling an audience, for example, that they must exert increased effort or that they must be very active is not really telling them what they are expected to do. By contrast, saying to an audience that they could distribute handbills at the student union at nine o'clock the next morning is saying something specific. Asking an audience to vote for a candidate because she or he is in favor of enlarging educational opportunities is vague. Asking an audience to vote for a candidate because he or she supports a $5 million increase in the federal loan program for students is specific.

Clarity and Precision

Mark Twain once observed that there is no such thing as a synonym; he admonished writers to seek the right word, not its "second cousin." Twain's advice is also good for public speakers. Precise words are important because they allow us to communicate our meaning as accurately as possible.

If you wanted to describe someone walking down the street, how would you do it? Specifically, what verb would you choose? This would depend entirely on the kind of image you wanted to create. If you wanted to portray the person as being in a hurry, you might use a verb such as *raced, hustled,* or *hurried*. But each of these is different. Which is faster? Which is more informal? To take a different example, suppose you wanted to describe a negative feeling about something. You might say you *disliked* it, but if you felt more strongly, you might choose a verb such as *hated, detested,* or *loathed*. Which conveys the most accurate description of your feeling? In general, you will be more efficient with your language if you choose words precisely. Why say "walked slowly," when you can say "ambled"? Why say "loved very much," when you can say "adored"? Precise language is both clear and compact.

Avoiding Clichés, Empty Words, and Distracting Language

Effective public speakers try to avoid using **clichés**—trite, overused expressions. At one time, these expressions were probably fresh and interesting. "The bottom line" conveys a clear enough meaning, but the phrase has been used so much that it doesn't show any originality and may have lost the precise meaning it was supposed to have. Because of overuse, clichés are tired and lifeless, and they are less likely to engage listeners' thoughts and hold their interest. Table 12.1 lists some clichés to avoid.

clichés expressions that are trite and overused

Also avoid **empty words**—those that add nothing but length to your sentences. For instance, why say "a number of," when you can say "several" or "many"? You might say "because" instead of "due to the fact that," "after" instead of "subsequent to," "about" rather than "in connection with," and "I must" instead of "it will be necessary for me to."

empty words words that add length but no additional meaning

Even though we might think of a speaking situation as an enlarged conversation, there are stylistic differences. A conversation is more interactive. We don't always finish sentences, we may be interrupted from time to time, or others in the conversation may verbalize reactions. Casual conversations are often

TABLE 12.1 Common Clichés to Avoid

After all is said and done	Last but not least
Easier said than done	All in all
Ignorance is bliss	In the final analysis
It goes without saying	Crystal clear
Few and far between	Between a rock and a hard place
More than meets the eye	Busy as a bee
Light as a feather	Cut to the chase

littered with unnecessary language that may be acceptable in that setting but not in a public speaking situation. We might say to a friend that "he was, like, very tall and, you know, well built." But that kind of language distracts and clutters in a public speech and definitely should be avoided.

If you can avoid empty words, clichés, and distracting language in your speaking, you will say more, say it more efficiently, and speak more clearly, and your audience will benefit through greater knowledge and understanding.

Constructing Sentences to Promote Clarity

Individual words must be clear, and so should sentences. Construct sentences with well-chosen words, but arrange those words so that the sentences they form are direct and easy to follow.

For good oral style, construct sentences so that the subject and the verb are close together. This makes the sentence easier to understand, and it sounds more natural. Consider the following sentence, in which the subject and verb have been separated: "This new program, which has been tried at other colleges similar to our own and has been enormously popular, is worthy of your support." Surely the sentence would be more understandable if it were reworked to say: "This program is worthy of your support. Other colleges like our own have tried it, and it has been enormously popular."

circumlocutions the use of an unnecessarily large number of words to express an idea

active voice sentence construction in which a subject performs an action

Another important issue is to keep sentences relatively short, with some appropriate variety. Shorter sentences are easier for listeners to follow. Also avoid needless repetition, unnecessary modifiers, and **circumlocutions**, such as: "The reason why I think this plan will work is because. . . ." Use the **active voice** whenever possible to eliminate unnecessary words. Consider the following examples:

"Great frustration with the new graduation requirements has been expressed by students throughout the university." *(passive voice)*

"Throughout the university, students have felt frustrated with the new graduation requirements." *(active voice)*

We will further explore the use of active language a little later in this chapter.

PORTFOLIO 12.2

Express Yourself Well

Look at the working outline for your forthcoming speech. Read through it as if you were an audience member, using the suggestions in Keep in Mind 12.2 to check your use of language. Circle problem areas and rework them so that you will present a clearer, more effective message.

Another consideration is to use only necessary modifiers. There are two kinds of modifiers: those that comment and those that define. **Commenting modifiers** include *very, most,* and *definitely.* These modifiers tell us nothing new; instead they try to boost the meaning of the word they modify. Yet if you select your words precisely, they should be able to stand alone without the assistance of such modifiers. By contrast, **defining modifiers** provide information that the noun standing alone cannot convey. They tell us something we need to know. Depending on whether an idea is described as *innovative, brilliant, outdated,* or *preposterous,* we will respond to it quite differently.

commenting modifiers modifiers that boost the meaning of a word but reveal nothing new

defining modifiers modifiers that provide new, needed information

Repetition and Restatement. Speakers may have to repeat certain words, phrases, or ideas to make them stick in listeners' minds. Clarity of oral style, in contrast to clarity of written style, may demand that a speaker use more **repetition** and **restatement** than a writer would use. Repetition is especially effective when the speaker wants the audience to remember specific, often vivid or especially meaningful, words or phrases. The speaker would most benefit from using restatement if he or she wanted to emphasize or clarify an idea by discussing it in several different ways. Of course, speakers should not overuse these devices, but, when used carefully, they help speakers reinforce main ideas and make important expressions memorable.

repetition repeating, word for word, key elements presented in a message

restatement restating, with slightly different language or sentence construction, key elements presented in a message

Perhaps one of the most famous uses of repetition was in a speech given by Winston Churchill in the early days of World War II when Britain stood alone against Germany. In refusing to consider negotiating with the enemy, Churchill said, "We shall defend our island, whatever the cost may be. We shall fight on the beaches. We shall fight on the landing grounds. We shall fight in the fields and in the streets, and we shall fight in the hills. We shall never surrender."[1] Another famous speech, Ralph Waldo Emerson's "American Scholar," uses restatement in a memorable way: "We will walk on our feet; we will work with our hands; we will speak our own minds. The study of letters shall be no longer a name for pity, for doubt, and for sensual indulgence. . . . A nation of men will for the first time exist, because each believes himself inspired by the Divine Soul which also inspires all men."[2]

transitional language words and phrases a speaker provides that signal movement and direction within a speech and the relationship between its parts

Transitional Language. As a speaker, you aim to help your audience follow, remember, and understand. One device that helps promote a clearer style is the use of **transitional language**, which continually points the audience in the proper direction. For example, as a speaker amplifies a particular point, he or she might say, "I've been telling you that a diet that is not properly supervised can be very dangerous for you. Let me give you an example of just how dangerous it can be by telling you about a college student named Joan." The move by the speaker from the generalization to the specific example is thus clearly delineated through the use of transitional language. Similarly, signposting, as discussed in Chapter 8, may direct listeners to each new idea through words such as *first* and *finally.* If you didn't do the Internet exercise in Chapter 8 (see page 186), you may want to go back to it and get more practice devising transitions.

KEEP IN MIND 12.2

Language and Clarity

Following are some ways to make language clear:

- Use familiar words.
- Avoid technical language.
- Define acronyms.
- Be concrete and specific.
- Communicate precisely.
- Avoid clichés, empty words, and distracting language.
- Construct simple, direct sentences.
- Use restatement and repetition.
- Use good transitions.
- Think clearly.

Clarity of Thought. The speaker who wants to use clear language must begin with clear thinking. If a speaker first understands what an idea is, it will be much easier for him or her to convey that idea to an audience. When a speaker has not thought out an idea clearly, the result will likely be confusion for the listeners.

Apart from the ideas that are discussed, language can have a force of its own. When used to promote interest, it can help make the speech persuasive and effective.

MAKING LANGUAGE INTERESTING TO LISTENERS

Preview As speakers, we can keep listeners interested by using active language—language that is lively and vivid—and figures of speech. We can also use effective rhetorical questions and parallelism.

Using Active Language

One of the things that always interests people is action. The way we choose language and the way we put it together can create a type of action for our listeners. We can create the illusion of action and help listeners understand more precisely what we have in mind in several ways. As noted above, simple and precise words and sentences help contribute to active speech.

Consider, for example, the way President Lyndon Johnson urged members of Congress to support him in passing the Voting Rights Act of 1965. When Johnson delivered this speech at a Joint Session of Congress, the United States was engulfed in great racial turmoil. In Alabama, in particular, bloody confrontations between police and civil rights protesters (both black and white) were regularly televised. In the United States, the rhetorical climate was one of great tension and urgency. In the following passage, there are no exceptional or unusual words and there is no particularly striking sentence construction, but the clarity and forcefulness of the language suggest action:

> The bill I am presenting to you will be known as a civil rights bill.
>
> But in a larger sense, most of the program I am recommending is a civil rights program. Its object is to open the city of hope to all people of all races, because all Americans just must have the right to vote, and we are going to give them that right.
>
> All Americans must have the privileges of citizenship, regardless of race, and they are going to have those privileges of citizenship regardless of race.
>
> But I would like to caution you and remind you that to exercise these privileges takes much more than just legal right. It requires a trained mind and a healthy body. It requires a decent home and the chance to find a job and the opportunity to escape from the clutches of poverty.
>
> Of course people cannot contribute to the nation if they are never taught to read or write; if their bodies are stunted from hunger; if their sickness goes untended; if their life is spent in hopeless poverty, just drawing a welfare check.
>
> So we want to open the gates to opportunity. But we're also going to give all our people, black and white, the help that they need to walk through those gates."[3]

Lively Language. Language also promotes a feeling of action when it is lively. Language that gives the most realistic and specific description of events, people, and ideas is the most lively. Pete, a student enrolled in a speech class, was given the assignment of making a speech of tribute. He decided to pay tribute to one of his teachers from the past. Here is a portion of his remarks: "Mr. Harrison was an excellent teacher that I had in high school. He was always well prepared and tried to enlighten the class when he had the opportunity. He tried to understand student needs and the values we held and to adapt accordingly to our experiences. He was certainly a good teacher and served as such a role model for me that I decided to become a teacher, too!" This passage lacks liveliness and color. Listeners don't get a clear picture of Mr. Harrison as a teacher or a person.

In the same class, another student, Andy, also chose to pay tribute to one of his teachers. It's fairly obvious that this speech excerpt is more real, creates more suspense, is more specific, and, as a whole, is livelier. Using this kind of language makes the audience want to listen.

> When I first went into class a tall man with slightly gray hair sat at the front of the room on the desk. He smiled and handed me a card to fill out. When I gave it back to him, he smiled again and said, "Thank you," in a quiet voice. But it was a funny thing. I knew somehow that that quiet voice was a powerful one, too, one that I was going to like to listen to, one that would sort of fill the room, but not batter at your ears. He looked relaxed sitting there, but I could tell he was watching everyone that came in, studying them, sizing them up. This was a lit. class, and I figured there was going to be a lot of BS about books that nobody had really read. But as I watched this guy I got a feeling that phonies were not going to get away with anything, that you had to know what you were talking about here. When he got up to talk, I actually felt excited, like something was going to happen. I was a little scared, scared that this guy would be tough, but more scared that maybe he wouldn't be, maybe I was wrong. English always bored me, but I really hoped maybe this time it would be worth it. When he started to talk he looked right at me and at everybody. He made some kind of joke. But then he started to talk to us, right to us, and I thought to myself, "My God, this might be OK after all."

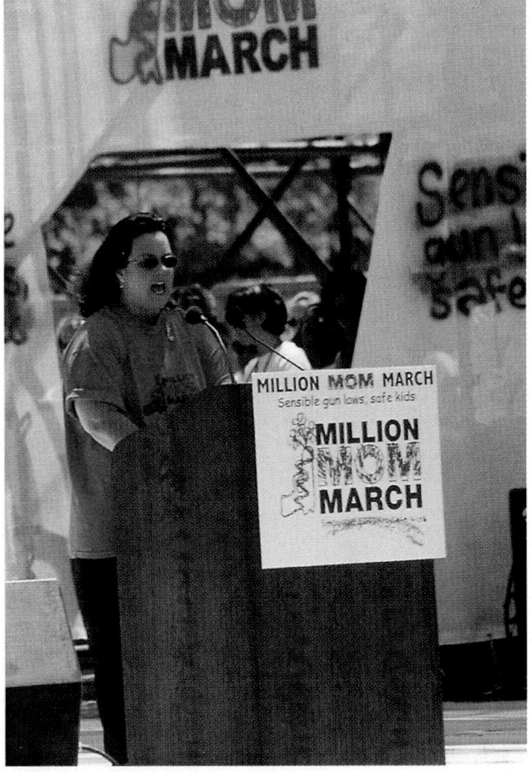

Talk show host Rosie O'Donnell is known for her lively and vivid use of language. Here she addresses the Million Mom March, a rally designed to help people visualize the dangers of guns to children. (Cleve Bryant/PhotoEdit)

Vivid Language. Listeners' emotions are often engaged through the use of vivid descriptions of pleasant or unpleasant situations. In Chapter 9, we noted that telling a story about real people tends to promote identification between the audience and the subject. The simple narrative can make us feel ashamed or angry or experience a host of other emotions.

Montel, a public speaking student, began a speech by describing an automobile accident in vivid detail. He explained how the victims of the accident were rushed to the nearest hospital and how one of the victims was examined very quickly, put on a stretcher, and left in a hallway unattended. He described the patient's deteriorating condition as the hours passed, and how doctors and nurses hurried by, some occasionally stopping for a quick look and then going on. As he told the story, the sense of frustration, surprise, and anger in the audience was apparent. Everyone wondered why on earth something wasn't being done for that patient. Montel concluded his story by explaining that the accident, which took place several years ago, involved a black woman who had been taken to a hospital in a predominantly white neighborhood. The example was so vivid and the emotions aroused were so real that the speaker had little more to do to finish his speech on the evils of racism.

sensory appeals language that encourages sensory reactions

In using vivid language, speakers often try to appeal to listeners' senses. Through **sensory appeals**, audience members are encouraged to see, hear, smell, taste, or feel something. Notice how the following speaker helps the audience visualize the violence he associates with animal rights protesters:

> Here are a few protest activities conducted in the name of animal rights. A few months ago PETA's vegetarian campaign coordinator from the Washington headquarters was in Denver attempting to unload a truckful of manure in front of the Colorado Convention Center. She was protesting against the World Meat Congress that was meeting there. Signage on the side of the truck said, "Meat Stinks." Police arrested her before she completed the job. At a dog show, PETA protesters opened the cages of several of the show dogs and turned them loose; they also put anti-freeze in the water bowls of some cages. One of the protesters said, "A dead dog is better than a caged dog." Add to this such incidents as PETA protesters throwing paint or blood onto fur coats worn by women walking down the street. . . .
>
> There's another animal rights group, the Animal Liberation Front, that has been blamed for the firebombing of an animal-research lab at Michigan State University. Police reported an estimate of $200,000 in damages and the destroying of 30 years' worth of primary research data. . . . Last year, the Animal Liberation Front planted incendiary devices in four downtown Chicago department stores.
>
> Another dimension of the fight for animal rights was provided by vegetarians who broke into the shop of a German butcher. They smashed equipment worth $21,000 and painted the message "Meat is murder, animal killer," on the shop windows. Subsequently, they slashed the butcher's tires and left a phone message, "Yesterday your store, tomorrow you.[4]

There is no doubt that listeners who are exposed to such a vivid and detailed narrative have a strong likelihood of identifying with it. With the bulk of the appeal resting on visual images, the result is a persuasive presentation.

Of course, how audience members respond to a particular speech will depend on their own values and beliefs. If, for instance, a listener who was an animal rights activist heard this speech, she might reject the speaker's comments, viewing them as exaggerated or misrepresented in some way. In this case, vivid language could actually undermine the speaker's purpose. But if the speaker was so effective that he was able to convince the listener that she had been misinformed, he might yet succeed.

Much depends on the speaker's ability to marshal excellent arguments and on the listener's ability to be open to new and alternative viewpoints. In this situation, as in so many others, speaker and listener depend on each other for a mutually satisfying outcome.

To assess the use of language to communicate information, go to **Next Step: Mastering the Six Cs of Language Effectiveness** in **Lesson 7** of the **VideoLab** CD-ROM and complete the quiz.

Using Figures of Speech

Language that is striking or impressive can create interest and contribute to understanding. For centuries, students of rhetoric have studied what are called **figures of speech**; these are special ways of using language to heighten the beauty of expression or the clarity of ideas. It is not important for the beginning student of public speaking to understand and identify all the technical names for the different figures of speech. But both listeners and speakers should be aware of some special ways of using the language. A word of caution: don't try to use "big words" or "fancy expressions" just to sound impressive. Be sure that you know the precise meaning of the words you use. **Malapropisms** are words that might sound right but have a different meaning from that intended. For instance, one speaker asserted, "After dinner, we would all conjugate in the lounge"; he obviously meant "congregate." He would probably have been better off saying "gather" or "meet."

figures of speech special uses of language that heighten the beauty of expression to make it clearer, more meaningful, and more memorable

malapropisms words used inappropriately that sound like the word that should be used

Simile. Language can be used to compare things. A direct comparison can be made between things that an audience might not see as being similar. This kind of comparison, a **simile**, is introduced by using the word *like* or *as*. "A day in the life of the college student," one student began her speech, "is like a day at an amusement park. You have ups and downs; you can get spun around; you can do new things you've never done before; you can have a lot of fun; and you can end by throwing up."

simile a direct comparison established by using the word *like* or *as*

More eloquently, Winston Churchill used a simile when he compared the future to a mighty river: "For my own part, looking out upon the future, I do not view the prospect with any misgivings. I could not stop it if I wished; no one can stop it. Like the Mississippi, it just keeps rolling along. Let it roll. Let it roll on full flood, inexorable, irresistible . . . to broader lands and better days."[5] By using this comparison, Churchill suggested that the future is a powerful, uncontrollable force.

Metaphor. Another kind of common comparison is the **metaphor**, which compares two objects that the audience might think of as being quite dissimilar. (The technical distinction between a metaphor and a simile is that *like* or *as* does not appear in a metaphor.) One freshman college student, facing her first set of finals at the end of her first semester, described her feelings through a metaphor: "I think I understand the principles of swimming, but I'm about to find out by jumping into the deep end of the pool; I just hope I don't drown." In a moving tribute to the murdered Mahatma Gandhi, Jawaharlal Nehru said, "A glory has departed and the sun that warmed and brightened our lives has set and we shiver in the dark."[6]

metaphor an implicit comparison in which two dissimilar objects are compared

These images create a certain feeling or mood in the audience. In this way, they make an important contribution to the audience's total understanding of a speech.

Antithesis. Language can be used to make contrasts between words or ideas. The special device known as **antithesis** is a way of putting two things together that have sharply different meanings. Through antithesis, ideas can be reinforced and compelling contrasts in thought can be suggested. One student speaker argued, "Right on this campus, we see the forces of life and personal sacrifice contending with the forces of death and personal profit." This speech attacked

antithesis placing two images together that have sharply different meanings those who would risk the effects of pollution in order to make money. The antithesis pitted life against death and sacrifice against profit in such a way that those who put money first were allied with death.

irony the use of language to imply a meaning that is totally opposite the literal meaning of a word or expression

Irony. Other stylistic devices can be used to make ideas more believable or understandable. Through **irony**, a speaker can strongly imply a meaning that is opposite that which is stated: "As we all know, doctors who have taken the Hippocratic Oath care a great deal about their patients and don't care anything at all about how much money they can make."

When using irony, the speaker's delivery should convey a tone of skepticism to clarify and reinforce the language. In addition, irony usually works best when listeners and speaker share similar attitudes toward the topic being discussed.

alliteration a repetitive pattern of initial sounds in a sequence of words, used to gain attention and reinforce an idea

Alliteration. A speaker who uses a repetitive pattern of initial sounds that can hold the audience's attention and reinforce the idea is using **alliteration**. One student speaker said, "For some, the university, instead of being a passport to plenty, is the doorway to doom." In his 1989 inaugural address, George Bush used alliteration when he said, "The President is neither prince nor pope."[7]

Poets commonly use alliteration and other figures of speech. Edgar Allan Poe wrote of the "silken, sad, uncertain, rustling of each purple curtain"[8] to capture the sound of curtains being blown about by an open window. Whether used in a poem or a speech, alliteration, if not forced or overdone, is memorable and pleasing to the ear.

personification a description of an inanimate form or thing as if it were human

Personification. The speaker who uses **personification** gives the characteristics of human beings to nonhuman forms or things: "This city can be a very hostile place. It can ignore you, it can frighten you, and it can punish you very severely if you ignore its unwritten rules." This student speaker then went on to talk about such urban problems as loneliness, homelessness, and crime.

oxymoron an expression that presents, in combination, seemingly contradictory terms

Oxymoron. Through an **oxymoron**, a speaker can combine seemingly contradictory expressions, such as *thunderous silence* or *cheerful pessimist.* Other oxymorons that were circulated by email in the 1990s included *act naturally, found missing, advanced BASIC, safe sex,* and *government organization.* Recently we attended a play titled *The Male Intellect: An Oxymoron?* a delightful comedy about the differences between men and women. As in the title of this play, public speakers often point to a contradiction that they use intentionally to emphasize the contrast between two things.

rhetorical questions questions posed by a speaker that are intended to stimulate thought and interest, not an actual oral response

Memorizing the definitions of these figures of speech is not nearly as important as recognizing this basic principle: choosing language that is effective in promoting your meaning and conveying your feelings helps better connect you with your audience.

 CONNECTING TO THE NET

There are many more figures of speech than we have described here. For a much more extensive list, including definitions and examples, go to **http://college.hmco.com/communication/andrews/public_speaking/2e/students/** and click on *Connecting to the Net.* From there, follow the link to Figures of Speech.

Using Rhetorical Questions

Speakers sometimes ask listeners questions. When they do so, they are usually not looking for an immediate response or expecting to initiate a dialogue with the audience. Instead, by using **rhetorical questions**, they are trying to pique the audience's curiosity and stimulate thinking. As we noted in Chapter 10, rhetorical questions may be used to gain the audience's attention during the speech's introduction. But they can also be used in other places in the speech. Here is an example of a speaker who used a rhetorical question as a punch line for his introduction:

> O'Hare Airport in Chicago was about one hour away from being fogged in for the night. One plane would be leaving for New York in thirty minutes. Five seats were left; six people bought tickets. No other planes would leave that night.
>
> John Jones, laborer, had won a trip to Europe and the boat left that evening.
>
> Mark Johnson, serviceman, back from two years overseas, is returning to his wife and baby in New York.
>
> Marie Wilson is hurrying to the bedside of her father, a heart attack victim, who is dying.
>
> Thomas Roberts is scheduled to attend a father-son banquet in New York with his son, who has been having some problems.
>
> Sam Brown, rock star, is on stage at Madison Square Garden that evening before 15,000 fans.
>
> Barbara Wright, retired schoolteacher, is being honored that evening at a class reunion.
>
> Which of the six would you leave behind?[9]

Rhetorical questions are effective because when someone asks us a question, we start to think. In most communication contexts, when we are asked questions, we are being invited to participate. Questions trigger guesses, speculation, and other forms of thought. In short, questions activate our brains.

Rhetorical questions can also be used as transitions, as noted in Chapter 10. As with other aspects of language, they must be chosen carefully. Imagine how interested you would be if a speaker asked you such an unimaginative question as: "Now, what are some reasons we should all wear seat belts?" or "Why is smoking really bad for you?"

The effectiveness of any rhetorical question depends on its wording, its timing, and the way the speaker develops the response to the question. Having posed the question, the speaker is, of course, obliged to answer it.

PORTFOLIO 12.3

How Interesting Are You?

Return to your working outline. This time check your wording to ensure that it is active, lively, and vivid. Also consider what figures of speech might be appropriate, as well as rhetorical questions or parallelism. Sketch out the possibilities for a few of these techniques, making sure that none appear forced or overdone.

parallelism the use of a series of sentences with similar length and structure to signify the equality of ideas

Using Parallelism

Some speakers use **parallelism** to suggest equality among their ideas. When used effectively, parallelism can bring force, clarity, rhythm, and interest to a speech. Using either parallel construction or phrases of about equal length also emphasizes the similarity of ideas. Franklin Roosevelt spoke forcefully about the plight of many Americans. The following example shows how several features of good oral style can work together. As well as having parallelism in its overall structure, this Roosevelt quotation contains repetition (at the beginning of each line and in the last line).

> I see millions of families trying to live on incomes so meager that the pall of family disaster hangs over them day by day.

KEEP IN MIND 12.3

Making Language Interesting

Here are some ways to make language interesting:

- Use active language.
- Use lively language.
- Use vivid language.
- Use figures of speech.
- Use rhetorical questions.
- Use parallelism.

The language you choose and the way you use it can make a difference in the way your audience responds. Becoming conscious of language and learning to use it effectively are critical parts of your growth as a speaker.

I see millions whose daily lives in city and on farm continue under conditions labeled indecent by a so-called polite society half a century ago.

I see millions denied education, recreation and the opportunity to better their lot and the lot of their children.

I see millions lacking the means to buy the products of farm and factory and by their poverty denying work and productiveness to many other millions.

I see one-third of a nation ill-housed, ill-clad, ill-nourished.[10]

Go to **Drill 7.2: Identifying Language Techniques** on the **VideoLab** CD-ROM and view the video clips. Afterward, take the quiz to assess your knowledge of the speaker's use of figures of speech and word choice.

USING LANGUAGE APPROPRIATE TO THE SITUATION

Preview We can outline some of the underlying features of effective oral style, but we cannot judge language without knowing something about the situation in which the speech is to be delivered. The setting, the context, and the occasion all may call for language to be used in different ways. Audience expectations are also critical.

All of us know that we use different conventions in language for different people and contexts. We all know that the words we choose when talking to our friends tend to be vastly different from the ones we choose when talking to our parents, to employers, or to teachers.

Appropriateness and Context

One of the most dramatic examples of contrasting uses of language was demonstrated by the publication of the famous Watergate tapes. These recorded conversations illustrated the startling differences between public and private choices of language made by President Richard Nixon and many of his advisers.[11] One of the things that shocked some people was not so much the use of specific expletives, but the fact that those words were used by the president of the United States in the Oval Office of the White House. To many people, who had surely heard expletives before and perhaps even used some of them themselves, their use in the White House did not seem fitting.

Contextual Factors Affecting Audience Perceptions. The question is this: what language is best suited to the context in which your speech occurs? Within this context, you yourself are an important element. Language that seems most appropriate in a particular speaking context may differ from your normal conversational language. In general, you will probably think about, choose, and use language more carefully in a public speech than you would in a private setting. The language you choose to introduce an important visiting speaker will be more formal than the language you use when giving a book report in class.

At the same time, though, a good speaker is not going to "fake" language to sound like someone else. For example, it would be absurd and inappropriate for a well-educated speaker to use poor grammar or coarse language because he or she thought that the nature of the audience called for it. Such an action is not only unethical, but it also would probably be interpreted as condescending and insulting rather than adaptive. It would also be unwise

Language choice depends partially on the context in which speaking occurs. Language appropriate to a religious service, for example, will be very different from language chosen in a more informal, less ritualized setting. (Ilene Perlman/Stock Boston)

for a speaker to assume the slang and special cultural or technical language of an audience or group when such language choices do not come naturally to her or him.

Certain aspects of a situation—the audience, the topic of the speech, and the occasion or setting in which the speech takes place—also have an impact on language choice. Martin Luther King, Jr.'s speech to the civil rights march in Washington, D.C., on August 28, 1963, is probably the best example of language use that grows out of all the constituents of a situation. His first words in the speech were, "Five score years ago a great American in whose symbolic shadow we stand today signed the Emancipation Proclamation."[12] He said this standing on the steps of the Lincoln Memorial. It was well calculated to remind the audience of Lincoln, his Gettysburg Address, and, by extension, the long and bloody struggle over slavery and racial prejudice.

Spotlight on Language Reflecting the Situation shows how one speaker adapted his presentation to the demands of a special context. Following the 1992 Los Angeles riots (in response to the acquittal of four white police officers in the beating of black motorist Rodney King), Rev. David Owen delivered a powerful sermon that both grappled with the tragic state of a nation still at war over race and honored the memory of Martin Luther King, Jr. After describing his dream, Rev. Owen went on to explain how, for a while, he lost faith in his dreams for America. After considerable inner struggle, he was eventually able to regain it. We were part of the audience who listened to Owen's powerful presentation. His effective oral style, the power of his language, and his ability to ground his sermon in the tension-ridden national context resulted in a moving and memorable presentation.

SPOTLIGHT ON... **Language Reflecting the Situation**

Excerpt from "I Had a Dream" by David Owen

When I first saw the fires in Los Angeles I remembered a much earlier dream—another dream of America, her cities and her people—a dream of faith and hope rather than desolation and fear. . . .

I also glimpsed that dream in my grade school where I was helped to understand that America is a country composed of many different kinds of people. In other countries, I was told, opportunities were often restricted to an elite few. But here in our American democracy all people were free, all people were considered equal, the rules for pursuing happiness were fair, and liberty and justice were offered to all. It was such a beautiful dream:

Give me your tired, your poor,
Your huddled masses
yearning to breathe free,
The wretched refuse of your teeming shore,
Send these, the homeless,
tempest-tossed, to me . . .

I rightly sensed that only a brave and confident country could dream such a dream.

As I grew older, I began to see that the dream was not yet fulfilled for all. During my sixteenth summer I worked for a bottling company in Milwaukee and spent some days delivering cases of soft drinks to the poorest—mostly black—neighborhoods of our city. In early morning deliveries we regularly woke homeless men who had spent the night on storeroom floors of neighborhood bars. In the basements of restaurants and grocery stores we often groped for empty cases in darkness, shaking the cases before picking them up so as to scare the rats away. . . . The stench in my nostrils from certain stores and restaurants stayed for days. I didn't understand all that I was experiencing, but I knew that it was a different America than I had previously seen.

After a few years I began attending meetings of CORE—the Congress of Racial Equality. We met on Sunday evenings in a storefront church within the black community. It was a small group. Typically fifteen blacks and a few whites attended. As we arrived and when we left plainclothes policemen photographed us from an unmarked car across the street. On other occasions they stood on the sidewalk photographing us more openly. The police were beginning to treat us as subversives. I did not understand why. I did not see myself as subversive. I had a dream.

One summer night marching with a group of black youth who were seeking a Fair Housing law for the city, we crossed the long 16th Street Viaduct to Milwaukee's southside. No blacks lived there. Crowds of whites were waiting. First they hurled obscenities—then rocks and bottles. The police added tear gas. Despite such opposition, the youth marched for 200 straight nights. With hundreds of other people I walked such gauntlets with them many times. It seemed important. I had a dream. . . .

The dream went on for more than ten years, carrying me to Montgomery, Alabama, with Dr. Martin Luther King . . . to Senators' offices and the basements of black churches in Washington, D.C.; to midnight strategy sessions with friends, and secret meetings in hotel rooms with officials of the Justice Department, and marches and demonstrations of many kinds. . . . It all seemed quite natural. I believed what my parents and church had taught me. . . . I believed in America. I believed in that day spoken of by Martin Luther King "when all God's children would be able to join hands and sing." I had a dream. From Maine to Mississippi, let freedom ring!

David Owen, "I Had a Dream" (speech delivered at St. Mark's United Methodist Church, Bloomington, Ind., May 31, 1992). Reprinted by permission.

Audience Expectations. Most of us do not appear in public speaking settings that are as dramatic or overriding as the context in which David Owen or Martin Luther King, Jr., found themselves. No matter where we are, however, we need to ask ourselves what the audience knows and thinks about the topic. Similarly, we should consider the level of linguistic sophistication the audience holds, how serious or casual the constraints of the setting are, how formal or informal the situation is, and what the physical limitations and relationships are between us and our listeners in this particular situation.

In a public speaking class, one speaker began this way: "I'm planning to say something today that is very important. It's of great interest and significance—not only to us here in this room, but to people everywhere. I just hope I can say it in a way that is fitting and proper." Conveying much the same idea, a minister in a church preceded his sermon with the old prayer, "May the words of my mouth and the meditations of our hearts be always acceptable in thy sight, O Lord our strength and our redeemer."[13] Obviously, reversing those two openings would be inappropriate, even though the essential idea of both is the same.

The public speaking class is a much more informal type of situation than a church. It calls for, among other things, different stylistic choices. The wise speaker thinks carefully about what an audience expects of him or her and makes reasonable, ethical, and appropriate adjustments to meet those expectations. This does not mean that you simply tell the audience what you think they expect you to say. Rather you develop your speech with an understanding of audience expectations in a specific context, taking them into account and respecting them.

Appropriate Language as Ethical Language

Sometimes when we think of speaking appropriately, we are thinking of speaking in a way that seems to "fit" the speech situation. But another dimension of appropriateness also involves using language with a concern for ethics. We have already hinted at some possible ethical concerns.

PORTFOLIO 12.4

Appropriateness

Contemplate your message in your forthcoming speech. Is any of the language you are considering questionable in terms of its appropriateness to the audience and setting? What alternative expressions might you use that would preserve the integrity of your message but present it more appropriately?

Promoting Mutual Respect. Using language the audience considers offensive or tasteless is not likely to get the desired response. But, more than that, *knowingly* using such language suggests that the speaker lacks concern or respect for the audience. As in any communication situation, mutual respect is the hallmark of ethical communication.[14]

Most speakers also have certain expectations for the way they hope to be treated by their audiences. They expect to be made to feel welcome, they expect not to be interrupted while they are speaking, and they assume that any audience member who chooses to challenge them (during the time for questions) will do so respectfully and without resorting to personal attacks. These expectations go both ways. As partners in the communication process, both speakers and listeners have the right to expect mutual respect, civility, good taste, and sensitivity to feelings.

sexist language language that demeans an individual or group on the basis of gender

Avoiding Offensive Language. Some listeners are offended by what they consider to be obscenities or "bad" language. The speaker who curses, even in jest, may suggest a lack of respect for some listeners' beliefs. Even though no offense is intended, the outcome may undermine the communication. Both the speaker and the listeners must recognize that language can produce strong associations with beliefs and values and thus can arouse strong emotions.

Ethical speakers must also guard against the use of **sexist language**—or any language that is demeaning to any group, culture, or individual. We are not

KEEP IN MIND 12.4

Using Language Appropriately

- Adapt to the context and occasion.
- Understand audience expectations.
- Speak within an ethical framework.
- Respect the audience.
- Avoid offensive language.
- Use emotional language ethically.

SPOTLIGHT ON... Avoiding Sexist Language

Speak in the plural whenever possible. If you say "Managers are often. . . . They try to motivate," you don't have to worry about portraying the manager as a man or a woman. The more you can use the plural, the more gender-neutral your language will tend to be.

Switch to "he or she" when you must use a singular subject. You might say, "A student who majors in business will choose between taking a foreign language, taking culture studies courses, or studying abroad. He or she will have to . . . ." This strategy works well as long as you don't overdo it.

Eliminate gender inflections. Any of us can learn to say "chairperson" rather than "chairman," "mail carrier" in place of "mailman," and "server" instead of "waitress."

Avoid using gender markers. It is always inappropriate to highlight a person's gender (or sexual orientation) when referring to his or her profession. Eliminate expressions such as "my female dentist," "that lesbian tennis player," or "the woman manager." Of course, the same rule applies to racial markers; equally offensive is "the Hispanic doctor" or "that black lawyer."

Don't hesitate to use gender-specific pronouns when they are appropriate. If you are referring to a person who is part of a group, all of whom are either male or female, you should refer to the person with an accurate pronoun. For instance, a former president of the United States would be "he" since we have had no female presidents. Similarly, a mother is "she," as is a Buddhist nun.

just talking about being "politically correct." We are talking about the speaker's attitude toward the listeners and toward others in society. Most of us know that women do not want to be referred to as "girls" or "chicks." Similarly, men don't want to be referred to as "boys" or "studs." Homosexuals will rightly take offense at being called "fags" or "dykes." See *Spotlight on Avoiding Sexist Language* for some guidelines in this regard.

Go to **Drill 7.3: Revising for Language Effectiveness** on the **VideoLab** CD-ROM and view the video clips you find there. As you watch the speakers, concentrate on identifying the ways in which their use of language could be improved.

Using language that may be perceived as racist, sexist, or offensive in some way will present some real problems, whatever the speaker's intentions or level of awareness. When, during the 1992 presidential race, Ross Perot was addressing a nearly all–African American audience and referred to them as "you people," he was poorly received by his audience, and his comment was repeated countless times by members of the press, as well as by his opponents. In short, whatever the speaker's intentions or attitudes, audience perceptions of appropriateness are critical.

Using Emotional Language Ethically. The ethical public speaker will never use language in an attempt to get the audience to respond in a kind of emotional frenzy, without thinking through an argument or carefully examining the speaker's evidence. As we have made clear, emotional appeals are quite appropriate and often necessary to move an audience to action. **Ethical emotional appeals** have a substructure of strong evidence and sound reasoning. The speaker assumes that audience members are thinking critically and constructively, and he or she will do nothing to get around their inclination and right to do so.

ethical emotional appeals appeals that seek an emotional response while simultaneously providing good reasons to justify the reaction sought

Figure 12.1 presents some specific questions that listeners (and speakers) might ask themselves in trying to make judgments about the quality of a speaker's style. Good oral style is effective, appropriate, and ethical.

FIGURE 12.1 The Characteristics of Good Oral Style

Here is a checklist you can use to evaluate your own or someone else's oral style:

- ___ Does the speaker seem to convey clear thoughts?
- ___ Does he or she use relatively simple, familiar words?
- ___ Are the speaker's words precise, concrete, and specific?
- ___ Does the speaker avoid technical words and acronyms if possible and/or define them for listeners?
- ___ Does he or she avoid empty words and clichés?
- ___ Does he or she use only necessary modifiers?
- ___ Is the speaker's language active, lively, and vivid?
- ___ Does the speaker use figurative language to stimulate and please listeners?
- ___ Does the speaker use parallelism to add interest and emphasize the equality of ideas?
- ___ Are the speaker's sentences relatively short and simple?
- ___ Does the speaker use the active voice?
- ___ Does he or she use rhetorical questions to stimulate listeners and challenge them to think?
- ___ Does the speaker emphasize ideas through restatement and repetition?
- ___ Does he or she emphasize main points through good transitional language?
- ___ Is the speaker's language well adapted to the speaking context?
- ___ Does the speaker appear to use language ethically, avoiding offensive language, respecting the audience, and using emotional appeals appropriately?

Go to **Lesson 6's Screening Room** on the **VideoLab** CD-ROM to view the speech on Native American symbols and evaluate the speaker's use of language in light of the characteristics of good oral style listed in Figure 12.1.

STYLE AND THE AUDIENCE'S RESPONSE

Preview When a speaker has good style, listeners are likely to be moved. Critical listeners will be aware that style in language can have an impact. They will look for sound arguments, good evidence, and substance of thought—regardless of the speaker's style. They will avoid overreacting to style in either a positive or a negative sense.

It should be apparent by now that style can have a strong impact on listeners—almost apart from the ideas that are being expressed. That is, the way in which ideas are expressed can be as important as the ideas themselves in influencing the listeners' reactions, since a clear speaking style enhances the speaker's ethos. As we have pointed out, the ethical speaker will be sensitive to the potential for such influence and will do everything possible to ensure that he or she does not deliberately use style to evoke unthinking emotional responses or to hide weak evidence or a flawed argument. Nevertheless, listeners need to be vigilant.

Style Substituted for Argument

labeling using emotionally charged language to identify something in an attempt to influence another person's perceptions

Speakers have been known to dismiss an idea not by dissecting it, analyzing it, or examining its weaknesses or strengths, but simply by **labeling** it. For example, a speaker might contend that an idea is too "socialistic," "radical," or "conservative." Such a speaker substitutes style for argument. Here's one example: instead of pointing to the shortcomings of a plan one speaker opposed, he simply said, "This is another one of those liberal ideas; it's just what you would expect, and it hardly merits our consideration." In this case, by using the word *liberal* with a disapproving tone, the speaker suggested that there was something wrong with being liberal (without specifying what he viewed as wrong).

What is the listener to do when confronted with this kind of "argument"? Good critical listeners will ask, *On what basis will I respond? What does the speaker mean by "liberal idea"? What are the implications?* In this example, is there evidence that this is a liberal idea? And, if so, is there evidence that the idea is either good or bad? If the listener finds himself or herself saying, "If this is liberal, I don't want to have anything to do with it," without questioning the speaker's meaning and asking for support for the assertion, then he or she may be falling prey to a stylistic substitution for argument. After all, a liberal idea may be fair, progressive, unprejudiced, and generous; or it may be lax, loose, and lenient. Clearly, depending on the speaker's intended meaning, the listener would evaluate the idea in strikingly different ways.

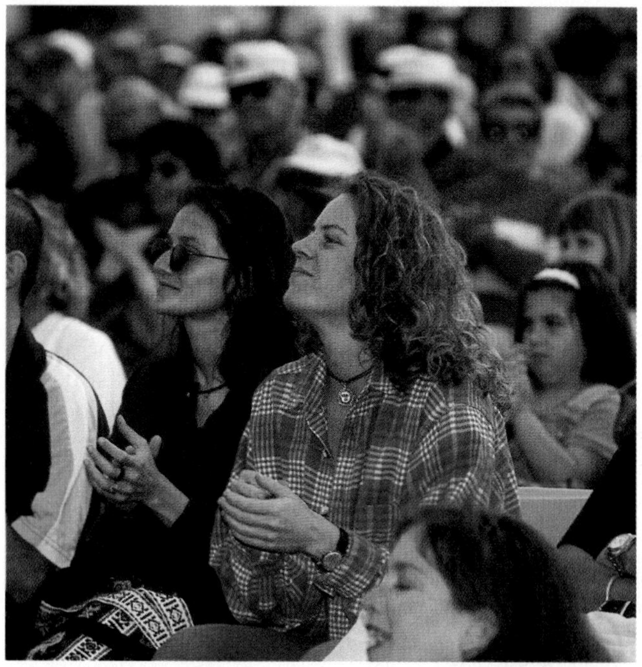

Good listeners, while obligated to listen critically, are partners in the communication process. They should attempt to empathize with the speaker, attending carefully to what he or she says. (David Young-Wolff/PhotoEdit)

Stylistic substitutions can occur in other ways. For instance, a speaker might use a false analogy (to be discussed further in Chapter 16) and try to condemn a proposal by saying, "This would make as much sense as playing tennis without a net." Listeners must ask themselves whether this comparison is really a good one. Of course, tennis would be a much different game without a net, but how does that relate to the proposal being criticized? Sometimes speakers attempt to short-circuit the listeners' reasoning process by using "clever" analogies and undefined words that are rich in connotative meaning and high in ambiguity. When this happens, the listeners' job is to refrain from judgment until the speaker is able to provide some clarification, perhaps after the speech.

In Chapter 9, we discussed the need for supporting ideas with evidence. Listeners should keep the same principle in mind when they are faced with persuasive language use. Here, too, listeners must be wary of accepting the speaker's word alone, even if that word is most aptly and interestingly chosen.[15] It is always reasonable for listeners to ask for evidence. A good speaker will anticipate being asked to provide support for his or her ideas.

Ethical Listening

From the listeners' perspective, there is also the burden of listening ethically. Listeners should reflect thoughtfully on the speaker's intentions. Occasionally a speaker will unintentionally say something offensive. For instance, one of us once had a student who insisted on calling her "ma'am." She did not especially care for this term since it reminded her that she was moving toward middle age. However, she tried to take into account the student's military background and recognized that he meant to show respect. Similarly, a returning male student in his early sixties always referred to the female members of his much younger audience as "ladies." These students wisely recognized that he used the term out of respect for them, not to demean them in any way.

In short, while audience members need to think and listen critically, they also need to extend some degree of empathy and understanding to the speaker. Listeners should not tolerate offensive or manipulative language, but neither should they be hypercritical or overly judgmental. As partners in the human communication process, speakers and listeners should accept some possibility of human error on both sides.

KEEP IN MIND 12.5

Audience Response

Listeners have a responsibility to

- detect when style is substituted for argument.
- listen ethically.
- recognize a sense of partnership in the human communication process.

Now that you have nearly finished reading this chapter, go to **Lesson 6 Coach: Tips to Remember** on the **VideoLab** CD-ROM and watch the speech clip. Then, read through the list of reminders concerning effective language usage. How well does this speaker measure up?

SUMMARY

In this chapter, we have seen the role that style plays in the presentation of a speech. You may have a perfectly prepared speech—one that is clearly and strategically organized, filled with excellent information and ideas, and appropriately reinforced through the use of sound evidence and reasoning. To make the speech truly effective, however, you must use language that is appropriate for the topic and the audience.

The overarching purpose of having a good speaking style is to promote the audience's understanding through the use of effective language. At the foundation of good language use is clarity. In general, using language that is familiar to listeners, as well as concrete, specific, and precise, will help you achieve a good speaking style. It's also important to avoid crowding sentences with clichés and empty words or constructing sentences so that they are tediously long, overly complex, and hard for listeners to follow.

Besides being clear, your language should be interesting to the audience. Listeners are likely to find active language more engaging than passive language, and most will see your style as striking or impressive if you use figurative language such as metaphors, antithesis, alliteration, and other language devices.

Finally, your language should be appropriate to the situation—well adapted to the speech setting, the listeners' expectations and levels of understanding, and the constraints of the occasion—and ethical. Some speaking situations call for more formal language than others, and one mark of a good speaker is his or her ability to demonstrate some flexibility in style across diverse speaking contexts. Using language ethically entails showing respect for the audience, striving never to offend them, using good judgment and good taste, and always encouraging the audience to respond thoughtfully rather than impulsively.

In short, your style can have a strong impact on listeners—apart from the ideas you are communicating. From an ethical perspective, both speakers and listeners must beware of the possibility of substituting style for argument. A speaker may use emotionally charged words, and the listeners may respond without carefully examining the substructure of evidence and reasoning underlying the speaker's powerful style. It is both the speaker's and the listeners' responsibility to be careful in using and responding to language.

QUESTIONS FOR REVIEW AND REFLECTION

1. What is meant by "style" in public speaking? How does it differ from other notions of style?
2. Contrast denotative and connotative language. How might charged language present challenges to listeners?

3. What are some ways that a speaker can strive to make his or her language clear?
4. What is wrong with using expressions such as "it goes without saying," "last but not least," and "due to the fact that" when you speak?
5. Why is active language more interesting to listeners than passive language?
6. Provide a good example of each of the following and explain how it makes an idea more effective:
   a. Simile
   b. Metaphor
   c. Antithesis
   d. Irony
   e. Alliteration
   f. Personification
   g. Oxymoron
   h. Parallelism
   i. Rhetorical question
7. To be effective, a speaker must speak appropriately. What are three key guidelines for using language appropriately in a public speech?
8. What is the relationship between using language appropriately and using it ethically?

ENDNOTES

1. Winston Churchill, "Dunkerque," in *Blood, Sweat and Tears* (New York: G. P. Putnam, 1941), p. 297.
2. Ralph Waldo Emerson, "The American Scholar," in *American Literature,* ed. Franklyn Snyder and Edward Snyder (New York: Macmillan, 1935), p. 459.
3. Lyndon B. Johnson, "The Voting Rights Act of 1965," in *Great Speeches for Criticism and Analysis,* ed. Lloyd Rohler and Roger Cook (Greenwood, Ind.: Alistair Press, 1988), pp. 231–232.
4. Lee W. Baker, "The Ethics of Protest: Is It Right to Do Wrong?" in *Contemporary American Speeches,* 8th ed., ed. R. L. Johannesen, R. R. Allen, W. A. Linkugel, and F. J. Bryan (Dubuque, Iowa: Kendall/Hunt, 1997), pp. 178–179. *Vital Speeches of the Day* 62, Lee W. Baker, "The Ethics of Protest," (February 1, 1996), p. 255.
5. Churchill, "The War Situation," in *Blood, Sweat and Tears,* p. 351.
6. Quoted in Jane Blankenship, *A Sense of Style: An Introduction to Style for the Public Speaker* (Belmont, Calif.: Dickenson, 1968), p. 70.
7. Quoted in Davis Newton Lott, ed., *The Presidents Speak* (New York: Henry Holt, 1994), p. 362.
8. Edgar Allan Poe, "The Raven" in *The Viking Book of Poetry of the English Speaking World,* vol. II (NY: Viking, 1959): 866.
9. John D. Garwood, "Back to the Basics: A Commitment to Excellence," *Vital Speeches of the Day* 46 (Feb. 6, 1980): 42.
10. Quoted in Blankenship, *A Sense of Style,* p. 101.
11. See Dennis S. Gouran, "Communicative Influences on Decisions Related to the Watergate Coverup: The Failure of Collective Judgment," *Central States Speech Journal* 34 (1984): 260–268.
12. Martin Luther King, Jr., "I Had a Dream," in *Great Speeches for Criticism and Analysis,* ed. Lloyd Rohler and Roger Cook (Greenwood, Ind.: Alistair Press, 1988), p. 325.
13. Psalms 19:14.
14. See Richard L. Johannesen, "The Emerging Concept of Communication as Dialogue," *Quarterly Journal of Speech* 57 (December 1971): 373–382, and Maurice S. Friedman, *Dialogue and the Human Image: Beyond Humanistic Psychology* (Newbury Park, Calif.: Sage, 1992).
15. For an excellent book on style, see Blankenship, *A Sense of Style.*

Go to **Lesson 7's Screening Room** on the **VideoLab** CD-ROM to view the speech on corporate welfare. Once you have watched the speech, take the quiz aimed at assessing the effectiveness of the speaker's language. You may also want to read through the authors' assessment of this speech on pages 306–308.

Darryl begins his speech with strong, active language. He takes what is for many the connotative meaning of welfare—"free ride," "lazy," "slackers"—and compares it with "hardworking" people who "struggle" to achieve the "American dream." Then, in an ironic twist, he reveals that he is talking about corporate welfare.

Darryl seeks to increase the clarity of his message by being concrete and specific, naming corporations and giving the dollar amounts of subsidies.

Notice that Darryl's sentences in this preview are short and direct—clear and easy to understand. He uses lively, active language in describing the intensity of his feelings about this giveaway. The use of the "fat cats" metaphor suggests negative connotations.

In describing social welfare and corporate welfare, Darryl uses vivid language to heighten the contrast. A concrete comparison reinforces clarity, and a rhetorical question directs listeners' attention to what follows.

Darryl Neher was a graduate student in speech communication when he gave this speech at Indiana University in 1998.

Corporate Welfare

Darryl Neher

I loathe welfare for everything it is. I mean, basically, it's a free ride for the lazy. It creates this culture of dependency that takes money from us hardworking American men and women who struggle to pay our way through school, raise our families, and basically strive for the American dream. It drives me absolutely nuts that Congress will do nothing about these slackers and take them off the public dole. I mean, it's about time these huge corporations, like McDonald's and E & J Gallo, start carrying their own weight and stop expecting us to pay their bills.

Did that confuse you a little bit? I mean, when I referred to Gallo and McDonald's as being fat on corporate welfare money? Well, I shouldn't be surprised, because as Mark Zepezauer and Arthur Naiman suggest in their book *Take the Rich Off Welfare,* most Americans have no idea that the federal government hands out over a hundred and fifty billion dollars a year to corporations. I was one of those people who didn't know until just recently. It was when I started reading article after article after article about companies like McDonald's, for example, who received two million dollars to market Chicken McNuggets in third-world countries from federal subsidies. It made no sense. It was only then that welfare took on a whole new meaning for me. And I hope after this speech, you get a similar new perspective.

Now, to try to reassess the meaning of welfare, I'm going to do three things. I'm going to provide a definition of what corporate welfare is. And then we're going to look at exactly how far-reaching corporate welfare is as well as its magnitude in terms of dollars. The third step is to look at the three biggest fat cats that I am most personally offended by, and hopefully it'll get your blood boiling a little bit, as well.

But the most important thing is this first step of finding a definition. In 1996, the Cato Institute published a policy paper that suggested that's the biggest problem with understanding corporate welfare. Everybody has a different formula. Well, the Cato Institute themselves identify corporate welfare as directed subsidies or benefits directed to very specific industries and businesses. If you look at the Center for Study of Responsive Law, they identify corporate welfare as something that directs not only subsidies, but also tax breaks, loopholes, certain benefits that come from trade tariffs—a whole range of issues that other definitions don't consider. If you really want to get to brass tacks in this issue, let's make a comparison. When we talk about social welfare, we're talking about Aid to Families with Dependent Children. We talk about food stamps, housing subsidies, Pell Grants, student loans, earned income tax credits. What do these things have in common with corporate welfare? One fundamental philosophy: we're taking federal tax money from our public coffers and giving it to specific organizations for their economic benefit. That's corporate welfare.

Now, how we define corporate welfare has a really dramatic impact on how we look at the amount of the money being given away. How big is corporate welfare? Well, even in the modest definition offered by the Cato Institute, corporate welfare is anywhere between sixty billion and seventy-five billion dollars of federal subsidies each year. If we go to the Center for Study of Responsive Law and use their definition, it's a hundred and sixty-seven billion dollars.

Those numbers are so huge we might have a hard time understanding them, so let's make a comparison here, to put it into perspective. In August of 1996, when President Clinton signed into law far-reaching welfare reform, one particular program came under attack. That was AFDC, Aid to Families with Dependent Children. AFDC had been described by David Rosenbaum of the *New York Times* as the centerpiece of "costly hodgepodge welfare programs." Radio host Rush Limbaugh claimed the AFDC was the central program that allowed "the poor to become the biggest piglets at the mother pig and her nipples. They're the ones who get all the benefits in this country. They're the ones that are always pandered to."

To make almost incomprehensible numbers easy to understand and to discredit the critics of social welfare, Darryl again uses comparisons and specific examples, employing active and vivid language.

But is that really the case? Let's look at the AFDC numbers. AFDC cost taxpayers, according to Zepezauer and Naiman, only eighteen billion dollars in 1996—one percent of the federal budget. Now you do the math. Even under the Cato Institute's estimates of corporate welfare, of sixty to seventy-five billion dollars, AFDC could have been paid for with corporate subsidies four times. Now, if you use the subsidies identified by the Center for Study of Responsive Law, AFDC could have been paid for for nine years. We're talking about subsidies that would have gone to families who live below the poverty level, which for a family of four is fourteen thousand dollars a year. That would have reached five million people, the majority of them children.

Let's do more math. Michael Moore, the author of *Downsize This!* points out that AFDC and food stamps comprised fifty billion dollars in subsidies in 1995. That accounts for four hundred and fifteen dollars a year out of our pockets—every person in the United States. Now let's equate that to a trip to McDonald's every day. Basically, we'd have to sacrifice one Diet Coke at McDonald's in order to pay for AFDC and food stamps. What about corporate welfare? Using that 170 billion dollar number, it would cost you and me each $1,388 to subsidize these corporations. And on our trip to McDonald's, not only would we have to sacrifice that Diet Coke, we'd lose the whole Value Meal, even if it had been super-sized. Four dollars and eighty-one cents a day—that's what it would cost us.

If those numbers don't boil your blood enough, let's look at some of these fat cats who have really abused the system. Let's take a look at someone like Lockheed Martin, a defense manufacturer. They received only a paltry twenty-five thousand dollars in a tax write-off in 1996. But what did the tax write-off come for? Entertainment expenses that were grounded in twenty thousand dollars worth of golf balls. That's your tax money at work.

As Darryl drives his point home with more specific examples, he effectively uses repetition of the phrase, "That's your tax money at work." He also reinforces his point by repeating the essential facts from each example in a summary paragraph.

Then we have the Walt Disney corporation, a company whose profits are over one billion dollars per year. They received a three-hundred-thousand-dollar federal subsidy in order to research bigger and better fireworks for their theme parks. That's your tax money at work.

But probably the biggest and most insulting federal subsidy of all that I came across happened between 1990 and 1994, where General Motors received 110.6 million dollars in federal technological subsidies under the auspices of a jobs program. During that time period, their profits skyrocketed.

And what happened? They laid off 104,000 of their workers—twenty-five percent of their U.S. workforce. That's your tax money at work.

Corporate welfare is a big problem for us. All of us. We're talking the transferral of federal money—your tax money that you give the federal government—to support corporations that make millions, if not billions, of dollars a year. And what happens? Lockheed Martin buys golf balls with your money. Disney improves fireworks for theme parks that you may never be able to afford to attend. And GM makes the best of a job development program where they can fire employees, increase profits, and keep your tax money.

As he comes to his conclusion, Darryl chooses very simple, straightforward language in suggesting the steps to take. His simple words suggest that the steps themselves are easy enough for everyone to carry out. Ending with another reference to the "fat cats," Darryl associates his position with "progress" and all the positive connotations it suggests.

It's all pretty depressing, but it doesn't have to be demoralizing. There are three really simple things that I want to leave you with right now. Think, read, and spread the word.

We've already started the first part. You're thinking about this problem. Welfare is taking on a whole new meaning for you.

The second part is equally as important. Start reading. For a basic place to start, go to the Internet. Go to your favorite web server and type in "corporate welfare." You will unleash a plethora of sites that will explain exactly what corporate welfare is about and identify many, many more of these programs that are taking your tax money and abusing it.

But the third thing is probably the most important. It's up to you to spread the word. I didn't know about corporate welfare at one time; you didn't know about it before today; other people don't know about it right now. Let them know what's going on. Don't let the corporate fat cats get away with this. If we can continue to let people know what's going on, we can rethink the meaning of welfare. It's the only way we can start, and it's the only way we can make progress. Let's keep the fat cats at bay.

Using Presentational Aids in Public Speaking

13

CHAPTER OBJECTIVES

After studying this chapter, you should be able to

1. **understand the diverse ways that presentational aids can help you as a speaker.**
2. **follow basic guidelines for creating and using presentational materials.**
3. **identify the sorts of presentational options available to speakers.**
4. **create computer-generated presentational aids.**
5. **recognize the importance of practicing with presentational aids.**

CHAPTER SURVEY

Functions of Presentational Aids

Guidelines for Preparing and Using Presentational Aids

Presentational Aid Options

Presentational Aids in the Computer Age

Practicing with Presentational Aids

Visual material has a powerful impact on how we react to information. Everyone had heard of police brutality and was aware that it existed, but when people saw the videotapes of Los Angeles police beating Rodney King in 1991, there was intense national indignation. And the feeling of loss felt by many British people was brought home most vividly by the pictures of thousands of flowers placed at the gates of London palaces in memory of Princess Diana in 1997. More recently, the terrible images of a small Palestinian boy dying in his father's arms or an Israeli soldier killed and beaten by a mob shocked television viewers around the world. These, of course, are very dramatic examples. But the use of presentational aids can have an impact in less spectacular situations—such as in a public speaking classroom. Presentational aids are an important communication tool.

Presentational aids must be used carefully, however. Using presentational aids effectively calls for careful thinking, strategic planning, and rehearsal. There is nothing magical about presentational aids. They assist us only if they function as intended and if we are able to present them effectively.

FUNCTIONS OF PRESENTATIONAL AIDS

Preview When used effectively, presentational aids can help a speaker be better received and can help audience members follow a speaker's ideas. In addition, they can provide emphasis, offer support, promote clarity, encourage emotional involvement, enhance retention and recall, assist with good delivery, bolster a speaker's credibility, and engage multiple listener senses. With all these possible benefits, a speaker will do well to learn to use them effectively.

presentational aids visual or audio-visual materials that help clarify, support, and/or strengthen the verbal content of a speech

Both speakers and listeners can benefit from the effective use of **presentational aids**. Presentational aids engage the senses (for most public speaking purposes, what we see and what we hear) and help clarify, support, and strengthen the speech. From the speaker's perspective, such aids can

- help support and highlight key ideas.
- facilitate understanding.
- encourage emotional involvement.
- assist with delivery.
- enhance the speaker's ethos.

Listeners also benefit from the effective use of presentational aids. From the listeners' perspective, presentational aids can

- help separate important from less important information.
- add interest and color.
- aid in comprehension and retention.

Let's turn to some specific ways in which presentational aids will be important to you as a speaker and a listener.

Providing Emphasis

One challenge for every public speaker is to find ways of helping the audience distinguish what is really important from what is less important. Research has shown that even a simple list can visually reinforce key ideas, as shown in Figure 13.1. In this visual, the speaker is highlighting the three major consequences of excessive drinking that she intends to address in her speech. A list, of course, is not a particularly impressive presentational aid, and other, more sophisticated aids may be required by the speech (or your instructor). Nevertheless, a list can help your audience follow your speech and remember the main points. A list featuring graphical icons—such as a dollar sign to designate "wasteful spending"—can be even more memorable than a list of key words.[1]

Let the material dictate the format best suited to achieve the desired emphasis. For example, suppose you wanted to stress the rising number of people who were testing HIV positive in your community. You could rattle off a series of numbers: "Ten people tested positive for HIV in 1985; five years later, twenty-six tested positive; thirty-nine cases were reported in 1995; and the most recent data, for 2000, reveal that fifty cases were reported here in our community." But rather than leave it to your audience to visualize the trend on their

FIGURE 13.1 **Consequences of Excessive Drinking**

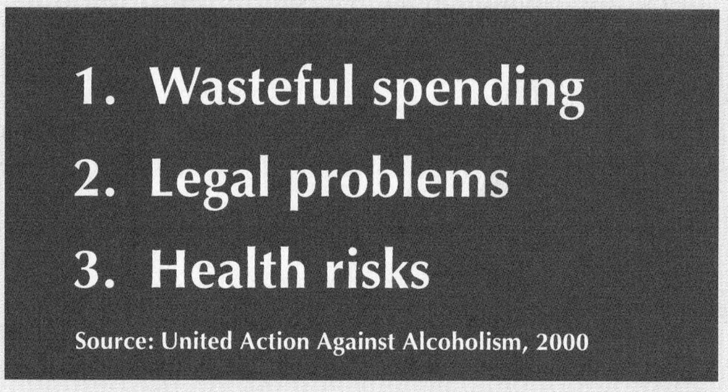

1. Wasteful spending
2. Legal problems
3. Health risks
Source: United Action Against Alcoholism, 2000

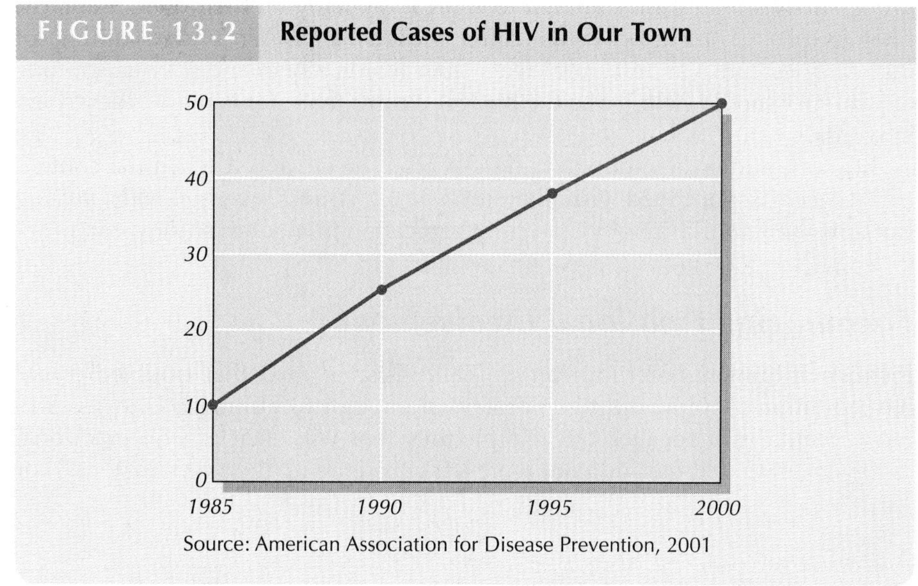

FIGURE 13.2 **Reported Cases of HIV in Our Town**

50
40
30
20
10
0
1985
1990
1995
2000

Source: American Association for Disease Prevention, 2001

own—and risk that some would fail to do so—you could assist them. In this case, a line graph (see Figure 13.2) could prove enlightening. Displaying such a graph would help the audience process the numbers in a way that underscored the upward trend.[2]

Providing Support

Presentational aids can also function as a form of evidence, helping to support your ideas. Suppose you have asserted that Britain's prime minister, Tony Blair, closely patterned his campaign after Bill Clinton's successful bid for the White House. You could support the assertion by noting how Blair employed key members of Clinton's campaign staff and used similar techniques. But the

Go to **Lesson 5's Screening Room** on the **VideoLab** CD-ROM to view the speech on smokeless tobacco. This speaker uses very limited visual support. Can you think of other or different ways that she might have used presentational aids to further enhance her speech?

most compelling evidence would be to show short video clips of Blair's and Clinton's speeches illustrating how closely Blair's themes and words matched Clinton's and how similar their speaking styles were.

Visual aids also can lend another type of support. When you present a graph, chart, drawing, or photograph that comes from a reputable source, you will, in effect, add credibility to your ideas. Moreover, you will show your listeners how a problem has grown, what poverty looks like on the face of a child, or how beautiful the Smoky Mountains are. They will not have to take your word for it; they can see for themselves.

Promoting Clarity

Effective presentational aids also promote clarity. Researchers have found that "human brains extract valuable information from audiovisuals more quickly and more easily than from purely verbal information," and do so with "a more error-free grasp of information."[3] As already noted, listeners who see a statistical trend via a graph are more likely to understand it—and to do so more immediately—than if they are left to chart it mentally on their own. Similarly, photographs of ancient Mayan ruins provide a clearer understanding of that early culture's architectural feats than words alone, and a visual outline of a budget should help make the budget clearer than if it is merely described in words.

In short, audience understanding can often be enhanced when the content of a speech is portrayed visually. *Spotlight on Visual Perception and Thinking* explains the importance of visual communication in modern society.

Encouraging Emotional Involvement

Pictures of human suffering from Somalia, Bosnia, and other troubled places have prompted public outrage substantial enough to influence U.S. involvement. Similarly, a speaker can use pictures that will elicit greater emotional involvement than if the audience were left to conjure up their own images.[4] For

SPOTLIGHT ON... Visual Perception and Thinking

Today, people get most of their day-to-day information through graphic images. In fact, some 99 percent of all the information we receive comes through the eyes from *objects* we see. . . .

We are a visual species. Television, graphic novels, picture magazines, and multimedia are just some examples of the visual media that we're exposed to. Icons abound—no-smoking signs, computer menus, traffic signs, the men's room, restaurant menus. . . . Are we reinventing communication with pictographs? Perhaps.

The point is that we do most of our thinking in terms of graphic images—visuals such as pictures, icons, and facsimiles. . . . We don't think much in words per se. Vision is the primary medium of thought. Simply, visual perception is visual thinking. Graphic images are the most powerful way of enhancing our perceptual thinking. And without such visual stimuli, productive thinking is impossible.

S. M. (Marty) Shelton, "Special Issue: Visual Communication: Introduction," *Technical Communication, Fourth Quarter* (1993): 617–618.

example, one of our student speakers sought to discourage the use of smokeless tobacco. The student displayed photographs of people who had had their jawbone removed because of cancer caused by dipping or chewing tobacco. The graphic displays drew audible responses from the audience that verbal descriptions, offered just prior to displaying the photos, had not.

A speaker, of course, must be mindful of her or his ethical responsibility to provide only representative examples. The speaker also must forewarn the audience of graphic content that some people may find offensive. As always, if you have any doubts about using such visual aids, be sure to consult your instructor in advance.

Assisting Retention and Recall

Presentational aids can make information and ideas more understandable and memorable. A 1989 University of Minnesota study concluded that people remember 43 percent more information when visuals are used than when they are not.[5] Subsequent research has supported these findings and suggests that effective presentational aids can make recall easier, faster, and more accurate than "memories of purely verbal messages."[6] If you want to leave a lasting impression on your audience, consider using good presentational aids.[7]

Helping with Extemporaneous Delivery

Most public speakers have difficulty developing an effective style of delivery. One of the chief hazards is overreliance on notes, which diminishes eye contact. There is no substitute for practice in improving this situation, but the use of presentational aids also can help.

Speakers who give workshop presentations soon learn how crucial presentational aids are in assisting their delivery. Presenters often project bulleted lists of key words onto a screen to orient the audience and bolster their comprehension. As the terms appear on the screen, they function as a speaking outline, reminding the speaker of what he or she wishes to address next. Some speakers also find that these prompts alleviate speaking anxiety.[8]

Of course, you should be aware of the risks of using such aids. For one, a speaker can use too many lists. Constantly displaying and quickly removing visuals can confuse the audience, just as leaving a visual up long after it is useful can bore or otherwise distract them. A speaker also should avoid visuals that feature too many words and simply duplicate his or her oral presentation. If you put your whole outline on a transparency, listeners will concentrate on the display instead of on you.[9] In addition, simply posting key words and not supplying a graph, chart, or other aid may diminish your effectiveness and tarnish your image. For this reason, your instructor may insist that you devise something other than a bulleted list as a visual aid.

Enhancing Your Credibility

Every speaker wants to be credible. As we discussed in Chapter 6, you will be seen as credible if the audience thinks you are competent and trustworthy, as well as enthusiastic and objective.

When you use good presentational aids, you do two things. First, you show the audience that you care enough about your presentation to prepare carefully. Colorful poster boards, well-constructed graphs, and effectively chosen video clips all serve to show listeners that you took pains with your preparation. By providing support for your ideas and showing your skill in assembling them, you project competence.

Second, you demonstrate your trustworthiness when you use presentational aids because you show your concern for the audience's understanding. In some cases, you are essentially letting them "see for themselves." You aren't asking them to rely exclusively on your judgment. In this way, listeners may see you as more open to scrutiny and more willing to let them share in determining the true nature of something. Thus, they are increasingly likely to see you as trustworthy and fair-minded, which enhances your ethos.

Engaging Multiple Senses to Promote Interest

As we've noted, from the audience's perspective, a speech that is well supported with presentational aids is often easier to follow and understand than one that is not. It is also more interesting. When you think of the problems with listening we discussed in Chapter 3, you will quickly recognize the value of presentational aids. By engaging multiple senses, presentational aids can help prevent listeners from feeling bored, distracted, or passive. Research indicates that visual aids bolster interest and involvement.[10]

Color. Researchers have reported that color adds interest.[11] Colorful poster boards, well-chosen video clips, and vivid graphs all attract attention. Most people prefer color to black-and-white—or at least most would like some color to break up black-and-white handouts, lists, and transparencies.[12]

Vivid colors are usually more striking than lighter shades. Contrast should be used to promote clarity.[13] See how color enhances the interest of the visuals portrayed in Figures 13.3 and 13.4.

Variety. Variety is one of the best ways to maintain audience interest. A presentation accompanied by varied graphs and perhaps a few pictures will likely be more interesting than one in which the speaker presents list after list on an overhead projector.

Not every presentation (particularly short presentations) will lend itself to such a variety of visual support. However, speakers should consider the presentational options available and then ask themselves if they might be able to strategically use some variety. As speakers, we must always ask ourselves, "How can I make my topic more appealing and more interesting to my audience?"

PORTFOLIO 13.1

Adding Emphasis, Clarity, and Life

Contemplate the information you are going to present in your next speech. Which information needs special emphasis? Which information could be made clearer? Do any of the areas seem dull or lifeless?

KEEP IN MIND 13.1

Functions of Presentational Aids

Presentational aids

- provide emphasis.
- support ideas.
- promote clarity.
- encourage emotional involvement.
- assist retention and recall.
- help with extemporaneous delivery.
- enhance the speaker's credibility.
- engage multiple senses.

FIGURE 13.3 **Source of Income**

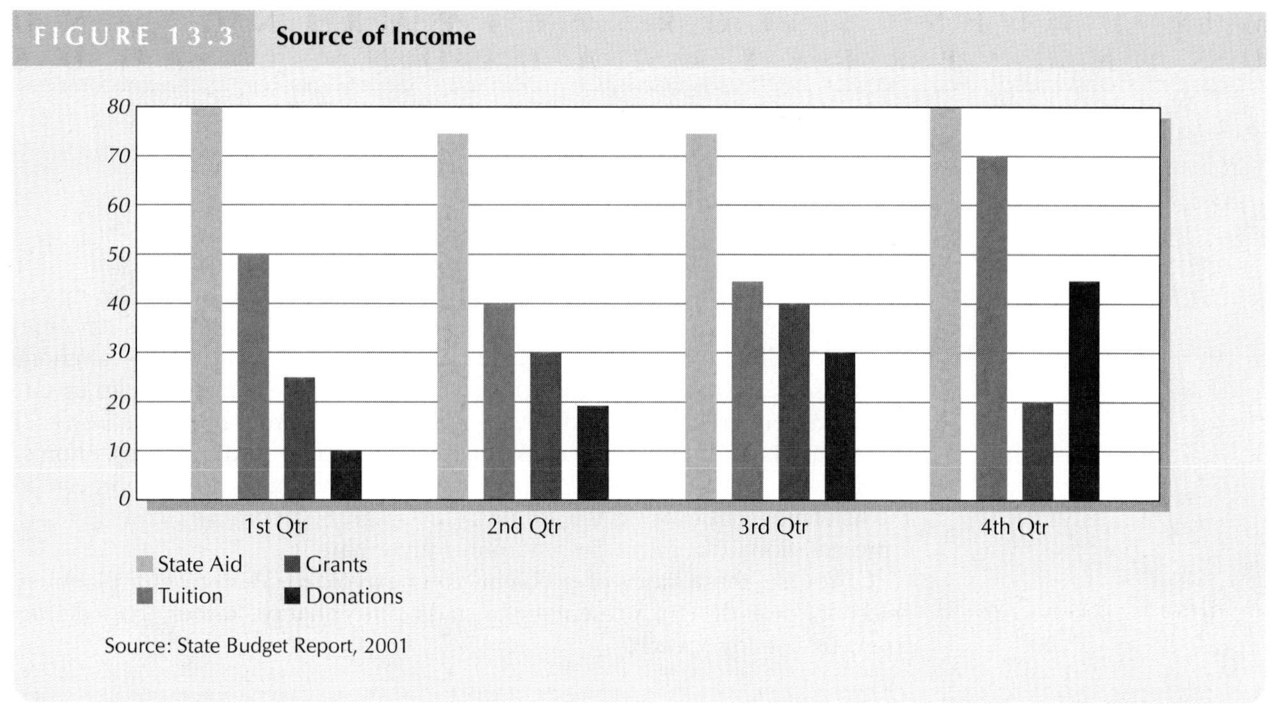

Source: State Budget Report, 2001

FIGURE 13.4 **Source of Income**

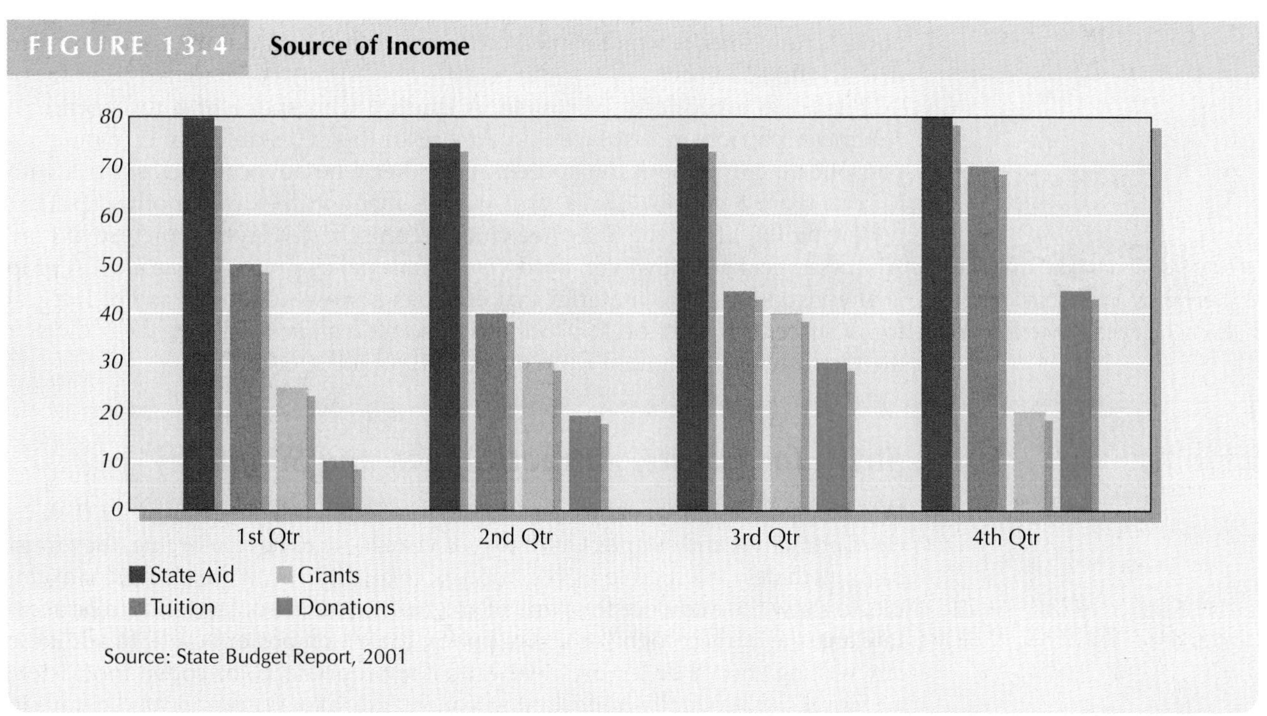

Source: State Budget Report, 2001

GUIDELINES FOR PREPARING AND USING PRESENTATIONAL AIDS

Preview Presentational aids must be carefully planned and prepared for maximum impact. In this section, we offer some basic guidelines for constructing and using presentational materials, ranging from practical tips to ethical considerations.

Just because a speaker commits to preparing and using presentational aids is no guarantee that such aids will contribute to his or her success. During our teaching careers, we have seen speakers use poster boards with smudges and misspellings, bring tiny objects to class and hold them up in the vain hope that those in the back will be able to see them, and place transparencies upside down on an overhead projector. One speaker actually brought a boa constrictor to class as visual support. The snake held the audience's undivided attention as it coiled and uncoiled around the speaker's arm, but in so doing it prevented the listeners from hearing the speaker's message. Such problems quickly turn a presentational aid into a presentational nightmare.

Of course, these kinds of problems can be avoided. With careful planning, selection, and design, presentational aids can enhance, rather than detract from, almost any speech.

Make Sure the Presentational Aid Is Truly an Aid

Visual or other sensory support can contribute to the success of almost any speech. As you contemplate your speech, note places where a presentational aid would help the audience understand what you're trying to say, add appropriate emphasis, encourage interest and emotional involvement, or help the audience remember what you've said. If a presentational aid doesn't fulfill one of these functions, it won't contribute to your speech, and it may serve only to distract the audience.

There are exceptions, of course. A student who spoke of a resurgence in American patriotism displayed an American flag to establish and maintain a patriotic air throughout the speech. A speaker who advocated closer ties with Mexico wore a poncho, pants, and sandals made in Mexico. Another speaker, reviewing the life of the Shawnee chief Tecumseh, displayed a picture of him. All these speakers, however, used visual material as **props**, not as aids. A prop is any visual or audio material that enlivens a presentation but is not integral to its success. It may be appropriate in some instances as long as it doesn't distract listeners' attention from the content of the speech.

prop visual or audio material that enlivens a presentation but is not a necessary element

Strive for Clarity, Attractiveness, and Simplicity

Whether you use a visual or audio presentational aid, you will want it to be clear, attractive, and simple. Obviously, if visuals are to be reinforcing, they must be immediately intelligible and of impressive quality. If you are trying, for example, to show the audience the parts of an engine, your visual aid should be accurate and the parts recognizable, not poorly drawn on poster board. In addition, any writing should be legible, neat, and, if appropriate, color-coded for clarity.

Simplicity is equally important. If you include a lot of complicated details in visual aids, they will only confuse the audience and obscure the point you're making. In general, it is best to show only the essentials and to illustrate only one idea in each chart, graph, or diagram.[14]

Remain Audience-Centered

Whenever you use a presentational aid, keep the audience in mind. To begin with, listeners must be able to see a visual aid. Problems in this regard are all too common. One speaker held up postcards while she talked about her trip to Paris. Another held up several different comic books while talking about his hobby of collecting comics. Only audience members in the first few rows could see these visuals. Many speakers use transparencies with print that is too small for most of the audience to see. Any visual must be displayed long enough for the audience to process the information and make sense of it, then put away when it is no longer relevant to the point you are making.

It should be obvious that no matter how potentially clever, well constructed, or compelling a presentational aid might be, if the audience cannot see or hear it, it will have, at best, no impact or, at worst, a negative impact. Audience members who must squint to see the print on a transparency or strain to hear the words on a recording can easily become frustrated and simply tune out the speaker.

Take all your listeners' needs into consideration. If necessary, walk around the room and show the visual at different angles, or hold it high so that those in the back can see. Strive for bold, legible printing or writing. Above all, make sure you do not obscure the presentational aid by blocking it with your own body or placing it incorrectly on an overhead projector. In addition, audio aids should be tested for sound levels that allow the people in the back to hear without blasting those in the front.

The effective public speaker uses presentational aids so that the audience knows what to focus on. It can be helpful to point to the part of the visual you are discussing without losing contact with the audience. If your visual has more than one part, you may need to direct the audience's attention to the part being discussed by pointing to it with your finger, a pencil, or a pointer. When using transparencies with a list, you might use a piece of paper to cover the part you are not yet ready to discuss. The goal is to think of how best to help the audience process the presentational aid in the manner intended.[15] As you direct the audience's attention to your visual materials, maintain contact with the listeners by the way you talk, your eye contact, and your bodily movement. Talk to your audience, not to the aid.

Make Sure the "Aid" Does Not Distract

Presentational aids attract attention. That's one reason you use them. But if you're not careful, they can take the audience's attention away from you and your ideas. If you set up a colorful poster board or an intriguing model at the beginning of your speech, many listeners will begin to focus on it right away, wondering what it is and how you are going to

 CONNECTING TO THE NET

To see examples of effective and ineffective presentational aids, go to **http://college.hmco.com/communication/andrews/public_speaking/2e/students/** and click on *Connecting to the Net.* From there, follow the link to Presentational Aids.

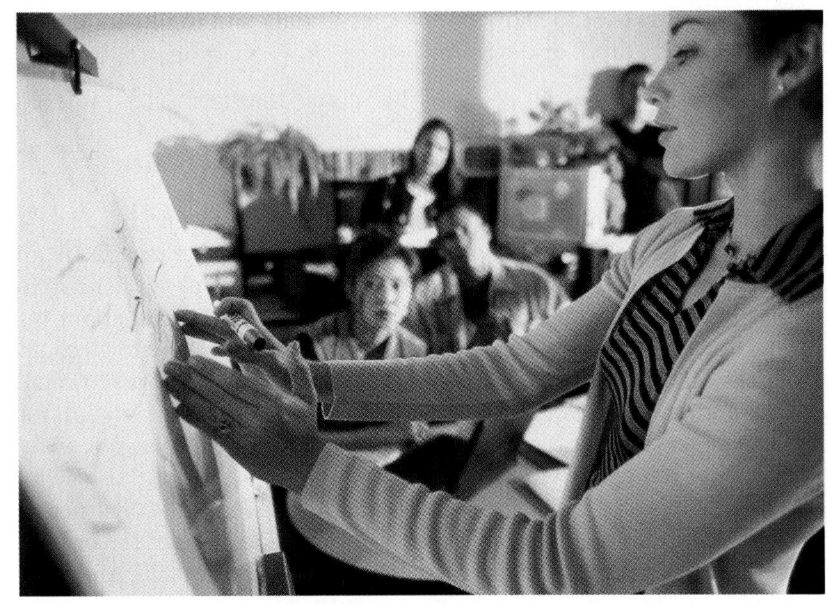

Charts and maps are often useful presentational aids. In this case, the speaker is able to highlight specific areas as she speaks, helping to direct listeners' attention to important information. (Zigy Kaluzny/Tony Stone Images)

use it. In addition, if your visual aid is not large enough, listeners may become discouraged or annoyed as they squint in an attempt to see the words, numbers, or images that you have displayed.

In general, the audience's attention will be drawn to visual images. This is wonderful news, as long as you keep the visuals out of sight until you are ready to refer to them. Similarly, as soon as you are finished discussing them, put them away or cover them.

Go to **Next Step: Evaluating the Use of Presentational Aids** in Lesson 6 of the **VideoLab** CD-ROM and view the three speakers using diverse presentational aids. After watching these clips, complete the quiz to assess how effectively each speaker used his or her aids.

Use Presentational Aids Ethically

Speakers often create their own visuals. You might create a bulleted list of key words or a simple graph to illustrate a statistical trend. The words will likely be your own, but you will need to reveal the source of the statistics—orally and with a written acknowledgment on the visual aid for the audience to see. Cite the source on the display simply by noting, for instance, "Source: American Cancer Society, 2000," or "Source: William Jones, *Getting Ready for the SATs, 2001.*"

Sometimes a speaker will discover an existing visual, such as a graph in *USA Today* or some other publication. In most settings, it is permissible to use this material (blown up and transferred onto a transparency, for example), but you must acknowledge the source orally and on the visual. Before using an existing visual, be sure to ask your instructor whether it is permissible to use it in the classroom; she or he may want you to design your own.

In any case, remember that citing the sources of presentational materials or of the content of aids you create is part of being an ethical public speaker.

KEEP IN MIND 13.2

Using Presentational Aids

Here are some guidelines for preparing and using presentational aids:

- They should support the speech.
- They should be clear, attractive, and simple.
- They should be audience-centered.
- They should not distract the listeners' attention.
- They should be used ethically.

PRESENTATIONAL AID OPTIONS

Preview Presentational support can range from the low-tech chalkboard to sophisticated computer-generated graphics. Many forms of support, such as graphs and charts, will reinforce your speech visually, whereas others, such as music, may provide reinforcing sounds.

What kind of aid should you use? The answer to this question depends on many factors. What are your speech topic and purpose? What are the listeners' expectations? What equipment is available in the room? Does the room lend itself to the kinds of visual or audio support you have in mind? If a room cannot be effectively darkened, for instance, you would be hard-pressed to use slides effectively. In making decisions about visuals, you have to know as much as possible about the context and setting in which you will give your speech.

Recognizing the Diversity of Presentational Options

Begin by examining the sorts of presentational aids available to you. In most speaking situations, the options are varied.

Chalkboard or Whiteboard. The chalkboard (now commonly replaced by a whiteboard) remains a useful device for speakers who have no other option for displays or who wish to compile a list working cooperatively with the audience. Most obviously, the chalkboard allows the speaker to highlight information visually and to put terms, diagrams, or sketches on the board as an explanation unfolds or a list develops. In addition, moving to and from the board allows the speaker to be active in communicating his or her ideas and can also help the speaker channel nervous energy.

Of course, the chalkboard has its limitations. Because it is so familiar to most audiences (including students), it may seem less interesting or original than other types of visuals. Poor handwriting and a tendency to look at the board rather than at the audience can also detract from effective communication. Speakers sometimes end up delivering their comments to the board rather than to the audience. These reasons alone discourage its use.

Even though you should select some means other than the chalkboard for enhancing your presentations, you still should know how to use the board effectively in case you encounter a speaking situation in which you have no other option or must use it as a backup. At minimum, make sure your handwriting or printing is legible, erase anything left on the board by the previous user, and practice using it in advance so that you do not lose contact with the audience when you write.

Poster Board Drawings. These common presentational aids can be constructed well in advance and can be either simple or sophisticated. They also can be colorful and engaging. The advantages end there, however. Aside from the time, effort, and artistic ability necessary to construct poster board drawings, they are clumsy to transport and handle. You must also make sure that you will be able to display them. For example, will a tripod be available? Will tape or thumbtacks be necessary? If you decide to use drawings, make sure to investigate and prepare adequately.

flipchart an oversize paper tablet that speakers can place on a tripod for use during a presentation

Flipcharts. A **flipchart** is essentially an oversize writing tablet, offering the same advantages and disadvantages of poster boards. Flipcharts are commonly used in business, conference, and workshop settings. In these settings, speakers often use flipcharts to record ideas generated during discussions or brainstorming sessions. If you have to use a flipchart, be mindful that you must have a tripod. Flipcharts are heavy and too unwieldy to be held or balanced on a chalkboard tray.

Handouts. Handouts are helpful if the audience needs to be able to recall information accurately for use at a later time, but they become more of a distraction than an aid when distributed during a speech. Select another means of visual assistance during your presentation—one that captures the essence of what you will provide later in the handout, as well as any specific information you must disclose during the speech. Tell the audience that you will be providing a comprehensive handout when you are finished speaking and that they need not write down detailed information during the speech.

If you plan to distribute multiple handouts at the conclusion of your talk, you may want to use different-colored paper so that listeners can easily find the information of interest to them. Let them know, for example, that the blue one contains the budget, the green one has important names and phone numbers, and the yellow one sketches out an agenda for a proposed conference.

Handouts can also be useful in promoting compliance. If you urge your listeners to send an email to a particular person or agency about a particular issue, for example, you can provide a handout with this information. By simplifying the task for listeners, you will increase the chances that they will follow through.[16]

Objects. Occasionally you will make a speech that involves the discussion of an object. If the object is large enough to be seen but small enough to carry with you, you may want to use it as a presentational aid. We have seen speeches effectively supported by objects such as tennis rackets, musical instruments, handmade clothing, antique vases, and fancy cakes.

Avoid small items that need to be passed around. Circulating something while you are talking can present problems. First, only one person will have the object while you are describing it; other listeners will be in the dark. Moreover, the act of passing something around will distract your listeners, taking their attention away from your speech.

Approach living things with caution. Pets, for instance, have been known to be stubborn, make unsolicited "contributions" to the presentation, and in other ways steal the show. In addition, they may be prohibited on the premises. Be sure to consult your instructor and not merely show up with a creature.

Be mindful, too, of other items that would certainly be prohibited, such as firearms and illegal substances or materials.

Models. Some speeches call for a model as a visual aid. An architect, for example, will likely need to use a three-dimensional model of a proposed building so that the audience will have a precise understanding of the structure. A paramedic might use a lifelike model of a person to train people how to administer CPR. A nursing student who wants to inform his or her public speaking class about the immune system might bring in one or more models of the human anatomy that will help explain the various parts of the system and how they function.

Obviously, constructing a three-dimensional model requires skill and effort. Many times our students have been able to borrow models, thus simplifying the task.

Transparencies and Overhead Projectors. Overhead projectors, particularly those used to display transparencies, are very common in classrooms and meeting rooms. They allow a speaker to project lists, figures, charts, graphs, and other information onto a large screen in supersize form.

A commonly used presentational aid is the overhead projector. Transparencies are easy to make and are inexpensive. They also serve as excellent backup if a speaker planning a more sophisticated presentation experiences unexpected technological problems. (David Weintraub/Stock Boston, Inc.)

Overhead projectors offer other advantages as well. First, transparencies can look professional and be easily created by computer. You simply print out the creation on transparency stock or have a paper printout photocopied on transparency stock. Existing material, of course, could simply be photocopied on transparency stock. In addition to being easy to produce, transparencies are easy to transport, allowing a speaker to use a large number (if necessary) in a single presentation. They also can be layered, so that you can actually build a graph or other aid as you provide the information in your speech.

As with other presentational aids, you should follow some basic guidelines when using an overhead projector and transparencies. First, avoid crowding too much information on a single transparency. It is better to have more transparencies and to keep each one clear and simple. Also, adjust the font or the size of the print so that it will be large enough for everyone in the room to read.

During the presentation, make sure you focus the projector clearly. When displaying transparencies, avoid "keystoning"—that is, producing that wide-at-the-top, narrow-at-the-bottom effect that occurs when the light is projected upward at too steep of an angle. You may also need to dim the lights in the front of the room to create enough contrast for the audience to see the transparencies. When presenting a bulleted list, use a cover sheet to expose one line at a time.

Avoid turning your back to the audience and talking to the screen, or staring down at the projector as you speak. Recognize that one great advantage of an overhead projector is its capacity for letting you never lose contact with the audience. You can face the audience at all times, simply highlighting items as you move along. In contrast to using a chalkboard or flipchart, you don't have to turn your back and write at any time. In fact, even if you bring a blank transparency to write on, you can still face the audience while, for example, you construct a list using listener input. Finally, make sure that you do not stand between the listeners and the projected image. It is very easy to unwittingly cast a large shadow on the screen.

Remember that an overhead projector calls attention to whatever is projected. When you are finished commenting on a projected image and have begun to discuss other issues, turn off the projector. Otherwise, the audience may be distracted by the image and not pay attention to what you are saying.

When used appropriately, an overhead projector is one of the most effective presentational aids available to you. Given its widespread use, you will want to become adept at using it.

Slides. Sometimes speakers develop presentations that they will likely deliver over and over again. A lifelong bird watcher, for instance, will often speak to audiences about migratory birds. A former Peace Corps volunteer in Africa will be called on to speak about the African people and their culture. These speakers often use slides to accompany their presentations. Slides are made from photographs or pictures and must be professionally prepared.

When using slides, it is critical to practice using them several times so that your comments and the slides are well coordinated. It is also useful to practice with the slide projector you will use during the presentation so that you can become familiar with any quirks associated with the equipment.

When you use slides in a speech, you will be speaking in a room that is at least partially darkened. This situation provides special speaking challenges. First, you must be extremely well prepared, since you may not be able to see your notes at all or will see them only dimly. Perhaps the wisest course is to use the slides to guide your comments. As each new slide appears, it will help you recall the information you want to share.

In addition, even though the room is somewhat darkened, the audience will be able to see you, especially after their eyes have adjusted to the dim lighting. It's important, then, for you to maintain eye contact with the audience—to gesture and speak with them directly. There is a natural tendency to ignore the audience and speak only to the slides appearing on the screen. But once you've determined which slide is being projected, you should turn to your listeners and talk with them.

Finally, slide presentations often last longer than other speeches. Make sure you know what the anticipated time frame is. Many speakers get carried away, keeping audiences for well over an hour or two. Given what we know about attention spans, and even with the added interest of visual support, speaking for much more than an hour is usually not the best plan. Ask about the available speaking time in advance and plan accordingly. Once your slides are set in place, it's awkward to hurry forward. It is far better to edit your slides before the speech.

Audio and Video Materials. Some topics cannot be explained by using only words. Recently, for example, one student wanted to discuss the nonverbal behaviors the parents of JonBenét Ramsey exhibited during an interview with Larry King and compare those behaviors with what scholars have identified as typical truth-telling versus lying behaviors. Showing video clips from the interview was essential to this speech. The speaker would have been hard-pressed to achieve the same effect by simply describing the behaviors.

In an increasingly media-oriented society, many listeners are attracted to presentations that use audio and video support. These sensory experiences, as we have noted earlier, help generate interest and involvement. Using them successfully, though, requires careful planning and preparation. In general, the more heavily your presentation depends on any form of technology, the more time and effort you must devote to creating what you will use and to making sure the appropriate equipment will be available. Also, the room in which you will be speaking must lend itself to using these aids effectively. Finally, you must make sure that the recording is cued to the proper place and that the equipment is set to the appropriate levels.

A speech that uses audio or video technology well can be extremely interesting and powerful. But if things go wrong—if pertinent clips cannot be located, the recorder malfunctions, or the tape breaks—the speaker may find it difficult to recover and achieve his or her purpose. Moreover, clips should be short, because they are illustrations of an idea. Showing a clip that takes up most of your speaking time is not using a presentational aid; it is substituting an audio-visual presentation for a major portion of your speech.

Using Visuals to Present Statistics

When you use statistical support, you will likely want to consider some sort of visual reinforcement, especially if you want the audience to grasp the importance of your figures and to remember them. Statistics lend themselves especially well to visual representation. Among the more common visual options are summary tables and various kinds of graphs.

Summary Tables. You can present statistical information clearly and concisely by displaying a **summary table**. This type of table allows you to analyze raw data and present conclusions in such a way that you clarify important relationships. Table 13.1 is a summary table. In this example, assume that the speaker is describing enrollment patterns at two colleges, Butler State and Midwestern College. He compares the number of students who are pursuing majors in the colleges' most prominent programs. His purpose is to show how one college is currently attracting students who are interested in liberal arts whereas the other is attracting students with a more professional or technical focus.

summary table an analysis of raw data presented in table format

Statistical summary tables may contain one main idea, or they may be more complicated and introduce more than one summary. Even with relatively sophisticated audiences, it is important to keep summary tables clear and reasonably simple. If more complicated summary tables are required, it's probably best to use several different tables; you might distribute a comprehensive handout showing these tables after you speak.

TABLE 13.1 **Summary Table**

Field of Study	Butler State (% students majoring)	Midwestern College (% students majoring)
Fine and performing arts	14%	04%
Humanities	32%	10%
Social sciences	22%	12%
Total (Liberal Arts)	68%	26%
Sciences and math	12%	19%
Engineering	(None)	21%
Business	11%	19%
Education	09%	14%
Total (Professional/Technical)	32%	74%

Graphs. Graphs are representations of numbers by geometric figures drawn to scale. Speakers often use graphs to make statistical information more vivid and to show relationships. Perhaps the most familiar and useful kinds of graphs are line graphs, bar graphs, pictographs, and pie graphs.

line graphs graphs in which one or more lines depict a trend or trends over time

Line graphs are especially useful for showing comparative relationships through time. Many business and professional presentations focus on information relating to time-based trends, as when comparing gross and net profits, production, or wages.

It is possible to place more than one line on a single graph, but it may be at the expense of clarity. If you plan to use multiple lines or curves, try to use strikingly different colors and restrict yourself to two or three lines. It's also important to recognize that a trend can be distorted (knowingly or unwittingly) by compressing or elongating the space allotted to time periods while keeping the other dimension of the graph constant. Ethical public speakers will not intentionally distort a trend simply to dramatize a particular point. Figure 13.5 is an example of a line graph.

bar graph a graph in which a series of bars depict comparative amounts of certain features or elements

Another kind of graph is the **bar graph,** often used to show quantity. A simple bar graph uses bars to indicate amounts and is well suited to presenting comparative statistics. Figure 13.6 depicts the same data as the line graph in Figure 13.5, but in a different way.

Bar graphs are particularly useful in that they can easily be made large enough for the audience to see and understand. As with a line graph, it is possible to depict a number of different statistical comparisons on the same bar graph, often through the use of different colors or shadings. Remember to keep it simple. As noted earlier, research cautions against the use of complex displays.

FIGURE 13.5 **Percent Minority Students**

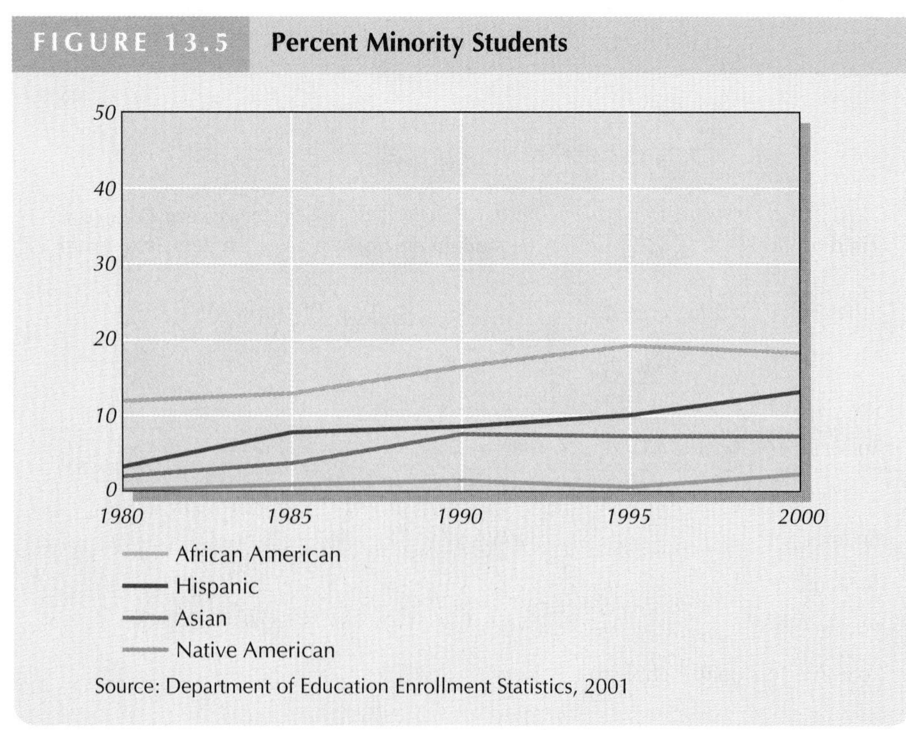

Source: Department of Education Enrollment Statistics, 2001

FIGURE 13.6 Percent Minority Students

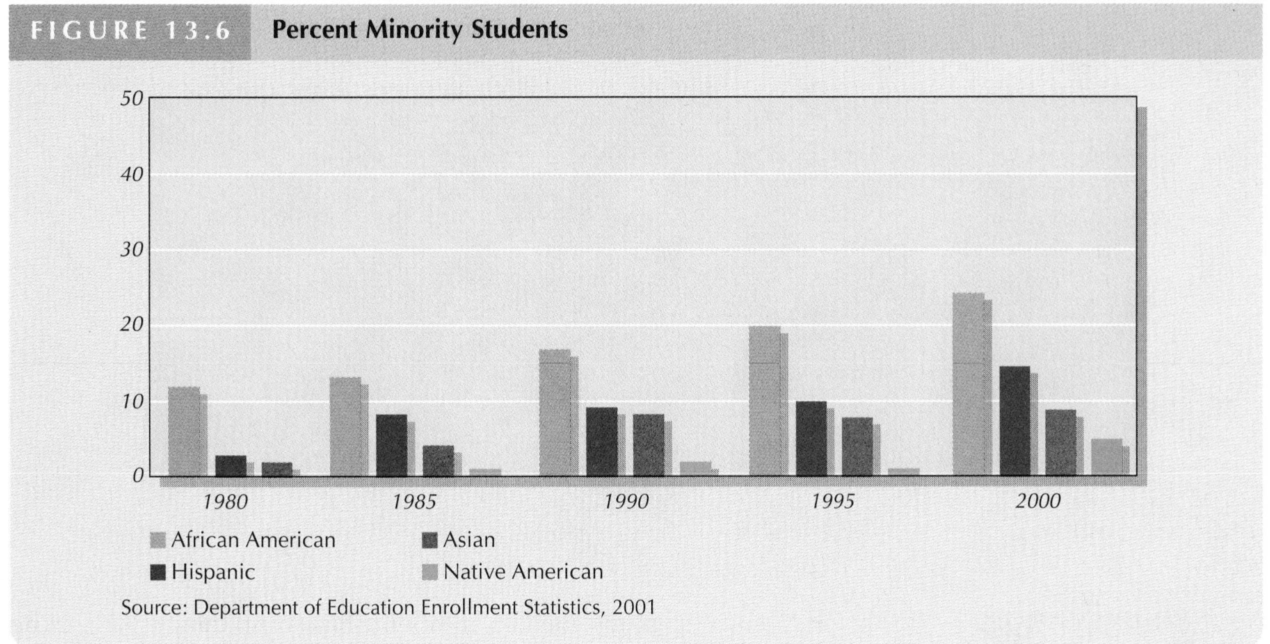

Source: Department of Education Enrollment Statistics, 2001

Listeners often find **pictographs** particularly interesting. In such a graph, pictures that relate to the content of the graph are used to form lines or patterns that convey information in the same way as other graphs do. Figure 13.7 shows how a pictograph can communicate information in an interesting, meaningful way.

The final type of graph is the **pie graph**, most often used to show numerical distribution patterns. When you are interested in showing how a total figure breaks down into different parts, you will probably want to use a pie graph. Suppose, for example, that you want to talk about ethnic and racial diversity

pictographs graphs that rely on a set of self-explanatory icons to depict growth or decline over time or between situations

pie graph a graph in the shape of a circle, where segments of the circle (cut into slices, like that of a pie) depict the relative size of a particular feature or element within the whole

FIGURE 13.7 Alcohol Consumption and Grades

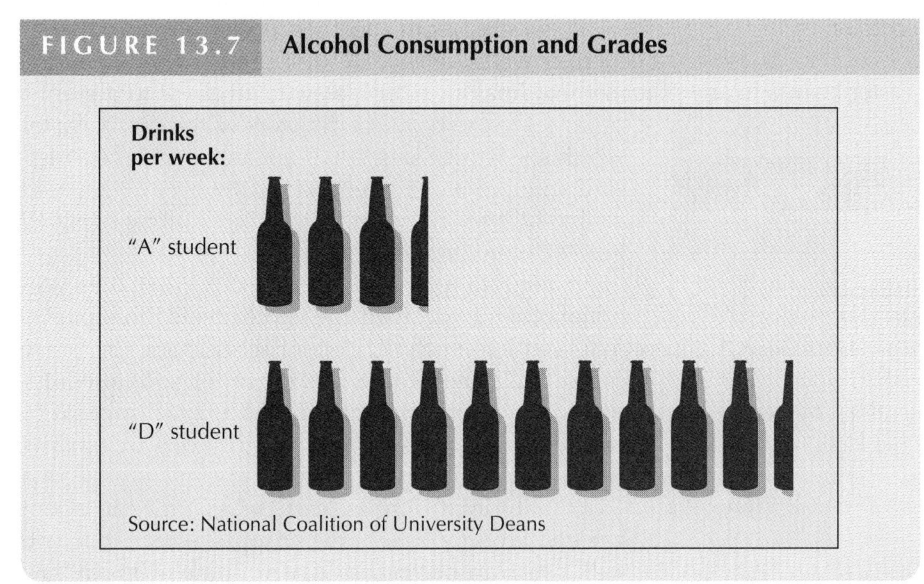

Source: National Coalition of University Deans

Go to **Lesson 3's Screening Room** on the **VideoLab** CD-ROM to view the speech on gun control and observe how this speaker uses presentational aids. Pay particular attention to the way he presents statistical information. In what ways did he present his statistics effectively? How could he have improved?

FIGURE 13.8 **Ethnicity at Center University**

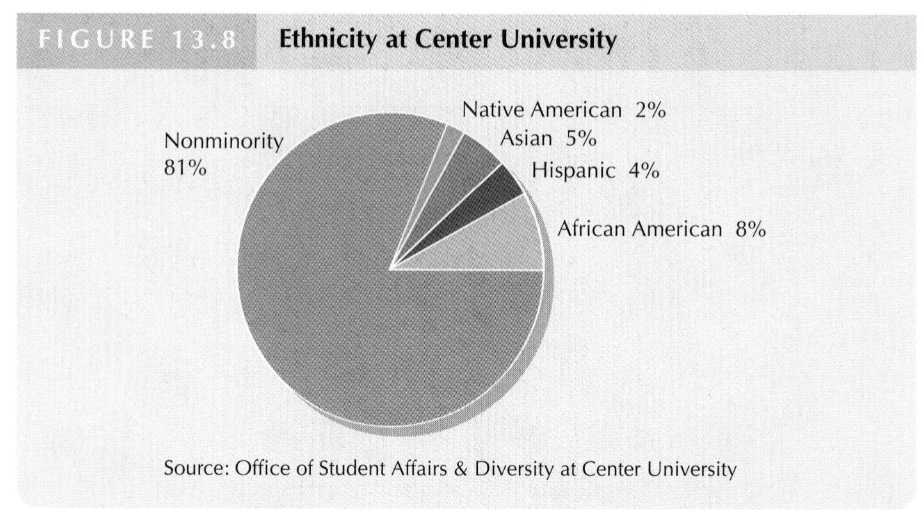

Source: Office of Student Affairs & Diversity at Center University

PORTFOLIO 13.2

Displaying the Numbers

Examine the working outline you are putting together for a forthcoming speech. What visual aids might you devise to help clarify the statistical information you will be presenting? Would a table work best? How about a graph? Sketch out your ideas, carefully considering which type of aid would work best.

on your campus—perhaps making the point that your campus is lacking such diversity. You might use a pie graph, such as the one depicted in Figure 13.8, to reinforce your point. Pie graphs are helpful in that they are relatively easy to construct. Because of their simplicity, they are instantly intelligible to the audience.

You might use several different kinds of graphs in a single presentation. When carefully constructed and used strategically, graphs can help you depict statistical information in ways that listeners will likely find understandable, interesting, and clarifying.

Choosing Presentational Aids with the Audience, Setting, and Occasion in Mind

Whenever you choose presentational aids, do so with the audience, setting, and occasion in mind. For example, for classroom speeches, poster board drawings are commonly used and generally well received. However, rarely would you use poster boards in any other setting. Imagine a businesswoman about to present a proposal to the board of directors of the company for which she works. She would not arrive with her briefcase and a pile of poster board drawings. She would probably use transparencies, computer-generated graphics, and handouts.

In general, you need to find out what presentational options are available and expected in a particular setting—including your classroom. In some cases, you may be able to arrange for special equipment. In others, you may have to alter your plans to accommodate the room's restrictions regarding equipment, lighting, or visibility.

Equally important is learning all you can about listener expectations. Some groups assume that you will use transparencies. If you come without any

KEEP IN MIND 13.3

Presentational Aid Options

- A wide range of options is available: chalkboard or whiteboard, poster board drawings, flipcharts, handouts, objects, models, transparencies, slides, or audio and video materials.
- Presentational aids are useful in presenting statistics. Summary tables, as well as various kinds of graphs, work well.
- Aids should be appropriate to the audience, setting, and occasion.

form of visual support, you might be seen as underprepared or unsophisticated. The classroom is no exception; know what is expected when you must give a presentation in a class.

Audiences often become accustomed to seeing presentational aids that help them learn, follow the main points, and distinguish important from less important information. A speaker who doesn't use presentational aids may be seen as less effective, less organized, and less interested in audience understanding.[17] In an increasingly visually oriented society, listeners expect good speakers to show them what they need to know.

Once you have carefully created a presentational aid to use as part of a forthcoming speech, go to the **Online SpeechStudio** and go through the **Checklist for Using Presentational Aids** to evaluate your efforts. Is there anything you need to change?

PRESENTATIONAL AIDS IN THE COMPUTER AGE

Preview By using computers, speakers can generate very sophisticated and professional-looking graphics. Audiences are becoming increasingly accustomed to polished visuals presented in attractive ways. In this section, we discuss the effective use of presentational software and electronic presentation systems.

If you've seen the movie classic *Star Wars*, you probably recall the scene near the end of the movie in which Luke Skywalker and his fellow warriors receive instructions on how to destroy the Death Star. The military strategist projects computer-generated graphics to provide an overview of the enemy's massive battleship, close-ups of its surface, and diagrams of its infrastructure. Without the visual display—complete with movement—the speaker would not have been able to provide this information to Luke and the rest of the force with such clarity, impact, and efficiency.

The visual displays that Luke and others seem to take for granted are no longer confined to science fiction but are becoming commonplace for us as well. We view full-motion weather maps, graphical depictions of what has happened on Wall Street, and computer-generated models of what likely occurred during an airplane crash. The technology is not limited to the mass media, but is often available for our own use because of the enhanced capacity of personal computers, the portability of the required hardware, and the simplification of presentational software. Businesspeople often display computer-generated slides at a meeting using a laptop computer and a portable projector, both of which are small enough and durable enough to be easily carried about, even taken along on trips. On campus, it is increasingly common for professors to deliver lectures using this technology and for students to use it in their presentations.

Direct and Indirect Uses

Many factors underlie the popularity of computer-assisted presentations. As already noted, user-friendly software packages (such as PowerPoint, AppleWorks, and Astound) have simplified the task of creating presentations, allowing for the easy creation of slides and the integrated use of images, sound, and video clips. In addition, such presentations no longer require multiple types of playback equipment. If a speaking site is equipped with the proper setup, all the presenter has to do is save the presentation on a disk and pop it into the computer on-site.

Another advantage is the ease and speed with which we can create professional-looking graphs, charts, diagrams, and other visual displays. Presentational software allows us to enter the information and select the type of graph, chart, or other device that is best suited to conveying the information. With creativity, we can even design our own graphics, such as the pictograph in Figure 13.7 on page 325 (see *Spotlight on Computer-Generated Visual Aids*). In addition, a presentational aid devised via computer can easily be modified or updated by simply editing or adding data, even during a live presentation.

Even though this technology has become increasingly attractive, it cannot always be used. Obviously, you must have access to the hardware and software needed to create such aids. Your school also must provide the proper equipment to present the aids you create. Many campuses simply do not have the funding necessary to purchase this equipment, set aside appropriate classroom space, and maintain an adequate staff to service the equipment.

Given these constraints, every student won't be able to deliver a computer-assisted presentation. Nonetheless, even if you cannot use computer technology directly during your speech, you can use it indirectly for your presentation. You can use the technology to construct a graph, table, or other visual display that you print out and use as a black-and-white or full-color transparency with an overhead projector. You will still reap the benefits of the technology and gain experience using it. Using computer technology in this way may actually work better in a classroom since the setup will require less time and many potential technical problems will be eliminated.

We hope that you will gain an appreciation for this new technology and will learn to function competently and comfortably at the cutting edge. Ultimately you will need to experiment with computer-assisted design to become competent with it.

PORTFOLIO 13.3

Let the Computer Do the Drawing

Review the sketches you made for Portfolio 13.2. Might you use PowerPoint or some other program to construct a graph you've sketched out? If you are not familiar with these programs and possibilities, ask for assistance at your school's computer center.

Tips for Preparing Computer-Generated Graphics

You may have to be proactive in gaining experience. Check to see if your campus offers training sessions on how to use presentational software and whether any labs on campus have presentational software on the server. If so, you can take advantage of the quickness and professional-looking results these programs offer. The lab might have a printer that can print out a slide on transparency stock. If not, you can print it out on paper and photocopy it on transparency stock. If you do not have access to presentational software, you may have another program (Microsoft Word, for example) that will allow you to create a table, chart, or graph that will work well once you place it on a transparency.

With the right software, you can use images downloaded from the Internet, copied from a collection of clip art, copied using a scanner, or loaded from a digital camera. For example, in a speech discussing skin cancer and malignant melanoma, one of our students downloaded pictures from a web site showing various warning signs and causes for concern. Within minutes, she located the pictures on the Internet and, with the click of a button, downloaded the images and imported them onto slides for her presentation.

FRAME OF REFERENCE

One of the most sophisticated presentational aids coming into widespread use is Microsoft PowerPoint. This speaker is making a professional sales presentation using this software.

SPOTLIGHT ON... **Computer-Generated Visual Aids**

How We Generated the Pictograph in Figure 13.7

To design this graph, we simply downloaded the image of a longneck bottle found on the Web, removed the brand name (using the program Photoshop), and then imported the altered image into a slide we were creating with PowerPoint. We also used Photoshop to cut the bottle in half. We simply copied the bottle in a new file and saved the new version once we had cut it in half.

Note the power of this visual aid to emphasize the content; it is much more powerful than merely reciting the statistics for an audience. How would you evaluate the power of this pictograph compared to the same information conveyed in a bar graph? (No pun intended!)

Using a picture or illustration from a clip art collection likewise involves just a few clicks of a mouse. Scanning an image of course requires a scanner. Then you just save the file and import it onto slides.

If you are producing color slides, you'll achieve the best results if you use a dark background and a light color for letters, numbers, lines, and other content. In our experience, we've found that a dark blue background with white content works best (see Figure 13.9). The contrast between dark and light helps prevent problems with **washout**.

washout the reduction in brilliance of an image being projected onto a screen due to interference by light or the possible loss of signal clarity between the computer and the projector

If you are relying on black-and-white images, you'll achieve the best results if you leave the background white and enter the letters, numbers, and such in black. If you produce a pie graph, bar graph, or some other image, you can use different fill patterns to set off individual elements (see Figure 13.10).

When selecting fonts for letters or numbers, keep in mind these guidelines. First, size the characters so that they can be read. In most fonts, you'll need to use at least an 18-point font, but you may need a 40- or 44-point font. You also might experiment with bold versus plain characters to see which provides the most clarity. In addition, you will want to choose a font that is easy to read. And be sure the font you select is supported by the computer you'll be using during your presentation. If it isn't supported, garbage may be all that appears on the screen.

Limit the content to one important graphic image or one idea per slide. Also, no more than five pieces of information of any kind (or any level of importance) should appear on a slide. You also will want to be concise. If you are using text, for example, keep the words and numbers to a minimum. Your audience should be able to process what is on the screen with a glance. Feature only those terms or expressions that categorize or highlight what you want to underscore. Or provide the spelling of an unfamiliar term or a definition for careful analysis.

Remember, as with all presentational aids, computer-generated graphics are there to support, emphasize, and clarify your key points. They are not a show unto themselves. Avoid graphics that are too cluttered or overpowering. Visual aids should not compete with or merely duplicate what is coming out of your mouth. They should support your presentation, not become your presentation.

When you use a visual aid, direct the audience's attention by emphasizing important information. In

PORTFOLIO 13.4

A Matter of Design

Look over the sketches you've made of potential presentational aids for your speech. Have you kept them all simple, including only the essential information pertaining to one idea per visual aid? Have you kept them free from distractions (such as a busy background or border)? Critique your sketches along these lines.

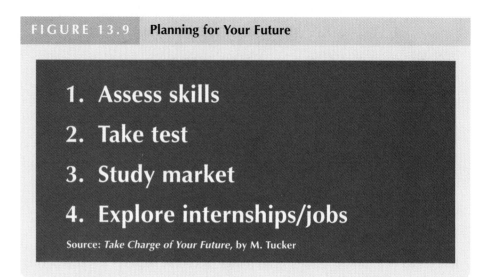

FIGURE 13.9 **Planning for Your Future**

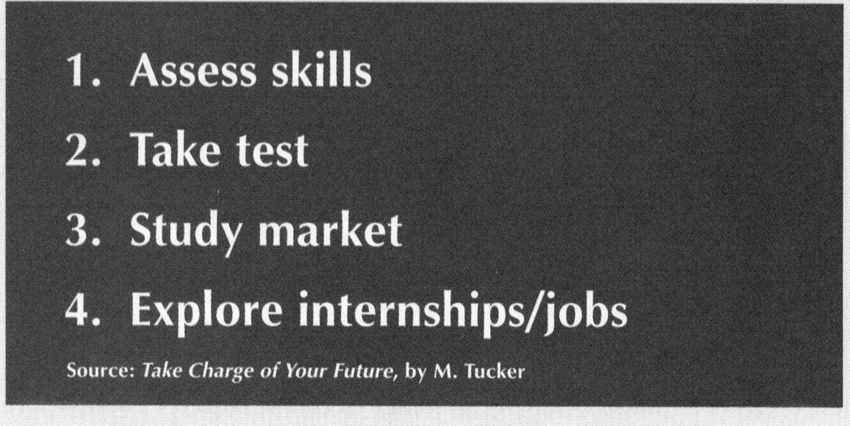

1. Assess skills
2. Take test
3. Study market
4. Explore internships/jobs

Source: *Take Charge of Your Future*, by M. Tucker

all likelihood, this will involve the construction of many slides or transparencies. For example, rather than project an entire bar graph, display and discuss it one bar at a time to help the audience process the information. If you are using a multiple-frame cartoon, introduce it one frame at a time. If you are using computer assistance directly, you can duplicate a slide several times and then work backward, deleting one element at a time so that, during your presentation, a click forward results in an added element. If you are using transparencies, you can either print out the slides that become progressively more complete and create multiple transparencies, or you can create one complete transparency and use a cover sheet to expose its elements one at a time.

In terms of design, keep everything simple, uncluttered, and consistent. Although the software may allow you to add various peripheral elements—such as shading, background patterns, movement, or highlighting—you should avoid too much distracting detail or too many effects. For example, if you are using computer assistance directly, you may be tempted to have a new element come flying and spinning in, accompanied by a dramatic sound, as you make a transition between slides. But it's best to keep things simple. Be mindful of what might be too cute and hence distracting. Likewise, moderation is the key in selecting or creating a background or border for your slide; avoid glitzy or distracting effects. Your visual displays should not upstage you as the speaker.[18]

One last piece of advice for anyone using computer assistance: make sure that you have a backup file saved on another disk. You might also have the slides printed on transparencies for use with an overhead projector. In this way, you can safeguard against potential disaster if the computer malfunctions or you encounter software or hardware incompatibility during the presentation.

KEEP IN MIND 13.4

Using Computer Assistance

The computer can be useful in generating graphics and serving as a presentational tool. Here are some tips for using it for your speech:

- Check out the facilities at your institution.
- If available, experiment with presentational software, such as PowerPoint.
- Downloaded Internet images may be a good source of visuals.
- Use color carefully to avoid washout.
- Select fonts carefully.
- Try to keep visuals simple, precise, and consistent.
- Back up essential files.

FIGURE 13.10 **Fast Food Sales in College Cafeteria**

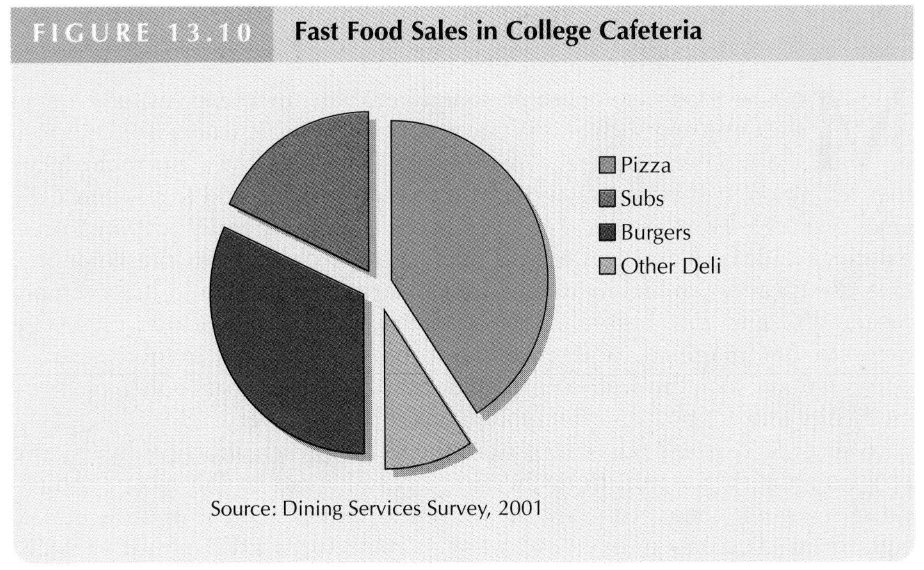

PRACTICING WITH PRESENTATIONAL AIDS

Preview Effective public speaking demands practice. And nothing is more important than practicing with presentational aids. The more aids you use and the more sophisticated those aids are, the more important such practice becomes.

Suppose you were planning to make a slide presentation and you accidentally put all the slides in the projector upside down. Wouldn't you prefer to discover your error in the privacy of your own living room rather than in front of an audience? What if you had a pile of transparencies that insisted on sticking to each other (as they often do)? Wouldn't it be better to figure out how to address that problem in advance (perhaps by putting sheets of paper between the transparencies) than to deal with it as you attempted to give your speech?

As we have pointed out before, if you are to be an effective public speaker, you must anticipate as much as possible. The audience may surprise you—but you shouldn't surprise yourself, especially if the surprise would embarrass you, make you feel or appear less than competent, or distract the audience as they try to think about your ideas.

Practice taking your audience through each visual aid, helping them process the information and glean the overall idea it suggests. Research indicates that listeners need and appreciate this assistance.[19] To ensure that your listeners have time to process what you have displayed, go through the information at a reasonable pace. First, give them an overview. For example, when presenting statistics about the increase in reported HIV cases in your community, you could say, "Let's see how HIV is on the rise in our community." Then you could reveal your source just prior to examining the data: "The State Board of Health reports that, in 1995. . . ." This will help listeners put the information in the proper context and lend support to it.

SUMMARY

Most public speakers use presentational aids. In an increasingly visual society, using such aids is one way of engaging listeners' senses. From the listeners' perspective, presentational aids can help them focus their attention, better understand and recall information and ideas, and fully enjoy a speech. From the speaker's perspective, using carefully prepared presentational aids is an excellent way to enhance a speech. By using presentational aids, the speaker can highlight main ideas, clarify and make information more meaningful and memorable, depict statistics, picture things that otherwise have to be imagined, and promote proper emotional involvement. If presentational aids are well constructed, they can also enhance the speaker's credibility and support an extemporaneous style of delivery.

Almost any speech can benefit from the use of presentational aids. Diverse options abound, ranging from the simple chalkboard to the most sophisticated computer-generated graphics. Most aids require the use of some sort of equipment—such as an overhead or slide projector, a DVD player or VCR, audio equipment, or a computer and high-lumen projector. The speaker must make sure that the speaking situation can accommodate the kind of technology, lighting, and equipment he or she needs.

Each aid should be carefully chosen and/or constructed, with the audience, the speech, and the setting in mind. Visual materials should be legible, attractive, clear, and visible to all members of the audience. Speakers should consider a broad array of options and then make judicious, conservative choices.

In many speaking contexts, professional as well as classroom, listeners expect speakers to have presentational support. Using presentational aids effectively requires practice.

QUESTIONS FOR REVIEW AND REFLECTION

1. What are some of the ways that using presentational aids can help speakers?
2. How do presentational aids assist audience members as they try to listen attentively to a speech?
3. Can you think of any topic for which no presentational support would be needed? Explain.
4. What are the major presentational options available to most public speakers? What are the potential advantages and disadvantages of each?
5. How might audience expectations influence your choice of presentational aids?
6. What aspects of the physical speaking environment should be considered in planning presentational aids to accompany a speech?
7. How have advances in technology influenced presentational aid options and their effective use?
8. What are the key principles to remember when preparing and using presentational aids?
9. Suppose you are making a speech on campus safety. You want to persuade your classmates that your campus is less safe than it was a decade ago. You

will discuss various kinds of crimes, including robbery, assault, and rape. As you reflect on this topic, what kinds of presentational aids do you think you might want to use? Try to think of at least three to five possibilities. Why would each be appropriate and potentially effective?

ENDNOTES

1. Michael P. Verdi and Janet T. Johnson, "Organized Spatial Displays and Texts: Effects of Presentation Order and Display Type on Learning Outcomes," *Journal of Experimental Education* 65 (Summer 1997): 303–317.
2. Maria L. Berg and James G. May, "Parallel Processing in Visual Perception and Memory: What Goes Where and When?" *Current Psychology* 16 (Winter 1998): 247–283. Also see Lih-Juan Chanlin, "Visual Treatment for Different Prior Knowledge," *International Journal of Instructional Media* 26 (1999): 213–219.
3. Doris A. Graber, "Say It with Pictures," *Annals of the American Academy of Political and Social Science* 546 (July 1996): 85–96.
4. Ibid.
5. Claire Morrison and William Jimmerson, "Business Presentations for the 1990s," *Video Manager* (July 1989), p. 18.
6. Graber, "Say It with Pictures," p. 86. Also see Carol L. Hodes, "Processing Visual Information: Implications of the Dual Code Theory," *Journal of Instructional Psychology* 21 (March 1994): 36–43.
7. Lih-Juan Chanlin, "The Effects of Verbal Elaboration and Visual Elaboration on Student Learning," *International Journal of Instructional Media* 24 (1997): 333–339.
8. Joe Ayres, "Using Visual Aids to Reduce Speech Anxiety," *Communication Research Reports*, (June–December 1991): 73–79.
9. Chanlin, "The Effects of Verbal Elaboration."
10. Hodes, "Processing Visual Information."
11. Elizabeth Keyes, "Typography, Color, and Information Structure," *Technical Communication, Fourth Quarter* (1993): 638–654.
12. It is important to remember that some listeners may be color deficient. There are ways of dealing with this problem. See William Horton, *Illustrating Computer Documentation* (New York: John Wiley & Sons, 1991), pp. 219–244.
13. There is considerable research on effective color combinations that consider hue, value, and saturation. See Edward Tufte, *Envisioning Information* (Cheshire, Conn.: Graphics Press, 1990).
14. Chanlin, "Visual Treatment for Different Prior Knowledge."
15. Shu-Ling Lai, "Influence of Audio-Visual Presentations on Learning Abstract Concepts," *International Journal of Instructional Media* 27 (2000): 199–207.
16. J. P. Dillard, ed., *Seeking Compliance: The Production of Interpersonal Influence Messages* (Scottsdale, Ariz.: Gorsuch-Scarisbrick, 1990).
17. An informal study conducted at Indiana University found that a particular instructor received much better course evaluations when she used multiple transparencies to outline her lecture's main points than when she gave the identical lecture without using visuals.

18. See, for example, L. Rieber, "Animation as a Distractor to Learning," *International Journal of Instructional Media* 23 (1996): 53–57.
19. Lai, "Influence of Audio-Visual Presentations." Also see Chanlin, "The Effects of Verbal Elaboration."

PART V

Particulars: Types of Public Speaking

Part V explains how speaker-audience connections work whenever you hope to gain understanding from your listeners or move audiences to feel strongly, agree with your position, or take action. This final section also describes speaking on special occasions and special applications of public speaking in the workplace.

14 Speaking to Inform

CHAPTER SURVEY

Functions of Informative Speeches

Types of Informative Speeches

Organizing the Informative Speech

How Audiences Learn from Informative Speeches

CHAPTER OBJECTIVES

After studying this chapter, you should be able to

1. **understand the different functions of informative presentations.**
2. **compare and contrast the different types of informative speeches.**
3. **describe the different ways that speakers can make information interesting and memorable to an audience.**
4. **organize and deliver an informative speech, following the guidelines for effective preparation and presentation.**
5. **understand the ethical issues of informative speaking.**

In business and many other professional settings, informative speaking is quite common. A floor supervisor might attempt to explain the reasons for a new job rotation schedule to a group of assembly-line workers. An attorney might enlighten a group of concerned citizens about the laws governing the release of convicted child molesters. An electrical engineer might demonstrate her plan for rewiring the high school to the school board, which must approve the funding. A teacher explains the steps involved in calculating the area of a geometric figure to her geometry class.

To test your skills and expand your understanding of informative speaking, go to **Lesson 8** of the **VideoLab** CD-ROM and walk through the videos, exercises, and tips provided.

Some informative speeches serve a dual function. You may transmit information to build a common ground of understanding before urging the audience to support a given point of view or to act in a certain way. Providing information thus becomes the foundation for persuasion. Nevertheless, when we speak of informative speaking in this chapter, we are thinking of a speech whose *major* purpose is to help the audience gain some understanding.

FUNCTIONS OF INFORMATIVE SPEECHES

Preview All informative speeches seek to gain audience understanding. Yet, they may function in different ways. Some speakers inform by offering audiences ideas and information. Others strive to shape perceptions. Still others articulate alternatives. Different types of informative speeches may describe, demonstrate, explain, or report on some process, problem, or phenomenon of interest.

Many of you will be called on to give informative presentations, not only in your speech class but also later in life. Sometimes when you give an informative speech, you will be imparting new information—helping the listeners understand something for the first time. On other occasions, you will take a familiar topic and present a different perspective or offer your own interpretation.

Although informative speeches function in a variety of ways, they all impart ideas and information. Audiences gain understanding by listening to, understanding, and contemplating what the speaker has to say.

Sharing Ideas and Information

Perhaps the most common function of an **informative speech** is to provide information or to share ideas. The speaker may decide that the audience needs to be briefed, taught, or informed about some data, program, issue, or problem. He or she aims to reduce ignorance, to provide insights, and to gain the listeners' cooperation in learning, growing, and understanding.

informative speech a presentation intended to help an audience gain understanding

For instance, a student speaker gave an informative speech about possible problems with eyesight that grow from the constant use of computers. He did not go on to urge students to return to the electric typewriter, nor did he ask them to modify the way they used their computers. Rather his specific purpose was, "I want my audience to understand the vision problems associated with extensive computer use." He informed the audience of various categories of eye problems and familiarized them with research findings related to the specific causes of such problems.

Shaping Perceptions

Sometimes speakers want to go beyond sharing information to influencing the audience's perceptions of events, issues, or problems. When informative speeches function in this way, they blur the distinction between informative and persuasive speaking. Although the speaker is still not asking listeners to do anything, he or she is hoping to shape their perceptions of events—and so perhaps to prepare them to change the way they think or behave. This kind of informative speaking may serve as the foundation for persuasion.

Go to **Lesson 4's Screening Room** on the **VideoLab** CD-ROM and view the speech on depression. Explain how this informative speech functioned (for instance, did the speaker attempt to articulate alternatives?). What was the speaker's specific purpose, and how effectively did he advance it?

For instance, a student in a public speaking class—a woman who was returning to school to complete her education after having dropped out to get married—decided to give an informative speech on the challenges of the first year of married life. She knew that most of the seniors in her audience were in their early twenties, many were dating someone seriously, and a few were engaged to be married. From casual conversations, she knew that most had a very starry-eyed view of marriage. So she decided to shape the audience's

Informative speeches aim at getting audience understanding through the sharing of ideas and information. This marine biologist from the Cabrillo Marine Aquarium is telling his listeners about the wonders of starfish. (David Young-Wolff/PhotoEdit)

perceptions with her informative speech. Her specific purpose was, "I want my audience to understand the complexities and responsibilities of the first year of married life." Again, she was not telling her classmates to abandon their dreams, to break up with their partners, or to live celibate lives. Instead she hoped to give them a new view of the realities of marriage—the issues to be negotiated; the decisions to be made; and the financial, relational, and personal challenges to be confronted.

PORTFOLIO 14.1

Eyeing the Alternatives

What contemporary issues concern you that must be considered in terms of various possible alternatives? Generate a list. Would any of the items you've listed make a good topic for an informative speech?

Articulating Alternatives

Most complex problems can be addressed in a variety of ways. Often we are not aware of our options, or we may know of only a few possibilities when in fact many others exist. Sometimes a speaker will give a presentation aimed at helping listeners grasp the number, variety, and quality of alternatives available to them.

For instance, a real-estate agent was recently hired by a city council to investigate possible properties that might work well as a recreation center for the young people of the community. The agent's job was to study the options and present them, fully and accurately, to the members of the council. His specific purpose was, "I want my audience to understand the best properties available for creating a youth recreation center." Preparing this kind of informative presentation required a great deal of careful research, a thorough consideration of all possible alternatives, and a willingness to present the information with accuracy and open-mindedness. The real-estate agent might have been tempted to promote one building that happened to be among his own company's listings. Instead, he wisely chose to acknowledge the various firms with which the different properties were listed and go forward with an accurate account of each.

KEEP IN MIND 14.1

Functions of Informative Speeches

- To share information and ideas
- To shape perceptions
- To articulate alternatives

TYPES OF INFORMATIVE SPEECHES

Preview Different types of informative speeches may describe, demonstrate, explain, or report on some process, problem, or phenomenon of interest.

As we noted earlier, the major purpose of any informative speech is to share knowledge and ideas with the hope of promoting the audience's understanding or competence. One common type of informative speech focuses on description.

The Speech of Description

Sometimes speakers want to describe a place, an event, or a person. By giving a **speech of description**, they hope to help the audience get a clear picture of their subject. Topics that might work well for this kind of speech include "The Workplace in the Year 2003," "The Great Smoky Mountains," "The New Hong Kong," and "Remembering the Winter Olympics of 1998."

speech of description an informative speech intended to provide a clear picture of a place, event, person, or thing

If you decide to give a descriptive speech, you will want to take great pains with your language. Precision, color, and clarity are essential. Usually you will want to use presentational aids. Slides, for example, might be very useful in showing the glories of nature, the cosmopolitan air of a major city, the ambiance of a university, the beauty of the churches of England, or even the ravages of war, disease, or poverty. However, avoid overrelying on visuals. Do the best you can to fully describe the subject of your speech without them, then add the visuals as a final clarifying touch, or use them to present images too complex or difficult to capture in words alone.

Many speeches with purposes other than informing listeners may use description. For instance, a speech of tribute or a eulogy (see Chapters 1 and 17) will usually include highly descriptive passages that celebrate someone's accomplishments or personal attributes. But unlike the informative speech, the primary purpose of these speeches is to move the audience, remind them of their values, and get them to honor the person who is the focus of the speech.

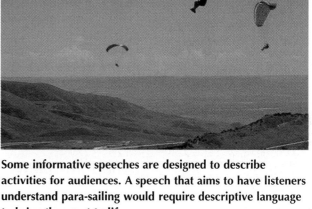

Some informative speeches are designed to describe activities for audiences. A speech that aims to have listeners understand para-sailing would require descriptive language to bring the sport to life.
(Lester Lefkowitz/The Stock Market)

The Speech of Demonstration

Sometimes speakers aim to teach an audience how something works or how to do something. On a popular morning show, Martha Stewart shows her television audience how to garden, decorate, and prepare gourmet meals. Viewers learn how to build an outdoor deck on *The New Yankee Workshop*. Any number of exercise experts tell us how to become more fit. Time management consultants run workshops on how to get organized. In each case, the speaker is demonstrating some sort of process.

speech of demonstration an informative speech intended to teach an audience how something works or how to do something

The **speech of demonstration** may be concerned with *application* or *understanding*. In some cases, the speaker wants the audience to apply certain principles or steps—to actually learn how to do something during the course of the speech. One student knew that students in her public speaking class would be required to make a PowerPoint presentation later in the semester. For her speech of demonstration, she brought in a laptop computer and portable projector and demonstrated how to set up the projector and use PowerPoint effectively to enhance a presentation. On other occasions, the speaker may be describing a more complicated process and hopes that the audience will simply grasp the process involved. A nurse in a hospital's cardiovascular unit uses a dummy to teach a group of heart patients the procedures that are involved in their surgery preparation, the surgery itself, and their subsequent recuperation. She wants her listeners to understand what to expect, not to undertake the procedures themselves.

After viewing portions of the milk additives speech in **Lesson 8's Screening Room** on the **VideoLab** CD-ROM, go to **Drill 8.1: Identifying Components of Informative Speaking** and evaluate the speech by completing the quiz.

Most speeches of demonstration involve the use of visuals to show, clarify, and make the information more memorable. Many use a sequential pattern of organization (discussing consecutive steps in a process). To make sure the audience clearly understood what was demonstrated, the speaker should allow ample time for questions.

The Speech of Explanation

speech of explanation an informative speech intended to help an audience understand complicated, abstract, or unfamiliar concepts or subjects

A speaker who wants to help the audience understand concepts that are complicated, abstract, or unfamiliar will give a **speech of explanation**. One of the more challenging types of informative speeches, the explanatory speech demands that the speaker be extremely knowledgeable about the topic and be able to explain it clearly to the audience.

A professor's lecture, for instance, is a speech aimed at explaining abstract or difficult concepts to students. Skilled teachers carefully define concepts being introduced, explain their importance or relevance, offer good clarifying examples, and give students the chance to show what they have learned through some kind of application exercise.

Conceptual Grounds

Are there any concepts that your classmates commonly do not understand and that you could help them grasp? Sketch out any speech possibilities that come to mind.

If you are giving a speech of explanation, you must be able to define the concept's main features or parts, explain its significance, and offer compelling examples that illustrate it. One student speaker gave a speech whose purpose was to help his classroom audience understand the meaning of *LD (learning-disabled)*.[1] As part of his speech, he offered the legal definition of LD, gave examples of some of the most common kinds of learning disabilities, and then explained how each might affect a student's ability to learn in particular kinds of classroom settings.

Speeches of explanation are among the most important speeches to make. Any speaker who can illuminate a concept for an audience that previously did not understand it has made a real contribution to their learning.

The Informative Oral Report

informative oral report a brief, informative presentation to assist a group's performance or decision-making

In professional settings, people are often called on to present an **informative oral report**. In some cases, these reports are given informally (perhaps even to one or two listeners) and may be quite brief. On other occasions, the speaker may be asked to prepare a more formal presentation, often technical in nature, to inform others in the organization of recent events, discoveries, or other vital information.

The need to give an informative oral report can arise in diverse professional contexts, but informative reports aren't limited to work situations.[2] Suppose you represented your fraternity or sorority at a state conference where new pledging regulations were introduced. At the next regular meeting of your fraternity chapter, the president might ask you to brief everyone on the new regulations. Or suppose you belonged to the student senate. You represented the senate at a meeting of the university's board of trustees, who were considering several different plans for increasing student tuition on your campus. Members of the senate would want to know about the trustees' plans, and they might ask you to report on the various options being considered.

Go to **Drill 8.3: Functions of Informative Speaking** on the **VideoLab** CD-ROM and read the review statements presented there. Then, assess how each statement is functioning in the context of an informative speech.

Informative reports often provide background that a group will use in making decisions or solving problems. Following a report (or even a series of reports), a group may go ahead with other business.

Although the primary purpose of a speech might be to report, explain, demonstrate, or describe, any speech can include a combination of these goals. For example, a speaker reporting on an innovative product would almost certainly devote part of his or her speech to describing the product and perhaps even take a few minutes to demonstrate how it works. Thus the various speech types are not always distinct.

KEEP IN MIND 14.2

Types of Informative Speeches

- Speech of description
- Speech of demonstration
- Speech of explanation
- Informative oral report

ORGANIZING THE INFORMATIVE SPEECH

Preview Several different strategies exist for organizing informative speeches. Although most of the organizational patterns described here can be used to arrange other types of speeches, they lend themselves particularly well to informative speeches. These patterns include chronological, sequential, spatial, categorical, causal, and problem-solution.

As we noted at the beginning of this chapter, many informative speeches are made in some kind of business or professional context. In such settings, they may include training sessions, workshops, briefings, and technical reports, as well as more standard speeches, such as those you are asked to deliver in your public speaking class. Regardless of the context or specific type of speech, organizing your remarks carefully is crucial.

In the following sections, we illustrate various organizational strategies by outlining a progression of main ideas that demonstrate how the pattern might be used. We do not include source citations in these outline segments, as you would do if you were developing a formal outline. For an illustration of a full-sentence outline that incorporates sources from the bibliography, see Chapter 10.

The same basic topic can be organized in a variety of ways. For purposes of illustrating this principle here, let us say that you are a native Chicagoan. You are attending a college that is located about five hours from Chicago, and you would like to make your classmates aware of the diverse places of interest in your hometown. Your topic is "It's a Wonderful Town: Chicago." Keep in mind that when you choose a topic that is already quite familiar to you, you will want to go well beyond your experiences and firsthand knowledge by doing careful research and enhancing what you already know.

Chronological Pattern

chronological pattern an organizational pattern in which ideas are arranged in a logical time order

One way you might organize your speech is by using the **chronological pattern**. For this speech, you might advance as your thesis, "Every month of the summer, there are plenty of interesting things to do in Chicago for visitors of all ages and interests." Your specific purpose is, "I want my audience to become aware of the diverse cultural, sports, and culinary experiences that people encounter when visiting Chicago during the summer months." You have chosen the summer months because this is the time when college students would be most likely to consider traveling. You would then proceed chronologically by highlighting events that take place during June, July, and August, and you would develop a main point for each of these summer months. Your first main point might be developed as follows:

I. In Chicago, the month of June features diverse activities that attract people from all over the world.

   A. For music lovers, there is the annual Blues Festival (June 8–11).

A topic for an informative speech may be organized in several ways, depending on the focus of the speech. For example, a chronologically organized speech about Chicago could emphasize the variety of activities available at different times of the year, whereas a spatial organization might emphasize the special attractions offered in different parts of the city. (Vito Palmisano/Tony Stone Images)

1. This year's theme is "Celebrate the Heritage and Tradition of Blues Music."
   a. It is dedicated to the centennials of Tampa Red and Pink Anderson.
   b. A special series of performances will pay tribute to the legendary Howlin' Wolf in honor of his ninetieth birthday.
2. This is the largest outdoor, free-admission blues festival in the world.
3. Every year, it attracts more than 650,000 purists, enthusiasts, and lovers of blues from all walks of life.

B. For art lovers, another June event is the annual Old Town Art Fair (June 10–11).
1. This fair is held in the historic landmark district of Chicago's Old Town Triangle, and the whole neighborhood gets involved.
   a. Each year, the fair is organized and operated by more than 750 neighborhood volunteers.
   b. Many neighbors open their gardens and patios for the Garden Walk.
   c. Local restaurants and concessions provide excellent food and refreshing drinks.
2. This art fair is the oldest outdoor juried art fair in the United States.
   a. Nearly 250 artists participate each year.
   b. More than 40,000 attendees browse and buy art, including paintings, sculpture, prints, photographs, fiber, glass, jewelry, ceramics, collage, and multimedia.
   c. An art auction features celebrity auctioneers, and a children's corner offers many hands-on artistic activities.

C. For everyone, there is the Taste of Chicago (June 30–July 9—this one really belongs to both months).
1. More than 70 of the city's favorite restaurants serve various specialty and ethnic dishes to more than 3 million people each year.
2. The food is matched with live music by famous performers on a multitude of stages throughout Chicago's Grant Park.
3. There's wonderful food and fun for everyone of all ages.
   a. Celebrity chefs demonstrate how they make their favorite and most exotic dishes.
   b. Experts demonstrate home decorating and gardening tips.
   c. A ninety-foot Ferris wheel and entertainment for children round out the fun.

If you are beginning to develop a speech using a chronological pattern of organization, go to the **Online SpeechStudio** and use the **Outline Worksheet for a Chronological/Sequential Pattern** to guide the construction of your outline.

Once you have completed a draft of your speech that is organized chronologically, go to the **Online SpeechStudio** and assess your outline draft by completing the **Checklist for a Chronological/Sequential Pattern**.

You might offer a transition into your second main point by saying, "For anyone who happens to visit the Taste of Chicago on July 3, beginning at 9:30 P.M., they have only to look up to catch Chicago's Independence Eve Fireworks Spectacular—a certain highlight of the city's special events in the month of July."

sequential pattern an organizational pattern in which the various steps of a process or a phenomenon are identified and discussed, one by one

Closely related to the chronological pattern is the **sequential pattern** of organization, in which you describe some process you want the audience to understand in step-by-step fashion. For instance, you might describe the steps involved in applying to graduate school, downloading software from the Web, or creating PowerPoint slides for use in a presentation. The sequential pattern is ideally suited to speeches of demonstration.

Spatial Pattern

spatial pattern an organizational pattern in which ideas are arranged with regard to their natural spatial relationships

Suppose that you prefer to use the **spatial pattern** as your organizing principle. For this speech, your thesis might be, "Even though Chicago is quite large, visitors can use public transportation to visit key spots all over the city." Your specific purpose would be, "I want my audience to understand the relative ease with which visitors can tour key sites of interest in Chicago." You would go on to highlight those points of interest according to space, beginning with Downtown Chicago and using a highlighting map as a presentational aid. Your first main point might be developed as follows:

I. Visitors could probably spend several weeks in Downtown Chicago and never see it all. But because of its central location and exciting features, it's a good place to start.

   A. Every great city has wonderful museums, and Chicago is no exception.

      1. Perhaps the first museum that one is likely to encounter Downtown (because of its centrality) is the Art Institute of Chicago, located on South Michigan Avenue.

         a. The Art Institute is one of the great museums of the world and the preeminent art institution in the Midwest.

         b. Its reputation is primarily based on its collection of impressionist and postimpressionist paintings—one of the largest and most important outside France.

         c. Among its holdings are such diverse masterpieces as Rembrandt's *Old Man with a Gold Chain*, Monet's *Six Versions of Stacks of Wheat*, and Picasso's *Mother and Child*. (*Note:* You would want to show these works as you referred to them.)

      2. Another Downtown museum of equal distinction is the Field Museum of Natural History, located at the south end of Grant Park.

         a. This museum is world-class in size and distinction, including 9 acres of exhibit halls and more than 20 million artifacts.

         b. Its exhibits and public programs specialize in anthropology, geology, zoology, and botany.

c. The Field Museum is particularly famous for its collections of dinosaur bones (including the most complete *Tyrannosaurus rex* skeleton found to date) and animal taxidermy (such as the lions from the film *The Ghosts and the Darkness*).

3. A third Downtown museum of great interest is the John G. Shedd Aquarium and Oceanarium, located at the very edge of Lake Michigan.

a. The Shedd houses the world's largest indoor aquarium, featuring some 8,000 aquatic animals.

b. More than 650 species are represented here, ranging from tiny, jewel-like lobsters to 1,500-pound beluga whales.

c. The Shedd Aquarium is devoted to conservation and the environment, and its educational programs reinforce those values.

B. Another highlight of Downtown Chicago is the Magnificent Mile—a flower- and light-filled promenade running along North Michigan Avenue.

1. The Magnificent Mile lies between Chicago's two most important waterways, the Chicago River on its south border and Lake Michigan on its north.

2. A walking tour along the Mile would feature such structures as the Michigan Avenue Bridge, the Wrigley Building, the Tribune Tower, Water Tower Place, the John Hancock Center, and the Drake Hotel. (*Note:* Depending on time constraints, you might elaborate on the history and significance of each of these buildings.)

C. Finally, a trip to Downtown Chicago would hardly be worthwhile without a stroll through Grant Park, the city's 319-acre "front yard."

1. From Lake Michigan on the east and Michigan Avenue on the west, the park is a segue from the lakefront to the bustling central city.

a. All of the museums we have discussed are considered part of Grant Park, but other features are worth our attention as well.

2. The centerpiece of Grant Park is the Buckingham Fountain.

a. Originally constructed in 1927, it was renovated and enlarged (doubled in size) in 1995. The fountain pumps more than 1.5 million gallons of water from Lake Michigan every day.

b. At night, a carefully orchestrated light show plays off the cascading water and creates a dazzling effect.

3. Another outstanding feature of Grant Park is the Petrillo Music Shell.

a. Music and drama festivals (such as the Blues Festival, the Jazz Festival, and the Gospel Festival) are performed there throughout the summer.

If you are developing your informative speech according to a spatial pattern of organization, go to the **Online SpeechStudio** and use the **Outline Worksheet for a Spatial Pattern** to guide you as you construct your outline.

b. Famous musical groups ranging from Benny Goodman's band to the Chicago Symphony Orchestra have performed at the shell.

4. As you might expect, Grant Park has something for everyone.

a. It has soccer fields, volleyball courts, softball fields, tennis courts, a bicycle/running path along the lake, and ice-skating for those with athletic interests.

b. The park also houses Soldier Field, home of the Chicago Bears and host to concerts, religious festivals, and, in 1994, World Cup soccer.

c. Every summer, the Taste of Chicago is held in Grant Park, offering food and fun to more than 3 million people.

Once you have developed an outline draft for your informative speech that is organized spatially, go to the **Online SpeechStudio** and evaluate your efforts by completing the **Checklist for a Spatial Pattern.**

After discussing these features of Downtown Chicago, your second main point might be the area north of Downtown, with a consideration of the Gold Coast, Old Town, Lincoln Park, and Lakeview/Wrigleyville.

Categorical Pattern

categorical pattern when ideas from several independent yet interrelated categories are used to advance a larger idea

As a final illustration, let's try approaching a speech about Chicago using the **categorical pattern** of organization. This time your thesis might be, "Because Chicago has so much to offer, it is an interesting place for visitors of all interests and ages." Your specific purpose is, "I want my audience to understand that Chicago is a great place to visit, regardless of your interests or age." You might then choose to organize your speech around categories such as music lovers, sports lovers, museum lovers, and those who love to eat. Here's how you might develop your first main point:

I. For music lovers, Chicago offers all kinds of music to lighten the heart and stir the soul—much of it free and open to the public.

A. First, for those who prefer jazz and blues, opportunities abound.

1. The annual Blues Festival, for example, is the largest outdoor, free-admission blues festival in the world.

a. Every year, it attracts more than 650,000 purists, enthusiasts, and lovers of blues from all walks of life.

b. This year's theme is "Celebrate the Heritage and Tradition of Blues Music," and the festival will pay tribute to the legendary Howlin' Wolf in honor of his ninetieth birthday.

2. Another famous summer music event is Jazzfest, a free outdoor music festival featuring national and international artists, along with Chicago's finest jazz and blues performers.

3. The annual Chicago Jazz Festival is a Labor Day tradition and is one of the city's oldest music festivals.

a. Performers range from local talent to national and international entertainers.

b. More than twenty-five performances on three stages in Grant Park attract jazz lovers from around the world.

B. Chicago also offers more than its share of musical events that are interwoven with broader celebrations of its ethnic and cultural diversity.

1. The Puerto Rican Fest, for instance, is a sizzling celebration of Puerto Rican culture and features live music, plays, games, food, and a parade.

2. The Irish American Heritage Festival incorporates Irish music, dance, and a sense of community—with one of this year's highlights being bagpipe marching bands.

3. The Chinatown Summer Fair—a one-day festival of food, art, and music—celebrates the depth and mystery of China's ancient culture right in the vibrant Chinatown neighborhood.

4. As a final example, the annual Viva Chicago Latin Music Festival offers an exciting variety of Latin music from around the globe: cumbia, tropical, merengue, salsa, ballads, ranchero, and mariachi.

C. Finally, there are a number of park concerts that are open to everyone.

1. The Grant Park Music Festival offers weekly performances between mid-June and mid-August.

a. This is the nation's only free, municipally funded, outdoor classical music concert series.

b. The city of Chicago is committed to this festival, as is evidenced by the fact that this is its sixty-sixth season.

2. In addition, Concerts in the Park celebrates its fifty-third year of providing free outdoor entertainment in neighborhood parks.

a. Performances are diverse, featuring some of the nation's top musicians performing jazz, reggae, blues, pops, big band, salsa, gospel, and classical.

b. These concerts take place in thirty-three parks across the city.

For your second main point, you would address sports lovers, making reference to Chicago as home to the Blackhawks, Bulls, Bears, White Sox, and Cubs, as well as noting major sporting events hosted in Chicago on a regular basis (such as the Big Ten Basketball Tournament).

By using the topic "Chicago" to illustrate three different patterns of organization, we hope that we have shown you that nearly any topic can be arranged in a variety of ways, depending on your specific purpose. We now turn to some other topics to illustrate two other strategies for organizing informative speeches.

If you plan to use a categorical pattern to organize your informative speech, go to the **Online SpeechStudio** and use the **Outline Worksheet for a Categorical Pattern** to construct your outline.

Once you have drafted the outline for your informative speech that is organized categorically, go to the **Online SpeechStudio** and assess your outline by completing the **Checklist for a Categorical Pattern**.

Causal Pattern

causal pattern an organizational pattern in which ideas focus on causes or effects or are arranged to reveal cause-to-effect or effect-to-cause relationships

Some informative speeches might follow the **causal pattern**, focusing on *causes only, effects only,* or moving either from *cause to effect* or from *effect to cause.* For instance, you may want your audience to understand the development of a specific event, problem, or idea. You may start with the effect, such as pointing to an increase in homeless people in your community, or you may begin by talking about the causes of homelessness, perhaps moving to the effects later. For this speech, you might advance this thesis: "Many factors have recently contributed to increased homelessness in our community." Your specific purpose would be, "I want my audience to understand the different factors that have contributed to homelessness in our community."

I. Several factors have contributed to the rise of homelessness in our community.

  A. First, more people are out of work than ever before.

    1. The closing of the Johnson plant this past winter left more than seven hundred people without jobs.

      a. Of those who lost their jobs, nearly one-third were close to retirement, and they were left without pensions or viable hopes for obtaining new jobs.

      b. Eighty of those who lost their jobs were single parents with small children.

    2. The local government's financial problems also resulted in more than one hundred government jobs being lost this year.

If you have decided to organize your speech using a cause-and-effect pattern, go to the **Online SpeechStudio** and use the **Outline Worksheet for a Cause-and-Effect Pattern** to construct your outline.

  B. In addition, illegal drugs have been introduced into the community at an alarming rate and have contributed to homelessness.

    1. Drug-related arrests increased by more than 15 percent this past year.

      a. The sharpest increases were in the possession and use of cocaine and heroine—two of the most dangerous illegal drugs.

      b. Last May, at one of our local high school proms, police arrested more than fifty underage drinkers.

    2. Several gangs have moved in from larger cities and are actively peddling drugs.

    3. Drug addiction can push people out of their homes and into the streets.

      a. Dr. Lori Heinz, head of our county's Welfare to Work program, estimates that close to 50 percent of the homeless are addicted to drugs and/or alcohol.

      b. The homeless are the least likely segment of society to receive treatment for drug problems, and this perpetuates a cycle of poverty and hopelessness.

  C. A final factor that has contributed to homelessness in our community is the fact that social agencies that help the poor have recently experienced financial woes.

1. Last summer, after two years of struggling, our largest homeless shelter closed.

2. The Community Kitchen used to serve two hot meals every day to anyone who was hungry. Now it serves only one meal, and it serves no meals on Sundays.

3. The Habitat for Humanity program no longer exists in our county.

   a. Five years ago, Habitat was building five to ten houses each year.

   b. The organization struggled with a decreased number of volunteers for several months before shutting down.

After describing some of these contributing causes, you would then, for the second main point, describe the effects of homelessness, including sickness and disease and the breakdown and demoralization of the family and the community.

When you have a good draft of your informative speech outline that you have organized according to a cause-and-effect pattern, go to the **Online SpeechStudio** and evaluate your outline by using the **Checklist for a Cause-and-Effect Pattern**.

Problem-Solution Pattern

The **problem-solution pattern** of organization may seem less obviously well suited to informative speeches. You may think, for instance, that you would be more likely to choose this organizational pattern for a persuasive speech than for an informative one, but that is not necessarily true. For example, suppose you wanted to talk about screening options for colon cancer. Your purpose would be not to advocate any particular solution, but to make listeners aware of alternatives available to them. For this speech, you might advance this as your thesis: "Because colon cancer is such a potentially deadly disease, becoming aware of screening options for early detection can help save lives." Your specific purpose might be, "I want my audience to understand the seriousness of colon cancer and become aware of the major screening alternatives that exist."

problem-solution pattern an organizational pattern in which a problem is identified and one or more specific solutions are described or proposed, depending on whether the speech is informative or persuasive

You would begin this speech by describing the nature of the problem. You would then define colon cancer as a major killer of men and women over age fifty, offer statistics to demonstrate its seriousness, and then talk about some of the likely causes and effects of the disease. After you have advanced listeners' understanding of the nature of the problem, you would be ready to move on to your final main point and consider early-detection options. In the third part of your speech, you would provide information based on this transition: "Now that we've seen the importance of early detection, let's explain the various tests currently available."

III. Several reliable screening alternatives exist.

   A. For those who are over fifty (and much younger if there is a history of cancer in their family), annual screenings begin with a hemocult test.

      1. Stool samples are taken at home and sent to the hospital for analysis.

2. Positive samples (that is, where blood is found in the stool) require follow-up tests.

B. One follow-up screening option is the barium enema, which completely cleanses your system, allowing doctors to take x-rays of your colon in order to look for signs of cancer.

   1. There are several advantages to this procedure.
      a. It allows doctors to see the entire colon.
      b. The test is noninvasive, with little risk to the patient.
      c. The test is less expensive than other screening procedures.
   2. However, there are some disadvantages to this screening method.
      a. Some patients find swallowing the barium to be an almost impossible, nauseating task.
      b. If trouble spots or polyps are found, the patient will need to undergo further testing.

C. Another screening option is the colonoscopy, which (following a thorough enema) is administered at the hospital while the patient is under sedation.

   1. What are the advantages of the colonoscopy?
      a. It is thorough—the doctor can examine the entire length of the colon using a tubelike scope.
      b. During the procedure, the doctor can remove small polyps and sample any suspicious tissue for a biopsy. Thus, no further screening procedures are required.
   2. Although some consider this test to be the most definitive, some disadvantages exist.
      a. The test is expensive, costing more than twice as much as other screening procedures.
      b. Because the procedure is invasive, there is some risk that the patient will suffer internal bleeding.

If you have chosen to organize your informative speech by using a problem/solution pattern, go to the **Online SpeechStudio** and use the **Outline Worksheet for a Problem/Solution Pattern** to assist you in developing your outline.

Once you have a good draft of your problem/solution outline, go to the **Online SpeechStudio** and assess your outline by using the **Checklist for a Problem/Solution Pattern**.

From here, you would proceed through other treatment options, making sure to offer a balanced assessment of each. You might conclude by mentioning a new screening option that is currently being researched—a stool sample combined with DNA screening. However, you should point out that even if studies using this screening method show promising results, the test will not be available to the public for a few years.

In choosing your organizational pattern, you should let your specific purpose be your guide. What pattern is most likely to produce the response you hope to get from your audience? What strategy is most likely to assist their awareness and understanding? Table 14.1 includes some guidelines.

KEEP IN MIND 14.3

Organizational Guidelines for Informative Speeches

- Recognize diverse organizational options, including the chronological, sequential, spatial, categorical, causal, and problem-solution patterns.
- Be aware that the same topic can be organized in more than one way.
- Choose the pattern that best fits your specific purpose.

TABLE 14.1 Guidelines for Choosing an Organizational Pattern

Pattern	Use When	Possible Topics
Chronological	you want to discuss an event, phenomenon, or concept over time.	Fashions for Women: 1960 to the Present Treating Breast Cancer: Major Breakthroughs Since 1975 The Civil Rights Movement of the 1960s
Sequential	you want to show a step-by-step progression.	How to Use PowerPoint Learning to Meditate
Spatial	you want to help the audience visualize something you are describing *and/or* you want to describe something by moving from point to point through space.	Traveling Through the Rocky Mountains Making the Most of a Day in Paris Exploring the Nile Getting Acquainted with the University's New Library Homes for the Future
Categorical	you want to emphasize the significance of the categories or divisions in some way *or* you are interested in a flexible approach to organization.	The Best Business Schools in the United States Choosing Your Next Car Techniques for Coping with Test Anxiety New Drugs for Treating HIV Dogs That Make the Best Pets Health Care Options for the Year 2001
Causal	you want your audience to understand those factors (causes) that have contributed to some outcome (effects) *or* you want your audience to understand the impact (effects) of some problem or phenomenon.	The Causes of Insomnia Why People Like to Live in Small Towns Understanding High Blood Pressure Why SAT Scores Are Declining El Niño's Effects on the Weather The Healing Effects of Pets
Problem-Solution	you want to make your audience understand a problem more fully, while acknowledging associated solutions, *or* you want to help your audience become aware of diverse solutions to a problem without advocating any one of them.	Academic Misconduct on Our Campus Addressing the Cholesterol Problem Strategies for Dealing with Iraq Obesity in the United States Options for Improving Your Vision Alcoholism and the College Student

HOW AUDIENCES LEARN FROM INFORMATIVE SPEECHES

Preview Listeners who are motivated to learn make the speaker's job much easier. Often, however, listeners are not as motivated initially as the speaker might hope, challenging the speaker to find ways to capture and maintain their interest and attention.

Go to **Drill 8.2: Identifying Organizational Patterns** on the **VideoLab** CD-ROM. Identify the organizational patterns suggested by these statements.

Speakers need to understand the strategies available for heightening listener interest and helping them learn and retain information.[3] A good place to start is by thinking about the extent to which listeners are motivated to listen.

THE WIZARD OF ID Brant parker and Johnny hart

By permission of Johnny Hart and Creators Syndicate, Inc.

The Role of Listener Motivation

Any teacher will tell you that forcing someone to learn is like taking a horse to water: you can no more make someone learn than you can make the horse drink. Much depends on the listeners and the understanding, beliefs, and attitudes they bring to the speaking situation. The ideal listener, as we discussed in Chapter 3, is the motivated listener, who is intrinsically interested in the topic, willing to work at listening, and eager to gain some new understanding. When listeners are motivated to listen and learn, the speaker's job is much more manageable.

Unfortunately, listening often takes place under less than ideal circumstances. Sometimes audience members do not have the background they need to be truly prepared to listen. Sometimes they resent having to listen to a presentation. At other times, they are simply bored. Under these circumstances, trying to impart information can be very challenging.

Usually when we are called on to make informative presentations, audience members are a mixed bag. Some are eager, some knowledgeable, and others less than motivated. Fortunately, there are things you can do to heighten listener interest and overcome, or at least reduce, initial inertia and apathy. The above cartoon depicts the king's way of motivating his listeners.

Capturing and Maintaining the Audience's Attention

A good place to begin is with thinking about how to interest listeners in what you are saying. Interest motivates learning.[4] In general, audience members will respond with interest to ideas and information that possess some of the qualities discussed below.[5]

Relevance. An audience of single parents struggling with child discipline problems, financial woes, and loneliness would probably be interested in hearing an expert speak about strategies for dealing with these problems. For an audience of happily married couples whose children are grown and have graduated from college, however, this subject would not be particularly relevant.

The first task, then, is to pick a topic that the audience perceives as relevant, as discussed in Chapter 6. You will want to deal with the matter of relevance right away, during the introduction of your speech. Why should your listeners want to hear about electric cars, the proposed community public transit system, or problems with voter registration? One student speaker established her topic's relevance by pointing out,

> Sometimes, as students, we get so busy that we don't pay attention to issues discussed in the state legislature that may directly affect our lives. I know this happens to me sometimes. But, today I want to familiarize you with a piece of legislation currently under debate in the legislature. It's called the Environmental Bill. *If* it is passed, our campus will become pedestrian-only—no more cars or buses. Do you take the IU bus to class? Do you car pool with your friends? Do you drive yourself to class? If so, you will be very interested in learning about the Environmental Bill—its advantages and disadvantages.

Of course, the issue of relevance needs to be addressed throughout the speech, not just during the introduction. If your listeners begin to think, *Wait a minute! What does this have to do with me?* they are probably not learning very much.

One way of stressing a subject's relevance is to emphasize its *usefulness* to the audience. Relevance and usefulness are often interrelated, but, usefulness is more practical and specific. Suppose the director of your college's placement office visited your class and spoke about the job market, carefully identifying the areas of greatest job growth and potential. Clearly this topic is relevant. It may be made more relevant, however, by stressing its usefulness. The speaker could do this by outlining the specific steps involved in using the university's placement service, how to develop a résumé, how to seek and incorporate references, and so forth. To the extent that listeners grow to understand how information is relevant and useful to them or to those they care about, they will likely become motivated to listen and learn.

Novelty. Listeners are often interested in things they find startling, unusual, or new. Novelty gains attention. Every semester, college speech teachers listen to speeches on the dangers of secondhand smoke, the importance of wearing seat belts, and the legalization of marijuana. Although there is nothing intrinsically "wrong" with these topics, speakers rarely offer much new information or insights about them. The topics are simply too familiar and tired.

Go to **Lesson 5's Screening Room** on the **VideoLab** CD-ROM and watch the speech on smokeless tobacco. In your judgment, how effectively does the speaker offer a novel approach to address the problem of secondhand smoke?

Whether information is seen as novel will depend on the audience and what they already know. If listeners know little about patient abuses associated with HMOs (organizations that manage health care), credit card fraud, or date rape drugs, such topics might generate interest. With any topic, some initial audience interest must exist—a readiness to learn or at least an openness to becoming interested. If a topic is seen as bizarre or irrelevant, the fact that it is also seen as new or unusual may not help very much.

Sometimes a speaker can approach a familiar topic in a novel or unusual manner and immediately gain the audience's interest. In general, when a speaker has personal, direct experience with a topic—due to personal experience, years of work experience, or achievements in the area—he or she will bring a fresh perspective that audience members may find interesting. For instance, we recently listened to a student named Julie speak about the problems with competitive gymnastics for young women. During that same semester, other students had chosen to speak on the same topic. However, Julie had participated in competitive gymnastics herself for several years and so brought her personal perspective to the subject.

Go to **Lesson 9's Screening Room** on the **VideoLab** CD-ROM and watch the first speech on women's gymnastics. To what extent and in what ways is the speaker able to incorporate her personal experience to create an element of novelty and maintain the audience's attention?

Importance. No one wants to waste a lot of time listening to someone talk about trivia. Even an amusing speech can lose an audience if no insights or bits of wisdom emerge. Not everyone agrees on what is worth knowing. However, speeches that deal with substantive topics, such as personal health, the economy, or education, are likely to be seen as worthy of the listening time invested.

As you select topics for informative speeches, make sure the subjects are significant. Suppose a speaker can provide insights into election irregularities during the presidential election of 2000. Or perhaps another can help us understand why Northern Ireland remains in a state of political turmoil. Or another can compare and contrast Hinduism and Buddhism as major world religions. In each case, the speaker has chosen a topic of substance, a topic that demands a good mind and thorough research, and a topic that requires real interest and commitment.

Variety. Most of us have had the experience of being bored during others' presentations. Speakers can be very predictable, constant, and dull. Longer presentations entail special challenges in this regard, since listener attention spans are often far too short.

Capturing Attention

Capture the audience's attention by emphasizing the subject's

- relevance and usefulness.
- novelty.
- importance.
- variety.

Speakers can help sustain the audience's interest by introducing some variety into their talks. Variety is not so much about the topic chosen for a speech as it is about the way the speaker presents it. Variety can come in many forms. One speaker may mix humor with more serious speech segments. Someone else may use presentational aids in imaginative ways to create visual variety. Another speaker may use variety in supporting material, including testimony, statistics, comparison, and narrative. Yet another may deliver a speech with varied movement, voice, and facial expressions. These are just a few of the options available to help sustain listener attention. With variety comes unpredictability, a certain level of suspense, and increased interest.

PORTFOLIO 14.3

Calculating Interest

Look over the list of topics you're considering for an informative speech to the class. Which appear most relevant to your classroom audience? Most useful? Most novel and important? How can you emphasize any or all of these qualities? Do any appear problematic along these lines? If so, what should you do? Which lend themselves to variety? How will you provide variety?

Combining the Factors. An effective speaker will use the attention-capturing factors just discussed in combination and in varying ways throughout his or her speech. For instance, a substantive topic may be of little interest to the audience unless the speaker is able to show its relevance. A novel topic may capture limited attention unless the speaker can show its importance. And no matter how effectively the speaker presents a topic, with varied support and commanding delivery, if its relevance has not been established, the speech will likely fall on deaf ears. Remaining mindful of the need to establish and maintain the audience's attention is an ongoing concern for every speaker.

Helping Listeners Learn

In Chapter 3, we discussed the audience's listening challenges, including ways to help them better attend to messages. If you are to give a successful informative speech, you have to present information that is, among other things, new to your listeners. However, new information can also be overwhelming if it is not presented effectively. Let's look at what you might do to help listeners learn better when you make an informative presentation.

- *Limit the number of details.* No listener can absorb list after list of facts and figures. Instead you can use statistical and other detailed information to support major ideas you want listeners to remember. Translating statistics into memorable or audience-specific terms can also help. Remember, not all topics are equally suited to a short presentation; choose wisely. Look at your specific purpose statement. Have you selected a purpose that is realistic, or is it too ambitious, given the time allotted for your talk? Decide what listeners really need to know to gain the kind of understanding you are hoping for. Ask yourself; "What is essential for my audience to understand, recall, and perhaps use?" Then avoid including extraneous information.
- *Pace yourself carefully.* One of the greatest barriers to learning is created when a speaker whizzes through information. Slow down to stress important concepts. Look for signs that listeners are following you. If they are taking notes, are they keeping up? If not, slow down and consider repeating key information. Nothing is gained if you cover a huge quantity of information in record time but nobody can keep up with your brisk pace.
- *Speak with a concern for clarity.* However motivated and interested listeners are in your topic, they cannot learn if you do not communicate clearly with them. To be clear, you will have to pitch your presentation to the appropriate level, neither above nor below listeners' heads. Careful audience analysis will help you choose the best approach. Being clear also means using excellent examples. Choosing and using words that are simple, precise, vivid, and accurate also will help. Always use good oral style so that your remarks are comfortable to listen to, intellectually accessible, and memorable.
- *Use restatement and repetition.* One of the main ways that all of us learn is by being exposed repeatedly to information. When information is restated or repeated, we tend to learn it better. As discussed in Chapter 12, restatement and repetition can be effective stylistic devices, and they are often used by great speakers. By providing emphasis, restatement and repetition make ideas and information stick in the minds of your audience.
- *Provide visual reinforcement.* Even if you speak clearly and pace yourself carefully, you will need to use presentational aids to highlight main points and to clarify and reinforce details that no listener could be expected to remember. Visually highlighting statistics is important, as is providing detailed budgets, financial projections, and other important data on handouts. Since most informative speeches cannot reasonably cover everything an

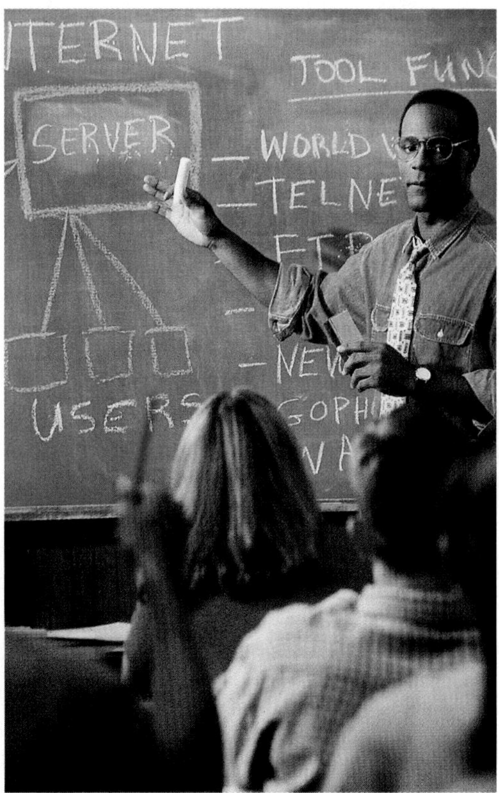

Listeners tend to absorb and remember information if more than one of their senses are involved. Visual reinforcement is one of the most common and most effective ways to help listeners learn. (Jose L. Pelaez/The Stock Market)

audience needs to know about, say, the particulars of a new computer system or the complexities of a proposed building project, you will need to provide those details in written form for listeners to ponder later.

You can use the **Informative Speech Evaluation Form** you find on the **Online SpeechStudio** to evaluate your fellow classmates' informative speeches.

- *Include time for questions.* Whenever people grapple with new ideas and information, they are bound to have questions. It's important, therefore, to build time for questions into your speaking schedule. If you have been given an hour, plan to devote at least fifteen minutes to questions—maybe more depending on the complexity and controversiality of your subject. The question period gives the audience a chance to clarify their confusion, seek further information, check their perceptions, and share ideas of their own. Not all speaking situations can accommodate time for questions (perhaps not even your public speaking classroom can do so), but whenever they can, they should.

- *Look for ways to involve listeners actively.* Learning experts agree that students (listeners) learn far more when they are actively involved in the learning process than when they remain passive.[6] Do all you can to engage your audience. Choose a topic that allows you to share relevant, important, or novel information (as discussed above) that you hope the audience will find intrinsically interesting. Beyond that, you may ask actual or rhetorical questions, test listeners with a pop quiz, ask them to write down objections or questions, or engage them in dialogue along the way.

  With a longer presentation, such as a workshop, you may build in all sorts of activities, such as small discussion groups or exercises. You may present a concept, illustrate it with a brief video example, and then follow up with an audience discussion. You may provide breaks, which build in time for informal chitchat. Be creative in thinking of ways to get the audience involved. A student speaker recently gave an informative presentation on the barriers faced by disabled students at the university. As part of her presentation, she asked listeners to try to exit the room in a wheelchair, to climb a stairway with a leg brace, and to brush their teeth using only one arm.

  In *Spotlight on Getting Listeners Involved,* HIV educator Mike Bryson describes his strategy for engaging the audience during his presentation. As you can see, Bryson's audience has a chance to get involved and to actually set the agenda for the speech.

KEEP IN MIND 14.5

Helping Listeners Learn

You can help listeners learn if you

- limit the number of details.
- pace yourself carefully.
- speak with a concern for clarity.
- use restatement and repetition.
- provide visual reinforcement.
- include time for questions.
- involve the listeners actively.
- assess listener learning.

Go to **Lesson 8 Coach: Tips to Remember** on the **VideoLab** CD-ROM. As you watch the brief video clip, read through the lists of "dos" and "don'ts." In light of them, how positively would you evaluate this speaker?

- *Assess learning, if possible.* Sometimes, when you are giving an informative presentation in a professional setting, you can take the time to check and see whether the audience is picking up on what you're "teaching" them. You may want to stop occasionally to ask them questions, as your college professors often do. You may introduce a theory and then ask them if they can think of examples. Or you may give them an example and ask them if it is good or bad. If you do this kind of checking along the way, you can adjust your remarks as you go. If there is confusion, you may want to repeat, offer new examples, or encourage listeners to ask questions so that you can better understand why they are confused.

Not every informative occasion presents assessment opportunities. You may have only ten minutes to talk. Or the speaking situation may be such that checking on audience comprehension and retention would be considered rude or inappropriate (if, for instance, you were a young employee called on to brief the top management team of the company for which you work). When the situation permits, however, take every chance to touch base with your listeners as the process unfolds.

Ethical Considerations

The ethical informative speaker has the highest regard for accuracy. In preparing an informative speech, you should seek a comprehensive understanding of the subject and examine evidence as broadly and objectively as possible. Read widely, think open-mindedly, be open to new information as it is discovered, and be willing to modify your initial thinking.

When you give an informative speech, do all you can to show the audience your concern for accuracy by substantiating your views with evidence, inviting the audience to investigate on their own, encouraging them to listen to you critically and constructively, and giving them sufficient time to quiz you and to express their concerns. When they do ask questions, respond honestly, indicating when you are uncertain or when you need to do further research.

To reinforce the value of ethical communication, you might want to think of yourself as a teacher. Ask yourself, "What have I learned from good teachers?" You know that good teachers have your best interests at heart. They go to great pains to make sure that you understand. They strive to be clear as they make abstract concepts concrete through excellent examples. They watch for your confusion and respond to it. They ask you questions to make sure you are following. They encourage you to apply what you are learning, and they give you plenty of chances to ask them questions. They would never lie to you, mislead you, or in any way knowingly deceive you. Striving for this degree of integrity lies at the heart of effective and ethical informative speaking.

FRAME OF REFERENCE

Audiences must be engaged emotionally to be persuaded. The ethical speaker has the good of the audience in mind when presenting thoughtful, moving arguments.

Go to **Next Step: Ethics and Informative Speaking** in **Lesson 9** of the **VideoLab** CD-ROM and assess your understanding of ethical considerations.

CONNECTING TO THE NET

As you can see, an informative speech always seeks to gain audience understanding. A good speaker knows that success depends in part on how much listeners feel involved in the topic. Go to: **http://college.hmco.com/communication/andrews/public_speaking/2e/students/** and click on *Connecting to the Net.* From there, follow the link to Informative Speaking. There you will find an informative speech that you can examine to see how well it measures up to the standards we have discussed in this chapter.

SPOTLIGHT ON... **Getting Listeners Involved**

From an Interview with Mike Bryson, HIV Educator

Whenever I make a presentation, I like to interact a lot with the audience. I tell them from the beginning that I hope they'll ask me questions—and I stop a lot and ask them what questions they have on their minds. Since I am talking about HIV-related issues, sometimes people are uncomfortable. They may find it hard to ask questions—to be singled out in any way. But I am patient and I keep on encouraging them to ask. I want them to set the agenda for my presentation because I have no way of knowing what their concerns are unless they tell me. I want to talk about what they want to hear. If they help me by guiding me, I can do that. I tell them this and eventually most audiences come through. When they do, then we really start to communicate.

SUMMARY

Informative speeches are commonly made in diverse business, professional, and classroom settings. The informative speaker aims at helping listeners understand. Some speakers do this by sharing ideas and information, others through shaping listeners' perceptions, and still others by articulating alternatives. Informative speeches may describe, demonstrate, explain, or report on some process, problem, or phenomenon of interest.

Various organizational strategies are available for arranging informative speeches. Speakers can use a chronological, sequential, spatial, categorical, causal, or problem-solution pattern depending on the speech's specific purpose. Most informative speeches can be approached in a variety of ways.

Every informative speaker must concern himself or herself with listener learning. Unfortunately not all listeners are intrinsically motivated to learn. If listeners are resentful, bored, or simply not convinced that they need to know what is being discussed, they can present real challenges for the speaker.

Even so, most listeners' attitudes can change, and many will improve if the speaker shows how ideas and information are relevant, useful, novel, and important, and if he or she uses presentational, stylistic, and content variety while delivering the speech.

The informative speaker should think about the learning process and strive to help listeners acquire information. Learning is more likely to take place if the speaker limits the number of details, paces himself or herself carefully, speaks clearly, uses restatement and repetition, and provides visual reinforcement. Audience members should also be given the chance to ask questions. The effective speaker will think of ways to actively engage the audience and to assess how much listeners have learned, if possible.

Finally, the ethical informative speaker will speak with accuracy and honesty. He or she will use reputable sources, openly acknowledge any existing bias, present alternatives in a fair-minded manner, and encourage listeners to ask questions if they have doubts or confusion. Informative speakers may want to use excellent teachers they have known as role models.

QUESTIONS FOR REVIEW AND REFLECTION

1. What is the overarching purpose of an informative speech? What are the three functions of informative speeches discussed in this chapter? Describe special issues and challenges associated with each.
2. What are some topics that might be appropriate for a speech of description? How important are visual aids to this kind of speech?
3. What is the difference between giving an informative speech that is geared toward understanding and giving a speech geared toward application?
4. What are some of the key points you will probably want to address in giving a speech of explanation?

5. Think of one context in which a student might be called on to give an informative oral report. What would be the keys to success in this situation?
6. Describe the role of listener motivation in the context of an informative speaking occasion.
7. What are some ways that speakers can make their ideas and information interesting to listeners? Which are the most important and why? Can you think of other ways of capturing the audience's attention?
8. The informative speaker's challenge is to help listeners learn. What are some techniques for doing this? Can you think of other ways to help that are not listed in the book?
9. As a public speaking student, when you are asked to make an informative speech, how will you make the audience believe that you are knowledgeable about your topic?
10. Choose a topic that you think would work well with each of the following organizational patterns: chronological, categorical, and problem-solution. List the topic and pattern, then justify your choice.
11. When you listen to someone make an informative presentation, how do you determine whether he or she is communicating ethically?

ENDNOTES

1. Lois Burke et al., *A Cornucopia of Strategies for Working with LD and ADD Students* (Columbus, Ohio: Ohio State University Office for Disability Services, 1999).
2. Laura J. Gurak, *Oral Presentations for Technical Communication* (Boston: Allyn & Bacon, 2000).
3. For a discussion of retention, see Robert L. Greene, *Human Memory: Paradigms and Paradoxes* (Hillsdale, N.J.: Erlbaum, 1992).
4. Abraham Maslow, *Motivation and Personality* (New York: Harper & Row, 1954).
5. See Jane Blankenship, *A Sense of Style* (Belmont, Calif.: Dickenson Publishing Company, 1968); Pamela J. Cooper, *Communication for the Classroom Teacher,* 5th ed. (Scottsdale, Ariz.: Gorsuch Scarisbrick, 1995); and James C. McCroskey, *An Introduction to Rhetorical Communication,* 7th ed. (Boston: Allyn & Bacon, 1997).
6. See, for example, Joan Middendorf and Alan Kalish, "The 'Change-up' Lectures," *National Teaching and Learning Forum* 5 (1996): 1–4; and Wilbert J. McKeachie, "Improving Lectures by Understanding Students' Information Processing," in *New Directions for Teaching and Learning: Learning, Cognition, and College Teaching,* ed. Wilbert J. McKeachie (San Francisco: Jossey-Bass, 1980).

The following informative speech was given by a student at a speaking contest at Ball State University in Muncie, Indiana. It contains extensive material on tissue engineering, a subject with which most audiences would not be familiar. Note the way Amy organizes the speech and develops ideas to promote audience understanding.

The Mouse That Heard

Amy Carpenter

The speech begins with a familiar reference followed by a statement designed to arouse interest and gain attention.

You've heard of the mouse that roared? Well, the mouse that *heard* has roared through the medical community. Never before had a body appendage been grown outside its natural surroundings until scientists at the University of Massachusetts and MIT were able to grow a human ear on the back of a little mouse.

Amy introduces the term *tissue engineering* and defines it. Then she stresses the significance of this research with testimony from an authority and statistical information.

The MIT mouse displayed the most noticeable of advances in a new medical field of tissue engineering. Tissue engineering, as defined by the magazine *Blood Weekly,* is a new line of research aimed at replacing body parts injured by disease, accidents, or birth defects by growing tissue in a laboratory until sufficiently developed to be transplanted back into the body. Gayle K. Knotten, Chief Scientist at Advance Tissue Sciences, notes that there is a tremendous need out there for transplantable organs and tissues, and people are only beginning to realize the potential for tissue engineering. In fact, as *Science News* reported, there are about 1.5 million Americans on waiting lists for donated tissues and organs today.

The transition to the body of the speech contains a brief preview of Amy's main ideas.

So to realize how you can benefit from our mutant mouse, we must first define what tissue engineering is, then we can look into what benefits are currently being derived from this technology, and finally we can probe into the future applications of this "body" of research.

In explaining what tissue engineering is, Amy first gives a technical definition and then restates it in simpler terms. She introduces the analogy to scaffolding that is used by experts and adds a common example of this analogy as she describes the work done on the Statue of Liberty.

To begin we must first examine what tissue engineering is and how it works. *Biomedical Materials* defines tissue engineering as "a manipulation of artificial implants, laboratory-grown tissues or cells, aimed at replacing or supporting the function of damaged or injured body parts." Basically, this says that it repairs those tissues that were once thought of as irreparable. This technology draws concepts from transplantation science, bioengineering, and genetic engineering to focus on the repairing and replacement of body tissue by controlling the cellular growth and development. Robert Langer, Chemical Engineer at MIT, explains that "the idea was to take biodegradable polymers, make scaffolding out of them, then grow that tissue on the scaffolding. As the scaffolding disappears, the tissue then would be ready to be implanted into the body." *Biomaterials* further explains, "Biodegradable plastics were crafted by computer-aided design into scaffolding beds which mimic the structure or in some cases the entire organ. As the cells divide and assemble, the scaffolding eventually disappears leaving behind only the new tissue to be transplanted into the body." This process is very similar to building construction. Take, for example, the facelift that was given to the Statue of Liberty. The scaffolding was set up to place a new layer of "tissue" onto the Statue. Once that tissue was in place, the scaffolding eventually came down, leaving behind only a fresh-looking Lady of Liberty.

Well, the next question then would be "wouldn't the tissue be rejected by the body?" This is where the process differs from the past. In previous attempts at tissue engineering, the tissue was grown *inside* of the body, where it received messages from the immune system inhibiting its growth. But when grown outside of the body, the tissue doesn't receive these messages and instead grows in a healthy environment. Ross Tubo, Chief Scientist at Ginseng Tissue Repair, explained it this way: "When transplanted back into the body, [the tissues] say, 'I recognize the neighborhood and now I'm going to build the house where I used to live.'"

Amy anticipates a question that might logically arise at this point as she elaborates on how the process works. She shows how the present process differs from the past, and, to further promote understanding, she quotes an expert source who uses an analogy to a common experience.

So how is this technology for transplant engineering being used?

A rhetorical question provides a transition to the next point.

This technology has already been used to grow cartilage, liver, ligament, muscle, and bone matter. In fact, according to *Chemical and Engineering News*, "The availability of having large quantities of transplantable tissues and organs along with the ability to elude the destructive power of a patient's immune system would have tremendous impact in improving health." In fact, the FDA is currently getting ready to approve this technique for the growth of cartilage and for the treatment of diabetes. According to *Blood Weekly*, doctors at Ginseng Tissue Repair were able to collect several donations of cartilage from different patients. From these donations, GTR grew larger amounts of cartilage, transplanted it back into the original donors, and deemed it as a successful treatment. Now lots of breakthroughs are being made with cartilage.

Here Amy develops the second point that she previewed in the introduction, then presents benefits of tissue engineering by offering specific examples taken from reliable sources.

Breakthroughs are also being made with the treatment of diabetes. William L. Chick of Biohybrid Technology has been able to engineer injectable insulin-producing cells that act just like a miniature pancreas. The treatment involves taking insulin cells from pigs, placing them into a capsule, then placing that capsule into the abdomen of the patient. The capsule eventually dissolves, leaving behind only the pancreatic matter to react with the body and produce insulin as needed. As Chick further notes in an interview with *Science* magazine, "This is a live-in, drug-delivery system. Each cell has a chemical mechanism which continuously monitors the blood glucose level only allowing enough insulin to be released to keep that blood sugar within its normal range. This is a much better system than continually injecting yourself with insulin." Currently, these cells are living from six months to a year, making a bi-yearly booster a necessity. Human trials have already begun at the University of Minnesota and if all goes well, 2.3 million Americans will be released from the encumbrance of life-style restrictions.

An extended specific example explaining how the process helps treat diabetes further develops Amy's point that this process is producing substantial benefits.

Tissue engineering, then, is already proving very valuable in the treatment of certain diseases. But what about the future?

Again, she uses a rhetorical question as a transition to her next point.

Pancreatic matter and cartilage are only the beginning. Eventually, entire organs will be engineered and there are several projects currently in the works. These include the construction of a liver, a heart valve, and a woman's breast.

Addressing the future, Amy presents her main idea: that entire organs will be engineered in the future. She lists three examples, each of which she will develop as a subpoint.

According to the *BBI Newsletter*, Cedars Sinai Hospital in Los Angeles have forged a liver. They've taken beads coated with collagen, placed liver cells into them, then run the blood of a patient through these beads until a traditional transplant could be performed. Some similarly engineered livers have already been transplanted into animals, but human trials remain a few years off.

Research progress made on liver construction is her first example of what's in store for the future.

Now while a liver's being constructed, breakthroughs are being made in the construction of a heart valve. C. K. Brewer, along with colleagues at the Harvard Medical School, has been able to create a heart valve leaflet which resembled the original material. When transplanted into the heart of a donor lamb, the leaflet functioned normally. Now the leaflet is the smallest function of the heart valve; therefore, theoretically constructing not only the entire

Her next example details progress made in constructing a heart valve.

valve, but the entire heart, should be possible. As Brewer observed in an article in *Popular Science,* "Conceptually, use of valves made from your own tissue would be more favorable than the most currently used state of the art replacements"—basically saying that tissue and organs made from your own cells would be more favorable and healthier for your body.

The third example explains breakthroughs in breast construction. Note that in all of these examples, Amy cites the credible sources from which she has drawn her examples.

And finally, breakthroughs are being made in the construction of a woman's breast. Each year 250,000 women suffer the devastating trauma of losing a breast to cancer. But Dr. David Moony of the University of Michigan along with Dr. James Martin of the Carolina Medical School have been able to take a woman's breast tissue and place it onto a scaffolding that has been molded into a realistic shape. As the tissue grows, the scaffolding would then be placed into the woman's body to finish growing in stages. As Moony told *Clinical Plastic Surgery,* "Generating a three-dimensional breast is difficult because the growth of the fatty tissue which makes up the breast isn't well understood." But doctors are hopeful to have an application within the next three years.

The conclusion briefly sums up the significance of the topic and the major points covered, and it makes a quick reference that connects the conclusion with the introduction.

The growing potential of tissue engineering promises great things for accident and injury victims and that list of 1.5 million Americans. By understanding what tissue engineering is, how it works, what benefits are currently being derived, and the future applications, we now have a better understanding of the impact this technology will have on human life. Now obviously we won't be growing ears out of our backs, but the mouse that heard has brought together concepts from transplantation, bioengineering, and genetic engineering to make a technology which truly roars.

The Persuasive Process

15

CHAPTER OBJECTIVES

After reading this chapter, you should be able to

1. **understand the kinds of persuasive issues.**
2. **formulate speech purposes that call for specific persuasive responses.**
3. **apply organizational strategies appropriate to persuasion.**
4. **find and use materials that will engage listeners' emotions.**
5. **understand and apply ethical guidelines in choosing persuasive appeals.**

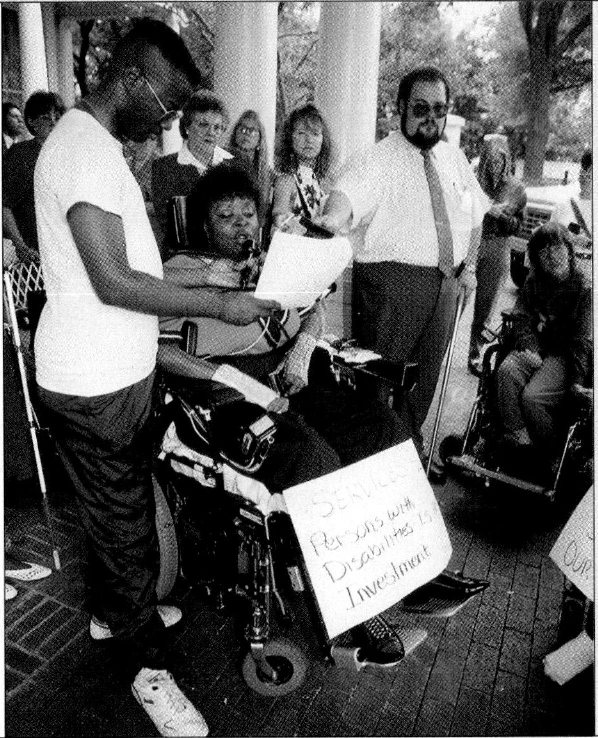

CHAPTER SURVEY

What Is Persuasion?

Persuasive Issues

Persuasive Purposes

Organizational Strategies in Persuasion

Appealing to Audience Emotions

A student urges his best friend to take a study break and come with him to a movie. A public health nurse goes to an elementary school to talk about drug use. A lawyer prepares to sum up the facts in the case by weaving them into a story she hopes the jury will find convincing. The president of the United States goes before a national television audience to urge support for the Gulf War. In everyday events and momentous undertakings, for average people and for world leaders, persuasion—attempts to influence the feelings, beliefs, or actions of others—plays a major role.

Persuasion permeates our lives. What to eat and wear, where to travel, what school to attend, how to vote—countless decisions are made on the basis of messages we receive, process, and act on. In situations ordinary and extraordinary, we find ourselves either the targets or the initiators of persuasion.

To test your skills and expand your understanding of the persuasive process, go to **Lesson 9** of the **VideoLab** CD-ROM and walk through the videos, exercises, and tips provided.

WHAT IS PERSUASION?

How we are persuaded is a question that has been studied by students of communication for centuries. The Greek philosopher Aristotle suggested that there are three principal ways in which things are proven

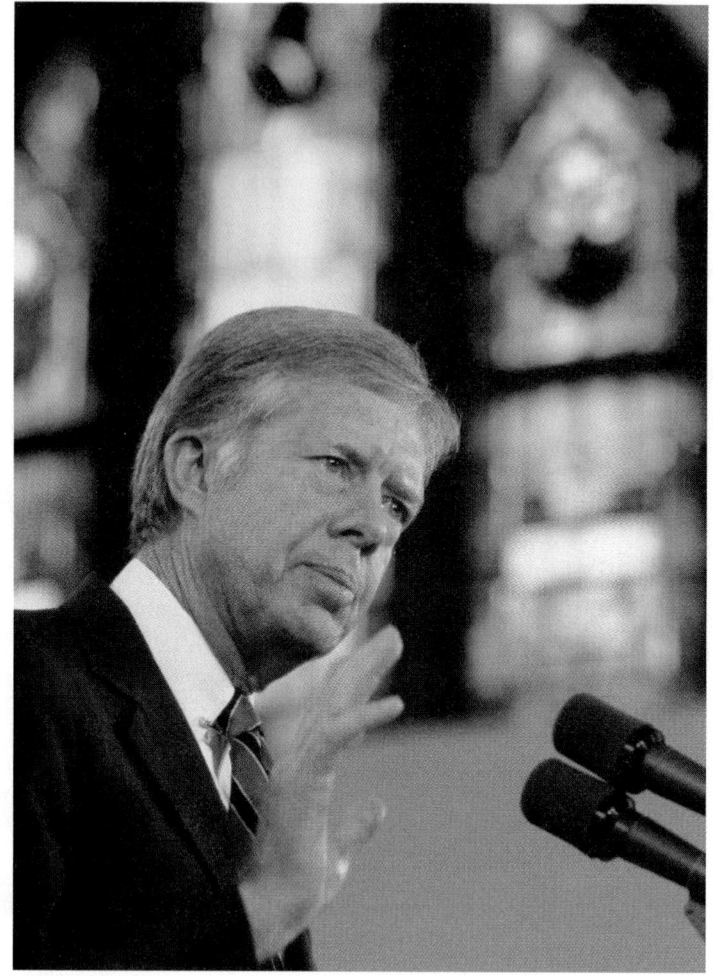

Former President Jimmy Carter has earned a reputation as a caring humanitarian. In 2002, Carter was awarded the Nobel Peace Prize. This strong ethos, when coupled with reasoned argument and emotional appeals, can produce a powerful persuasive message. (Wally McNarnee/Corbis)

ethos the audience's perceptions of a speaker's character, intelligence, and good will

pathos emotional content that influences our beliefs or actions

logos logical content that influences our beliefs or actions

to us. These "proofs" are usually referred to as **ethos** or ethical proof, **pathos** or emotional proof, and **logos** or logical proof. We are often persuaded to believe something or to take some action because of the following:

- We especially trust or have confidence in the person who is trying to persuade us. This person's *ethos* influences us. (We discussed ethos in detail in Chapter 6.)
- We recognize how what the speaker proposes will meet our needs and identify emotionally with the course of action proposed. How *pathos* functions persuasively is addressed in this chapter.
- We find the speaker's arguments sensible and compelling. How *logos* strengthens a speaker's ability to persuade is the subject of Chapter 16.

These three modes of proof are not mutually exclusive; persuasion rarely depends on ethos, pathos, or logos alone. A particular idea or assertion made by a speaker may appeal to listeners logically and emotionally at the same time. What we hope to do in this and the following chapter is to explain emotional and logical appeals, recognizing that they work together to promote effective persuasion. We begin our discussion of persuasion by investigating the kinds of issues that call for persuasion.

After viewing the video clips in **Drill 9.4: Aristotle's Persuasive Proofs** on the **VideoLab** CD-ROM, complete the quiz to test your understanding of persuasive proofs.

PERSUASIVE ISSUES

Preview Persuasive issues revolve around questions of fact (what is true), definition (what things mean), cause (why things happen and with what results), value (whether things are good or bad), and policy (what should be done in the future).

Is That the Truth?

Issues of fact address the question of what is true. Normally we use the word *fact* to describe something that is established without discussion—something that can be determined by simply consulting the proper reference, such as looking at a thermometer to see what the temperature is or checking the *TV Guide* to find out what time our favorite TV program begins. These "facts" are not what we seek to persuade other people about. When faced with a controversial issue, however, the "facts" are not likely to be proven as absolutely true or false. The persuasive speaker aims for listeners to accept her or his case as probably true.

issues of fact disagreement about what is or is not true

This kind of persuasive issue is one that we typically encounter. When a speaker asserts that HMOs do not provide adequate health care, the audience will ask whether that is true, and it is up to the speaker to prove that it probably is. So, too, listeners will ask, "Is that a fact?" when a speaker tells them that gays in the military are bad for discipline, that social security will yield better results if it is privatized, or that students who work part-time generally do better in school than those who don't work at all.

What Does That Mean?

Issues of definition center on the meaning of conceptions or terms that may be understood differently by different listeners. Often a speaker wants listeners to see things from a new perspective. A city council, for example, once debated a proposed zoning ordinance prescribing that houses in one area of town could be occupied only by "single families." The ordinance seemed designed to prevent landlords from renting houses in this particular neighborhood to groups of students. Much of the debate, however, revolved around the meaning of *family*. Some speakers at the public hearing tried to convince the council members that *family* should mean a married couple and their children, while others argued that such a definition was much too restrictive in today's society. All of these conflicting speakers were trying to persuade their audience that their definition of *family* was the best one. In many criminal trials, to cite another common example, the issue of fact (Did the defendant commit the crime?) is secondary to the issue of definition (He caused the death of the victim, but was his act self-defense, manslaughter, or murder?).

issues of definition disagreement about what something means

Why Did That Happen, and What Will Result?

issues of cause disagreement about what prompted something to transpire or is likely to transpire

Issues of cause raise questions of how things have come about as well as what is likely to happen because of events transpiring now. Speakers consider problems or trends and try to persuade listeners that these events—either undesirable or desirable—have their origins in situations that either can be changed or should be perpetuated. If something is wrong (or right), how did it get that way? If we continue on our present course, what will happen to us?

Political candidates seeking reelection, for example, attempt to persuade voters that good economic times are the result of policies they have pursued. Politicians out of power try to persuade audiences that unwanted events—the rise in the crime rate, for example—have been caused by elected officials who hold office. Interest rates are raised based on the assertion that doing so will result in reduced inflation. Some would argue that membership in a fraternity or sorority will lead to increased chances of success in the future, while others would persuade us that fraternities promote a lifestyle that results in antisocial behavior. These are all cases in which the issue centers on certain actions bringing about certain effects.

Is This Good or Bad?

issues of value disagreement about whether something is good or bad

Issues of value focus on moral or ethical issues that touch on what we believe and what we esteem. Most of us strive to do the right thing. We want to be good people and live up to our ideals. Being human, we often fail. But sometimes we can't make up our minds whether certain actions fit with our values or violate them; sometimes we don't realize that things we do contradict what we say and believe. Urging listeners to embrace certain values or to live up to ones they already hold is often the role of the persuasive speaker.

Speakers for animal rights, for example, attempt to persuade their audiences that the cruel treatment of animals for purposes of experimentation is morally wrong. Those opposed to affirmative action contend that it violates our commitment to equal treatment under the law. Pornography debates often bring about conflicting value issues: on one side, people assert that pornography is morally reprehensible because it degrades women; on the other side, people argue that to censor pornography is to attack freedom of speech, one of our most cherished political values.

Speakers who address issues of value address the tough questions of which values are more important or relevant in a given situation, what standards we use to judge what is good and bad, and to what authorities we might turn for guidance.

KEEP IN MIND 15.1

Different Types of Persuasive Issues

- *Issues of fact* answer the question, Is that the truth?
- *Issues of definition* answer the question, What does that mean?
- *Issues of cause* answer the question, Why did that happen, and what will result?
- *Issues of value* answer the question, Is this good or bad?
- *Issues of policy* answer the question, What are we going to do?

What Are We Going to Do?

issues of policy disagreement about what should be done

Issues of policy have to do with our actions in the future: there is something wrong in our world, and we need to correct it; we have a problem that needs to be solved; there is danger ahead that must be avoided, tendencies in society

Issues of policy focus on courses of action that may be taken in the future. When considering such issues, Congressional committees routinely hold hearings in which advocates for various solutions to problems are heard.
(Paul Conklin/PhotoEdit)

that are potentially harmful. In such instances, speakers address future courses of action by urging specific policies.

Since many see health care for the poor and the elderly as a serious problem, one might argue that universal health care must be achieved in the United States within the next decade, or that Medicare be replaced with a private health care system. A persuader concerned with the spread of AIDS might want to convince listeners that the wealthy nations should invest significant resources to stop the AIDS pandemic in Africa. A person who is worried about the effects of television on children might wish to argue that strict regulations concerning children's programming be adopted by the federal government.

Once you have decided on the issue you want to address in your speech, you have created a tentative thesis statement. Now your task is to decide precisely how you want your audience to react. You need to devise a specific purpose for your speech that will spell out the response you want to evoke.

Go to **Drill 9.2: Identifying Persuasive Issues** on the **VideoLab** CD-ROM and complete the quiz that asks you to identify different kinds of issues or questions that might be addressed in persuasive speeches.

PERSUASIVE PURPOSES

Preview Persuasive speaking aims at influencing the feelings, thoughts, and behavior of listeners by eliciting strong feelings, gaining agreement, or inducing action.

Speeches to Stimulate

In a **speech to stimulate**, you want to get your audience to feel more strongly about something with which they might already be in agreement. You want to reinforce or strengthen ideas or beliefs that listeners already have rather than create new beliefs.

speech to stimulate a speech intended to reinforce ideas and beliefs already held by the audience and to intensify their feelings

There are times when public speakers hope to overcome apathy or to promote involvement or awareness in their listeners. All of us can think of ideas or

FRAME OF REFERENCE

In a speech to actuate, the speaker hopes to get listeners to take specific action. Actively involved, responsive listeners are more likely to act on the speaker's recommendations.

principles that we would not object to but that don't seem to make much difference in our thoughts or actions. We may subscribe to political convictions, religious beliefs, or moral values, but not always have them uppermost in our minds. In such instances, speakers will likely concern themselves with issues of value. Many people, for example, are nominal Democrats or Republicans, yet they would be unable to identify their party's candidates for state or local offices, they don't seem to care very much which party wins, and they might not even vote at all.

The speaker who would like all the Democrats or all the Republicans to support the party (by working door to door, giving money, or voting) knows that people must feel personal motivation before they will be prepared to give such support. Part of the total communication in a political campaign, therefore, is aimed at getting those who already agree with the party's positions and candidates to feel strongly about their political allegiance by emphasizing common values. Speeches to stimulate play an important role in firing up the party faithful.

There are many other examples. Religious speakers often try to get audiences to feel more strongly that the principles to which they may pay lip service are important to their lives. The teacher who attempts to get students (who are already committed to furthering their education) to feel more strongly that completing their degree is essential, the president of a campus organization who tries to create more enthusiasm among members for the group's goals, and the basketball coach who addresses fans are all speaking to stimulate. Communication with the aim of reinforcing existing feelings or beliefs is based on the assumption that the listener and the speaker are already in substantial agreement. The coals are glowing, but they need to be fanned if they are to burst into flame.

One student in a public speaking class chose the topic "Ways to Improve Higher Education." She believed that the audience, though apathetic, would agree with her ideas, so she gave a speech to reinforce existing beliefs. Seeing her topic as a policy issue, she formulated the thesis, "To maintain a well-educated society, costs of higher education must be kept low." Her specific purpose was, "I want my audience to feel more strongly that the costs of higher education must be kept as low as possible." This purpose stated what the speaker hoped the audience would feel when she finished speaking. It was limited in scope and could be handled within the confines of the situation.

Speeches to stimulate often aim at creating a mood or feeling that might influence the atmosphere in which other forms of persuasion later occur. When President Bill Clinton gave his first inaugural address in 1993, he did not outline specific legislative initiatives or make concrete proposals for action. Rather he attempted to create a positive mood that would serve as a backdrop for actions that he would later propose. Emphasizing shared values, the new president sought, as most presidents do in inaugural addresses,[1] to underscore our common determination to solve tough problems and to cooperate in bringing about necessary change. He said,

> Though our challenges are fearsome, so are our strengths. Americans have ever been a restless, questing, hopeful people, and we must bring to our task today the vision and will of those who came before us. From our Revolution, to the Civil War, to the Great Depression, to the civil rights movement, our people have always mustered the determination to construct from these crises the pillars of history.

PORTFOLIO 15.1

Providing a Boost

Are there any beliefs, feelings, or values that you and the class likely hold but that are in need of a boost? For example, do Americans have the same work ethic that helped to build our nation into one of the greatest countries of all time?

Identify any such areas that could use a boost and sketch out your ideas for a speech that would stimulate a renewal. Discuss with your instructor any possibilities you'd like to pursue as a speech to the class.

> Thomas Jefferson believed that to preserve the foundations of our nation we would need dramatic change from time to time. Well, my fellow Americans, this is our time. Let us embrace it.
>
> Our democracy must be not only the envy of the world but the engine of our own renewal. There is nothing wrong with America that cannot be cured by what is right with America. And so today we pledge an end to the era of deadlock and drift, and a new season of American renewal has begun.[2]

Speeches to stimulate are often the forerunners of persuasive efforts to convince or actuate. They must intensify feelings or reinforce existing predispositions so that listeners are made aware of the relevance and importance of the beliefs, feelings, and values they already hold.

The Speech to Stimulate

The speech to stimulate

- encourages listeners to feel more strongly.
- reinforces existing ideas and beliefs.
- helps the audience to overcome apathy.

Speeches to Convince

In a **speech to convince**, you aim to secure the agreement of your listeners. We have all at times wanted someone to agree with our point of view. The issue might be one of fact, such as whether Michigan or Ohio State plays the toughest football schedule. It might be an issue of value, such as whether a recent Woody Allen film is as innovative as the critics say it is. It could be an issue of policy, such as when one tries to convince listeners that the battered woman syndrome is a legitimate legal defense. Whatever the case, we have all had experience with this kind of persuasion.

speech to convince a persuasive speech in which the speaker attempts to secure audience agreement with his or her point of view

That does not mean, of course, that we all know how to convince others. Sometimes we seem to succeed, and sometimes we don't. Although the study of persuasion does not assure anyone of success, it does increase our chances of being effective. One way to give ourselves a better chance of success is to identify the precise persuasive goal that we have in mind. This goal, like all goals in communication, is shaped by the situation.

Take, for example, a persistent issue of policy. In 1993, the opening days of the Clinton administration, the new president proposed to lift the ban on homosexuals serving in the military. Faced with stiff resistance from the Joint Chiefs of Staff, some powerful members of Clinton's own party in Congress, and the Republican opposition, the president agreed to some temporary measures and a waiting period during which congressional hearings would be held. During that time, the American people could be "educated" on the issue. Both sides hoped to convince Americans that one or the other course was the right one to pursue. In Congress and throughout the various media forums open to advocates, they sought to gain popular agreement with their position. In this instance, the American people were not really called on to take direct action, since the government and the military would have to do that. But the weight of popular agreement with one side or the other would serve as a powerful and persuasive inducement to act. In this particular rhetorical situation, messages designed to gain agreement were most appropriate.

It is important to understand what is reasonable and possible to accomplish in a persuasive speech. Dramatic shifts of opinion and ideas are very rare. Sometimes it is better to try a very small step that can be taken than to attempt a large one that is doomed to falter. Consider, for example, the student who came up with this specific purpose:

- I want my audience to agree that vehicles with internal combustion engines that burn fossil fuels should be banned from our roadways and only zero emission vehicles, such as electric cars, should be allowed.

PORTFOLIO 15.2

Can We Agree?

Do you have a particular view on something that may not be shared by your classmates? Might you be able to get them to accept your point of view? List any plausible topics for a speech to convince. You may wish to discuss a topic with your instructor.

Such a speaking purpose would have been very difficult to accomplish in one relatively short speech. So he rethought his projected topic and came up with an issue of fact and an issue of policy, which he turned into two, more limited persuasive goals:

- I want my audience to agree that electric-powered vehicles are more environmentally friendly.
- I want my audience to agree that internal combustion engines that burn fossil fuels threaten our environment.

All speech purposes should be stated as the desired audience response, so you should think of the speech to convince in terms of *gaining agreement from listeners on a specific point.* If you set out "to persuade my audience about nuclear power," you haven't focused on the specific response you want. Consider the wide range of options:

- I want my audience to agree that nuclear power should be attempted on a much larger scale than at present.
- I want my audience to agree that nuclear power should be rejected as a viable energy alternative.
- I want my audience to agree that the development of nuclear power should be given first priority in our national energy conservation program.

It is only when you have made a clear choice as to the issue you wish to address, translated this issue into a specific purpose, and developed a thesis statement that you can then go on to develop the speech.

campaign a series of messages aimed at moving listeners closer to a specific position or course of action

Many successful persuasive efforts are really part of an overall **campaign**—a series of persuasive messages aimed at moving listeners toward a specific position or course of action. Only rarely does a single persuasive message do much to move listeners significantly. More typically, as listeners attend to a series of messages, they are more likely to be persuaded than if they are exposed to an isolated persuasive message. A speech to convince, then, may not explicitly ask for direct action but will often aim at influencing listeners' perceptions so as to dispose them to take certain actions.

KEEP IN MIND 15.3

The Speech to Convince

The speech to convince

- seeks to gain agreement from the audience.
- is focused on a realistic, specific purpose.
- is often part of a persuasive campaign.

Speeches to Actuate

speech to actuate a persuasive speech in which the speaker attempts to get the audience to take specific, overt action

In a **speech to actuate**, you want your audience to take direct, observable action. Every day we encounter appeals, pleas, suggestions, and demands that we act in certain ways. Politicians exhort us to get out and vote. Health experts tell us to eat right and exercise. Advertisers entice us to purchase their products and services. Girl Scouts ask us to buy their cookies.

Normally, persuasion has action as its ultimate goal. Political office-seekers give speeches and buy radio and television commercials hoping to convince electors of the soundness of the candidates' positions and motivate citizens to vote. (Associated Press)

All persuasive speeches have some sort of action as the ultimate goal. This action may be a change of feeling or perception or a more perceptive activity. But everyone who plans a speech to actuate has a very definite and concrete goal in mind: a direct action that needs to be taken. Any response short of the requested action does not accomplish the speaker's goal.

Suppose, for example, that you are particularly eager to see a certain candidate elected to the state legislature. Your friend, whom you know to be not particularly partisan, is persuadable. After spending considerable time trying to get your friend to commit himself to your candidate, and after sensing that you have finally gained the agreement of your friend, you will be disappointed to hear him say, "Well, I guess you're right. Of course, I can't vote anyway because I never registered." Agreement, though somewhat satisfying, isn't all that you had in mind—you wanted a vote that would count in the election.

In planning a speech to actuate, you need to determine the precise action that you wish to see listeners take. If your topic is "Volunteerism," for example, here are some possible reactions you might want:

- I want my audience to pledge to spend two hours a week as a volunteer.
- I want my audience to join the National Association of Volunteer Workers.
- I want my audience to help serve at least one meal this month at the Community Kitchen.

Clearly, these are all different purposes, yet all reflect the speaker's intention to aim for direct, clearly specified, action. You will not be happy if the audience only learns something about the role of volunteers in charitable organizations or if they merely agree that volunteers are important.

The speech to actuate yields tangible results. You know that you have not done well if you ask twenty people to make sizable donations and you end up

SPOTLIGHT ON... **Inducing Action**

Will You Give Blood?

Early in our research careers we conducted a study in which we assembled a group of people who had all indicated rather strong negative attitudes toward the idea of giving blood to the Red Cross. We subsequently asked them to listen to a powerful persuasive speech, delivered by a young hemophiliac who made a poignant plea for blood donations.

Immediately following the speech, we administered another attitude questionnaire. Interestingly enough, impressive reversals in attitude seemed to have occurred. In fact, over 70 percent of those previously opposed to giving blood now indicated that they *would* donate blood if given the opportunity! Yet, when those same individuals were confronted with official Red Cross blood donation sign-up cards (as soon as the attitude questionnaires were collected), informed that the Bloodmobile would be in town during the following month, and told that transportation would be provided to and from the Bloodmobile, *nearly 80 percent* of those with "changed" attitudes declined to commit themselves to the *action* of donating blood. We concluded from this study that moving listeners is difficult; inspiring them to act is even more demanding.

Patricia Hayes Andrews and John E. Baird, Jr., *Communication for Business and the Professions,* 6th ed. (Madison, Wis.: Brown & Benchmark, 1995), pp. 359–360.

PORTFOLIO 15.3

Let's Do It!

Is there a particular action you'd like to influence your classmates to take? What precisely is that action? Is it feasible? How can you make it easy for them to do as you request? Sketch out your ideas for a possible speech to actuate and discuss it with your instructor.

with only two dollars. One cannot always tell whether listeners will actually do what is hoped for, but the speech to actuate is not one that aims only for a mental or emotional response.

Taking action often demands that listeners exert energy, give up time, or spend money. If listeners are to respond by actually doing something, they must feel that the action is feasible, important, and, as much as possible, convenient. Students might consider it feasible to work two or three hours a week as a volunteer in a literacy program or at a halfway house, but they would likely consider it out of the question to participate in a program to help the homeless that requires them to miss six weeks of school and absorb travel and living expenses for that period.

A famous historical example of a successful speech to actuate is the reaction to Richard Nixon's "Checkers speech" in 1952. Faced with charges of maintaining an illegal secret campaign fund, Nixon went on television to plead his case to the nation. He began by denying the charges made and explaining the nature and uses of the campaign fund. But then he did something "unprecedented in the history of American politics"—he promised to give a complete financial history to the audience. Nixon concluded by asking viewers to write and send telegrams to the Republican National Committee supporting his retention as the party's vice-presidential nominee. The overwhelmingly positive response helped keep Nixon on the ticket.[3]

KEEP IN MIND 15.4

The Speech to Actuate

The speech to actuate

- aims for an overt, observable action from listeners.
- stresses the feasibility and importance of the proposed action.
- directs the audience toward the specific action.

As far as you can, you should also make it easy for listeners to take the action you're recommending. If you want listeners to write letters, you might distribute a sample letter with the mailing addresses of those to whom it should go. If you are urging the audience to volunteer with a particular agency, you ought to provide them with names and telephone numbers of contact people at the agency. If you are urging them to vote, you need to provide them with information (preferably written out and distributed) about polling places or procedures for

TABLE 15.1 Persuasive Purposes

Persuasive Purpose	Possible Topics	A Sample Specific Purpose
Speeches to stimulate reinforce existing attitudes and beliefs.	The Importance of an Education Our Most Basic Freedoms A Healthy Lifestyle Driving Responsibly High Tuition: You Can Make a Difference	I want my audience to feel more strongly that it is important to get a good education.
Speeches to convince seek to gain audience agreement.	Participate in the Political Process Peace Can Happen in the Middle East Year-Round Schooling Is Desirable Everyone Should Study Abroad for a Semester	I want my audience to agree that a portfolio system of grading is better than traditional grading systems.
Speeches to actuate get listeners to take action.	Volunteer Time to Promote Literacy Subscribe to the Campus Literary Magazine Buy Your Clothes at a Thrift Shop Start an Investment Club Join a Support Group for Working Students	I want my audience to attend the rally protesting tuition hikes.

obtaining an absentee ballot. No matter what the course of action intended, you should ask; "What can I do that will make it as easy as possible for listeners to do this?"

Since different audiences hold different values, some topics and types of speeches are more appropriate for certain audiences than for others. Some audiences may already accept as true certain ideas or beliefs, while other audiences are skeptical. In addition, more limited purposes are more likely to be accomplished than broad goals, a consideration that is critically important. Table 15.1 summarizes the three kinds of speeches discussed in this section and gives examples of topics for each type.

ORGANIZATIONAL STRATEGIES IN PERSUASION

Preview The basic organizational patterns discussed in Chapter 10 include several options for persuasive speeches. Some patterns, however, seem particularly suited to developing certain persuasive issues, and the pattern known as the motivated sequence is especially useful in moving listeners toward some ultimate action.

The organizational patterns described in Chapter 10 apply when organizing a persuasive speech. You may wish to review the organizational patterns—chronological, spatial, categorical, causal, and problem-solution—that were explained in detail in that chapter. Following are some suggestions for applying these patterns to speeches revolving around the various issues we have discussed.

Organizing Strategies for Issues of Fact

Issues of fact are usually developed categorically if you want to state your position and give reasons for supporting it. For example, suppose you wish to advocate increased telecommuting as a business strategy. The thesis posits an issue of fact: "Telecommuting has direct benefits for all involved." The specific purpose for your speech to convince would be: "I want my audience to agree that telecommuting benefits companies, employers, and the public." The main ideas, organized categorically, would enumerate the benefits to be derived.

I. Telecommuting increases the company's ability to recruit top people while reducing operating costs.

II. Employees who are telecommuters have more time at home and spend less money on work-related expenses.

III. If fewer people commuted to work each day, traffic congestion, air pollution, and the consumption of foreign oil would be reduced.

It is sometimes useful to employ the chronological pattern of organization to fit a particular issue of fact. The chronological pattern might serve you well, for example, if you wanted your audience to agree that the costs of proper medical care were excluding many people from such care. By showing the growing expenses and how this increase has affected groups over time, you could establish the fact at issue.

Organizing Strategies for Issues of Definition

Issues of definition are typically developed categorically as well. A categorical pattern that stresses comparison and contrast may be particularly well suited to definitional issues. Suppose, for example, that you want to argue that capital punishment is murder. That issue hinges on what you mean by murder. Your thesis is: "Capital punishment is indistinguishable from murder." Your specific purpose is: "I want my audience to agree that capital punishment is a form of murder." The main ideas, organized categorically, would emphasize comparisons between the two concepts in order to establish their similarity in meaning.

I. Murder occurs when one person or group kills another person, as does capital punishment.

II. Murder is premeditated, as is capital punishment.

III. Murder is against the law, as capital punishment violates the commandment "Thou shalt not kill."

The categorical pattern also could delineate criteria for establishing meaning. If, for example, you wish to argue that "racial profiling" is unjust, each main idea could describe a characteristic of "justice" in order to contrast the practice of racial profiling with these criteria.

Organizing Strategies for Issues of Cause

Obviously, the causal pattern works well with this kind of issue. Suppose you are concerned about the effects that the wave of mergers of large companies can have on the economy and believe that the monopolies will be harmful. Confronting this issue of cause, your thesis could be: "The economic consequences of monopolies will harm us as consumers." Your specific purpose for this speech to convince is: "I want my audience to agree that monopolies are harmful to them." Thus the main ideas would detail the effects of monopolies.

I. Monopolies make markets inefficient by supplying fewer products than are needed by consumers.

II. Monopolies intimidate entrepreneurs, reducing the chances that new companies will be formed.

III. Once a monopoly takes over a market, consumers are no longer assured of the quality of products and services.

You could also organize from effect to cause, depending on your topic. If, for example, you wish to examine the reasons for a lack of diversity at your school, you might go backward from this effect to seek causes such as high tuition, a lack of need-based scholarship, and a belief by minorities that they are unwelcome.

If you plan to approach your persuasive speech by using a cause-and-effect pattern, go to the **Online SpeechStudio** and use the **Outline Worksheet for a Cause-and-Effect Pattern** to help you construct your outline.

Once you have a good outline draft for your persuasive speech that is organized according to a cause-and-effect pattern, go to the **Online SpeechStudio** and assess your outline by completing the **Checklist for a Cause-and-Effect Pattern.**

Organizing Strategies for Issues of Value

Issues of value are often approached by reminding listeners of accepted standards of ethical judgment or behavior and then applying them to a given case. Take, for example, the question of euthanasia, sometimes called mercy killing. You might want to give a speech to convince based on the thesis, "The medical community should support euthanasia for terminally ill patients when it is in the patient's best interest and at the patient's request," and the specific purpose: "I want my audience to agree that the medical community should support euthanasia." The main ideas, organized categorically, would reflect the criteria for good medical care as applied to euthanasia.

I. Since medical care should aim to cure a patient, different procedures should apply when there is no cure.

II. Since medical care should try to ease suffering, the possibility of ending intense, uncontrollable pain by ending life should be considered.

III. Since medical professionals should honor the wishes of their patients, those patients who desire euthanasia should be allowed to make that decision themselves.

You could also organize a speech categorically, focusing on the reasons why something is good or bad. Take, for example, the concern many parents have about maintaining moral values in a technological society. You might develop a speech arguing that television has adverse psychological and intellectual effects on children by listing the reasons that too much TV viewing by children is bad (TV programming suggests that violence is a normal response, it sets no moral standards, it offers no intellectual challenges).

Organizing Strategies for Issues of Policy

Advocating courses of action for the future is a major persuasive goal. From how we should raise money to support a local organization to whether or not the United States should intervene in foreign disputes, we are constantly called on to make or support decisions that have the potential to influence the way we live our lives—in small or very significant ways. The way we organize such speeches can vary widely. Virtually every pattern of organization can be adapted to deal with policy questions.

A categorical pattern is appropriate in addressing most persuasive issues, and it can always be used when confronting policy questions. A student gave a speech on road rage in which his thesis was: "Road rage can be reduced if authorities take appropriate action." His specific purpose was: "I want my audience to agree that states can combat road rage through new programs and procedures." The main ideas for such a speech might be as follows:

I. Heavy traffic and increased stress contribute to road rage.

II. States can reduce road rage with educational programs that help motorists avoid becoming victims of it.

III. States can enact legislation that forces those involved in road rage incidents to undergo special training courses in anger management.

IV. States can enact harsh penalties that include significant jail terms for repeat offenders.

A very common organizational pattern used to develop policy questions is the problem-solution pattern. If, for example, children have been injured at a particular street crossing and you see this as a serious problem, you might wish to organize a speech that has as its thesis: "The installation of a traffic light will save lives. Your specific purpose would be: "I want my audience to agree that a traffic light should be installed at Hawthorne and Third Streets." Your main ideas would detail the problem, look at possible solutions, and defend a new traffic light as the best solution.

I. Pedestrians crossing Hawthorne Street at Third Street have sustained a variety of injuries that could have been fatal.

II. Efforts to slow traffic by installing a warning sign have not reduced the risks.

III. Putting in a speed bump will disrupt the flow of traffic, is a costly process, and will not provide a perfectly safe crossing for pedestrians.

IV. A traffic light is the only safe and sure solution to the problem.

The chronological pattern may be the best pattern to use when you want to review past actions to show the way we are headed in the future. If, for example, you wished to argue against U.S. intervention to help solve an international problem, you might review the limited success experienced over time in

Lebanon, Somalia, and Bosnia, leading to the conclusion that the effort was not worth the cost.

The causal pattern would be a good one to use if you wanted to show that the present policy will lead to undesirable results and must be changed. You might, for example, want to assert that welfare reform legislation has harmed those it was intended to help, describing significant aspects of the legislation and then showing that these provisions have resulted in more women and children below the poverty level, failure of job training to lead to skilled jobs, and the removal of the "safety net" for the truly needy.

The Motivated Sequence as an Organizing Strategy

A particularly effective sequence for persuasive speeches is the **motivated sequence.**[4] This pattern is a popular one for professional persuaders because it fits so well with the way we see and think about things. When you see an ad in a magazine or a commercial on television—maybe a picture of a person, a setting, or an unusual sight—it arouses your interest; it captures your attention or piques your curiosity. The ad suggests that something in your life could be changed: you could be thinner, you could make more of your life, or you could drive a car that would impress your friends. The commercial makes you vaguely dissatisfied. It then offers a product or service that will meet the need that the ad itself has created and helps you visualize the benefits of the product or service: maybe you can see yourself thirty pounds thinner, in front of a radar screen, or driving a flashy car. Finally, the ad hopes to move you to action: enroll in the weight-loss program, "be all that you can be," or get behind the wheel.

motivated sequence an organizational pattern for a persuasive speech that is based on psychological studies of what motivates human interest and behavior

After viewing the entire speech on milk additives, go to **Lesson 9 Next Step: Using Monroe's Motivated Sequence** on the **VideoLab** CD-ROM and take the quiz to better understand how an informative speech can be transformed into a persuasive one.

Once you have drafted your outline, go to the **Online SpeechStudio** and use the **Checklist for the Motivated Sequence Pattern** to evaluate how effectively you have used the motivated sequence.

This is a very popular organizational pattern with other speakers as well. It lends itself particularly well to speeches that hope to produce action in their listeners. In the previous section on purposes, we pointed out that reinforcing beliefs or gaining agreement may serve as a prelude to action: before you can get listeners to do something, they have to see its importance and be convinced that action is warranted. The motivated sequence helps speakers integrate these goals in a way designed to parallel the audience's thought patterns.

When using this pattern of organization, you go through five basic steps:

1. *Arouse:* capture the audience's attention and focus on a problem.
2. *Dissatisfy:* make them understand that this is a serious problem that needs their attention and action.
3. *Gratify:* tell them that it is within their power to remedy this situation.
4. *Visualize:* show them exactly how much they can improve the situation.
5. *Move:* appeal to them to take a specific action.

If you plan to develop your persuasive speech by using the motivated sequence, go to the **Online SpeechStudio** and use the **Outline Worksheet for the Motivated Sequence Pattern** as you construct your outline.

Suppose you are a personnel manager at a corporation, and you want your listeners to fund a program to address the problem of alcohol abuse in the company. Figure 15.1 traces how you might organize your remarks using the motivated sequence.

The motivated sequence works especially well when the topic demands both logical and emotional proof. This pattern allows you to engage the audience's emotions and urge them to act. It provides a balanced treatment of the problem and the solution, although you can choose to shorten the problem

FIGURE 15.1 Using the Motivated Sequence

1. Arouse

"Every morning he wakes up with an aching head, mild nausea, and a distinct feeling of remorse. He swears he is going to live his life differently today. He calls his supervisor and says he'll be a little late for work. His hands quivering, he sips some black coffee. If only his mind would clear! He needs to have a clear head at work! He looks at his bloodshot eyes and ruddy face. He wonders how many people know how much he drinks . . ."

2. Dissatisfy

"This is a sad story of one lonely man—an isolated case. Or is it? Actually, this story could be the story of many men and women in almost every organization—including our own. Over 8 million workers nationwide suffer from alcohol abuse. Earlier this year, our own company survey revealed that nearly 10 percent of our fellow workers are struggling with alcohol. Does this problem affect their happiness? Of course! Does it affect their productivity? You bet it does. Some believe that U.S. businesses lose hundreds of millions of dollars every year because of illnesses, mistakes, accidents, and depression attributable to alcohol and drug abuse. For us, here in Centerville, that loss likely totaled about 2 million dollars just last year! And the problem just keeps on growing . . ."

3. Gratify

"What can we do? Is there an affordable solution to this growing problem? The good news is "Yes, there certainly is!" Two years ago the J. Johnson Company in Chicago tried a new approach to combating alcoholism that cost only about $200,000 by the end of the first year. It involved counseling, support groups, health and fitness education, and dietary planning. It's a multi-dimensional approach to this old, old problem. And it's working. By the end of the first year, half of the 4,000 employees who had admitted to problems with alcohol at J. Johnson declared themselves to be alcohol-free. By the end of the second year, another 500 joined their ranks."

4. Visualize

"Can we model this program here in Centerville? I am confident we can. Since our company is smaller, we would need to invest about $100,000. We already have a facility—on the fifth floor—where several offices and a lounge stand unused. The relative isolation of this area is a real advantage. Besides that, we already have nearly a dozen people who have volunteered to help with organizing support groups and with dietary and other aspects of health education. If we can hire a director and slightly renovate the fifth floor, we'll be ready to go! Based on our survey, we have over 500 employees who want to do something about their alcohol problem and are waiting for a program to help them."

5. Move

"All we have to do is act. We have nearly a million dollars in our Educational and Support Initiatives Fund this year. I am asking for one tenth of that. With a relatively small investment, we could make a real difference in the lives of our employees. You can do something to make that lonely man with shaking hands regain his pride, his self-respect, and his productivity. I urge you to support this program—for the good of those who are suffering and for the welfare of us all."

Go to **Lesson 2's Screening Room** on the **VideoLab** CD-ROM. Does the speaker aim to stimulate, convince, or actuate? What organizational pattern does she use, and how effectively does she use it?

component if you think your audience is already aware of it. With the specific example given in the previous paragraph (alcohol abuse in the company), the challenge will likely be to convince the audience that a general problem of society is something that they should tackle because it is right and because they are more affected than they might imagine. Any speaker who uses this pattern must be very knowledgeable about the details of the solution being proposed.

If you plan to use a refutational pattern to organize your persuasive speech, go to the **Online SpeechStudio** and use the **Outline Worksheet for a Refutational Pattern** to assist you in constructing your outline.

Refutation as an Organizing Strategy

In persuasive situations, there are always varying points of view. What makes persuasion necessary is the fact that agreement does not exist. Often it is essential that a speaker consider and refute arguments that contradict her or his own. Failing to recognize arguments on both sides of the issue might suggest to an audience, particularly an audience familiar with those arguments, that the speaker is overlooking, ignoring, or deliberately trying to hide arguments that would be disadvantageous to his or her case.

Once you have completed an outline draft, go to the **Online SpeechStudio** and use the **Checklist for a Refutational Pattern** to help you evaluate how effectively you have used the refutational organizational pattern.

To deal effectively with counterarguments, a speaker can arrange ideas in a sequence in which those in favor of a proposition are contrasted with those opposed to it. This **refutational sequence** lends itself to the speech to convince. It is suited to a speech that deals with the acceptance or the rejection of a specific program, policy, or idea. If a speaker is discussing a constitutional amendment to limit government spending, that speaker could use the refutational pattern to lay out the arguments in favor of the amendment as opposed to the arguments against the amendment. By weighing both sides of the issue, the speaker can then come to a decision for or against it.

refutational sequence an organizational pattern in a persuasive speech that helps listeners weigh both sides of an issue by contrasting the ideas for and against that issue

This method should be viewed cautiously by listeners and approached honestly by speakers. If a speaker is unethical, discussing both sides of an issue may have the appearance of impartiality when, in fact, the speaker is distorting arguments he or she disagrees with.

As an example of a refutational arrangement, let's look at a speech with the specific purpose: "I want my audience to agree that the best kind of state-sponsored student loan program is one that provides for a 100 percent state guarantee of loans." Each main idea would be developed to substantiate the contrasting plans.

I. The state senate and the house of representatives have passed two different student loan bills, one that provides a 100 percent guarantee of loans and one that provides a 95 percent guarantee.

II. The 100 percent plan would make more loans available to more students and would qualify the state for 100 percent federal reimbursement for any defaulted loans.

III. The 95 percent plan would make financial institutions more cautious in lending and could result in the saving of tax dollars.

IV. But the drastic reduction in loans that would result from the 95 percent plan would defeat the purpose of the program, and many worthy students would be unable to raise the money to attend college.

It is apparent that a variety of organizational patterns will fit different kinds of persuasive speeches. What is important to remember is that you can systematically decide what is best.

KEEP IN MIND 15.5

Organizational Strategies for Persuasive Speeches

- Persuasive issues of fact, definition, cause, value, and policy may lend themselves to different organizational patterns.
- The motivated sequence consists of these basic steps: arouse, dissatisfy, gratify, visualize, move.
- A refutational sequence will help you deal with counterarguments.
- The right pattern depends on your thesis and your specific purpose.

- Consider what kind of issue your topic addresses.
- Devise a thesis appropriate to the persuasive issue.
- Craft a specific purpose that clearly designates the response you want.
- Choose the organizational pattern that will best help you accomplish that purpose.

APPEALING TO AUDIENCE EMOTIONS

Preview For persuasion to take place, listeners' emotions must be engaged. Persuasive speakers appeal to listeners' emotions by using affective language; by referring to shared values; by using specific, vivid detail; by using visualization; and by using comparisons with the familiar.

Listeners who have little or no emotional involvement in a speech are unlikely to respond to your message. Appealing to an audience's emotions is fundamental to being a successful persuader, since a person is unlikely to be stimulated or roused to action if he or she can't relate to the problem being discussed or see the necessity of doing anything about it. People who are not emotionally involved just don't care. People who don't care can't be persuaded.

Fear, pride, anger, reverence, compassion, excitement—strong feelings are powerful motivators. Successful speakers know that listeners can be motivated only when their emotions are engaged. In the following passage from a speech given by President Ronald Reagan, he argues for the passage of a highly controversial defense budget that would provide for a strategic defense system against Soviet missiles (popularly known as "Star Wars"). He stresses that the issues are "timely and important" because they relate to matters that directly affect everyone—matters that strike at very basic human emotions evoked by "peace and national security." Fear of war and massive destruction, responsibility for one's children, patriotic duty, and the American way of life are all called up in support of the president's plan. Listeners are reminded that a budget debate isn't just a wrangle over numbers—it's about how to survive in a "dangerous world."

Go to **Drill 9.1: Identifying Components of Persuasive Speaking** on the **VideoLab** CD-ROM and view the two speeches on women's gymnastics. Assess their relative strengths by taking the quiz.

> The subject I want to discuss with you, peace and national security, is both timely and important. Timely, because I've reached a decision which offers new hope for our children in the 21st century, a decision I'll tell you about in a few minutes. And important because there is a very big decision you must make for yourselves. This subject involves the most basic duty that any president and any people share, the duty to protect and strengthen the peace.
>
> At the beginning of this year, I submitted to the Congress a defense budget which reflects my best judgment of the best understanding of the experts and specialists who advise me about what we and our allies must do to protect our people in the years ahead. That budget is much more than a long list of numbers, for behind all the numbers lies America's ability to prevent the greatest of human tragedies and preserve our free way of life in a sometimes dangerous world.[5]

How, specifically, do you go about getting an audience emotionally involved in a speech? In Chapter 11, we described ways of involving listeners, and we stressed the importance of attracting and holding listeners' attention

Appeals to our emotions are the basis for most advertising. The insurance ad capitalizes on our love for our children and our need to provide for their futures. The anti-smoking ad dramatizes the harmful effects of cigarette smoking by a striking comparison with a substance that everyone would recognize as a deadly one.
(left: Michael Newman/PhotoEdit; right: Reprinted with permission CDC The Centers for Disease Control)

and establishing common ground. Let's consider now how you, as a persuasive speaker, can put these principles into action.

Using Affective Language

affective language language that elicits an emotional response

Affect is emotion, and **affective language** is strong language that plays on emotions or feelings. Many of us, for example, get a different feeling when someone talks of his or her "home" than of "the place where I live." Consider the emotional impact of these statements:

"I see things differently from Bob."

"I think Bob's statement is not quite accurate."

"What Bob is saying is somewhat misleading."

"Bob is a liar."

To say someone "lied" is to use strong, affective language. As a persuader, you must choose language carefully, thinking about how words may influence feelings. Eugene Debs, the four-time Socialist party candidate for president of the United States, opposed American involvement in World War I. In 1917, the Sedition Act put serious restrictions on freedom of speech in wartime, and many antiwar speakers were jailed. Debs tested the law by giving a speech in which he fiercely attacked the government and the Wall Street interests he held responsible for the war. He was arrested, tried, and convicted. At his sentencing, he defended freedom of speech and gave one of the most moving appeals for social justice in American history.

> Your Honor, years ago I recognized my kinship with all living beings, and I made up my mind that I was not one bit better than the meanest on earth. I said

> then, and I say now, that while there is a lower class, I am in it, while there is a criminal element, I am of it, and while there is a soul in prison, I am not free. . . .
>
> I am thinking this morning of the men in the mills and the factories; of the men in the mines and on the railroads. I am thinking of the women who for a paltry wage are compelled to work out their barren lives; of the little children who in this system are robbed of their childhood and in their tender years are seized in the remorseless grasp of Mammon and forced into the industrial dungeons, there to feed the monster machines while they themselves are being starved and stunted, body and soul. I see them dwarfed and diseased and their little lives broken and blasted because in this high noon of our twentieth-century Christian civilization money is still so much more important than the flesh and blood of childhood. In very truth gold is god today and rules with pitiless sway in the affairs of men.
>
> Your Honor, I ask no mercy and I plead for no immunity. I realize that finally the right must prevail. I never so clearly comprehended as now the great struggle between the powers of greed and exploitation on one hand and upon the other the rising hosts of industrial freedom and social justice.
>
> I can see the dawn of a better day for humanity. The people are awakening. In due time they will and must come to their own.[6]

You can see in this example how Debs uses moving language to describe the plight of the poor and to contrast the "powers of greed" with "the rising hosts of industrial freedom and social justice."

Identifying Shared Values

values those things that are considered good and desirable

Listeners are more likely to be emotionally engaged when their own values are involved. You should aim to identify **values** that you and your audience hold in common and show how your ideas and beliefs relate to those values.

When Geraldine Ferraro was nominated for vice president of the United States in 1984, she was the first woman ever to be nominated for that office by a major political party. In her acceptance speech, she set out to identify her values and those of her running mate, Walter "Fritz" Mondale, with basic American values.

> We are going to win, because Americans across this country believe in the same basic dream.
>
> Last week, I visited Elmore, Minnesota, the small town where Fritz Mondale was raised. And soon Fritz and Joan will visit our family in Queens. Nine hundred people live in Elmore. In Queens, there are 2,000 people in one block. You would think we would be different, but we're not. Children walk to school in Elmore past grain elevators; in Queens, they pass by subway stops. But, no matter where they live, their future depends on education—and their parents are willing to do their part to make those schools as good as they can be. In Elmore, there are family farms; in Queens, small businesses. But the men and women who run them all take pride in supporting their families through hard work and initiative. On the Fourth of July in Elmore, they hang flags out on Main Street; in Queens, they fly them over Grand Avenue. But all of us love our country, and stand ready to defend the freedom that it represents.[7]

Ferraro's message seeks to unite small-town and big-city values in a larger context of American values.

Using Vivid Detail

Using vivid detail helps us visualize a situation. Listeners relate much more directly to concrete stories and examples than they do to abstractions. Charities that wish to raise money for medical research for children, for example, often choose a "poster" child who represents thousands of afflicted children. The one child is real—a person potential donors can see and to whom they can relate—and thus the children's plight is more likely to be emotionally involving.

Persuasive speakers engage audiences' feelings by reinforcing generalizations with vivid, emotional details. Senator Robert Dole, the 1996 Republican candidate for president, urged leaders of the entertainment industry to reduce the violence and sexual content in popular films, television, and music. In this excerpt, Senator Dole gives a series of vivid examples that would have been emotionally charged for many parents.

> A line has been crossed—not just of taste, but of human dignity and decency. It is crossed every time sexual violence is given a catchy tune. When teen suicide is set to an appealing beat. When Hollywood's dream factories turn out nightmares of depravity.
>
> You know what I mean. I mean "Natural Born Killers." "True Romance." Films that revel in mindless violence and loveless sex. I'm talking about groups like Cannibal Corpse, Geto Boys and 2 Live Crew. About a culture business that makes money from "music" extolling the pleasures of raping, torturing and mutilating women, from "songs" about killing policemen and rejecting law. The mainstreaming of deviancy must come to an end, but it will only stop when the leaders of the entertainment industry recognize and shoulder their responsibility.[8]

The details in this passage are concrete and specific, calling up vivid images that are meant to shock.

Using Visualization

In an effort to make messages more concrete, speakers often employ **visualization**. Descriptions that evoke images that people can understand and imagine help audience members to "see" how a speaker's plan is to be put into action or what the results of a proposal might be. Visualization stirs the imagination, gets the audience thinking, and involves listeners in the process of constructing the speaker's message.

visualization envisioning for an audience what might or could transpire

By visualizing events, a speaker can demonstrate for an audience that a problem or crisis really exists, just as pictures can bring home the reality of a situation. Mothers Against Drunk Driving, for example, has done more than tell people that many young people have been killed by drunk drivers. For instance, they ran an ad campaign that showed pictures of real young men and women whose lives had been lost as a result of alcohol-related accidents.

Visualization can also compare or contrast the present with a projected future, as, for example, Martin Luther King, Jr., did in his famous "I Have a Dream" speech, in which he visualized what a racially integrated America would be like. In a speech at the Democratic National Convention in 1992, Mario Cuomo used the metaphor of a parade to help the audience visualize what he believed would be the result of a Democratic victory in the election.

> A year ago, we had a great parade in New York City to celebrate the return of our armed forces from the Persian Gulf. I'm sure you had one, too. But as joyous as those parades were, I'd like to march with you in a different kind of celebration—one, regrettably, we cannot yet hold.
>
> I'd like to march with you through cities and rural villages where all the people have safe streets, affordable housing, and health care when they need it.
>
> I want to clap my hands and throw my fists in the air, cheering neighborhoods where children can be children, where they can grow up and have the chance to go to college and one day own their own home.
>
> I want to sing—proud songs, happy songs—arm in arm with workers who have a real stake in their company's success, who once again have the assurance that a lifetime of hard work will make life better for their children than it's been for them.
>
> I want to be part of a victory parade that sends up fireworks, celebrating the triumph of our technology centers and factories, outproducing and outselling our overseas competitors.[9]

The language Cuomo chose helped listeners to "see" in their mind's eye the picture he hoped to project.

Comparing Actions

Speakers often relate new plans or proposals to familiar actions. Sometimes controversial, complicated proposals, when compared with familiar situations, sound like the only sensible, fair thing to do.

Before the United States entered World War II, the British were fighting virtually alone against Nazi Germany. Hard-pressed for war materials and without sufficient funds to buy all they needed, the British were desperate. President Franklin Roosevelt supported a plan called lend-lease to provide the British with American ships and other equipment on credit. The plan was highly controversial because the American public generally favored neutrality. The president explained the lend-lease bill by using a familiar illustration to compare the situation to that of two neighbors.

> Well, let me give you an illustration: Suppose my neighbor's home catches fire, and I have got a length of garden hose four or five hundred feet away; but, by Heaven, if he can take my garden hose and connect it up with his hydrant, I may help him to put out his fire. Now what do I do? I don't say to him before the operation, "Neighbor, my garden hose cost me $15; you have got to pay me $15 for it." What is the transaction that goes on? I don't want $15—I want my garden hose back after the fire is over. All right. If it goes through the fire all right, intact, without any damage to it, he gives it back to me and thanks me very much for the use of it. But suppose it gets smashed up—holes in it—during the fire; we don't have to have too much formality about it, but I say to him, "I was glad to lend you that hose; I see I can't use it any more, it's all smashed up." He says, "How many feet of it were there?" I tell him, "There were 150 feet of it." He says, "All right, I will replace it." Now, if I get a nice garden hose back, I am in pretty

CONNECTING TO THE NET

As you can see, the persuasive process revolves around different kinds of issues but is always based on the speaker's effort to get a desired response from an audience. A good speaker knows that success depends in part on how much listeners feel involved in the topic. Go to: **http://college.hmco.com/communication/andrews/public_speaking/2e/students/** and click on *Connecting to the Net.* From there, follow the link to Persuasive Process. There you will find a persuasive speech that you can examine to see how well it measures up to the standards we have discussed in this chapter.

> good shape. In other words, if you lend certain munitions and get the munitions back at the end of the war, if they are intact—haven't been hurt—you are all right; if they have been damaged or deteriorated or lost completely, it seems to me you come out pretty well if you have them replaced by the fellow that you have lent them to.[10]

The fundamental principle to remember is that to be persuasive, you must engage your audience's emotions. Changing beliefs or inducing action is unlikely if listeners don't care one way or the other.

Go to **Lesson 6's Screening Room** on the **VideoLab** CD-ROM and view the speech on Native American symbols. What devices does the speaker use to appeal to the audience's emotions? How effectively and ethically does she advance her appeals?

Ethical Considerations in Emotional Appeals

Examples of emotional appeals are very common in our everyday lives, especially in advertising. Yogurt commercials show an elderly man and his even older mother to suggest that eating yogurt will help us live longer, appealing to our concern for our well-being. Athletic teams wear shoes with a famous trademark on them so that we will identify with the athletes and perhaps think that by buying the shoes, we, too, will be heroes. Political ads show a candidate in friendly exchange with people in a nursing home and appeal to our sense of love and responsibility for aging parents or grandparents by implying that the politician will support programs to assist them. Advertisers know that successful marketing of a product often depends on audiences' emotional reactions.

Emotional appeals, though important, can also be manipulative, and this is a danger to be avoided. In discussing the importance of emotional appeals, Aristotle stressed the relevance of the emotion to the topic at hand and did not call on speakers to try to manipulate listeners by playing on inappropriate emotional appeals. When feelings such as fear, anger, love, rage, and guilt are invoked, the results can be powerful and to some extent unpredictable. Ethical public speakers recognize and respect the power of emotions and seek always to appeal to listeners' emotions in ways that honor the dignity and humanity of all their listeners and encourage a thoughtful consideration of the proposed courses of action.

In speaking persuasively, you should seek never to exaggerate or to use language that is so evocative that listeners are tempted to overreact. Vivid stories about brutal crimes, the agonies of deadly viruses, or the horrors of war may or may not be appropriate—it depends on the specific speaking situation. However, we all know that speakers can go too far. In striving to stir audience emotions, speakers can use rude, crude, or tasteless language, often in the name of getting everyone fired up and ready to act. Apart from the very real possibility that such tactics may backfire, the ethical speaker seeks to avoid overwhelming his or her listeners with emotions so strong that they can hardly think.

When in doubt, you can apply one general test to any emotional appeal you are about to use: underneath the emotional appeal, is there a sound argument—a substructure of evidence and reasoning—that can withstand the test of critical scrutiny? You do not want your audience members to respond unthinkingly, but rather with their minds and emotions working

Feeling Like You Do

How should your audience feel in relation to what you'll be saying in your forthcoming speech? How will you get them emotionally involved? Is the feeling you wish to elicit substantiated by sound argument? Identify any problems that might exist when the appeal is subjected to critical scrutiny and what corrective measures you will take.

KEEP IN MIND 15.6

Involving the Emotions

Involve your audience's emotions by

- using affective language.
- appealing to shared values.
- giving specific, vivid details.
- employing visualization.
- comparing plans or proposals to what is familiar.
- maintaining an ongoing concern for ethics.

SPOTLIGHT ON... Ethical Communication

1. Do not use false, fabricated, misrepresented, distorted, or irrelevant evidence to support arguments or claims.
2. Do not intentionally use unsupported, misleading, or illogical reasoning.
3. Do not represent yourself as informed or an "expert" on a subject when you are not.
4. Do not use irrelevant appeals to divert attention or scrutiny from the issue at hand. Among the appeals that commonly serve such a purpose are: "smear" attacks on an opponent's character; appeals to hatred or bigotry; derogatory insinuations—innuendoes; God and Devil terms that cause intense but unreflective positive or negative reactions.
5. Do not ask your audience to link your idea or proposal to emotion-laden values, motives, or goals to which it is actually not related.
6. Do not deceive your audience by concealing your real purpose, by concealing self-interest, by concealing the group you represent, or by concealing your position as an advocate of a viewpoint.
7. Do not distort, hide, or misrepresent the number, scope, intensity, or undesirable features of consequences or effects.
8. Do not use "emotional appeals" that lack a supporting basis of evidence or reasoning, or that would not be accepted if the audience had time and opportunity to examine the subject themselves.
9. Do not oversimplify complex, gradation-laden situations into simplistic, two-valued, either-or, polar views or choices.
10. Do not pretend certainty where tentativeness and degrees of probability would be more accurate.
11. Do not advocate something in which you do not believe yourself.

Richard L. Johannesen, Reprinted by permission of Waveland Press from Johannesen, *Ethics in Human Communication,* 4th ed. (Prospect Heights, Ill.: Waveland Press Inc., 1996), pp. 287–288. All rights reserved.

Go to the **Online SpeechStudio**, where you will find the **Persuasive Speech Evaluation Form**, which you can use to assess your classmates' persuasive speeches.

together. In seeking listener involvement, commitment, and action, the ethical speaker cannot sacrifice respect for the listeners or fail to recognize and honor their right to think things through and to make up their own minds.

In *Spotlight on Ethical Communication,* scholar Richard Johannesen offers a summary of ethical standards for human communication. He points out that these criteria are rooted in the values of American representative democracy. Although several of these "rules" go well beyond the specific issue of using emotional appeals ethically, they provide an overarching framework for considering ethics in the context of persuasive speaking.

SUMMARY

Persuasion is an integral part of our lives. In your work and your personal life, you will constantly be called on to be persuasive and to respond to persuasive messages.

When you plan to give a persuasive speech, it is essential that you know what you hope to accomplish. Understanding persuasive issues of fact, definition, cause, value, and policy will help you design a specific purpose that calls for a persuasive response: to reinforce attitudes, beliefs, and values (speech to stimulate); to gain agreement (speech to convince); or to induce specific actions (speech to actuate).

Although almost all organizational patterns may be adapted to persuasive speeches, considerations of purpose, audience, topic, and setting will help you organize your speech appropriately. To be persuaded, listeners must have their needs met, must be engaged, must care about the topic, and must see the relevance of what you propose to their lives. By using affective language, appeals to shared values, specific details to support your ideas, visualization, and comparisons to what is familiar, you appeal to listeners' emotions. However, emotional appeals should not replace sound argument. As an ethical speaker who respects your listeners, you will not ask them to respond unthinkingly or fail to respect their right to think things through and to make up their own minds.

QUESTIONS FOR REVIEW AND REFLECTION

1. Distinguish between a speech to stimulate, a speech to convince, and a speech to actuate.
2. What organizational strategies are most useful in persuasion?
3. What basic human needs should an audience address?
4. Why is it important to engage listeners emotionally?
5. How does a speaker involve the emotions of the audience?
6. What ethical problems are associated with the use of emotional appeals? How can an ethical speaker use such appeals?

ENDNOTES

1. See Kurt W. Ritter and James R. Andrews, *The American Ideology* (Annandale, Va.: SCA Bicentennial Monographs Series, 1978), pp. 40–68; and Karlyn Kohrs Campbell and Kathleen Hall Jamieson, *Deeds Done in Words: Presidential Rhetoric and the Genre of Governance* (Chicago: University of Chicago Press, 1990), pp. 14–36.
2. William Jefferson Clinton, "Inaugural Address," in *The Presidents Speak,* ed. Davis Newton Lott (New York: Henry Holt, 1994), p. 367.
3. Richard M. Nixon, "The Checkers Speech," in *Contemporary American Voices,* ed. James R. Andrews and David Zarefsky (New York: Longman, 1992), pp. 41–48. See also Roger Morris, *Richard Milhouse Nixon: The Rise of an American Politician* (New York: Henry Holt, 1990), pp. 757–850, for a complete account of the Nixon speech and the situation surrounding it. Another famous historical example is the extent to which the debate over ratification of the Panama Canal treaty in 1978 hinged on public opinion. For an extensive account of that debate, see J. Michael Hogan, *The Panama Canal in American Politics* (Carbondale, Ill.: University of Southern Illinois Press, 1986).
4. This pattern is based on Monroe's Motivated Sequence; see Alan H. Monroe, *Principles and Types of Speech* (Chicago: Scott Foresman, 1935).
5. Ronald Reagan, "National Security," in *Contemporary American Voices,* ed. James R. Andrews and David Zarefsky (New York: Longman, 1992), p. 349.

6. Eugene Debs, "Statement to the Court," in *American Voices: Significant Speeches in American History*, ed. James R. Andrews and David Zarefsky (New York: Longman, 1989), pp. 415–416.

7. Geraldine Ferraro, "Acceptance of the Democratic Nomination for Vice President," in *Contemporary American Voices*, ed. James R. Andrews and David Zarefsky (New York: Longman, 1992), pp. 365–366.

8. Robert Dole, "Sex and Violence in the Entertainment Industry," in *Contemporary American Speaker*, 8th ed. R. L. Johannesen, R. R. Allen, W. A. Linkugal, & F. J. Bryan (Dubuque, IA: Kendall-Hunt, 1997), pp. 245–246.

9. Mario M. Cuomo, "Nominating Address," *Vital Speeches of the Day* 58 (August 18, 1992): 619.

10. Franklin D. Roosevelt, *Selected Speeches, Messages, Press Conferences and Letters*, ed. Basil Rauch (New York: Holt, Rinehart & Winston, 1960), p. 271.

The following five-minute speech to actuate offers the thesis that eating foods containing olestra is both beneficial and satisfying. The speaker's specific purpose is to get his listeners to eat products containing olestra.

Go to **Lesson 5's Screening Room** on the **VideoLab** CD-ROM and watch the speech, "The Case for Olestra." After viewing the speech, complete **Drill 5.2: Identifying Keys to Good Persuasive Organization**.

The Case for Olestra

Josh Boyd

If you've ever tried fat-free potato chips or tortilla chips, you know that they taste suspiciously like salty cardboard. If you're interested in reducing the amount of fat in your diet, this is a problem. Today, I want you to try a delicious solution: snacks made with Procter & Gamble's new fat substitute, olestra. P&G makes olestra by combining sugar with fatty acids from vegetable oil to make a new kind of cooking oil. What they get from that combination is a molecule that tastes like regular oil but is too big to be digested. As a result, you get all the taste of fat without keeping any of it in your body.

Josh begins by arousing interest through allusions to a common experience and by briefly describing how this new product is made. He also suggests that a common need—to reduce fat in one's diet—can be achieved without sacrificing taste.

Maybe you've heard that olestra is a bad or even dangerous additive. Maybe you're curious about what it's really like. Today, I'll answer your questions and give you three reasons why you should eat snacks made with olestra.

This transition previews what is to come and indicates a categorical organization in which the reasons to act are enumerated.

First, snacks made with olestra taste great. During P&G's development of olestra, people reported that products made with it had the same "mouth feel" of regular fat. So unlike other fat-free snacks you might have tried, snacks cooked in olestra don't feel extra dry or not crispy enough in your mouth; they feel just like normal snacks feel.

I *know* about olestra's great taste—I lived in the central Indiana test market that had olestra snacks a year before most parts of the country. Olestra chips really do taste like regular chips. And they're available in a nice variety of brands. P&G makes fat-free Pringles, and it has licensed olestra to Frito-Lay; this means that you can also buy Ruffles, Lay's, Tostitos, and Doritos made with oil that adds zero fat grams but keeps all the flavor.

The first reason is supported by a comparison and by the use of personal experience. This personal experience is also a way that the speaker builds credibility, since he uses and has enjoyed this product himself without any ill effects.

A second reason for you to eat fat-free snacks made with olestra is that they're safe. Some people doubt this—the Center for Science in the Public Interest has bitterly opposed olestra, and hey, there's even a warning label on snacks made with it [shows this on a bag]. It talks about loss of vitamins and possible digestive side effects.

But let me set your mind at ease about those things. Most of the side effects of olestra happened in early studies, when olestra had the consistency of a very light oil like mineral oil. Since then, it's been "stiffened" and most of the side effects have gone away. To deal with the loss of some vitamins, P&G fortifies snacks made with olestra with extra amounts of those vitamins.

These concerns aside, olestra has also survived long and rigorous testing. The Food and Drug Administration checked olestra for 24 years before approving it. The FDA's Dr. Helen Thorsheim observed that studies of olestra took up over 150,000 pages and included more than 150 safety studies.

As Josh moves to his second point, he confronts possible objections and refutes the assertion that this product has harmful effects through the use of expert testimony. He uses affective language by describing the testing as "rigorous" and "thorough" and repeating "safe" and "safety."

These weren't just animal studies, either—98 different studies done with human subjects established olestra to be safe. Dr. William Klish, a professor of pediatrics and the head of pediatric nutrition at Texas Children's Hospital, called olestra "one of the most thoroughly tested ingredients to hit the market," and added, "I wish all ingredients were tested this thoroughly."

And just this January, a study in the *Journal of the American Medical Association* again found olestra to be safe. In a double-blind study of over a thousand people, half of the participants were given unmarked bags of regular chips and half were given unmarked bags of chips made with olestra. Participants were then interviewed over the next three days—people who ate *regular* chips reported more problems than people who ate olestra chips.

So olestra is safe to eat.

The third reason to use olestra appeals to something we all value: our health. The fact that we can be healthy and derive pleasure at the same time is emphasized. Again, testimony by authorities is used.

Not only is olestra tasty and safe; a third reason you should eat snacks made with olestra is that they will make your diet healthier. How? By reducing the fat in your diet. Organizations such as the American Heart Association and the American Cancer Society recommend limiting the fat in your diet to reduce your risk of various diseases. But if you've ever tried a low-fat diet, you've found out that you have to make some big changes. With olestra, that's no longer true.

Here's how it works. A one-ounce serving of regular chips has 10 grams of fat. A one-ounce serving of chips made with olestra—same brand, same taste—has zero grams of fat. So if you usually eat potato chips with your lunch or for a snack while watching TV, for example, just changing your chips will reduce your fat intake by 10 grams a day! The American Dietetic Association endorses olestra as a way to reduce fat and calories in your diet. And Dr. Wayne Callaway of George Washington University makes the commonsense point that it's much easier to stick to a low-fat diet if it still tastes good!

The brief conclusion makes the action Josh wants his listeners to take explicit and summarizes the reasons for doing so.

I've brought some chips made with olestra for you to try, and I hope that all of you will make olestra snacks part of your diet. Why? Because they taste great, they're safe, and they'll help you eat healthier. So if you want to deal with the problem of high fat in your diet without giving up taste, get rid of that salty cardboard and try the olestra solution.

Arguing Persuasively

16

CHAPTER OBJECTIVES

After studying this chapter, you should be able to

1. **construct a sound, persuasive argument.**
2. **understand how inductive and deductive reasoning function in the construction of arguments.**
3. **identify fallacies in reasoning.**
4. **understand how rationalization affects reasoning.**

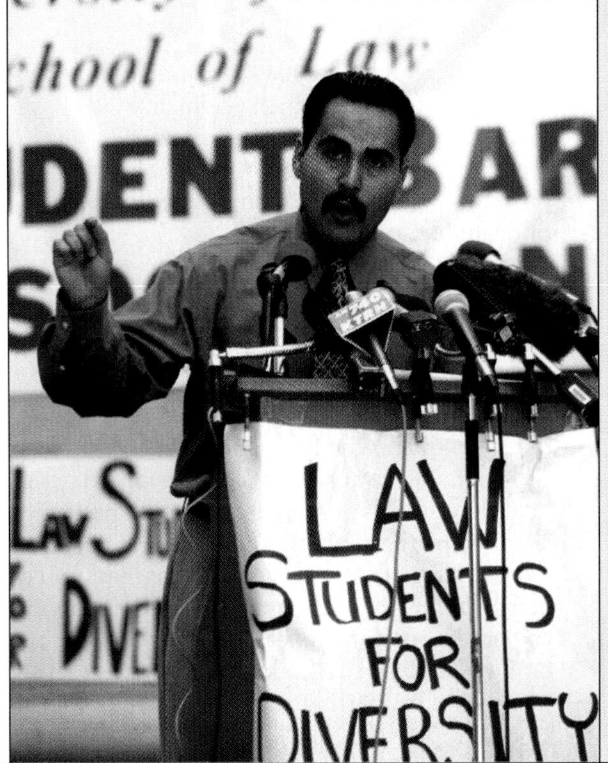

CHAPTER SURVEY

Decisions you make in life are based on a variety of factors. Sometimes you might be strongly influenced by a friend, a mentor, or a trusted group to act in a certain way: that is, ethos is the primary influence. Sometimes you are swayed by your feelings, and your emotional involvement moves you to action: in that case, pathos is given the most weight in your decision. No one form of proof always predominates or affects all people the same way. Obviously some means of persuasion are more effective than others, some are more effective with certain audiences, and some are not effective at all. But to be persuaded, most listeners need to feel that what you ask them to do or believe makes sense. Human beings have the ability to reason, and although we do so imperfectly at times, we are capable of being persuaded by logical argument: logos. What constitutes a good argument is the subject of this chapter.

To test your skills and expand your understanding of arguing persuasively, go to **Lesson 9** of the **VideoLab** CD-ROM and walk through the videos, exercises, and tips provided.

CONSTRUCTING AN ARGUMENT

Preview An argument is based on premises that must be acceptable to the audience. It is advanced by a speaker who makes claims supported by evidence that justifies the audience's acceptance, that is relevant to the claim, and that is sufficient to support the claim.

We all know that there are good and bad arguments. Too often we tend to decide which is which on the basis of how closely those arguments match our own opinions or beliefs—that is, a "good" argument is one with which we agree. Of course, we know that we are not always right. All of us have been "talked into" something that proved to be disappointing, unpleasant, or even disastrous.

The Components of an Argument

argument a position you advance as you lead from a premise to evidence to a claim or conclusion

The process of "talking someone into something" is the process of constructing an **argument**. The ultimate judges of whether an argument is good or bad are the speaker and the listeners.

A persuasive argument consists of a claim supported by evidence grounded in a premise. It is audience-centered. Persuasive arguments do not demonstrate absolute truth or falsity. You wouldn't construct an argument to prove that the temperature of a room is eighty degrees; you'd just look at the thermostat. You might, however, engage in an argument about whether keeping the room at a cooler temperature is healthy. The outcome of a persuasive argument depends on how well you are able to get listeners to accept your claims. Let's examine this notion by starting with premises.

Premises

premise an acceptable generalization for a particular context or audience

The **premise** is an acceptable generalization that grows out of the context in which the public communication occurs. The first test of any premise is whether it is accepted as true by an audience. In the United States, for instance, most listeners might agree that everyone is entitled to fair and equal treatment under the law. Yet within our country, some groups accept without question the premise that police routinely give preferential treatment to certain racial groups or social classes, whereas other groups contest such a premise. We might feel confident that an audience in our society would accept the idea that individual rights are important and should be protected, but people in a different culture might not question the assumption that individual rights have to be sacrificed for the good of the community. And even within American culture, some listeners will need no proof for the assertion that education is important to everyone, whereas others will never be convinced that education is worth the time or money. Premises, then, are audience specific.

Quite often premises are not even stated by the speaker; they are invisible underpinnings, like the pilings sunk into the ground to support a bridge. And like the pilings, they need inspection to make certain they can sustain the weight of the argument. The speaker has an ethical responsibility to test the firmness of these foundations. Indeed, when we speak, unless we are very careful, we might not even be aware of what our own premises are. This lack of awareness is a mistake, for when we speak, we want to be absolutely sure of the integrity of our own thinking. If we don't examine our own premises, we cannot be sure that we aren't asking the audience to act on the basis of values that we ourselves find questionable.

Consider this example. Colleen had an important decision to make. She had been offered a job by two competing companies, both major firms. She was already working at Vine Consulting part-time and knew that its managers valued her skills at conflict negotiation, one of the traditional strengths of the company. However, she had seen some dubious ethical practices by its management team and had heard of internal disputes that made her uneasy. Management had treated her well, but Colleen had seen that they devalued and marginalized older, loyal employees and did not tolerate dissent. White and Associates, on the other hand, was a well-known company with a stable, solid reputation, but it did not regard conflict negotiation as central to its business. Some friends who knew the situation and distrusted the CEO at Vine advised her not to stay there.

Ineffective Tools of Persuasion (*The Far Side* ® by Gary Larson © 1987 FarWorks. All rights reserved. Used by permission.)

Colleen went over the pros and cons carefully. She was influenced to some extent by ethos, since she was suspicious of Vine's management and aware of the advice of her friends. The pathos, or emotional proof, moved her to distrust Vine's leaders because their arrogance and insensitivity violated her personal values. To Colleen, these reasons suggested that she should avoid the job with Vine, but they didn't say much about why she should take the job with White. Then she asked herself whether it made sense to make such an important decision without considering why she wanted a job at all. Of course, she wanted to make a good living, but more than that, she wanted a career in which her special interests and skills would be valued by the company.

Colleen finally persuaded herself to take the job with Vine by framing this argument: She accepted as her premise the notion that any company for whom she worked would see her abilities as a conflict negotiator as central to the business. Vine Consulting valued conflict negotiation highly, whereas White and Associates saw such activity as something they should engage in but as not essential to their operation. Therefore, Vine was the company she wanted to work for. In reaching this decision, she followed the substance and form of *logos*, or logical proof. That is, she established a premise that her audience (herself, in this case) accepted, considered the relevant information in the light of this premise, and reached a conclusion.

In the end, Colleen made a decision based on the premise that professional goals and interests should be the basis for accepting employment. Would everyone have held the same premise to be true? Undoubtedly some people would have worked from the premise that working for good, honest people or that a pleasant, friendly working environment should be the basis for accepting employment. These different premises stem from different values—or, at least, different priorities in ordering values. An ethical speaker will try to understand the premises from which she or he argues.

PORTFOLIO 16.1

A Tour of the Premises

Sketch out the persuasive speech you are considering presenting to the class. What premises underlie your claims? Are each of the premises valid and acceptable to your audience?

Critical listeners should seek to know and question the premises that speakers advance. As a member of an audience, you need to try to understand the premises on which an argument is built—premises that the speaker assumes you will accept without serious questioning. By trying to understand these assumptions, you can protect yourself against arguments that may sway you because of their logical appearance.

Claims and Evidence

claims alleged truths put forward by a speaker

evidence fact and opinion used to support a particular perspective

Assuming that a speaker's premises are valid, you can then turn your attention to the **claims** being made. Claims are assertions put forward by a speaker as true and are supported by **evidence** that attests to the accuracy of such claims.

Claims are directly related to the persuasive issues discussed in Chapter 15. If the issue centers on whether or not a thing is true, the speaker will make *claims of fact.* If the issue is meaning, he or she will make *claims of definition. Claims of cause* are appropriate when the issue is why something happened and what the likely results of your actions will be. The question of whether something is good or bad is addressed by *claims of value.* Finally, an advocate for a future course of action will make *claims of policy.* The types of evidence used to support these claims are discussed in Chapter 9. Some forms of support seem particularly well suited to substantiating certain claims. Let's consider each of these claims and the most appropriate forms of evidence to support them.

Arguments are constructed on sound premises that the speaker must understand and believe. The Dalai Lama of Tibet, winner of the Nobel Peace Prize, exemplifies a speaker whose beliefs and experiences make his ideas more convincing. (Don Farber/SYMGA)

Claims of Fact. When attempting to persuade an audience that something is true, factual evidence is most effective: statistics, specific examples, testimony by authorities, and comparisons can all be used to support claims of fact. When hearings were being held by a public utilities commission on a proposal to reduce fees that long-distance telephone companies have to pay to local companies, one student tried to determine the benefits consumers would derive from the plan. After researching the issue, he decided that consumers would save little, if any, money. The factual claim and supporting material he used looked like this:

Reductions of fees for long-distance telephone companies will not result in lower costs for consumers.

A. According to the *New York Times,* documents filed by AT&T indicate that basic rates on One Rate plans would increase by 66 percent. *(statistic)*

B. According to the Consumers Union, new per-minute fees would go up every day except Sunday, resulting in higher bills for low-volume callers. *(authority)*

C. A customer who made 45 minutes of long-distance calls on Saturday would pay $4.95 under the old plan and $13.05 under the new plan. *(example)*

D. Even if the companies changed to a flat 19-cents-per-minute rate, the cost would still go up to $8.55. *(example)*

Claims of Definition. When you are trying to establish the meaning of a controversial or potentially controversial term for an audience, the principal type of evidence used to support such claims of definition is authority. We often look to

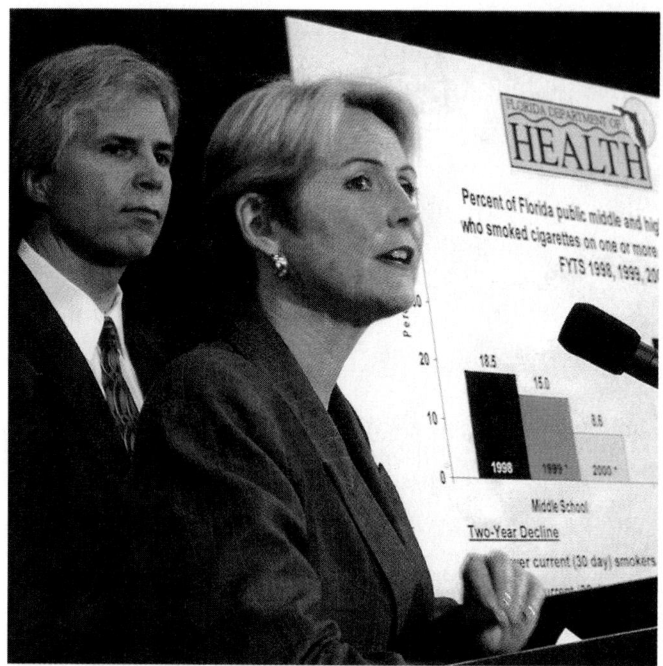

Statistical evidence is one effective way to support a claim. Here the Florida Tobacco Project Director supports her claim that the project is beginning to get results by showing that Florida's middle school smokers dropped by almost one-half in one year. (Associated Press)

definitive sources for meaning, as well as to people whom we believe are knowledgeable and reliable. We also find examples helpful in establishing meaning. A student concerned with the ways information is collected and stored on the Internet decided to examine the debate over privacy. Before she argued that actions to protect privacy should be taken, she needed to consider what is meant by privacy in this context. Her definitional claim was developed like this:

As U.S. citizens, we all believe we should enjoy the right of privacy.

A. According to the *Oxford English Dictionary,* the most authoritative dictionary of the English language, privacy is defined as "the state or condition of being alone, undisturbed, or free from public attention, as a matter of choice or right; freedom from interference or intrusion." *(authority)*

   1. We would all agree, for example, that, if your roommate opened and read your mail, such an action would be a violation of your privacy. *(example)*

   2. People who work at home expect other members of the family to respect their privacy and not intrude on their working hours. *(example)*

B. Our right to be free of government intrusion has been established by rulings of the U.S. Supreme Court. *(authority)*

   1. In landmark cases regarding contraception and abortion, the Supreme Court has ruled that citizens have a constitutional right to privacy. *(authority/example)*

   2. In 1999, the Supreme Court upheld a California law that prohibited commercial information services from obtaining police records that are available to journalists. *(authority/example)*

C. In *The Language and Journalism,* Ruth K. Kent defines the right of privacy as "the right of a citizen not to have details of his life explored in the press. . . . The right of privacy also prevents the use of a person's name or picture in an advertisement without his permission." *(authority)*

1. Dustin Hoffman successfully sued an advertiser for using a picture of him in his role in *Tootsie* without his permission. *(example)*

2. If I were running for student body president, I couldn't list as supporters the names of everyone in this class in an ad in the student newspaper unless you had given me permission beforehand. *(example)*

Claims of Cause. When you are trying to persuade an audience that certain past actions or events resulted in present conditions, factual data, such as statistics and testimony by people with authority, are an excellent way to prove these claims of cause. Analogies and examples are useful ways to establish points of comparison between past events and present situations. A student at a small college, concerned about the quality of her education, considered the causes of the problem. In her introduction, she described the decrease in graduates going on to graduate or professional schools, the decline in the number of internships obtained by students, and the dissatisfaction evidenced in student evaluations. Here is an example taken from her speech that shows the kind of evidence used to establish one claim of cause:

One reason that the quality of instruction is decreasing here is that the traditional close relationships between faculty and students are breaking down.

A. Fewer faculty are being hired, so student-teacher ratios are higher.

B. Ten years ago, there were 273 faculty positions. Five years ago, there were 260. Today there are 243. *(statistics)*

C. That means that ten years ago, there was about one faculty member for every 18+ students, five years ago about one faculty member for every 19+ students, and today about one faculty member for every 20+ students. *(statistics/comparison)*

D. To make matters worse, several positions are held by temporary faculty.

1. Twenty-eight faculty positions are filled by 41 part-time or adjunct instructors. *(statistics)*

2. According to Dr. Marjorie Biggs, president of the local chapter of the American Association of University Professors, part-time faculty usually hold jobs at more than one institution, often have to commute long distances, and are unsure of whether their jobs will continue from year to year. "Under those conditions," Dr. Biggs said, "they can't be expected to have much loyalty to the institution or to put in extra time and effort with their students at one of their jobs." *(authority)*

3. One part-time English instructor told me that she has three different jobs that cause her to drive about forty miles each day three days a week. She can't hold any more than the minimum number of office hours, and, given the time it takes to grade papers and prepare lessons, she doesn't have time to answer a lot of student email messages. *(example)*

Claims of Value. Ethical issues—matters of right or wrong, good or bad—are often resolved by appeals to common values. Statistical material may be used to show how seriously values are being ignored or distorted. People with authority help establish the rightness or wrongness of actions. Certainly one of the most powerful supports for claims of value is the narrative example, which tells a story or gives details of a specific case.

One student used as a narrative example her uncle, who had undergone what was supposed to be a routine operation but had been seriously disabled as a result. This student studied the issue of medical malpractice, trying to determine how serious a problem it is. Alarmed by what she found out, she decided to speak on this topic. In her introduction, she first told her uncle's story, then reinforced the value Americans place on good health care and the belief that hospitals are places where we are cured and cared for. As her first main idea, the speaker put forward and developed the following claim:

Malpractice violates the trust we place in health professionals.

A. People are seriously hurt by medical malpractice.

   1. A doctor who was known to have an addiction to prescription sedatives and was accused of performing the same operation twice on a man's leg was still hired by a hospital whose chief of staff knew of the doctor's reputation. *(example)*

   2. A young woman named Rose Prindilius was given labor-inducing drugs and then left for seventeen hours without a doctor's supervision. The result was a baby born with the umbilical cord wrapped around her neck, causing severe brain damage. *(example)*

   3. Cynthia Hendrick went to see her doctor twice with severe abdominal pains and was given antibiotics for a urinary tract infection. When she ended up in an emergency room two weeks later, it was discovered that she had a burst appendix that had abscessed. She later discovered that her HMO had implemented a cost-cutting policy forcing a delay in tests that should have been performed earlier. *(example)*

B. Because malpractice is so widespread, the trust we have in doctors and hospitals seems misplaced.

   1. According to a Harvard Medical School study published in the *British Medical Journal,* medical malpractice is the eighth leading cause of death in the United States. *(authority/statistics)*

   2. In an article in *Business and Health,* Gail Dutton reports that at least 44,000 and possibly as many as 98,000 people are killed each year by mistakes made in medicine. Even that smaller number is higher than the death toll from car accidents, breast cancer, or AIDS. *(statistics/comparison)*

   3. The General Accounting Office, a nonpartisan congressional research agency, reported that nearly thirty out of every one hundred patients are misdiagnosed and that mistakes such as overdosing, underdosing, and prescribing medications to which the patient is allergic or that react negatively with other medications are common. *(authority/statistics/example)*

good friend, is not rich, and makes people laugh support the claim that he would be a strong leader? Josh's qualities as a friend might or might not be related to his ability to exert leadership.

Third, the amount of evidence used must be sufficient to support the claim. What we have been talking about up to this point is largely a matter of the *quality* of evidence. There is also the matter of *quantity*. If you were trying to explain to your family how hard you have to work to get an education, you would likely do more than tell them you have a lot of reading to do or that you have to give a speech next week. You would surely give them all the details of the books you have to read, the papers you have to write, the exams you have to study for, the oral presentations you have been assigned, and so forth. In other words, you would present evidence that is not only true and relevant but also sufficient. Of course, what constitutes a sufficient amount of evidence depends on the audience's judgment. A claim that listeners see as highly controversial or about which they are skeptical calls for more evidence than one that audiences find easier to believe or less contentious.

Safe and Sound

Look at the sketch you constructed for Portfolio 16.1 and each of the claims you wish to advance. For each one, is your evidence sound enough to promote audience acceptance? Is the evidence truly relevant to the claim? Is the evidence sufficient to substantiate the claim?

Louis gave a brief speech in class on the benefits of aerobic exercise. One claim he made was that swimming was both healthy and enjoyable. Since Louis's speech could not exceed five minutes, the amount of evidence he could use was limited. He chose a claim that would not be highly debatable and therefore would need a minimal amount of evidence, but still enough to meet the standard of sufficiency. Notice how he brought evidence to bear to support his claim. Even though that claim was not highly contested, Louis wisely did not rely simply on an assertion.

> There's no doubt that swimming is good for you. Experts agree that swimming improves flexibility, coordination, and strength, and ranks just below running for aerobic benefits. Dr. Robert McMurray of the University of North Carolina's Human Performance Lab points out that swimming instantly increases blood flow to your heart. And in a study of swimmers, Dr. Eric Orwoll, chief of endocrinology at the VA Medical Center in Portland, Oregon, found that they had more calcium and phosphorus in the spine and arm bones than did their sedentary counterparts. He concluded that "resistance exercise, like swimming, should give you the same kind of effect as weight-bearing exercise."
>
> And there are a lot of people who seem to find swimming both healthy and fun. A Lou Harris poll, for example, reported that 26 million people swim three or four times a week. The American Red Cross, which offers swimming courses throughout the country, reports that they have issued more than 70 million water safety certificates.

The best argument, then, is one in which the claims are most adequately supported by the evidence and which grows out of an intellectually and emotionally acceptable premise. The best argument is not always the most effective one, just as the best product is not always the one that sells the most. As we have stressed, audiences make judgments about arguments, such as what is sound or sufficient evidence. Unfortunately, consumers—consumers of products and consumers of arguments—can be and are being duped. Intellectual hucksters are harmful and dangerous. The ethical responsibility of the

✔ KEEP IN MIND 16.2

Testing Evidence

Speakers and listeners can test the quality of evidence by answering these three questions:

- Is the evidence sound enough to justify the audience's acceptance of the claim being made?
- Is the evidence relevant to the claim being made?
- Is the evidence sufficient to warrant the claim being made?

speaker is to carefully apply the principles that demonstrate the proper use of evidence. It is the listener's responsibility to evaluate carefully and critically the relationship between evidence and claims.

INDUCTIVE AND DEDUCTIVE REASONING

Preview The process of reaching a sound conclusion may be *inductive,* when a speaker argues from particulars to a generalization, or *deductive,* when a speaker moves from a generally acceptable premise through particular instances to a claim consistent with the premise.

Sound reasoning is not automatic. Not everyone examining the same evidence will draw the same conclusion from it. The two ways in which we normally reason—from particular instances to generalizable conclusions or from a general principle to specific cases—are called inductive and deductive reasoning.

Inductive Reasoning

inductive reasoning examining a set of specific instances or making a series of observations and drawing from those examples a general conclusion

Inductive reasoning requires that you examine a set of specific instances or make a series of observations, then proceed to draw a general conclusion based on them. Here is an example:

Fact 1: My sister is weaker than my brother.

Fact 2: My mother is weaker than my father.

Fact 3: I am weaker than my boyfriend.

Conclusion: Males are stronger than females.

As this example suggests, we use induction every day, often without realizing it. We point out, for example, that Democrats are liberal, professors are intellectual, women are sensitive, and accountants are quiet. Most of these generalizations come from induction. Although we must guard against stereotyping and allowing the conclusions we draw to become unthinking, rigid categories (as we pointed out in Chapter 5), we cannot avoid reasoning inductively.

For example, a speaker who argues that overexposure to loud music results in impaired hearing is basing her conclusion on specific examples of people who have suffered hearing losses. Whether she is right depends on the number of cases she has observed and the representativeness of the sample she is discussing. Could the people to whom she is referring have had their hearing damaged in some other way? Is there any chance of hereditary weakness? Are there dramatic instances to the contrary? We can never be absolutely certain. The best the speaker can do is to convince her audience through the weight of evidence that the outcome is likely.

probability the extent to which we can predict something based on past experiences or observations

The process of induction, then, relies on **probability**. It relies on past experiences or observations to predict what is likely to happen. Induction typically moves from particulars to a generalization. In the following excerpt from a student speech titled "Controlling Pests," you can see how Maria relies on specific examples (particulars) to reach her conclusion (the generalization). In this portion of her speech, Maria reasons inductively.

> We have seen that insects cause a tremendous amount of damage to crops and that pesticides are not always effective or safe in combating this problem. So what do we do? Well, pests can be controlled naturally in several ways.
>
> First, by altering the genetic makeup of plants, we can produce crops that are resistant to diseases and pests. An article in *BioScience* reported that "some insect pests that attack the foliage of the eight to ten most widely grown crop plants are controlled by the use of plants bred to be genetically resistant to them." Second, biological control through such natural enemies as microorganisms helps in pest management. As Biologist James Cook indicated, of 850 natural enemies of insect pests and weeds, 40 percent are providing some level of biological control of targeted insects and weeds. And, third, decoys are a common organic method of controlling pests. Decoys are plants that, planted among crops, attract the insects first. The insects can then be detected and destroyed before they attack the crops. A common decoy, for example, is yellow nasturtiums planted at the base of a tomato plant to attract aphids, who are attracted to the color yellow. Once on the flowers, they can be detected and destroyed.
>
> So we can see that natural ways of combating pests can be effective.

When we reason inductively, we draw conclusions based on specific instances, facts, or observations. Go to **Next Step: Understanding Inductive Reasoning** in Lesson 9 of the **VideoLab** CD-ROM and identify the specifics in the speech clip that lead to the speaker's general conclusion.

Using inductive reasoning, Maria has sought to prove that natural means of pest control are effective. That is, she has reached a generalized conclusion based on particular examples of organic methods.

Deductive Reasoning

We are using **deductive reasoning** when we begin with a generally accepted premise and apply that premise to a specific situation or person. A classic example of deductive reasoning, called a **syllogism**, might look something like this:

deductive reasoning applying a generally accepted premise to a specific situation or person

syllogism a classic, formal argument in which one presents a major premise, a minor premise, and then a conclusion

A. All ministers are pious. *(major premise)*

B. Reverend Smith is a minister. *(minor premise)*

C. Therefore Reverend Smith is pious. *(conclusion)*

Most of us do not think or talk this formally, but we often rely on informal deductive reasoning when trying to be persuasive. Suppose you are urging a friend not to quit school, so you advance this argument: "You'll get a good job when you graduate from college." In a formal sense, you are arguing as follows:

A. People with college degrees get good jobs.

B. If you don't quit, you will graduate from college.

C. Therefore you will get a good job.

Frequently, as in this example, we don't actually go through all the steps with the audience. We expect the listeners to fill in the missing premise. This "rhetorical syllogism"—a syllogism adapted to persuasive argument—is called an **enthymeme**. This is often how we construct arguments in our daily lives: "He is so rude. He never thanks me for anything I do for him." This argument leaves out the premise, "Failing to thank people for favors done is rude."

enthymeme a classic form of argument in which a premise is omitted with the expectation that the audience will supply the premise

Of course, as in all aspects of persuasion, much depends on the audience. Most people would accept the premise that not thanking people is rude. Sometimes, however, some listeners might contest the implied premise. "She's so snobbish. She belongs to Alpha Alpha Alpha Sorority," is based on the premise that sorority women are snobbish. Some people might accept this premise, but it is likely to be rejected by members of sororities in general and certainly by members of Alpha Alpha Alpha.

If the premises are true or accepted as true by the audience, they are the starting point for a deductive argument, which then offers particulars linking the premises with the generalized conclusion. Examine the following passage in which a student questions the use of SAT scores in college admissions. In this excerpt, you can see how Rick, the speaker, offers the basic premise that college admissions ought to be fair. It can be assumed that such a premise would seem sensible to his listeners. So he then proceeds deductively toward a conclusion. He gives particulars designed to show that the SATs, upon which admissions are based, are not fair. If this evidence is convincing, relevant, and sufficient for the audience, it will support the generalization that he reaches: the SATs should not be used in admissions decisions until they are revised.

> If you're like me, you're probably glad you got into college. Some of you may have had no trouble while others might have sweated out admission decisions. No matter how we got here, I think we would all agree that the way decisions are made to admit students should be fair. We all ought to get an equal chance and be judged by the same standards. Well, you may be shocked to realize that that just isn't happening.
>
> All of us took the SATs to get into this school. Well, that's fair, isn't it? You might be shocked to know that the SATs work against women. A report by the University of California at Berkeley showed that women earn higher grades in college than men with identical SAT scores and claimed that "women are in fact better students than the SATs predict and are therefore typically underrepresented proportionately." And how about minorities? David Wilmouth, author of "Should the SATs Be a Factor in College Admissions?" argues that racial bias accounts for the consistently lower scores achieved by minorities. Surely how much money you have shouldn't determine whether or not you should be admitted to college, right? The *Phi Delta Kappan* did a study that demonstrated a direct correlation between poor SAT scores and school-age poverty, leading them to conclude that "poverty is the single best predictor of how well a student will do on the SAT."
>
> This situation should not go on. The SATs need serious revision, and until that happens they should not be used to determine college admission.

When we reason deductively, we begin with a widely accepted "truth" and apply it to a specific situation. Go to **Next Step: Understanding Deductive Reasoning** in Lesson 9 of the **VideoLab** CD-ROM and watch the speech clip. Then complete the exercise to see if you can identify the speaker's major and minor premises, as well as his conclusion.

KEEP IN MIND 16.3

Inductive and Deductive Reasoning

- Inductive reasoning typically proceeds from particulars to a generalization.
- Deductive reasoning moves from a generally acceptable premise through particular instances to a claim consistent with the premise.
- No form of persuasive argument leads to absolute conclusions.

Of course, in any argument there is always room for error. Conclusions based on either inductive or deductive reasoning are not absolute. The audience will ultimately judge whether a speaker makes a good case for his or her claims. Table 16.1 compares inductive and deductive patterns of argument.

TABLE 16.1 Inductive and Deductive Patterns Compared

Following are extracts from the introductions of two speeches urging changes in the registration system.

Inductive ***(based on an unstated premise, the argument proceeds from particulars to a claim)***	**Deductive** ***(moves from a generally acceptable stated premise through particular instances to a claim consistent with the premise)***
Unstated Premise: Because of its importance to us, registration should be efficient and accurate.	***Premise:*** Because of our academic interests, our finances, and our convenience, it is very important that we be able to register for and get the classes we need to graduate.
Particular: For students who preregister, there is a 9% error rate, so that some students are enrolled in the wrong classes or incorrectly informed that classes are closed.	***Particular:*** My roommate had to stay an extra semester in order to get a required course he needed to graduate. He found out well into the semester that the course he was told was closed was, in fact, underenrolled.
Particular: In the last preregistration period, I was disconnected from my telephone registration four times and had to make several calls before I could get on the system again.	***Particular:*** My roommate isn't the only one who has had this kind of problem. Nine percent of all registration transactions are errors of some kind.
Particular: A survey conducted by the student newspaper found that 68% of the students were dissatisfied or highly dissatisfied with the present preregistration system.	***Particular:*** I did a quick email survey of this class and found that 11 out of 20 of us have had some problems with preregistration.
Claim: It is very clear that our preregistration system has serious problems.	***Claim:*** We are not being served well by the present registration system, which must be completely overhauled.

FALLACIES IN REASONING

Preview Arguments can be unsound when flaws in reasoning, or fallacies, occur. Common fallacies occur when speakers draw irrelevant conclusions, employ insufficient evidence, make faulty assumptions, and indulge in personal attacks.

As we have pointed out, any claim is only as good as the evidence that supports it. Many things can go wrong during the reasoning process, leading one to draw a faulty conclusion. Following are some common **fallacies** in reasoning that ought to be avoided, both by speakers and by listeners.

fallacies flawed arguments

These frequently occurring fallacies are often known by the Latin names given to them by scholars centuries ago. The fallacies may be described as those that

- result from conclusions that are irrelevant to the premise *(fallacies of relevance).*
- stem from inadequate evidence *(fallacies of inadequate evidence).*
- are based on false assumptions *(fallacies of false assumptions).*
- arise when claims are answered or supported by personal attacks *(fallacies of personal attack).*

Fallacies of Relevance

Appeal to Ignorance *(Ad Ignorantium).* Speakers will sometimes try to convince audiences that because a certain proposition has not been proven wrong, it must be right. If a friend told you that she was getting thought waves from a boy in her math class urging her to ask him out, could you prove that she wasn't? If you couldn't, that would not, of course, prove that she *was* getting these extrasensory messages. Yet many speakers seem to believe that such an argument is correct. A legislator, for example, offered the following argument:

> I am convinced that my bill to require teachers to lead children in saying the pledge of allegiance every day in school will instill stronger feelings of patriotism and loyalty to our country. So far, no one has been able to prove that I'm wrong about this. So, if I'm right, why would anyone here oppose making our kids more patriotic?

No one might be able to prove that saying the pledge won't make children more patriotic, but that does not support the conclusion that saying the pledge *will* result in increased patriotic feelings.

The *ad ignorantium* fallacy may be viewed from the opposite angle as well: just because something has not been proven to be true does not prove that it is false. Because no one has been able to prove that there is life on other planets does not necessarily mean that there isn't. In the following argument, a student reached a fallacious conclusion after an accurate review of the evidence:

> So we've seen that, while there are instances which seem to suggest that some children act violently after watching television and some studies indicate that television violence can desensitize children to violent acts, no one has been able to establish a direct link between TV and violence. We can only conclude that television does not produce violent reactions in children.

Because we can't prove that TV causes violent behavior does not mean that we have proven it doesn't cause such behavior.

Appeal to Popular Beliefs *(Ad Populum).* Sometimes known as the *bandwagon effect,* this fallacy occurs when a speaker urges listeners to endorse ideas or attitudes primarily because many other people are supporting them. Although we may have been admonished not to "follow the crowd," many of us are tempted to do so in certain situations, and public speakers sometimes take advantage of this inclination, urging listeners to endorse a plan, buy a product, or embark on a course of action simply because "everybody is doing it." Knowing that other people support an idea or product is one piece of information we might want to be aware of, but that knowledge is not terribly persuasive by itself. Often we hear polling data used to support action: "Since this plan is approved by 63 percent of Americans, it should be adopted." Whether approved or not, any plan that cannot be supported with good reasons should be viewed skeptically. In the following excerpt, the speaker makes an effort to secure listeners' approval with an *ad populum* fallacy:

> All of us, as good Americans, know that in time of war we must support our men and women in uniform, no matter how we feel about the war. The time for dissent has passed now that the people have spoken, and all loyal citizens will do their best to help our country defeat our enemies.

Because there is popular support for the war does not mean that the war is justified or is likely to be in our best interest.

The Disconnected Conclusion *(Non Sequitur).* This fallacy occurs when an argument is introduced or a conclusion drawn that has no logical connection to what has gone before. You may be trying to get a friend who is in academic trouble to study harder. Your urging may produce the response, "Well, I don't see you getting all A's." This assertion doesn't relate to the issue at hand: how your friend can improve his grades. A student who maintains, "That astronomy teacher doesn't know very much about physics. He can hardly speak English," has produced a *non sequitur:* whether or not the instructor can speak English may relate to how effective he is as a teacher, but it is irrelevant to the claim that he doesn't know anything about physics. In the excerpt that follows, the speaker's final conclusion is not relevant to the evidence she presents and is a *non sequitur:*

This ad is based on a disconnected conclusion (a *non sequitur*). The sex appeal of the models, "covered" by a cell phone, has nothing to do with the implied claim that this company will provide superior service. (Bill Aron/PhotoEdit)

> There really is no good reason to prevent first-semester students from joining sororities. It will help us to make friends early in our college careers and get over the natural feelings of homesickness. Besides that, living in a house helps you become more responsible and develops your social skills. And the food at the house, as everyone knows, is so much better than dorm food. So, being in a sorority won't affect your adaptation to college academic work.

The reasons the speaker offers may be good reasons for allowing first-year students to join sororities, but they do not support her conclusion that joining a sorority won't affect one's academic adjustment to college. That conclusion doesn't follow from the evidence; it just isn't relevant to the support the speaker offers.

Appeal to Tradition *(Ad Verecundiam).* You have probably heard this fallacy expressed many times as, "We've never done that before." Perhaps you've tried to convince a friend to study with you and have been rejected on the basis that she has always studied alone. Perhaps you've tried to get other members of an organization to which you belong to have a car wash to raise money, only to be answered with, "We always have a raffle." People often like to do things they've always done because they're more comfortable with the familiar. But this kind of a response doesn't really reflect the proposal being made and is irrelevant as to whether the idea is a good one or not. Consider this excerpt as an example:

> The proposal to change orientation procedures for new employees has some serious problems, as I see it. They have always begun the orientation by filling out the proper forms. Being introduced to their superiors first, before we get the paperwork over with, has never been tried before. This new orientation would not follow the pattern we've used for years. I don't think we ought to get into something that's untried.

Anything new, of course, will be "untried." This objection doesn't offer specific, well-supported objections that are relevant to the plan itself.

The Red Herring. This argument attempts to throw the audience off track when a speaker does not want the quality of the argument examined. (The term *red herring* comes from an old practice of using the scent of smoked herring to train hounds to hunt.) A red herring raises irrelevant, often highly emotional issues aimed at gaining listeners' hasty support. You and a friend, for example, might be arguing over whether prayer in public schools should be allowed. Your friend asserts, "The real issue here is whether we are going to allow atheists to determine what happens in our schools." Yet you, and many others who oppose prayer in schools, may be deeply religious and still uphold the principle of separation of church and state. The issue is not atheism, but your friend hopes to get some support by reducing the situation to simplistic and largely irrelevant terms. The following excerpt offers another illustration of the red herring fallacy:

> My client is a fine, upstanding citizen who has spent his life in community service. He was a Boy Scout leader, sang in the church choir, and coached Little League. This man has lived here all his life and never has been charged with a crime before. Would such a man be likely to have embezzled money from his employer?

Perhaps he wouldn't be likely to do so, but his attorney has not addressed that issue here. The man's guilt or innocence must be established by an examination of the evidence. The introduction of his presumably exemplary life is a red herring, not relevant to whether he actually committed the crime with which he is charged.

The Straw Man. If a speaker describes a false, easy-to-refute argument as one that is made by his opponents, then proceeds to demolish it, he is said to be setting up a straw man. This is a fallacy when the argument that the speaker represents as his opponent's is distorted and misleading. For example, if you were trying to convince a friend that it would be a bad idea to cheat on a test, and he asserted, "You think everyone should be perfect, that we all have to do the right thing all the time. Well human beings aren't like that. Sometimes we do things that we're not proud of but have to do to get ahead." That statement includes a distortion of your argument. You would find it very hard to defend the proposition that we should all be perfect or that human beings could act in such a way that they never failed to do the right thing. You made the point that cheating is unethical—a point that is hard to refute. So your friend set up a straw man—everyone should be perfect—that is easier to knock down. Following is an excerpt that illustrates the straw man argument:

> We need to continue to find ways to reform the welfare system so that our tax dollars are not wasted on those who just want a free handout. Opponents of reform believe that anyone who doesn't care to work shouldn't have to. They argue that if a woman wants to have children out of wedlock, knowing that the state will give her enough money to take care of them, that's her right, and we have the obligation to support her with our taxes.

The argument that this speaker imagines his opponents making is, of course, an easy one to refute—few taxpayers want to give money to people who refuse to work or to support those who expect that others will take care of them. Opponents of welfare reform, however, have never made such arguments. They have expressed concern for single mothers whose pay will hardly cover childcare and the possibility that many children will fall below the poverty level. They have raised a variety of objections to specific reform plans and suggested that creating more jobs is a better solution to welfare problems. The speaker does not address these arguments. Instead he creates a straw man that will be easy to knock down.

These fallacies—appeal to ignorance *(ad ignorantium)*, appeal to popular beliefs *(ad populum)*, the disconnected conclusion *(non sequitur)*, appeal to tradition *(ad verecundiam)*, the red herring, and the straw man—are flawed because the conclusions they draw are not relevant to their premises.

KEEP IN MIND 16.4

Fallacies of Relevance

Several fallacies result when conclusions are based on irrelevant supporting evidence.

- In the *appeal to ignorance (ad ignorantium),* a speaker asserts that because a proposition has not been proved to be wrong, it must be right.
- In the *appeal to popular beliefs (ad populum),* a speaker urges acceptance of ideas because everyone else supports them.
- In the *disconnected conclusion (non sequitur),* the conclusion offered by a speaker has no logical connection with what has gone before.
- In the *appeal to tradition (ad verecundiam),* a speaker's conclusion, instead of addressing the issue, is based on the assumption that things should always be done as they have been in the past.
- The *red herring* is used by a speaker to divert listeners' attention from the real issue to one with which they are more likely to agree.
- The *straw man* is a false, easily refuted argument that a speaker sets up as that of his or her opponents and then easily demolishes.

Fallacies of Inadequate Evidence

False Cause *(Post Hoc).* This very common fallacy occurs when a speaker confuses a chronological relationship with a causal one. Simply because one event follows another does not prove that the first caused the second. Because your roommate smokes and gets better grades than you does not mean that smoking results in better grades. Politicians often fall into the *post hoc* fallacy. The incumbent congressman asserts that his support of gun control has resulted in less violent crime. His opponent maintains that the congressman's failure to support tax relief has led to economic problems for local businesses. This example also illustrates the important point that most problems and their outcomes have multiple causes. Too often we have a tendency to oversimplify. Seeking simple solutions to complex problems can lead to the *post hoc* fallacy. Here is another example:

> Here's a very important reason to go to college: the more education you get, the more money you will make. So if you want to ensure a comfortable lifestyle and an income that will provide your family with all their needs, as well as the luxuries that we would all like to enjoy, you had better get an advanced education.

It is true that, on average, people with college degrees tend to make more money than those without them. But notice that this argument asserts that if you go to college, you will do well financially. All college graduates are not alike, however. How well you do financially also will depend on your personal characteristics and goals. Furthermore, all college programs are not alike. Graduates with an M.B.A. may do better financially than graduates with a degree in education who become teachers, and those with an M.B.A. from a prestigious school may do better than those with a degree from another school. And, of course, a woman with an M.B.A. from Harvard may earn less money than a man with no college education who took a small convenience store and turned it into a nationwide chain. The point is that going to college does not automatically lead to material success. A speaker who asserts anything to the contrary may be committing a *post hoc* fallacy.

The Hasty Generalization. This fallacy occurs when a speaker jumps to a hasty conclusion on the basis of inadequate or unrepresentative observations. This is perhaps the most common inductive fallacy. A person observes a limited number of college students, senior citizens, Catholics, or kindergartners, then draws a sweeping generalization about others of the same category. Often a speaker is quoting the research of others who have drawn such conclusions, so he or she needs to know as much as possible about the sample size, representativeness of the sample, and objectivity of those who collected the data and drew the conclusions. Here is an example from a student speech:

> Last spring I spent three weeks as an observer in one of these poor schools. What I saw was lazy teachers and lazy students. Everyone seemed to be going through the motions. Students weren't

KEEP IN MIND 16.5

Fallacies of Inadequate Evidence

These fallacies occur when conclusions are drawn without sufficient evidence to support them.

- The *false cause (post hoc) fallacy* occurs when a speaker maintains that because an action preceded an event, the action caused the event.
- The *hasty generalization* is a false conclusion based on inadequate or unrepresentative observations.

> motivated to learn and teachers were just too tired and frustrated to try to get anything out of these kids. I don't believe that pouring money into poor schools will help them much. People just won't do things they don't want to do.

It is unlikely that the student really did observe "everyone" in the school. What he saw was a small sample of teachers and students. Further, they were from one particular school. To generalize from this limited experience about all teachers and students at "poor schools" is to reach an unwarranted, fallacious conclusion.

These two fallacies—the false cause *(post hoc)* and the hasty generalization—occur when conclusions are drawn without sufficient evidence to support them.

Fallacies of False Assumptions

False Alternatives. This fallacy results when a speaker bases her or his argument on the assumption that only a very limited number of alternatives exist. When only two options are presented, this fallacy may be referred to as a *false dilemma.* If someone at a party asks, "Are you going to have a drink, or are you some kind of prude?" you have been presented with only two alternatives designed to make you do something you might not want to do. You don't want a drink, but you don't want to be labeled as a prude either. The assumption that you have to choose one or the other is false. Obviously you can refuse a drink without condemning others for drinking, or you can refuse a drink and still be a sociable person. In trying to persuade listeners to take a particular position, a speaker sometimes poses a very undesirable alternative to the one the speaker is urging them to accept. Consider this example:

> The budget deficit, while reduced in recent years, is always a serious threat. The only way to make sure that it doesn't grow out of hand is to cut programs. Some people may be hurt by this, but we have no choice—either we cut programs, or we run the risk of huge deficits building up again.

There are certainly other choices possible. One choice is to do nothing and see if the deficit really does grow. Another is to raise taxes to prevent a deficit. Another is to combine small cuts in some programs with modest tax increases. It may be that cutting programs is a good solution, but that must be proven. To offer either huge deficits or program cuts as the only alternatives is to present a false dilemma.

Begging the Question. This fallacy rests on circular reasoning: arguments go in circles, with no proof for the assertions advanced; rather the conclusion is assumed by the premise. Suppose, for example, that someone asserts, "Jane Marshall is brilliant." You ask, "How do you know?" The person replies, "She belongs to Phi Beta Kappa." Then you ask, "What does it take to get into Phi Beta Kappa?" If the person responds by saying, "You have to be brilliant to be elected to Phi Beta Kappa," you have a clear case of circular reasoning. To demonstrate brilliance, one might refer to Jane's problem-solving ability, her communication skills, or her creativity. In short, one would offer specific evidence to prove the assertion instead of begging the question by assuming that the two assertions can be used as proof of each other. Here is another example:

> A good reason for keeping capital punishment is that it deters crime. Potential criminals will think very carefully before committing murder if they know that they will be executed if they are caught. Therefore the murder rate is reduced when capital punishment is in place.

This speaker maintains that capital punishment deters crime. What is his evidence? Just his assertion that potential criminals will be deterred by capital punishment. In other words, when forced to support his contention, the speaker makes the same claim in different words.

The Faulty Analogy. This flawed reasoning results from the false assumption that two objects being compared are comparable when, in fact, they are not similar enough to warrant the comparison. A skeptical manager might argue, "It's silly to talk about letting workers make decisions about their own jobs. You might just as well talk about giving horseracing back to the horses!" The comparison between workers and horses here is scarcely justified. There might be perfectly good reasons why workers should not make some of their own decisions, but this analogy fails to present any of them. Speakers often use false comparisons to make an issue that they support seem much more desirable to listeners, as in the following example:

> Gun control is not a new idea. Keeping guns out of the hands of the people has been tried before. In Nazi Germany, guns were confiscated to prevent any groups from taking actions that might have undermined Hitler. In Cuba, Castro has tried to make sure that no one but his own Communist followers have guns. Whenever dictators want to stifle opposition, they take away people's guns. Now we have men and women in Washington who want to pass gun control legislation to take away your guns.

The clearly implied comparison is based on the assumption that political supporters of gun control legislation are similar to dictators, a wildly improbable analogy. One of the many obvious ways that this comparison breaks down is that our political leaders can be voted out of office in the next election. Although there may be valid arguments against passing specific gun control legislation, the speaker has not presented them here.

The Slippery Slope. The faulty assumption behind this fallacy is that every action taken will lead to another action, until the first action can be viewed as the same as the most extreme one. That is, if you take the first step down the slippery slope, you will soon find yourself sliding to the bottom. Again, some opponents of gun control afford a good example of this fallacy when they argue that allowing the government to ban any kind of weapons at all will lead to confiscation of all guns. The following example illustrates the slippery slope fallacy as it was used in a student speech:

> The Board of Trustees is considering raising tuition next year. This is a very dangerous action and threatens to undermine the very foundation of public education. A state university is supposed to serve the interests of the citizens of the

> state; if this tuition increase is put in place, it will be the first step in an ever-increasing spiral of rising costs for us. Eventually, everyone who is not rich will be excluded from our state universities and only the elite will have the opportunity to get a college education.

This argument assumes that the proposed increase will ultimately lead to the worst-case scenario. The increase might indeed result in a hardship for some students, and better alternatives to rising costs might be found, but the extreme case envisioned by this speaker is not warranted by the evidence presented.

These fallacies—false alternatives, begging the question, the faulty analogy, and the slippery slope—result from false assumptions and therefore suggest incorrect or misleading conclusions.

KEEP IN MIND 16.6

Fallacies of False Assumptions

Fallacies that result from false assumptions suggest incorrect or misleading conclusions.

- The *False alternatives* fallacy results when a speaker suggests that only a very limited number of alternatives exist when, in fact, other alternatives are possible.
- *Begging the question* is based on circular reasoning, in which the conclusion is assumed by the premise.
- The *faulty analogy* occurs when a speaker compares two things that are not similar in relevant ways.
- The *slippery slope* results when a speaker assumes that every action will lead to another action, until the most extreme result is predicted as likely.

Fallacies of Personal Attack

Attack Against the Person *(Ad Hominem).* This fallacy is well known. Examples abound during political campaigns when opponents attack each other's character, integrity, or intelligence. This kind of attack is fallacious when it diverts attention away from the issues or is used to substitute for a discussion of proposals, ideas, or plans. You might propose, for example, that your organization take on a community service project, such as helping illiterate adults learn to read. Someone could quite legitimately argue that such a project is too time-consuming or that there aren't enough members interested in that particular service. But if someone opposes your idea by saying, "Well, Jane hasn't been a member of this organization for very long, so I don't think we should take her suggestion seriously," that person is not discussing the proposal at all, but rather is committing the *ad hominem* fallacy. Here is another, more complex example:

> The congressman's attack on the president's behavior is hypocrisy of the worst sort. The congressman has, for many years, had an affair with a woman who is not his wife and has an illegitimate child. Who is he to say that anyone else has violated the moral code observed by most people in this country?

Now it might be true that the congressman is a hypocrite. Likewise the congressman probably has done things in his private life that many would find immoral or offensive. Indeed the congressman might have drawn the above response because of his own personal attacks on the president. But this response does not get at the issue of the president's behavior. It is an *ad hominem* fallacy because it does not deny or defend the president's action, but instead attacks the person who raised the issue.

Guilt by Association. This fallacy arises when someone judges the quality of an idea or the worth of a person or program solely on the basis of its association with other ideas, persons, or programs. For some people, any idea that

To give you the opportunity to see if you can identify different kinds of fallacies, go to **Recognizing Fallacies in Reasoning I** on the **Online SpeechStudio** and complete the exercise.

Go to **Recognizing Fallacies in Reasoning II** on the **Online SpeechStudio** to further test your ability to detect fallacies.

comes from someone they dislike is bad. If you view yourself as politically liberal, you might be tempted to discredit the views of Pat Buchanan, Jesse Helms, or William F. Buckley, Jr., because of their conservative images. Much research has shown that we frequently rate an idea, painting, essay, or speech much higher if we are told that it came from a person we feel has high credibility than if it is attributed to a neutral or negative source.[1] This illustrates the power of ethos that we discussed earlier. It is very important, however, to focus on the quality of an idea or argument being advanced rather than either accepting or dismissing it because its source has associations that we see as positive or negative. You can see this fallacy operating in the following example:

> How can we believe that this proposal is made with our best interests in mind? Mr. Morgan says it will save us a lot of money. But Mr. Morgan belonged to an investment club in which the investors lost almost everything. One member of that club was actually indicted for fraud, while a few others pulled out just in time to make a lot of money at the expense of their fellow members.

It is most likely that Mr. Morgan was not the one indicted for fraud, nor was he one of the members who pulled out, or the speaker would probably have said that. In all likelihood, Mr. Morgan was one of the unfortunate investors who lost a lot of money. But the speaker is suggesting that Mr. Morgan's plan—which is not discussed—is suspect because of Mr. Morgan's former associates.

✔ KEEP IN MIND 16.7

Fallacies of Personal Attack

Certain fallacies are used by speakers to sidestep the issues involved and misdirect the listeners' attention through personal attacks.

- The *attack against the person (ad hominem)* diverts attention away from the issue by direct attacks on the character, intelligence, or integrity of an opponent.
- *Guilt by association* arises when a speaker attacks the worth of a person or his or her ideas based on that person's associations.

Arguments that are based on personal attacks—the *ad hominem* attack and guilt by association—are flawed because they sidestep the issues involved and misdirect the listeners' attention.

The fallacies we've discussed are not the only reasoning problems you may encounter, but they are some of the most common. By becoming familiar with them, you should better understand the kinds of flaws that can occur in arguments. Understanding these fallacies is the first step toward identifying them in the speeches of others and avoiding them in your own speeches.

RECOGNIZING AND AVOIDING THE USE OF FALLACIES

Preview To uncover fallacies—and thus to protect yourself against them and avoid using them yourself—you can use a model of argument that will help you see faulty relationships between the evidence and the conclusions based on that evidence.

It is important to remember that as a listener, you should be skeptical of arguments, examining them carefully for defects. As a speaker, you have an ethical and logical obligation to produce sound arguments. You must examine the structure of arguments you hear very carefully and look for flaws when you construct your own.

A simplified version of the Toulmin model, based on the work of the philosopher Stephen Toulmin, can help you spot fallacies.[2] This model suggests that there are three basic components of an argument: the **data**, or evidence; the **claim**, or the conclusion drawn from the evidence; and the **warrant**, a statement, usually implied and not spoken, that justifies moving from the data to the claim. Diagrammed simply, an argument should look like this:

data evidence or supporting material

claim a conclusion arrived at by contemplating particular evidence

warrant a belief or assumption that justifies accepting a claim

As an example, here is an excerpt from a speech on how the justice system works for minorities:

> Our justice system means justice for all. But it doesn't really work that way in practice. A federal investigation of the New Jersey State Police found conclusive evidence of racial profiling. The *New York Times* reported a story of an African American businessman who was stopped as he got off a commuter train and searched in the train station although the police were looking for a suspected robber described only as "a young black man." According to an ACLU survey, African Americans are four times more likely to be stopped by police in a large city than are whites.

The data in this argument are racial profiling in New Jersey, a businessman is searched without cause, and a survey shows racial bias in police stops. This leads to the claim that our justice system does not provide justice for all. Is that claim warranted? It is if you believe that justice requires that all people be treated alike, regardless of race. Diagrammed, the argument would look like this:

DATA
- New Jersey State Police engage in racial profiling.
- New York police stopped a man only because he was black.
- Police in major cities stop African Americans more than whites.

CLAIM
- The justice system does not provide justice for all.

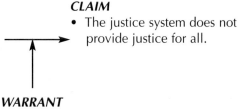

WARRANT
- Justice requires that all people be treated alike.

How can this model help you to recognize and avoid fallacies? By analyzing the data and the claim, you can determine the implied warrant—what you have to agree with in order to accept the conclusion based on the evidence. As examples, consider each of the kinds of fallacies we have discussed and see how the model can work to help you.

Fallacies of Relevance. An automobile ad suggests that a certain car is the best car in the country because it is the most widely sold.

DATA
- More people buy this car than any other.

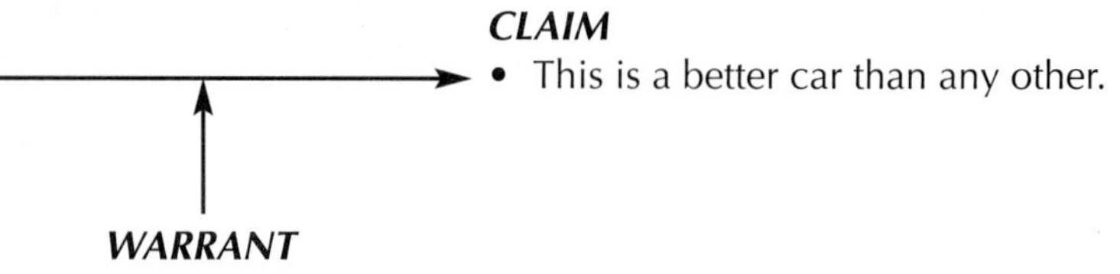

CLAIM
- This is a better car than any other.

WARRANT
- The more cars that are sold, the better the car.

The flaw here is obvious. There could be a lot of reasons, aside from quality, that this car sells well. It might be a lot cheaper than others, for example, so more people can afford it. The warrant for this claim is an *ad populum,* or bandwagon, fallacy.

Fallacies of Inadequate Evidence. A member of the city council argued that a zoning exception not be granted because the last exception granted to a builder led to another request by that builder for another exception.

DATA
- A past request was followed by an additional request for an exception.

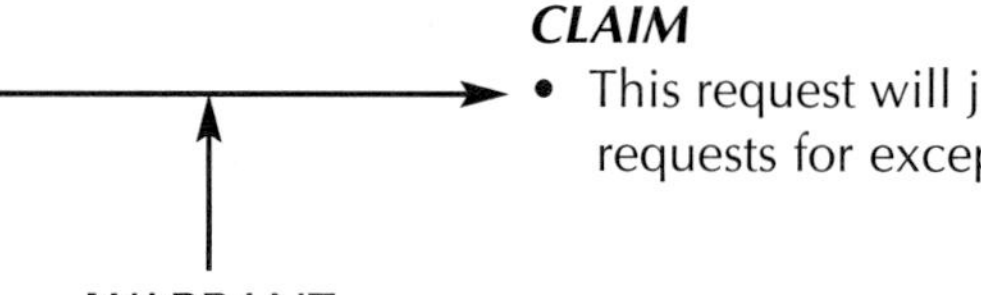

CLAIM
- This request will just lead to more requests for exceptions.

WARRANT
- Exception requests are always followed by more requests.

Go to **Lesson 2's Screening Room** on the **VideoLab** CD-ROM and view the speech on child protection. Analyze the nature and quality of the speaker's arguments by identifying her premises, warrants, and claims. To what extent and in what ways are her arguments sound, effective, and ethical?

This argument is flawed because the speaker seems to be basing his claim on one example. There is no evidence, and little likelihood, that every builder will act in the same way. The warrant for this claim is a hasty generalization.

Fallacies of False Assumptions. As you are planning your schedule for next semester, Mike, a biology major who lives in the same dorm as you do, drops in. He suggests that you not take a history course you're thinking of taking because he found it very boring.

DATA
- Mike found the history course boring.

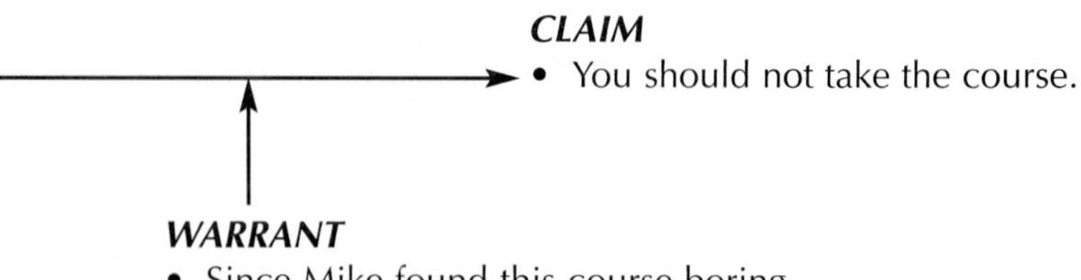

CLAIM
- You should not take the course.

WARRANT
- Since Mike found this course boring, you will, too.

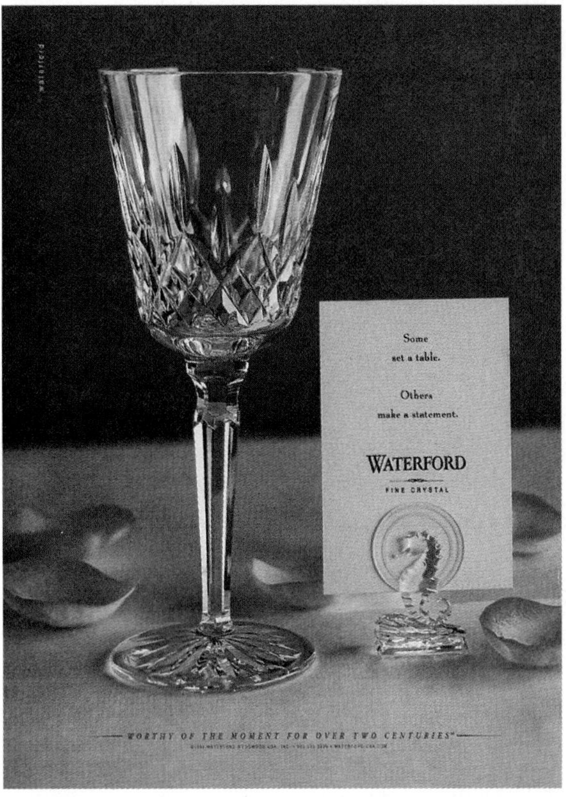

By asserting that this product "makes a statement" whereas all other choices are ordinary and lacking in good taste, this ad presents false alternatives. (Reprinted with permission of Waterford Crystal)

For a final opportunity to assess your ability to detect and analyze fallacies in reasoning, go to **Drill 9.3: Find the Fallacies** on the **VideoLab** CD-ROM and complete the exercise.

The problem here is Mike's assumption that you and he have the same interests. You may be considering the course because you enjoy history, whereas you don't care much for science. This warrant is based on a false analogy.

Fallacies of Personal Attack. A political speaker attacked his opponent for her opposition to gun control, a position taken by radical militia groups, asserting that such people are dangerous terrorists.

PORTFOLIO 16.3

A Genuine Argument

Look at the sketch you constructed for Portfolio 16.1. Are any of your claims derived from faulty or fallacious reasoning? What correctives might you undertake? Make a note of any problems you detect and any solutions you will pursue.

DATA

- Gun control is advocated by militias and by my opponent.

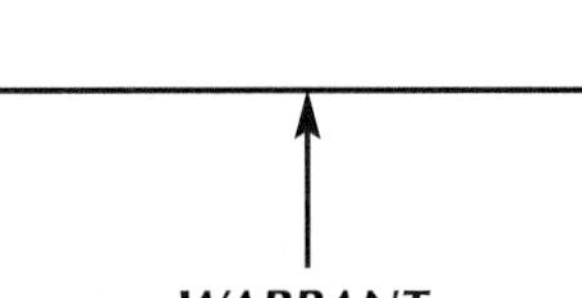

CLAIM

- My opponent and militias are dangerous terrorists.

WARRANT

- Since my opponent takes a position held by terrorists, she is sympathetic to terrorism.

KEEP IN MIND 16.8

Recognizing and Avoiding Fallacies

To detect fallacies,

- uncover the warrant that leads from the data to the claim.
- evaluate the warrant to see if it justifies the claim.

If the warrant does not support the claim, the fallacy will be exposed.

It is clear that the only way to accept the conclusion that both are terrorists is to accept the flawed warrant that just because they agree on one issue, they must be similar in all other respects. This warrant is obviously guilt by association.

Searching for the warrants in arguments can be a very useful way to uncover hidden assumptions and beliefs that are not reasonable when examined. Identifying these warrants will assist you in detecting fallacies in the messages you hear and avoiding fallacies in constructing your own arguments.

RATIONALIZATION AND REASONING

Preview Sometimes speakers rationalize, substituting or adding stated reasons for real reasons. Listeners should recognize their own rationalizations so that they can make more informed judgments. Rationalizations that lead to arguments that are not well thought out and appropriately developed are unethical.

We have all been in situations where our real reason for doing something is not what we publicly express. You might, for example, have gone to a meeting or participated in an activity that you say interests you, but in reality you went because a person you wanted to get to know better would be there. Similar situations abound in our lives. You might, for example, buy something that is very expensive because you want it, like it, or want to indulge yourself, but later say that you bought it because it will save you money in the long run. A popular cartoon once showed a young boy writing a letter to a medical school. After going through a long section in which he attested to his desire to help others, his wish to be useful to society, and his need to serve the community, he ended up with something like, "And besides all that, I really want to make a bundle."

Rationalization in Public Speaking

Public communication offers numerous examples of this process at work. Speakers often give lofty, highly principled, and highly abstract reasons for promoting policies or plans that are less idealistic than they sound. They appeal to the purity or integrity of the U.S. Constitution, urge us to launch a campaign to check the rising tide of crime in the streets, or urge us to adopt policies that promote self-help as opposed to government aid. Sometimes these speakers are honest and straightforward in their arguments; at other times, they use such arguments to mask racism or selfish motives. Welfare reform, for example, may be advocated by some speakers because it is simply a way of reducing their taxes. Other speakers might promote tax reform to guarantee that everyone pays a fair share or to preserve the rewards of one's labor, both of which are commendable. But sometimes these are merely acceptable ways of arguing on behalf of those who want to pay as little as possible to support the needs of society.

The process that we have been discussing—finding good or acceptable reasons for taking action or supporting ideas that one is inclined to take or support in any case—is called **rationalization**, substituting or adding stated reasons in place of the underlying real reasons.

rationalization supplying stated reasons for certain actions or beliefs in place of the actual, underlying reasons

Motivations for Rationalizing

Why do we rationalize? We probably rationalize because of how we believe certain public arguments will affect our image—the image that we have of ourselves and the image that others have of us. For example, if we like to think of ourselves as practical and hardheaded, we may not wish to admit, even to ourselves, that we bought a new car because we like its color and sporty design. In such a case, stating the salesperson's arguments about gas mileage, record of repair, and comparative costs allows us to preserve our self-image.

It's also quite conceivable that we might want to do something that we perceive as being in contrast to the norms or practices of a group with which we identify, so we try to find reasons for that behavior that are acceptable to the group. One professor who identified himself with what he considered to be the moderate-to-liberal intellectual community decided to vote for a gubernatorial candidate who was conservative and decidedly not intellectual. The real reason for his choice may well have been that the opposition candidate was personally distasteful to him or that he was really much more conservative than he would admit. But he justified his action by asserting that the candidate of his choice was a great friend to education in the state. If one judged the candidate by his support of the university's basketball team, this was true; by almost any other criterion, it was not. The professor perceived his vote for the candidate as being something that had to be justified in terms of the accepted norms of the group with which he identified.

Rationalization has profound and far-reaching implications for both speaker and listener. For the speaker, as we pointed out in Chapter 5, one important task in analyzing the audience is understanding the kinds of allegiances, loyalties, and associations that audience members have and therefore the kinds of motivations and pressures to which they might be vulnerable. As you prepare to speak, you must be aware that audiences may demand a good, sound argument not only to be convinced or motivated—they may be that already—but, in a sense, also to be armed with weapons necessary to defend their decisions.

The lifelong Democrat, for example, may be ready to switch parties because he feels that would be in his best economic interest. Yet he hesitates to abandon long-professed principles for what he fears might appear to be crass or selfish reasons. He needs reasons—other than personal self-interest—to act. A Republican speaker seeking his vote will provide those reasons. There are many motivations for change: the Democratic voter's beliefs could well have changed over the years; he might be convinced that his own party has deviated from its original principles; he might just think that it's time to give the other party a chance. Nevertheless the wise speaker will recognize that the audience may be looking for a rationalization—another motivation for the speaker to provide them with a good, sound, sensible argument.

For the listener, the most important fact about rationalization is that he or she does it. Rationalization is simply a part of our behavior. It is a way in which we manage the world around us. There are times when we must rationalize in order to cope with our lives. But in a public speaking situation, the more we can understand about our own reactions to messages, the better we are at judging and acting on those messages.

PORTFOLIO 16.4

Identifying the Real Reasons

What really compels you to advance a certain position? Do you have the best intentions of others at heart? Are you being honest with yourself about your own motivations? Attempt to identify and assess your reasons for speaking and how those reasons influence what you say.

As we respond, we should try to understand the basis of our response. Ultimately we may decide that it is not politic, polite, or safe to explain to others the real reasons for our actions. We may never want to tell someone that we bought a car because it was fire-engine red and "hot." Nonetheless we can make more informed decisions if we at least recognize the basis of each decision. Maybe if we say honestly to ourselves, "I really want to buy that car because of its look," we might give ourselves a chance for internal rebuttal—a chance for another part of ourselves to say, "Is its appearance worth the gas guzzling?" How we resolve that question can depend on many factors, such as our perception of environmental problems, our commitment to the ecology, our realistic assessment of our own finances, or our basic value system. Rationalization is, after all, a way of smoothing over conflict. The critical listener will often encourage self-conflict in order to make the best decision.

Undoubtedly any discussion of rationalization raises ethical questions. On the most basic level, we cannot ask, "Is rationalization right or wrong?" Rationalization simply is; it is a psychological process. The real question is whether rationalization can be misused or misdirected by speakers and listeners in the public speaking situation.

All of us know that at times people are offered what appear to be "good reasons" to encourage them to do things that are harmful or socially undesirable. Some people tend to act on the basis of prejudice, ignorance, and narrow-mindedness, grasping at more "respectable reasons" for doing what is essentially wrong. Other people have basically good instinctive feelings that direct them to act in ways that are beneficial to the community in which they live. These people may need to be assured, through argument, that their instinctive responses are indeed good ones. The resolution of such issues will hinge on how speakers or listeners see themselves and the world in which they live. That is, their personal values will ultimately determine the way in which rationalization is used.

In the context of this chapter, however, there is one rule related to ethics and rationalization, and to reasoning in general, that seems sensible: a sound argument is one that is clearly thought out, well developed, and supported by evidence, and that reaches a sensible conclusion. An argument that is an obvious effort to promote reasonable and logical thought could hardly be conceived of as being unethical. However, an argument that is unsound, is based on faulty or insubstantial evidence, and comes to a conclusion that is misleading or myopic does not promote clear thinking, and to offer such an argument is clearly unethical.

✔ KEEP IN MIND 16.9

Rationalization

- Rationalization substitutes or adds stated reasons for real reasons.
- We rationalize because we see certain public arguments as more advantageous to us than private ones.
- Speakers may rationalize when they provide listeners with acceptable reasons for doing what they want to do.
- Listeners should recognize their own rationalizations so they can make more informed judgments.
- Arguments that are not well thought out and appropriately developed are unethical.

SUMMARY

In presenting a reasoned rhetorical argument, you carefully examine the premises on which the argument is based. Moving from those premises, you use evidence that is justified, relevant, and sufficient to support sound claims. While all claims may be substantiated by the principal forms of support discussed earlier in this book, different types of claims suggest the use of different evidence. Claims of fact are usually supported by statistics, specific examples, testimony by people with authority, and comparisons. Claims of definition rely primarily on authority. Claims of cause are best supported by statistics, authority, and analogies. Claims of value are best established by appeals to common values and narrative examples, although statistics and authority also can be useful. In supporting claims of policy, statistics and authority are especially effective, along with specific examples, comparisons, and definition.

You may proceed *inductively* by examining a set of specific instances from which you draw a general conclusion, or *deductively* by beginning with a generally accepted premise and applying that premise to a specific situation.

As a speaker, you need to understand and avoid common fallacies that result from conclusions that are irrelevant to the premises, that stem from inadequate evidence, that are based on false assumptions, or that arise when claims are answered or supported by personal attacks. As a listener, you should look for fallacious reasoning and always assume a skeptical attitude as you evaluate arguments.

In the process of putting together a good argument or reacting to an argument presented to you, be aware that people typically rationalize, embracing what they consider publicly acceptable reasons for a belief or action in place of other, less admirable or sensible reasons they may have. Rationalizing is not always a bad thing, but speakers need to recognize ethical limits in encouraging listeners to do so.

Go to **Lesson 9 Coach: Tips to Remember** on the **VideoLab** CD-ROM and view the speech clip. Use the lists of "dos" and "don'ts" to remind yourself of the basic principles of effective public speaking.

QUESTIONS FOR REVIEW AND REFLECTION

1. What makes a good argument? Provide an example.
2. How can you determine whether a claim is warranted by the evidence?
3. Contrast each of these types of claims: fact, definition, cause, value, and policy.
4. What is the difference between inductive and deductive reasoning?
5. Name the different categories of fallacies, explaining why each results in faulty reasoning. Provide an example of a specific fallacy for each category.
6. Provide one example of how the Toulmin model can be used to recognize and avoid fallacies.
7. What is the meaning of rationalization? What is the relationship between it and reason?
8. Should speakers and listeners try to avoid rationalizing? Why or why not?

ENDNOTES

1. Jack L. Whitehead, "Factors of Source Credibility," *Quarterly Journal of Speech* 54 (1968): 59–63.
2. Stephen E. Toulman, *The Uses of Argument* (Cambridge: Cambridge University Press, 1958). See also Wayne Brockriede and Douglas Ehninger, "Toulman on Argument: An Interpretation and Application," *Quarterly Journal of Speech* 46 (1960): 44–53.

The following persuasive speech was given in 1997 by Joseph McNamara, former chief of police of San Jose, California, to the Commonwealth Club of San Francisco. You will see that Mr. McNamara doesn't cite the sources for the evidence he offers. Given his experience and the fact that he is a fellow of a highly respected research institute and an established author, he relies on his ethos to ensure his audience's acceptance of the reliability of his sources. The speaker tries to show that solutions to the drug problem are effective only if they actually prevent drug use, and by that criterion the government's drug war has failed. He also argues that not only has the program failed, but it has produced additional negative results.

The introduction uses three rhetorical questions. The first leads into a startling statement based on statistical evidence. McNamara suggests the fight against drug use should be aimed at protecting our health, a basic need. This unstated premise is that solutions are effective only if they actually prevent drug use. The second question refines the problem and asserts that efforts to prevent drug distribution are ineffective and costly. The third question introduces the next section's chronological narrative.

The Drug War: Violent, Corrupt, and Unsuccessful

Joseph McNamara

What is the principle behind the United States international war on drugs? It is a blurry picture. There is no clear line between the dangerous molecules that are made illegal and the safe molecules that we decide may be used under proper supervision. The most dangerous drugs of all are alcohol and tobacco, which kill close to a million Americans a year. If we look at all illegal drugs, cocaine, heroine, LSD, and PCP, it is estimated that they kill between 3,000 and 20,000 Americans a year. It is quite clear that we are not reacting to the danger of drugs.

Why have we waged this enormously unsuccessful and costly war against drugs? About two centuries ago certain groups in the United States began lobbying efforts to attach a criminal and a moral stigma to drug use. They succeeded in getting drugs outlawed. How did we get into this situation?

The quick historical summary supports a claim that legislation to prevent drug use was introduced for moral reasons, and not at the insistence of medical authorities. This assertion, following the premise, further suggests that the program is a failure.

England used to rule the world and waged two wars to force China to accept opium. The use of opium was popular in England at the time and without the stigma that it has today. So opium was sold to China and subsequently caused problems there. When the American missionaries came to China they found the effects very destructive. They began to lobby England and other countries to stop trading opium, and they began to campaign aggressively in America. The *Congressional Record* is quite clear. Drugs were not criminalized in part because of complaints from the police or medical authorities. They were criminalized because religious groups got their version of sin put into the penal code. In 1914 they succeeded in getting the Harrison Act passed, which is the cornerstone of the legislation in the United States.

Here Chief McNamara appeals to listeners' safety needs. His statement that he is not in favor of drug use and believes in regulation builds his ethos and implies that he wishes to avoid extremes—both of the pre-1914 situation and of the war on drugs.

Prior to 1914, the United States had a drug problem in the sense that many people were using drugs without being aware of the dangers. But there was no international black market, no organized crime involving drugs, none of the terrible violence and world-wide corruption that we see today. Since drugs were criminalized we have all those things. Estimates are that the per capita use of drugs is twice what it was before drugs were criminalized. I am not in favor of drug use. I think all drugs possess danger and require regulation. What I am suggesting is that we have two extremes. On one side we have the U.S. war on drugs; on the other side we have pre-1914 total market freedom for any drugs. Neither of these extremes is the answer but in between there are a lot of things that could occur.

The war on drugs cannot succeed. About $500 worth of cocaine or heroin in a source country, Mexico, Bolivia, Colombia, Peru, will bring as much as $100,000 on the streets of an American city. All the cops and prisons and armies of the world can't stop this; it is an economic force that is simply unstoppable. The profit is there because of prohibition. You all know what happened when the United States, from 1920 to 1933, prohibited alcohol. We had violence, corruption, the formation of an organized criminal structure which is still with us today. Because our thinking about these substances is frozen a century ago we are unable to rationally look at what the drug war is doing to America.

The body of McNamara's speech begins by asserting that the economic force of drugs is so great that the traffic cannot be stopped.

The war on drugs has not reduced drug use. The United States says that it will reduce or eliminate foreign production of drugs. If you have followed the news over recent months you know that this is ludicrous. The fact is that many of these countries are poor, and drug profits are greater than their gross domestic product. During the presidential campaign, George Bush went to a summit with the presidents of Peru, Argentina, Brazil, and Colombia. They told him bluntly that they were not going to destroy their countries in a civil war because we Americans can't control our demand for drugs. That is a very legitimate point. This problem exists because millions and millions of Americans are willing to spend billions and billions of dollars to purchase something even though it is illegal, even though they have been told that it is dangerous for their health.

Here McNamara begins specifying how the drug war has failed. He examines each government strategy in turn, starting with an assertion that foreign governments cannot and will not reduce production.

The entire illicit supply of drugs for the United States could probably be grown in about 50 square miles, almost anywhere in the world. With that in mind, the government's contention that they can stop foreign production of drugs is ridiculous. The government has to lie to itself; it decertifies Colombia for aid because Colombia wasn't trying hard enough to prohibit drugs, and then they increased aid. These countries hate our hypocrisy, our overbearing methods; they think this is an American problem and that we are very disrespectful of their sovereignty and indeed we are.

He appeals to common sense by ridiculing the notion of halting production of a crop that could be grown in such a small space nearly anywhere.

Strategy two was that since we can't stop production of drugs, we seize them at the border. The government estimates that they seize about 10 percent. One indication of how unsuccessful this is, is that despite seizures of tons of cocaine and heroin, the street price remains stable. The supply already here is so great that even vast seizures of drugs do not cause a rise in the price. Early in the drug war, the government said that tough enforcement increased the price of drugs and made them harder to get. Those on the front lines of policing said that it didn't make it harder, but it made it more expensive and made drug users commit more crimes to get money for the drugs. That strategy of interdiction also fails because of our vast borders, the enormous volume of international trade, and what is left of the Constitution's prohibitions against unlawful search and seizure.

McNamara cites the stable price of heroin and cocaine and the impossibility of patrolling our vast borders to demonstrate that seizing drugs at the border isn't working. He further invokes his ethos as he refutes the claim that drugs are harder to get.

The third aspect of the government's strategy is massive incarceration. We now have 1.6 million people under penal sanction in the United States, the greatest number in our history. Many are in for long, mandatory sentences of 5, 10, 15 years in prison. Many serve 80 percent of that time. Judges increasingly do not have discretion. This imprisonment falls most heavily on minorities. There is an old racist stream that runs through drug prohibition. The *Congressional Record* when the missionaries were calling for making drugs illegal is quite explicit. They talked about their efforts to Christianize the "yellow heathen" and to save the "Inferior races." There was also testimony that these substances made black men rape white women. In 1937, the

McNamara uses statistical evidence to take on the government incarceration strategy. He shows that prisons are more crowded than ever, then combines historical testimony and statistics to highlight racist undertones in U.S. drug policy. Note McNamara's effective use of specific examples to bolster his claims.

Marijuana Tax Act made marijuana illegal with the same racist commentary and the same inflated erroneous rhetoric that these drugs cause violence. The government's own study indicates that only 4 percent of homicides take place because someone is out of their mind on drugs. The other violence associated with drugs is the drug trade, the commerce between drug dealers, and the culture of drug dealing. Drug arrests of nonwhites are four to five times greater than for whites, despite the fact that about 80 percent of drug crimes are committed by whites, and this is reflected in the prison population.

We have this ominous future before us, people doing mandatory sentences who some day will get out. What chance are they going to have in life? We have drug-free work places so nobody with a drug record could get a job to begin with. We now have drug-free housing; if your son or nephew gets busted for pot someplace else, you will be evicted from public housing. We have created this monster for ourselves; we virtually have ensured that people that we have punished for drug use can never rehabilitate themselves.

Arguing the program causes worse problems, he turns to instances of corruption, offering a striking specific example. McNamara appeals to his audience by describing the ways in which their rights could be trampled on and their property seized by describing the seizure process.

The other problem is the enormous corruption. We invaded Panama because President Bush called General Noriega an "international thug." As soon as the troops had secured the city a Drug Enforcement agent put handcuffs on General Noriega, who is now residing in a federal prison for 40 years. A year later that same DEA agent was himself arrested for stealing $720,000 in laundered drug money. The corruption has reached into our federal law enforcement; all throughout our nation we see the police corrupted, and the legal system paralyzed. Another heavy penalty we pay for the hysteria about these substances is that we have authorized seizure of private property. Remember that under criminal law if you are accused by the police of a crime, you are presumed innocent until you are proven guilty in court.

Not so with seizure. Law enforcement authorities can seize a property if they suspect that it is used in a criminal enterprise, and you have to go to court to prove that you are innocent. They have seized more than $4 billion, without criminal conviction occurring in most cases. With the mere presence of suspicion, large amounts of cash, an "Informant" who said that you were involved with drugs, etc., they can take your house, your business, your car, and they have done this over and over again.

McNamara now returns to examining government strategies to prevent drug use and argues that DARE has failed.

Drug education is another thing that the government talks about. The government has spent unprecedented amounts of money trying to educate young children not to use drugs. The DARE program (Drug Abuse Resistance Education) runs about $1 billion a year. It is taught by uniformed police officers in schools throughout the country, often financed by federal grants. Two studies commissioned by the government showed that DARE was ineffective. The government did not print or publish this study, which created an uproar in the research community. DARE had a constituency, and the government didn't want to lose that constituency by admitting that DARE had failed.

Returning to his introduction, he mentions alcohol and tobacco again and offers his solution: that other drugs be treated in the same manner as these two and repeats his claim that criminalized drugs are not as harmful as smoking and drinking.

We should declare the war is over. The mere word itself gives a connotation that anything goes, that all kinds of violations of search and seizure laws, all kinds of misconduct make sense, that the police can do anything because we are waging war against evil substances. We could immediately treat marijuana as we treat alcohol and cigarettes. There has never been a recorded death by marijuana, there has never been a recorded homicide caused by smoking pot. Prominent politicians and leaders, Bill Clinton and Newt Gingrich, have talked about how they experimented with pot. Now brain damage aside, neither of them went on to heroin or to commit armed bank robberies as far as we know.

We need to step back. Prohibition ended when President Hoover appointed a commission to study how Americans could be more law-abiding. The commission repealed prohibition a few years later. Anyone who looks objectively at America's drug war will see that it is racist, violent, corrupt and unsuccessful. That is why I think a commission for investigating the situation is needed.

17 Speaking on Special Occasions

CHAPTER SURVEY

The Functions of Ceremonial Speeches

The Speech of Introduction

The Acceptance Speech

The Speech of Inspiration

The After-Dinner Speech

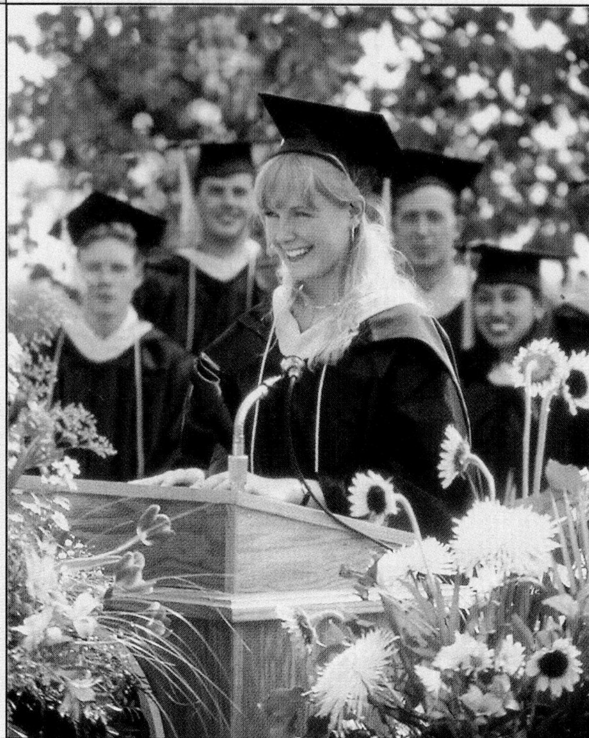

CHAPTER OBJECTIVES

After studying this chapter, you should be able to

1. **understand the diverse functions of ceremonial speeches.**
2. **identify and describe several different types of ceremonial speeches.**
3. **prepare and deliver at least one kind of ceremonial speech.**

It is hard to live in this society without listening to some speaker, somewhere, introduce or pay tribute to someone, present or accept an award, or give a speech to motivate or inspire. These ceremonial speeches are usually associated with very important occasions: weddings, funerals, graduation ceremonies, awards banquets, conference closing ceremonies, and major political events.

Ceremonial speeches may differ in tone, length, specific purpose, and level of challenge to the speaker. For instance, some speakers might find it relatively easy to offer a toast but would find the idea of delivering a eulogy more daunting. Even so, most ceremonial speeches share certain basic functions.

To expand your understanding of speaking on special occasions, go to **Lesson 10** of the **VideoLab** CD-ROM and walk through the videos, exercises, and tips provided.

THE FUNCTIONS OF CEREMONIAL SPEECHES

Preview Ceremonial speeches are often presented in formal situations and may be associated with important cultural rituals. Through these speeches, we may celebrate our values and beliefs, applaud or remember our role models and heroes, and strive to offer our listeners encouragement and inspiration.

Speeches that are given on ceremonial occasions are rich in ritual and symbolic importance. As we honor others, pay tribute to those we love or have lost, and celebrate our accomplishments, we are participating in **rituals** that bind us together as a community, a group, or a country. Ceremonial speaking uplifts us, comforts us, and reinforces our beliefs in ourselves and in one another.

rituals formal or ceremonial acts performed regularly by a group of people

Celebrating Values and Beliefs

Most ceremonial speeches articulate and reinforce common **values**. What has brought us together? What defines us as a group? Which of our victories or accomplishments are we most proud of? What are the principles we cherish? What do we believe in most deeply?

values those things that we consider good and desirable

In their inaugural addresses, U.S. presidents remind us of our common beliefs. John Kennedy did so eloquently when he said, "Let every nation know, whether it wishes us well or ill, that we shall pay any price, bear any burden, meet any hardship, support any friend, oppose any foe to assure the survival and the success of liberty."[1] Similarly, Dwight D. Eisenhower concluded his second inaugural address by saying, "May the light of freedom, coming to all darkened lands, flame brightly—until at last the darkness is no more. May the turbulence of our age yield to a true time of peace, when men and nations shall share a life that honors the dignity of each, the brotherhood of all."[2] Americans share the values emphasized in these ceremonial speeches: liberty, freedom, and peace. Other cultures may share different values, such as interdependence and collectivism, and speakers in those cultures would speak to those values.[3]

Go to **Lesson 10's Screening Room** on the **VideoLab** CD-ROM. After watching the speech, a tribute to Don McLean, assess the speaker's effectiveness by taking the quiz. You may want to reread page 21 in Chapter 1 to review the speech-of-tribute guidelines.

Honoring Heroes

Those members of our organizations, communities, and nation who personify and illuminate our values are our **heroes**. By holding them high, praising their accomplishments and special qualities, and remembering how they lived their lives, we are reminding ourselves of our own values. Heroes are our role models, and so we shower them with honors, decorate them in time of war, choose them as our commencement speakers, and mourn them when they die.

heroes people we admire and look to as personal role models

When Ronald Reagan eulogized the space shuttle astronauts killed in the *Challenger* explosion in 1986, he referred to them as "seven heroes . . . who were daring and brave and [who] had that special grace." Eulogizing Martin Luther King, Jr., Robert Kennedy said, "King dedicated his life to love and to justice between fellow human beings." In a speech class, a student giving a speech of tribute said of her grandfather, "I admired him for his courage and strength. He was my anchor when my parents divorced. He comforted me and loved me and made me believe that I would survive. My grandpa was always my hero, but he was also my best friend." In each of these cases, exceptional individuals were honored because they embodied human qualities admired by the speaker and presumably shared by the audience.

If needed, review the McLean tribute in **Lesson 10's Screening Room** on the **VideoLab** CD-ROM. Also, watch the speech of introduction in **Lesson 1's Screening Room**. Then, consider how these speeches function to celebrate beliefs and values, honor heroes, and/or offer inspiration and encouragement. Are there other functions served by these speeches? Elaborate.

Offering Inspiration and Encouragement

When speakers present awards or pay tribute to individuals, deliver commencement speeches, or give motivational speeches, they offer encouragement and inspiration to listeners. A life well lived provides an example for us all—a

National heroes personify and illuminate our values. The Unknown Soldier, buried at Arlington National Cemetery, symbolizes military men and women who die in the service of the country. (Stacy Pick/Stock, Boston, Inc.)

For an enhanced understanding of key values that are shared across cultures, go to **Drill 10.2: Identifying Universal Values** on the **VideoLab** CD-ROM.

Review the list of universal values discussed in **Drill 10.2** on the **VideoLab** CD-ROM. Then, go to **Drill 10.3: Applying Universal Values** and complete the quiz to assess the speaker's appeals to universal values.

tangible example that shows us that hard work, determination, and the desire to succeed pay off. Many speakers who give acceptance speeches (accepting an award or honor) may say to the audience, "You can do this, too! I have every confidence." The commencement speaker admonishes the graduating class to "reach for the stars." After-dinner speakers may use humor to achieve similar goals. Even the eulogy can remind us that ordinary people like us can have quite an impact on others' lives. Beyond reinforcing or celebrating values or people, the ceremonial speech can help us articulate goals, give us a clearer vision of the future, and challenge us to do our best. In *Spotlight on a Commencement Speech,* Sister Georgie Anne Geyer seeks to inspire her listeners, the graduating class of Saint Mary-of-the-Woods College, by asking them to look inward, see what they love, and then follow their dreams with conviction and joy.

SPOTLIGHT ON... A Commencement Speech

There is really only one thing that I know to tell you graduates—only one thing—and that is FOLLOW WHAT YOU LOVE! Follow it intellectually! Follow it sensuously! Follow it with generosity and nobility toward your fellow man! Don't deign to ask what "they" are looking for out there. Ask what you have inside. . . . Doing what you love, whether it is having children, working in a profession, being a nun, being a journalist, is all encompassing, all engrossing; it is like a very great love affair occurring every day. It is principle and creation, you know why you are here, your personal life and your professional life is all one. It is not fun, not games, not winning or losing, not making money or having your 15 minutes on television; it is what no one can ever, ever take away from you, it is . . . pure joy. . . .

So, seize the moment joyfully. Follow not only your interests, which change, but what you are and what you love, which will and should not change. And always remember these golden days.

Georgie Anne Geyer, "Joy in Our Times," *Vital Speeches of the Day* 55 (August 15, 1989): 668.

Ceremonial speeches take many different forms. In Chapter 1, we discussed three commonly encountered ceremonial speeches: speeches of tribute, toasts, and eulogies. In the remainder of this chapter, we'll consider other important types of ceremonial speeches: the speech of introduction, the acceptance speech, the speech of inspiration, and the after-dinner speech.

KEEP IN MIND 17.1

Functions of Ceremonial Speeches

Ceremonial speeches

- celebrate beliefs and values.
- applaud and remember heroes.
- offer inspiration and encouragement.

THE SPEECH OF INTRODUCTION

Preview Almost every speaker has to be introduced. Even if the audience is already familiar with the person about to address them, they will expect someone to stand and make a few introductory comments. In many instances, the guest speaker is not well known to listeners, and so the speech of introduction provides essential information.

In Chapter 1, we discussed several first speaking assignments. In addition to offering different kinds of tributes, one option was to introduce a classmate to the rest of the class. In this chapter, we return to the speech of introduction and consider it in the context of introducing a speaker who is about to make a presentation to a group of listeners.

Many people who introduce speakers have no idea how to approach a **speech of introduction**. They may prepare very little, if at all, hastily scratching down a few notes about the speaker during lunch or quickly underlining a few points on the speaker's résumé. Some cop out completely by saying, "I'm delighted to welcome our speaker tonight, a person who needs no introduction." Others go to the opposite extreme, giving a lengthy introduction that tells the audience more than they want to know or can absorb. Some introducers end up reading large portions of résumés—much to the audience's chagrin.

speech of introduction a short speech that serves to introduce the principal speaker

Purposes of the Speech of Introduction

The effective speech of introduction will do three things. First, the introducer will extend a warm welcome to the speaker, making him or her know that everyone is pleased to have him or her as a guest. Second, the introducer should take pains to establish the speaker's ethos by emphasizing key educational or professional accomplishments, noting awards and honors, and discussing the kind of expertise, knowledge, and experience the speaker brings to the topic he or she is addressing. Finally, the introducer should provide listeners with information they need to prepare them for the speech that follows. At the very least, they should be told the specific topic or title of the speech, and they also may need to know that the speaker will take questions afterward or will be available to interact with them at a reception following.

In short, the speech of introduction sets the stage for the speaker and the speech. The introducer must keep the spotlight on the speaker and resist the urge to speak at great length. In *Spotlight on the Speech of Introduction,* a student officer of the Future Farmers of America (FFA) extends a warm welcome to a motivational speaker.

SPOTLIGHT ON... **The Speech of Introduction**

In FFA [Future Farmers of America], we are constantly striving to make a difference in the lives of students and in each other. The man you are about to hear from makes a difference in the lives of most of the people whom he meets.

Dr. Rick Rigsby hails from the Lone Star State of Texas where he is an Assistant Professor in the Department of Speech Communication and Theatre Arts at Texas A&M University. After graduating from California State University, he became a television news reporter and sports reporter for a CBS television affiliate. In 1990, he earned his Ph.D. from the University of Oregon.

Along with his responsibilities as a professor of communication, he also serves on the coaching staff of the Texas A&M Fightin' Aggies football team and as a preaching associate at Aldersgate United Methodist Church.

Dr. Rigsby's first contact with FFA took place last year at the State FFA Presidents' Conference, and to put it mildly, we fell in love! Since then, he's devoted much of his time traveling all around the country and speaking to FFA members. In fact, back in December, our national office team had a chance to meet with him as he assisted with our communications training. I guess the best way to describe this man is by saying that he arrived as Dr. Rick Rigsby, but when he left, he was our friend, Brother Ricky!! Seldom have I met a man who cares more deeply for people. With that, I want to ask your assistance in giving a warm welcome to the man who can change our lives—Dr. Rick Rigsby!

Speech given at the FFA State Convention.

Tips for Preparing and Presenting the Speech of Introduction

Presenting an effective speech of introduction requires an understanding of its nature and purpose and, like other speeches, careful preparation. Here are some practical guidelines:

 PORTFOLIO 17.1

Introductions and Revelations

Think back on speeches of introduction you have heard. Which were the most enjoyable? Why? Which were the least enjoyable? Why? Divide a sheet of paper into two columns, listing the most and least enjoyable elements of these speeches. Then compare your lists with the observations and pointers we offer. In what ways do your experiences reflect our advice? What can you add to the discussion?

- *Do your homework.* As with other kinds of speeches, preparing carefully for a speech of introduction is important. Study the materials the speaker has provided, such as a résumé. Call and chat with the speaker if the information he or she has given you is unclear or incomplete. Make sure you understand exactly what the speaker plans to talk about.
- *Look for connections between the speaker and the audience.* Most speakers have accomplished many things, been many places, and won several awards. You clearly cannot cover them all. You will want to highlight information that would be important for any group to know. But you also will need to look especially for ways to introduce this particular speaker to this particular group of listeners. What do they have in common? What values do they share? When you are able to make these connections, you will assist the speaker in establishing common ground with the audience.
- *Jot down some notes.* Prepare a brief, preferably key word, outline. Make sure that you record accurate information. You'll want to get the right names of awards the speaker has won, schools he or she has attended, and so forth. The audience might not know the difference if you mispronounce the speaker's title or say she attended Yale when she really went to Harvard, but surely the speaker will.

- *Deliver the introduction effectively.* You should deliver your introduction using a direct, extemporaneous style. You will want to sound welcoming and comfortable with your knowledge about the speaker. If you know the speaker personally, your tone should convey warmth and pleasure. If you do not know the speaker, you should still sound as if you are excited to have the chance to hear him or her talk and convey your interest in the topic. Of course, the sentiments you communicate should be genuine. It would be best if you agreed to introduce only those speakers whom you regard positively.
- *Stay focused on the speaker.* The clear purpose of the speech of introduction is to introduce the speaker, not give yourself the chance to deliver a speech of your own. Some introducers end up sharing stories about how they met the speaker or talking about common experiences they have shared. It may be fine to share a brief anecdote of this sort, but don't get carried away. You may be tempted to try to impress the audience with how well you know this person, but when you succumb to this temptation, you have lost your speaker focus.

Evaluating Introductions

The speech of introduction should

- welcome the speaker.
- establish the speaker's ethos.
- prepare the audience for the speech to follow.

THE ACCEPTANCE SPEECH

Preview Those who receive an award are often called on to make an acceptance speech. In accepting an honor, the speaker usually expresses a sense of gratitude, acknowledges others, and recognizes the deeper meaning of the award. Often brief, the acceptance speech should be carefully planned and delivered with language that is fitting to the occasion.

We all enjoy receiving an award or being honored. When we are honored, we typically find ourselves in a public setting with an audience watching us receive our award. Sometimes we are not expected to do anything except smile appreciatively at the audience while saying "thank you" to the person handing us the award. On other occasions, however, we may be expected to make a short **acceptance speech**.

acceptance speech a typically brief speech expressing gratitude for an honor or award

Purposes of the Acceptance Speech

In making an acceptance speech, you will want to convey a sincere sense of gratitude to those who have honored you. Your expression of thanks should be spoken with a tone of modesty, grace, and sincerity. Suppose the leaders of your hometown have just named you one of the outstanding alumni of your local high school. Imagine yourself receiving this award in front of several of your former teachers and classmates, your parents, and a number of community leaders. You might begin by saying,

> Thank you so much for honoring me with this wonderful award. I have always felt very fortunate to have grown up and been educated in such a fine, supportive community. I will always treasure this very special honor because it comes from you—the people who have meant the most to me throughout my life.

FRAME OF REFERENCE

In accepting an award, the speaker hopes to convey a sense of gratitude to the audience. On receiving an award as an outstanding speaker, Scott McKain pays tribute to the organization that presented him with the award as well as the special people who helped him in his career.

If sincere, this expression of thanks should be very well received.

In your acceptance speech, you will also want to acknowledge others. This does not mean that you must come up with a lengthy list of everyone who ever contributed to your life in any way. But you do need to thank those who have helped you along the way, and especially those who are most closely associated with this particular award.

A young woman, Patti, once won a state speech contest. In honor of her victory, the mayor of her community presented her with the Mayor's Key to the City at a formal meeting of the city council. In accepting her award, Patti acknowledged someone by saying,

> I would never have received this honor—in fact, I would never have even *entered* this speech contest—had it not been for the encouragement of my history teacher, Dorothy Killion. It was Ms. Killion who found out about the contest and encouraged me to enter it. She has been a source of inspiration for me ever since I entered high school, and today I am especially grateful for her faith in me. Without her, I would not be receiving this honor.

Patti could have given credit to many other people, but she chose the person who had most directly contributed to this particular award.

Finally, in delivering your acceptance speech, acknowledge the deeper meaning of the award, using language that fits the formality and dignity of the occasion. If you were accepting the Outstanding Alumni Award mentioned above, you would probably want to reflect on the values that your school and community stand for and affirm your commitment to those values and your appreciation of them. You might comment on what it means to you to be part of a community where education is truly celebrated, where people understand the meaning of being a good neighbor, and where diversity is valued. When you share your sense of the award's deeper meaning, you show your understanding of its significance, and you honor your listeners and others responsible for giving you the award.

Tips for Preparing and Presenting the Acceptance Speech

Even though most of us will make an acceptance speech only a few times in our lives, when we do, the event will be very important to us, and we will want to do an excellent job. Here are some guidelines to follow:

- *Learn as much as you can about the award.* Knowing about the award—its history and meaning—can help you prepare your comments concerning its deeper meaning to you. If you are the first person to receive this award, you may want to mention that fact. If other people you admire have received this award previously, mentioning them and your admiration for them would be fitting.

- *Plan and practice your speech in advance.* Make sure you know how you are going to convey your gratitude, whom you want to acknowledge, and what you want to say about the award's true meaning. You can make a few notes. Practicing several times will help you deliver your speech with little reference to them. Speak as conversationally as possible.

- *Make your language fit the occasion.* Acceptance speeches are usually delivered in formal settings, and your language should reflect a sense of dignity. Telling jokes and using slang are not appropriate. This is a time to speak formally, even eloquently, if possible.

- *Make your speech brief.* Most acceptance speeches should be very brief, probably no longer than three to five minutes. The speech could be even shorter, as long as it contains the key elements discussed here. Your listeners will expect you to be brief. However important your award is, the audience will no doubt have other business to conduct, and perhaps a keynote speaker is yet to come. So a carefully crafted, brief acceptance speech is usually expected and appreciated.

  Like other speaking occasions, certain situations may call for a longer acceptance speech. The person who is nominated by the Republican or Democratic party to run for president of the United States, for instance, will be expected to make a much longer acceptance speech. Those who are awarded the Nobel Prize traditionally deliver longer speeches. But most of us will not confront these types of speaking situations.

- *Adapt to audience expectations.* Although we can make some generalizations about acceptance speeches, each speech will grow out of a particular situation and may present you with diverse audience expectations. It's important for you to understand these expectations and adapt accordingly.

  In *Spotlight on the Acceptance Speech,* Scott McKain adapted his speech well to a unique situation. Scott received a prestigious award for excellence in professionalism and public speaking from the National Speakers Association. The entire evening's program was devoted to five award presentations, and each recipient was *expected* to speak for several minutes (longer than the typical acceptance speech). Scott clearly knew his audience well and chose to conclude his speech by offering them hope and encouragement, seeking to inspire them to excel. In a sense, he combined the acceptance speech and the speech of inspiration, which is discussed in the next section.

PORTFOLIO 17.2

"And I'd Also Like to Thank. . ."

Which of the pointers provided in the text regarding the acceptance speech make good sense to you, in light of your viewing of an awards ceremony you've seen on television or attended in your community? What, if anything, would you modify in the text?

KEEP IN MIND 17.3

Functions of the Speech of Acceptance

The speech of acceptance should

- express a sense of gratitude.
- acknowledge others.
- recognize the deeper meaning of the award.

SPOTLIGHT ON... The Acceptance Speech

This honor, this recognition, this award is *so* meaningful and so special. Yet, what I find myself thinking on this night is not so much of the wonderful honor, but of the wonderful *people* who have been so gracious, so kind, so incredible to me during the 15 years that I have been a professional speaker.

I would certainly like to thank the selection committee because I know what a challenging and difficult and awesome job it is—and I know how seriously you take it, and that adds to my appreciation of this wonderful honor. . . .

There are some special people I would like to thank as well. Mark Mayfield and I have traveled around the country speaking as all of you do, but Mark and I also do a team presentation together for a lot of chapter meetings. Mark and I talk about the importance of having a speaker "buddy"—someone with whom you can share, someone you can call in the middle of the night, someone you can talk with, share with, and Mark is the guy who has served that role for me. But Mark has also been one of my *best friends* for the past 25 years. And Mark, I *appreciate* everything that you have meant in my life and thank you so much for that. . . .

The next one is tough. There was a young woman who left an incredibly difficult situation, a relationship that was emotionally and physically abusive. To take the steps she took—I don't know that kind of courage—she turned her life around. She got a job, and because of her physical attractiveness and charisma, she was able to date some very successful people—bankers, lawyers, entrepreneurs. And then, a guy came along and said he wanted to be a speaker. . . . When I asked her to marry me, I said, "Wouldn't it be so great if we could make it *together?*" We married after knowing each other 10 weeks—and that was 15 years ago! And so, Sherri, the next time you smile that smile and crinkle your nose and your eyes flash and you giggle and say, "I made him all he *ever* was," please know that I told my 2,000 best friends that *I* know it's true.

And, finally, my mentor is not here tonight—except in spirit. The reason I have had the chance to be here tonight is because I had the great good fortune to know a speaker named Grady Nutt. . . . Grady became one of my dearest, closest friends—an inspiration in my life. He did *so many things* to make my life so wonderful! Grady was the most incredible speaker I have ever heard. He could double an audience over in laughter—yet, he could set them straight with insight and truth and perceptions beyond which I have not known. I wanted to *be* Grady Nutt!! He helped my career in so many ways, but never more than when he took me aside one week before he died in a plane crash returning home from a speech. He said, "Scott, if you hope to be the next Grady Nutt, the best you can hope for is second place. Be the best Scott you can be!"

I have this fear that tonight there are many of you who are first-timers and new in this business who are sitting there, and you've not only been inspired, not only been motivated—you've been *terrified!!!* (laughter) You've seen wonderful speakers, you've seen wealthy speakers, you've seen rich speakers talking to you about how they've spoken in Paris and how they've spoken in Israel and how they've spoken around the world—and *you're* hoping you can speak, next week, somewhere close to home! The advice I would like to give you, for what it's worth, is the advice that Grady gave to me: "Be the best *you* that you can be!" You've got a corner on that market!

. . . I think of when Kevin Costner was accepting the Oscar for *Dances with Wolves.* He held that most famous award in his hand. He looked at it and he looked at the crowd and he said, "You know when we get together, in this same room, the same time next year . . . when we get together—there are going to be a lot of you who don't even remember who won the awards." "But," he said, "you have given my friends and my family and me a night we shall *never* forget." Thank you for making that memory for me.

Scott McKain speech

THE SPEECH OF INSPIRATION

Preview The minister who speaks at a youth conference, the motivational speaker who talks to community volunteers, and the commencement speaker who addresses a group of graduating seniors all want to inspire their listeners. So, too, do keynote speakers at political conventions, as they celebrate and strive to reinforce the party's fundamental principles.

The **speech of inspiration** is aimed at arousing listeners' feelings of appreciation, commitment, and motivation to pursue worthy goals or embrace lofty values. Inspirational speeches are given in diverse settings, ranging from academic and business to political and religious.

speech of inspiration a speech intended to inspire appreciation, commitment, and motivation to pursue worthy goals or embrace lofty values

Purposes of the Speech of Inspiration

Speeches of inspiration provide encouragement, offer a new perspective, and motivate listeners to do things differently or see life in a new light. They also remind listeners of their own values and reinforce shared beliefs. Speakers who inspire help listeners feel uplifted—their minds refreshed, their convictions clarified, their emotions stirred, and their spirits renewed.

Spotlight on the Speech of Inspiration presents an excerpt from one of the great keynote speeches, delivered in 1984 at the Democratic National Convention by Governor Mario Cuomo of New York. In this part of his address, Cuomo seeks to inspire his listeners to embrace the values of the Democratic party—a commitment to inclusiveness and diversity—and to remember how fortunate they are to be part of a nation that has upheld such values. In this excerpt, Cuomo moves toward his conclusion with a compelling story.

Not everyone can be an inspirational speaker. This kind of speaking grows from one's life history, philosophy, and desire to inspire and motivate others. Often the speaker will have an extensive background with a problem, an issue, or a goal. A person who has overcome great adversity (such as a physical disability), conquered a major problem (such as

 PORTFOLIO 17.3

The Inspiration Factor

Who inspires you? What motivational speaker, or "regular" speaker who presented a motivational speech, has affected your outlook and degree of enthusiasm? What was it about her or his message that got to you? What was it about his or her delivery that fired you up?

Make a quick list of the speaker's content and presentational style. Then read the tips we provide. How does what you've listed reinforce what we've presented in the text? What supplemental insights can you add?

A speech of inspiration can motivate listeners to pursue worthy goals. Here Milton Creagh encourages his audience of young students to avoid drug and alcohol abuse. (Associated Press)

SPOTLIGHT ON... The Speech of Inspiration

It's an old story. It's as old as our history. The difference between Democrats and Republicans has always been measured in courage and confidence. The Republicans believe that the wagon train will not make it to the frontier unless some of the old, some of the weak are left behind by the side of the trail. The strong, the strong they tell us will inherit the land! We Democrats believe in something else. We Democrats believe that we can make it all the way with the whole family intact. And we have more than once—ever since Franklin Roosevelt lifted himself from his wheelchair to lift this nation from its knees. Wagon train after wagon train, to new frontiers of education, housing, peace; the whole family aboard; constantly reaching out to extend and enlarge our family, lifting them up into the wagon on the way. Blacks and Hispanics and people of every ethnic group, and Native Americans—all those struggling to build their families and claim some small share of America. For nearly fifty years we carried them all to new levels of comfort and security and dignity, even affluence. And remember this—some of us in this room today are only here because this nation had that kind of confidence. And it would be wrong to forget that.

Mario Cuomo, "Keynote Address," in *Great Speeches for Criticism and Analysis,* 2nd ed., ed. Lloyd Rohler and Roger Cook (Greenwood, Ind.: Alistair Press, 1993), p. 67. *Vital Speeches of the Day* 50: Mario Cuomo, "Keynote Address to the Democratic National Convention," (August 15, 1984), p. 647.

alcoholism), or devoted his or her life to working with a social malady (such as poverty or child abuse) is an excellent candidate for inspirational speaking.

Tips for Preparing and Presenting the Speech of Inspiration

If you are in the position of giving a speech of inspiration, here are some guidelines to follow:

- *Establish your credibility.* As an inspirational speaker, you must have a positive ethos with the audience. There can be no doubt about your commitment in the minds of the listeners. Often the audience will already know of your commitment, or the person who introduces you will remind them. But if this does not happen, you will need to make your convictions clear. We can feel inspired only by those who are living the life they are asking us to live, whose successes empower them to offer us

THE WIZARD OF ID **Brant parker and Johnny hart**

By permission of Johnny Hart and Creators Syndicate, Inc.

encouragement, and whose philosophy we can strongly identify with.

- *Reinforce the values you share with the audience.* Speakers cannot motivate or inspire listeners if they share no common bond of values, aspirations, and goals. You can usually assume that you and your listeners believe in the same fundamental ideals and share many aspirations. Nevertheless, during your speech you should celebrate those values, stimulating the audience to remember and honor them. In some inspirational speeches, such as sermons, you will ask listeners to recommit to a life that more fully honors those things in which you all believe.

CONNECTING TO THE NET

The most famous examples of speeches of inspiration in the United States are the inaugural addresses of our presidents. To study some of these addresses, go to: **http://college.hmco.com/communication/andrews/public_speaking/2e/students/** and click on *Connecting to the Net*. From there, follow the link to Presidential Inaugurals.

- *Deliver your speech with enthusiasm and conviction.* No one can be inspired by a speaker who delivers a speech without much enthusiasm. Perhaps more than any other kind of speaker, the inspirational speaker should use a dynamic, engaging delivery—with plenty of movement, excellent eye contact, and vocal and facial expressiveness. Projecting a confident, enthusiastic style is essential to maintaining credibility and inspiring the audience. For most inspirational speeches, brevity is also a virtue.

KEEP IN MIND 17.4

Functions of the Speech of Inspiration

The speech of inspiration should

- offer encouragement, insights, or motivation.
- help listeners feel uplifted, refreshed, or inspired.
- reinforce shared values, goals, and aspirations.

THE AFTER-DINNER SPEECH

Preview Sometimes speeches are given after lunch or dinner, perhaps in the context of a business meeting or conference. Although many after-dinner speeches seek primarily to entertain listeners, they may convey a more serious, memorable message as well.

Most **after-dinner speeches** are enjoyable to listen to, but not all after-dinner speakers will see their primary goal as entertainment. When, for example, Alan Greenspan presents an after-dinner address to a group of distinguished economists, he may not be very amusing. In fact, in this situation the audience may be far from relaxed as they wait to hear his pronouncements on the future of the U.S. economy. In some situations, then, after-dinner speeches are informative or persuasive.

after-dinner speech a speech presented after a meal that attempts to stimulate enjoyment while informing or persuading

Purposes and Challenges of the After-Dinner Speech

Because after-dinner speeches are often delivered after the listeners have eaten either lunch or dinner, or sometimes at the conclusion of a long conference, most are brief. The speaker needs to establish a theme, set a mood, or convey a

After-dinner speakers, though they may aim to convey an important message, should be sure to make the speech entertaining and enjoyable. (John Coletti/Stock, Boston, Inc.)

message. Although humor is often used, beneath the humor is usually a memorable message. The language should be lively and colorful, and the delivery spontaneous and direct.

After-dinner speeches can be challenging. Humor is hard to plan; professional humorists are likely to employ teams of writers, and even they can and often do flop. Also, what may seem funny to you or to a few of your friends one night may not seem so funny the next morning.

For example, a student was preparing to give a report in class on a famous debate of the eighteenth century in the British House of Commons. The night before his presentation, he amused himself and his roommates with the idea that the debate could be reported the way Dick Vitale, the sports announcer, would report it. The next morning at 8:30, however, what had seemed so funny the previous night sounded strained and overdone in the classroom. Instead of being enjoyable, the experience was embarrassing for everyone.

Spotlight on the After-Dinner Speech features a delightful after-dinner presentation by Mark Mayfield, a motivational speaker, to a large audience. His humorous stories were enhanced by an engaging, audience-centered style of delivery. It's important to recognize that this segment is part of Mayfield's introduction. The body of the speech uses much humor but simultaneously conveys a compelling message about laughter and life.

Enjoyment Versus Humor

Creating enjoyment, it should be pointed out, does not always mean being funny. In fact, many after-dinner speeches include a lot of informative material. And however lighthearted they may be, many, like a good fable, have a

SPOTLIGHT ON... **The After-Dinner Speech**

I'm just a wee bit nervous about this, uh, platform. Let me tell you why. This happened years ago. I'm doing a meeting and it was a dinner event and we had a temporary riser much like this—and we had the head table up there—and everybody who could correctly spell their own name was at this table—crammed up there like sardines.

Halfway through the course of the meal the gentleman to the far right of the speaker decides to get slightly more comfortable—so he scoots his chair a tad to his right, but it's enough of a tad to move the right rear leg of his chair off the platform. Now, you all know what happens when a chair sits on three legs! It doesn't!!! He fell off the right side of the platform. Now, put yourself in his shoes. What is the first thing that you do when you fall from an elevated place? You reach for something—that's right!! This guy's a normal fellow—he *grabs the tablecloth!* (mimics this) Now, as he goes to the ground, he *yanks* everybody's half-eaten meal onto our laps up there!

Now, put yourself in *these* people's places. What is the first thing that you do when you spill food on your lap? You *jump up!* That's right!! But, let me tell you something—*before* you jump up, you know what you do? You scoot your chair back! This is 100% true: the entire head table just disappeared!!

Now, you probably think that this was the apex of the entertainment—no, no, no! See, this was an awards program and the first award they were going to present is to a gentleman who's a rather tall chap—in fact, he's about 6′7″. How do I know that? Well, this was an older hotel and the ceilings were low—and they had ventilation fans. The distance between the ventilation fan blade and the top of the riser was 6′5″! You do the math—okay?

Now, he gets called for this award—this is a complete surprise to him. He's coming to the front, paying no attention . . . POW!!! Steps up and gets nailed by the fan blade—right here (points) on the forehead. Have you ever been hit by a fan blade here? One thing happens. You bleed! A lot! Now, you've got to picture this—this guy is receiving an award. He's got blood covering his face, his white shirt is red, his handkerchief is blood-soaked—he receives an award for working twenty years without a time loss accident!!! So, I'm telling you, I'm a little nervous about this stage up here. . . .

Mark Mayfield, "Mirthmaking."

moral at the end. For the audience, enjoyment comes from being relaxed and interested in the point or moral being communicated, not necessarily from being amused.

Furthermore, different people enjoy different things. Some people like to solve puzzles and play word games. Some people like historical adventure. Some people like to watch television, and their interests might range from sitcoms to documentaries to sports. Some people invariably find a cream pie smashed in a comic's face to be uproariously funny. What people enjoy is not always easy to predict, and the clues you can get from audience analysis may or may not be helpful.

Obviously, listeners will bring diverse tastes and preferences to any speaking situation. Even so, if you think about it, you can probably guess with some accuracy what kind of music many college students find enjoyable, what sorts of television programs most people watch, what movies are popular, what the serious interests are of those in particular majors, and so forth. A speaker could give a speech with such specific purposes as the following:

- I want my audience to enjoy my account of how King Tut's tomb was first discovered.
- I want my audience to enjoy my explanation of how horror movies are made.
- I want my audience to enjoy a description of my motorcycle trip through the Middle East.

PORTFOLIO 17.4

The Heart of the Spectacle

Think back on speeches you might have listened to in an after-dinner setting. Which were the best ones? Did the speaker merely rattle off joke after joke, or was he or she simultaneously getting at something worthy of your attention? What does this tell you about the most effective qualities of an after-dinner speech?

In all of these cases, the listeners may learn something or may even be actuated in some way, such as going to see a horror movie or taking a trip to Egypt, but that is not what the speaker hopes to accomplish. What he or she really wants is for each listener to have a good time listening to the speech. That means, of course, that the speech will have to be developed differently from a speech with another kind of purpose. Many after-dinner speeches are developed inductively, as the speaker shares amusing, meaningful, or interesting stories. Of course, the strategy used depends, as always, on the speaker's specific purpose.

Tips for Preparing and Presenting the After-Dinner Speech

If you have the talent, inclination, and opportunity to develop and deliver an after-dinner speech, here are some tips to keep in mind:

- *Seek to stimulate enjoyment in your audience.* As with all speeches, audience analysis is essential. What will listeners most enjoy? How can you connect with them and those things that would amuse them? You may plan to share some interesting and amusing stories. Occasionally, some of your humor may be spontaneous. You may also gesture, move, and use your voice and other aspects of your delivery to reinforce listeners' enjoyment of your presentation. You will want to use an engaging, extemporaneous delivery.
- *Keep your presentation brief.* The after-dinner speech is usually best received if it is not too long and drawn out. Expectations and customs will vary from audience to audience, but generally a speech of twenty minutes or so should be well received. However, stay in touch with the audience response. Build your speech flexibly so that you can add more humorous stories (if things are going very well) or omit some (if you are starting to lose the audience).
- *Communicate a memorable message.* Most audiences expect to walk away from a speech with something to think about, remember, or use as a basis for further thought or action. However much they may enjoy themselves, they will appreciate a more enduring message. Humor—perhaps in the form of an amusing story—can be quite memorable, and most good anecdotes have a serious point. Besides, when listeners are enjoying themselves, perhaps even laughing at their own human foibles, they tend to become less defensive and more responsive to change. Thus the listener who is enjoying himself or herself may also be learning and growing.

 KEEP IN MIND 17.5

Functions of the After-Dinner Speech

The after-dinner speech should

- stimulate enjoyment in the audience.
- use humor effectively.
- convey a meaningful message.

Table 17.1 reviews the guidelines for presenting the speeches discussed in this chapter.

TABLE 17.1 Tips for Ceremonial Speeches: A Checklist

Type of Ceremonial Speech	Tips
Speech of Introduction	Do your homework. Look for and stress connections between the speaker and the audience. Jot down some notes; develop a key word outline. Deliver the introduction effectively. Stay speaker focused.
Acceptance Speech	Learn as much as you can about the award. Plan and practice your speech in advance. Make your language fit the occasion; use dignified language. Make your speech brief. Carefully adapt to audience expectations.
Speech of Inspiration	Establish your credibility. Reinforce the values you share with your audience. Deliver your speech with enthusiasm and conviction.
After-Dinner Speech	Stimulate enjoyment in your audience through engaging content and delivery. Keep your presentation brief. Communicate a memorable message.

Ceremonial speeches come in diverse forms and serve varied purposes. To test your understanding of ceremonial speeches, go to **Next Step: Ceremonial Speaking** in **Lesson 10** of the **VideoLab** CD-ROM and complete the exercises.

Go to the **Online SpeechStudio,** where you will find the **Ceremonial Speech Evaluation Form** that you might want to use the next time you listen critically to a ceremonial speech.

SUMMARY

The principles of effective communication we have discussed throughout this book are applicable to a wide variety of speaking contexts. Even so, certain speaking occasions may present special challenges. In this chapter, we have examined public speaking for ceremonial occasions.

Most of us will give ceremonial speeches at various times throughout our lives. When we give these speeches, the occasions are usually important and often rather formal. Through ceremonial speaking, we reinforce shared beliefs and values, applaud or remember heroes, and strive to encourage and inspire our audience.

Ceremonial speeches are varied in purpose, formality, and context. They include speeches of introduction (in which we introduce someone who is about to give a speech), acceptance speeches (in which we accept an award or honor), inspirational speeches (in which we attempt to encourage or motivate the audience), and after-dinner speeches (in which we seek to interest and entertain the audience).

Ceremonial speeches should be carefully planned, crafted with the demands of the occasion and audience expectations in mind, and delivered with a style fitting to the occasion—usually extemporaneously. Though important, most ceremonial speeches are relatively brief. However, there are exceptions, such as commencement speeches, inaugural addresses, and other political speeches.

For a reminder of the rules of effective ceremonial speaking, go to **Lesson 10 Coach: Tips to Remember** on the **VideoLab** CD-ROM, view the video clips, and review the list of "dos" and "don'ts."

QUESTIONS FOR REVIEW AND REFLECTION

1. What are the basic functions of ceremonial speeches?
2. What three components should a speech of introduction include? What are the potential pitfalls when delivering this kind of speech?
3. Suppose you discover that you are going to receive an award and you have to give a brief acceptance speech. What are some key elements you would include in your speech?
4. Support or refute this statement: "Acceptance speeches should always be brief." Explain the basis for the position you are taking.
5. What are the keys to an effective speech of inspiration?
6. Describe the role of humor in the after-dinner speech. How would you distinguish humor from enjoyment?

ENDNOTES

1. John Fitzgerald Kennedy, "Inaugural Address," in *The Presidents Speak,* ed. Davis Newton Lott (New York: Henry Holt, 1994), p. 313.
2. Dwight D. Eisenhower, "Second Inaugural Address: The Price of Peace," in *The Presidents Speak,* ed. Davis Newton Lott (New York: Henry Holt, 1994), p. 310.
3. R. Cohen, *Negotiating Across Culture: Communication Obstacles in International Diplomacy* (Washington, D.C.: Institute of Peace, 1991).

Communicating in the Workplace

18

CHAPTER OBJECTIVES

After studying this chapter, you should be able to

1. **recognize the importance of group work in contemporary organizations.**
2. **identify the strengths and weaknesses associated with group work.**
3. **participate in a team meeting, following the principles of effective group communication and leadership.**
4. **plan and present a group presentation to an audience.**
5. **recognize some special kinds of public presentations given in business and professional settings.**
6. **prepare and deliver a sales or proposal presentation to a small group.**

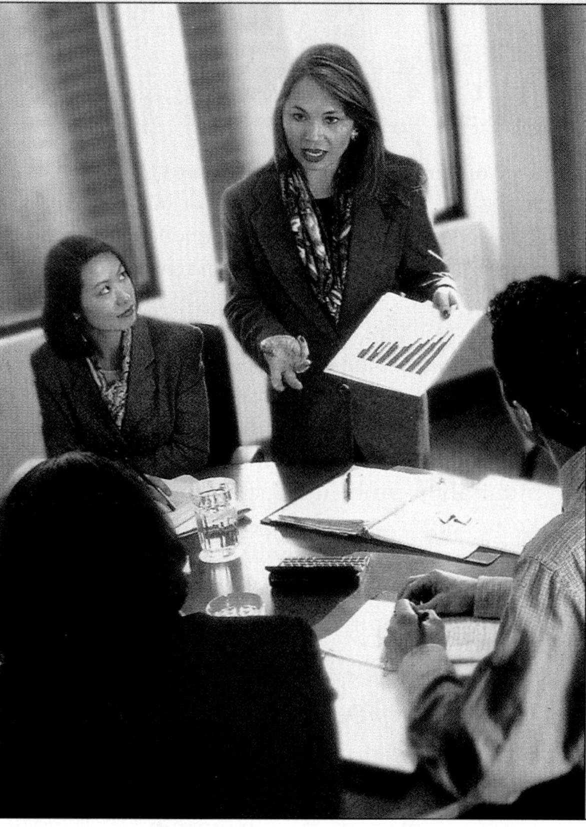

CHAPTER SURVEY

Perhaps as you have read this book, you have asked yourself the question, "Will I *really* be asked to make speeches after I graduate from college and move on with my career?" The chances are very good that you will be called on to make public presentations throughout your life, as a professional in various work situations (as a manager, accountant, health care professional, attorney, or teacher) and as a citizen in your community (as a member of a school board, parent teacher organization, church group, city council, or volunteer organization). If you occupy a leadership position, you will speak more. If you simply belong to an organization, you will be asked to report, provide information, and offer impromptu assessments in all kinds of meeting contexts.

You will also be expected to know how to interact effectively in groups. Nearly everyone participates in meetings, task forces, teams, and other groups as part of professional life. As organizations have become increasingly team-based, their leaders are seeking employees who feel comfortable working in this group-oriented environment. Thus, knowing how to be a team player, how to interact effectively with others to complete projects, and how to provide leadership in group contexts are increasingly valued skills in the twenty-first century.[1] This final chapter explores some of the special communication opportunities and responsibilities that are very much a part of modern business and professional life.

COMMUNICATING IN GROUPS

Preview Increasingly, contemporary organizations are using groups to solve problems, make decisions, monitor quality, and engage in a host of other activities. When groups have effective leadership and team members who understand group dynamics and are committed to making the group work, they can make tremendous contributions to the workplace.

Teamwork has become the buzzword of business. Most modern management theories advocate using teams or groups to solve problems, make decisions, determine quality standards, and engage in a host of other activities. Yet not all groups are effective. Many are plagued by serious communication problems, lack of commitment, and a poor understanding of how groups should work. When groups do function effectively, they can be tremendous sources of creativity, commitment, and motivation. Understanding how to make groups work well is vital in the contemporary professional world.[2]

Groups: Pros and Cons

Participating in groups can be frustrating. Group members may arrive late, refuse to do their share of the work, dominate the group's interactions by talking incessantly, or take the group off on irrelevant tangents. Group meetings can be time-consuming. We may find ourselves wishing that we could just work on a problem on our own; the group may seem to be wasting valuable time. Group members may also show little ability or willingness to listen to others, while appointed leaders may not be up to the task of leading.

The group is a dynamic unit in which issues, data, timelines, and personalities get stirred together, sometimes yielding an unproductive, unpleasant brew. It is little wonder that Irving Janis, a group scholar, once observed that "groups, like individuals, have shortcomings. Groups can bring out the worst as well as the best in man. Nietzsche went so far as to say that madness is the exception in individuals but the rule in groups."[3] Given this kind of indictment, why are groups increasingly used in academic, professional, and business settings?

Sometimes groups work extremely well together, as you can see from the *Spotlight on Hot Groups*. Groups can be creative. They bring together individuals with different interests and areas of expertise, providing an arena where problems can be approached from a variety of perspectives and decision-making can be improved.[4] In addition, working in groups can be enjoyable.

When group members are allowed to make decisions that have an impact on their lives, they may feel empowered and more willing to work hard to put the solution into action. Those who have had some input into an organization's

SPOTLIGHT ON... Hot Groups

Scholar Harold Leavitt argues that companies sometimes need groups that managers can't control. These so-called "hot groups" are lively, high-achievement, dedicated groups, whose members are turned on to exciting and challenging tasks.

Hot groups are typically characterized by:

- Total preoccupation with the task at hand
- Intellectual intensity, integrity, and lively argument
- Emotional intensity
- Fluid role structure
- Small size

Hot group members are best described as:

- Connective individualists—independent individuals who are also team players

When are hot groups most likely to pop up?

- When organizations permit openness and flexibility
- When leaders encourage independence and autonomy
- When organizations hire great talent and then give individuals plenty of elbow room
- When the organizational culture is committed to truth seeking
- When a state of crisis or keen competition with other groups exists

Key individual roles within hot groups:

- *Conductors,* who lead the orchestra—obvious movers and shakers
- *Patrons,* who support it—working behind the scenes to protect, coach, listen, and offer suggestions
- *Keepers of the Flame,* who sustain the group through time—nourishing new ideas, new solutions, and new partners in a long chain of hot groups

Harold J. Leavitt and Jean Lipman-Blumen, "Hot Groups," *Harvard Business Review* 73 (Fall 1995): 109–116.

decision-making are likely to feel committed to helping implement the decision, policy, or plan. If group members study effective group communication, they can usually learn to function effectively in small group contexts. One good place to begin is by considering group leadership.

Group Leadership: What Are the Options?

In most work groups, one person is the leader. He or she may be responsible for preparing an agenda and for dealing with the logistics of the meeting, such as arranging a meeting time and place. He or she also will be expected to get the group started, keep everyone on track, guide the discussion, see that some record of the meeting is kept, and close the meeting on time.

An important element of group leadership is the extent to which the leader shares power with the group members. Some leaders take total control of the meeting and decision-making, simply telling everyone else what is going to happen, who is going to do what, and so on. Other leaders are just the opposite; they allow a great deal of participation by the group members, both in interacting and in making decisions.

Regarding the concept of shared or conserved power, we can identify four basic approaches to conducting meetings.

Autocratic Leadership. This highly directive approach to leadership occurs when a leader does virtually all the talking and decides everything (or virtually

Presidents may have demonstrated different styles of leadership but all have relied on extensive input from groups of advisers when forming policy or making important decisions. (SYGMA)

everything) the group will do. **Autocratic leadership** results in meetings that consist primarily of announcements made by the leader, followed by questions group members may have for the leader. In other words, communication is almost exclusively downward (from leader to group member), and shared decision-making is virtually nonexistent.

autocratic leadership a style of leadership in which the leader is the principal voice and decision-maker

Consultative Leadership. When the leader uses a **consultative leadership** style, he or she encourages input from group members, while retaining the authority to make the final decision. In effect, the leader "consults" with group members, asking for their thoughts and ideas concerning problems, decisions, actions, and so on. Group members participate in the interaction, and they have some influence on the leader's thinking. However, they have power only to the extent that they can persuade the leader to adopt their suggestions or proposals.

consultative leadership a style of leadership in which the leader encourages suggestions and proposals

Democratic Leadership. A leader who embraces the **democratic leadership** style adheres to the principle of "one person, one vote." The leader simply facilitates the meeting; he or she has no more power than anyone else. Group members interact spontaneously while making decisions and solving problems together.[5]

democratic leadership a style of leadership in which the leader facilitates meetings in such a way that group members interact and solve problems together

Laissez-faire Leadership. Using the **laissez-faire leadership** style, a leader has virtually no role in the meeting. If, for example, a supervisor asks an employee to conduct a meeting while the supervisor sits at the back of the room, or if the boss announces in advance that he or she will not attend a particular meeting so that a less inhibited discussion might occur, he or she is practicing laissez-faire leadership. If this leadership style is to be effective, it ought to be occasional and strategic. Since the laissez-faire leader gives away power, the group takes on both control and responsibility for its actions.

laissez-faire leadership a style of leadership in which the leader cedes control to the group in an attempt to promote creativity and responsibility

What Determines the Best Leadership Style?

No one approach to leadership is always best. Each situation must be examined to determine which leadership style will be most effective. Several factors should be considered when selecting a style (and corresponding meeting agenda).

Do you think you can identify your typical leadership style? Does your style vary, depending upon the situation? To assess your leadership preference(s), go to the **Online SpeechStudio** and complete the **What Kind of Leader Are You?** self-inventory.

- *Group expectations* are important. Every group has its own culture and history. What sort of leadership does the group expect you to provide?
- *Group purposes* should also be taken into account. What is the group trying to achieve? Learning, socializing, or team building require minimum leader control, while communicating specific information to the group is much more directive.
- *Group methods* are another consideration. Some group processes, such as brainstorming or rating problem priorities,[6] require strict procedural control, while others, such as discussing a problem's underlying causes, can be done with virtually no leadership.
- *Time* is also a consideration. Participation takes time, while announcements can be given quickly. If a decision must be made at once, autocratic leadership may be required.
- *Group members' skills and maturity* should also be considered in choosing a leadership style. Experienced, mature group members require less guidance and control than do new, inexperienced members. Moreover, the more people participate, the better they become at participation. Thus, gradually giving more and more participation to group members is one way of increasing the skills and maturity of the group.
- *The leader's own skill and confidence* are also important. In general, directive leadership is easier to exert than consultative or democratic leadership. The latter two require skill in listening, handling conflict, controlling group interaction, and so on. Thus, as leaders become more skilled, they tend to become more participative over time.
- *The need for group support* and *the group's interest and involvement in the issues under discussion* are final considerations in choosing the most appropriate leadership style for a given situation. Some decisions need the active endorsement of the group. In addition, participation in decision-making increases the commitment of those making the decision. Simply being told what to do or how to do it minimizes commitment and motivation. And, of course, the more controversial, involving, and interesting the issue being discussed, the more the members of the group will want, and should be encouraged, to participate.

Power and Leadership

Appointed leaders are very important in groups. Leaders establish the climate, set the rules (at least initially), and have many opportunities to exert their influence. In organizational settings, appointed leaders are powerful people. The leader may be the department head, the chairperson of the board, or even the CEO. The leader's status can be intimidating to other group members. Suppose you don't agree with the senior partner in your law firm or the dean of your school. Would you feel free to tell him or her?

SPOTLIGHT ON... **Avoiding Meeting Pitfalls**

Practical Tips for Leaders

Appointed leaders spend a lot of time planning and conducting meetings. Here are seven common meeting pitfalls and brief suggestions for how to avoid them.

- *Lack of clarity about the meeting's purpose:* Why is the group meeting? It's easy to hold weekly staff meetings, for instance, whether or not they are needed. The effective leader should be able to answer this question, "What are the results this meeting should produce?"
- *Goals that could be accomplished by means other than a meeting:* There is nothing magical about holding a meeting, and sometimes the wisest course is to avoid meeting in the first place. Meetings that are routinely held for the exclusive purpose of sharing information and project updates should be canceled in favor of emails and information-sharing software, such as Lotus Notes.
- *Inadequate preparation on the part of the leader:* For a meeting to work well, the leader needs to address a number of issues in advance: What is the purpose? Who is coming? How long will the meeting last? Where is the best place to meet? What is the agenda? What problem-solving approach will work best? What information will participants need in advance of the meeting?
- *A haphazard decision-making process:* Meetings are the forum in which team-based organizations make some of their most important decisions. Yet, many committee members do not really understand how to approach decision-making, and meetings can be sloppy and unproductive. The leader needs to be savvy about group process and to select a decision-making agenda that is well suited to the issues the group is addressing.
- *Jumping to conclusions:* In reaching a decision, groups rarely establish criteria or standards by which solutions will be evaluated. Instead, they are quick to jump into a consideration of solutions, long before they understand the problem. The leader should choose a problem-solving agenda that requires the group to define and explore the problem, to reflect on its causes and effects, *before* looking at possible solutions.
- *Overdeveloped egos:* Some meetings end up not being about problem solving at all. Ideas may not be accepted on their merits but on the competing interests of people at the table. The leader must anticipate ego issues, recognize that some participants bring their own agendas to the meeting, and create and reinforce norms that keep conflicts focused on issues.
- *Insufficient follow-up:* Meetings typically end with people being assigned to carry out various tasks. Such assignments must be accompanied by some sort of time frame and procedures for reporting back to the group. The minutes of the meeting should completely and accurately reflect what actions the group took and who was assigned various responsibilities for implementing the solutions agreed upon.

Edward Prewitt, "Pitfalls in Meetings and How to Avoid Them," *Harvard Management Update* (June 1998), pp. 9–10.

Official leaders can encourage those of lesser status to express their views candidly, or they can make them painfully aware of the price associated with disagreement. When Irving Janis studied group decision-making, he looked at groups of individuals who worked with and advised U.S. presidents. Based on his research, he concluded that leaders needed to take some direct actions to make their groups healthy and effective. He suggested, for instance, that leaders insist on the critical evaluation of ideas and information, that they occasionally ask the group to meet and talk about controversial issues in their absence, and that they ask to hear the case against any course of action the group is preparing to take.[7] The *Spotlight on Avoiding Meeting Pitfalls* offers some helpful advice to leaders.

Most leaders are in a position to empower others. They can insist on hearing from everyone. They can ask other group members to help with specific leadership functions. They can listen intently, ask probing questions, insist on hearing dissenting points of review, encourage conflict, and make sure they do

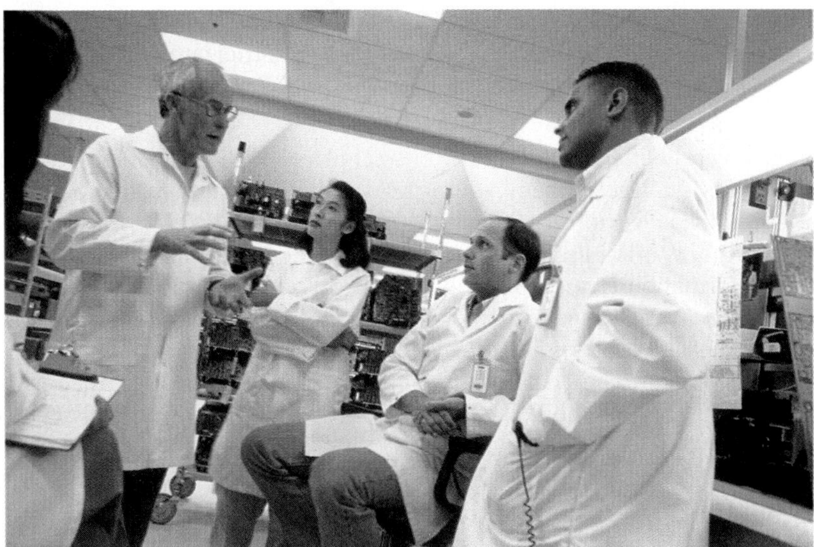

Each group member, as a part of a team, plays an important role in promoting successful interactions. (Walker Hodges/Tony Stone Images)

not dominate the conversation. They can create a climate of shared leadership, shared problem solving, and shared responsibility for the outcome of the group's deliberations. Although there are many situational factors to consider in choosing a leadership style, many groups work more effectively if leadership and decision-making are shared.

Becoming an Effective Team Member

Whether you are in an official leadership position or not, you can choose to behave in ways that enhance the group's interaction.

Prepare for Each Meeting Carefully. This means doing your homework so that you are knowledgeable about the issues to be addressed. When you offer your ideas, you'll want to be able to support them with good evidence and information. Bring notes with you, as well as copies of relevant documents that you might need to reference during the meeting. Being prepared also means developing a positive attitude toward other group members. In what ways do you anticipate that others will be able to contribute? What special experiences or knowledge will you want them to share?

Keep an Open Mind. Come prepared to listen to others and to contribute to a group decision. Of course, you will already have thought seriously about the issues to be discussed, but that doesn't mean that you have made up your mind before the meeting even starts. Remain open to others' perspectives. Encourage the expression of different points of view. If others persuade you, don't hesitate to change your mind.

Listen Constructively and Critically to Others. When someone else is talking, listen to that person with the intent of seeking an understanding of his or her point of view. Even if you don't agree with it, give it fair consideration. At the same time, don't hesitate to question someone whose information seems vague or whose ideas are not clearly articulated. Good group members take each other seriously, have a healthy respect for each other, are not afraid to challenge each other, and expect to be challenged in return.

PORTFOLIO 18.1

Expanding Your Reach

Read through the various constructive roles in Figure 18.1. Which of the roles have you most commonly played? What other roles should you take on in order to expand your repertoire as well as benefit the group? Contemplate these matters and experiment the next time you're in a group situation.

Play Several Different Roles. Group scholars have identified nearly twenty positive roles that group members can play, ranging from information giver to harmonizer (see Figure 18.1). Sometimes group members get in a rut and basically do only one or two things. For instance, a dominant person might primarily give ideas and information and control the flow of conversation. That person needs to be more balanced, also seeking others' ideas and offering appreciation when someone comes up with a good plan of action. When roles are shared in groups, everyone benefits. The group is healthier, the appointed leader's task is more manageable, and all participants should be more satisfied with the group's interactions.

Pay Attention to Nonverbal Communication. Often when we think of people working together in groups, we focus on what they say. But it is important to watch how they are acting, too, and to recognize how important **nonverbal communication** can be. For example, pay attention to eye contact. When a group member is involved in the discussion, he or she will look at others and return their gaze. Someone who refuses to establish eye contact is suggesting a lack of involvement, preparation, or interest—or perhaps a level of discomfort with what is happening. Being aware of this kind of nonverbal behavior and its implications is the first step toward acknowledging it and perhaps making some needed changes.

nonverbal communication facial expressions, gestures, vocal qualities, and physical movements that reinforce or contradict one's verbal messages

groupthink when a group's critical appraisal of ideas and willingness to express concerns are hindered by its desire for consensus

Similarly group members should be seated so that everyone has good visual access to everyone else and so that those who want to make a contribution can easily catch the eye of the chair and be "called on." A group that meets around a round table is signaling equality of status and interaction potential. By contrast, a group whose appointed leader sits at the end of a rectangular table reinforces status roles and makes it less likely for all group members to interact as equals. Monitoring these nonverbal cues is very important.

KEEP IN MIND 18.1

Communicating in Small Groups

If group work is to be productive, here are some things to remember:

- Understand the pros and cons of working together in teams.
- Consider diverse approaches to leadership.
  —Recognize factors that influence the choice of leadership style.
  —Tap the talents and resources of group members.
- Each group member should approach the team's meeting by
  —preparing carefully.
  —keeping an open mind.
  —listening constructively and critically to others.
  —playing several different roles.
  —paying attention to nonverbal communication.
  —encouraging constructive conflict.
  —treating others ethically.

Encourage Constructive Conflict. Some groups are intolerant of dissent or of conflict in any form. If someone disagrees with the group's majority, he or she may be treated like some kind of traitor. The group may put a lot of pressure on this individual, urging him or her to "come around" and "not rock the boat." Cohesive groups that are closely bonded and that have worked together over a long period of time are sometimes especially likely to expect everyone in the group to agree. In fact, some highly cohesive groups are susceptible to **groupthink**, in which group members' striving for consensus overrides their ability to critically appraise ideas and proposed courses of action.[8] The problem with this approach to decision-making is that group members do not feel free to express their concerns. As they monitor their doubts, they lapse into silence. They

FIGURE 18.1 **Constructive Roles in Groups**

Task Roles

Initiator—proposes new ideas, procedures, goals, and solutions; gets the group started

Information giver—supplies evidence, opinions, goals, and related personal experiences relevant to the task

Information seeker—asks for information from other group members, seeks clarification when necessary, and makes sure that relevant evidence is not overlooked

Opinion giver—states her own beliefs, attitudes, and judgments; is willing to take a position, although not without sensitivity to others' views

Opinion seeker—solicits opinions and feelings of others and asks for clarification of positions

Elaborator—clarifies and expands the ideas of others through examples, illustrations, and explanations—a valuable role so long as elaborations are task-relevant and reasonably brief

Integrator—clarifies the relationship between various facts, opinions, and suggestions and integrates the ideas of other members

Orienter—keeps the group directed toward its goal, summarizes what has taken place, and clarifies the positions of the group

Evaluator—expresses judgments about the relative worth of information or ideas; proposes or applies criteria for weighing the quality of information or alternative courses of action

Procedural specialist—organizes the group's work; suggests an agenda, outline, or problem-solving sequence

Consensus tester—asks if the group has reached a decision acceptable to all; suggests, when appropriate, that agreement may have been reached

Building and Maintenance Roles

Supporter—praises and agrees with others, providing a warm, supportive, interpersonal climate

Harmonizer—attempts to mediate differences, introduces compromise, and tries to reconcile differences

Tension reliever—encourages a relaxed atmosphere by reducing formality and interjecting appropriate humor

Gatekeeper—exerts some control over communication channels, encouraging reticent discussants, discouraging those who tend to monopolize the discussion, and seeking diversity of opinion

Norm creator—suggests rules of behavior for group members, challenges unproductive ways of behaving, and gives a negative response when someone violates an important group norm

Solidarity builder—expresses positive feelings toward other group members; reinforces sense of group unity and cohesiveness

Dramatist—evokes fantasies about persons and places other than the present group and time; may test a tentative value or norm through hypothetical example or story; dreams, shows creativity, and articulates visions

Working for others can be challenging, yet, nearly all of us will work under someone else's supervision a good deal of the time. To get a sense of the kind of leader you would prefer to work for, go to the **Online SpeechStudio** and complete the **What Kind of Follower Are You?** self-assessment.

are suffering, and so is the group. Healthy groups not only tolerate dissent and constructive conflict, but they welcome it.[9]

A critical role the leader can play is to encourage anyone who seems to have doubts (within reason) and to discourage anyone who appears intolerant

SPOTLIGHT ON... Creating the Conditions for Constructive Team Conflict

Is conflict always healthy? Not necessarily. It depends on how it's handled. The key is to keep healthy conflict from degenerating into dysfunctional interpersonal conflict and hostility.

Scholars from Stanford University who have studied many teams have observed:

> Without conflict, groups lose their effectiveness. . . . The alternative to conflict is usually not agreement but apathy and disengagement. Teams unable to foster substantive conflict ultimately achieve, on average, lower performance. . . .

By contrast, teams who handle conflict constructively tend to:

- work with more, rather than less, information and debate on the basis of facts
- develop multiple alternatives to enrich the level of discussion, debate, and argument
- share commonly agreed-upon goals
- inject humor into the decision process
- maintain a balanced power structure
- resolve issues without forcing consensus

Kathleen M. Eisenhardt, Jean L. Kahwajy, and L. J. Bourgeois III, "How Management Teams Can Have a Good Fight," *Harvard Business Review* 75 (Spring 1997): 77–85.

of dissent. Group members may need to be reminded that the group will make better decisions if conflicting views are aired. Reinforcing turn taking can help, too. The decisions the group makes will be better if they are truly shared and if they have emerged through a process of constructive argument and collaborative conflict.[10] The *Spotlight On Creating the Conditions for Constructive Team Conflict* offers some suggestions for how teams can constructively handle conflict.

Go to the **Online SpeechStudio,** where you will find a **Group Discussion Participation Evaluation Form** to use the next time you observe a group working together to solve a problem or make a decision. This form focuses on the performance of one individual within the group.

Go to the **Online SpeechStudio** to find another evaluation form—the **Individual and Group Discussion Evaluation Form**—that you can use to assess the performance of an entire group, as well as the individual members who are a part of it.

Treat Others Ethically. Ethical group members are less interested in winning an argument than in achieving a consensus based on mutual understanding and respect. They are as eager to listen and learn as to offer opinions and advice. Ethical group members insist on accuracy of information and are willing to take extra time and put up with additional meetings for the sake of a better, more fully informed decision.

Ethics involve developing a sense of responsibility for the good of the group as a whole. Since groups are usually embedded in a larger organization, the ethical group member will be mature enough to recognize that other organizational groups may have different priorities and that no matter how hard this group works or how well it performs, others also work hard and have legitimate needs to be fulfilled. In short, the ethical group member is a good thinker, a good listener, a hard worker, and a responsible member of the organizational community.

GROUP PRESENTATIONS

Preview Most of the time, group meetings are private affairs. Committees deliberate, decisions are made, and problems are solved behind closed doors. But sometimes individuals join with others to make group presentations before an audience. These are public presentations, and they share some similarities with individual speechmaking. Yet because a group is involved, issues of planning, coordination, and format require special attention.

How frequently will you be asked to make group presentations? No one can answer that for sure, but students at some universities often make group presentations in class, business and professional leaders are called on to participate in panels addressing various issues of relevance to the community, teams present proposals to prospective clients, and anyone who attends a conference will occasionally participate in a group presentation.

These presentations take a variety of forms and are conducted for a variety of "publics." As organizations have become increasingly consumer-oriented, many have turned to public forums to interact with community groups, stockholders, customer groups, and others. One large manufacturer of hospital supplies, for example, conducts seminars on managing hospital resources for hospital executives across the country. During these seminars, attendees listen to short speeches by experts in many areas of management, watch as these experts discuss issues with one another, and then ask questions related to their own concerns. Similarly many companies have started conducting such meetings for their own employees to increase the visibility of their executive group and to promote interaction among employees and management. These meetings involve public speaking in a group setting and plenty of general group interaction.

Whether planning and presenting a group presentation is more or less difficult than making an individual speech will depend in part on how knowledgeable and responsible group members are. Knowing basic principles of both group communication and public speaking can be very helpful.

Panel Discussions

In business and professional settings, speakers may be asked to participate in **panel discussions**, in which they interact directly and spontaneously under the guidance of a moderator. Here are some tips for preparing for and participating in panel discussions:

panel discussions public discussions in which participants on a panel interact spontaneously under the guidance of a moderator

- *Know the group.* Find out who the other panel members are and what organizations or positions they represent. Having this information, as well as anticipating the group's size, will help you tentatively plan what you want to say and how much you want to talk.
- *Obtain an agenda for the discussion.* The moderator should have some plan for how he or she wishes to organize the panel discussion. Having an agenda gives you some idea of what to expect and what issues the panel will address. Use the agenda as your guide to prepare for the discussion. Your goal is to be able to make a substantive contribution. Make a few notes, although most of your remarks should be fairly spontaneous.
- *Participate actively while sharing the floor with others.* The moderator may start with a brief statement or open question, and you can feel free to jump in and comment whenever you are ready. Make your comments succinct. Take turns with other panel members. The best panel discussions are lively and dynamic.
- *Use good interpersonal skills.* Listen to others attentively. If you do need to interrupt, do so politely and tactfully. Build on others' comments, if appropriate. Establish good eye contact with listeners while also communicating directly with other panelists. Cooperate with the moderator.

- *Come prepared to answer questions.* Panel discussions are typically followed by a question-and-answer period. Good discussions that are lively and informative should stimulate listener questions and comments. Often listeners interact extensively with panel members following a discussion. It is almost as if the audience has become part of the group.

Symposium Presentations

symposium presentation a formal presentation by a group in which each member presents prepared remarks about the topic being addressed

Go to the **Online SpeechStudio,** where you will find the **Symposium Presentation Critical Reaction Form** that you can use the next time you listen to a symposium presentation. Notice that the form allows you to assess the group's overall performance, as well as the contributions of individual members.

Another kind of group presentation is the **symposium presentation.** In comparison with the panel, the symposium is more formal. Although the group addresses a broad topic, each member prepares and presents an individual presentation. Group members do not interact directly; rather they are introduced by the moderator, and they take turns speaking one by one. Here are some tips for preparing for a symposium:

- *Know your assigned topic.* Understand what you are expected to talk about as well as the topics of other symposium members. Make sure you don't cover ground that others will cover. Once you understand your role, prepare your symposium presentation just as you would any other speech.
- *Respect group norms.* Stay within the time limits you have been given so that everyone will have a fair chance to speak. When you are not speaking, listen attentively to others. You are part of the group but also part of the audience. If reasonable, adapt your style of delivery to that of others in the group. If others remain seated while they speak (and if you are comfortable doing so), remain seated as well, unless you have a compelling reason to deliver your remarks standing.
- *Maintain a cooperative attitude.* Being asked to speak as part of a group can raise competitive feelings. Although the tendency to wonder, *Who is going over best with the audience?* is understandable, it is better to stay focused on communicating as effectively as you can and to hope that everyone in the group makes an effective presentation so that the whole symposium is a success.
- *Be prepared to respond to questions.* Like the panel, the symposium presentation is always followed by questions. In this case, listeners are more likely to direct their questions to one individual than to pose general questions for anyone in the group to answer. In this sense, the questioning may be a little more focused and formal, but it is just as important. Symposium members, perhaps even more than panelists, function as experts on their specific topics, and the audience expects to learn a good deal from them.

Team Presentations

team presentation a presentation devised and delivered by a team of organizational members to a group of leaders, seeking their endorsement or support

The **team presentation** is designed to influence an audience of key decision-makers. Because a group is involved in planning and delivering the presentation, however, careful coordination among team members is essential. Teams may grow from almost any kind of organizational context. In the Indiana University School of Business, for example, teams of students study a problem

No matter what form it takes, the team presentation should be clearly focused and cohesive. Each member of the team must be competent to carry out her or his part in the group's presentation. (A. Ramey/PhotoEdit)

that has challenged a local business. Using principles they have learned in class, they work together throughout the semester to create a strategic plan and, at the end of the term, to present their solution to the leaders of the business. As another example, video production teams from various companies make presentations to a potential client—one of the largest pharmaceutical companies in the Midwest. They are competing to be selected as the producer of a big-budget promotional video for the pharmaceutical company. As a third example, a team of administrators from a university makes a presentation to a prospective funding agency, asking the agency to support an innovative curriculum that relies on team-teaching and interdisciplinary internships. The agency has limited funds, so the administrative team is competing with teams from many other colleges and universities.

What will separate successful from unsuccessful teams in these and other situations? Some tips follow:

- *Recognize the significance of the presentation.* Team presentations are often used to decide whether a group or an entire company is competent and trustworthy enough to perform an important task or take on a major responsibility. On some occasions, the team is seeking a key endorsement or financial support. In many instances, the team or organization's livelihood will depend on how effectively the group makes its case. Each team member needs to understand the stakes involved in this speaking situation.[11]

- *Devise a well-coordinated, clearly focused presentation.* If the team presentation is to be effective, team members must work together collaboratively throughout the process. What is the specific purpose of the presentation? What are the needs, interests, and values of this particular audience? How should the work be divided? What examples and other supporting material can best illustrate the value of the team's proposal?

What can the team do to establish their competence and skill? What kind of visual support will the group want to use? How can the proposal be best introduced and concluded?

As you can see, these questions are the same as those addressed by any individual public speaker. But the individual seeks answers on his or her own. The team members, by contrast, spend time working together to make strategic decisions, to choose ways to integrate and coordinate what they are doing, and to make sure they are supportive of each other throughout the process. With team presentations, issues of group dynamics interact with principles of public speaking.

- *Create a professional presentation.* The team will need to put forth considerable time, effort, and money to make sure their presentation reflects well on the team and the organization and clearly demonstrates their commitment to the project, solution, or proposal. Presentational aids should be designed with the utmost care and professionalism. In most settings, group members should dress professionally and with a level of formality that speaks to the importance of the occasion.
- *Seek ways to reinforce listeners' perceptions of the team's cohesiveness and competence.* If the audience is thinking of hiring a particular team of people to carry out a project, they will be very concerned with how smoothly the group works together. What better way to convey a sense of excellent teamwork than by giving an outstanding team presentation? Team members should remain attentive to and respectful of other members of the group throughout the presentation. Transitions between individuals should show how their work is related. During the presentation, group members should make regular references to each other's efforts and comments. One team member might say, "As Paul mentioned, he and I work closely together when we are choosing the background music for our productions. Let me give you an example of how this worked with our last project."

  In short, team members should reinforce and be mutually supportive of one another. They should use verbal and nonverbal communication (head nods, smiles, supportive gestures) in ways that demonstrate their respect for, interest in, and enthusiasm for one another's ideas and contributions.
- *Devote substantial time to answering questions.* Responding to listener questions is a critical part of the team's success. Especially when the stakes are high and when audience members are being asked to endorse the team's ideas, proposal, or project, they expect and deserve to be given the chance to seek more information, to challenge assumptions, to ask for additional examples, and to do all they can to convince themselves that the action they are about to take is judicious. Thus,

KEEP IN MIND 18.2

Guidelines for Group Presentations

Panel Discussions

- Know the group.
- Obtain an agenda for the discussion.
- Participate actively while sharing the floor with others.
- Use good interpersonal skills.
- Come prepared to answer questions.

Symposium Presentations

- Know your assigned topic.
- Respect group norms.
- Maintain a cooperative attitude.
- Be prepared to respond to questions.

Team Presentations

- Recognize the significance of the presentation.
- Devise a well-coordinated, clearly focused presentation.
- Create a professional presentation.
- Seek ways to reinforce listeners' perceptions of the team's cohesiveness and competence.
- Devote substantial time to answering questions.

team members must reserve ample time for audience questions, welcome listeners' feedback and expressed concerns, and respond with a focus on brevity and honesty.

The team presentation is a type of symposium presentation. For an evaluation form that you can use to assess a team presentation, go to the **Online SpeechStudio** and look for the **Team Presentation Critical Reaction Form**. Once again, you will find both a group and an individual evaluation form.

PROPOSAL PRESENTATIONS

Preview When we think of making a public speech, we usually imagine ourselves speaking in front of a fairly large audience. In professional settings, however, people often speak to smaller audiences in diverse meeting contexts. The proposal presentation is typically given in this kind of situation.

So far in this chapter, we have discussed communicating in groups, group leadership, and making presentations as part of a group. There are times, however, when individuals make presentations to small groups, as is the case when they make proposal presentations.

A **proposal presentation** is usually developed by some member of an organization, often at a supervisor's request, and delivered to a small group of decision-makers. Sometimes proposals are presented to small groups of peers, but more often they are given to groups of superiors. Most of the time, then, proposal presentations are presented to groups of important decision-makers—organizational representatives with great demands on their time and energy. When you give a proposal presentation, you are persuading—pitching a specific proposal to decision-makers with the power to accept or reject it.

proposal presentation a presentation typically delivered to a small group of decision-makers and seeking their endorsement of what is proposed

Preparing for the Proposal Presentation

To be persuasive, proposal presentations must be carefully crafted and audience centered. They are usually given by speakers who are proponents of change and innovation. Successful speaking begins with a proposal worth presenting. It is equally critical for the speaker to engage in painstaking audience analysis, considering the listeners both as individuals and as decision-makers who play specific roles within a particular group.

The Organizational Context. As you craft a proposal presentation, keep in mind that organizations present a structured, hierarchical context for interaction. First, your boss has probably invited you to speak. Although receiving such a request is a compliment, it can also be somewhat intimidating. What's more, you will likely be speaking to those who are well established within the organization. In most cases, they will have more formal authority than you do and have the power to endorse or reject your proposal.

What are the implications for you in this kind of situation? First, as we discussed in Chapter 2, communicating with those of higher status may make you apprehensive. Anticipate this possibility and review the strategies for managing speech anxiety. Beyond that, considerable research has shown that **upward communication** can be problematic in organizational settings.[12] Speakers who are keenly aware of the higher status of their listeners may be tempted to downplay negative information and to exaggerate positive information,

upward communication communicating with someone of higher status perhaps to please their audience and present themselves in the best possible light. A commitment to ethical communication, however, requires honesty in this speaking situation, just as in any other.

specialization a trend in organizations for members to have deep expertise in a given area, often accompanied by a narrowness of focus

Another organizational trend is toward **specialization**. Organizations have increasingly hired those with depth of expertise.[13] Yet sometimes expertise is accompanied by a narrow focus. As a result, the speaker may face a group of listeners who have their own niche, speak their own jargon, and have their own agendas. Adapting to this kind of audience can present a special challenge.

Analyzing Your Listeners as a Dynamic Group. In most speech contexts, audience members may or may not know each other. However, the typical audience for a proposal presentation consists of listeners who are part of a group that works together. They know whom they most respect and whose views they can ignore. Some listeners are more influential than others; some are better liked. As a small group audience, then, they have a dynamic quality. They are interdependent, and they will negotiate their decision about your proposal as they interact with you and with each other before, during, and after your speech.

You will more likely make a successful proposal presentation if you consider your audience as a dynamic group. Think about who the group's leaders are. Understand that power and status are not always the same (the vice president who clearly has status may or may not have power), and be aware of how this particular group makes decisions. Do you have to convince all of them or simply a majority? Are the listeners empowered to make the decision, or do they serve in an advisory capacity to some "higher" authority? Consider such group-related questions as part of your audience analysis.

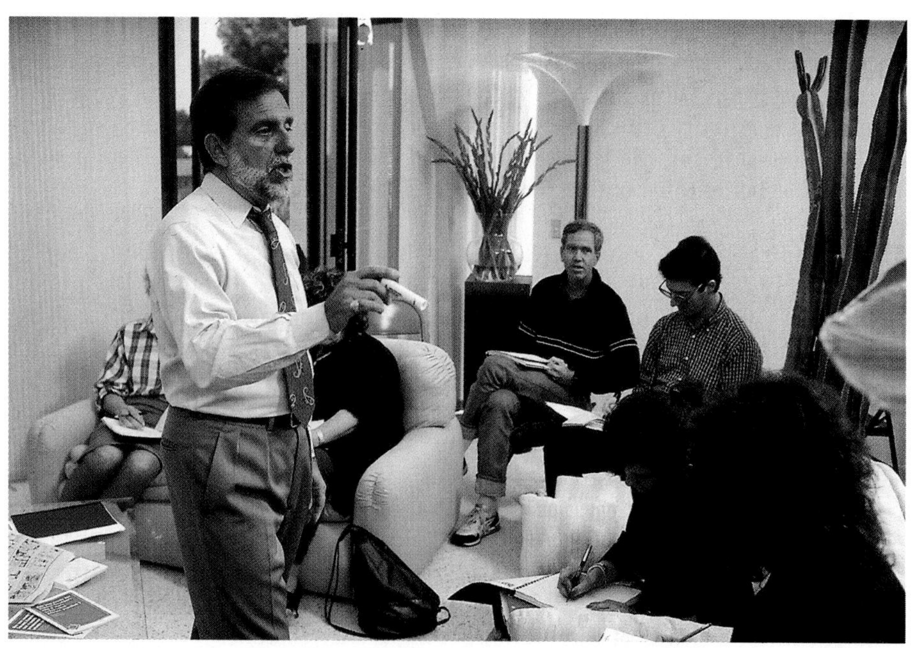

A good presentation takes into account the organizational context of the presentation and is geared toward the needs and roles of the listeners. (Michael Grecco/Stock, Boston, Inc.)

Organizing the Proposal Presentation

Three patterns of organization are especially well suited to the proposal presentation: the scientific problem-solving pattern, the state-the-case-and-prove-it pattern, and the motivated sequence. The proposal presentation is a speech to actuate. We have already discussed the motivated sequence in Chapter 15; you may want to refer to that chapter to refresh your memory. Like the motivated sequence, the two patterns presented here could be used with any speech whose goal is to get the audience to take some concrete action.

The Scientific Problem-Solving Pattern. This pattern of organization is based on John Dewey's Reflective Thinking Sequence,[14] often used by groups engaged in solving problems or discussing questions of policy. The **scientific problem-solving (SPS) pattern** addresses these questions:

scientific problem-solving pattern an organizational pattern often used in problem solving that can also be used, in whole or in part, to structure a speech inductively

1. How shall we define and limit the problem?
2. What are the causes and extent of the problem?
3. What are the effects of the problem? Who has been hurt?
4. What are the criteria by which solutions should be judged?
5. What are the possible solutions and the relative strengths and weaknesses of each?
6. What is the best solution?
7. How can we put it into effect? (Optional; these details may be decided by the group later.)

Usually you will want to use the SPS pattern if you assume either that the audience is not very well informed about the problem or that the audience may be resistant to the course of action you are proposing. The SPS pattern works well with uninformed listeners because it allows you to educate them about the problem in some detail before presenting solutions. Suppose you were addressing a complex legal issue, a challenging ethical dilemma, or a complicated pollution problem. The listeners may need the information you present in order to proceed wisely.

The SPS pattern also allows you to present a problem inductively. You are not leaping to any conclusions. Rather you are carefully considering, together with the audience, different aspects of the problem and an array of different solutions before moving to the one you think is best. This pattern shows your audience that you have examined the problem with a fair and open mind. After such careful scrutiny, you are asking your listeners to follow your lead in supporting a particular course of action.

The State-the-Case-and-Prove-It Pattern. Another organizational option for proposal presentations is almost the opposite of the SPS pattern. When using the **state-the-case-and-prove-it pattern**, you develop a central thesis with supporting arguments. Typically, the pattern consists of a brief introduction followed by a thesis statement, several contentions with appropriate elaboration and support, and a conclusion that summarizes the basic arguments and calls for action. The basic organizational approach looks like this:

state-the-case-and-prove-it pattern a speech pattern in which the speaker advances a thesis followed by several contentions with appropriate elaboration and support

I. Introduction/State Thesis
II. Contention One
  Evidence
III. Contention Two
  Evidence
IV. Contention Three
  Evidence
V. Summary/Appeal

Unlike the SPS pattern, the state-the-case-and-prove-it pattern should be used when your listeners already know there is a problem or an issue that needs to be addressed. When the listeners are already convinced that something needs to be done, you can assume a common base of information and understanding. This is a friendly, well-informed audience. Any speaker who tries to ignore an audience's experience and knowledge risks boring, frustrating, and possibly insulting them.

As an example of this pattern, you might say that the audience is aware that new federal regulations are requiring organizations to become more proactive in addressing the childcare and eldercare needs of employees. You would then go on to propose a specific response to this federal mandate. You would devote most of your speaking time to showing why your particular approach—to convert a little-used company library into a daycare facility—responds to the new regulations and would be an excellent, cost-efficient facility as well. At the end, you would briefly summarize your ideas and appeal to the board for their support.

The state-the-case-and-prove-it pattern is solution-heavy. The speaker who uses it must be relatively certain that the audience already believes that something needs to be done about a problem or a situation that is well understood. The speaker's goal, then, is to persuade the audience to support his or her particular solution. Doing this requires considerable focus on the solution and the reasons for its excellence. The listeners want to act; the speaker's challenge is to get them to realize that the proposed course of action is the one they want to pursue.

✔ KEEP IN MIND 18.3

Proposal Presentations

Here are some tips for preparing and delivering a proposal presentation:

- View the organization in a communicative context.
- Undertake a detailed analysis of the small group audience.
- See the listeners as members of a dynamic small group.
- Choose an appropriate organizational pattern:
  - —Scientific problem-solving pattern
  - —State-the-case-and-prove-it pattern
  - —Motivated sequence
- Deliver your proposal effectively by using these strategies:
  - —Be extemporaneous.
  - —Use presentational aids.
  - —Respect time limits.
  - —Know the group's culture.

Delivering the Proposal Presentation

Because of the relatively intimate communication environment in which proposals are often presented, effective delivery is crucial.

- *Use extemporaneous delivery.* You will likely be delivering your presentation in a boardroom environment, perhaps standing (or even seated) at one end of a conference table. You must be direct, flexible, and spontaneous. Your eye contact should include everyone, and you should gesture and move as naturally as possible.
- *Use presentational aids.* When presenting proposals, visuals help the audience follow you,

remember your ideas, and picture your plan. Make sure your aids look professional and that you use them with ease. Check out the room in advance to make sure the equipment you need is there. As we discussed in Chapter 13, computer-produced aids are becoming the norm.

- *Respect time limits.* This group is probably meeting for some time, and you are only a part of the agenda. If your presentation takes more time than the group has allowed, the members may resent being put off schedule. Leave ample time for questions.
- *Know the group's culture.* You want to fit in with the culture of the group as much as possible. If this group dresses somewhat casually, so should you. Also, anticipate the group's interaction style. For instance, does this group ask questions during the presentation? Some groups like to make the presentation more interactive. The more you know about your group of listeners and their general expectations, the better able you will be to deliver your proposal effectively.

Proposal presentations are often given to groups of key decision makers in business and professional settings. If you are listening to proposal presentations as part of your public speaking class, you can go to the **Online SpeechStudio,** where you will find a **Proposal Presentation Evaluation Form** that you may find helpful.

SALES PRESENTATIONS

Preview The key to success for any organization is sales; unless someone can sell the organization's services or products to someone else, that organization will not survive. Many sales occur when organizational representatives speak to prospective customers or clients, trying to persuade them to try, buy, or otherwise use a specific service or product. Although some of these sales transactions take place in informal, interpersonal contexts, many involve formal presentations.

Like the proposal presentation, the typical sales presentation is given before a small group. Unlike the proposal presentation, however, the **sales presentation** is given to individual customers or another organization rather than occurring within the organization. The speaker acts as a representative of the organization and its products or services.

sales presentation a speech given to potential customers or clients in an attempt to sell them products or services

Successful sales presentations depend on several things: knowing your own product or service, understanding the organization to which you are selling, and being sensitive to the characteristics, needs, and values of the group to whom you are speaking.

Preparing for the Sales Presentation

As in any speaking situation, the most important work occurs before the actual presentation. You must first learn as much as you can about your audience and the situation in which you will be speaking. Use that information to organize and outline your presentation. Then prepare supporting materials, such as visual aids.

Typically you will not be well acquainted with the group to whom you are selling. However, you will probably have some contact with at least one member

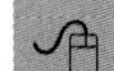

CONNECTING TO THE NET

Want to access articles on team presentations, sales presentation, and related topics? Go to: **http://college.hmco.com/communication/andrews/public_speaking/2e/students/** and click on *Connecting to the Net.* From there, follow the link to Resources from SalesDoctors.

of that group, if only to schedule your presentation. During that initial contact, try to learn as much of the following as you can:

1. Who will make the decision concerning purchase of the service or product?
2. Who will be attending the meeting? Learn how many people are coming (so you know what to expect and how many copies of handouts you need to bring) and what positions these people hold.
3. If the decision-maker is not scheduled to be part of the meeting, find out why. Meetings that do not include the decision-maker are typically not very productive for the sales presenter.
4. How long will the meeting last? Tailor your presentation to fit the allotted time.
5. Why is this organization considering purchasing this product or service? In other words, what are the organization's needs?
6. What criteria will be used to make the decision? The person making the arrangements with you may not know this information, but if you can find out, you will know what things to emphasize in your remarks.
7. What physical arrangements and equipment are or can be available?

Using this information to shape your presentation will enable you to provide a much more efficient, effective view of your service or product.

Organizing the Sales Presentation: The INPC Model

INPC model a sales presentation that follows four steps: introduction, need, presentation, and close

Any pattern of organization that can be used with a speech to actuate can be used with a sales presentation. However, we find the **INPC model** particularly effective. This model involves four steps: introduction, need, presentation, and close, as Figure 18.2 illustrates.

Following the INPC model, you should do several things in your *introduction.* First, identify who you are and what organization you represent. Indicate how long your organization has been in the business (if appropriate), your organization's specialties or notable achievements, and some customers who use your products or services. This information will help your listeners feel that they are dealing with an experienced, reputable organization and sales representative. Next, briefly state the purpose of your presentation. Finally, establish the climate for your presentation. Informal, extemporaneous presentations are usually effective. You may want to say, "I intend to be fairly informal in my remarks, so please feel free to ask questions whenever you like. I'll ask you any questions I have as well." This kind of statement encourages two-way communication between you and the group, and it contributes to a relaxed atmosphere for everyone.

Clearly, some *need* must exist; otherwise you would not have been asked to make the presentation in the first place. To establish the need, you might begin by describing the organization's needs as you see them based on what you have learned through your research. Attempting to sell her consulting services to an organization, one speaker said,

> One of our specialties is diversity training. This area is fairly new, and you may wonder if you really need to make an investment in this kind of training right now. As you think about that question, you might want to consider the fact that

FIGURE 18.2 The INPC Model for Organizing the Sales Presentation

- Introduction
  - Establish your identity and credibility.
  - Establish your purpose.
  - Establish the climate for interaction.
- Need
  - Describe this organization's needs.
  - Describe the typical organization's needs.
- Presentation
  - Provide an overview of the product or service.
  - Show or describe key product features.
  - Tie features to listener needs to show benefits.
- Close
  - Summarize benefits.
  - Summarize reasons to choose your product and organization.
  - Ask for questions.

your company has become incredibly diverse in the last three years. You have more women in management positions and more racial and ethnic diversity *than any comparable company in your industry!*

You also might refer to typical needs you have found in comparable organizations. It is important to watch the audience very carefully while you describe your perceptions of their needs. By watching their reactions, you may be able to tell which needs seem most important to them.

Once you have established the need, you can begin the actual *presentation* of your product or service.

1. Provide an overview of the product or service and how it works or is performed, taking the group through a step-by-step sequence: "If you decide to work with us on diversity training, we'll want to conduct a very detailed needs assessment. We will tailor our workshop to your specific needs. We will plan to offer the workshops in the fall at times convenient to you."

2. Describe particularly important features of your product or service in relation to the audience's needs: "One key to effective diversity workshops is having excellent presenters. We have some of the best in the business; most have won awards in the area. We also have special expertise in harassment issues and intercultural communication. Since you have so many women in your work force and such a culturally diverse group, you will want to emphasize those areas."

PORTFOLIO 18.2

Applying Principles and Adapting to the Situation

Study the INPC model in Figure 18.2. In what ways does it mirror what you've learned about speechmaking so far? After noting the similarities, contemplate how the same principles of effective speechmaking can apply to various presentational situations.

3. Explain the benefits of your product or service to this particular group: "When diversity workshops are well done—and ours will be—they lead to a more cohesive and compassionate work force, higher morale, and often better productivity."

Finally, the *close* should offer a substantive, memorable conclusion to your sales presentation. Summarize the benefits you have already described. Go over why this group should choose you and the organization you represent, reminding the audience of your organization's stature and track record. You might say, "Our company was the first to offer diversity training. Since we began, we have worked with more than two thousand organizations. Our consultants have achieved national recognition. Last year, the President's Task Force on Diversity in the U.S. Workforce honored us with its annual Excellence in Education Award." Since products and services are often quite similar, the unique qualifications of your organization may be the determining factor that gets you the sale.

We all listen to sales presentations throughout our lives. Some are delivered on television, others are given in one-on-one situations, and still others are presented as more formal speeches. The next time you listen to a sales presentation, go to the **Online SpeechStudio** and use the **Sales Presentation Evaluation Form** you find there to evaluate it.

When you have finished speaking, invite questions. Even though your listeners may have asked questions along the way, they will likely think of more after you've finished your remarks. This question phase is critical. It gives you the opportunity to provide additional information, clarify confusion, speak directly to listener needs, and overcome objections that are raised. By handling questions effectively, you not only maintain the positive impression you have created up to this point, but you also advance your cause significantly.

KEEP IN MIND 18.4

Sales Presentations

Here are some tips for preparing and delivering a sales presentation:

- Learn as much as you can about the audience and the situation, including the following:
  - —Who is the key decision-maker?
  - —Who will be attending the meeting?
  - —Why won't the decision-maker be attending the meeting (if this is the case)?
  - —How long is the meeting to last?
  - —Why is the organization interested in this particular product or service?
  - —What criteria will be used to make the decision?
  - —What physical arrangements and equipment are available to assist with the presentation?
- Use the INPC model to organize the presentation, following these four steps:
  - —Introduction
  - —Need
  - —Presentation
  - —Close
- Deliver the presentation by using these strategies:
  - —Speak informally, directly, and spontaneously.
  - —Use excellent presentational aids.
  - —Remain especially alert to audience members' nonverbal reactions to your speech.
  - —Reserve plenty of time for audience questions.

Delivering the Sales Presentation

When making a sales presentation, your delivery should be spontaneous and flexible. Although these qualities are valuable for all kinds of public speaking, they assume heightened importance in the sales presentation. As you seek to persuade your listeners to invest in your product or service, watch their reactions carefully. Be sensitive to them and flexible in the way you respond.

Be on the lookout for signs of approval, confusion, skepticism, indifference, or resistance. When you see that listeners are responding well to your message, you may choose to make a shorter presentation and let the group get on with formally making a decision about your product or service. With less positive reactions, you will need to do things such as give another example to clarify, offer strong proof of your claims, ask direct questions about group needs and interests, or respond directly to their concerns. Watching for, interpreting, and responding to feedback from your small group audience can make your sales presentation much more effective.

SUMMARY

Organizations are increasingly using teams or small groups to solve problems and make decisions. Groups possess strengths (the potential for creativity, commitment to decisions, and social enjoyment) and weaknesses (being potentially time-consuming, intolerant of diversity, and dominated by a few members). Leaders should select their leadership approach by taking certain situational factors into consideration. Leadership styles range from autocratic to laissez-faire.

The appointed leader is in an excellent position to influence the group in positive ways. When leaders choose to share power and responsibility with other group members, they contribute to a healthier, more productive climate. Effective team members prepare carefully for each meeting, maintain an open mind, listen critically and constructively to others, play multiple communication roles, are attentive to nonverbal communication, encourage constructive conflict, and treat others ethically.

Sometimes professionals are called on to make public presentations as part of a group. Some of these group presentations take the form of a panel (complete with spontaneous interaction under the guidance of a moderator), and others are organized more formally in the form of a symposium (with each group member making a short speech). On other occasions, groups make team presentations (usually designed to influence an audience of key decision-makers). After group presentations are made, listeners usually ask questions. The question-and-answer period often leads to an extensive sharing of ideas and information and a great deal of interaction between speakers and members of the audience. During the coming years, communicating effectively in group settings such as these will only continue to grow in importance.

Finally, the workplace creates a context in which some special kinds of public presentations are given. For example, organizational employees may be called on to present proposals and to make sales presentations. Both of these persuasive presentations are typically delivered to a small group of decision-makers who will choose whether to invest in the proposal or purchase the product or service offered by the speaker. Like other speeches, these presentations need to be prepared carefully, delivered using an extemporaneous style, and organized appropriately, using one of the patterns well suited to persuasive speeches. Each should be carefully timed, with plenty of opportunity for audience questions. Presentational aids are a must. These kinds of persuasive presentations are among the most important speeches given in the workplace.

QUESTIONS FOR REVIEW AND REFLECTION

1. What are some of the advantages and disadvantages of working together in groups?
2. Describe the following leadership styles and explain the circumstances under which each style might be used appropriately:
   a. Autocratic
   b. Consultative

   c. Democratic
   d. Laissez-faire

3. When you work in groups, which leadership style do you prefer the leader to use? Why? Which style do you typically use? Why?
4. What are some qualities that distinguish an effective group member from one who is less of a contributor? In light of your list, how would you evaluate your own group participation the last time you worked with others in this way?
5. Compare and contrast these forms of group presentations:
   a. Panel discussions
   b. Symposium presentations
   c. Team presentations
6. In what ways might a small-group audience differ from a larger, more general audience? How do the differences influence the way you prepare and present a proposal for a small group?
7. Under what circumstances would you choose to use each of the following patterns of organization for a proposal presentation? Why?
   a. Motivated sequence
   b. Scientific problem-solving pattern
   c. State-the-case-and-prove-it pattern
8. What are the basic steps in the INPC model for organizing and delivering a sales presentation?
9. In this chapter, we have emphasized the role of the question-and-answer period that follows each presentation. Do you think that responding to questions is especially important in business and professional settings, or do you think that it is equally important in all speaking contexts? Explain your answer.

ENDNOTES

1. See, for example, Harry Dent, *The Roaring 2000s* (New York: Simon & Schuster, 1998), pp. 3–38; and Charles J. Stewart and William B. Cash, Jr., *Interviewing: Principles and Practices*, 9th ed. (Boston: McGraw-Hill, 2000), pp. 263–264.
2. See C. E. Larson and F. M. J. LaFasto, *Teamwork: What Must Go Right/What Can Go Wrong* (Newbury Park, Calif.: Sage, 1989); and Jon R. Katzenbach and Douglas K. Smith, "The Discipline of Teams," *Harvard Business Review* 71 (March–April 1993): 111–120.
3. Irving Janis, *Groupthink*, 2nd ed. (Boston: Houghton Mifflin, 1982), p. 3.
4. A. J. Salazar, "Understanding the Synergistic Effects of Communication in Small Groups: Making the Most Out of Group Member Abilities," *Small Group Research* 26 (1995): 169–199.
5. Susan E. Kogler Hill, "Team Leadership Theory," in *Leadership: Theory and Practice*, ed. Peter G. Northouse (Thousand Oaks, Calif.: Sage, 1997), pp. 159–183.
6. See, for example, A. Paul Hare, *Groups, Teams, and Social Interaction* (New York: Praeger, 1992); and Randy Y. Hirokawa and Marshall Scott Poole, eds.,

Communication and Group Decision Making, 2nd ed. (Thousand Oaks, Calif.: Sage, 1996), in which a number of articles deal with idea-generation techniques, such as brainstorming.

7. See Janis, *Groupthink;* and Irving Janis and Leon Mann, *Decision Making: A Psychological Analysis of Conflict, Choice, and Commitment* (New York: Free Press, 1977).
8. Janis's original formulation of groupthink appeared in Irving Janis, *Victims of Groupthink: Psychological Studies of Foreign Policy Decisions and Fiascoes* (Boston: Houghton Mifflin, 1972). For additional studies of groupthink, see, for example, Rebecca J. Welch Cline, "Groupthink and the Watergate Cover-up: The Illusion of Unanimity," in *Group Communication in Context,* ed. Lawrence R. Frey (Hillsdale, N.J.: Erlbaum, 1994), pp. 199–223.
9. See, for example, Gay Lumsden and Donald Lumsden, *Communicating in Groups and Teams: Sharing Leadership,* 3rd ed. (Belmont, Calif.: Wadsworth, 1999).
10. See Joseph P. Folger, Marshall Scott Poole, and Randall K. Stutman, *Working Through Conflict,* 3rd ed. (New York: Longman, 1997).
11. See Thomas R. Leech, *How to Prepare, Stage, and Deliver Winning Presentations* (New York: American Management Association, 1993), p. 278, which emphasizes how significant a team presentation can be.
12. See, for example, Janet Fulk and Sirish Mani, "Distortion of Communication in Hierarchical Relationships," *Communication Yearbook 9* (Beverly Hills, Calif.: Sage, 1986), pp. 483–510; and Phillip K. Tompkins, *Organizational Communication Imperatives: Lessons of the Space Program* (Los Angeles: Roxbury, 1993), for a discussion of how failed upward communication contributed significantly to the space shuttle *Challenger* disaster in 1986.
13. Peter F. Drucker, "The Coming of the New Organization," *Harvard Business Review* 66 (January–February 1988): 45–53; and Peter F. Drucker, "Managing Oneself," *Harvard Business Review* 77 (March–April 1999): 65–74.
14. John Dewey, *How We Think* (Boston: Heath, 1910).

Evan Broom, sales manager, Sanders and Company of Indianapolis, Indiana, gave the sales presentation that follows. Broom is speaking to the representatives of two companies that are planning a merger. This speech is designed to sell the approach that Sanders and Company will take to facilitate the merger; especially focusing on communication. Broom builds his company's credibility by carefully detailing how their investigation of client needs and strengths led to the proposed plan.

Employee Communication Plan for a Merger Announcement

Evan Broom

Although Evan might have begun with a statement to establish his company's credibility, he holds that information until later in the speech. He does quickly outline the purpose and describes the needs of his client in terms of the tasks assigned by the client.

Hi, and thanks so much for having us here this morning. We're very excited about our presentation this morning and the opportunity to share with you our employee communication plan for your company's merger.

You've given us a very specific task, and the task was made up of several components. First, to come up with a communication plan unifying two competitors. And these two competitors, the number three competitor in the market and the number five competitor in the market, will now come together to be the number one leader in this industry. And we need to give both of these companies, number three and number five, a feeling of equal status so that all employees come into the new company not feeling as though one's been bought by the other, but as if they're all part of a new team. We need to take the employees of Eye-tech and Prosmarc and bring them together under the new company of EyeMarc.

Evan begins his overview of the services his company will provide by describing how they arrived at their plan. In doing so, he elaborates on the client's needs, comparing those needs to practices throughout the industry.

First, I'd like to share with you a little bit about our methodology. How did we arrive at the recommendation that we're going to present today? First, we conducted an employee survey with employees of both companies. We analyzed the geographic issues with your nationwide and global workforce. We looked at work site logistics. And we did some industry benchmarking—what's worked well before. And we've checked all of this against your merger strategy.

Let's briefly look at what we learned in the employee survey. Many employees within both companies feel disconnected from their current company as far as communication. They're hungry for news about the company and there's tremendous uncertainty because they know that something's up—they don't know what. Relative to the geographic issues, you have a coast-to-coast workforce and foreign manufacturing, as well. And you have everything from large offices and large manufacturing to small field offices. Regarding work site logistics, it runs the complete range, from administrative, manufacturing, research. You have multiple shifts. But fortunately, many of the facilities, in fact, most of the facilities, have large meeting rooms, or some large place to gather the employees together. Relative to industry benchmarking, we're going to learn in our presentation later today about some of the best practices in the industry—what's worked well with other companies that have similar demographics to your employee base and to your company.

We've looked at all of your needs and checked that against the strategy. Is our plan in alignment with your corporate goals? Is there a speed to market—can we get this message out quickly? What are the development priorities within the organization, and how can communication help those? Resource allocation—money and time from within the company. We've taken a look at what's available within your organizations to help put this together and what do you need from outside.

In this section, Evan outlines the key questions that his plan will answer for the client. These questions bring into sharp focus how the plan will meet the company's needs.

Let's look briefly at our recommendation. We've proposed using satellite business television to link up all of your facilities, coast-to-coast and even foreign manufacturing, using the power of satellite business television, and we'll refer to that today as "BTV." In fact, let's refer to it as EyeMarc TV, just for fun.

The major portion of the speech describes the key features of the plan as it relates to the client's needs.

Looking at the BTV event, business television utilizes satellite technology. From a studio location, we will beam by satellite to all of your locations nationwide to unify your global workforce with a simultaneous live announcement. It will be high-energy television. This will be a television show announcing this, and the CEO and the other leaders of the company will be part of this television program. In essence, we're building for you a private television network, for this day, for this event. And it will have the feeling of an event.

Now, why do we feel capable of helping you pull this off? Well, we have the technical expertise to take on what some would consider a risky project. And we'll share with you how we can minimize that risk. We have the creative resources to make this an engaging experience, to make this a fun program, to make it a high-energy program for your employees. We have the logistic partners globally, that can take care of all of the needs at each location that you have, whether it's a large facility or a small. And we have the depth and experience. We've done this before. We are not uninitiated to this. However, we know that you are. This will be your first experience in this, and we'll guide you every step of the way. And you have our commitment that our backup plans will have backup plans, and we know that you're making a large investment with this, and we'll make sure that it goes well.

Evan has saved the description of his company's expertise until this point, where he blends it with a summary of the benefits to the client.

So what are the next steps? What do we need to do with the rest of our day today? I hope to give you a few minutes to do a little looking through our executive summary. And let's do a little crystal balling and see what are the unique opportunities that we can bring with this project. We need to consider today what will be our operational plan—how will we turn this idea into reality? We have the financial overview to look at so that you know what the cost will be on this project and whether the companies will be able to move forward in this plan. And certainly today, we'll hope to have some type of commitment to proceed, either with the plan as we have it, or with the plan as we alter it.

Evan ends with a preview of what will happen next. Since he refers his listeners to the executive summary they will read, there is no need for him to summarize at this point. He also indicates that questions will follow the reading of the summary.

So let me give you a few moments to review the executive summary, and then we'll come back to answer questions and move on from there. Thanks.

Peer Evaluation and Feedback

APPENDIX A

When you think of taking a public speaking class, you likely focus on your role as speaker. What will you speak about? How effectively will you prepare and deliver your speeches? What kind of grade will you earn? While it's natural to think of your performance as a speaker, it's also important to remember the other significant role you will play throughout the course—as a listener and respondent to your fellow classmates. You will, in fact, devote far more time to listening than to speaking during the course of the semester. You may give only five or six speeches, but you will listen to as many as 150 speeches. What you do during this listening time will influence what you learn from the class, as well as how much your peers benefit from your presence as a member of the classroom audience.

WHAT AUDIENCE ROLES MIGHT YOU PLAY?

As in any listening context, you will want to function as a good **critical listener.** Return to Chapter 2 and review the requirements for critical listening. In brief, to be a good critical listener, you will want to follow some of these guidelines:

- Through your nonverbal communication, show the speaker that you are engaged.
- Take notes as you listen.
- Identify the speaker's main points.
- Look for evidence.
- Examine the speaker's reasoning.
- Minimize distractions.
- Suspend judgment.

Your instructor may ask you to focus on different specific aspects of your peers' speeches at different times, but you should be prepared to listen as comprehensively as possible and to *practice listening as an **active process.*** Since critical listening takes a lot of effort, you will need to work at it. Not only will you need the skills outlined above, you will also need to come to class rested and ready to make substantive contributions to the classroom community.

One excellent way to practice critical listening is to listen to speakers outside the classroom. Go to the **Online SpeechStudio,** where you will find the **Guidelines for Evaluating an Outside Speaker** you might use.

Equally important, you will want to come to class prepared to function as a **supportive listener.** In a classroom environment, where everyone is relatively new to public speaking and where many are nervous about how well they will be received, behaving supportively is especially important. After all, you and your peers are "in this together." One day you may be a peer evaluator, asking questions and offering feedback, and the next day you will be standing in front of the class, as the speaker and the recipient of others' feedback. When you put yourself in the speaker's role, you know how important it is to feel that your peers want you to succeed. Being supportive does not mean checking your critical thinking skills at the door. Rather, as a supportive listener, you will want to

- show the speaker that you are interested and engaged through your nonverbal communication,
- maintain an open mind, especially when listening to controversial topics,
- show your interest by asking thoughtful questions,
- offer constructive, balanced verbal feedback (when given the opportunity).

We all recognize supportive listeners when we see them. They often nod or smile while we are speaking. They appear to be alert and interested, rather than fighting off sleep. They jot down a few notes. When given the chance, they ask good, constructive questions. Their verbal feedback is thoughtful, fair, and balanced (relating both positive and improvement-oriented comments).

The critical listener and the supportive listener are mutually reinforcing, often overlapping, roles. When performed in tandem, they contribute to an enlightened, challenging, and positive public speaking environment.

OFFERING PEER FEEDBACK

Early in the semester, your instructor may function as the sole source of feedback for all speakers. As the semester progresses, however, chances are that each of you will be invited, and often required, to function as a **peer critic**. Although the word *critic* may suggest a negative connotation, geared toward identifying the flaws in someone else's speech, nothing could be further from the truth. Whenever you are asked to serve as a peer critic, you will want to follow these general guidelines:

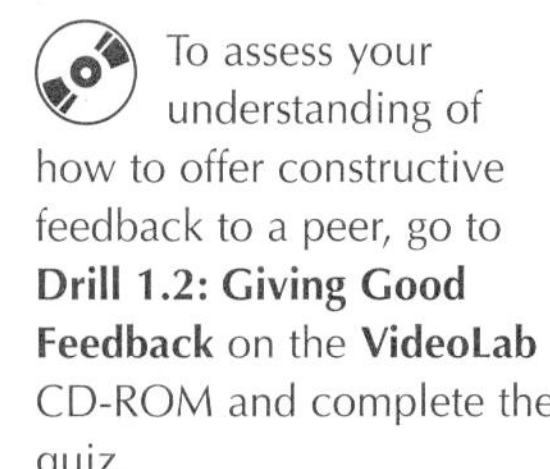
To assess your understanding of how to offer constructive feedback to a peer, go to **Drill 1.2: Giving Good Feedback** on the **VideoLab** CD-ROM and complete the quiz.

- *Offer balanced feedback—citing strengths as well as areas for improvement.* You might praise the speaker, for example, by pointing to the engaging ways that she incorporated personal experiences in ways that contributed to her positive ethos. At the same time, however, you might note that she could have further enhanced her speech by better identifying her various information sources.
- *When you identify an area for improvement, also suggest one thing the speaker might do to improve.* If you asked for better documentation, for instance, you might then go on to note, "When you talked about your advocated

plan of action to promote the welfare of women, you mentioned the name of a politician who agreed with you, but I had never heard of her. It would be good if you could identify her, and if her credentials are impressive, tell us that, too. If she chaired a panel on domestic violence, for instance, she would become even more credible. You could also tell us how recent her testimony is."

- *Be specific*. For instance, rather than saying, "You need to be better organized," you might say, "I think we would have been better able to follow your speech if you had used a preview in your introduction."
- *Focus on a limited number of issues*. If you identify ten areas for improvement, you may impress your instructor with your critical thinking skills, but you will likely overwhelm the speaker. At most, offer two or three suggestions for improvement.
- Avoid commenting on potentially offensive issues, particularly when offering oral feedback. For instance, if a speaker is wearing an outfit that exposes a great deal of skin or is sporting a hat that hides much of his or her eyes, you would not want to embarrass the speaker by discussing your perceptions during an in-class feedback session. You might choose to express your concern on a written feedback form. Check with your instructor if you are at all uncertain. (See Figure 1 for a sample peer-critic feedback form.)

Go to the **Online SpeechStudio,** where you will find a **Peer Evaluation Form** to guide you as you listen critically and constructively to your fellow classmates' speeches.

For a more structured evaluation form that can be used to guide your assessments, both inside and outside the classroom, go to the **Online SpeechStudio** and view the sample **Speech Evaluation Form**. Consider using this feedback form during the next round of in-class speeches.

To complete this form in electronic format, go to the **Peer-Critic Feedback Form** on the **Online SpeechStudio**.

FIGURE 1 **Peer-Critic Feedback Form**

1. **List at least three of the speaker's main strengths. Why is each important or valuable?**
2. **List two ways that the speaker might improve his or her speech. Why do you feel these improvements are needed?**
3. **For each improvement area you have identified, offer one or two specific suggestions for how the improvement can be made.**

DIFFERENT FORMATS FOR PEER FEEDBACK

Many options exist for structuring the approach and format for peer feedback. In some cases, all members of the classroom audience will be invited to offer feedback; on other occasions, a single peer critic or panel of critics will be identified by the instructor. Here are some common approaches your instructor may use:

1. *Everyone who is not speaking is assigned the role of critical listener with an emphasis on questioning.* With this method, everyone listens carefully and after the speeches have been delivered, each speaker will respond to listener questions. Your role as peer listener here is to identify some appropriate questions to ask. You may want to ask the speaker such questions as "Can you give us another example of that kind of approach?" "How do you see that plan working here on our own campus?" "Where could I go to read more about these kinds of innovations?"

2. *The instructor invites all listeners to offer comments on the speeches—either pausing after each speech or waiting until all of the speakers have spoken on a particular day.* Using this format, the instructor may ask you and your peers to respond to these questions: "What did you like best about the speech(es)?" "What areas for improvement can we identify?" "What are some steps the speaker(s) might take to improve?" The instructor will likely participate in this conversation as well, particularly in identifying improvement strategies.

Occasionally, you may be asked to offer feedback on a specific aspect of a speaker's delivery. Go to the **Online SpeechStudio** for the **Guide for Evaluating Voice and Articulation**.

3. *Different listeners may be assigned a specific task.* For example, one person or group may be asked to focus on the speaker's content, another on the speaker's organization, and a third on the speaker's delivery. This approach narrows and focuses each peer critic's task, making critical listening a bit more manageable. (See Figure 2 for a sample critique form that focuses on the speaker's delivery.)

4. *The instructor may assign you to a panel of peer critics.* On a particular speaking day, you and two or three others from the audience will serve as "critics for the day." The instructor will give you specific instructions for the format she or he wants you to follow. In all likelihood, you will have some feedback forms to complete. Following the speeches, you may be asked to present your feedback (possibly in front of the class) in a kind of panel format, or you may be asked to give your written comments directly to the speakers. The instructor may look at your comments before passing them on to the speakers, and you may be asked to sign your name or to complete the forms anonymously. Finally, sometimes your instructor will use a combined approach, so that you and your peer-critic panel provide both oral and written feedback. (See Figure 3 for a sample peer-critic panel assignment.)

These are not the only approaches to involving you and your classmates in peer feedback, but they do suggest a range of alternatives you may encounter. Whether you are working on your own or with a group of your classmates, you will want to follow the guidelines for critical and supportive listening discussed earlier.

FIGURE 2 **Delivery Feedback Form**

Please evaluate the speaker's delivery by completing the scales that follow:

The numbers represent:

	Poor 1	2	3	4	5 Superior
1. Eye contact	**1**	**2**	**3**	**4**	**5**
2. Use of notes	**1**	**2**	**3**	**4**	**5**
3. Use of voice	**1**	**2**	**3**	**4**	**5**
4. Gestures	**1**	**2**	**3**	**4**	**5**
5. Bodily movement	**1**	**2**	**3**	**4**	**5**
6. Facial expression	**1**	**2**	**3**	**4**	**5**
7. Poise	**1**	**2**	**3**	**4**	**5**
8. Conversational tone	**1**	**2**	**3**	**4**	**5**

Comments: **Provide at least two specific comments, identifying particular strengths and weaknesses, and, in the case of the latter, specify how they might be corrected.**

To complete this form in electronic format, go to the **Delivery Feedback Form** on the **Online SpeechStudio**.

OTHER WAYS OF OFFERING FEEDBACK

Many instructors enjoy creating a collaborative learning environment—one in which you and your fellow classmates work together throughout the course. Although you may think of your instructor as being the "expert" (and no doubt he or she is!), even so, in public speaking classes, each and every person's views and reactions are important. You and your classmates are the target audience. Since each speech is geared toward getting a specific audience response, how you, as audience members, react to the speaker's arguments and ways of organizing and presenting information and ideas becomes paramount. Speakers will analyze and adapt to you. If they don't, they will not achieve their speaking goals.

There are numerous ways that you may be asked to collaborate with your peers. You may work in small groups to brainstorm possible speech topics, in pairs to look over each other's working outlines, or in pairs or in groups to evaluate the presentational aids that each of you is planning to use. If you come upon an article or a web site that you know relates to someone else's topic, you can send him or her an e-mail message to share the source. You can also get together outside of class, whether your instructor requires you to do so or not. For instance, a few days before the day of your speech, you and a

Go to the **Online SpeechStudio**, where you will find a **Practice Presentation Feedback Form** that you can use during a practice speaking session with your working group.

To complete this form in electronic format, go to the **Sample Assignment for a Peer Critic Panel** on the **Online SpeechStudio**.

FIGURE 3 **Sample Assignment for a Peer-Critic Panel**

Your five-person peer critique panel will listen to all of the speeches on the day to which you are assigned. Before coming to class, decide how you want to divide the work. For instance, one of you may want to focus on the ways the speakers involved the audience, another might comment on how the speakers used such elements as previews, transitions, and summaries to provide structure and organization to their speeches, a third might focus on the kinds and quality of evidence the speakers used, a fourth might comment on the speaker's delivery and use of presentational aids, and a final critic might examine how effectively the speakers responded to audience questions.

There are other ways of organizing your panel; for instance, one person might focus on general strengths, another on general areas for improvement, and the other three could each offer two concrete suggestions for improvement. Yet another strategy might involve some of the approaches outlined above, but one critic might pose additional questions for the speakers to answer.

Once your group has decided on how you want to approach this assignment, you will come to class prepared to listen carefully to the speakers, taking good notes on your area of focus. At the conclusion of the speeches, you will be given 5 minutes to confer with your fellow panelists. Then, you will come to the front of the room, seat yourselves as a panel, and proceed to share your feedback with the class. You will have 10 minutes to offer your feedback. The remainder of the class will be devoted to others' responses, including those of the speakers, who may want to respond to questions or other issues.

This assignment is worth 20 points, 15 based on the panel as a whole and 5 points based on your individual comments.

small group of peers can get together and practice giving your speeches to one another. Not only is this kind of oral practice in front of a live audience very helpful, but when the actual speaking day arrives, each of you will feel more confident because part of the audience is your "working group" and is particularly supportive of you. (See Figure 4 for a sample activity you can use as you collaborate with your peers.)

FIGURE 4 **Sample Collaborative Activity: Evaluating a Partner's Presentational Aids**

As you look over the presentational aids that your partner plans to use during his or her next speech, evaluate them in light of some of the criteria that follow:

1. **Are the presentational aids attractive?**
2. **Are they sufficiently large? Check font size.**
3. **Are the aids simple—not cluttered?**
4. **Are they well constructed, with a professional look?**
5. **Do they clarify or illuminate the speaker's ideas?**
6. **Will the aids likely assist with extemporaneous delivery?**
7. **Will the aids promote audience recall of important information?**
8. **Are the aids really needed?**

Once you have given the speaker your feedback, ask him or her to show you how each aid will be used during the speech. Doing this will entail practicing parts of the speech. Be sure to meet in a room with appropriate computer support if your partner plans to use computer-generated graphics as presentational aids.

Once you have worked through your partner's presentational aids, offering constructive feedback, reverse roles and repeat the above.

To complete this form in electronic format, go to the **Sample Collaborative Activity: Evaluating a Partner's Presentational Aids** on the **Online SpeechStudio**.

Speeches for Review and Analysis

APPENDIX B

INFORMATIVE SPEECH

Meredith Mira, Student

Milk: Does It Do a Body Good?

Go to **Lesson 8's Screening Room** on the **VideoLab** CD-ROM and watch this speech. Then go to **Drill 8.1: Identifying Components of Informative Speaking** and take the quiz to test your knowledge of informative speaking.

Meredith Mira was a first-year student in a beginning public speaking class at Indiana University when she gave this speech.

Some pour it on their cereal every day. Many drink it with their evening meals. All mothers feed it to their newborn babies. What is this substance I'm referring to? I think you all know. It's milk, of course. Pure, white milk.

Well, at least it used to be pure. For in November of 1993, the Food and Drug Administration, or the FDA, approved the sale of milk from cows that had been treated with a genetically engineered hormone in order to increase their milk production. This hormone, referred to as RBST, is an artificial version of a naturally occurring hormone in cows called BST. RBST supplements this natural process, and allows the cow to produce ten to twenty percent more milk. But the question is, does it really do a body good?

Now the product seems simple enough, but, in fact, it has become the subject of a major controversy. Monsanto, the chemical company that created RBST, says that it's virtually identical to naturally occurring RBST, and is completely safe, as well as economically efficient. However, activist groups such as the Pewfrume Campaign, disagree. They claim that the health consequences of RBST are severe, and the economic effects are going to be negative. Today, I'd like to consider the reasons behind this controversy, beginning with how RBST affects the cows, moving on to how these effects can have human consequences, and finally concluding with the economic impact RBST will have.

Let's begin with the root of the controversy: the cow. Now, the use of RBST prolongs the amount of time that the cow produces milk. The wear and tear of this overproduction leads to an increase in udder infections, which, in turn, leads to an increase of antibiotics to fight these infections. Now, keep in mind: udder infections are not uncommon, but the increased risk of udder infections could have human consequences.

As quoted in the *New York Times,* anti-biotechnology activist Jeremy Rifkin stated, "Studies have shown that RBST-injected cows suffer from an increase in udder infections, so cows on RBST are also likely to be shot up with larger doses of antibiotics, which may find their way into your milk." The fear is if people drink milk that's laced with antibiotics, bacteria within that person will build up an immunity to those antibiotics, therefore rendering life-saving drugs useless. Dr. Cara Mahmed, as Head Scientist of the National Resource Council, feels that unless quick action is taken, we are going to have an epidemic of untreatable stomach ailments, many of which will end in death.

Now the FDA and the Monsanto chemical company agree that both udder infections and antibiotic treatments are legitimate concerns, but they don't feel that RBST poses a serious threat in either of these cases. You see, they say that RBST's role in causing udder infections is actually quite minimal, compared with the other things that are going on on a farm. In fact, the simple shift in seasons from summer to winter is nine times as likely to cause an udder infection than the use of RBST. And as for antibiotics, the FDA concludes that all milk is subjected to rigorous federal tests, and that if there was any antibiotics in it at all, it would all be discarded, thus ensuring safe and wholesome milk.

So as you can see, there is a major controversy concerning antibiotics as treatment for udder infections, and the implications for human health are severe. But an even more serious risk is that people who drink RBST milk are under a greater risk of developing breast and colon cancer.

Now the function of RBST is to stimulate the extra production of a growth-like factor called IGF-1. IGF-1 increases the milk yield, but it also poses a threat of cancer to humans. According to Dr. Samuel Epstein, Professor of Occupational and Environmental Medicine at the University of Illinois, IGF-1 is a growth factor for human breast cells, maintaining their malignancy, progression, and invasiveness. Cancer researcher Dr. George Trash supports this claim with his study, published in a 1995 issue of *Cancer Research.* He found that even minute amounts of IGF-1 protects tumor cells from chemotherapy, thus stimulating cancer growth.

Now, RBST proponent and Food Safety Specialist, Donna Scott, disagrees with both of these views. She says, "Protein hormones are animal species specific. What triggers cell activity in a dairy cow can't do so in a human."

So we have now seen that RBST possibly causes severe health problems, ranging from antibiotic immunity to cancer growth. But what will this increase in milk do to our pocketbooks? Let's consider the economic impact.

Opponents feel that an increase in milk will actually have a negative impact on the economy, while proponents feel that this increase will positively affect our economy over time. Opponents begin their argument with the fact that we already have a fifteen percent surplus of milk. If we have so much milk, why do we need to produce any more? Furthermore, overproduction does not equal lower prices. You see, the government artificially props up the price of milk. They set a minimum standard, and then they buy up the surpluses with your money—the taxpayers' money.

Now proponents agree that prices initially will rise. However, they'll soon decline over time because of increased efficiency. You see, using RBST allows farmers to get more milk using fewer cows, eventually allowing the government's set minimum price to fall. Many people feel that with the fluctuations of the economy, only time will tell what RBST will do.

Now we have considered every factor in the cycle of production, from actually injecting the cow with RBST to selling it at the grocery store. So, how pure do you think milk is now? The answer seems to be an ambiguous one, with strong arguments on both sides of the table. Today, I have given you the key components to personally solve this controversy. We have come to realize that RBST can result in an increase in udder infections, which could eventually cause antibiotic residue to end up in your milk. We have shown that the stimulant known as IGF-1 is thought to be cancer-causing; however, proponents disagree. And finally, we have examined the economic implications, and found that they span a large spectrum, from both the positive to the negative.

You now have the pieces to the puzzle. You, as a consumer, have the power to decide. Milk: does it really do a body good?

PERSUASIVE SPEECH

Holly Carolyn Baxter, Student

Enabling the Nondisabled

Holly Carolyn Baxter gave this speech in May 1998 at Indiana University. She was seriously injured in a car accident and is interested in the problems of the disabled.

Do you remember watching Superman on television or reading Superman comic books and thinking how great it would be to be the man, or in my case, the woman of steel? Unfortunately, I found out that sometimes you need to be careful what you wish for, because those wishes can come true.

No, I can't fly like Superman, lift up the corner of my car to change a flat tire, or even peer into my professor's mailbox to catch a glimpse of the next exam, but thanks to a careless driver and a bit of bad luck three years ago, I ended up breaking fifty-two bones and becoming the woman of steel: steel plates, steel rods, and steel screws, that is!

I was forced to face the fact that I, like everyone else, was not invincible. After spending over a year using a wheelchair, I was amazed at the attitudes people had and how I was treated. One woman proceeded to lecture me on why I should have worn a seatbelt, even though I had been, and another woman pushed me out of her way like a shopping cart.

After these experiences, I became interested in what we as college students can do to start to alleviate these problems. To investigate this issue, let's wheel on by the issue of who is disabled, crutch on over to how we use stereotypes as a crutch, and crash into what we as college students can do to start to alleviate these misguided stereotypes.

Let's wheel on into who has a disability. According to the United States Census Bureau in 1997, fifty-four million Americans are considered to have a disability. This is one in five people. An additional 1.2 million Americans with disabilities are in institutions and not counted as part of Census Bureau data. Of these figures, 12.6 million are children under the age of 18. Amazingly, over 75 percent of these Americans were not born with a disability, but rather acquired it later in life, much like I did after my car accident.

So, who is considered to have a disability? The Americans with Disabilities Act of 1990 says that someone is considered to have a disability if he or she has "a physical or mental impairment that substantially limits one or more major life functions, has a record of having such an impairment, or is regarded as having such an impairment." Major life functions include: seeing, speaking, breathing, caring for oneself, working, hearing, walking, performing manual tasks, and even simply, learning.

We've wheeled on through who is considered to have a disability, so let's crutch on over to how we use stereotypes as a crutch.

Most of us are simply uncomfortable with unfamiliar situations. We've all been to that party and wondered: How do we act? What do we say? Walter Lippmann in 1922 said that when we are unfamiliar with a situation, we often rely on stereotypes to form our attitudes. These incorrect stereotypes often make us feel that we can discount people with disabilities as something we will never have to deal with. Unfortunately, that was what I used to think, too.

Carling put it best in 1962, when he said, "People expect a cripple to be crippled; to be disabled and helpless; to be inferior to themselves, and they will become suspicious and insecure if the cripple falls short of these expectations." Amazingly, Edelsky and Rosengrant found in 1981 that nondisabled people are often surprised to discover that people with disabilities are attractive, bright, or competent, or have families, jobs, or hobbies.

Now that we have seen how we use stereotypes as a crutch, let's crash on into what we as college students can do to help.

The first step to alleviating stereotypes is to simply change the way we use language. We can avoid terms such as: *cripple, handicapped,* or *invalid* and instead use *individual with a disability*. We can avoid the term *normal* implying that those with disabilities are abnormal, and instead use *nondisabled, abled,* or if we want to be completely honest, *temporarily nondisabled*. We can avoid terms such as *victim* or *afflicted with,* and instead realize that people live with disabilities, not suffer through them. Finally, we can dispel the longest standing stereotype of all: *confined to a wheelchair* or *wheelchair-bound*. I quickly learned that wheelchairs are neither confining nor binding when you are unable to use your legs; rather they are freeing and offer a sense of independence. Thus, we can say that a person uses a wheelchair much like many of us use eyeglasses, and let's face it, have you ever heard someone say, "That person over there who is confined to eyeglasses or contact lens–bound?"

Well, we've wheeled on through who is considered disabled, crutched on through how we use stereotypes as a crutch, and crashed into what we as college students can do to start to alleviate these stereotypes.

So, in the future, be careful what you wish for, because those dreams can come true. I no longer dream of being the woman of steel, but I do dream of a society where people are not judged by their ability to run, see, or hear, but in the historic words of Martin Luther King's dream, "by the content of their character."

AWARD ACCEPTANCE

Neal Malicky, President of Baldwin-Wallace College

Confessions of a Recovering Bigot

Neal Malicky, an educator and educational administrator, was given the National Conference of Northern Ohio's Humanitarian Award in 1996. He gave the following speech accepting the award at a meeting of that organization (formerly known as the National Conference of Christians and Jews) on November 6, 1996.

I am very grateful to the National Conference for the high honor of the Humanitarian Award. I do not feel deserving of this award, but I accept it with deep gratitude, great humility, and on behalf of many people in education who work to make this a more just society.

It's a privilege to share this evening with Jackie Woods, whose dynamic leadership I admire greatly. I am deeply indebted to Rena Blumberg for her overly generous introduction. Many of you know Rena does everything at a single pace: full speed. Thank you, Rena.

I appreciate friends and colleagues from Baldwin-Wallace College who have shared this evening with us, and, of course, my family: Margi, Mike, Eric, and David and my sister, Joyce, who are here, and others who are here in spirit. If the true measure of wealth is gratitude, I am wealthy tonight. I want also to recognize with deep personal appreciation my colleagues from other universities, including several presidents who are here, who labor with dedication and conviction to teach students that acceptance and respect for individual differences is the mark of the educated person and the quality necessary for a society to survive.

What can a person say in receiving an award of this magnitude? There is no way that it can be deserved so I cannot talk about what might have been done to merit it. Neither can I say how I might live up to it because although I will strive to do so, undoubtedly, I will fail to fulfill all that I hope to do, as all of us do.

I have decided to share a few very personal reflections which reveal some inner thoughts about the subject of prejudice and discrimination as it raises its ugly head in my life and perhaps in yours. It emerges in strange and unexpected ways, never welcome or invited, but like an intruder it barges into our lives with its coarse and offensive rejection of our humanity. For when we discriminate against another of God's children our own humanity is lessened and our self-worth is lowered. We are damaged just as much as we damage others.

Our need to eliminate prejudice from our lives is necessary for our survival as humans, else we become what we hate.

I would like to share with you four brief vignettes: simple reflections which suggest a person's inner struggle with this complex and vexing quest to become fully human.

I have titled this "Confessions of Four Recovering Bigots."

I don't know why I said it. I had no idea the impact it would have. I'm not even sure I knew what it meant. How could I at 5?

We did our own work in our house. Then mother got sick, and she stayed sick for a long time. A heart ailment, the Dr. said. With three little kids and Dad off to work, she needed help. So Dad said, "let's get someone to help out." It was arranged.

Mrs. Johnson came quietly. Mom gave her instructions about what to do, and she went about doing it. I watched. It wasn't the work I watched. It was her! She was different. And in our house. And then, I said it!

"You're a ______ aren't you!" (And I used a word I had heard on the playground, the N word.)

She didn't reply. She didn't have to. I could tell by her look I had said the wrong thing. The word meant little to me, but it meant a great deal to her. Though resting in the next room, Mother heard me, and that word meant a great deal to her, too. I hadn't seen her move so fast in weeks.

"You naughty boy," she said. "Where did you learn that word?" She took hold of my ear and led me to the bathroom sink where she followed her personal method of cleaning up language by washing my mouth out with soap!

The soap tasted bitter, caustic. It didn't belong in the mouth. That's why she put it there. The assumption Mom followed was that cleaning the mouth with such an unpleasant taste would clean it also of unacceptable words. It seemed to work.

I never used that word again.

Often, over the 57 years between that day and now I have thought about what it meant to call Mrs. Johnson that name. Why did it mean so much to her? And to mother? And, why, for half a century has it brought such a feeling of shame whenever I hear it?

Dan ran a small business. He worked hard and treated his employees fairly; he was aggressive, and a good citizen.

"I don't have any problem with these folks, but they're costing me money," Dan thought.

They shouldn't expect us to wait for them all the time.

Why do they expect all these extras? All that signing; expensive ramps, elevators, special toilets, wide hallways.... Is that fair to the rest of us? Why do we need to take care of them?

Why can't they just keep up?

Susan is a good mother, and she loves to shop. It's fun! It distracts her mind and lets her look freely at beautiful things.

But sometimes, even when shopping, secret thoughts emerge.

Why do they talk so loud? It sounds like gibberish.

Why do they dress so funny? All kinds of strange stuff.

Why do they have so many kids? Not one or two like most Americans. But six or eight or more!! More cost to all the rest of us. I'll bet they're on welfare, or will be.

If they come to America, why don't they act like Americans?

When our ancestors came here they learned English, worked hard, went to church, built homes, and became American. These folks speak Spanish, or Vietnamese, or whatever, sleep in hovels, live on the dole, and don't care about being American.

Why don't they act like Americans?

Why don't they act like us?

Robert and Marie were the ideal couple: good jobs, a stable home, successful kids, and stalwart members of their church. They had worked hard to overcome their prejudices, but this is where they draw the line, or at least they always did.

People are born with their race or nationality. They grow up with their religion. They don't choose to be disabled. But surely they decide to do this. Don't they?

Besides, it's wrong! At least they always thought it was. Doesn't the Bible say so?

Then they met Delores and Lauri.

They seemed very normal, both of them. They were nice people, talented, friendly with their neighbors, successful in their work, good parents, loving in their relationships, and lesbians.

They also found out about Donald.

Robert worked with Don. He was very professional, cooperative, kind, and gay.

Robert had no idea about Don's sexual orientation. They had traveled together, even roomed together. It never occurred to him.

Then a more important thought came to Robert. Why should it have occurred to him? Delores and Lauri were everything a person could be as employees, friends, neighbors. Why should their choice to live with each other rather than with a man make a difference?

Don was an able, caring person. Why should it matter that he lived with Charles?

Why should it matter at all?

Where do five year olds learn such words? Or good people have such thoughts?

We don't invite thoughts like these. They explode into our quiet lives and shatter our image of ourselves with nuclear force. Where do they come from? What do we do with them?

When we were younger we sang from *South Pacific*, that "You've got to be taught to hate and fear."

It's half right. You do have to be taught to hate and fear, but many forces in our society are teaching those messages today. The other half needs our attention. We've got to be taught to overcome those fears which lead us down the road to prejudice, and bigotry, and to becoming less than human.

In a previous era the bigot may have peeked out through slits in white sheets, cowering under the cover of night while wreaking hatred and havoc on weak victims. Today's racist may dress well and rationalize racist behavior with phrases like: "You can't let him have that job because, after all, he's...."; Or, "We know those people are good at...but not at...."

Or, "They've come a long way, but they're not ready for...."

American society will become increasingly diverse in the next century, and we must go beyond shallow rationalizations if we are to provide full opportunity for each and justice for all. In our homes and schools, in our churches, synagogues, temples, and mosques, wherever we are, we must be teachers and examples of what it means to overcome our bigotry; of what it means to be human.

And people of faith, in whatever religious tradition, affirm that we are all children of one Father and Mother Creator, and, therefore, brothers and sisters one with another. People of faith and conviction more than others must become people of courage, teaching by word and example that we can overcome our bigotry and create justice in society.

When that sickening feeling emerges within us from an unsought pang of bigotry; or when we feel that shudder of fear as we see another form of discrimination emerge in our society, we must fight against it with the strength of our conviction and the power of our faith. When we do, we may feel that lump in the throat that reveals our best selves and our true humanity. Then, we will become part of the solution, and not be part of the problem.

Let us pledge to ourselves and to each other that we will generate the conviction to eliminate the prejudices that are within us, thus enhancing our own humanity. And let us muster the courage to help overcome the obstacles to justice and equality that are present in our society, thus enriching the lives and opportunities of others and fulfilling the dream for America.

There is no higher commitment for people of faith and conviction, no greater challenge for Americans, no finer opportunity to fulfill our calling as children of God.

Vital Speeches of the Day 62: Neal Malicky, "Confessions of a Recovering Bigot," (March 15, 1997), pp. 351–352.

COMMENCEMENT ADDRESS

David D. Ho, M.D., AIDS Researcher

Science as a Candle of Hope

Dr. David M. Ho is a leading researcher in the fight against AIDS. He gave the following address at commencement ceremonies at the California Institute of Technology, Pasadena, California, on June 13, 1997.

Thank you, it's great to be back. Good morning, President Everhart, Dr. Moore, and members of the Trustees and faculty. To the graduates and their families and friends, my heartfelt congratulations! It is indeed a momentous day in your lives.

What an incredible honor it is for me to return to Caltech as the commencement speaker. As a young boy growing up in southern California, this was my dream school. Caltech is where my scientific interests were inspired by the genius of extraordinary men like Feymann, Gell-Mann, and Delbruck.

It is also the very place where I first learned to tackle research with a multi-disciplinary approach not limited by arbitrary boundaries that separate biomedical sciences from physics, chemistry, engineering, and mathematics. I will forever be indebted to you.

I am here today because I have been given a great deal of praise and recognition for recent advances made in AIDS research. Achievements in research seldom belong to a single individual. Science is a richly collaborative endeavor, and my personal recognition is merely symbolic for the many important discoveries and contributions made by a cadre of talented scientists in the field. As Newton aptly put it, "If I can see farther, it is because I stand on the shoulders of giants."

The recent media attention focused on AIDS research has provided a unique opportunity to educate the public at large about a plague of staggering dimensions, and to advocate to our leaders a proper course of action. It is also gratifying to see that the media is willing, on occasions, to prominently feature scientists for accomplishments that move our society forward. However, on a personal note, I find the media spotlight is hot enough to bake, and as Einstein had cautioned, "the only way to avoid the corruption of praise is to keep on working."

I feel extremely privileged to work on AIDS. As a young physician in Los Angeles in 1981, I was fortunate enough to witness the beginning of the visible part of the AIDS epidemic. Over the course of a year, young men, one after another, were presented to the hospital with a multitude of opportunistic infections, leading to death within days to weeks. It was evident that their immune system was damaged. But, by what? Their medical histories strongly suggested the possibility of a sexually transmitted agent that caused immunodeficiency. And yet, any description of a similar syndrome was nowhere to be found in the medical literature. The disease was obviously new!

In this manner, AIDS appeared insidiously and mystified doctors and scientists alike. No one could have predicted that 16 years later, we would face a global epidemic of HIV infection that is arguably the plague of the millennium.

Today, HIV continues to spread at an alarming rate of 8,500 new cases per day, and more than 50 million infections are expected by the year 2000. For a biomedical scientist, what could represent a greater opportunity than to conduct research on a lethal microbe that threatens the health of the entire world? Members of the class of '97, as you move on in life, be prepared to take advantage of the opportunities that are bubbled up by serendipity. Then have courage and conviction in pursuing your goals and ideals.

You have chosen a noble profession, one filled with excitement. Nothing is more thrilling to me than the process of scientific discovery. When the wonder of nature is revealed, one is left breathless and awestruck. Imagine the joy and intellectual satisfaction that must have pervaded this campus when the positron was discovered, when the nature of the chemical bond was revealed, when the redshifts of the spectra of galaxies were observed, or when that which makes the sun shine was understood. Allow me a more modest but personal anecdote.

Beginning in 1991, my colleagues and I had the privilege of working with structural biologists and medicinal chemists to test small chemicals that might intercalate into the catalytic site of the HIV protease, an enzyme essential for the production of infectious progeny virus. So overwhelming was the excitement that overtook us when substances were found to potently inhibit the protease enzyme, thereby blocking viral replication in the test tube.

Three years later, we again had the privilege of being the first to administer one of these chemicals to infected patients. Unmatched were the joy and amazement as we watched the level of HIV fall, ever so dramatically. At first, little did we know that we were sitting on top of a fundamental discovery in AIDS research. But, shortly thereafter, by simply asking why does the virus fall and why does it fall in that manner, it quickly dawned on us that HIV must be turning over rapidly, in a dynamic equilibrium with the host. Using data from our patients and working together with mathematicians, we proved that HIV replication in vivo was rapid and remorseless. In the course of only a few weeks, the old paradigm that HIV was largely a latent virus was completely shattered. So incredible was the ensuing intellectual satisfaction that I now fully appreciate the meaning of a line in the book, *The Ascent of Man*. It reads, "when the answers are simple, then you hear God thinking."

Despite the breakneck speed of scientific discoveries in the field, AIDS patients already faced a decade and a half of horror and disappointment. But, because of science, there is now hope. In the past two years, with new knowledge and new therapies, it has become possible to control HIV so effectively that the virus is no longer detectable in the infected person. This dramatic attack on the virus is associated with a substantial clinical benefit to the patient. For the first time in this dreadful epidemic, the tide has begun to turn against the virus. Although a cure is still not in hand, as stated in *Time* magazine, the worst fear, the one that seeded a decade with despair, the foreboding sense that the AIDS virus might be invincible, has finally been subdued. After 15 years of cursing the darkness of AIDS, a candle of hope has been lit by science.

AIDS, however, is not over. Worldwide, most infected persons cannot access the promising new therapies, and much remains to be done in controlling the spread of this epidemic. It is my deepest hope that the recent scientific advances will inspire government, academia, and the private sector to remain vigilant and to re-double our efforts to bring an end to this tragedy. Prevention is the ultimate key to controlling the epidemic, and vaccine science must now take center stage, as was declared by President Clinton last month. And, fortunately for us, Dr. David Baltimore is now heading up the national effort in this area. Of course we also look to his leadership, as the next Caltech President, to deliver our school, boldly and proudly, into the next millennium.

Recently, my thoughts have taken me on a number of self-reflective journeys. Let me humbly share a few with the graduates. In our experiments attempting to eradicate HIV from an infected person, I have learned that success in research, as is the case in most endeavors, required bold decision making and a willingness to take informed risks. As so eloquently stated by Harold Shapiro of Princeton, "an excessive zeal to avoid all risks is in the end, an acceptance of mediocrity and an abdication of leadership." You must take on the toughest challenge but view it as the greatest opportunity, for every noble work is at first seemingly impossible. Have the courage to risk failure, for as T. S. Eliot once said, only those who risk going too far can possibly find out how far one can go.

In the best tradition of Caltech, always maintain, unwaveringly, a deep commitment to excellence. It is okay to stay small, as long as you stay in the forefront. As you enter a career in science or engineering, never permit the excellence of your work to be compromised.

I remember with a great deal of fondness my mates from the class of '74. Just like you, what a bunch they were. Stay young at heart. But, should you need to grow, do not suppress your individuality nor insist on conformity. Continue to let imagination and creativity percolate throughout your lives, both personal and professional.

I have also reflected on the contribution of my heritage to my career. Were it not for the profound Asian respect for intellectual achievements and scholarly endeavors, a scientist I might not be today. Moreover, values of drive and dedication, imprinted during early childhood, have continued to serve me well. In any culture, there is simply no substitute for hard work. I have been an American for so long that I have nearly forgotten that I am also an immigrant. From time to time, I can still sense the desire that burns in the belly of a new immigrant, the desire to carve out a place in the new world, in the land of opportunities. To this day, I maintain an underdog mentality that motivates me to a higher level of work ethics.

Uncharacteristically, let me begin to close with a political comment. Throughout its history, America has continually benefited from the drive, labor, and creativity of immigrants, many in the fields of science. Just look among the graduates today. Thus, today, one prevailing view that immigrants constitute a constant drain on our society is simply baseless, wrong and shameful, especially in this nation of immigrants.

Graduates, as future scientists and engineers, it is likely that you will from time to time, be underappreciated, underrecognized, and, very likely, underpaid by our society. You will have to take solace and satisfaction in knowing that your work has helped to build a better, safer, and healthier world. A world with hope. Members of the class of '97, it matters not whether you work on numbers, atoms, molecules, machines, organisms, the earth, or the cosmos. Through science and technology, any one of you can cast a giant shadow on our planet. As Margaret Mead so nicely stated, "Never doubt that a small group of committed citizens can change the world. Indeed, it is the only thing that ever has."

Congratulations again and my best wishes!

Vital Speeches of the Day 62: David Ho, "Science as a Candle of Hope," (August 15, 1997), pp. 660–662.

SPEECH OF INSPIRATION

Frances J. McClain, Professor of Music

The Music in Your Soul: A Celebration of Life

Address by Frances J. McClain, Livingstone Professor of Music at Queens College, delivered at the fall convocation to students, faculty, and staff of Queens College, Charlotte, North Carolina, September 18, 2001.

The horrific terrorist attack on our country taught us how, in a single minute, we can be hurled from order into chaos, from joy into sorrow, and from life into death. Shouldn't we, therefore, learn to appreciate life more, to view each day as the blessing it is, and to celebrate each day to its fullest? So then, on this fall convocation at Queens College, let us celebrate life and this day. As students, faculty, and staff, let us observe this occasion as a time of new beginnings, new goals, and new opportunities for the attainment of worthwhile endeavors.

As a music therapist, I know that the power of music can not only comfort and console us, it can also inspire, unify, and uplift our spirits. So I thought, wouldn't it be appropriate if I could place the concept of celebration within a musical framework? Now we all know that most celebrations—whether weddings, parties, dances, receptions—are more festive, more engaging, more memorable with just the right type of music. After all, most of us love, or at least like, music. WE MOVE, SOOTHE, AND GROOVE TO IT, RIGHT?

In fact, music is not just a part of our lives, it is a part of our language as well. Don Campbell, the author of *The Mozart Effect,* states that "Music is rapidly becoming the common tongue of the modern world." Musical metaphors now dominate our language. For example:

- When people are in agreement, we are in tune, or in harmony with each other.
- When we want to make a good impression, we want to set the right tone, strike a sympathetic chord, or communicate on the same wavelength.
- When you hear good news, it is music to your ears!
- And when we don't know what to expect, we play it by ear.

And of course, the list could go on.

So then, like the musical qualities we have adopted into our language, there are also music qualities and characteristics we can utilize in our lives. Now when I speak of musical qualities, I am not referring to how well you may or may not sing or play, or what you know or don't know about music, or what type or style of music you like or dislike, or how much you loved or hated your music lessons. Regardless of this, you all have some of the same elements in you that are in music. And these musical qualities, which emanate from the soul, are essential to the celebration of life!

Think of what you respond to most in the music you enjoy—not the lyrics, but the music itself. Is it the melody, the harmony, the rhythm, the tempo, or the dynamics? Whichever of these elements it is, each of us has some of these same musical qualities in us and we can use them daily.

Melody.

First of all, like music, each of us has a unique melody. Just as we identify a song by its melody, each of us is identified by our melody, which I like to think of as our musical personality.

For example, some personalities are like melodies. Some of you are quiet, soft, and lyrical. Others are rhythmic and energetic. Some are majestic and somber. Yet others may be whimsical and funny. Still others are cool and mellow. And truthfully, some of you are like the new styles of music, you are just way out there.

Regardless, your melody is your own sound, your own style, your essence, your identity. You know this is true because when a person tells us something about someone else, we often say that sounds just like him or her. In other words, we recognize the melody of that individual. Whatever the sound or style of your melody, use it to celebrate life. Like the film classic with Julie Andrews, you have your own Sound of Music. So find a job, a career, a hobby, a dream that suits your music—that will let you play your melody to its fullest.

You know, you can't really be happy when you're playing someone's song. Mama Cass Elliot, a singer my colleagues remember from their youthful days, phrases it this way: "Make your own kind of music. Sing your own special song. Make your own kind of music, even if nobody else sings along."

In the work setting especially, you need a job that will allow you the joy of expressing your melody, your creativity. As Duke Ellington, the famous African-American jazz composer and performer, said, "People who make a living doing something they don't enjoy wouldn't even be happy with a one-day work week." So find an atmosphere and environment that welcomes and nurtures your melody.

Harmony.

Just as the melody is the solo or single line, the harmony involves other voices or instruments that complement and add beauty to the melody. Bringing harmony does not only refer to singing a particular voice part, such as soprano, alto, tenor, or bass, or playing given notes on a particular instrument. It also refers to how you bring various people and ideas together. You truly celebrate life when you are able to help individuals work together, care about each other, and share with each other.

I suspect that some of you as RAs in the dorm and officers of various clubs and organizations may get plenty of practice this year in the art of harmony—of getting people to work cooperatively together and to live peacefully together, to support, complement, and genuinely care about each other.

So take heart, and remember the words of Jesus when he said, "Blessed or happy are the peacemakers, for they shall be called the children of God."

Rhythm.

Well, besides melody and harmony, there is also rhythm. Many of you may respond to the rhythm of music because it organizes the music. It brings energy and vitality to the music. The rhythm gives us the beat that causes us to clap our hands and tap our feet.

Some of you have the gift of rhythm. You know how to get people organized, energized, enthusiastic, and motivated. For some of you, it will be your energy, your encouragement that will keep people from giving out or giving up. The enthusiasm you display can truly be contagious and can inspire others to go the extra mile.

Like the rhythm of nature and the rhythm of our own bodies, some of you will show a dependability and regularity in everything you do. You won't miss a single beat in anything you do to achieve your goal.

Tempo.

Now just as a melody has rhythm, it also has a tempo. The element of tempo refers to the speed or pace of the music—how fast or slow the music will go. As you know, a fast tempo can stimulate us to move in a certain way, to put pep in our step, give us a boost, and energize us. In contrast, a slow tempo can help us relax, reduce stress, slow down our heart rate, help us focus more, cause us to be more introspective.

As you celebrate life, you will learn the art of tempo. Things happen to us at different times and tempos. They are not always at the expected or desired time. Some things come quickly, others far more slowly. Learn to accept and appreciate where you are right now in your life.

Some of you know how to use the element of tempo. You know how to move quickly or slowly, depending on what is needed. During this year, you may be asked to move quickly on a decision, or to do a job in a very short period of time. You will be asked to step in—at a moment's notice. And some of you will be successful because you will be able to quickly assess a situation, make a plan, stay with it, and keep a steady tempo until the task is completed.

Yet others may need to move a little slower. Perhaps take the time to listen, weigh the issues, or think through a problem. You will be successful because you were patient, because you waited, because you did not act in haste.

Some of you have perhaps already decided that the tempo of four years to complete a degree is a little too fast for you. It doesn't fit your melody—so you are going to slow down the pace. Don't be afraid to make this decision if it is appropriate for you. Remember that sometimes by slowing down the pace, we can avoid decisions or actions that could later on have detrimental results. The tempo of life can become so hectic, so complex that we can't enjoy where we are for thinking about where we want to be or think we should be. So perhaps we could all benefit by slowing down a little.

On the other hand, however, sometimes you can slow down the tempo of life a little too much. In fact, there is a proverb that I like from the book *Leaves of Gold* that states, "Laziness travels so slowly that poverty soon overtakes him." A word to the wise!

In all sincerity, concerning the tempo and timing of life, remember the words of King Solomon in Ecclesiastes: "To every thing there is a season, and a time to every purpose under heaven."

Dynamics.

Well after melody, harmony, rhythm, tempo, the last element is that of dynamics, which refers to the volume—the loudness or softness of your melody.

Over the years, I see freshmen come in quiet, reserved, and a little shy about using their melodies and in leading others. But by the senior year, they crescendo to become leaders with loud, vibrant, and stimulating melodies. Therefore, I encourage you to use the opportunities at Queens to turn up your volume, to grow, and to be a leader. So when it is your time to be heard, be a strong soloist, sound off. Raise the volume. Show others the love and passion you have for something. Don't be afraid to put yourself out there for a cause. As Martin Luther King would say, "Be a drum major for justice."

However, when others need to be heard, let your melody float softly into the background. Those of you who have ever sung in a choir, played in a band or orchestra know how the beauty of the music can be destroyed by just one person playing or singing louder than everyone else. So learn to blend, to complement, to sustain the efforts of others. Like the element of dynamics, learn when to be loud enough to be heard and soft enough to hear others.

Well, in summary, I sincerely hope you will

- use your unique melody in a very meaningful way throughout your life;
- blend your voice with others to create harmony;
- find a rhythm that organizes and energizes your life;
- select a tempo that is comfortable for you and your goals;
- decide when the dynamics of your melody should be loud or soft.

When you discover and develop your musical qualities, your life will truly take on a new dimension that will honor your Creator and enhance your interactions with others.

In closing, I say thank you and may God bless as you use the music in your soul to celebrate life!

Vital Speeches of the Day 68: Frances J. McClain, "The Music in Your Soul: A Celebration of Life," (November 1, 2001), pp. 59–61.

SPEECH OF TRIBUTE

Bill Clinton, President

Dedication of the Roosevelt Memorial

President Clinton gave the following speech of tribute at the dedication of a memorial commemorating the life of President Franklin D. Roosevelt, who led the United States out of the great economic depression of the 1930s and served as president during World War II. The speech was given at West Potomac Park in Washington, D.C., on May 2, 1997.

Thank you very much. Senator Inouye, Senator Hatfield; Your Highness; my longtime friend, David Roosevelt, and the members of the Roosevelt family; Mr. Vice President; to all those who have worked to make this day a reality. Let me begin by saying to Senator Inouye and Senator Hatfield, the United States proudly accepts the Franklin Delano Roosevelt Memorial.

Fittingly, this is the first occasion of its kind in more than 50 years. The last time the American people gathered near here was in 1943 when President Franklin Roosevelt dedicated the memorial to Thomas Jefferson. Today we honor the greatest President of this great American century. As has been said, FDR actually wanted no memorial. For years, none seemed necessary—for two reasons: First, the America he built was a memorial all around us. From the Golden Gate Bridge to the Grand Coulee Dam; from Social Security to honest financial markets; from an America that has remained the world's indispensable nation to our shared conviction that all Americans must make our journey together, Roosevelt was all around us.

Second, though many of us never lived under his leadership, many who did are still around, and we have all heard about him from our parents or grandparents—some of us, as we pass WPA or CCC projects along country roads; some of us as we looked at the old radios that our parents and grandparents kept and heard stories about the Fireside Chats and how the people felt. Today he is still very real to millions upon millions of Americans, inspiring us, urging us on. But the world turns and memories fade. And now, more than a half-century after he left us, it is right that we go a little beyond his stated wishes and dedicate this memorial as a tribute to Franklin Roosevelt, to Eleanor, and to the remarkable triumphs of their generation.

President Roosevelt said, "We have faith that future generations will know that here, in the middle of the 20th century, there came a time when men of goodwill found a way to unite and produce and fight to destroy the forces of ignorance and intolerance and slavery and war." This memorial will be the embodiment of FDR's faith, for it will ensure that all future generations will know. It will ensure that they will all see the "happy warrior" keeping America's rendezvous with destiny.

As we stand at the dawn of a bright new century, this memorial will encourage us, reminding us that whenever America acts with certainty of purpose and FDR's famous flexibility of mind, we have always been more than equal to whatever challenges we face.

Winston Churchill said that President Roosevelt's life was "one of the commanding events in human history." He came from privilege, but he understood the aspirations of farmers and factory workers and forgotten Americans. He electrified the farms and hollows, but even more important, he electrified the nation, instilling confidence with every tilt of his head and boom of his laugh. His was an open, American spirit with a fine sense for the possible and a keen appreciation of the art of leadership. He was a master politician and a magnificent Commander-in-Chief.

And his partner was also magnificent. Eleanor Roosevelt was his eyes and his ears, going places he could not go to see things he would never see to come back and tell him how things actually were. And her reports were formed as words in his speeches that touched little people all across America who could not imagine that the President of the United States knew how they lived and cared about them. She was his conscience and our nation's conscience.

Franklin Roosevelt's mission was to change America to preserve its ancient virtues in the face of new and unprecedented challenges. That is, after all, America's mission in all times of change and difficulty. The depth and sweep of it was unprecedented when FDR asked a shaken nation to put its confidence in him. But he had no doubt of the outcome.

Listen to what he said in September of 1932, shortly before he was elected for the first time. He proclaimed his faith: "Faith in America, faith in our tradition of personal responsibility, faith in our institutions, faith in ourselves demanded we recognize the new terms of an old social contract. New conditions imposed new requirements upon government and upon those who conduct government." That was his faith. He lived it, and we are here as a result.

With that faith, he forged a strong and unapologetic government, determined to tame the savage cycles of boom and bust, able to meet the national challenges too big for families and individuals to meet on their own. And when he restored dignity to old age, when he helped millions to keep their farms or own their homes, when he provided the simple opportunity to go to work in the morning to millions, he was proving that the American Dream was not a distant glimmer, but something every American could grasp. And then that faith of his infused all of his countrymen.

With that faith he inspired millions of ordinary Americans to take responsibility for one another—doing their part, in his words, through the National Recovery Administration, reclaiming nature through the Civilian Conservation Corps, gathering scrap, giving up nylons, and eventually storming the beaches at Normandy and Okinawa and Anzio.

With that faith, he committed our nation to lead the world, first as the arsenal of democracy, and then at the head of the great crusade to free the world from tyranny. Before the war began, the four freedoms set the foundation for the future and made it clear to the whole world that America's goal was not domination, but a dominion of freedom in a world at peace.

With that faith as the war neared an end he would never see, he traced the very architecture of our future, from the G.I. Bill to the United Nations. Faith in the extraordinary potential of ordinary people sparked not only our victory over war, depression, and doubt, but it began the opening of doors and the raising of sights for the dispossessed in America that has continued down to the present day. It was that faith in his own extraordinary potential that enabled him to guide his country from a wheelchair. And from that wheelchair and a few halting steps, leaning on his son's arms or those of trusted aides, he lifted a great people back to their feet and set America to march again toward its destiny.

He said over and over again in different ways that we had only to fear fear itself. We did not have to be afraid of pain or adversity or failure, for all those could be overcome. He knew that, of course, because that is exactly what he did. And with his faith and the power of his example, we did conquer them all—depression, war, and doubt.

Now, we see that faith again alive in America. We are grateful beyond measure for our own unprecedented prosperity. But we must remember the source of that faith. And again, let me say to Senator Inouye and others, by showing President Roosevelt as he was, we show the world that we have faith that in America you are measured for what you are and what you have achieved, not for what you have lost. And we encourage all who face their difficulties and overcome them not to give into fear, but to believe in their possibilities.

And now again we need the faith of Franklin Roosevelt, in an entirely different time, but still no ordinary time, for in this time new livelihoods demand new skills. We have to fight against the enormous, destructive influences that still grip the lives of too many of our young people. We must struggle to make our rich racial, ethnic, and religious diversity a source of strength and unity when such differences are the undoing of millions and millions around the world. And we must fight against that nagging old doubt.

It is a strange irony of our time that here, at the moment of our greatest prosperity and progress in so many years—in 1932, one in four Americans was out of work; this morning we learned that fewer than one in 20 Americans are out of work, for the first time in more than two decades. And at this time, when the pinnacle that Roosevelt hoped America would achieve in our influence and power has come to pass, we still, strangely, fight battles with doubts—doubts that he would treat with great impatience and disdain; doubts that lead some to urge us to pull back from the world at the very first time since Roosevelt's time when we actually can realize his vision of world peace and world prosperity and the dominance of the ideals for which he gave his life.

Let us honor his vision not only with this memorial today, but by acting in the way he would tell us to act if he were standing here, giving this speech, on his braces, looking at us and smiling at us and telling us we know what we have to do. We are Americans. We must have faith. We must not be afraid. And we must lead.

The great legacy of Roosevelt is a vision and a challenge—not a set of specific programs, but a set of commitments—the duty we owe to ourselves, to one another, to our beloved nation, and increasingly, to our fellow travelers on this small planet.

Now we are surrounded by the monuments to the leaders who built our democracy—Washington, who launched our great experiment and created our republic; Jefferson, who enshrined forever our creed that it is self-evident that we are all created equal, with unalienable rights to life, liberty, and the pursuit of happiness; Lincoln, who gave his life to preserve Mr. Washington's republic and to make real Mr. Jefferson's words. And now, Franklin Roosevelt, who saved freedom from tyranny, who restored our republic, who defined Mr. Jefferson's creed to include freedom from want and fear. Today, before the pantheon of our democracy, let us resolve to honor them all by shepherding their legacy into a new century, into a new millennium.

Our mission is to prepare America for the time to come, to write a new chapter of our history, inspired always by the greatest source of hope in our history. Thomas Jefferson wrote the words, but Franklin Roosevelt lived them out every day. Today I ask you to remember what he was writing at Warm Springs when he died, that last speech: "The only limit to our realization of tomorrow will be our doubts of today. Let us move forward with active faith."

My fellow Americans, every time you think of Franklin Roosevelt put aside your doubts, become more American, become more like him, be infused with his strong and active faith.

God bless you. God bless America. And may God always bless the memory of Franklin Delano Roosevelt.

Vital Speeches of the Day 62: Bill Clinton, "Dedication of the Roosevelt Memorial," (June 1, 1997), pp. 482–484.

EULOGIES

John McCain, Senator

Eulogy in Honor of Mark Bingham

U.S. senator John McCain delivered this speech on September 22, 2001, in honor of Mark Bingham, one of the passengers aboard hijacked United Airlines Flight 93 on September 11, 2001. Mark Bingham met Senator McCain during McCain's 2000 presidential bid. The normally apolitical Bingham liked what he saw in McCain: a willingness to fight for principles. In this speech, the tables are turned, as it's now McCain who considers Bingham his personal hero for taking on the suicide hijackers who commandeered the plane that would eventually crash outside of Pittsburgh, Pennsylvania.

I didn't know Mark Bingham. We met once briefly during my presidential campaign, yet I cannot say that I knew him well. But I wish I had. I wish I had. You meet a lot of people when you run for president. I was fortunate to have had the support of many Americans who were, until then, strangers to me. And I regret to say, that like most candidates I was preoccupied with winning or losing. I had not thought as much as I should have about what an honor, what an extraordinary honor it was to have so many citizens of the greatest nation on earth place their trust in me, and use our campaign as an expression of their own patriotism. They were the best thing about our campaign, not me. Had I been successful, my greatest challenge would have been to prove myself worthy of the faith of so many good people.

I love my country, and I take pride in serving her. But I cannot say that I love her more or as well as Mark Bingham did, or the other heroes on United Flight 93 who gave their lives to prevent our enemies from inflicting an even greater injury on our country. It has been my fate to witness great courage and sacrifice for America's sake, but none greater than the selfless sacrifice of Mark Bingham and those good men who grasped the gravity of the moment, understood the threat, and decided to fight back at the cost of their lives.

In the Gospel of John it is written, "Greater love hath no man than this, that a man lay down his life for his friends." Such was the love that Mark and his comrades possessed, as they laid down their lives for others. A love so sublime that only God's love surpasses it.

It is now believed that the terrorists on Flight 93 intended to crash the airplane into the United States Capitol where I work, the great house of democracy where I was that day. It is very possible that I would have been in the building, with a great many other people, when that fateful, terrible moment occurred, and a beautiful symbol of our freedom was destroyed along with hundreds if not thousands of lives. I may very well owe my life to Mark and the others who summoned the enormous courage and love necessary to deny those depraved, hateful men their terrible triumph. Such a debt you incur for life.

I will try very hard, very hard, to discharge my public duties in a manner that honors their memory. All public servants are now solemnly obliged to do all we can to help this great nation remain worthy of the sacrifice of New York City firefighters, police officers, emergency medical people, and worthy of the sacrifice of the brave passengers on Flight 93.

No American living today will ever forget what happened on September 11, 2001. That day was the moment when the hinge of history swung toward a new era not only in the affairs of this nation, but in the affairs of all humanity. The opening chapter of this new history is tinged with great sadness and uncertainty. But as we begin, please take strength from the example of the American we honor today, and those who perished to save others in New York, Washington, and Pennsylvania. The days ahead will be difficult, and we will know more loss and sorrow. But we will prevail. We will prevail.

Pay no heed to the voices of the poor, misguided souls, in this country and overseas, who claim that America brought these atrocities on herself. They are deluded, and their hearts are cramped by hatred and fear. Our respect for Man's God-given rights to life, liberty, and the pursuit of happiness assures us of victory even as it made us a target for the enemies of freedom who mistake hate and depravity for power. The losses we have suffered are grave, and must not be forgotten. But we should all take pride and unyielding resolve from the knowledge that we were attacked because we were good, and good we will remain as we vanquish the evil that preys upon us.

I never knew Mark Bingham. But I wish I had. I know he was a good son and friend, a good rugby player, a good American, and an extraordinary human being. He supported me, and his support now ranks among the greatest honors of my life. I wish I had known before September 11 just how great an honor his trust in me was. I wish I could have thanked him for it more profusely than time and circumstances allowed. But I know it now. And I thank him with the only means I possess, by being as good an American as he was.

America will overcome these atrocities. We will prevail over our enemies. We will right this terrible injustice. And when we do, let us claim it as a tribute to our liberty, and to Mark Bingham and all those who died to defend it.

To all of you who loved Mark, and were loved by him, he will never be so far from you that you cannot feel his love. As our faith informs us, you will see him again, when our loving God reunites us all with the loved ones who preceded us. Take care of each other until then, as he would want you to. May God bless Mark. And may God bless us all.

Thank you.

Senator John McCain: *Eulogy in Honor of Mark Bingham*, delivered September 22, 2001, San Francisco, California. Downloaded from *http://mccain.senate.gov/bingham.htm.*

EULOGIES

Linda Farrow, United Airlines MEC President

Tribute to the Flight Crews Lost on September 11, 2001

On September 11, 2001, thirty-five American Airlines and United Airlines crew members were killed in the terrorist attacks on the World Trade Center. Linda Farrow delivered this eulogy in their honor at memorial services in Chicago, Illinois, and Newark, New Jersey.

It seems like years, but it was only a few weeks ago that the columnists were lamenting the lack of heroes in America and that our heroes were superficially famous stars of movie screens and sports arenas.

Now newspapers throughout the land devote pages to listing our heroes. Few were famous before that infamous Tuesday. Most of our heroes came out of ordinary homes in cities and suburbs, going to work, just as they had done a thousand times before. But on that day, they were called upon to make the ultimate sacrifice. And they did.

The American author F. Scott Fitzgerald said, "Show me a hero and I will write you a tragedy."

The skies, the skyscrapers, the police stations, and the firehouses were filled with heroes on

September 11, and the tragedies were written to a scale even greater than the buildings destroyed that day.

In our industry, among those assembled here as well as those on the line right now, we have our own heroes, taken from our ranks but remembered now and forever.

When the winds of war blew across our land, our flying partners were in the eye of the storm. Not one of them knew when the day began that they would be the first casualties of this new war.

More than a century ago, a philosopher was asked, "What, then, is our duty?" And his answer was, "It is what the day requires."

Our flying partners, like thousands of flight attendants around the world, went to work that fateful day, prepared to board flights and shepherd our passengers to their destinations.

For a few hours, in a small space in the sky, we share our passengers' hopes and dreams. We hear of their successes and disappointments. We see the famous and the unknown, the rich and the refugees. We see people fleeing war and famine, who lean toward the cabin windows, searching for their first sight of our nation's shores as we bring them to their new homeland. We see couples at the beginning of their lives together, grandparents on the way to see their first grandchild, and children, from six to sixty, going to visit with their parents.

We help America and the world do its business, flying brokers and bankers across the continents. We carry salespeople to their clients and bring them back to their families when the deal is done. We have flown the nation's soldiers into battle zones, and returned to take them home at battle's end.

All the while, we are together, bound by our unique job, by our training and by our dedication to our passengers' safety. At the beginning of our careers and every year until we take off our wings, we train to keep our passengers safe. We comfort them in turbulence, support them when they're ill, and evacuate them in emergencies. That is why those of us who wear the wings are not coworkers, or associates, but flying partners.

Every day that we board the aircraft, we are dependent upon one another to protect ourselves and our passengers.

Our flying partners on our Flight 93 and Flight 175, as well as on American Flight 11 and Flight 77, saw something on that Tuesday morning that none of us have ever encountered. That day our flying partners saw an evil so great that the human eye could not recognize it. Even now the mind cannot encompass it. In the end they must have known that this evil of such immense proportions would defeat their efforts to protect their passengers and themselves. Heroic efforts were made aboard those planes by flight attendants, who spent their last precious minutes alerting our companies to the threat and trying to protect others. Many more heroic acts took place that day and are known only to God.

In the airline industry tragic accidents are so rare they are known only by flight numbers. But how shall this tragedy be known? It was not an accident but a planned attack on America and on us. Never before has the industry lost so many crews, passengers, and airplanes in so short a time. History might refer to this by the date, September 11, but whatever history calls it, we can be certain that it will always be known by the heroic acts of hundreds and thousands of ordinary people.

Among those flight attendants were veterans with thirty and forty years of experience and some who had been in the skies for less than a year. We had college graduates, former police officers, and mothers and fathers who had every expectation of returning to their families. They all shared a love of flying. They all knew that there was something about this job that gets into your soul and calls you to it. Our heroes, whose names we are learning, are the flight attendants who have been taken from our ranks at United.

Lorraine Bay joined United forty years ago and was the most senior of the flight attendants who died that day. She was on Flight 93.

Sandra Bradshaw was one of those who called from Flight 93, alerting the world to the tragedy unfolding above us. It was a call to say good-bye to her husband and children too.

Robert Fangman joined United just last November and was assigned to Boston in January. He was on Flight 175 and leaves behind his mother and six siblings.

Wanda Green, on Flight 93, had twenty-nine years of seniority and had been planning to retire in the coming months. She leaves her parents, two children, a brother, and a twin sister.

Amy Jarret, twenty-eight years old, was on Flight 175. In her father's eulogy, he said, "I don't know what happened up there, but she would have been one of those people trying to do the right thing."

Amy King and Michael Tarrou were engaged and had left their home in Stafford Springs, Connecticut, that morning to work Flight 175. They were together when it was flown into the World Trade Center. Michael leaves a daughter.

Ceecee Lyles had been a police officer in Fort Myers, Florida, before joining United. She is another of the flight attendants who called from Flight 93. Her husband alerted authorities. Ceecee leaves her husband and four children.

Kathryn Yancey Laborie had been with United for seven years when she boarded Flight 175. Her father, in words similar to those used by many of the flight attendants' families, said, "She loved to fly." She leaves her parents and two brothers.

Alfred Marchand left the police force in Alamogordo, New Mexico, after a twenty-year career, and pursued his love of travel and flying. He joined our ranks less than a year ago and was on Flight 175. He leaves his wife, his son, two stepsons, and his mother.

Alicia Titus had been with an Internet firm but decided that she really belonged with us when she discovered her love of travel. Her father said that he had no doubt "Alicia died while trying to do good in the midst of evil," on Flight 175. She was engaged to be married and leaves her parents and a sister.

Deborah Welsh had been with Eastern and Kiwi Airlines before coming to United five years ago. She was on Flight 93. She leaves her husband, who said of her, "She'd want us to make sure the planes keep going. She loved this industry."

Each of them had plans for the future, whether it be marriage or retirement. Each of them had families to raise or be with. Each had hopes for tomorrow. Every one of them did what the day required.

Martin Luther King, Jr., said, "The ultimate measure of a man is not where he stands in moments of comfort, but where he stands at times of challenge."

We stand with our fallen flying partners as we return to our flights and our passengers, knowing they gave the full measure in their time of challenge.

In their last moments, in that small space in the sky, those flight crews saw evil. It is our prayer and our faith that they now see the face of God and are at peace forever. We pray that their families and all of us who are their flying partners will find comfort in that.

Hold them in your hearts and minds and prayers.

Thank you for coming here today to honor the lives and the memory of these heroes, our flying partners.

Linda Farrow, United Airlines MEC President: *Eulogy for the Flight Crews Lost on September 11, 2001.* ORD and EWR Memorial Services, September 2001. Speech written by Glenn Avery and delivered by Linda Farrow

INDEX